Sentences may pertain to states or processes or events. How do they do this? It is their aspectual properties which allow users of natural languages to express their perspective on the temporal structures they are talking about: on boundedness, ongoing activity, uniqueness, habituality, indeterminacy and many other often subtly encoded forms of temporality. Henk Verkuyl here presents a unified formal system to account for these properties. He explains the many forms of aspectuality in terms of the opposition between terminativity and durativity. He then describes and explains the way in which terminative aspect is compositionally formed by the merging of temporal information inherent in the verb and atemporal information expressed by its arguments. His theory also covers a large number of different durative constructions in a uniform way, combining insights and tools from Montague Grammar and generative grammar (in the broad sense which also includes the localistic framework).

A theory of aspectuality draws together into a coherent whole the author's thinking on the subject over the last twenty years, and will interest all those working on aspectuality and quantification. It promises to be a major new contribution to our understanding of the subject.

A theory of aspectuality

In this series

35 MARTIN ATKINSON: *Explanations in the study of child language development*
36 SUZANNE FLEISCHMAN: *The future in thought and langauge*
37 JENNY CHESHIRE: *Variation in an English dialect*
38 WILLIAM A. FOLEY and ROBERT VAN VALIN JR: *Functional syntax and Universal Grammar*
39 MICHAEL A. COVINGTON: *Syntactic theory in the High Middle Ages*
40 KENNETH J. SAFIR: *Syntactic chains*
41 J. MILLER: *Semantics and syntax*
42 H. C. BUNT: *Mass terms and model-theoretic semantics*
43 HEINZ J. GIEGERICH: *Metrical phonology and phonological structure*
44 JOHN HAIMAN: *Natural syntax*
45 BARBARA M. HORVATH: *Variation in Australian English: the sociolects of Sydney*
46 GRANT GOODALL: *Parallel structures in syntax: coordination, causatives, and restructuring*
47 JOHN M. ANDERSON and COLIN J. EWEN: *Principles of dependency phonology*
48 BARBARA A. FOX: *Discourse structure and anaphora*
49 LAUREL J. BRINTON: *The development of English aspectual systems*
50 DONNA JO NAPOLI: *Predication theory*
51 NOEL BURTON-ROBERTS: *The limits to debate: a revised theory of semantic proposition*
52 MICHAEL S. ROCHEMONT and PETER W. CULICOVER: *English* focus constructions and the theory of grammar
53 PHILIP CARR: *Linguistic realities: an autonomist metatheory for the generative enterprise*
54 EVE SWEETSER: *From etymology to pragmatics: metaphorical and cultural aspects of semantic structure*
55 REGINA BLASS: *Relevance relations in discourse: a study with special reference to Sissala*
56 ANDREW CHESTERMAN: *On definiteness: a study with special reference to English and Finnish*
57 ALESSANDRA GIORGI and GIUSEPPE LONGOBARDI: *The syntax of noun phrases: configuration, parameters and empty categories*
58 MONIK CHARETTE: *Conditions on phonological government*
59 M.H. KLAIMAN: *Grammatical voice*
60 SARAH M.B. FAGAN: *The syntax and semantics of middle constructions: a study with special reference to German*
61 ANJUM P. SALEEMI: *Universal Grammar and language learnability*
62 STEPHEN R. ANDERSON: *A-Morphous Morphology*
63 LESLEY STIRLING: *Switch reference and discourse representation*
64 HENK J. VERKUYL: *A theory of aspectuality: the interaction between temporal and atemporal structure*

Supplementary volumes

AYHAN AKSU-KOÇ: *The acquisition of aspect and modality: the case of past reference in Turkish*
MICHEAL O SIADHAIL: *Modern Irish: grammatical structure and dialectal variation*
ANNICK DE HOUWER: *The acquisition of two languages from birth: a case study*
LILIANE HAEGEMAN: *Theory and description in generative syntax. A case study in West Flemish*

Earlier issues not listed are also available.

A THEORY OF ASPECTUALITY

THE INTERACTION BETWEEN TEMPORAL AND ATEMPORAL STRUCTURE

HENK J. VERKUYL

Professor of Linguistics
Research Centre for Language and Speech, Utrecht University

CAMBRIDGE
UNIVERSITY PRESS

Published by the Press Syndicate of the University of Cambridge
The Pitt Building, Trumpington Street, Cambridge CB2 1RP
40 West 20th Street, New York, NY 10011-4211, USA
10 Stamford Road, Oakleigh, Melbourne 3166, Australia

First published 1993

Printed in Great Britain at the University Press, Cambridge

A catalogue record for this book is available from the British Library

Library of Congress cataloguing in publication data

Verkuyl, H. J.
A theory of aspectuality: the interaction between temporal and atemporal structure / Henk J. Verkuyl.
p. cm. – (Cambridge studies in linguistics; 64)
Includes bibliographical references and index.
ISBN 0-521-44362-8
I. Title. II. Series.
P281.V43 1993
415–dc20 92-33563 CIP

ISBN 0 521 44362 8 hardback

TAG

Contents

PART II: NOUN PHRASE STRUCTURE

Preface

The idea that aspectuality, roughly, the property which makes it possible for a sentence to signal whether or not it pertains to something bounded, can be characterized compositionally by a system of rules of interpretation has been around for some time now. However, its articulation appears to be difficult. Not only is it an area of investigation in which several disciplines are deeply involved – linguistics, logic, cognitive science, computer science and philosophy – the phenomena are also very hard to capture because the systematic formal study of temporality as expressed by sentences of natural languages is relatively new. Of course, there is a tradition in which at least a lot of valuable data and generalizations have been made available. However, when it comes to making a theory, soon one is bound to recognize that a lot of preparatory work is to be done before one can even think about theory formation. The picture is also complicated by the fact that the formal semantic study of discourse structure has developed very rapidly in the past ten years, so that all of a sudden all sorts of relatively new factors are drawn into an area of investigation whose scope was mostly restricted to sentences only. A lot of sorting out has to be done against the currents of shifting fashions.

The present study is characterized by a set of restrictive assumptions determining its focus. The first one is that theory formation can be compared with building a house, so there should be some solid ground for its foundations. As set theory has proved to be very solid as the foundation for many sciences, it seemed to me that it might be helpful to use it for a field of study in which quantification over temporal and atemporal entities is central. I have chosen to work in the framework of the Theory of Generalized Quantification, a model-theoretic enterprise which became popular in linguistics through the work of Richard Montague in the sixties and in its current form by the work of Jon Barwise, Edward Keenan, Johan van Benthem, Dag Westerståhl and many others in the seventies and eighties. The second assumption is that the formal machinery of generalized quantification may be compatible with and even incorporate valuable insights of generative grammar, taken here in a broad sense. For example, the localistic tradition in linguistics has been very important and fruitful for getting an insight into the way change and states are expressed. One of the purposes of this study is to show that localistic insights, as developed in recent work by Ray Jackendoff and in my own work, can be incorporated into standard type-logical representations. In fact this can be done by one elegant formula. In this way, the approach to change in which verbs are taken as dynamically contributing to the build-up of temporal structure is made central. Also aspectual asymmetry as defended in this study is very well compatible with the fundamental asymmetry between arguments of the verb which is inherent to the NP VP distinction in Chomskian syntax.

The third assumption is that one should not start with the roof before the first floor is ready: if terminative aspect, that is, the property of a sentence to pertain to a bounded temporal entity, is built up compositionally, as will be defended, then one should be able to select the proper building bricks and put them together into a certain coherent structure. Starting to construct at a level too high will not do. In other words, a theory of aspectuality based on composition should operate from bottom to top and make sure that it can deal with the basic things before it proceeds to sky high. No attention will be given to aspectuality of texts, in spite of interesting work in this area, such as Kamp and Rohrer (1983), Hinrichs (1986a, 1986b), Partee (1984) and Caenepeel (1989) among others, because so many things need to be done at the lower floors before one may feel safe to proceed. In fact, the present study will be restricted to the study of the interaction between the verb and its arguments, as it was in the papers which form the foundation of the present study, my papers on aspect during the mid-seventies and the eighties. Until recently, I focussed on the formalization of terminative aspect, considering durative aspect as the aspectual 'garbage can', and my original attention was to continue restricting this focus, negation excepted. The formalism of Generalized Quantification Theory (GQT), however, has forced me into being explicit also about all sorts of things which happen to fall under the label of durativity. Subsequently, the present study has also become a theory about large parts of the durative garbage can: it will formally describe at least eight ways in which durativity can be obtained, among which are bare plurality, Progressive Form, habituality, negation, different argument structure, etc.

The fourth assumption is that even though I am very happy with working in an interdisciplinary context, the present theory is fundamentally linguistic even though a lot of logical machinery is being employed. It explains, for example, why I have never liked 'reading-itis', the wish to assign as many readings as possible to a sentence without taking into account that a sentence might simply be used to underinform and that it is better to provide for means to describe underinformation precisely and formally. It also explains why I did not deal with aspectual matters in terms of scopal change. In my view, the temporal analysis of a sentence like *Two girls dropped a bag* can be given without making an appeal to structures which are paraphrased by 'There is a bag such that two girls dropped it'. Of course, for certain logical purposes scopal change turns out to be very helpful, but as soon as the temporality of sentences is central, all the toy tools of logicians should be reconsidered and not be taken for granted. In this way, the present book also appears relevant for logicians interested in natural language. There are many more assumptions, but these will be made clear while proceeding. Summarizing, this study will concern the principles governing the compositional nature of sentential aspect and the characterization of the semantic factors putting it together.

The book is organized as follows. Part I contains a general introduction to the scope of this study. It also contains an overview of the literature led by the question of how useful the so-called aspectual Verb classes, invented by Zeno Vendler, are for aspectual theory. Part II deals with the (atemporal) quantification expressed by Noun Phrases. It begins with a brief introduction to some key notions of the Theory of Generalized Quantification. The main question raised then is: can this theory deal with the solid aspectual notion of Specified Quantity (roughly, finite cardinality or bounded portion of matter)? It can, but it will be argued that this can be done best at a certain type-logical level assumed for NPs in my 1981 paper 'Numerals and Quantifiers in X-bar Syntax and their Semantic Interpretation'. Not only does such a treatment of NPs give a precise delineation of the notion of Specified Quantity, it also makes it possible to capture a set of phenomena in which NPs, for example, the bare plural, denote an Unspecified Quantity. Moreover, Specified Quantity NPs turn out to have a systematic Unspecified Quantity interpretation, which makes it possible to 'isolate' a well-organized field in the realm of genericity and reassign it to the area of aspectuality: the intriguing phenomenon of definite and indefinite plural and singular 'bareness'. Part II contains a section also including parts of a paper written by Jaap van der Does and myself on the semantics of plural NPs. The PLUG-grammar resulting from this joint work will be used as the basis for a further temporal extension in Part III.

Part III contains a critical analysis of the approach to the logic of change based on Von Wright's analysis, in which change is taken in terms of a transition between two points of evaluation. The main question became: what happened between these two points? This misguiding question was not posed at all in the localistic tradition mentioned above, to its benefit. This tradition takes change dynamically in terms of construction of temporal structure, thus providing automatically for the fiercely desired answer, the unavailing hunt for which led to a massive turning away at the beginning of the eighties from interval semantics to event semantics. A sketch of the localistic framework based on joint work by Joost Zwarts and myself on Jackendoff's Conceptual Semantics shows that Jackendoff's conceptual syntax can be modelled in terms of set-theoretical notions. Later on, the localistic 'heritage' is translated into the type-logic employed in the extended PLUG-grammar, called PLUG^{+}. Then a critical examination of the contribution of event semantics to aspectual theory is given. It will be rejected as a means to explain aspectual phenomena, not as a means to operate at higher levels of language structure. Furthermore, an analysis is made of the notion of aspectual perspective. It is argued that terminative aspect should be seen as a signal that a sentence is used 'at the rock-bottom of extensionality', so to say. It signals which sort of temporal structure is taken as basic and by this the notion of boundedness is restricted to just one model (i.e. to one time structure). Concomitantly, many forms of durativity signal that a sentence should not be understood with respect to a single model (or domain). Finally, the PLUG^{+}-grammar is developed. It characterizes the aspectuality of a large set of sentences. The grammar covers terminative sentences, a variety of durative sentences, among which are sentences with a progressive form, habituality, partially affected arguments, etc.

The aspectual theory taking shape in the present study has been prepared in a number of articles written between 1974 and 1991. Part of their content has been incorporated, of course, though it turned out to be easier to rewrite rather than simply to copy. However, sometimes it was easier to copy while making some small adaptations. Thus, chapter 2 is a slightly revised and extended version of a part of Verkuyl (1989), chapter 7 contains a part of Verkuyl and Van der Does (1991), whereas a part of Verkuyl and Zwarts (1992) has gone into chapter 10.

Acknowledgments

There are many who I would like to thank for their contribution. First of all, of course, Jaap van der Does and Joost Zwarts. Without them the present study would not have had its present depth and scope. In particular, my work with Jaap van der Does on plurality forced me into deciding on the overall formalism and brought me back to my 1981 paper, which turned out to be very profitable for the analysis of the notion of Specified Quantity. Joint work with Joost Zwarts on Jackendoff's Conceptual Semantics served as a basis for me to draw localism formally into GQT and to make the 'translation' from uninterpreted conceptual structure into type-logical interpretations. As a result, I was able to capture the localistic tradition in one function which is made part of the type-logical GQT-formalism. The present work also includes traces of joint work with Franciska de Jong and Leonoor Oversteegen in the early and mid-eighties, so I would also like to thank them.

A crucial role was played by Kees Vermeulen, our 'home-mathematician' at the OTS, with whom I had a nice deal. For him, going through the present work was part of an enterprise of getting him acquainted with linguistic analyses of natural language. In exchange I had the good fortune of being corrected on the formalism, when it did not do what I hoped it would do or when it did what I did not like it to do. Part of the dynamic machinery of chapter 3 has been given a formal definition as a result of our frequent interaction.

I would like to thank Johan van Benthem, Martin van de Berg, David Dowty, Jan Tore Lønning, Manfred Krifka, Alex Lascarides, Godehard Link and Remko Scha for their comments on the plurality theory, and Nicholas Asher, Hans Kamp, Reinhard Muskens and Ralph Naumann for comments on some of the temporal issues. Johan van Benthem commented on most of my aspectual and quantificational papers. I have stocked up his written annotations and I will now finally give my answers to fundamental questions he raised, so I thank him for asking them. Mentioning Johan nearly automatically involves mentioning Jeroen Groenendijk, Dick de Jongh and Martin Stokhof. This enumeration completes the non-linguistic part of the Gamut quintuple.

Working as one of its members has profoundly influenced the course of my scientific interest. It has (they have!) determined the force with which I have tried to meet the standard of rigorous explicitness. Furthermore, I would like to thank readers of many earlier versions of this book (or of parts thereof), in particular the 'Groningen-group' consisting of Arie Molendijk, Leonie de Smet, Rita Landeweerd, Henriëtte de Swart, Co Vet, Helen de Hoop and Mark Kas. The present book deviates quite drastically from what they had to go through, also due to their detailed criticism. I also would like to thank Frank van Eynde for his insightful comments. On the generative side, I profited from discussions with Peter Coopmans and Martin Everaert on idioms, from my contacts with Ad Neeleman and Fred Weerman on the Complex Predicate Analysis, as well as from a discussion with Gennaro Chierchia. In particular, I would like to thank Johan Kerstens for his critical and detailed comments on the prefinal draft of this book, which he read from the beginning to its (then) end. I can only hope that my critical and detailed comments on the prefinal draft of his book will have helped him as much. All these comments have led to considerable improvements. In this connection, I would also like to thank many of my students. Some of them have already been mentioned, but I would like to add Joyce Bommer and Rini de Jong.

I also thank Adrie Barentsen, Andrej Danchev, Krasimir Kabakčiev, Nel Keijsper, Bozena Rozwadowska, Maaike Schoorlemmer and Maria Stambolieva for discussions about the subtleties of Slavic aspect. Wim Stokhof played an important role by refusing to take the Dutch equivalent of one of the crucial sentences, *Judith ate three sandwiches*, as terminative. Even though I disagree with this observation, it forced me into rethinking some of the fundamental issues that I had taken for granted, and it led me into formalizing the notion of partial affectedness, which had been left implicit in my 1972 thesis. He also was so kind as to organize a small seminar in the Institute for Languages and Cultures of South-East Asia and Oceania at Leyden University, so that the present theory could be put to the test with respect to a number of languages. I thank the participants for providing valuable material.

Finally, my visit to Amherst in the second part of 1986 was an enormous impetus to get this book written. The biannual Amsterdam Colloquia were very important for the development of my aspectual theory. A lecture series at the Bulgarian Academy of Science in May 1989 and lectures at the European Summer School for Language, Logic and Information at Groningen in 1989 and at Leuven in 1990 also helped me very much. I was also happy to participate in workshops organized by Mario and Andrée Borillo from IRIT in

Toulouse in 1990 and 1991. I profited very much from the discussions with the participants in these activities.

The list of acknowledgements is in fact much longer: it includes all those who are mentioned in the papers I have written. I thank them again here.

I Issues of compositionality

INTRODUCTION TO PART I

The aim of this book is to present a theory about aspectual properties of sentences in natural language. These are properties allowing sentences to express temporal structure with respect to which they are interpreted. Sentences may pertain to states or processes or events, they may express boundedness, duration, repetition, semelfactivity, frequency, habituality, and many other forms of temporality. The question put in its simplest and crudest form is: how do they do this? The answer to this question will be given in terms of the opposition between terminative aspect (roughly, the expression of boundedness) and durative aspect (roughly, the expression of unboundedness). More particularly, it will be given by presenting a theory about the way terminative aspect is compositionally formed on the basis of semantic information expressed by different syntactic elements, in particular the verb and its arguments. It will be argued that an aspectual theory is explanatorily adequate only if it treats the opposition between terminative and durative aspect structurally. The focus of the theory proposed in the present study will be on the interaction between the temporal and atemporal information contributed by constituents involved in aspect construal.

Part I is introductory in the sense that it will try to clarify crucial issues which are involved. In chapter 1, some preliminary notions will be explained, identifying step by step the scope of this study. The provisional picture emerging is that of a simple 'aspectual feature algebra'. The claim is that, on the basis of semantic information associated with specific syntactic elements, it can be predicted whether or not a sentence is terminative. The semantic information associated with the verb (the feature playing a role in terminative aspect construal will be called [+ADD TO] and it expresses (roughly) progress in time) will amalgamate with the semantic information associated with the argument NPs of the verb (the feature involved in terminative aspect will be called [+SQA] and it expresses (roughly) a Specified Quantity of the entities introduced by the head noun of the NP). The use of features is temporary and just for conceptual convenience: it is much easier to give first an overall idea of the aspectual theory by using a sort of informal 'feature algebra', and then proceed by replacing the features by expressions of a standard formal language, as will be done in Part II and Part III.

The compositional approach on the basis of semantic information scattered over constituents in the sentential structure is in conflict with the idea of aspectual classes, such as Vendler's popular verb classes. Vendler (1957) proposed a quadripartition – States, Activities (unbounded processes), Accomplishments (bounded processes) and Achievements (point events) – breathing new life into an old Aristotelian classification (actually a tripartition) of situational types. The classification is non-linguistic, as it concerns situational categories, but linguistic criteria are used to distinguish the classes from one another. This made Vendler's work of interest to linguists: they started to distinguish State verbs, Activity verbs, Accomplishment verbs and Achievement verbs. Among linguists accepting this division, the idea seems to be that, even though the specific linguistic criteria may vary across different languages, every language can produce congenial criteria so as to give Vendler's quadripartition a solid grounding as part of an aspectual theory.

In my view, Vendler's classification runs afoul of the evidence emerging from the linguistic tradition in the first half of this century that aspect is essentially a non-lexical property of sentence structure, both in non-Slavic and Slavic languages. Yet many formal semanticists use it as part of their aspectual theory. These two things cannot be married: if aspect formation is a process at a structural level it is hard to see how a lexical division can be maintained. It will be shown in chapter 2 that theories appealing to Vendler classes are hampered if they set out to treat aspect as something that is to be assigned to complex structure. In chapter 2.10, it will be made clear why in a theory of aspect construal the interaction between atemporal and temporal structure must be given a central place.[1]

1 *The Plus-principle*

1.0 Introduction

To evade the notorious terminological problems connected with the definition of aspect, I shall simply say at this point that central to the present theory is the conviction that, in English, sentences like (1)–(4) differ in a number of important respects and that an aspectual theory is called for to describe and explain these differences.[2]

(1) Judith ate a sandwich
(2) Judith ate sandwiches
(3) Judith ate bread
(4) Judith ate no sandwich

One may analyse these sentences atemporally, as numerous generations of linguists and logicians have done, exclusive of (2) and (3). One way to do this is to represent the meaning of (1) and (4) in terms of a formal atemporal logic, say first-order predicate logic (including propositional logic). For example, one could express the difference in meaning with the help of the following logical formulas:

(5) $\exists x(\text{Sandwich}(x) \wedge \text{Eat}(\text{Judith},x))$
(6) $\neg\exists x(\text{Sandwich}(x) \wedge \text{Eat}(\text{Judith},x))$

This is how linguists of the sixties and the early seventies thought logicians were bound to represent the meaning difference between these sentences.[3] However, it is evident that (1)–(4) express temporality: they pertain to something going on in time or being the case during a certain period of time preceding the point of speech. This is not expressed by (5) and (6). In the past twenty-five years, linguists and logicians have started to realize that there is a temporal perspective from which these sentences may be studied and that representations like (5) and (6) should be replaced or at least extended.[4] Different sorts of formal means have been introduced to account for the properties which are temporally relevant, some of which will be discussed in this study.

The properties relevant for the study of terminative and durative aspect can be isolated on the basis of tests. A well-known test to separate (1) from (2) and (4) is to combine the sentences with two sorts of temporal adverbial:

(7) #Judith ate a sandwich for an hour
(8) Judith ate a sandwich in an hour

(9) Judith ate sandwiches for an hour
(10) ?Judith ate sandwiches in an hour

(11) Judith ate bread for an hour
(12) ?Judith ate bread in an hour

(13) Judith ate no sandwich for an hour
(14) ?Judith ate no sandwich in an hour

In (7), the semelfactive reading is excluded in which Judith ate and consumed one sandwich. If (7) can be given an interpretation, it must mean that she repeatedly ate a sandwich or that she ate *from* one sandwich during a period lasting an hour. If they do not want to reject (7), people feel themselves forced into a repetition or into stretching out an event, for example by taking (7) as expressing that it took Judith an hour to eat a sandwich. Forced repetition or forced stretching will be indicated throughout this study by the symbol #. It is important to stress here that aspectual theory should focus on the question of which property it is that blocks the normal single-event reading of (1). And more fundamentally: what is actually blocked? On the other hand, in (9), (11) and (13) 'normal' interpretations are possible: like (2), sentence (9) reports about an eating which is presented as a process going on unboundedly; the same applies to (11), whereas (13) reports about a state just as in (4).

The sentences (8), (10), (12) and (14) form a second aspectual test: (8) says that Judith completed the eating of a sandwich within an hour. That is, one may read (1) such that its meaning is compatible with *in an hour*: the event of her eating a sandwich is completed in a period which is shorter than an hour. On the other hand, (10), (12) and (14) have question-marks. Again (2)–(4) behave differently: they cannot occur with adverbials like *in an hour*, which evidently require something bounded. Sentence (10) is as bad as *Judith walked in an hour*, so if *Judith walked* pertains to something unbounded, (2) must also pertain to something unbounded, just like *Judith ate bread* and *Judith ate no sandwich*. In chapter 2, more attention will be paid to aspectual tests like these. Here they merely serve to identify and demarcate the area of the present study.

The specific semantic effects resulting from combining (1)–(4) with the two temporal adverbials reveal that it is necessary for anyone who sets out to describe the differences and correspondences between (1)–(4) to take into account the temporal structure of these sentences. In my view, this is what an aspectual theory is about, or should be about. Intuitively, the theory involves temporal quantification, as is suggested by the use of such (still impressionistic) phrases as 'single event reading', 'repetition', 'process going on', etc. Central to the aspectual theory of the present study will quantification indeed be, both temporal and atemporal, as the difference between (1) and (2) must at least partially be attributed to a difference between *a sandwich* and *sandwiches*.

The study of aspectual properties turns out to be relevant for the analysis of multiple quantification expressed in sentences like:

(15) Two girls ate five sandwiches
(16) The three men lifted four pianos

which have received a lot of attention in the literature, mostly in terms of an atemporal binary relation between members of a set of two girls (three men) and a set of five sandwiches (four pianos), as for example in Kempson and Cormack (1981), Scha (1981), Gil (1982), Link (1983, 1984) and Lønning (1987b).[5] These authors did not observe that the sentences (15) and (16) are terminative, and if they did, they did not bother to give this semantic property its place as a part of their analysis. This kept them from trying to explain why (17) and (18) do not exhibit the same quantificational behaviour as (15) and (16).

(17) Two girls ate no sandwich
(18) The three men did not lift four pianos

In (16), for example, it is possible to have three different liftings in mind involving twelve different pianos altogether, but also one lifting in which three men and four pianos were involved. The interpretation of (16) seems to range over a scale from a purely collective extreme (all the three men lifted four pianos together at one time) and a purely distributive extreme (each of the men lifted four different pianos at different times one after the other). Two facts must be explained with respect to sentence (18). The first one is that if (18) is taken contrastively (say, by continuing with ... *but six*), it remains terminative. The second one is that under a non-contrastive reading one is not bound to interpret (18) as pertaining to values between the two extremes. It is simply denied that there was a lifting of four pianos and one is not forced to commit oneself to a possible way of non-lifting between the two extremes. In other words, under a non-contrastive reading there is no point in giving (18) a collective or a distributive interpretation (for some discussion see Lønning 1989).

One of the questions posed in the present study is how the opposition between terminative and durative relates to the opposition between distributive and collective. It will be shown that there is a close relationship and that the answer must be found in looking at the interaction between temporal structure induced by the verb and the atemporal structure expressed by its argument NPs. The need to include the analysis of atemporal quantifiers in the aspectual theory will lead to the treatment of terminative sentences like *Judith ate three sandwiches*, *Two girls ate some sandwiches*, *At least one man lifted four pianos*, *At most three children came in* and *Many children came in*. These sentences are interesting from two points of view: (i) they contain so-called generalized quantifying expressions, like *some*, *at least one*, *many*, etc.; and (ii) some of them contain two quantifying NPs so there is some need to account for their interaction. In other words, what does a sentence like *Two girls ate three sandwiches in an hour* really express? This question will be dealt with in chapter 7.4.

It will also be necessary to develop a theory about the way the verb which introduces temporal structure relates to the atemporal quantifying expressions which constitute its arguments. One of the problems connected with the analysis of atemporal quantification appears to be that in the literature sentences under analysis are mostly sentences expressing states, such as *600 Dutch firms use 5000 American computers*, *Every doctor likes some female patient* and *Four squares contain three circles*, or that sentences containing verbs expressing progress in time are treated as if they pertain to eternal states. This excludes taking into account temporal structure, even though in the informal explanation of the sentential meaning often an appeal is made to events, or situations, etc. The method involved comes close to allowing all mathematically proper combinations of members of a Cartesian product. Relations are mathematically, that is purely extensionally, treated as sets of pairs <x,y> where x and y are the elements between which the relationship holds. On this view, there is no room for the contribution of the verb itself to what is expressed by the sentences whose main predicate it is. Yet, temporal structure seems to be relevant in cases in which the arguments of a predicate can be related to different events. For example, in (16) it is evident that each of the men could have lifted the same pianos, be it on different occasions. It also appears to be evident that if two men are involved in lifting the same piano, they are involved in one and the same event as far as the piano is concerned (though each man might think that he is the only agent involved). In general, one should rather think of sets of pairs of the form <x,<i,y>>, where i pertains to a temporal parameter generated by the verb itself. This formal machinery will be discussed in chapter 13.

There is a complication of the main issue that should be involved right from the start. In Dutch there are sentences like (19):

(19) Judith at een boterham op
lit.: Judith ate a sandwich up

Verbs like *eten* (eat) allow some additional morphological means to strengthen the expression of terminative aspect, as shown with the help of (20) and (21):

(20) Judith at een boterham toen ik binnenkwam
lit.: Judith ate a sandwich when I came in

(21) Judith at een boterham op toen ik binnenkwam
lit.: Judith ate a sandwich up when I came in

So, in Dutch there are verbs like *opeten* (eat up) and *opdrinken* (drink up).[6] Whereas many Dutch speakers are willing to interpret (20) as saying that Judith was eating a sandwich when I came in, (21) is to be interpreted as strongly suggesting that Judith started eating up a sandwich after I had come in, a phenomenon described in Hinrichs (1981), Kamp and Rohrer (1983), Partee (1984), Oversteegen (1989), among others. On the other hand, it is clear that (1) is terminative, as can be seen from its behaviour in (7) and (8), and so is its Dutch counterpart *Judith at een boterham.* Moreover, (20) may be given the same interpretation as (21). One might say that (19) is the strong terminative version of (1), but it is also clear that an aspectual theory cannot ignore the phenomenon of the 'strengthening' or the 'weakening' of terminativity.

In this respect, sentences like (22) are also very important for an aspectual theory, because this theory must explain why they may express completion but also allow non-completion:[7]

(22) Jan liep naar de winkel
John walked to/towards the store

(23) Jan liep in vijf minuten naar de winkel
John walked to/towards the store in five minutes

(24) Jan liep naar de winkel, maar halverwege werd hij geraakt
John walked to/towards the store but halfway he was hit

Like sentence (1) it meets the *in*-test in (8), as shown by (23), so one may say that (22) is terminative, but still one might say (24), allowing for the event to be interrupted (Oversteegen 1989). In view of these observations, a central place in the present study will be given to verbs like *eat*, *walk*, etc., because they represent the 'medial category' of verbs contributing to terminative aspect as contrasted with on the one hand stative verbs like *hate*, *be dead*, *concern*, *believe*, etc., which do not contribute at all, and on the other hand verbs like *buy*, *die*, *stab*, etc., which do not appear to allow interruption of the sort exemplified in (24).

Indeterminacy as to completion is not only restricted to prepositions such as the Dutch *naar* (to/towards), it also may show up in sentences like (25):

(25) John read a book for two hours

Fillmore (1971) observed that this sentence may have an interpretation in which John read just a part of the book, so actually he was reading a book for two hours. Hence, *John read a book* is not terminative and, contrary to what is predicted by the *for*-test in (7), there is no aspectual repetition in (25). Dowty (1986) takes this example as an indication that the approach of Verkuyl (1972), which predicts that *John read a book* is terminative, is wrong. In chapter 14, I will show that the aspectual theory expounded here, while adopting the approach attacked by Dowty – who misrepresents it, as pointed out in the introduction to Part II – can handle sentences like (25) correctly, in the same way as it will treat (20), (21) and (22).

An important part of aspectual theory is the question of how to deal with sentences like (26):

(26) Judith was eating a sandwich

Sentences like (26) are durative. So, a natural question is: if we take (26) as a change of (1), what has changed? This question has been raised many times in the past twenty years in the study of the Progressive Form.[8] Some say that there is an aspectual difference between (26) and (1) which is quite different from the one between (1) and (2)–(4). This difference roughly coincides with a difference between 'subjective' and 'objective' in the following sense. By choosing *was … ing* a speaker is said to place the hearer 'in the middle' of the eventuality described, whereas the event described in (1) is said to be presented 'from the outside' and hence as bounded. This opposition is considered to be subjective. On the other hand, (1) would be 'objectively' terminative because any event 'to eat a sandwich' when executed by one person is inherently bounded. This is (objectively) inherent to the nature of the event, whereas 'to eat sandwiches' is inherently and objectively unbounded. The difference between 'subjective' and 'objective' forms of aspectuality is often expressed by a terminological distinction between aspect and aktionsart.

In spite of the clear difference between sentences like (2)–(4) and (26), I find the distinction between aktionsart and aspect distracting, in particular the identification of aspect with 'subjective' and aktionsart with 'objective'.[9] For example, the very distinction between a subjective and an objective way of presenting a sentence would break down as soon as one assumes that the speaker's choice of constituents like *a sandwich* and *Judith* in sentences like (1) is a subjective way of conveying information. As Galton (1984) pointed out convincingly: one may describe one and the same situation as a state, a process or an event. The same point is made by Comrie (1976). The speaker could have chosen other ways of presenting the same information. The distinction between subjective (aspect) and objective (aktionsart) remains impressionistic as long as there is no way to make the difference sufficiently explicit.

Moreover, it seems to me that the distinction between aspect and aktionsart in terms of 'subjective' and 'objective' is actually an ontological wolf in linguistic sheep's clothing. It is not a matter of coincidence that the distinction has become popular in the Slavistic tradition in which aspect predominantly has been taken as a morphological-lexical matter: lexical-semantic considerations often slip into ontological considerations. The better strategy appears to account in detail and formally for the relationship between (1) and (2)–(4), and for the relationship between (1) and (26) and to decide then how the formal machineries involved relate to one another. In chapter 3.5, formal descriptions will be given of (1)–(4), (19), (22), (25) and (26). It will be concluded there that there is nothing against making a practical distinction between aspect and aktionsart, but that the opposition does not play any theoretically significant role. To give an example, in Bulgarian (see Danchev 1992) one has not only to deal with the opposition between sentences like (27) and (28), but also between (27) and (29):

(27) Judit izjade edin sandvič
Judith ate (Aor.) a sandwich

(28) Judit jadeše edin sandvič
Judith ate (Imp.)/was eating a sandwich

(29) Judit jadeše sandviči
Judith ate (Imp.) sandwiches

These oppositions can be dealt with without having to appeal to notions like aspect or aktionsart. The term *aspectuality* seems to capture the whole area covered by the two notions.

By the above remarks it stands to reason that aspectuality is taken notionally in the present study: English does not grammaticalize aspectual differences, at least not systematically in the way Slavic languages do. Nor does Dutch. On the other hand, I have the firm belief that the present theory may contribute to a better understanding of aspectual phenomena in languages in which aspect is grammaticalized. This conviction is based upon the fact that our theory makes a number of correct predictions on the basis of English and Dutch with respect to Slavic languages, as will be pointed out in chapter 2.4 and in chapters 13 and 14.

1.1 Inner and outer aspect

More terminology needs to be fixed. In view of the aspectual differences between (1) on the one hand and (2)–(4) on the other, sentence (1) is called *terminative*, whereas sentences (2)–(4) are called *durative*. However, sentences like (8) are not terminative, and (9), (11) and (13) are not durative in the same sense, because the role of the temporal adverbials in aspect construal is different from the role of other constituents. In the literature there has been some discussion about this issue. Vet (1976: 150), for example, pointed out that the *for hours*-test discussed above seems to hold for sentences like (30) and (31):

(30) #The whole day Judith ate sandwiches for hours

(31) #The whole day Judith ate a sandwich for hours

According to him, (30) expresses aspectual repetition of the same sort as (7): if one is forced to interpret sentence (30), one is bound to say that for twenty-four hours it was such that there were several non-consecutive periods lasting some hours each. During each of these periods Judith ate sandwiches. Thus the effect of applying *for hours* to (2) appears to yield a bounded quantifiable event, say ⟦Judith ate sandwiches for hours⟧, the denotation of (7). Sentence (30) blocks the possibility of having one such event. For Vet this seems to show that the sentence *Judith ate sandwiches for hours* itself is terminative, *the whole day* being a durational adverbial operating on it.

Vet's idea has received some support. Lindstedt (1984, 1985), for example, yielded to a temptation which in my view should be shunned. He proposed that the Finnish equivalents of sentences like

(32) During almost all his life Pekka read the paper for one week each year one hour a day

fit in the alternating mould P(I(P(I(P(I))))), where *Pekka read the paper* is taken duratively (=I), *Pekka read the paper one hour* is terminative (=P), *Pekka read the paper one hour a day* is durative, and so on. So the resulting aspect of sentence (32) is terminative, according to Vet, the main idea being that aspect stacks all the way up alternatingly from *Pekka read the paper* to (32) as a whole.

An objection to this sort of analysis is that it assumes that I and P remain constant at higher levels of structure. It is as if the mayor of New York City does not have the same job as the governor of New York (which is true) but would have the same job as the president of the United States. After all, there seems to be quite a difference between (7) on the one hand and (30) and (31) on the other, and between *Pekka read the paper for one week* and (32). Does the quantification involved pertain to the same sort of entity at each level at which a P takes an I or an I takes a P? They do not. In my view, the principles involving aspectual composition in *Judith ate sandwiches for hours* from *Judith ate sandwiches* and *for hours* differ so much from those involved in *Judith ate sandwiches* from *Judith*, *ate* and *sandwiches*, that it would be misleading to apply the notion of terminativity both to the former and to the latter, until it can be proven that one should do so. The only way to find out is first to account explicitly for *Judith ate sandwiches*, then for the adverbial *for hours*, and finally for the combination of the two constituents, and subsequently step by step for the other combinations. Thus, if there were some alternating scheme of the form P(I(P...(P(I)))) for sentences like (32), it would have to be modified, for example into the scheme $P_n(I_n(P_{n-1}...(I_2(P_1(I_1)))))$, where each subscript i represents a syntactic node immediately dominated by a node of level i+1. The use of a subscript, say i+1 for P_{i+1}, would indicate that the P_{i+1}-operator in spite of its assigning a P-property to an I-node also has aspectual properties that are only available at the i+1-level and not at the i-level or any lower level. Lindstedt does not provide such a scheme.

There are two empirical observations justifying scepsis with respect to an alternating P/I-proposal without an added (subscript) proviso. First, note that (30) expresses the same sort of quantification as (31). That is, the whole day it was the case that there were several periods lasting hours during which the predication holds good. But it does not appear to make a difference whether *for hours* operates on the terminative (1) or the durative (2). The combination of either sentence with *for hours* yields the same result: something bounded. From a compositional point of view this is undesirable: it would be wrong to say that (7) and (9) differ in meaning but to deem irrelevant this difference in (30) and (31). The second point is that semantically there is a difference between *for an hour* and *for hours*, the former pertaining to just one hour, the latter to an unbounded set of hours. Yet there is no aspectual difference between (30) and (33), on the one hand, and (31) and (34) on the other:

(33) #The whole day Judith ate sandwiches for an hour
(34) #The whole day Judith ate a sandwich for an hour

Here again something happens which does not occur at the lowest aspectual level: there should be an aspectually relevant difference between (7) *#Judith ate a sandwich for an hour* and *#Judith ate a sandwich for hours*, just like there is a difference between (1) *Judith ate a sandwich* and (2) *Judith ate sandwiches*. But there is no such difference. This strongly suggests that aspectual theory should distinguish between aspectual levels: the aspectual level of (1) is different from the level of (7) and this is different from the one in (32). Given the prospect of emptying the content of the notion of aspect if it is taken for granted that aspect of (1), (7) and (31) is formed in the same way, the most sound strategy seems to be to start from the very bottom of a sentential structure to the top with the working hypothesis that aspect differs at each structural level unless the evidence is otherwise.

In Verkuyl (1987a), a distinction was introduced between *inner* and *outer* aspects. Inner aspect is formed in (1)–(4), outer aspect in (7)–(14) and in the sentences (30)–(34). The present study is crucially focussed on the composition of inner aspect. It does not deal with the description of sentences like (30)–(34), nor with sentences like (7)–(14), in the absence of a sufficiently articulated theory of adverbial modification. In general, one might say that the study of inner aspect concerns the relationship between a verb and its arguments.

1.2 [±ADD TO] and [±SQA]

Verkuyl (1972) took into account the traditional (mainly non-structuralist and German) literature on aspectuality in the period between 1875 and the 1950s. Its thesis was that linguistic aspectual research had clearly and increasingly been developing into the conviction that aspect was a structural phenomenon. This is more visible in non-Slavic languages, such as Dutch and English, where it is not systematically expressed by morphemes but in the form of information scattered over certain constituents of the sentence, in particular the verb and its arguments.

Gruber's so-called Thematic Framework, developed in 1965 and 1967, made it possible for me to express this structural approach to aspectuality by putting heavy stress on localism as a means of accounting for the expression of different sorts of temporal structure in natural language (Gruber 1976). This framework assumes a fundamental bipartition into verbs expressing movement and verbs expressing no movement. The term 'movement' covers all sorts of literal and metaphorically taken movement in different semantic fields such as position in place and time, possession, identity, and circumstance (Jackendoff 1976, 1983, 1990; Verkuyl 1976, 1978).[10] The entity moving is called the *Theme* (whence the term 'Thematic' for the whole system). Most movements are directional in the sense that they presuppose or express a Source and a Goal. The distance between Source and Goal is called a Path (of the Theme). Thus, for any movement or change in a domain of interpretation a thematic kernel pattern of Theme, Source and Goal can be discerned: it consists of a Theme moving from a Source to a Goal (which together constitute a Path). In logical terms, the movement from Source to Goal is to be described as an additive or cumulative process: structure is built up monotone increasingly from a point zero. This runs counter to the dominant logical approach of the seventies and eighties in which the interval between Source and Goal was taken as a whole and checked on its internal structure (closed under subset). This approach will be dealt with extensively and critically in chapter 10.

In Verkuyl (1972), sentences like the following were used to make a distinction between durative and terminative sentences:[11]

(35) They ate cheese (dur.)
(36) They ate from the cheese (dur.)
(37) They ate sandwiches (dur.)
(38) They ate three sandwiches
(39) They ate a sandwich

(40) They drank whisky (dur.)
(41) They drank from the whisky (dur.)
(42) They drank a litre of whisky
(43) They drank a glass of whisky
(44) They drank a draught from the whisky

(45) He played from Schumann's cello concerto (dur.)
(46) He played music (dur.)
(47) He played a piece from Schumann's cello concerto
(48) De Machula played the cello concerto by Schumann
(49) De Machula played some of Boccherini's cello sonatas

(50) She knitted Norwegian sweaters (dur.)
(51) She knitted at a Norwegian sweater (dur.)
(52) She knitted (those) ten Norwegian sweaters

(53) He walked (dur.)
(54) He walked a kilometre
(55) He walked to the station
(56) He walked from the Mint to the Dam

This set of data led to the thesis that the aspectuality of the terminative sentences is compositionally formed. The line of argument is that *eat* being constant in (37)–(39), the aspectual difference between these sentences must be attributed to a difference between the NPs *sandwiches*, *three sandwiches* and *a sandwich*. This difference was explained in terms of quantification and the delimitation of mass: *sandwiches* in (37) pertains to an Unspecified Quantity of sandwiches, *three sandwiches* in (38) and *a sandwich* in (39) to a Specified Quantity of sandwiches. PPs like *from the cheese* in (36) and *from the whisky* in (41) were accounted for by assuming an empty head ø so that a structure like $[_{NP}ø[_{PP}$from$[_{NP}$the whisky$]]]$ was treated as an (argument–)NP of the verb *drink* in (41). In this way, a complex NP like *a draught from the whisky* in (44) could be taken as its specified counterpart, the head NP now being lexically filled and expressing a Specified Quantity of whisky, just like (42) and (43). Likewise, the aspectual difference between *a piece from Schumann's cello concerto* in (47) and *music* in (46) was explained in terms of the notion '(Un–)specified quantity of music'. The material shows the close relation between the aspectual behaviour of bare plurals and mass nouns.

As to the PP *to the station* in (55) several options along the line of Gruber (1976) were considered, one option being to treat *to* as an element incorporated into the verb *walk*, so that *the station* in (55) would end up as the complement of *walk-to*, that is, as the second argument of this verb. Finally, though the relation between *a kilometre* in (54) and the spatial PP *from the Mint to the Dam* in (56) was left unanalysed, it was clear that the intuitively clear notion of 'Specified Quantifity' should capture it.

In Verkuyl (1972), a generalization was made over verbs like *walk*, *drink*, *eat*, *play*, *knit* and so on, but this was done rather informally. The semantic element associated with *walk* was MOVEMENT, with *drink* and *eat* TAKE, with *play* PERFORM, with *die* TRANSITION, with *knit* ADD TO. These semantic (quasi–)characterizations of verbs expressing change have in common that they all pertain to something going on in time. As can be seen from the following passage, the category ADD TO emerged to refer to the dynamic semantic information distinguishing verbs like *eat*, *walk*, *drink*, *knit*, etc. from *not eat* and from verbs like *want*, *hate*, etc.

> Speculating further on the possibility of relating MOVEMENT + QC (= Quantifying Complement) to the node CONSTRUCT we could say that the predicate 'ADD TO' is of great relevance to both categories. If we say at some moment t_m, where $t_i < t_m < t_j$, that Katinka is constructing something, we could equally well say that she is adding something to what has been constructed during the interval (t_i, t_{m-1}). One can only say *Katinka breit nu aan die trui* (Katinka is working now at that sweater) if she had already begun knitting. It is not possible to say this sentence at t_i: something must have resulted from Katinka's knitting before we can use *breien aan* (work on). As far as MOVEMENT + QC is concerned, we could say that moving from some point P_i to another point P_j, where the distance between P_i and P_j, is the interval (P_i, P_j), can also be conceived in terms of the predicate 'ADD TO'. If someone is walking at P_m, where $P_m \in (P_i, P_j)$ such that $P_i < P_m < P_j$ ..., we can say that he is adding some distance measuring units to the interval (P_i, P_{m-1}). It is not possible to use the sentence *Hij wandelt nu* (He is walking now) if he is at P_i. (1972: 95f.)

In later work, the abbreviatory feature [+ADD TO] was used to stand for categorial nodes like MOVEMENT, TAKE, ADD TO, etc., to account for the dynamicity expressed by the verb.[12] Furthermore the Gruberian complex category of Specified Quantity of A has been replaced by an abbreviatory feature [+SQA]. It is one of the purposes of this study to provide a detailed model-theoretic analysis of the semantic information represented by [+SQA] and [+ADD TO].

At this point it seems appropriate to react to Dowty's unjustified claim that my 1972 approach is basically syntactic (Dowty 1986: 40; and after him Hinrichs 1986a; Krifka 1989b). I think it was (generative–)semantic.[13] This means that it looks as if nodes like MOVEMENT and SPECIFIED QUANTITY OF belong to syntax, as they are part of the representational language used in that framework. However, there are several places in Verkuyl (1972) in which explicit reference is made to crucially semantic notions. For example, on page 73, SPECIFIED and UNSPECIFIED were explicitly called *semantic categories* and careful reading of pages 54–73 shows that indeed a meaning opposition was intended. Dowty's misleading interpretation of my 1972 framework will be discussed in more detail in the introduction to Part II.

The basic idea of aspectual compositionality was and still is that only a combination of a [+ADD TO]-verb with one or more of its argument [+SQA]-NPs yields a compositionally formed (and hence semantic) terminative inner aspect. In the other cases, the overt or covert NPs such as *sandwiches* and *bread* necessarily lead to durativity.[14] Thus, three sorts of aspectual situations are predicted, where [–ADD TO] stands for 'no movement', and [+ADD TO] for 'movement'. These three situations are exemplified in (57)–(64):

Compositional scheme

a. **[–ADD TO] and [±SQA]** ('No movement') ⇒ durativity

(57)	John is ill	
(58)	Judith wants to eat a sandwich	

b. **[+ADD TO] and [–SQA]** ('Movement with leaks') ⇒ durativity

(59)	Den Uyl gave *badges* to a congress-goer	leak at Theme
(60)	*Nobody* gave a badge to a congress-goer	leak at Source
(61)	Den Uyl gave a badge to *congress-goers*	leak at Goal

c. **[+ADD TO] and [+SQA]** ('Bounded movement') ⇒ terminativity

(62)	The patient died	
(63)	Den Uyl gave a badge to a congress-goer	
(64)	Judith ate three sandwiches	

The Gruberian outlook is mentalistic: (62)–(64) express terminative aspect, because they contain the right elements for providing an 'ontological clue'. Here the notion of aspectual perspective comes in. That is, by the choice of the verb and the determiners, (62)–(64) all go about a temporal entity which is conceived of as bounded. By convention one might agree that these bounded entities are to be called *events*. If one does so, then metaphors compete to take over the job of sharpening the contours of this intuitive concept: events can be compared with an island perceived in the flow of time, or with a big whale jumping up in the ocean: they are discernible by their bounds. Or, pursuing the leak-metaphor, one might be tempted to think of a wine-cask having a couple of stopcocks which must be closed in order to assure a specified quantity. All these metaphors concur with the idea of terminative aspect as a marked category. On the other hand, the verb in (59)–(61) does express 'movement' but there are no bounds to form a discernible 'island', or there is an aspectual leak in at least one of the NPs because it denotes an unspecified quantity. The mentalistic tradition clearly does play a role in the Gruberian framework and related research (Bach 1981, 1986; Chierchia 1984: 26ff.; Verkuyl 1985b; Jackendoff 1983, 1990).

In my view, the existential introduction of an event e as part of the domain about which we talk with the help of (62)–(64), is only licensed by a particular choice and arrangement of words in sentential structure. In this way, one basic element of the Gruberian approach is made visible: events are not primitives. They are construed by language, in particular by the choice of the elements we put together in a sentence to speak about the world and to order it. The choice of verbs like *want* in (58) signals that the main predication is not about something bounded but rather about a state (of mind). The choice of verbs like *eat* in (64) indicates that one wants to talk about something that was going on, a process, whereas the choice of certain NPs, such as *Judith* and *three sandwiches*, expressing 'a specified quantity' makes this process bounded. It is the interaction of atemporal and temporal structure that is crucial to a proper understanding of what aspect is about.

In the present study the idea of an aspectual 'leakage' in the sense demonstrated by (59)–(61) is maintained in spite of the abolition of the thematic roles Theme, Source and Goal. Verkuyl (1988) argued that these roles may be confusing rather than explanatory, because there is no clear way to define them unequivocally. In chapter 10 an extensive reanalysis will be given of the localistic framework. It will be rephrased into the model-theoretic framework maintaining its virtues. Without going into the details of this translation, it will be clear that the italicized NPs in (59)–(61) can simply be taken as the argument NPs of the verb in question. For the time being, it will be sufficient to interpret aspectual leakage in terms of certain properties of argument NPs.

A natural way to combine the ideas of compositionality and constructivity is given by the ontological classification in Figure 1, which is inherent to the Compositional Scheme underlying (57)–(64), but which remained implicit in Verkuyl (1972) as it did not focus on a classification of sorts of eventualities.

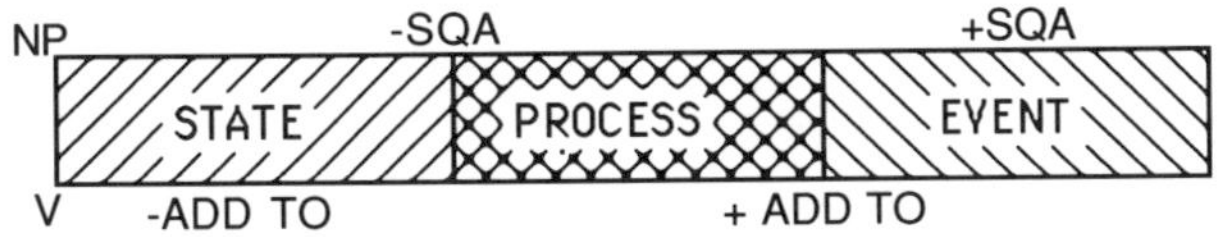

Figure 1 States, Processes and (terminative) Events are construed by combining semantic information expressed by the verb with semantic information expressed by its argument NP(s)

The contribution of the verb to terminative aspect is [+ADD TO], where [+ADD TO] stands for the property of additivity informally introduced above. Together with the semantic information [+SQA] contributed by its argument NPs, this property can be said to map onto an event. Thus, terminative aspect is a way to signal that we are speaking about what we conceive of as events, temporal entities that can be counted and quantified over. The [+ADD TO] together with [–SQA] yields an unbounded process; [–ADD TO] is sufficient to obtain states.[15] Durative aspect is a way to signal that we want to talk about something going on in time unboundedly or about something not going on in time. There are three partitions cutting across Figure 1:

> an ontological tripartition: state vs. process vs. event;[16]
> a lexical bipartition: [–ADD TO] (state) vs. [+ADD TO] (change);
> a structural bipartition: durative (state/process) vs. terminative (event).

A useful analogy urges itself upon us to express the idea of compositionality. Terminative aspect can be seen as a molecule built up from the atoms [+ADD TO] and [+SQA]. The terminative molecule, [+T], in sentences like (64) *Judith ate three sandwiches* is a 'triple-atom' molecule, as represented in (65a):

(65)	a.	Judith ate three sandwiches	[+SQA] + [+ADD TO] + [+SQA] = [+T]
	b.	Judith ate sandwiches	[+SQA] + [+ADD TO] + [–SQA] = [–T]
	c.	Judith ate no sandwich	[+SQA] + [+ADD TO] + [–SQA] = [–T]
	d.	Judith wanted nothing	[+SQA] + [–ADD TO] + [–SQA] = [–T]
	e.	Nobody ate a sandwich	[–SQA] + [+ADD TO] + [+SQA] = [–T]
	f.	Nobody ate sandwiches	[–SQA] + [+ADD TO] + [–SQA] = [–T]
	g.	Nobody ate a sandwich	[–SQA] + [+ADD TO] + [+SQA] = [–T]
	h.	Judith wanted a sandwich	[+SQA] + [–ADD TO] + [+SQA] = [–T]
	i.	No one wanted a sandwich	[–SQA] + [–ADD TO] + [+SQA] = [–T]

Only if all atomic features are positive, as in (65a), can the composite molecular feature be [+T]. That is, only (65a) has terminative aspect, all molecules with one or more minus features being durative. As long as features will be used to speak about aspectual composition, I will use the term *Plus-principle* to refer to the requirement that all aspectual 'atoms' involved are plus-values. Of course, one is to present more than metaphors, however useful these may be to reveal underlying assumptions.

One way to get to more standard expressions is to see (65) as a sort of semantic feature algebra, which serves as a point of departure. On our way to more precise model-theoretic representations, this intermediate station serves its purpose well, because it enables us to underscore some important points of the methodological strategy being employed in this study. First of all, if (65a) is the point of departure, the most important claim is that any sentence of the form [NP [V NP]] meeting (65a) should be terminative. In this sense, a theory based on the Plus-principle makes itself vulnerable because there are (apparent) counterexamples, as we shall point out shortly, which may invalidate the claim of [+T]-composition. Our theory must give a satisfactory answer, or it will have to be rejected. Secondly, (65) suggests that the formation of [–T] is more complex in the sense that both the verb and its arguments may have minus-features. This means that a theory along the lines of (65) takes durativity to be essentially different from terminativity. Durativity is rather the aspectual 'garbage can' (the more sophisticated term is default), as can be seen in (2)–(4) and (26), where four sorts of durativity are made visible. In this sense, terminativity is more well behaved. Our theory is not a theory about durativity, though it will speak out on a number of durative constructions. Thirdly, the idea of an aspectual algebra is useful to ask elementary but relevant questions about the syntactic structure carrying aspectual information. In the algebra of numbers the plus-operator is binary. So, if (65) contains algebraic-like expressions with two plusses, one should ask oneself whether or not the plus-operation is associative. In other words, does the equation (66)=(68) hold?

(66)	([+SQA]	+	[+ADD TO])	+	[+SQA]
(67)	[[Judith		ate]		three sandwiches]
(68)	[+SQA]	+	([+ADD TO]	+	[+SQA])
(69)	[Judith		[ate		three sandwiches]]

This question amounts to asking whether aspect construal takes into account syntactic structure. Suppose that (66) equals (68). Under associativity, it should make no difference for a bottom-to-top interpretation of (64) taking into account its syntactic phrase structure, to start out with (67) or (69). In either case, one should obtain terminative aspect on the basis of the plus-features. However, on the basis of (67), the Subject+Verb-group [Judith ate] cannot reasonably be interpreted as [$+T_{SUBJ+VERB}$], because *Judith ate* taken as a phrase is durative rather than terminative. This would lead to a situation in which the minus-feature [–T] of *Judith ate* is combined with a plus-feature [+SQA] of *three sandwiches* to yield the terminative [+T] of (65a).[17] The construal of the terminative aspect on the basis of (69) gives a different situation: the verb and its direct object NP form a complex plus-feature assigned to the VP and this combined with the subject NP yields again a [+T]. We may conclude that (66) does not equal (68), but also that (69) is a more plausible structure for the expression of terminative aspect than (67), the latter running counter to the idea of terminative aspect as being formed on the basis of plus-features only. In other words, the equation (66)=(68) implies that there would be no system in aspect construal. Therefore, I will adopt an asymmetric construal of terminative aspect along the lines of (69). This means that (66) does not hold and that the aspectual algebra in (65) is to be replaced by the stacked version given in (70):

(70) a. ate three sandwiches $[+\text{ADD TO}] + [+\text{SQA}] = [+\text{T}]_{VP}$
b. ate sandwiches $[+\text{ADD TO}] + [-\text{SQA}] = [-\text{T}]_{VP}$
c. wanted a sandwich $[-\text{ADD TO}] + [+\text{SQA}] = [-\text{T}]_{VP}$
d. wanted sandwiches $[-\text{ADD TO}] + [-\text{SQA}] = [-\text{T}]_{VP}$

e. Judith ate three sandwiches $[+\text{SQA}] + [+\text{T}_{VP}] = [+\text{T}]$
f. Judith ate sandwiches $[+\text{SQA}] + [-\text{T}_{VP}] = [-\text{T}]$
g. Nobody ate a sandwich $[-\text{SQA}] + [+\text{T}_{VP}] = [-\text{T}]$
h. No one wanted sandwiches $[-\text{SQA}] + [-\text{T}_{VP}] = [-\text{T}]$

An asymmetrical approach has far-reaching consequences.[18] One of these consequences is that terminative VP-aspect, abbreviated here as $[+\text{T}]_{VP}$, differs quite substantially from terminative (inner) S-aspect. As long as features are used to speak about VP-aspectuality and S-aspectuality, $[\pm\text{T}]_{VP}$ and $[\pm\text{T}]$ will be used, respectively. Recall that the features used here are just convenient preliminary abbreviations that will be replaced by formal representations.

One immediate advantage of thinking of aspectual composition in terms of a feature algebra is that it leads to the need of being interested in the way the lexical information, provisionally labelled [+ADD TO], will be amalgamated with the structural [+SQA]-information carried by the NP into structural aspectual information [+T], where [+T] represents terminative aspectuality. Perhaps it is appropriate to make the general point visible. Let me indicate where structural considerations should occupy us, and where lexical considerations are in place.

It can be seen easily in Figure 2 that the verb expresses lexical information, and that terminativity at the VP-level is seen as structural by a merger of structural NP-information obtained by the merger of lexical information expressed by DET and N. Likewise, Figure 2 raises the question central in Part II: how and when does NP-structure express [+SQA]-information? It means a detailed

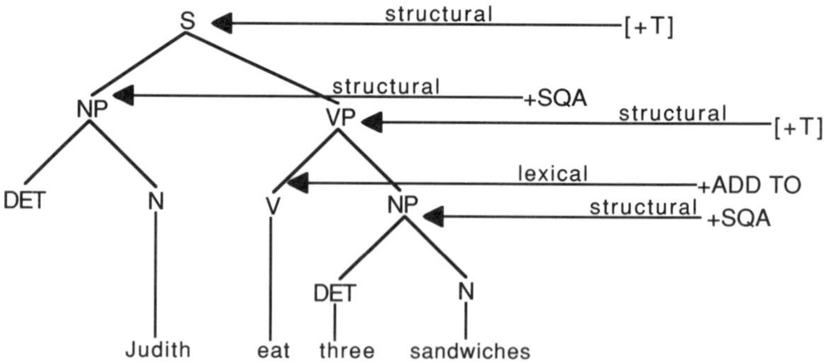

Figure 2 Aspect construal involves a compositional amalgamation of lexical and structural semantic information, here still abbreviated as features

investigation of the role of the determiner, which turns out to require far more structure than is given in Figure 2. Figure 2 also raises the question central in Part III: what is the interaction between NP-structure, the V and the VP?

1.3 Aspectual asymmetry

The present theory distinguishes between aspectual *layers*, as it sees a difference between aspectual construal at the different levels of grammatical structure. The basic idea is: a VP-node differs structurally from the S-node, so if there is VP-aspect, it differs from S-aspect, unless there is evidence to the contrary. Verkuyl (1971) proposed that terminativity be assigned to the sentential node S (minus the durational adverbial), leaving the position in earlier work that it be assigned to VP. The move from the VP-level to the S-level was prompted by the observation that the subject-NP plays a decisive role in aspect construal, as shown by the difference between the odd and even sentences in (71)–(76).

(71) For years water came in from the rock
(72) #For years *a litre of water* came in from the rock

(73) For hours *people* walked out of the house
(74) #For hours *the person* walked out of the house

(75) For months *patients* here died of jaundice
(76) #*These two patients* died of jaundice for months

The history of this move from the VP-level to the S-level is visible in the organization of my dissertation: the principles of aspect composition were mainly described from the point of view of VP-aspect.[19] Its final chapter added the insight that the subject NP is also involved in the formation of *inner* aspect. However, this does not entail that we have to accept (75) as the model for aspect construal. Figure 2 is compatible with the observation that in (71), (73) and (75) the subject NP co-determines the sentential aspect.

Is there linguistic evidence for the thesis that aspect is construed asymmetrically along the lines of Figure 2? One way to find it is just to seek alliance with a syntactic framework in which a fundamental asymmetry is assumed with respect to the VP (e.g. Chomsky 1981: 127ff.). However, I do not want to be dependent on a particular choice in a particular syntactic theory. If the interpretive mechanisms involved in aspectual composition are sufficiently supported, the best candidate for a marriage would be a syntactic theory in which asymmetry is independently assumed on syntactic grounds.

Is there any independent linguistic evidence for aspectual asymmetry? There is. Firstly, one can easily say *to eat a sandwich in five minutes* as contrasted with ?*to eat sandwiches in five minutes*. In other words, the *in*-test for terminativity applied to the sentence (1) in (8) applies already at the level of VP. The same applies to the *for*-test used in (7): *to walk for an hour* is well formed, #*to walk a mile for an hour* cannot be interpreted or must be interpreted as expressing forced repetition. This aspectual behaviour is not displayed by any combination of the subject NP and the verb: whereas *eat a sandwich* is to be interpreted as pertaining to something bounded, *Judith eats* can either not be interpreted or it must be interpreted duratively.

The second argument for aspectual asymmetry concerns idiomatic expressions. They are interesting for the study of aspect because idiomatic expressions lack properties that must be present in their non-idiomatic counterparts, or have properties that are lacking. From the latter point of view, idiomatic phrases are (on their way to being) petrified. Thus, it is often impossible to move a phrase out of an idiomatic expression, as shown by (78) and (79):

(77) John kicked the bucket
(78) *The bucket was kicked by John
(79) *What did you say that John kicked?

Thus, the petrification can be made visible, syntactically. Semantically, it is to be expected that NPs like *the bucket* will lose their referential force, either partially or completely. On the literal interpretation of (77), it should be possible to continue with … *and Mary kicked three buckets*. This is excluded on the idiomatic reading. Likewise, *John kicked a bucket* does not have an idiomatic counterpart.[20] No idiomatic expressions involving a two-place predicate seem to exist that can be analysed as the result of a fusion of the verb and its subject NP (Keenan 1976; Coopmans and Everaert 1988).[21] That is, there is no idiomatic expression of the type [NP^s V] with a two-place predicate V such that [[NP^s V] NP^o] is the complete idiomatic sentence, s and o being superscripts for subject and object, respectively. This means that idioms show asymmetrical behaviour. Actually, we can in a way repeat the first argument for aspectual asymmetry here. It is *to kick the bucket*. The VP itself is already an idiomatic expression.

Asymmetry of idiomatic expressions can be used as an argument for aspectual asymmetry, only if their difference with non-idiomatic expressions can be analysed as a difference of aspect. Given the terminative VP-scheme [+ADD TO] + [+SQA], there are, in principle, two places where idiomatic expressions might differ aspectually from their non-idiomatic counterparts. One possible difference might be effected by a difference of meaning in the verb. It may lose its [+ADD TO]-force so that [$-T_{VP}$] results. Another possibility is that the NP might change from [+SQA] to [–SQA]. In this case, the purely extensional (referential) meaning of the NP in a certain model should undergo a change.

As far as Dutch is concerned, for a non-idiomatic terminative VP a tendency can be observed to have its terminativity affected when it is used idiomatically. The judgments are quite subtle but visible.[22] The best way to proceed is to apply the standard aspectual tests. The *for hours*-test does not appear to observe the difference between an idiomatic expression and its non-idiomatic counterparts.

(80) Zij gaf hem een veeg uit de pan
lit.: She gave him a smear from the pan
She took a swipe at him

(81) #Zij gaf hem urenlang een veeg uit de pan
lit.: She took a swipe at him for hours

(82) Hij maakte van een mug een olifant
He made from a mosquito an elephant
He made a mountain out of a mole hill

(83) #De hele tijd maakte hij van een mug een olifant
lit.: The whole time he made from a mosquito an elephant

One cannot interpret (81) as pertaining to just one smear from the pan: she had a smack at him repeatedly. The same seems to hold for (83), although it might pertain to a situation in which he made a lot of fuss about just one point.

However, there are some cases which I am tempted to interpret as being focussed on the process-part of the event rather than on its termination:

(84) Hij zette zijn beste beentje voor
lit.: He put his best leg forward
He made a determined effort

(85) De hele middag zette hij zijn beste beentje voor
lit.: The whole afternoon he made a determined effort

(86) Hij deed een boekje over haar open
lit.: He opened a book about her
He showed her up

(87) Hij deed urenlang een boekje over haar open
lit.: He opened a book about her for hours

For example, (85) is correct as expressing that he behaved very well the whole afternoon. It certainly does not mean that he put his best foot forward several times during the afternoon in a non-literal sense. The same applies to (87): for hours he gave negative information about her.

As to the *in an hour*-criterion, there appears to be a tendency for the idiomatic expressions to behave duratively rather than terminatively:

(88) ?In tien minuten gaf zij hem een veeg uit de pan
lit.: She gave him a smear from the pan in ten minutes

(89) Hij bedekte het met de mantel der liefde
lit.: He covered it with the cloak of love
He drew a veil of love over it

(90) ?In een uur bedekte hij het met de mantel der liefde
lit.: He covered it with the cloak of love in an hour

Recall that a terminative phrase taking an *in*-adverbial is interpreted as located within the bounds of the interval introduced by the NP of the adverbial. That is, *He ran a mile in an hour* means that if the event 'he ran a mile' took place during the interval R and *an hour* denotes the interval H, then $R \subset H$. But if (88) can be interpreted, it would mean that it took her ten minutes before she took a swipe at him. Likewise, (90) does not mean that it took an hour for him to draw a veil of love over it. Again, a regular interpretation is blocked.

As said above, judgments are quite subtle and difficult in this area. Certainly, this is due to the fact that it is unusual to modify idiomatic expressions with *for*- and *in*-adverbials. If these observations are supported, however, a conclusion can be drawn: the thesis of aspectual asymmetry is at least compatible with the data from idiomatic expressions: idiomaticity in transitive verbs is always located in the VP and never in the combination of subject and verb. That the interaction of [V NP^o]-idioms with *for*- and *in*-adverbials differs from their non-idiomatic counterparts can also be seen as a support for the thesis.

The third argument for aspectual asymmetry comes from languages in which morphology plays a much more prominent role in the encoding of aspect. Adri Barentsen (pers. comm.) pointed out that in Slavic languages there is some systematic relationship between the occurrence of a direct object and the presence of perfective aspect. In Russian, some perfective prefixes (in a certain set of minimal pairs such as *pisat' – napisat'* (to write), *čitat' – pročitat'* (to read), *pit' – vypit'* (to drink)) require an object NP, whereas imperfectivity allows for the absence of this NP.

(91)	a. *Ja pročital I have read	b. Ja čital I have been reading
(92)	a. Ivan pročital poeziju Ivan has read the poetry	b. Ivan čital poeziju Ivan has read poetry
(93)	a. Ivan pročital stixotvorenija Ivan has read the poems	b. Ivan čital stixotvorenija Ivan has read poems

One does not say (91a) but rather (91b). The perfective verb is also much happier with a [+SQA]-object and so it is strange to say (92a) and not (92b), because *poeziju* is [–SQA]. Also, (93a) must be interpreted as saying that Ivan has read *the* poems, that is poems that are known in the context of use, whereas (93b) means that Ivan has read poems. These data strongly suggest that *pro-* in (92a) and (93a) requires a [+SQA]-object. One could say that by the absence of articles in Russian NPs, the verb contains clues as to [+SQA]- or [–SQA]-information expressed by its argument-NPs (Kabakciev 1984a, 1984b). In chapter 13.6 and 13.7, the behaviour of perfectivizing prefixes will be discussed in more detail. In general, Russian two-place predicates extend the information expressed by the perfective prefix to the object rather than to the subject. This can be taken as an argument for the contention that aspect formation is asymmetrical.[23] A fourth and a fifth argument will be given in the next section.

1.4 The scope of this study

The scope of this study can be determined with the help of Figure 2, which is simplified to Figure 3, where [+ADD TO] is aspectually relevant semantic information carried by V. It roughly expresses a going on in time, and [+SQA] is the structural information associated with the NP, expressing 'Specified Quantity of A', where A is the denotation of the head noun N of the NP. The complex semantic information associated with $[+T]_{VP}$ is the terminative VP-aspect; [+T] is the terminative S-aspect at the sentential level.

The leading question of this study is: under what conditions do sentences of the form (1)–(4), that is, of the form [NP [$_{VP}$ V NP]], meet the conditions of Figure 3 and under what conditions do they not meet them? In other words: what is the semantics of (1)–(4) and how do these sentences express their aspectual properties? These questions are quite restrictive as they seem to limit the scope of aspectual theory to sentences with transitive verbs only. Not all sentences of a language having terminative inner aspect happen to be of the form [NP[$_{VP}$ V NP]]. Yet, it appears methodologically fruitful to use the scheme in Figure 3 as the point of departure because it opens ways that would remain closed otherwise. For example, sentences like:

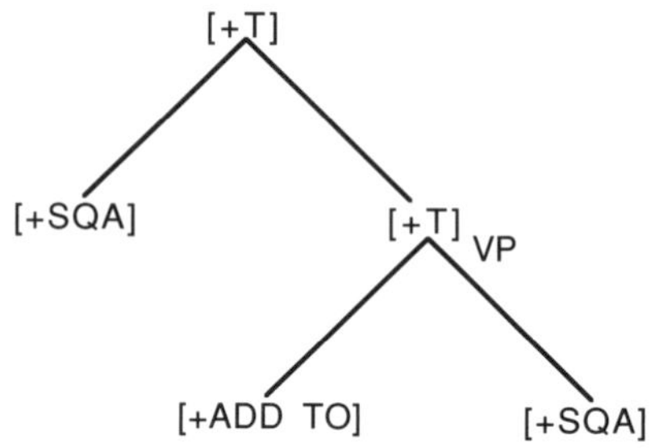

Figure 3 This basic pattern underlies the asymmetric composition of verbal and nominal aspectual information

(94) John walked
(95) John died

immediately become a problem given Figure 2. It would be rather dubious not to treat *walk* and *die* as [+ADD TO], but if we do that, the compositional machinery yields the wrong result making [+T] out of [+SQA]+[+ADD TO] both for the durative (94) and for the terminative (95). This is wrong. One could save a lot of trouble, of course, by stipulating that verbs like *die* are lexically characterized as [+T_{Lex}], so that at the VP-level *died* in (95) is $[+T]_{VP}$. Likewise, one could take, like Verkuyl (1972), the non-ergative verb *walk* as a two-place verb having a [–SQA]-complement in the case of (94), whereas it has a [+SQA]-complement in the case of *John walked a lap*, *John walked to the store*.

We can do better than that, I think. Figure 3 is very much compatible with the view that sentences like (95) can be analysed as ergative sentences, which means that *die* is to be taken as a verb whose external argument is empty. Thus, in generative terms (95) could be given the structure (96):

(96) $[[_{NP}\text{John}]_i\ [_{VP}\text{die } e_i]]$

where e_i is the trace of the internal argument *John*, which has the internal argument position at d-structure. It moves to the position of the subject (because it does not receive case). The resulting aspectuality is basically $[+T]_{VP}$-aspectuality, because the transition from $[+T]_{VP}$ to [+T] is not affected by any semantic information from the external argument position. As far as *walk* is concerned, we will provide for a solution in chapter 14 accounting for both its transitive and intransitive use: there is no 'transition' from [–ADD TO] to [+ADD TO], because the neutral verb stem *walk* will be in a position to choose between being inserted into an intransitive [–ADD TO]-frame and a transitive [+ADD TO]-frame. At this stage, however, Figure 3 forces us methodologically into rejecting *ad hoc* solutions and it proves to be a good guide to a better understanding of the issues involved.

At this point the fourth argument for aspectual asymmetry, due to Bommer (1989), can be discussed. She observed that sentences like (97) are terminative, as shown in (98):

(97) Two sandwiches were eaten

(98) Two sandwiches were eaten in an hour

Bommer argues convincingly that passive sentences like (97) show ergative behaviour, which means that (97) is to be analysed as not having an external argument. In other words, (97) is analysed along the lines of (99), where the NP *two sandwiches* is 'moved' from its position in the VP and indicated by its 'trace' e_i to its front position:

(99) $[[_{NP}$Two sandwiches$]_i$ $[_{VP}$be eaten $e_i]]$

If this analysis can be maintained (see also Beedham 1982), then again it points to taking the VP as a unit at which aspectuality can be construed.

Figure 3 also has the advantage of making a compositional aspectual theory vulnerable in the proper way. That is, it forces us into seeing that sentences like (100) and (101)

(100) John pushed the cart

(101) John stroked the cat

(at least superficially) fulfil their requirements: all NPs in these sentences are [+SQA]. To say that *push* and *stroke* would be [–ADD TO]-verbs would run counter to our idea that they express a going on in time. Hence it is predicted that (100) and (101) are terminative, were one to stick to Figure 3. However, they are clearly not terminative. Here again, it seems reasonable to assume a more complicated verbal structure, as illustrated in Figure 4, where XP is some constituent, say a particle, or a prepositional phrase, or a prefix, bringing about a complex verb that behaves aspectually in the same way as a VP. Sentences like (100) have systematically a terminative completion as demonstrated in:

(102) John pushed the cart away (over the ridge, aside, etc.)

which suggests that *push* in (100) can be seen as an 'incomplete verb', just like *stroke*. As I do not want to blur the concept of [+SQA], one should not label *away* as [+SQA], but rather say that the semantic interpretation of *away* may be treated in terms of the presence of semantic information expressing the same sort of information as [+SQA] does in NPs. If so, one might say that *push away*

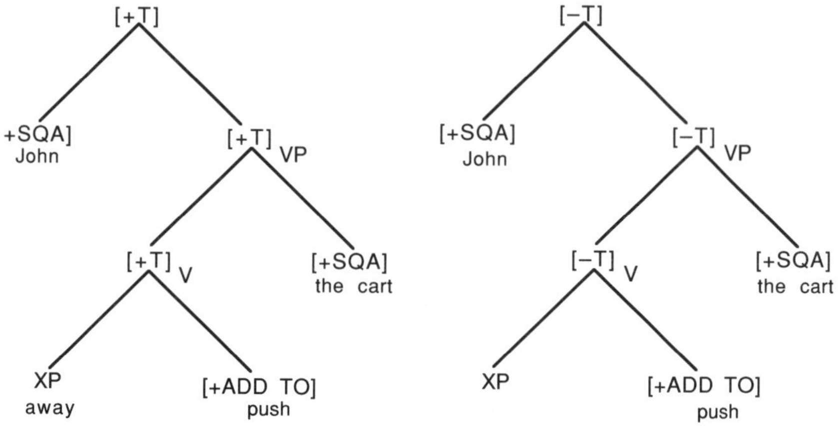

Figure 4 'Push'-verbs can be shown to be apparent counterexamples to the Plus-principle, if one assumes that both *push away* and *push* are complex verbs, the former terminative and the latter durative

is a terminative verb complex, whereas *push* is a durative verb complex: [−T]=[ø + [+ADD TO]]. A more complete analysis of constructions like (100) will be given in chapter 14. It will be shown not only that (100) and (101) are apparent rather than real counterexamples to the Plus-principle, but also that a choice between apparent or real is due to the crude nature of ±-features. The semantic analysis of [+SQA]-NPs in Part II and of [+ADD TO]-verbs in Part III will reveal that the sentences like (100) and (101) are useful for the present aspectual theory: they contribute to a better understanding of the semantics of the internal Θ-role as they require that more systematic attention be paid to the role of the XP in Figure 4 in establishing verbhood.

At this point it has become possible to add the fifth argument for aspectual asymmetry. It takes advantage of the well-known fact that in certain languages resultatives occur only as a form of modification of the second argument NP. Consider the following Dutch sentences:

(103) Mirjam wreef mijn voeten warm
lit.: Mirjam rubbed my feet warm

(104) Mirjam wreef mijn voeten
lit.: Mirjam rubbed my feet

(105) #Urenlang wreef Mirjam mijn voeten warm
lit: #For hours Mirjam rubbed my feet warm

In (103), the predicate adjunct *warm* may modify *Mirjam*. In that case, the adjunct constitutes a secondary predication modifying the main predication:

Mirjam rubbed my feet and doing that she was warm. There is another interpretation saying that Mirjam rubbed my feet while they were warm. On both interpretations (103) is durative, just like (104): Mirjam could have rubbed my feet for hours. However, there is also a resultative interpretation – actually the most natural interpretation of (103) if it is written – which is paraphrased as: Mirjam rubbed my feet and as a result my feet became warm. Two facts are important: (a) on this interpretation (103) is terminative, as shown in (105), with *warm* as a resultative; (b) the resultative adjunct does not modify the subject: Mirjam does not necessarily become warm by rubbing my feet. The only NP that can be modified in (103) is the internal argument NP *mijn voeten* (my feet). There is no *a priori* reason why the adjunct should not modify the external (subject) NP in two-place resultative constructions. Yet this is universally not the case, to my knowledge. The adjunct crucially contributes to aspect by secondary predication on the internal argument-NP.

The examples (103)–(105) are interesting because they meet the requirements for plus-values. *Mirjam* and *mijn voeten* (my feet) are [+SQA], and it is not reasonable to say simply that *wrijven* (rub) is [–ADD TO]. Yet (104) is durative. So, here again is an apparent counterexample to Figure 3, for two reasons: (a) in (104) there are only plus-features and still the result is [–T]; and (b), (103) would be a case in which [–T] would change into [+T]. Again Figure 4 suggests a way out: *wrijven* (rub) may be considered an 'incomplete' verb whose inherent [+ADD TO] takes an empty particle. In other words, *warm wrijven* (to rub warm) is a complex [+T]-verb. In chapter 14, these cases will be discussed in much more detail. It will be shown that they are not real counterexamples at all.

Figure 4, as a natural extension of Figure 3, seems to apply to overt three-place predicates as well, as shown by sentences like (63) *Den Uyl gave a badge to a congress-goer*, discussed in some detail in Verkuyl (1976). Here *give* is an [+ADD TO]-verb taking its direct object to form a [+T]-constituent *to give a badge*, which takes the indirect object NP *a congress-goer* to form a [+T]-construction again, *to give a badge to a congress-goer*, etc. In this connection, it is revealing that *the cart* in Figure 4 behaves like an indirect object. Verbs like *push* and *stroke* allow for prepositions typical of indirect object constructions, as will be shown in chapter 14.1.

1.5 Conclusion

Given the above strategy on the basis of Figure 3, the main tasks of the present study can be described as follows:

a precise account of what [+SQA] stands for semantically: Part II;
a precise account of what [+ADD TO] stands for semantically: Part III;
a precise account of the interaction between the atemporal information expressed by [+SQA]-NPs and the temporal information expressed by [+ADD TO]-verbs: chapter 13.

The compositional outlook on aspect construal in terms of these three tasks runs counter to approaches to aspect based on aspectual classes. Therefore, a sort of overview of the literature from the point of view of how useful it might be to discern aspectual classes, is called for in this introductory part. It serves two purposes: (a) to extend the scope of the subject matter and the depth of theory formation by discussing relevant literature; (b) to underscore the importance of a compositional approach by showing how approaches based on Vendler's aspectual classes all show a systematic fault by not taking seriously the need to look at aspect construal as a structural process.

2 *Aspectual classes and aspectual composition*

2.0 Introduction

Aspectual classes appear to play an important role in the linguistic and philosophical literature these days, judging from the many references to Vendler's 'Verbs and Times'. In the literature on aspect, it is hard to find a contribution that does not refer to this philosophical essay.

What did Vendler actually propose? The question is of some importance because it is a rather striking feature of his analysis that he kept the quadripartition at the lexical level. He used the term 'term' to denote verbs, even though he seemed to be aware of the fact that his categories are complex in the sense that, for example, the direct object appears to co-determine whether or not a transitive verb belongs to one of the four categories. His inclination to stay at the lexical level enforces the idea that what he really did was to propose ontological categories: if knowledge of the world and knowledge of a language tie up intimately at some place, they do that at the lexical level and not so much at the structural level (Putnam 1978; Dowty 1979; Partee 1980).

Vendler's classification, however, turned out to relate to linguistic work on aspect. Some of his criteria were well known in the literature on the imperfective and perfective aspect in Slavic languages. As said earlier, the implication that each of his lexical classes can be used in the theory of aspectuality actually constitutes a setback. Yet, Vendler-classes are highly popular: many semanticists use the quadripartition as part of their aspectual theory. In my view, these two things cannot be married as they are incompatible: if aspect formation is a process at a structural level it is hard to see how a lexical division can be maintained. Closer analysis of recent contributions to aspectual theory reveals (a) that people say explicitly that they like Vendler's proposal, and (b) that they do not use his classes if they express linguistically relevant generalizations. My examination of Vendler's proposal will lead to the conclusion that he mixed up some of his criteria: he did not distinguish well between criteria based on (some sort of) agentivity and criteria based on purely temporal properties of situations such as boundedness, uniqueness, etc. Thus, it follows that Vendler's quadripartition has nothing to say about aspect construal. To avoid misunderstanding, even though my discussion of Vendler's paper is critical, it does not take away much from my long-standing admiration for this essay.

In section 2.1–2.4, Vendler's proposal will be analysed in detail. It will be shown that it is based on a cross-classification involving two parameters. In section 2.5–2.9, some proposals based on Vendler and Kenny will be examined with respect to their claim that they use aspectual classes explanatorily. They do not, as I shall point out. None of the authors discussed use 'their Vendler-classes', because when it comes to aspectually relevant generalizations, classes are simply grouped together. The analysis of their proposals makes it possible to focus more closely on the real parameters involved. These parameters are discussed in section 2.10. In section 2.11, I will briefly discuss a temporal ontology using Vendler classes and containing operators relating them.[24]

2.1 Vendler's time schemata

Vendler used the following 'time schemata' to characterize his verb classes:[25]

(106) STATE: *A loved somebody from t_1 to t_2* means that at *any* instant between t_1 and t_2 A loved that person.
ACTIVITY: *A was running at time t* means that time instant t is on *a* time stretch throughout which A was running.
ACCOMPLISHMENT: *A was drawing a circle at t* means that t is on *the* time stretch in which A drew that circle.
ACHIEVEMENT: *A won a race between t_1 and t_2* means that *the* time instant at which A won the race is between t_1 and t_2.

This is Vendler's own wording. I have underlined the terms *instant* and *stretch* to mark one of the two crucial parameters involved, the other being the one italicized by Vendler himself, viz. the (in)definiteness of the temporal unit involved, expressed by *any*, *a* and *the* in (106).

With Galton (1984) and Hoeksema (1984), I share the opinion that Vendler's division must be analysed as a partition in which the four classes are intended to be on an equal footing. Many authors ignore this feature of Vendler's division. Essentially, (106) induces a matrix: States and Processes share the property of pertaining to non-unique, indefinite temporal entities; States and Achievements pertain to instants, whereas Activities and Accomplishments are conceived of as *processes going on* at time stretches; and finally

Table 1 *The four 'Vendler-classes' can be derived from two underlying parameters, here taken as features* [± *Process*] *and* [± *Definite*]

	–Process	**+Process**
–Definite	State	Activity
+Definite	Achievement	Accomplishment

Achievements and Accomplishments involve unique, definite temporal units.[26] This is captured in Table 1. Anticipating the discussion of the criteria pertaining to the opposition Stretch vs. Instant below, I have italicized the phrase *processes going on* because it is crucial to the interpretation of the opposition Stretch vs. Instant: processes going on in time require there to be stretches to 'go on in'. In view of this, the division based upon (106) will be constructed as Table 1.

Vendler's criteria pertaining to the vertical division in Table 1 will be called the Continuous Tense Criteria (CTC); the horizontal division will be examined under the heading of Definiteness Criteria (DC). In the next two sections, these criteria will be investigated.

2.2 Continuous Tense Criteria

These criteria involve the opposition between continuous and non-continuous tense. The most important one is *ProgF*: Accomplishment verbs and Activity verbs can have a Progressive Form, whereas State verbs and Achievement verbs cannot have it. This is illustrated by the following data, where the judgments are Vendler's:

(107) a. *I am knowing, she is loving him, he is possessing the house, he is ruling the country (States)
b. He was running, she is swimming, they are pushing the cart (Activities)
c. She is running a mile, he is drawing a circle, he was eating a sandwich (Accomplishments)
d. *She was recognizing him, he was reaching the top, she was winning the race (Achievements)

The sentences in (107a) and (107d) are starred to indicate that they are meant to exclude the Progressive Form. ProgF seems to be based on the parameter [αProcess] in Table 1, which in its plus-value [+Process] pertains to processes going on in time. As Vendler put it: 'running, writing and the like are processes going on in time, that is, roughly, that they consist of successive phases following one another in time' (p. 99).

ProgF has not been accepted as a solid criterion by a great many authors, who noted that sentences such as (108) and (109) are acceptable (e.g. Leech 1971: 1–27; Comrie 1976: 37f.; Vlach 1981: 279ff.; Mourelatos 1978: 417):

(108) I am living in Amherst
(109) I am assuming that you will come tonight
(110) The dead man is hanging there to deter the population
(111) Mr Smith is standing by the Nile
(112) You are looking well
(113) He is being ill

(114) She is winning this game
(115) He is dying
(116) She was reaching the top
(117) Look at the screen, the Challenger is exploding now
(118) He is discovering now that he is a homosexual
(119) Manufacturers were beginning to find it difficult to meet the dates

Putting aside the observational inadequacy of ProgF, however, one can easily see that it does not do what it is assumed to do. This becomes clear from the choice of examples like (107a)–(107d), which shows that ProgF is factually based on another criterion, namely the opposition between expressing or not some specific sort of agentivity which is absent in (107a) and (107d), showing up in (107b) and (107c) though. But examples like (120)–(124) are non-agentive; (122) and (124) cannot even be taken as quasi-agentive:

(120) The weather is developing a strange pattern
(121) Colgate is starting to score some coups of its own
(122) Imports are increasing in price as a reflection of the weakening dollar
(123) Two years ago these operations were not making any money
(124) We are at a point here where small things are mattering

The problem appears to be that ProgF is used to cover two quite different semantic factors. It is said to pertain to successive phasal progress in time, but it is also tied up with the concept of agentivity. Thus, it is strongly suggested that these two factors are identical, which they are not; or that they are closely related, which they are not either. In Table 2, it is shown (a) that the concept of agentivity is not essentially tied up with the use of the Progressive Form, and (b) that the use of the Progressive Form is not essentially tied up with the crite-

Table 2 *The use of the Progressive Form is independent of the question of whether a verb expresses Agentivity or Progress in time*

	Agentive	*Process*
He is running	+	+
He is ignoring me	+	–
Prices are increasing	–	+
Small things are mattering	–	–

rion of Progress in time, though it is more closely related to temporality. Emmon Bach (pers. comm.) pointed out that in stories the Progressive Form can pertain to States in such a way that the objects which are in a given state are temporarily experienced by the narrator (Galton 1984; Dowty 1979). Thus, a sentence like *The village was lying in the valley* seems to report a state of a village as seen by the narrator who is telling the story as if he just had entered the valley. The use of the Progressive Form tends to actualize its ephemeral nature: the state is reported from the point of view of the narrator. It would be natural to say that the lying-state of the village is presented here as temporarily present.

Let us now have a look at the negative side of ProgF: States and Achievements. Undoubtedly, the important role of agentivity in the analysis of temporal phenomena in the work of both Vendler and Kenny (1963) is due to Ryle (1949), who also led them back to Aristotle. In this perspective, it is clear why Vendler put States and Achievements in one category: to distinguish Achievements from Accomplishments, he argued that the former have State-like properties. However, do States and Achievements form a natural class?

It can be observed that **She is loving him* in (107a) is rejected on different grounds from **She was recognizing him* in (107d). In the latter case one could say, following Vendler's description of Achievements for the moment, that there is some temporal unit but there is no room within the bounds of a point, because there are no bounds: points are atomic. In the case of States, some sort of universal quantification over a certain time stretch is assumed. Galton makes the same point from a slightly different angle by pointing out that Vendler's

> state-verbs lack continuous tenses because their meaning is already necessarily continuous in nature, so a continuous tense would be superfluous; while achievement-verbs lack continuous tenses because their meanings, involving as they do the idea of punctuality, are incompatible with continuity. (1984: 71)

Vendler introduces other Continuous Tense Criteria to strengthen his case, but as formulated most of these turn out to be tests for agentivity. A clear example is the so-called *do*-criterion applied to the difference between *Do you know that she is ill?* (answer: *Yes, I do*), and *Do you run?* where *Yes, I do* expresses an intention. Clearly, this criterion cannot be used in non-animate cases like (120)–(124). Yet, the *do*-criterion has an important place in Vendler's exposition. Dowty (1979) does not have it.[27]

Connected with the use of *do*, there is a criterion that I shall call *AgMod*, as it boils down to Agentive modification by adverbials, as in (125).

(125)	a.	*John deliberately knew the answer	(State)
	b.	John deliberately pushed the cart	(Activity)
	c.	John deliberately painted a circle	(Accomplishment)
	d.	*John deliberately found a penny	(Achievement)

This seems to work quite well, as in the case of adverbials like *attentively*, *studiously*, *carefully*, etc., but now consider (126)–(129):

(126) The sun had (*deliberately) evaporated four gallons
(127) The lightbeam (*deliberately) passed the house
(128) The mummy was (*deliberately) dried out by the drought
(129) The washer (*deliberately) ejected these dishes

Even though *deliberately* is incompatible with the sentences in (126)–(129) , I think Vendler would have to put *evaporate*, *pass*, *dry out* and *eject* in the category of Accomplishments. Dowty (1979) would have no problem either in accepting these verbs as non-agentive Accomplishments. Again it seems as if one of the CTC, AgMod, has to do with voluntary agency rather than with continuous tense. This is exactly the reason why Mourelatos (1978) used the term 'Developments' in order to comprise both (agentive) Accomplishments and non-agentive cases.

The same objection applies to verbs like *stop* and *start* which are said by Vendler (but not by Dowty) to take only Activities and Accomplishments as shown in (130):

(130) a. ??She stopped/started knowing the answer
b. She stopped/started running
c. She stopped/started drawing a circle
d. ??She stopped/started finding her sister

Again one could say that some sort of (voluntary) agency seems to be involved in (130b) and (130c) rather than a process taking time: it is rather odd to say

The mummy stopped drying out, even though *dry out* is not a State or an Achievement term. Consider also (131)–(134):

(131) Stop being a fool, being naughty, being a workalcoholic
(132) Stop being ill, being eight feet long, being loved
(133) He is being a fool, naughty, a work-alcoholic
(134) He is being ill, eight feet long, loved

where both (131) and (132) without the verb *stop* pertain to states of affairs or habits or dispositions. *Stop being ill* is somewhat strange given the current insights into the causes of illness: one does not have control over illness. The meaning of *love* seems to express that the one who loves as well as the one being loved have no agentive control: it seems to happen, just like recognizing some object.

Strictly speaking, *stop/start* cannot be a criterion, because there is no Progressive Form in the sentences of (130). This is no hair-splitting. If one does not allow the *-ing*-forms in (130a) and (130d), one should be able to explain why phrases like *Knowing that he was ill...*, *Finding her sister...*, are perfectly acceptable.

Summarizing, one can say that Vendler seems to be guided by at least one of the following principles, where CTC stands for ProgF, for *do*, for AgMod, and for *stop/start*:

(135) If a verb is positive with respect to CTC, then it belongs to the set of Activity verbs or Accomplishment verbs.
(136) If a verb belongs to the set of Activity or Accomplishment verbs, then it is positive with respect to CTC.

Of course, Vendler is only committed to (135), as the antecedent of (135) refers to linguistic criteria. But it would be nice for him if both (135) and (136) held. This is not the case, in two directions. Firstly, (135) does not hold, which becomes clear as soon as we take its contraposition: many State verbs and Achievement verbs allow for the Progressive Form, as shown by (109) and (99c). Even if a verb is negative with respect to CTC, it can be a (non-agentive) Accomplishment verb, as shown in, for example, (120).

Secondly, it has become clear that (136) does not hold either. This too can be shown by contraposition: there are verbs thrown out by CTC which are Activities or Accomplishment by any other account, because they take time, as shown by (120)–(124) and by (126)–(129).

Vendler's criterion Progressive Form turns out to be actually focussed on some unclear concept of agentivity. Vendler seems to follow here the linguistic tradition which coined the term 'Aktionsarten' for the phenomena at issue: the ways actions are conceived of. This term itself suggest that agentivity plays an important role. However, important for what? Human actions are extremely important for philosophers. But are they linguistically important as well? And if they are, do they concern aspect? The answer should be negative, I think. It is a rather bad but understandable habit of linguists to choose mainly sentences pertaining to animate beings such as John and Mary, or Jack and Jill, at the expense of non-animacy. However, the concept of agentivity may overlap greatly with the concept of processes going on in time, because most of the time we speak about human actions. But this does not mean at all that these concepts can be equated.

2.3 Definiteness Criteria

Returning now to Table 2, I would like to review Vendler's arguments for a horizontal division on the basis of the Definiteness features. The characterizations in (106) should set Accomplishments and Achievements apart from Activities and States, but Vendler restricted himself mainly to the opposition between Accomplishments and Activities. The few words he spent on the difference between Achievements and States complicate the picture considerably, as will be pointed out shortly.

Vendler characterized the differences between Activities and Accomplishments by two different sorts of linguistic criteria: (A) those based on co-occurrence, which I shall call *FIT*-criteria; (B) those based on entailment.

A. FIT-criteria.

The first sort of criteria concern certain restrictions on co-occurrence of verbs with certain adverbials or verbs. I shall refer to these criteria with the letters **F** for *for*-adverbials, **I** for *in*-adverbials and **T** for the verb *take*, as exemplified by the following sentences:

(137)	He ran for half an hour	**F**
(138)	#He ran a mile for half an hour	
(139)	?He ran in half an hour	**I**
(140)	He ran a mile in half an hour	
(141)	?It took him half an hour to run	**T**
(142)	It took him half an hour to draw the circle	

The peculiar feature of sentences like (138) is not only that a single-event reading is blocked, but that in many cases an interpretation is invoked in which repetition of the event or a peculiar sort of stretching of the event, in this case 'He ran a mile', is forced upon us. As said before, one of the basic problems of aspectual theory is how to explain the blocking of the singular event reading and the tendency to assign a repetitive reading.[28]

The **F**-criterion is the most well-known litmus-test in the study of aspectuality. It has had a long history in the literature. It also has a reasonably clear intuitive interpretation: the duration expressed by the adverbial is incompatible with the concept of a unique definite event that is discernible by its bounds. An agentless variant of **F** not discussed by Vendler – it was proposed in Verkuyl (1972) – is what I call the Conjunction-criterion **C**:

(143) The VAX printed a paper on Saturday and on Sunday
(144) The VAX ran on Saturday and on Sunday
(145) The postman delivered a parcel on Saturday and on Sunday

In (143) one can be sure that there were two printings, one on Saturday, the other one on Sunday. In (144), the VAX may have been running twice having stopped working at night, but it may also have been working constantly throughout the weekend. *The postman delivered a parcel* in (145) is an example of what Vendler would call an Achievement: as in (143), there were two deliveries.[29] Vendler's Accomplishments and Achievements form a natural class with respect to **C**.

The **I**-criterion seems to have the same range as **F**, though again **I** as presented by Vendler is tied up to the concept of agentivity: tasks are carried out by some agent in x many time units. Thus,Vendler says that *He did it in twenty seconds* is the appropriate answer to *How long did it take to draw the circle?* But it is quite possible to apply **I** to non-agentive cases. Many linguists consider **I** to be equivalent to **F**. I doubt it. Note, for example, that (139) can have a meaning: 'It took him (less than) half an hour before he started to run.' The same interpretation can be given to (141).

The **T**-criterion is quite dubious. Its form, *It took X y time to ...*, requires that the value of X be a term expressing some sort of agency. At least that is how **T** works: it excludes Achievements, as Vendler says explicitly on page 10. It is therefore important to see that it is **T** that seems to have prevented Vendler from staying in the right aspectual track. If he had only used **F** and **I**, and not **T**, he would have been forced to recognize that both Achievements and Accomplishments meet **F** and **I**, as shown by comparing the Accomplishments in (138) and (140), with the Achievements in (146) and (147). Now he ignores this relation, thus leaving an important part of aspectual theory out of his scope.

(146) #She won the race for half an hour
#The bomb exploded for half an hour
#He reached the top for half an hour

(147) She won the race in half an hour
The bomb exploded in half an hour
He reached the top in half an hour

Dowty (1979: 58) also accepts (147) as well formed. So, again Vendler seems to have mixed up criteria pertaining to agentivity with criteria pertaining to the properties of temporal entities, such as the possibility of discerning intervals as temporal units that can be counted. But more importantly, Vendler did not acknowledge that Accomplishments and Achievements form a natural class indeed, as they are supposed to be by the Definiteness-parameter in (106).

Turning now to the difference between States and Achievements, one can observe that Vendler introduced a new opposition. He says:

> verbs like *knowing* and *recognizing* do not indicate processes going on in time, yet they may be predicated of a subject for a given time with truth or falsity. Now some of these verbs can be predicated only for single moments of time (strictly speaking), while others can be predicated for shorter or longer periods of time. One reaches the hilltop, wins the race, spots or recognizes something, and so on at a definite moment. On the other hand, one can know or believe something, love or dominate somebody, for a short or long period. (p. 102)

This opposition apparently pertains to a difference between a moment (having a minimal length) and a (convex) set of moments, having length. It does not coincide with the opposition between [+Process] and [–Process] underlying the vertical division in Table 1, because this concerns (non–)continuous tense. What (148) seems to add to Table 1 is given in Table 3. The first two columns in Table 3 give the same information as expressed by Table 1. They have 'an air of completeness': all four classes are distinguished from one another with

Table 3 *Vendler used in fact a third parameter,* [±*Momentary*], *which blurs the clear picture of Table 1*

	Process	**Definite**	**Momentary**
States	–	–	–
Activities	+	–	–
Accomplishments	+	+	–
Achievements	–	+	+

the help of just two parameters. Yet Vendler wants to distinguish States from Achievements by a redundant opposition based on length. Note that [+Process] implies [–Momentary].

Clearly, the redundancy of the Momentary-parameter shows up in an overlap with the Definite-parameter, as can be seen by considering the criterion used to defend [–Momentary] for States given by Vendler:

(148) For how long did you love her? For three years

(149) How long did you believe in the stork? Till I was seven

These are exactly the criteria separating Activities from Accomplishments: they are variants of **F**. Vendler misleadingly suggests that all verbs expressing [–Momentary] meet (148) and (149), but this is not so, because Accomplishments fail the test: #*For how long did you draw the circle?* is not well formed in the single-event reading on Vendler's own account. Thus, the (148) and (149) should be headed under [–Definite].

Table 3 explains why some authors discussing Vendler's partition adopted more or less these three parameters, as I shall point out below.

B. *Entailment-criteria*

Vendler used some important criteria based on entailment relations. He seems to return here to the well-known Aristotelian division discussed in Book IX of *Metaphysics* between verbs expressing incomplete movement (process, energeia) and completed movement (actuality, kinesis).[30] Vendler says:

(150) If it is true that someone is running or pushing a cart now, then even if he stops in the next moment it will be still true that he did run or did push a cart. On the other hand, even if it is true that someone is drawing a circle or is running a mile now, if he stops in the next moment it may not be true that he did draw a circle or did run a mile. In other words, if someone stops running a mile, he did not run a mile; if one stops drawing a circle, he did not draw a circle. But the man who stops running did run and he who stops pushing the cart did push it. (p. 100)

Dowty (1979: 57) noticed that if one replaced the verb *stop* by an appropriate tense, Vendler could be said to have given in (150) two criteria at once, given in Dowty's formulation as (151) and (152).

(151) *Homogeneity*
If V is an activity verb, then *x V-ed for y time* entails that at any time *x V-ed* was true. If V is an accomplishment verb, then *x V-ed for y*

time does not entail that *x V-ed* was true during any time within y at all.

(152) *Imperfective*
If V is an activity verb, then *x is* (*now*) *V-ing* entails that *x has V-ed*.
If V is an accomplishment verb, then *x is* (*now*) *V-ing* entails *x has not* (*yet*) *V-ed*.

The intent of both criteria is clear: if you 'get into' the interval during which an activity takes place, *Homogeneity*, as I will call it, says that you can be sure to find the same sort of action at any part of the interval. Criterion (152) has also been proposed by Kenny (1963) to separate Activities from what he calls Performances, roughly the union of Accomplishments and Achievements. I refer to it as *Imperfective*, because it has played an important role in the discussion of the so-called Imperfective Paradox: if you are drawing a circle, you have not drawn a circle, whereas if you are walking now, you have walked.

As to (151), it seems to me that it correctly renders what Vendler tries to express in the second part of (150). Yet (151) must be rephrased because one cannot base entailment on sentences like #*He drew a circle for an hour*. This sentence is not well formed in the single-event reading and it is this reading that is relevant to (150). But apart from that, what about sentences like (153)–(155)?

(153) For hours Judith ate sandwiches
(154) For some time she browsed in that book
(155) She stopped waltzing

By all criteria, *to eat sandwiches* in (153) must be taken as an Activity term (one can do it for hours, one cannot do it in an hour, one can stop it, etc.). But it is clear that at the first sandwich, (151) does not apply at all. In order for someone to browse through a book in (154) she must at least have turned more than one page. And Dowty's (155) raises a problem if she stopped after one or two steps. Dowty (1979: 171) is aware of this problem (one has to do at least three steps before one can waltz), but he does not return to (151) in order to repair it.

As to *Imperfective*, Parsons (1985) follows Bach (1981) by raising some doubts, though he says that the intuition behind it seems to be correct. His point is that if one says *She is knitting a sweater*, she might have knitted another sweater than the one she is knitting, but the criterion is said to hold good if one can exclude other sweaters. I do not think his point is correct because in the case of an *accusativus effectivus* quantification should be thought of at the type level rather than at the token level, as was pointed out in Verkuyl (1972: 85–97). There is a more severe problem with (152), however, which will be discussed in chapter 9.3 and solved in chapter 13.8: there are counterexamples to the Imperfective Paradox. For example, it does not work for *He was drawing some circles.*

Though these sorts of objections are certainly relevant, I would like to restrict myself here to observing that (150) and its close approximations, (151) and (152), have been formulated with the help of active sentences. At least, both criteria must be rephrased to accommodate sentences like (156)–(158):

(156) a. #John got dressed for hours
b. #The wall was pulled down for hours
c. #Mookie got hit for half an hour
d. #John was released the whole afternoon

(157) a. John got dressed in a minute
b. The wall was pulled down in five minutes
c. Mookie got hit in ten minutes
d. John was released in two hours

(158) a. John got dressed on Monday and on Tuesday
b. The wall was pulled down on Monday and on Tuesday
c. Mookie got hit on Monday and on Tuesday
d. John was released on Monday and on Tuesday

That is, all these sentences can be said to contain Accomplishment or Achievement terms according to the criteria **FIC**, two of which are proposed, both by Vendler and Dowty. However, one cannot apply *Homogeneity* and *Imperfective* to (156)–(158). So again, it seems to be the case that a specific linguistic criterion is associated with an unclear amalgamation of different factors such as agentivity and more purely temporal aspects. Of course, one could say that (156)–(158) can be 'transformed' in such a way that their active counterpart can be captured by (151), but that is virtually impossible in the (a) and the (c) cases. My conclusion is that neither (151) nor (152) is a reliable criterion, and certainly not in their less clear formulation (150).

Reconsidering the nice quadripartition in Table 1, one would have wished that Vendler had been using formulations that had precisely cut the set of verbs on the basis of two binary oppositions. By adding a new sort of parameter based on length, he created redundancy problems, as shown in Table 3 From the point of view of aspectual analysis, Vendler's use of the criterion **T**, deprived him of the possibility of really contributing to aspectual theory: he did not recognize that his Achievements should take time in order to receive the proper aspect. Again the notion of length seems to play a negative role here: in order to widen the gap with Accomplishments, Vendler deprived Achievements of length by compressing moments into points. In doing so, he mixed up two parameters.

2.4 On the alleged punctual nature of Achievements

To set Achievements apart from the other three classes, Vendler used a criterion which I shall call Present Perfect Now (PPN). Vendler observed that in the case of pure Achievement terms 'the present tense is almost exclusively used as historic present or as indicating immediate future' (1967: 103). Thus, (159) is not used to report an actual finding but rather to predict that he is going to win. Instead one has to use (160) to report the actual winning.

(159) (Now) he wins
(160) (Now) he has won

However nice at first sight, this criterion is not convincing: one broadcast of a game will do to convince oneself that reporters often use the simple present in Achievement situations (catch the ball, hit the ground, score, etc.). In a game, the loser can give up by saying *You win* rather than *You have won*. In the linguistic literature, facts like these are well registered. They take away much of the force of Vendler's contention. But I would like to counter Vendler not on the basis of observational adequacy. So let us agree with him, for the sake of the argument, that the Present Perfect is more appropriate than the present in pairs like (159) and (160). But then the question arises: what about the pairs in (161)–(164)?

(161) ?She hates him up till now
(162) She has hated him up till now
(163) ?She walks already for an hour now
(164) She has already walked for an hour now

These are cases in which the Present Perfect reports an actual hate (State) or walk (Activity) more appropriately than the Simple Present. The phenomenon that the Present Perfect pertains more fittingly to the present situation than the Present itself is not restricted to Vendler's Achievement terms. A possible answer to my objection here is that (161)–(164) contain adverbials that are absent in (159) and (160); but note that (162) and (164) report on an actual state and activity, respectively, both taking place at the moment of speech as in (160).

To my knowledge, it has gone unnoticed that the distinction between Accomplishments and Achievements is completely lexical. This is quite different from the opposition among the other three categories: (165) shows that there are differences between Activities and Accomplishments in which the complement-NP is involved and not only the verb; the same applies to States vs. Accomplishments in (166), and to States vs. Activities in (167).

(165)	**Activities**	**Accomplishments**
	She ate *sandwiches*	She ate *a sandwich*
	She wrote *at the letter*	She wrote *a letter*
	She ate *from* the cheese	She ate *the cheese*
(166)	**States**	**Accomplishments**
	She ate *no sandwiches*	She ate *a sandwich*
	She wrote to *nobody*	She wrote *a letter*
(167)	**States**	**Activities**
	She ate *no sandwiches*	She ate *sandwiches*
	She wrote to *nobody*	She wrote *to her mother*

Such examples cannot be produced with respect to the opposition between Accomplishments and Achievements. This is a severe blow for those who want to defend the distinction on structural grounds: it is really the only opposition that is completely lexical. And this means that the way is open to quite arbitrary judgments concerning the right class.

As an illustration for these objections against the lexical basis for the distinction between Achievements and Accomplishments, I would like to discuss here a counterargument against PPN based on modern technology, because it shows that some intriguing problems of lexical semantics are involved in Vendler's analysis. Compare (168) with (169).

(168) Now John types/has typed the letter p
(169) Now John types/has typed that (business) letter

To type x means that x is made visible by print or on the screen of a word processor, say. I can safely assume that Vendler, applying PPN, would characterize *type the letter p* as an Achievement term, whereas *type that letter* in (169) would be taken as an Accomplishment term, just like *write a letter*. Vendler says:

> When I say that it took me an hour to write a letter (which is an accomplishment), I imply that the writing of the letter went on during that hour. This is not the case with achievements. Even if one says that it took him three hours to reach the summit, one does not mean that the 'reaching' of the summit went on during those hours. (p. 10)

According to this, if one says that it took him five minutes to type the letter p, one does not mean that the 'typing' of the letter went on during those minutes, whereas if one says that it took him five minutes to type that (business) letter, one could very well mean that the 'typing' of the letter went on during those five minutes. Note also that another one of Vendler's criteria applies to (168) and not to (169):

(170) At what time did you type the letter p? At noon sharp
(171) At what time did you type that (business) letter? *At noon sharp

According to Vendler, the difference between (170) and (171) would have to be taken as an indication that *type the letter p* is an Achievement term. Applying PPN, if we give a report about John's actual typing of the p in a split second, we could use the Present Perfect, probably even better than the Simple Present. This does not hold for (169) if John is typing a letter that Sue gave to him to type and mail.

Note again, with an eye on (165)–(167), that the difference between (168) and (169) is not structural, but lexical (letter $\in$ Alphabet vs. letter $\subseteq$ Alphabet). This observation is compatible with the fact that in modern technology the reverse argument is also possible in two respects: (a) the typing of the letter p on the screen of a word processor can take a while due to some *PleaseWait* command so that it takes time before the p has become visible and has been typed out; (b) the typing of a business letter may take just a moment: if it is standard, it can be produced by hitting one single key. If things are going that quickly it would mean that both *type a letter p* and *type a (business) letter* are members of one and the same category and that they manifest themselves as either Achievement terms or Accomplishment terms dependent on something which has nothing to do with language itself. One can easily imagine situations in which writing and typing a letter is a heterogeneous process of assembling all sorts of information stored in a data base. In that case, writing or typing a letter would have a structure like reaching the top of a mountain or winning a race: only at a certain point can the letter be said to be written or produced. But sentences like (170) and (171) can also pertain to old-fashioned typewriting. On Vendler's account each of them would be ambiguous: he would have to put both *type* and *write* in two of his classes.

It is worthwhile (and necessary) to apply the same argument to the well-known example (172).

(172) John drew a circle

John can draw a circle without actually drawing its parts with a pencil. On a sophisticated computer there are keys to touch in order to reach a result. One does not even have to see an incomplete circle on the screen. By hitting the last key in a series of drawing tasks on the keyboard, the circle can be produced at once, which would make it analogous to reaching the top, or winning the race. By introducing logical names one can easily draw a circle by hitting one key only. PPN would certainly apply positively if we have to report about what is happening on the screen in these split seconds. It might be mistaken to restrict the meaning of *draw a circle* in (172) to the way we learn about drawing circles with the help of a pencil or with the help of compasses (which can be turned around very quickly). After all, all sorts of new techniques can be introduced changing the sort of muscular actions involved but leaving intact the concept of drawing, which might turn out to be focussed on the product rather than on the use of arms or pencils to bring the drawing about. I am afraid that Vendler's use of *draw a circle* concerns the 1950s stereotype of the verb *draw* rather than its real range of possibilities. We do not assign new meanings to words like *type*, *draw*, *write*, etc. if we use them in connection with new technological techniques, unless there is too much tension between the old technique and the new one, as in the case of *write* and *type*(*writing*), some decades ago. We do not use *draw a circle* figuratively if John produced a circle on the screen with the help of a click on the Apple mouse. The meaning of verbs like *draw*, *write*, etc. is such that new techniques can be captured by them, indicating that it was accidental up till now that *draw a circle* pertains only to events taking more than one moment. The length of the event does not seem to be a linguistic matter.

To summarize, the validity of Vendler's criterion, dubbed Present Perfect Now, is damaged by observational problems. There are a great many cases where the Simple Present can be used to report actual winnings and findings. But it also suffers more serious setbacks due to the fact that from the point of view of language the length of (a time unit involved in) an event does not qualify as a meaning element that distinguishes certain verbs from others. Thus there is no reason to distinguish *to walk a mile* from *to walk a yard* linguistically on the grounds that a mile consists of feet, whereas a foot does not consist of miles, or on the grounds that one can walk a foot in a split moment. One need not introduce giants (who can walk a mile in a second) and dwarfs (who I am told need time to walk a foot) to compress miles to points and extend feet to long distances. The typewriting example shows that it is not necessary to step into the world of fiction to make this point. In other words, the opposition between a point and an interval as far as length of temporal units is concerned is not identical to the opposition between an instant and a stretch from the point of view of one unit taking time as against a set of units taking time.

Given these considerations, there appear to be no grounds for distinguishing Achievement terms from Accomplishment terms. I would also like to conclude that Vendler's quadripartition is perhaps relevant for philosophical (ontological) purposes, but not for the study of structural meaning involved in aspectual composition.[31]

2.5 Mourelatos' merger of Vendler and Kenny

In this and the following section, attention will be paid to a philosophical tradition that has also made its way into aspectual theory: namely, the proposals based on Kenny's, or rather Aristotle's, classification of temporal types. Mourelatos (1978) speaks about the 'Vendler–Kenny scheme of verb-types', suggesting that Vendler's and Kenny's classifications are closely related. However, Vendler's partition is based on a quadripartition, whereas the Kenny-scheme is a partial ordering. The different ways in which the classifications are constructed suggest that they are not as much related as suggested. For example, it seems to be the Aristotle–Kenny line rather than the Vendler line which brought about the currently quite popular tripartition of Eventualities (Bach's term) into States, Processes and Events.[32] Kenny (1963) made a split between verbs having non-continuous tense (States) and verbs having continuous tense (Activities and Performances). In this sense, Kenny is much more faithful than Vendler to Aristotle's division in *Metaphysics* IX 1048, 18–35, who distinguishes Actualities (States) from Incomplete and Complete Movements (ed. Ross).[33]

Mourelatos (1978) did three things: (a) he merged Vendler and Kenny into one division of situational types; (b) he extended the classifications such that they apply both to agentive and non-agentive cases; and (c) he coined useful terms for situational types corresponding with sentences. His proposal is captured by Figure 5. The merger of Vendler and Kenny is more Kennyan than Vendlerian: the Kenny tree constituting the upper two layers in Figure 5 is simply extended with Accomplishments and Achievements as subclasses of the performances. However, Mourelatos rightly undid Vendler's analysis from its agentive bias by distinguishing supersets in which Vendler's non-States would fit as proper subsets. And finally, he proposed that the main partition in Figure 5 involve States, Processes and Events, suggesting that the distinction between Developments and Punctual Occurrences is at least a secondary division.[34]

It is interesting that Mourelatos focussed on the Progress-parameter: non-States occur, they take time in a dynamic way. As far as Vendler's Definiteness-parameter is concerned, Mourelatos interprets this in terms of an opposition [±Count], where [+Count] is similar to Vendler's [+Definite], but in which [–Count] applies only to [+Process]. Mourelatos seems to concentrate

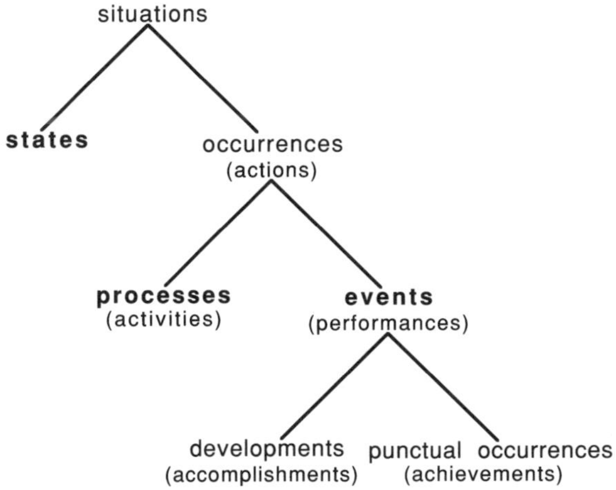

Figure 5 Mourelatos' merge of Vendler and Kenny is more Kennyan than Vendlerian, because three of Vendler's categories are now taken together in one category: occurrences

on the quantification over temporal entities: events can be counted, processes cannot. Mourelatos' analysis can be compared with Vendler's by considering Tables 3 and 4. The striking difference is of course the value assigned to Achievements in the leftmost column of the two tables. It should be observed, though, that Mourelatos has not given any linguistic argument for the distinction between the four classes he distinguishes.

2.6 Dowty's reductionist approach

Dowty reproduced Vendler's criteria in a more linguistic fashion, presenting them in a systematic and neat way. Though he is aware of many observational problems for the criteria proposed by Vendler, Dowty accepts them as basi-

Table 4 *Mourelatos' classification can also be reduced to a matrix. It is based on three-valued parameters*

	Occur (process)	**Count** (definite)	**Punctual** (momentary)
States	–	ø	ø
Activities	+	–	ø
Accomplishments	+	+	–
Achievements	+	+	+

cally sound, trying to incorporate the aspectual classes, as he called the Vendler-classes, in his grammar. He proposed a 'reductionist analysis': Activity verbs, Accomplishment verbs and Achievement verbs are constructed out of one or more Stative predicates and operators like BECOME and CAUSE. If V_n is an n-place predicate and $a_1, \ldots, a_n$ its argument(s), the four classes are roughly represented as:

States	$V_n(a_1, \ldots, a_n)$
Activities	$\text{DO}\,(a_1, V_n(a_1, \ldots, a_n))$
Accomplishments	$\text{DO}(a_1,V_n(a_1, \ldots, a_n))$ CAUSE BECOME $(V_n(a_1, \ldots, a_n))$
Achievements	$\text{BECOME}(V_n(a_1, \ldots, a_n))$

'Roughly', I say, because Dowty subdivides each category, but these subdivisions are not important for the present discussion (Dowty 1979: 123ff.). Note that the pattern for States returns in each of the three other classes. Thus, Activity is a relation between an argument and a State upon which the DO-operator has a certain semantic effect. In this way, the interpretation of the Vendler-classes is made dependent on the model-theoretic interpretation of BECOME, CAUSE and DO as connected with States.

The resulting classification is represented in Table 5 which is constructed from three of the 'five partially cross-classifying semantic distinctions' underlying Dowty's final scheme that is seen by him as a revision of Vendler's classification (Dowty 1979: 184).[35] Let us consider in more detail the interrelationships between the classes. The basic division seems to be the one between States, which have just one point of evaluation, and non-States, which have two points. This distinction is given its shape by the absence or presence of the operators DO, BECOME and CAUSE. Dowty assigns two points of evaluation to Achievements, changing [–Occur] into [+Occur] (or, [–Process] or [+Process]), just like Mourelatos. Thus, his idea seems to be that processes going on in time are changes, but that the concept of change between two

Table 5 *Dowty's aspectual matrix is also based on a partial ordering*

	Process	**Definite**	**Complex**
States	–	ø	ø
Activities	+	–	ø
Accomplishments	+	+	+
Achievements	+	+	–

points of evaluation cannot be equated with the concept of the length of a stretch between two points.

The second parameter is Definiteness: a change can be indefinite or definite. In Dowty (1979), it is not made clear how a predication of the form DO (a_1, $V_n(a_1, \ldots, a_n)$) is to be interpreted, in spite of the meaning postulate for Activity verbs on page 362, which adds to the confusion, because there an agent undergoes a Q(x) to ¬Q(x) transition, where Q is some location in a three-dimensional space. However, in Dowty (1986: 42) it is clear that a proposition of the form DO (a_1, $V_n(a_1, \ldots, a_n)$) is true at an interval only if it is true at most subintervals above a certain minimal size. This does not hold for definite changes. These are characterized by their having a BECOME-operator, which makes the interval of change closed. Dowty's Definiteness-parameter does not deviate crucially from Vendler's and will be discussed in much more detail in chapter 9.2. The third division involves the presence or absence of CAUSE together with BECOME. Accomplishments require that these two operators go together, which accounts for the label [+Complex] to characterize this class, Achievements being Singulary or [–Complex].

It must be acknowledged that Dowty has presented one of the most detailed and precise grammars of the English verbal system thus far. Yet the question must be raised whether the incorporation of the Vendler-classes in his grammar provided it with more explanatory value than it would without them. I think it did not. The places to look for are places in which each of the classes is used to explain certain aspectual phenomena assuming a one-to-one relation between an aspectual class and a certain aspectual phenomenon that asks for an explanation. There are no such places. I shall clarify this point. In aspectual theory, the difference between the (a) and (b) sentences of (173) and (174) must be explained.

(173) a. John slept for an hour

b. ?John slept in an hour

c. $\exists i_1[\text{PAST}(i_1) \wedge \text{an\_hour}'(i_1) \wedge \forall i_2[i_2 \subseteq i_1 \rightarrow \text{AT}(i_2, \text{sleep}'(j))]]$

d. $\exists i_1[\text{PAST}(i_1) \wedge \text{an\_hour}'(i_1) \wedge \exists i_2[i_2 \subseteq i_1 \wedge \text{AT}(i_2, \text{sleep}'(j))] \wedge \forall i_3[[i_3 \subseteq i_2 \wedge \text{AT}(i_3, \text{sleep}'(j))] \rightarrow i_2 = i_3]]$

(174) a. John awakened in an hour

b. #John awakened for an hour

c. $\exists i_1[\text{PAST}(i_1) \wedge \text{an\_hour}'(i_1) \wedge \exists i_2[i_2 \subseteq i_1 \wedge \text{AT}(i_2, [\text{BECOME awake}'(j)]) \wedge \forall i_3[[i_3 \subseteq i_2 \wedge \text{AT}(i_3, [\text{BECOME awake}'(j)])] \rightarrow i_2 = i_3]]]$

d. $\exists i_1[\text{PAST}(i_1) \wedge \text{an\_hour}'(i_1) \wedge \forall i_2[i_2 \subseteq i_1 \rightarrow \text{AT}(i_2, [\text{BECOME awake}'(j)])]]$

Dowty (1979: 332–336) gives a description of sentences like (173a) and (174a): the meaning of *for an hour* represented in (173c) requires that for all intervals i_2 which are part of the set of intervals called an-hour′ it is true that John slept at i_2. *In an hour* in (174c), however, requires that there be an interval i_2 where the predication is satisfied and i_2 is unique. The uniqueness condition $\forall i[[i \subseteq i' \wedge \text{AT}(i,\phi)] \rightarrow i=i']$ requires 'that the verb is true at a *unique* subinterval (though still not necessarily a proper subinterval) of the measured interval' (1979: 335). The same would apply to (175).

(175) Judith ate three sandwiches in an hour

For Dowty, (64) *Judith ate three sandwiches* is an Accomplishment: the eating of three sandwiches occurred at a unique subinterval of i_1, which might be i_1 itself. That (173b) and (174b) are not well formed follows from their representations (173d) and (174d).

According to Dowty, formula (173d) is strange because it assigns to *sleep* a uniqueness condition which it does not require. Formula (174d) says that for all subintervals i_2 of i_1, John became awake, which indeed is a strange interpretation suggesting a repetition. It would mean that if there are five intervals i_2, John would have become awake five times. Dowty (1979: 336) says:

> Thus the semantics given here for *for*-adverbials and *in*-adverbials explain why *for*-adverbials are appropriate for states and activities (i.e. both these classes of predicates are true of most or all subintervals of an interval of the predicate's truth) but not for accomplishments and achievements (since they are 'non-subinterval predicates') and, conversely, why *in*-adverbials are appropriate for accomplishments and achievements (since they can satisfy the 'uniqueness' requirements in the semantics of *in*) but not for activities and states.

This passage clearly shows that in his analysis of the aspectual blocking of the single-event reading *John awakened* in (174c), Dowty appeals to a division between Activities and States, on the one hand, and Accomplishments and Achievements on the other. So again we are in a situation where aspectual phenomena are not explained by Vendler-classes because Accomplishments plus Achievements covers the set of structural phenomena which fall under the label of terminative aspect.[36]

My conclusion is that Dowty did not show that he needs four Vendler-classes for structural purposes.

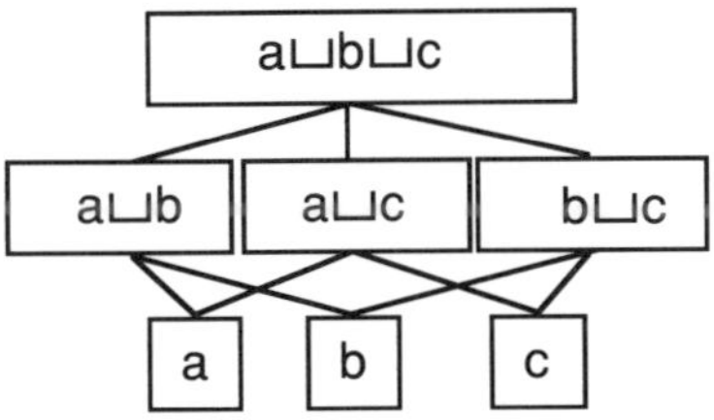

Figure 6 From atomic individuals one may construct i-sums on the basis of the summation operation joining them

2.7 Hoeksema's cross-classification

Hoeksema (1984) can be characterized as an attempt to give a faithful interpretation of Vendler's cross-classification in Table 1. There are some terminological differences: [αDefiniteness] is called [αCount], whereas [αProcess] is called [αDuration]. There are also big differences, such as the application of model-theoretical tools by Hoeksema. He assumes models containing a set W of so-called possibilities (actual and possible events). The summation operation $\sqcup$ is defined on W, giving join-semilattices.[37] For convenience, in Figure 6 we give a simple lattice structure which has the three elements a, b and c. In this structure, so-called i-sums are constructed on the basis of the atomic individuals a, b and c. The supremum or top element in this set is the uniquely specified three-membered i-sum $a \sqcup b \sqcup c$. In models with more than three entities, $a \sqcup b \sqcup c$ would be just one of the three-membered i-sums. The ontological assumptions about lattice structure lead to the belief that quantification over sets can be abolished. The i-sums are all taken as individuals. For example, if a is John and b is Mary, $a \sqcup b$ is the individual John+Mary.

Hoeksema postulates that the set W of possibilities contains instants as well as non-instants, where x is an instant if and only if for all y, if $y \subseteq x$, then $x \subseteq y$, that is, x has no proper parts; and furthermore, that 'every member of W has instantaneous parts' (1984: 215). This amounts to saying that there is no null-element: there are minimal atomic parts in each event. Hoeksema defines four features as in (176), where $X \subseteq W$:

(176) –Count: $\forall x,y \in W((x \in X \& y \in X) \Rightarrow x \sqcup y \in X)$
+Count: $\forall x,y \in W((x \in X \& y \in X) \Rightarrow x \sqcup y \notin X)$
–Duration: $\forall x,y \in W((x \in X \& y \subseteq x) \Rightarrow y \in X)$
+Duration: $\forall x \in W((x \in X \Rightarrow \neg \forall y(y \subseteq x \& x \subseteq y))$

Table 6 *The four Vendler-classes may be derived on the basis of two parameters, but here the features involved are interpreted model-theoretically*

	[–Duration]	[+Duration]
[–Count]	$(x\in X \& y\in X) \Rightarrow x \sqcup y\in X)$ $(x\in X \& y\subseteq x) \Rightarrow y\in X)$ **States**	$(x\in X \& y\in X) \Rightarrow x \sqcup y\in X)$ $x\in X \Rightarrow \neg\forall y(y\subseteq x \& x\subseteq y)$ **Activities**
[+Count]	$(x\in X \& y\in X) \Rightarrow x \sqcup y\notin X)$ $(x\in X \& y\subseteq x) \Rightarrow y\in X)$ **Achievements**	$(x\in X \& y\in X) \Rightarrow x \sqcup y\notin X)$ $x\in X \Rightarrow \neg\forall y(y\subseteq x \& x\subseteq y$ **Accomplishments**

The feature [–Count] is interpreted as the property of being closed under finite union, which is characteristic for monotone increasing structures (see DEF 2.2.4). [+Count] forbids the sum of x and y to be part of the same event of which they are part. The property labelled as [–Duration] is the property of monotone decrease (see DEF 2.2.7); [+Duration] stands for the property of not being an instant. This means that all members of X must have proper parts. These four properties of event types square as shown in Table 6.

The [–Duration] feature for States seems plausible. It provides for monotone decrease, whereas [–Count] adds the so-called property of closure under finite union: if two sets are members of X their union is also a member of X. However, monotone decrease is equivalent to (177):

(177) $x \sqcup y\in X \Rightarrow (x\in X \& y\in X)$

(178) $(x\in X \& y\in X) \Leftrightarrow x \sqcup y\in X$

By the conjunction of (177) and [–Duration], States are required to meet condition (178), which makes them Ideals (Zwarts 1981). Ideals are the monotone-decreasing counterparts of filters. I do not know whether Hoeksema is aware of this result of conjoining [–Count] and [–Duration]. He does not comment on it.

As to Activities, suppose that Activities would have been conditioned such that for all $x\in X$, x would be an instant. In that case, [–Count] would lead to the obviously trivial condition applying only to cases where $x=y$, because that would be the only circumstance under which [–Count] would hold. So, [+Duration] seems to be necessary to prevent just that situation. It seems more proper to condition [–Count] such that it requires that $x\neq y$. In that case, [+Duration] would simply follow from [–Count].[38] As to Accomplishments, the interaction of the features [+Count] and [+Duration] also raises problems. [+Count] allows only for non-monotone structures, but [+Duration], in order for it to be of any use, presupposes monotonicity. I shall demonstrate this point. Suppose $x \in X$ and $y \subseteq x$ and $y \in X$. Then, of course, $x \sqcup y \in X$, because if $y \in X$, $x \sqcup y = x$ and $x \in X$. Suppose now that $x \in X$, $y \subseteq x$ and $y \notin X$. Then there are three possible situations: $|x|>1$ or $|x|=1$ or $|x|=0$. If $|x|>1$, then [+Duration] is empty, because any set having two members meets it; the same applies to $|x|=1$, because $\emptyset \subseteq x$, and $|x|=0$ is excluded by [+Count], because any summation of $\emptyset$ with an element of X is an element of X. Thus, I conclude that [+Duration] is unnecessary, as it operates trivially. The same applies to Achievements. Again, [+Count] requires a non-monotone structure, to the exclusion of any structure of the form $x \sqcup y$ as a member of X, as shown in the previous paragraph. But this means that the antecedent of [–Duration] is always vacuous, making the consequent always (trivially) true: the condition $y \subseteq x$ amounts to saying $x \sqcup y = x$.

One of the virtues of Hoeksema's approach is that he set out to explain certain linguistic regularities in Dutch morphology in terms of his classification. The suffix *-ing* in Dutch differs from the prefix *ge-* aspectually, as shown in (179) and (180).

(179)	*de leving (the living)	State
	de wandeling (the walk)	Activity
	de ontmoeting (the encounter)	Accomplishment
	de ontploffing (the explosion)	Achievement

(180)	*het geblijf (the staying)	State
	het geren (the running)	Activity
	*het gebouw van een huis (the building of a house)	Accomplishment
	*het gewin van de race (the winning of the race)	Achievement

However, as shown by the asterisks, the model-theoretic explanation of this phenomenon has to appeal to sets of classes, that is, to the parameters involved rather than to pairs of features from (176). In the case of *-ing*, the generalization is that its interpretation is a function whose domain is restricted to Accomplishments, Achievements and Activities 'with definite endpoints', a notion not properly defined by Hoeksema. Given the fact that 'with definite endpoints' is incompatible with [–Count], the generalization seems to be that the domain is open to [+Count] structures. In the case of *ge-*, the interpretation function in question is restricted to Activities, that is, to the feature [–Count].

In my view, the empirical data can be accounted for without an appeal to the cross-classification in Table 6. On the contrary, this classification seems to prevent a better understanding of the phenomena at issue, because it suggests that the Vendler-classes are of explanatory value, whereas it turns out to be the case that at best some of the features from which they are constructed contribute to the appropriate generalizations.

2.8 Carlson's extension

Carlson (1981) does not start with classes. Rather, he selects three parameters based on three pretheoretically chosen grammatical criteria and forms six aspectual classes from them, four of which are given a Vendlerian name. The three criteria are given here slightly adapted to circumvent expressions from the game-theoretical framework in which Carlson works.

> Criterion 1: A sentence ϕ is [+point] iff ϕ has a truth value at moments.
>
> Criterion 2: A sentence ϕ is [+extended] iff ϕ has a truth value with respect to extended periods.
>
> Criterion 3: If ϕ is [–continuous], then if ϕ is true in periods P, P′ and P″, and $P' \neq P \neq P''$, $P \cup P' \cup P''$ is a period only if P is a moment and $P' = P''$.

I am not very much interested here in the exact analysis of the six classes, because most of the differences between them are lexical. Moreover, the judgments about the sentences supporting Carlson's classification are quite subtle, not to say untransferable to Dutch, where their counterparts do not hold. So, I will focus on the features as they construct the four Vendler-classes.[39] Carlson would characterize them as in Table 7, which does not really differ much from Mourelatos' and Dowty's schemes. This point will come back shortly, in section 2.11, where I shall also discuss the theoretical importance of Carlson's strategy of taking aspectual classes as derivatives, or at best ontological cate-

Table 7 *Carlson's three parameters yield six aspectual classes, four of which are Vendler's classes. Carlson's other categories, Dynamic (+ + +) and Momentaneous (– – +) are not discussed here, as they play no role in the argumentation*

	Extended	**Continuous**	**Point**
State	–	+	+
Activities	+	+	–
Accomplishments	+	–	–
Achievements	+	–	+

gories that may provide some footing for a linguistic analysis of sentences expressing change in time.

2.9 Ter Meulen's hierarchy

Ter Meulen assigns to all verbs of a language a set of processes: 'primitive, unstructured chunks of the temporal domain' (1983: 179) from which VP-interpretations are constructed, which are intervals and moments. She characterizes the four Vendler-classes at the VP-level by interpreting every VP as a set of subsets of P ($[\![VP]\!] \subset \wp(P)$), where P is the set of processes p partially ordered by a strict precedence relation <. A process p_1 is part of p_2 ($p_1 \leq p_2$) if p_1 is located in the partial order on P within the 'bounds' of p_2: a day is a part of a week; writing the letter *p* is part of writing the word *part*, etc.

Table 8 shows how Ter Meulen conceives of the relationships between the Vendler-classes, where $X \subseteq P$. States are defined as monotone increasing (see DEF 2.2.4). Activities are on a par with structures having the same properties as (181):

(181) $Q_A = \{\{b\}, \{a,b\}, \{a,b,c\}, \{b,c,d\}, \{a,b,c,d\}\}$

This means that they are weaker than filters: (181) is not closed under finite intersection, because $\{b,c\}$ is not an element of Q_A. Again, there is not one argument explaining why or making it plausible that Activities should be weaker than filters. Condition c still allows for (181). Thus, Accomplishments do not meet the requirements for filters (see DEF 2.2.5). Condition d, an existential version of monotone decrease, makes Achievements filters, but also ultrafilters (see DEF 2.2.6). From a classificatory point of view, Ter Meulen offers a highly suspicious quadripartition: the classes are not mutually exclusive. Achievements are Accomplishments, which are Activities, which are States. The classification in Table 8 turns out to be simply modelled after the hierarchy of generalized quantifiers discussed in chapter 4.2, where ultrafilters are filters which are monotone-increasing structures. That a classification has this rather peculiar sort of structure should evoke scepticism which can only be taken away by forceful empirical argumentation. My scepticism is not taken away. I have three sorts of objections to make: firstly, there is hardly any linguistic argumentation for this division; secondly, the idea of a hierarchy is implausible in view of the negation of non-States; and thirdly, the classification does not explain anything.

As to the first objection, there is no linguistic problem that might be solved by Ter Meulen's choice of temporal structure. This enhances the idea that she

Table 8 *Ter Meulen organizes the Vendler-classes into a stacked inclusion-relation: beginning with States, each class is formed by having one more semantic property than its predecessor*

	States
a.	$\forall x \in X \forall y \in P(x \leq y \Rightarrow y \in X)$
	Activities
a.	$\forall x \in X \forall y \in P(x \leq y \Rightarrow y \in X)$
b.	$\forall x, y \in X \exists z \in X(z \leq x \& z \leq y)$
	Accomplishments
a.	$\forall x \in X \forall y \in P(x \leq y \Rightarrow y \in X)$
b.	$\forall x, y \in X \exists z \in X(z \leq x \& z \leq y)$
c.	$\forall x \in X(x = x_1 \cup x_2 \Rightarrow \text{either } x_1 \in X \text{ or } x_2 \in X)$
	Achievements
a.	$\forall x \in X \forall y \in P(x \leq y \Rightarrow y \in X)$
b.	$\forall x, y \in X \exists z \in X(z \leq x \& z \leq y)$
c.	$\forall x \in X(x = x_1 \cup x_2 \Rightarrow \text{either } x_1 \in X \text{ or } x_2 \in X)$
d.	$\forall x \in X \forall y \in P(y \leq x \Rightarrow y \in X)$

is offering an ontological rather than a linguistically relevant classification. The scarce linguistic evidence adduced is based upon entailment. In defence of her monotone-increasing definition of States she says that (182) holds as a property of States (1984: 267).

(182) John was ill last week $\models$ John was ill on Wednesday.
(183) John was ill on Wednesday $\models$ John was ill last week.

However she also says: 'if some state holds in a part of a temporal domain p_1, it continues to hold in p_2, that has p_1 as part' (1983: 180). This is a rather unclear formulation. It looks as if Ter Meulen is defending the validity of (183), which she probably would not do if *last week* were to mean 'the whole week that preceded this one'. Presumably Ter Meulen means that if John was ill last Wednesday, then one can say that John was ill during some time last week. What she really seems to be saying is that if something holds at a certain time, it will also hold as part of a larger period. But this holds for non-States as well. If I say that his car hit that pole on 18 March 1985, then his car hit that pole in 1985 and in the eighties of this century, and so on. Is persistency, then, what States are about? Galton (1984: 24) observes: 'a state is dissective in the sense that any stretch of time in which a particular state obtains can be broken down into substretches in each of which that state holds', an opinion also held by Vendler, Taylor (1977) and Hoeksema (1984). That is, the view upon states is 'downward', as in (182); that is, monotone decreasing.

Why is it increasing in Ter Meulen's view? I think, because she has been caught by the *prima facie* attractiveness of 'filtering down' to an ultrafilter. Her analysis is primarily preoccupied with the notion of homogeneity, a notion which is only relevant to non-States. Activities are relatively homogeneous; condition c makes Accomplishments more heterogeneous, because it says that no part of a set of processes X has the same structure as X. Condition d is simply putting a heavier constraint on this by requiring that X is not divisible. In this sense, Ter Meulen is close to Taylor (1977). However, by her wish to 'filter all the way down' from States to Achievements, she is forced to define States in such a way that condition a in Table 8 carries over to Activities.

The second type of objection is the following. Negation of non-durative aspect blurs the very distinction between terminative and durative aspect, as shown in (184) and (185). The positive sentences *He handed a cup of tea* and *She won* are terminative, whereas their negative counterparts are durative.

(184) a. #He handed a cup of tea for hours
b. He didn't hand a cup of tea for hours

(185) a. #The whole afternoon she won
b. The whole afternoon she didn't win

This fact brings Ter Meulen into severe problems, because if monotone increase is part of non-States, then negation of these three classes cannot result in monotone increase. One may rather expect monotone decrease. This is a problem for all classifications discussed thus far.

Finally, Ter Meulen's proposal lacks any explanatory value. It does not contribute to a better understanding of what aspect is about. None of the four classes is used to explain a linguistic phenomenon. And if so, then one starts to be puzzled. For example, Ter Meulen (1984: 270) points out that 'conjunction and disjunction of indivisible entities have all the expected Boolean properties:

(186) John and Peter walked to school ⊨ John walks to school and Peter walks to school

(187) John walked to school ⊨ John or Peter walked to school'

If *walks* in (186) is read as *walked*, both (186) and (187) surely are valid. But if one drops *to school* in this entailment to obtain Activities, their validity will not change. And if one adds *like to* before the verb *walk* to get a State, the entailment still holds.

My conclusion is that Ter Meulen's proposal fails to make clear why a Vendler-classification based on hierarchy in this way could possibly be of interest for aspectual theory.

2.10 Moens' temporal ontology

At the close of this chapter, some attention will be paid to Moens (1987), who proposed a temporal ontology in which the Vendler-classes are incorporated (see also Moens and Steedman 1987; Lascarides 1988). Moens distinguishes five classes:

(188)

	Moens	*Vendler*
	State	State
	Process	Activity
	Culminated Process	Accomplishment
	Point	–
	Culminated Point	Achievement

For Moens this aspectual classification is not verbal but sentential, or rather propositional. On the other hand, one needs to have entrance to the internal structure of these classes because all sorts of transitions may take place. That is in sentences like (189)–(192):

(189) John walked
(190) John walked to the store
(191) John was walking
(192) John was walking to the store

Moens assumes there to be some basic form to which operators are applied yielding the ultimate meaning. Thus, they are analysed as (193)–(196).

(193) Past(John walk)
(194) Past(John walk to the store)
(195) Past(PROG(John walk))
(196) Past(PROG(John walk to the store))

Now, ⟦John walk⟧ belongs to the category Process (Pr), whereas ⟦John walk to the store⟧ belongs to Culminated Process (Cp). Though Moens observes that the Cp in (193) is compositionally derived, he does not give a precise grammar, so he simply characterizes (John walk to the store) as belonging to Cp. It should be observed that even though Moens speaks about (188) in terms of a temporal ontology, he also underlines the fact that the five categories represent a perspective on how the world is structured by a particular choice of constituents. In that sense, Moens and I do not differ very much about the role of ontological considerations in grammar.

According to Moens, the PROG-operator takes only Processes. So, in order to obtain (192), one should make a Pr out of a Cp, as is done in the formalization of Moens' system in Lascarides (1988). This is done by taking PR and CP as operators, so that (195) will be represented as (197), and (196) as (198).

(197) Past(PROG(John walk))
(198) Past(PROG(PR(John walk to the store)))

The idea behind this is that Cp's focus on the end-point of the interval, whereas the operator PR, when applied to a Cp-proposition, brings you to the process part. Underlying this is the conviction that the structure of propositions is to be related to a so-called Nucleus, which is an elementary event structure of the following form (Tichy 1980, 1985; Löbner 1988):

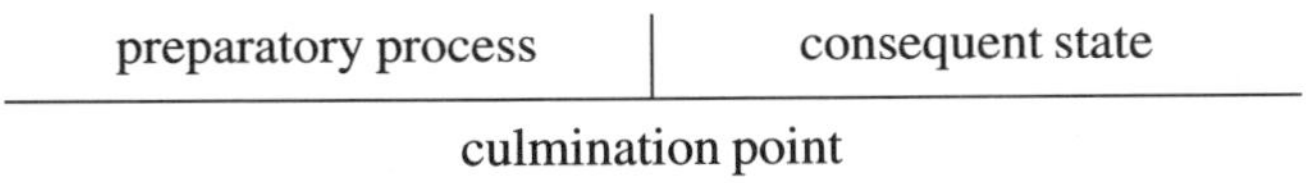

All propositions expressing temporal structure and all the operators changing membership of one of the classes are defined in terms of this schema. For example, the Cp-proposition (John walk to the store) is changed into a Pr-proposition focussing on the preparatory process. This makes it possible to apply PROG. Likewise, CP applied to (John ran) would yield CP(John ran), which expresses a culminated process, for example in sentences like *John ran in four minutes* (this morning), which pertain to a habit. The CP-operator explains why the durative *John ran* may occur with an *in*-adverbial, which should not be possible, given the aspectual tests discussed in section 2.3. I will come back to this point in chapter 13.8, and argue there that such an operator is not necessary at all for the sentence under analysis (see also Naumann 1991).

Moens (1987) and Moens and Steedman (1987) give an illustration of what they call an *aspectual network*,[40] shown in Figure 7. I have added [±SQA]- and [±ADD TO]-specifications in order to see how these can be matched.

There are three classes: States, Processes and Culminated Processes (=Events). Moens assumes that the latter two are extended intervals, and he also assumes that there are atomic counterparts to them. So he distinguishes between Points (wink, tap, hiccough) and Culminations (recognize, spot, win the race). I am not sure whether or not my [−ADD TO] would apply to Point and Culmination in an extended Figure 7 in which room would be made for atomic entities.

Figure 7 contains some ingredients which are important to discuss at this point. First of all, Moens does not operate on the basis of contributions of the

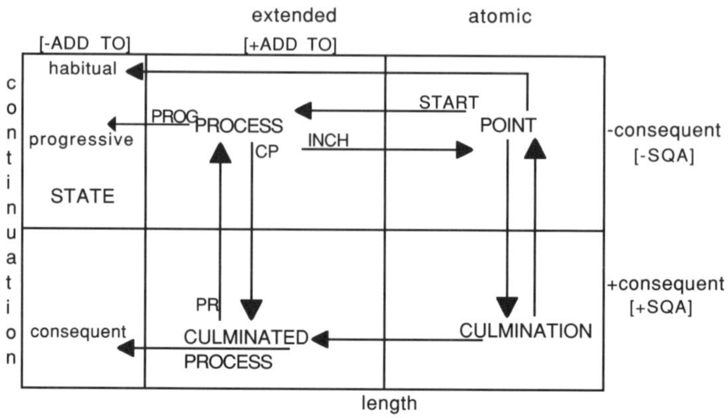

Figure 7 Moens' aspectual network can be interpreted in terms of the features [±ADD TO] and [±SQA]

NPs to the interval structure: he is focussed on interval properties such as length (extended vs. atomic) and continuation (±consequent). This makes his approach only partially congenial to the present study: there is congeniality in so far as the aspectual theories are based on the conviction that intervals do play a role. However, the difference is that Moens is operating much more on time intervals, whereas in my theory intervals are taken more abstractly as mathematical, in particular numerical structures which are related to time structure only by a mapping brought about by tense (see chapter 13.8). Moreover, the dynamicity expressed by [+ADD TO]-verbs is assumed holistically, so to say, by reference to the developmental phase. I do not exclude the possibility that it might be shown that [–consequent] may be interpreted as [–SQA] and [+consequent] with [+SQA], but Moens gives no indication that this might be so. In fact, he takes the compositional construal of sentential aspect for granted. Another point at which I take a different route is the treatment of the Progressive Form: no PR-operation will be assumed to prepare (John walk to the store) for receiving PROG.

It should be observed though that Moens' system contains a lot of interesting insights that are very useful for extending the scope of the aspectual theory developed in the remainder of the present study.[41] As observed earlier, I have excluded some phenomena, such as outer aspect, and I do not pay attention to verbs like *start*, *begin*, *end*, etc. as Moens (1987) and Freed (1979) did, among others. Thus, Moens' scope is larger, so the idea of a network in which certain operators interact may work very well at a somewhat higher level of analysis. Compared with the microscopic study of inner aspect, Moens' system has

Table 9 *Comparison of the matrix features used by different scholars to characterize their aspectual classes*

Vendler	Hoeksema	Mourelatos	Dowty	Carlson
±Process	±Duration	±Occur	±Change	±Extended
±Definite	±Count	±Count	±Definite	±Continuous
(±Momentary)		±Momentary	±Complex	±Point

inevitably macroscopic features. This means that for some microphenomena Moens has no answer, that for some phenomena Moens' answers can be compared with the answers given in the present study, and that for some phenomena Moens gives answers which fall outside the scope of the present study. In particular, it will be possible to compare Moens' and Lascarides' treatment of the Progressive Form.

2.11 Conclusion

The purpose of this concluding section is to show that in spite of what the authors discussed in the present chapter claimed to do, they did not really use aspectual classes but rather underlying parameters to make their case, and to sort out which sort of parameters they used. Table 9 contains a survey of the parameters involved in the construction of aspectual classes as discussed above. I will leave out Moens' as well as Ter Meulen's position, because their systems have complications amply discussed but not relevant at this point. I shall ignore the differences between the parameters, but rather focus on what they appear to have in common, as far as the positive values are concerned. *Grosso modo*, the parameters in Table 9 pertain to the following properties of temporal structure:

The *transition* from one point to the other. This property is expressed in its positive value by Vendler's [+Process], by Hoeksema's [+Duration], by Mourelatos' [+Occur], by Dowty's [+Change] and by Carlson's [+Extended]. In some way or other the going on in time is expressed, although in some cases (Dowty, who is following Taylor (1977) in this respect) the dynamic part is suppressed.

The *boundedness* in the sense that the interval characterized by progress is definite: it can be the input to some quantificational operation, say frequency, repetition, semelfactivity, and so on.

The *length* of the interval. Though the scholars mentioned in Table 9 are not very clear in this respect, there is a tendency to make a difference between a point and a set of points (an interval), or between a singleton (an interval having one element) and an interval.

At first sight, Dowty's [+Complex] seems the linguistic odd thing out in the sense that he needs it only to distinguish Accomplishments from Achievements. Given the fact that a point precludes internal complexity, the length of an interval presumes it. So [–Complex] equals [+Punctual].[42]

Now, a couple of remarks are called for. Firstly, it may be asked why most of the scholars discussed here focussed on aspectual *classes* rather than on aspectual *parameters*. Dowty, for example, goes a long way to evade an explanation of the basic questions of aspectual theory in terms of his parameters. Hoeksema introduces them and tries to eliminate them in favour of the Vendler-classes which he turns out not to use. It is only Carlson who goes in the opposite direction: he pays lip service to the aspectual classes, and then he tries to explain aspectual phenomena in terms of his features, interpreting them model-theoretically. I have no explanation for the tendency to stick to aspectual classes. Secondly, the striking thing is that none of the parameters is systematically related to constituents of natural language, except for the verb. That is, the parameters are all related to the verb itself, implicitly or explicitly. This is quite suspicious and in my view it gives away a philosophical bias rather than a linguistic point of view. In other words, it shows that one is speaking about ontological categories rather than linguistic categories.

Thirdly and more or less following from the second point: all parameters involved are temporal parameters, in some way or other. This is quite unattractive and unnatural from the point of view of aspectual composition in which atemporal entities are involved. So the question is: why this restriction to temporal properties of the domain structure? The answer I would like to give is that the terminative aspect of sentences like (64)

(64) Judith ate three sandwiches

is built up as an assemblage of temporal and atemporal information. It is the quantificational information associated with *Judith* and *three sandwiches* which can be held responsible for terminativity. Of course, Mourelatos, Hoeksema and others mentioned countability as a factor crucial to terminative aspect, but they attribute the [+Count]-information to the verb. Let us therefore rearrange Figure 1 as Figure 8. Thus, the classification in Figure 8 can be made

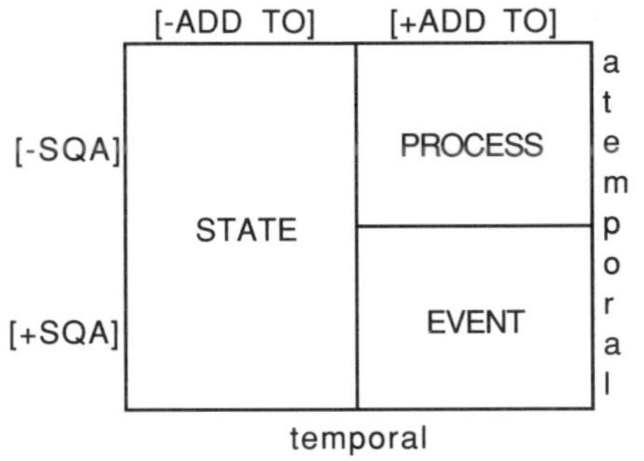

Figure 8 Three types of eventuality can be construed with the help of the verbal and nominal features [±ADD TO] and [±SQA]

on the basis of the two parameters involved. It can be seen that the [–ADD TO]-specification of the verb giving it its stative character is to be treated as a property which does not have aspectual interaction with the NP in sentences like (64). Sentences like (199) and (200) are both durative:

(199) Jessica hated three yuppies
(200) Jessica hated yuppies

and they show that the direct object [+SQA]-NP in (199) remains 'neutral', in the sense that it does interact aspectually with the verb, as in the terminative sentence (64), which would become durative if *three* is dropped.

The difference between the parameters involved in Figure 8 is that one of them is temporal, the other one atemporal. That aspect construal is an interaction between parameters of a different sort has been ignored in the model theoretically oriented literature of the seventies and eighties. The scheme in Figure 8 provides the natural means to account for a compositional approach to aspect: [+SQA] can be related to the NP, [+ADD TO] to the verb. In this way, the approaches discussed in this chapter are improved on. In my view, the above remarks also explain the failure of interval semantics to remain attractive for the analysis of change as expressed by natural language. One simply got on the wrong track by focussing too much on the construction of temporal domain structure rather than on the question of how language can be seen as a means to construe structure by the choice of the constituents that make up a sentence.

CONCLUSION TO PART I

As observed before, the present aspectual theory focusses on the interaction between temporal and atemporal structure in sentences like (1)–(4). This interaction can be (crudely and provisionally) captured by an aspectual 'feature algebra' based on two parameters discussed above and collected in Figure 8. However appealing this compositional machinery may be, it fails to give a satisfactory account of why it is that an NP is [+SQA] or [–SQA]. For example, to assign [+SQA] to both *a sandwich* and *three sandwiches* is correct but it does not explain anything unless we know what these NPs share. This extends, of course, to NPs like *many sandwiches*, *at least three sandwiches*, *most sandwiches*, etc. which also may express [+SQA]-information. A detailed enquiry is also necessary because certain NPs look as if they are [+SQA], whereas they are to be interpreted as [–SQA]. One needs to know more about the NPs themselves in order to make sure that the process of compositional interpretation proceeds as it should. Therefore, Part II will focus on the atemporal side of Figure 8. Two results are aimed at. The first one is to indicate exactly under which conditions NPs are [+SQA] or [–SQA]. This means that the representation of NPs should contain or lack certain information which is interpreted as contributing to terminative or durative aspect. The second one is to indicate exactly where atemporal structure 'meets' temporal structure. The basic intuitive idea is that terminative sentences require a mapping between the [+SQA]-information and the [+ADD TO]-information. In more refined analyses, the representation of NPs should provide for points of attachment for the verb to accomplish some mapping relation between temporal and atemporal structure. These two issues will be central in Part II.

II Noun phrase structure

INTRODUCTION TO PART II

In this second part, one of the central issues will be the question of whether or not the intuitive notion of Specified Quantity of A ([+SQA]) can be captured by the Theory of Generalized Quantification. As it is possible to circumscribe this notion quite precisely at the informal level, it should be possible to give it a formal interpretation in terms of existing or new notions of this theory, where it may serve its purpose as explaining part of the compositional machinery involved in the interpretation of sentences expressing terminative aspect. The same applies *mutatis mutandis* to the notion of Unspecified Quantity ([–SQA]).[1]

It may be helpful to begin the search for a formal articulation of the notion of (Un–)Specified Quantity of A by having a closer look at its informal characterization in Verkuyl (1972):

> The node SPECIFIED calls for some further explanation. Nodes like FINITE or BOUNDED would come close to the meaning of SPECIFIED; however, UNSPECIFIED cannot be identified with INFINITE. The category SPECIFIED could be characterized as 'giving the bounds of the temporal interval in question'; the category UNSPECIFIED as 'not giving the bounds of the temporal interval in question'. Since the expression 'giving the bounds of an interval' involves referential information, SPECIFIED is provisionally located in the Determiner. The point is that *het concert* (the concerto) and *een concert* (a concerto), when occurring in sentences like *De Machula speelde het celloconcert van Schumann* (De Machula played Schumann's cello concerto) refer to bounded or finite intervals on the Time axis. Only because these intervals are bounded can we isolate them as temporal entities distinguishable from sortlike entities; and only because they are bounded can we count them. (p. 59)

> At this point it will have become clear that what we have been doing here is to analyze such categories as COUNT into more elementary categories scattered over the whole Noun Phrase, whereas Chomsky (1965) assigned the syntactic feature [+Count] to the Noun. It is of importance to bear in mind that the node COUNT (i.e. the categories into which COUNT can be analyzed) plays a crucial role in the description of the Aspects. Its presence accounts for the fact that sentences containing a Nondurative Aspect can express frequency if they also contain Durational Adverbials. Nodes which exclude count, e.g. Mass, do not cause repetition, as we see from *De Machula speelde urenlang muziek* (De Machula played music for hours). (p. 59)

> By levering up the distinction between COUNT and NONCOUNT to the level of the NP we can better explain the opposition between *#De Machula speelde urenlang het celloconcert van Schumann* (De M. played Schumann's cello concerto for hours] and (i) *De Machula speelde urenlang celloconcerten van 19e eeuwse componisten* (De M. played cello concertos by composers of the 19th century for hours) with respect to the diversity of Noun Phrases which

> can replace their underscored constituents. The presence of such Numerical elements as *een*, *twee* (two), *sommige* (some), *enkele van* (some of), etc. indicates that the NP refers to entities which can be quantified. If these elements are absent as in the case of *De Machula speelde urenlang muziek* (De M. played music for hours), (i), etc. we simply cannot count. Countability is a matter of reference and hence it should be accounted for at the level at which constituents can refer to things. (p. 61)[2]

> Thus the difference between the categories DURATIVE and NONDURATIVE can be explained in terms of set theoretical notions. It has become clear that the semantic information 'UNSPECIFIED QUANTITY OF X' or 'SPECIFIED QUANTITY OF X' pertains directly or indirectly to the Time axis. That is, the quantities of X involved are expressible in terms of linearly ordered sets of temporal entities. (pp. 96–97)

If one abstracts from the terminological idiosyncrasies, the notion 'Specified' in the above quotations is closely tied up both with the notion 'Count' and with the notion of temporal boundedness: it requires that the temporal interval during which some activity is going on be bounded by the interaction with an NP whose reference is such that its members can be counted, in principle. Crucial is the idea that there is some mapping between the information of the NP and information contributed by the verb in the sense that a *specified* NP makes the interval introduced by the verb bounded. This idea will be pursued in the present study in an attempt to account for the semantic interaction between V and NP.

Much of the terminology in the quotations was branded by generative grammar, in particular by Gruber's system of polycategorial syntax in which NPs like *the sandwich* and *a sandwich* were given structures like:[3]

(1) $[_{NP}[_{NP}[_{DET}\text{DEF SPECIFIED}]\ [_{N}\text{QUANTITY}]]\ [_{PP}[_{P}\text{OF}]\ [_{NP}[_{MASS}\text{BREAD}]]]$

(2) $[_{NP}[_{NP}[_{DET}\text{INDEF SPECIFIED}]\ [_{N}\text{QUANTITY}]\ [_{PP}[_{P}\text{OF}]\ [_{NP}[_{MASS}\ \text{BREAD}]]]$

Gruber was a semanticist rather than a syntactician, so one might see in this sort of representation an attempt to analyse NPs and Ns into semantically more primitive elements. The mass NP *bread* and the NP *a slice of bread* would receive the following representations, respectively:[4]

(3) $[_{NP}[_{NP}[_{DET}\text{INDEF UNSPECIFIED}]\ [_{N}\text{QUANTITY}]]\ [_{PP}[_{P}\text{OF}]\ [_{NP}[_{MASS}\text{BREAD}]]]$

(4) $[_{NP}[_{NP}[_{DET}\text{INDEF SPECIFIED}]\ [_{N}[_{QUANTITY}\ \text{slice}]]\ [_{PP}[_{P}\text{of}]\ [_{NP}[_{MASS}\ \text{bread}]]]$

From (1)–(4) it should be obvious that the difference between terminativity and durativity cannot be equated with a difference between Definite and Indefinite. Consider the following sentences:

(5) Judith ate those three sandwiches
(6) Judith ate three sandwiches
(7) Judith ate sandwiches
(8) Judith ate that sandwich
(9) Judith ate a slice of bread
(10) Judith ate bread
(11) Judith ate lots of bread

Both (5) and (6) are terminative, just like (8) and (9). Yet each pair contains a definite NP and an indefinite NP. The same applies to the difference between Singular and Plural. Both (5) and (7) have a plural direct object NP and yet there is a clear aspectual difference between them, whereas there is no aspectual difference between (5) and (8). According to Verkuyl (1972), it is the element SPECIFIED that should account for the aspectual difference.

That definiteness and indefiniteness cannot be the explanatory concepts was apparently overlooked by Dowty (1979), who introduced Principle D as a general principle holding for sentences like (7) and (8):[5]

> *Principle D*:
> If a sentence with an achievement verb contains a plural indefinite NP or mass noun NP (or if a sentence with an accomplishment verb contains such an NP as object), then it has the properties of a sentence with an activity verb. (p. 63)

Dowty suggests that Principle D is proposed in or compatible with Verkuyl (1972), and then he goes on to explain that I gave this principle the form in (12):[6]

(12) $*[_{\text{VPnon-durative}}\ [_{\text{V}}\text{AGENTIVE}] + [_{\text{NP}}\text{PLURAL INDEFINITE/MASS}\ ]]$

Now, there is some sort of filtering device that I used, namely the one given in (13):

(13) $[_{\text{S}}[_{\text{NP}}\pm\text{SQA}] + [_{\text{VP}}[_{\text{V}}\text{VERB}] + [_{\text{NP}}\pm\text{SQA}]]]$

It says, in a somewhat simplified form, that if one of the NPs is [–SQA], the sentence is durative, whereas the sentence is non-durative (in the present terminology, terminative) if the following conditions are fulfilled: (a) each NP is [+SQA]; (b) 'VERB must stand for subcategorial nodes ... such as MOVEMENT, PERFORM, TAKE, ADD TO, CHANGE, DO, etc.; and (c) [13] does not apply to negative sentences' (1972: 106).[7] As demonstrated in chapter 1.2, (13) can better be explained in terms of a 'feature algebra' rather than be taken as a filter, but this constructive use of (13) remained implicit in Verkuyl (1972).

I agree with Dowty that (13) taken as a filter cannot *explain* aspect construal, but the simple fact is that in the framework of generative grammar around 1970 there were no formal means to do the job properly. However, I sharply disagree with Dowty that (12) should express what (13) is intended to express. It is not so much the node AGENTIVE which is problematic, although I think that agentivity is not an important factor at all in aspectuality (in fact, it causes a lot of trouble), but it is Dowty's use of syntactic features like INDEFINITE and PLURAL which clearly misrepresents my position. My real position has always been that aspect construal is a semantic process and not that it should be a syntactic process as has been wrongly attributed to me by Dowty (1979, 1986), and after him by Hinrichs (1986a) and Krifka (1989b).[8] The root of these misrepresentations is the fact that Dowty attributed Principle D and (12) to me. In fact, I do not accept (12) and Principle D even as being correct at the descriptive level. I also think that the fact that Dowty relies on the notions of ±indefiniteness and ±singular in his own Montagovian framework prevents him from getting at the right characterization of aspectuality, as will be argued in chapter 9. Running ahead of the argumentation in that chapter, I will restrict myself here to sketching the main line of argument against the validity of Principle D which has remained a guiding principle for Dowty (1979), in order to show that we need different features from (IN)DEFINITE or SINGULAR/PLURAL that can be held responsible for the [±SQA]-behaviour of NPs. In general, my argument shows that the [+SQA]-notion cannot be explained in terms of the existential or universal quantifier, as argued by Dowty.

Principle D was put to work by Dowty to account for the difference between the terminative sentence (14) and the durative sentences (15) and (16) where *the buried treasure* is DEF SG and *fleas* INDEF PL.[9]

(14) John discovered the buried treasure in his back yard
(15) John discovered fleas on his dog in his yard
(16) John discovered crabgrass in his yard

One might be tempted to believe that at this informal level of description, the notion of '(in)definiteness' should not be taken too literally, but when it comes to a more formal treatment, Dowty attempts to explain the difference between the contribution of NPs to terminative aspect in sentences like (14) and (15) in terms of scope differences of quantifiers involved: the definite NP *the buried treasure* is analysed as a definite description, roughly as ιx.(x is treasure ∧ x is buried), whereas the indefinite plural *fleas* is analysed as ∃x.x is flea. According to Dowty, this explains the aspectual difference between (17) and (18).

(17) #For six weeks John discovered the buried treasure
(18) For six weeks John discovered fleas on his dog

Sentence (17) says that John repeatedly discovered the unique x such that x is a buried treasure, whereas (18) can report about a period of six weeks during which John discovered fleas. Dowty analyses *for six weeks* in terms of universal quantification over times and a two-place AT-operator, so that the aspectual difference between (14) and (15) can be explained in terms of a difference in scope behaviour:

(19) $\forall t \in$ Six weeks AT(t, John discovered ιx ...)
(20) $\forall t \in$ Six weeks $\exists$x.AT(t, John discovered x ...)

Though Dowty is not very clear about it, it must be assumed that in (19) the definite description behaves like a proper name, so that it cannot be in the scope of $\forall t$, whereas the existential quantifier $\exists x$ in (20) will be in the scope of the universal quantifier so that for every relevant t there will be an x such that John discovered x (1979: 79f.).[10]

The contribution of the NP to terminative aspect is much more complicated than Dowty suggested. For example, Dowty may indeed account for the difference between (14) and (15) with the help of Principle D, but it does not help to explain the difference between (14) and the terminative sentence (21).

(21) John discovered a buried treasure in his back yard

Moreover, the explanation of the occurrence of enforced repetition discussed later on cannot be captured in terms of scope behaviour: if (21) is analysed in terms of an existential quantifier, one ends up with (20) as the representation of *#For six weeks John discovered a flea on his dog*. But (20) is the representation of (18). So, in this sense Dowty's Principle D is a significant step back with respect to my 1972 analysis of Specified Quantity (see chapter 2.6) as summarized by scheme (13).

More generally, the quantifiers of standard first-order predicate logic are not sufficient to express the information intended by the node SPECIFIED in the representations (1)–(4). There is no way to use $\forall$ and $\exists$ either apart or together (as in the iota-operator ι) such that one representational unit may express what the direct object NPs in sentences like (5), (6) and (8) have in common and what they share with NPs like those in (22), among others.

(22)	a. some of the sandwiches	d. a pound of bread
	b. not all sandwiches	e. both sandwiches
	c. a slice of bread	f. that sandwich

g. most sandwiches
h. all the sandwiches
i. more than half of the sandwiches
j. many sandwiches

However, some of the NPs in (22), such as *more than half of the sandwiches* and *many sandwiches*, are not definable in terms of ∀ and ∃, as pointed out, for example, in Barwise and Cooper (1981).

The semantic theory that has extended the scope of quantification so as to treat quantifying expressions like (22) uniformly in terms of quantification over sets rather than over individuals is called the Theory of Generalized Quantification (GQT). This theory has been successful in many respects: in an amazingly short period of about a decade the age-old veil over the diversified group of numerical elements in many natural languages has been raised, at least enough to establish the belief that a better understanding of those puzzling elements has become possible. It would be unwise to express theoretically relevant insights on quantification without making use of the results of GQT.

There are two reasons for undertaking the enterprise of considering in detail how a strong intuitive notion like [+SQA] can be given a precise formal interpretation in GQT. The first one is that many of the analyses of GQT do not go deep into the syntax of prenominal structure, that is, the structure preceding the head noun of the NP. Thus quantifying expressions like *more than half of the*, *some but not all*, *some of the*, and even *all the* and *not the*, etc. are treated as simplex determiners. From a linguistic point of view this is intolerable, the more so because sufficient syntactic means are available, in particular from the generative tradition. It will be shown in the chapters constituting Part II that syntactic refinements lead to semantic refinements. The second reason is that the above pretheoretical exploration of the [+SQA]-notion cannot but lead to the conclusion that a quantificational theory is called for. Pretheoretically, the notion itself has been well established in the sense that we can make clear which empirical load it has. But it is in need of a theoretical framework in which it can be articulated formally so that it can contribute to a theory of aspect. It is the framework of GQT that I shall confront with the many subtleties of natural language triggered by the use of the [+SQA]-notion in the realm of aspectuality. It means that we confront an originally atemporal theory with a notion of NP-quantification which is underlyingly affected by temporal structure. Our goal is to see how GQT manages to overcome these difficulties.

3 *The tools of generalized quantification*

3.0 Introduction

This chapter contains a brief survey of the formal machinery employed in GQT, a theory which is generally considered as a further development of the treatment of quantification in Montague's PTQ. There is, however, a technically important difference between Montague's treatment of NPs and the GQT-treatment: the former uses the indirect method of translating expressions of natural language into type-logical expressions, which are then semantically interpreted as set-theoretical objects, whereas the latter uses the direct method. On the former, an English sentence like *All children came in* is translated into a logical formula, say *f*(*All children came in*), which is then interpreted. The essence of the direct approach is that *all*, *children* and *came_in* are directly taken as denoting semantic objects. This means that the syntactic structure of *All children came in* is mapped into constituents which are directly related to semantic objects of the domain. These objects belong to distinguished types (individuals, sets, functions, relations, etc.).

As its machinery will play an important role throughout the present study, I shall first introduce a type-logical language EL which itself is an extension of the standard predicate first-order logic including propositional logic. EL will be used as a formal logical language representing (the denotations of) expressions of natural language. It will play a role throughout the following chapters as a sort of checkpoint with respect to which elaborations of the system can be measured. Further, it is important to see where EL fails to capture the properties of sentences we are interested in.

There are two reasons for making the survey of EL given in section 3.1. Firstly, GQT is not so old and venerable that its body of thought is well established. Secondly, a large number of the readers of this study will be linguists and among them there are those who are not, or not thoroughly, familiar with GQT. Those who are not familiar may need some help from additional literature.[11] Those who are acquainted with the basics of GQT may wish to go through section 3.1 cursorily, the more so because it contains a small model with respect to which sentences and its constituents are interpreted. Most of the introductory books are rather abstract and it might be helpful to operate at a more concrete level. Thirdly, it is necessary anyway to have a formal grammar of aspect, so why not start to build it up from the beginning and extend it gradually? Finally, in transitive sentences with plural NPs some interesting form of 'low-level'-intensionality is visible. It is exactly for this reason that I want to first build up the formal language EL of extensional type logic from scratch, so to speak, so that one can clearly see where the intensionalized extensions come in, as will be demonstrated in chapter 13. Also, habituality and genericity involve a transition from extensionality to different sorts of intensionality, and the only way to reach for a better understanding of complex phenomena is to build things up from the very start. Those who are well acquainted with GQT may pick up the main line of this chapter in chapter 4.

3.1 Extensional type logic: EL

Type-logical languages are languages which systematically relate syntactic categories to types of semantic objects in the world (or a mental model thereof). Roughly, a semantic object of a certain type a is taken to be the denotation of a member of a certain linguistic category *a*. In other words, linguistic categories may be distinguished from one another due to the fact that they relate to different sorts of semantic objects. Type-logical specifications may be used to express relevant correspondences and differences.

The language EL is an extensional language. It is part of the make-up of the intensional language IL used by Montague for the analysis of quantifying NPs. One of the reasons for Montague to prefer type-logic to standard first-order predicate logic was a linguistic one. For example, in first-order logic sentences like (23)–(25) are represented as shown:

(23)	All children came in	(23′)	$\forall x[\text{child}(x) \rightarrow \text{came\_in}(x)]$
(24)	No children came in	(24′)	$\neg\exists x[\text{child}(x) \wedge \text{came\_in}(x)]$
(25)	Judith came in	(25′)	$\text{came\_in}(j)$

Linguistically, all three sentences are of the form [NP VP], but the semantic information associated with the NP in (23) and (24) is scattered over the entire formula. That is, *all* is analysed as corresponding to the part $\forall x[\ldots(x) \rightarrow \ldots(x)]$, whereas *children* and *came in* are treated equivalently, namely as predicates over the variable x; (25) is represented as $\alpha(\beta)$. Here all semantic information of the subject NP is expressed by β, which has the role of the argument of the predicate α. Montague used type logic to overcome this diversity by modelling (23′)–(25′) on one form, as will be pointed out shortly.

The domain of interpretation D of EL contains some basic types out of which more complex types of semantic objects are constructed. Let *e* and *t* be basic types, where *e* is the type of expressions pertaining to individuals and *t* is the type of expressions pertaining to truth values. One may then (provisionally) define the set of all possible types.[12]

DEFINITION 1

T, the set of types, is the smallest set such that:

a. *e*,*t* ∈ **T**

b. if a,b ∈ **T**, then <a,b>∈ **T**

Here any type <a,b> is to be taken as a function from semantic objects of type a to semantic objects of type b. This definition allows for the recursive construction of types, such as <*e*,*t*> (functions assigning individuals to truth values), <<*e*,*t*>,*t*> (functions from sets to truth values), <*e*,<*e*,*t*>> (functions from individuals to functions from individuals to truth values), <<<*e*,*t*>,*t*>,*t*>, <<*e*,*t*>,<*e*,*t*>>, etc. The basic idea behind the type-logical approach is that a member of a linguistic category is systematically interpreted in terms of its belonging to a semantic object of a basic or a derived type.

The vocabulary of EL consists of (at least):

DEFINITION 2

a. for every type a, a (possibly empty) set CON_a of constants of type a
b. for every type a, an infinite set VAR_a of variables of type a
c. the standard logical connectives ¬, ∧, ∨, →, ↔
d. the quantifiers ∃ and ∀, and the operator λ
e. the brackets (and)
f. the identity symbol =

There are variables and constants of different sorts. Notational conventions like the following will be used to indicate the type assigned to expressions:[13]

DEFINITION 3

Variables	Type	Constants	Type
x, y, z	*e*	j	*e*
X, Y, Z, U, W	<*e*,*t*>	child, came_in,...	<*e*,*t*>
P, *Q*, *R*, *S*	<<*e*,*t*>,*t*>	eat, …	<*e*,<*e*,*t*>>
		all, some, a, …	<<*e*,*t*>,<<*e*,*t*>,*t*>>

For convenience, types are often written as subscripts to expressions. Thus, if *child* is an expression of English, $\text{child}_{<e,t>}$ says that *child* is an expression whose denotation is taken as a semantic object of type <*e*,*t*>. Note that an expression of a standard predicate-logical form [child(x)] is of type t, its type-logical structure being $[\text{child}_{<e,t>}(x_e)]$. As $\text{child}_{<e,t>}$ denotes a function which applies to x, the resulting expression is of type t. In formulas, the brackets [and] will sometimes be used instead of (and), only for convenience.

A meaningful expression ME of EL is a member of $\cup_{a\in \mathbf{T}}\text{ME}_a$. The syntax of EL is (provisionally) defined as follows:

DEFINITION 4

a. if $\alpha\in \text{CON}_a$, then $\alpha\in \text{ME}_a$
   if $\alpha\in \text{VAR}_a$, then $\alpha\in \text{ME}_a$

b. if $\alpha\in \text{ME}_{<a,b>}$, and $\beta\in \text{ME}_a$, then $\alpha(\beta)\in \text{ME}_b$

c. if $\phi,\psi\in \text{ME}_t$, then $\neg\phi$, $\phi\wedge\psi$, $\phi\vee\psi$, $\phi\rightarrow\psi$, $\phi\leftrightarrow\psi\in \text{ME}_t$

d. if $\alpha,\beta\in \text{ME}_a$, then $\alpha=\beta\in \text{ME}_t$

e. if $\phi\in \text{ME}_t$ and $v\in \text{VAR}_a$, then $\exists v\phi, \forall v\phi\in \text{ME}_t$

f. if $\alpha\in \text{ME}_a$ and $v\in \text{VAR}_b$, then $\lambda v\alpha\in \text{ME}_{<b,a>}$

g. Every meaningful expression in EL is constructed by (a)–(f) in a finite number of steps.

A model **M** for EL consists of a domain set E and an interpretation function I: **M**=<E,I>, where I is a function assigning to each constant $c\in \text{CON}_a$ of the language some element I(c) of type a. The variables of EL are interpreted standardly by the assignment function g. In this way, the basic expressions of the language are interpreted by I and g. Composite expressions are standardly interpreted by the function $[\![.]\!]_{\mathbf{M},g}$. Given an expression α, $[\![\alpha]\!]_{\mathbf{M},g}$ is the denotation of α with respect to **M** and g.

On the basis of DEF 1 one may define the domains of interpretation corresponding to the various types.

DEFINITION 5

a. $\mathbf{D}_e=E$

b. $\mathbf{D}_t=\{1,0\}$

c. $\mathbf{D}_{<a,b>}=\mathbf{D}_b^{\mathbf{D}_a}$

Expressions of type *e* are interpreted as elements belonging to the domain of individuals $\mathbf{D}_e$. We shall say that $\mathbf{D}_e=E$, where E is the domain of individuals and that the domain of interpretation for expressions of type t is $\mathbf{D}_t=\{1,0\}$, that is, the set of truth values. Finally, the domain of interpretation of expressions of type

<a,b>, $\mathbf{D}_{<a,b>}=\mathbf{D}_b{}^{D_a}$. We follow the practice of writing Y^X for the set of all functions from type X to type Y. This means that $\mathbf{D}_{<a,b>}$ is seen as the set of functions from $\mathbf{D}_a$, the set of entities of type a, into $\mathbf{D}_b$, the set of entities of type b.

Functions of the form <a,*t*> are so-called characteristic functions of a set over another set. This means that if a constituent is interpreted as a set A which is a subset of B, it can also be treated as a function f_A over B mapping all elements of A onto 1 and all elements in the complement of A in B onto 0. In doing this, we split B by taking all those entities which are A to truth value 1 and all entities which are not A to truth value 0. In this way, any expression of type <a,*t*> denotes a set of entities of type a. Scheme (26) illustrates the domains to which the denotations of expressions of basic and composite types belong, both in terms of a functional domain and set domain.

(26)

Type	*Functional domain*	*Set domain*
e		$\mathbf{D}_e$=E
t		$\mathbf{D}_t$={1,0}
<*e*,*t*>	$\mathbf{D}_e \rightarrow \mathbf{D}_t$	$\wp$(E)
<<*e*,*t*>,*t*>	$(\mathbf{D}_e \rightarrow \mathbf{D}_t) \rightarrow \mathbf{D}_t$	$\wp\wp$(E)
<<<*e*,*t*>,*t*>,*t*>	$((\mathbf{D}_e \rightarrow \mathbf{D}_t) \rightarrow \mathbf{D}_t) \rightarrow \mathbf{D}_t$	$\wp\wp\wp$(E)
<<*e*,*t*>,<*e*,*t*>>	$(\mathbf{D}_e \rightarrow \mathbf{D}_t) \rightarrow (\mathbf{D}_e \rightarrow \mathbf{D}_t)$	$\wp(E) \times \wp(E)$
<<*e*,*t*>,<<*e*,*t*>,*t*>>	$(\mathbf{D}_e \rightarrow \mathbf{D}_t) \rightarrow ((\mathbf{D}_e \rightarrow \mathbf{D}_t) \rightarrow \mathbf{D}_t)$	$\wp(E) \times \wp\wp(E)$
<*e*,<*e*,*t*>>	$(\mathbf{D}_e \rightarrow (\mathbf{D}_e \rightarrow \mathbf{D}_t)$	$E \times \wp(E)$

The semantics of EL is given in definition 6.

DEFINITION 6

a. if $\alpha \in \text{CON}_a$, then $\llbracket\alpha\rrbracket_{\mathbf{M},g}=I(\alpha)$

if $\alpha \in \text{VAR}_a$, then $\llbracket\alpha\rrbracket_{\mathbf{M},g}=g(\alpha)$

b. if $\alpha \in \text{ME}_{<a,b>}$ and $\beta \in \text{ME}_a$, then $\llbracket\alpha(\beta)\rrbracket_{\mathbf{M},g}=\llbracket\alpha\rrbracket_{\mathbf{M},g}(\llbracket\beta\rrbracket_{\mathbf{M},g})$

c. if $\phi,\psi \in \text{ME}_t$, then

$\llbracket\neg\phi\rrbracket_{\mathbf{M},g}=1$ iff $\llbracket\phi\rrbracket_{\mathbf{M},g}=0$

$\llbracket\phi\wedge\psi\rrbracket_{\mathbf{M},g}=1$ iff $\llbracket\phi\rrbracket_{\mathbf{M},g}=1$ and $\llbracket\psi\rrbracket_{\mathbf{M},g}=1$

$\llbracket\phi\vee\psi\rrbracket_{\mathbf{M},g}=1$ iff $\llbracket\phi\rrbracket_{\mathbf{M},g}=1$ or $\llbracket\psi\rrbracket_{\mathbf{M},g}=1$

$\llbracket\phi\rightarrow\psi\rrbracket_{\mathbf{M},g}=0$ iff $\llbracket\phi\rrbracket_{\mathbf{M},g}=1$ and $\llbracket\psi\rrbracket_{\mathbf{M},g}=0$

$\llbracket\phi\leftrightarrow\psi\rrbracket_{\mathbf{M},g}=1$ iff $\llbracket\phi\rrbracket_{\mathbf{M},g}=\llbracket\psi\rrbracket_{\mathbf{M},g}$

d. if $\alpha,\beta \in \text{ME}_a$, then $\llbracket\alpha=\beta\rrbracket_{\mathbf{M},g}=1$ iff $\llbracket\alpha\rrbracket_{\mathbf{M},g}=\llbracket\beta\rrbracket_{\mathbf{M},g}$

e. if $\phi \in \text{ME}_t$ and $v \in \text{VAR}_a$, then

$\llbracket\exists v\phi\rrbracket_{\mathbf{M},g}=1$ iff there is at least one $d \in D_a$: $\llbracket\phi\rrbracket_{\mathbf{M},g[v/d]}=1$

$\llbracket\forall v\phi\rrbracket_{\mathbf{M},g}=1$ iff for all $d \in D_a$: $\llbracket\phi\rrbracket_{\mathbf{M},g[v/d]}=1$

f. if $\alpha \in ME_a$, $v \in \text{VAR}_b$, then $[\![\lambda v\alpha]\!]_{\mathbf{M},g}$=that function $h \in \mathbf{D}_a^{\mathbf{D}_b}$ such that for all $d \in \mathbf{D}_b$: $h(d)=[\![\alpha]\!]_{\mathbf{M},g[v/d]}$

This is fairly standard. Rule f says: if α is a meaningful expression of type a and v is a variable of type b, then any lambda-expression $\lambda v\alpha$ is interpreted, given a model **M** and a variable assignment g, as a function from the domain $\mathbf{D}_b$ into the domain $\mathbf{D}_a$ such that its application to a semantic object d yields the semantic object $[\![\alpha]\!]$, which is the denotation of α such that the value of the variable v is d (Gamut 1991: 105).[14] Note that $[\![\lambda v\alpha]\!]_{\mathbf{M},g}$ is a characteristic function if it is an element of the domain $\mathbf{D}_t^{\mathbf{D}_b}$.

As said earlier, Montague used type logic to model the semantic representation of the sentences in (18) on their syntactic form. In particular, rule f of the syntax of EL makes it possible to represent all NPs in (18) as follows:

(27) $\lambda X_{<e,t>}.\forall x(\text{child}(x) \rightarrow X(x))$
(28) $\lambda X_{<e,t>}.\neg\exists x(\text{child}(x) \wedge X(x))$
(29) $\lambda X_{<e,t>}.X_{<e,t>}(j_e)$

These expressions are of type *<<e,t>,t>*. Their type-logical structure can easily be computed: the variable X is of type *<e,t>*, whereas the expressions following the point behind λX are of type *t*. According to rule f, the type of the whole lambda-expression is *<<e,t>,t>*. This means that the expressions in (20) all denote a (characteristic) function having sets as input and truth values as their output: if they are applied to an expression of type *<e,t>* which denotes a set, for example, to *come in*, they yield either the truth value 1 or 0. The semantics of EL says that the denotation of (27) is (30):

(30) $[\![\lambda X.\forall x(\text{child}(x) \rightarrow X(x))]\!]_{\mathbf{M},g}$

It is that function $h \in (\mathbf{D}_e \rightarrow \mathbf{D}_t) \rightarrow \mathbf{D}_t$ such that $h([\![\text{came\_in}]\!]_{\mathbf{M},g})=1$ if and only if $[\![\forall x(\text{child}(x) \rightarrow X(x))]\!]_{\mathbf{M},g[X/[\![\text{came\_in}]\!]]}=1$.

Determiners are of type *<<e,t>,<<e,t>,t>>*. The determiners *all* and *no*, for example, have the following representations:

(31) $\lambda Y_{<e,t>}\lambda X_{<e,t>}.\forall x[Y(x) \rightarrow X(x)]_t$
(32) $\lambda Y_{<e,t>}\lambda X_{<e,t>}.\neg\exists x[Y(x) \wedge X(x)]_t$

Here again rule f lets the expressions apply to an expression of type *<e,t>* to form an expression of type *<<e,t>,t>*. Thus, the application of (31) to the expression *child* results in (27). Likewise, (32) represents a relation between the sets X and Y constrained by the condition that no x is an element of X *and* Y.

The type-logical approach of NPs of the form [Det N] is illustrated in Figure 9a, where Det is treated as a syntactic category taking an N (type <*e*,*t*>) to form an NP (type <<*e*,*t*>,*t*>). The type-logical structure of sentences of the form [[Det N] VP] is given in Figure 9b. This survey of the type-logical background

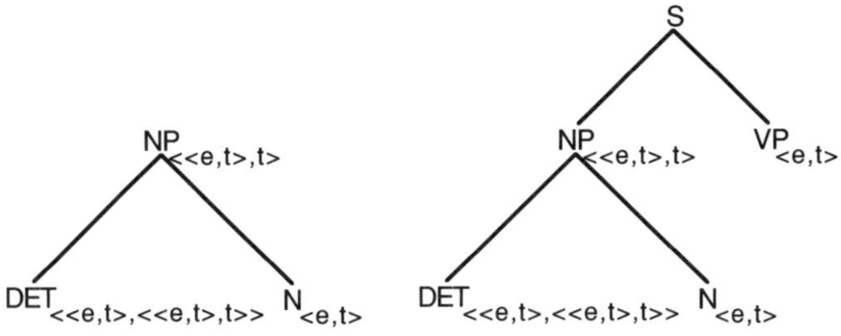

(a) (b)

Figure 9 A determiner forms an NP of type <<*e*,*t*>,*t*> by operating on N, as shown in Figure 9a; Figure 9b also shows that the output of this operation takes the VP as its input, yielding an S of type *t*

of the theory of generalized quantification should suffice to give a fair idea of its leading assumptions.

3.2 Generalized quantification

Barwise and Cooper (1981) is generally considered as the eye-opener for linguists and philosophers with respect to earlier work on generalized quantification in mathematical logic. They extended the empirical scope of logic considerably by investigating the properties of quantifying expressions like *both*, *many*, *few*, *at most n*, *several*, *more than half*, etc., which had escaped attention so far due to the ample attention for logical quantifiers such as *all*, *some*, *no* and *not all*. In the eighties, the definitions of these 'new' quantifying expressions and their classification have been subjected to closer scrutiny by linguists, philosophers and logicians.[15] In this section, I shall review some of the results in so far as they are relevant to the main issue of Part II.

A *model* **M** for a language L consists minimally of a domain E and an interpretation function ⟦.⟧ which assigns members of L to entities in the domain. So, **M**=<E, ⟦.⟧>. In the theory of generalized quantification, set theory is taken as the foundation of semantic interpretation. That is, models are specified in terms of set theory and other specifications are derived from that. The language in which generalized quantification is expressed will reflect this. To facilitate the exposition, I will discuss some English sentences like (35)–(40) with the help of a model $\mathbf{M}_1$, where the domain E consists of four individuals and where $\wp$(E), the power set of E, is the set of all subsets of E.[16]

(33) E={a,b,c,d}
⟦child⟧={b,c,d}
⟦cat⟧={a}
⟦dog⟧=∅
⟦came in⟧={a,b,c,d}

(34) $\wp$(E) = {∅,{a},{b},{c},{d},{a,b},{a,c},{a,d},{b,c},{b,d},{c,d}, {a,b,c},{a,b,d},{a,c,d},{b,c,d},E}

(35) All children came in
(36) No children came in
(37) The cat came in
(38) Three children came in
(39) Several children came in
(40) Not all children came in

Let us first interpret the lexical elements in these sentences minus the determiners. In (33), the denotata of the three nouns and the verb in $\mathbf{M}_1$ are all sets. There are three children in E and all elements of E came in, three of them being children, the fourth being a cat. There are no dogs in E. All sets in (33) are elements of $\wp$(E) as defined in (34).

If we interpret the linguistic expression *child* as the set of children {b,c,d} in $\mathbf{M}_1$, it is just another way of saying that b, c and d have the property 'child'. An immediate advantage of this treatment is that the full power of set theory can be used in the interpretation of sentences. Saying that an expression denoting a set of entities is of type <*e,t*>, is a convenient way of interpreting *child* as a characteristic function $f_{[\![child]\!]}$ of the set ⟦child⟧ over E. This function is spelled out for $\mathbf{M}_1$ as (41).

(41) $f_{[\![child]\!]}$={<a,0>, <b,1>, <c,1>, <d,1>}

Type-logically, $f_{[\![child]\!]}$ has as its domain E and as its co-domain the set of truth values {1,0}. More generally for N:

(42) $f_{[\![N]\!]}$: E→{1,0}

where for all d in E, d↦1 iff d∈ ⟦N⟧, otherwise 0. Note that (41) and ⟦child⟧ in (33) express the same information, but the use of the functional format has sometimes advantages over the use of the set format, or vice versa. It is now that we can see in (41) why *child* is of type <*e,t*>, its denotation being a set of ordered pairs, in each of which there is an individual d of type *e* as its left member and a truth value as its right member. Thus, the functional notation in (41) reveals its type-logical structure.

Montague's invention was to treat NPs as terms denoting collections of sets. For example, the NP denotation ⟦all children⟧ would be the collection (43):

(43) $\{X \subseteq E: [\![child]\!] \subseteq X\}$

(44) $\{X \subseteq E: [\![child]\!] \cap X = [\![child]\!]\}$

which is the set of all sets X such that for all individuals x in E, if x is in the set ⟦child⟧, x is also a member of X. An equivalent way of saying (43) is (44). Extending this format to the NPs in (35)–(40) one obtains (45)–(50), where $|\alpha|$ represents 'the cardinality of the set α'.[17]

(45)	⟦all N⟧	=	$\{X \subseteq E: [\![N]\!] \cap X = [\![N]\!]\}$
(46)	⟦no N⟧	=	$\{X \subseteq E: [\![N]\!] \cap X = \varnothing\}$
(47)	⟦the$_{sg}$ N⟧	=	$\{X \subseteq E: [\![N]\!] \cap X = [\![N]\!] \wedge \|[\![N]\!]\| = 1\}$
(48)	⟦(exactly)n N⟧	=	$\{X \subseteq E: \|[\![N]\!] \cap X\| = n\}$
(49)	⟦several N⟧	=	$\{X \subseteq E: \|[\![N]\!] \cap X\| \geq 2\}$
(50)	⟦not all N⟧	=	$\{X \subseteq E: [\![N]\!] \cap X \neq [\![N]\!]\}$

The definitions in (45) and (47) are identical, except for the extra condition that the cardinality of ⟦N⟧ is 1. The NP-denotations in (35)–(40) in $\mathbf{M}_1$ are spelled out in (51).

(51)

⟦all children⟧	=	{{b,c,d},{a,b,c,d}}
⟦no children⟧	=	{∅,{a}}
⟦the$_{sg}$ cat⟧	=	{{a},{a,b},{a,c},{a,d},{a,b,c},{a,b,d},{a,c,d}, {a,b,c,d}}
⟦two children⟧	=	{{b,c},{b,d},{c,d},{a,b,c},{a,b,d},{a,c,d}}
⟦several children⟧	=	{{b,c},{b,d},{c,d},{a,b,c},{a,b,d},{a,c,d}, {b,c,d},{a,b,c,d}}
⟦not all children⟧	=	{∅,{a},{b},{c},{d},{a,b},{a,c},{a,d},{b,c}, {b,d},{c,d}, {a,b,c},{a,b,d},{a,c,d}}

Type-logically, sets like (43) and (44) are characteristic functions from $\wp(E)$, the power set of E, onto the set of truth values {1,0}. The direct interpretation proceeds as follows:

(52) $f_{[\![NP]\!]}: \wp(E) \rightarrow \{1,0\}$

The function $f_{[\![NP]\!]}$ has as its domain the set of all subsets of E and it splits up $\wp(E)$ into a collection Q of subsets which are mapped onto 1 and into a collection Q′ of subsets which are mapped onto 0. The function $f_{[\![\text{all children}]\!]}$ in $\mathbf{M}_1$ can be spelled out as a set of ordered pairs, each pair consisting of a member from $\wp(E)$ and either 1 or 0, as in (53):

(53) $\{<\{b,c,d\},1>, <\{a,b,c,d\},1>, <\varnothing,0>, <\{a\},0>, <\{b\},0>, <\{c\},0>, <\{d\},0>, <\{a,b\},0>, <\{a,c\},0>, <\{a,d\},0>, <\{b,c\},0>, <\{b,d\},0>, <\{c,d\},0>, <\{a,b,c\},0>, <\{a,b,d\},0>, <\{a,c,d\},0>\}$

(54) $\{<\varnothing,1>, <\{a\},1>, <\{b\},0>, <\{c\},0>, <\{d\},0>, <\{a,b\},0>, <\{a,c\},0>, <\{a,d\},0>, <\{b,c\},0>, <\{b,d\},0>, <\{c,d\},0>, <\{a,b,c\},0>, <\{a,b,d\},0>, <\{a,c,d\},0>, <\{b,c,d\},0>, <\{a,b,c,d\},0>\}$

(55) $\{<\varnothing,1>, <\{a\},1>, <\{b\},1>, <\{c\},1>, <\{d\},1>, <\{a,b\},1>, <\{a,c\},1>, <\{a,d\},1>, <\{b,c\},1>, <\{b,d\},1>, <\{c,d\},1>, <\{a,b,c\},1>, <\{a,b,d\},1>, <\{a,c,d\},1>, <\{b,c,d\},0>, <\{a,b,c,d\},0>\}$

This amounts to saying that $f_{[\![\text{all children}]\!]}$ sends the two members of the collection of sets in (53) to 1 and all other elements of $\wp(E)$ to 0. More generally, $f_{[\![\text{all N}]\!]}$ in (45) maps a set X onto 1 if and only if $[\![N]\!]\subseteq X$. As $\{b,c,d\}\subseteq\{a,b,c,d\}$ in $\mathbf{M}_1$, sentence (35) is true. In (54) and (55), the functions $f_{[\![\text{no children}]\!]}$ and $f_{[\![\text{not all children}]\!]}$ are spelled out. In the ordered pairs, the left members of the pairs are sets, which means that they are of type $<e,t>$. Thus, the functional notation displays its type-logical structure $<<e,t>,t>$. In this way, it is demonstrated what it means to say that NPs denote (characteristic functions of) collections of sets: the sets in the pairs having a 1 constitute Q, the extension of the NP.

The condition $[\![N]\!]=1$ in (47) can be made part of the definition or it can be added as a presupposition, as in Barwise and Cooper (1981). In the former case both *The child came in* and *The dog came in* will be false, in the latter their truth value will be undefined in $\mathbf{M}_1$. This point will be taken up again in chapter 4.4 and in chapter 5.2, where sentences like *All dogs came in* are also discussed.

All sentences (35)–(40) are of the form $[[_{NP}\text{Det N}]\ \text{VP}]$. A determiner Det will be interpreted as a function $[\![\text{Det}]\!]$, often written as D_E:

(56) $D_E: \wp(E)\rightarrow\{1,0\}^{\wp(E)}$

D_E is not a characteristic function because its co-domain is not the set of truth values. It is a function from $\wp(E)$ into the set of (characteristic) functions from $\wp(E)$ into truth values. This is another way of saying that D_E applied to a set $[\![N]\!]$ yields the function $f_{[\![NP]\!]}: \wp(E)\rightarrow\{1,0\}$ spelled out in (52). More generally, if we write A for $[\![\mathrm{N}]\!]$, then $D_E(A)=[\![\mathrm{NP}]\!]$. If we write B for the extension $[\![\mathrm{VP}]\!]$, then $D_E(A)(B)=1$ iff $B \in D_E(A)$.[18] This makes it possible to define (57)–(62).

(57) $[\![\text{all}]\!](A)(B)=1$ iff $B \in \{X \subseteq E\colon A \subseteq X\}$

(58) $[\![\text{no}]\!](A)(B)=1$ iff $B \in \{X \subseteq E\colon A \cap X = \varnothing\}$

(59) $[\![\text{the}_{sg}]\!](A)(B)=1$ iff $B \in \{X \subseteq E\colon A \subseteq X \wedge |A|=1\}$

(60) $[\![\text{exactly n}]\!](A)(B)=1$ iff $B \in \{X \subseteq E\colon |A \cap X|=n\}$

(61) $[\![\text{several}]\!](A)(B)=1$ iff $B \in \{X \subseteq E\colon |A \cap X| \geq 2\}$

(62) $[\![\text{not all}]\!](A)(B)=1$ iff $B \in \{X \subseteq E\colon A \cap X \neq A\}$

This says, for example, that $[\![\text{all}]\!]$ is a function having members of $\wp(E)$, that is, sets, as its input and the function $[\![\text{all}]\!](A)$ as its output, which applied to B yields a truth value. Hence, saying that (35) *All children came in* is true is to say that $[\![\text{all children}]\!]([\![\text{came\_in}]\!])=1$ which says that (35) is true if and only if $[\![\text{came\_in}]\!] \in \{X\colon [\![\text{child}]\!] \subseteq X\}$, that is, iff $\{a,b,c,d\} \in \{\{b,c,d\},\{a,b,c,d\}\}$. This is true in $\mathbf{M}_1$. Sentence (36) *No children came in* is false because $[\![\text{came\_in}]\!] \notin [\![\text{no}]\!]([\![\text{child}]\!])$. Here A and B do not intersect at all.

It is sometimes convenient to treat the function $D_E(A)(B)$ as a two-place relation $D_E(A,B)$, which is often written as D_EAB, where $A=[\![\mathrm{N}]\!]$ and $B=[\![\mathrm{VP}]\!]$. The general format for expressing the relation D_E between A and B is given in Figure 10 (Van Benthem 1983b). In particular, D_E expresses information about the intersection between A and B. This shows up in the definitions of the determiners (they are given below in (39)) and in the definitions of the NPs in (45)–(50). Hence, our search for the definition of the [+SQA]-notion will be focussed on the intersection $A \cap B$.

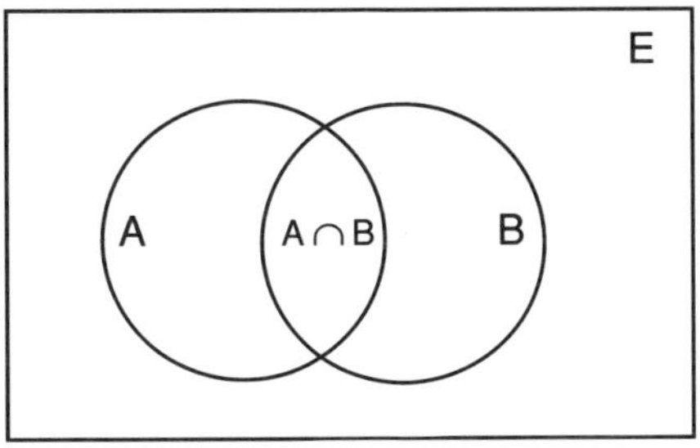

Figure 10 Any determiner can be defined in terms of an intersection $A \cap B$ between two sets A and B, given a domain of entities E

It is often convenient also to use a functional rather than a set-theoretical notation. So, rather than writing ⟦α⟧ as a set of entities of type a, one may write a λ-function of type <a,*t*>. This function is written in bold-face to distinguish it from the λ-expressions of EL. The left-hand side of (63)–(65) is equivalent to the right-hand side.[19]

(63)	⟦child⟧	⇔	λx.child(x)
(64)	⟦all children⟧	⇔	λX.⟦child⟧⊆X
(65)	⟦all⟧	⇔	λYλX.Y⊆X

Thus, λX.⟦child⟧⊆X does not denote a function but is a function. It remains possible to see its type-logical structure: in the metalanguage A⊆X is of type t, so the meta-linguistic expression λX.A⊆X is of type <<*e*,*t*>,*t*>.[20] If the variable x is of type *e*, and the variables X and Y are of type <*e*,*t*>, then the meta-linguistic expression (63) is also of type <*e*,*t*>; (64) is of type <<*e*,*t*>,*t*>, and (65) of type <<*e*,*t*>,<<*e*,*t*>,*t*>>. I shall sometimes use type-logical subscripts to facilitate the access to the type-logical build-up of a function, for example, $\lambda Y_{<e,t>}\lambda X_{<e,t>}.Y\subseteq X$ is a function of type <<*e*,*t*>,<<*e*,*t*>,*t*>>: it takes an argument of type <*e*,*t*> to yield something of type $\lambda X_{<e,t>}.Y\subseteq X$, which is of type <<*e*,*t*>,*t*>. The bold-face convention will be dropped if no misunderstanding with expressions from EL is possible. The function notation is convenient in derivations. In (66), a list of NP-denotations in two notations is given.

(66)

	⟦NP⟧	*Set notation*	*Function notation*
a.	⟦all⟧(A)	{X⊆E: A⊆X}	λX.A⊆X
b.	⟦both⟧(A)	{X⊆E: A⊆X∧|A|=2}	λX[A⊆X∧|A|=2]
c.	⟦the_{sg}⟧(A)	{X⊆E: A⊆X∧|A|=1}	λX[A⊆X∧|A|=1]
d.	⟦an⟧(A)	{X⊆E: A∩X≠∅}	λX.A∩X≠∅
e.	⟦not all⟧(A)	{X⊆E: A∩X≠A}	λX.A∩X≠A
f.	⟦no⟧(A)	{X⊆E: A∩X=∅}	λX.A∩X=∅
g.	⟦only⟧(A)	{X⊆E: A∩X=X}	λX.A∩X=X
h.	⟦not only⟧(A)	{X⊆E: A∩X≠X}	λX.A∩X≠X
i.	⟦exactly n⟧(A)	{X⊆E: |A∩X|=n}	λX.|A∩X|=n
j.	⟦at most n⟧(A)	{X⊆E: |A∩X|≤n}	λX.|A∩X|≤ n
k.	⟦at least n⟧(A)	{X⊆E: |A∩X|≥n}	λX.|A∩X|≥ n

The definitions of the corresponding determiners are given in (67):

(67)

⟦Det⟧	*Function notation*		⟦Det⟧	*Function notation*
a.	⟦all⟧	λYλX.Y⊆X	b. ⟦both⟧	λYλX.[Y⊆X∧|Y|=2]

c.	$[\![\text{the}_{sg}]\!]$	$\lambda Y\lambda X.[Y\subseteq X\wedge\|Y\|=1]$	h. $[\![\text{not only}]\!]$	$\lambda Y\lambda X.Y\cap X\neq X$
d.	$[\![\text{an}]\!]$	$\lambda Y\lambda X.Y\cap X\neq\varnothing$	i. $[\![\text{exactly n}]\!]$	$\lambda Y\lambda X.\|Y\cap X\|=n$
e.	$[\![\text{not all}]\!]$	$\lambda Y\lambda X.Y\cap X\neq Y$	j. $[\![\text{at most n}]\!]$	$\lambda Y\lambda X.\|Y\cap X\|\leq n$
f.	$[\![\text{no}]\!]$	$\lambda Y\lambda X.Y\cap X=\varnothing$	k. $[\![\text{at least n}]\!]$	$\lambda Y\lambda X.\|Y\cap X\|\geq n$
g.	$[\![\text{only}]\!]$	$\lambda Y\lambda X.Y\cap X=X$		

In view of our wish to be able to deal with transitive sentences like (68),

(68) Judith ate three sandwiches
(69) Mary mailed some letters
(70) Judith let in the cat

the model $\mathbf{M}_1$ must be extended. The extension is given in (51′).

(51′) $E'=\{a,b,c,d,\ \ldots,s_1,s_2,\ \ldots,le_1,le_2,\ \ldots,j,m\}$
$[\![\text{Judith}]\!]=j$
$[\![\text{Mary}]\!]=m$
$[\![\text{letter}]\!]=\{le_1,\ le_2,\ \ldots,\ le_m\}$
$[\![\text{sandwich}]\!]=\{s_1,\ s_2,\ \ldots,\ s_n\}$
$[\![\text{mail}]\!]=\{<m,le_1>,\ <m,le_2>\}$
$[\![\text{let in}]\!]=\{<j,a>,\ <j,b>,\ <j,c>,\ <m,d>\}$
$[\![\text{eat}]\!]=\{<m,s_1>,\ <j,s_2>,\ <j,s_3>,\ <j,s_4>\}$

We have now included Judith and Mary. The denotations of the two-place verbs reveal that Judith let in the cat as well as the children b and c, whereas Mary let in child d. Mary mailed two letters and Judith ate three sandwiches.[21]

The determiner of the direct object NP in the structure $[NP\ [_{VP}V[_{NP}Det\ N]]]$ expresses a binary relation. Its formulation is more complicated than in the case of intransitive verbs. A sentence like (68), for example, will be analysed in terms of a double application of the scheme in Figure 10. That is, $[\![\text{three}]\!]$ is a function operating on $[\![\text{sandwich}]\!]_{<e,t>}$ and the relation $[\![\text{eat}]\!]_{<e,<e,t>>}$ yielding the set of three-sandwich-eaters in E:

(71)
$$[\![\text{Three}]\!]([\![\text{sandwich}]\!])([\![\text{eat}]\!]) = \{e\in E{:}\,|[\![\text{sandwich}]\!]\cap\{d{:}<e,d>\in[\![\text{eat}]\!]\}|=3\}$$

This set, say S^3, is the set of those entities e in E which ate three sandwiches.[22] Hence, $S^3=\{\text{Judith}\}$, because Mary ate just one sandwich.

Barwise and Cooper (1981) define the denotation of the NP *Judith* – roughly $[\![\text{(the) Judith}]\!]$ – as the set of all subsets of E containing $[\![\text{Judith}]\!]$ as a member.[23]

(72) $[\![\text{(the) Judith}]\!]=\{X\subseteq E{:}\ j\in X\}$

Assuming that ⟦(the) Judith⟧ is a function operating on the set defined in (71), we get the following truth condition: (68) is true iff:

(73) $S^3 \in \{X \subseteq E: [\![\text{Judith}]\!] \in X\}$

In other words, (68) is true in $\mathbf{M}_1$ because $j \in S^3$. From chapter 7 on, the formal treatment of transitive verbs will become more and more central, due to the interaction of atemporal structure and temporal structure in the VP-denotation of sentences like (68).

3.3 Conclusion

This concludes the exposition of the main tools of the Theory of Generalized Quantification. EL underlies the formal representations used by GQT for the analysis of natural-language expressions.

4 *In search of* SQA

4.0 Introduction

Can the notion of [±SQA] be captured in terms of generalized quantification? This question was raised in Verkuyl (1987a) concerning what can be called Standard GQT. This subsumes all work on generalized quantification based on the assumption that NPs are of type <<*e*,*t*>,*t*>, that is, that they denote collections of sets. The answer given was roughly: a determiner Det of an NP yields a [+SQA]-NP if and only if the intersection of the two sets standing in the Det-relation is bounded, that is, finite and non-empty. This answer is not satisfactory: (a) it does not cover the question of whether or not the [+SQA]-property is related to any of the well known constraints on quantifiers, such as monotonicity, strength, properness, and so on; (b) there are apparent counterexamples which have not yet been dealt with; and (c) the conditions under which an NP may express [–SQA]-information were not sufficiently described.

The characterization of [+SQA] at the <<*e*,*t*>,*t*>-level will be summarized in section 4.1. It will be made clear that there is an interesting difference between the so-called mathematical meanings of *at least n* and *at most n* on the one hand and their meaning in sentences expressing temporal structure. In section 4.2, attention will be paid to some of the major constraints on Generalized Quantifiers having emerged in the eighties, in order to see in section 4.3 whether or not [+SQA] may be associated with one of them. Central to section 4.4 is the observation that the notion of [+SQA] has some overlap with the notions of strength and properness. However, these properties turn out to be neither sufficient nor necessary for the characterization of [+SQA]-information expressed by NPs. The discussion of properness and improperness in section 4.4 also prepares for the discussion in chapter 5.2 of the controversy between Russell and Strawson on definiteness. For aspectual theory this discussion is important because it must deal with the question of whether *The King of France crossed the street* is terminative, if there is no king of France. In general, the story of chapter 4 is: there seems to be no satisfactory way for GQT to deal with the [±SQA]-distinction as long as it treats NPs at the level of <<*e*,*t*>,*t*>.

4.1 SQA: Boundedness of A∩B?

Verkuyl (1987a) made an attempt to define the notion 'Specified Quantity of A' in the Standard Theory of Generalized Quantification. The basic idea was to identify it with the intersection A∩B in Figure 2 given certain conditions.

DEFINITION 1: An NP of the form Det N denotes a *Specified Quantity* of A in E relative to B iff A∩B is bounded.

DEFINITION 2: An NP of the form Det N denotes an *Unspecified Quantity* of A in E relative to B if: (a) $A \cap B = \varnothing$; or (b) $|A \cap B|$ cannot be determined.

DEFINITION 3: A set S is *bounded* if there is an $m \in \mathbf{Z}^+$ $(= \mathbf{N} \setminus \{0\})$, such that for all $x_i \in S$, $i \leq m$ (i a number assigned to members of S).

The durativity of sentences like (74)–(79) was accounted for on the basis of condition (a) in DEF 2:

(74) *No child* came in
(75) *Nobody* stumbled
(76) He lifted *nothing*
(77) Mary did*n't* mail *a single letter*
(78) *None of them* came in
(79) Mary mailed *no letter*

These sentences are all durative. They allow for durational adverbials, they cannot be combined with *in an hour*, they express a state in conjoined temporal adverbials, and so on:

(80) For hours *no child* came in
(81) ?*Nobody* mailed a letter in an hour
(82) Mary let in *none of the children* on Monday and Tuesday

As for (b) in DEF 2, bare plurals and quasi-partitives turn out to be [–SQA].

(83) There were *children* coming in
(84) Mary mailed *letters*
(85) Judith ate only *sandwiches*
(86) She ate *from the sandwiches*
(87) She read *a sort of books* which I never manage to finish

It is clear that these sentences are all durative even though the verb may contribute to terminative aspect:

(88) For hours *children* came in

(89) ?The children ate *from the sandwiches* in an hour

Note that (85) is also durative. Zwarts (1981) treated the Dutch equivalent of *only* as a determiner. Thijsse (1983) pointed out that the English *only* can be taken as a modifier of the quantifier, on the assumption that *only sandwiches* in (85) is analysed as $[_{NP}$only $[_{NP}$ ø sandwiches]]. I will continue to include *only* in the list of determiners but it will be thrown out in chapter 6.3, where independent evidence is given supporting Thijsse's contention. It should be observed that bare plurals and quasi-partitives have been treated unfeelingly in GQT. Part of this is due to the success of Carlson's 1978 analysis of bare plurals, but due to its ontological assumptions it is hard to translate this theory into terms of GQT. I shall discuss bare plurals in more detail in chapter 6.3.

As far as DEF 1 is concerned, the terminativity of sentences like (90) was characterized in terms of a bounded intersection $A \cap B$.

(90) a. The child came in
b. Both children came in
c. Three children came in
d. At least three children came in
e. Some of the children came in
f. Every child came in

In all these sentences, $A \cap B$ is non-empty and finite in the sense that in E it is possible to fix the cardinality of $A \cap B$, either actually or by virtue of having the knowledge of an omniscient entity. In this way, the notion of [+SQA] was captured.

DEF 1 expresses the idea that terminativity can only arise in a model where $A \cap B$ is non-empty and finite because E provides an upper bound. I made an appeal to the so-called Fixed Context Assumption (FCA) proposed by Barwise and Cooper (1981), which says that there is a fixed context determining the meaning of the basic expressions with respect to a given model. This assumption, which is open to different interpretations, can be interpreted as saying that speaker and hearer assume that the universe E about which they are talking has a certain cardinality at the moment of speech (as if one takes a picture of that situation fixing it, so to say). For example, the set of children is virtually infinite in the sense that members of this set fall out because they die or enter into adulthood. New members enter every minute because they are born. In normal conversation, however, there is some sort of fixing in the sense for the sentences in (90), one restricts ⟦child⟧ to the set of all children that exist or are taken into consideration at that moment, a set closed off at the moment of speech, so that its cardinality is a certain value m. The Fixed Context Assumption seems to be called for in sentences like:

(91) God counted the reals in a minute
(92) Albert repeatedly threw out **N**

where *God counted the reals* is terminative, whereas the reals are certainly infinite (I owe (91) to Gennaro Chierchia (pers. comm.)). A mathematician can repeatedly exclude the set of natural numbers **N** from certain calculations. I am not sure whether or not Barwise and Cooper had examples like these in mind, when they formulated the FCA, but it should be possible to treat an infinite set as something on which repeated operations are made possible: we humanize infinity, so to say, or freeze it, when we need it. This does not depend on the reals but rather on our conception of counting and throwing out things. In the present study, the Fixed Context Assumption will no longer be used to account for boundedness.

In Verkuyl (1972), it was pointed out that [+SQA] also pertains to mass NPs. DEF 1–3, however, do not capture terminative aspect in (93) and (94).

(93) Judith ate a slice of bread
(94) He drank a litre of whisky

They will be left out in the present section, but they will be included later on, in chapter 8.3. The main idea carries over quite readily due to the work of Link (1983), Bunt (1985) and others. For the present it suffices to say that if a portion of matter is bounded, it is $[+\text{SQA}]_m$, where m is the subscript for 'mass'. If it is empty or not determinable, it is unbounded:

(95) Judith ate nothing
(96) Judith ate cheese

However, at present, I shall keep things manageable by restricting myself to individuals and sets.

Summarizing, the large majority of the NPs occurring in terminative sentences can be described with [+SQA] interpreted as in DEF 1–3. Yet, it will become clear in chapter 6 that my 1987a analysis can be improved upon, thereby evading the problems signalled here. Also, the treatment of $A \cap B$ as 'undetermined' is left in the dark: no formal treatment was given. Moreover, the analysis of [+SQA] was not at all related to any of the global or local constraints on quantifiers. The next step is therefore to check whether the notion of Specified Quantity can be related to these constraints.

4.2 Constraints on Quantifiers

In Barwise and Cooper (1981), Van Benthem (1983b, 1986), Keenan and Faltz (1985), Keenan and Stavi (1986), Westerståhl (1984, 1985) among others, constraints on the semantic interpretations of determiners and NPs are systematically discussed. There are two lines of research: (a) the global one; and (b) the local one. We will briefly discuss both.

Global constraints are properties shared by all or most determiners. They play an important role in the literature as they express empirical hypotheses about universal properties of determiners and so they can be falsified or modified, or relativized. The most well known are:

(97) CONSERVATIVITY (CONS)
$D_E AB$ if and only if $D_E A(AB)$

(98) EXTENSION (EXT)
if $A,B \subseteq E \subseteq E'$, then $D_E AB$ if and only if $D_{E'} A(A \cap B)$

(99) QUANTITY (QUANT)
$D_E AB$ depends only on the numbers of entities in A, $A \cap B$ and E

CONS has been proposed by Barwise and Cooper (1981). According to Van Benthem (1986: 8) it 'accounts for the privileged role of the first argument in a determiner statement: it "sets the stage"'. It says that determiners pick out those B which are part of A, B–A being irrelevant, whereas A–B is relevant. EXT is a principle expressing that a determiner remains constant in all those models in which it establishes the relation between A and B. The notion of [+SQA] is compatible with both (97) and (99). The intuition behind QUANTITY is that $D_E AB$ is insensitive to the individual traits of the objects in A, B and E. It is just the numerical values that appear to count. QUANTITY also appears to be a background assumption for the analysis of the [+SQA]-notion, but as far as I can see it has no direct explanatory value for the analysis of aspectuality.

In the literature also, much attention has been paid to the internal set theoretical structure of the collections of sets which are quantifiers. Quantifiers can be distinguished from each other because they satisfy different 'local' constraints. One can hardly discuss generalized quantifiers without referring to them, so we can take advantage of the need to mention them by checking whether or not they are relevant for the discussion of the [+SQA]-notion.

DEFINITION 4: Q is *monotone increasing* if for any of its sets X in E the supersets of X in E are also members of Q, in all possible models. That is, if Q is monotone increasing, Q satisfies (100) in every model.

(100) $\forall X,Y \subseteq E((X \in Q \wedge X \subseteq Y) \Rightarrow Y \in Q))$
(101) $\forall X,Y \subseteq E(X \cap Y \in Q \Rightarrow (X \in Q \wedge Y \in Q))$
(102) $\forall X,Y \subseteq E((X \in Q \wedge Y \in Q) \Rightarrow X \cup Y \in Q)$

An NP is called monotone increasing if in every model in which its interpretation is defined, it expresses a monotone-increasing quantifier. An equivalent way of saying that Q is monotone increasing in M is to say that (101) holds good in M. That quantifiers like ⟦all children⟧ as defined in (45) satisfy (100) and (101) in $\mathbf{M}_1$ can be checked easily with the help of (100). The quantifier (50) ⟦not all children⟧ does not meet it: {b,c} is a member of Q, so {b,c,d}, being its superset, should be a member of Q too. But it is not. Monotone-increasing quantifiers have the property of being *closed under (finite) union.* That is, Q is monotone increasing only if (102) holds in every model. This property brings out the difference between ⟦exactly two children⟧ and ⟦several children⟧, the latter being closed under union: {b,c} and {b,d} are elements of Q and so is their union {b,c,d}. This does not hold good for ⟦exactly two children⟧.

So we have two pairs of cases, in which all four may contribute to terminative aspect; two of them are monotone increasing, two are not.

DEFINITION 5: A monotone-increasing quantifier Q is a *filter* iff Q satisfies (103):

(103) $\forall X,Y \subseteq E(X \cap Y \in Q \Leftrightarrow X \in Q \wedge Y \in Q)$

It can be seen quickly that ⟦*all children*⟧ is a filter, but also that ⟦*several children*⟧ spelled out in (49), is not a filter. It does not satisfy $\Leftarrow$ (see (107) below): {b,c} and {c,d} are members of Q, but {c} is not.[24]

DEFINITION 6: A filter is an *ultrafilter* iff it satisfies (104).

(104) $\forall X \subseteq E(X \in Q \Leftrightarrow E - X \notin Q)$

Proper names and definite descriptions like *the cat* are considered ultrafilters generated by individuals. We saw in (72) that the NP *Judith* denotes the set $\{X \subseteq E\colon j \in X\}$ generated by Judith (Barwise and Cooper 1981: 174). This amounts to saying that we want to collect all sets containing j as an element. And this is equivalent to saying that this collection meets the condition of containing no sets in which j does not occur. It is only sets containing j which meet (104), as (47) illustrates for the unique cat a in $\mathbf{M}_1$.

A sort of 'downward' constraint on the members of Q is called monotone decreasing. This family of quantifiers also shows some pyramidal structure.

DEFINITION 7: Q is *monotone decreasing* if for any of its sets X the subsets of X are also members of Q in all possible models. That is, if Q is monotone decreasing Q satisfies (105) in every model.

(105) $\forall X,Y \subseteq E((X \in Q \wedge Y \subseteq X) \Rightarrow Y \in Q)$
(106) $\forall X,Y \subseteq E(X \cup Y \in Q \Rightarrow (X \in Q \wedge Y \in Q))$
(107) $\forall X,Y \subseteq E((X \in Q \wedge Y \in Q) \Rightarrow X \cap Y \in Q)$

An equivalent way of saying that Q is monotone decreasing in M is to say that (106) holds good in $\mathbf{M}_1$. Monotone-decreasing quantifiers have the property of being *closed under (finite) intersection* (Zwarts 1981: 63). That is, Q is monotone decreasing only if (107) holds in every model. It can be checked easily in $\mathbf{M}_1$ that ⟦no child⟧ satisfies (105), ∅ being the subset of any set. The same applies to ⟦not all children⟧.

DEFINITION 8: A monotone decreasing quantifier Q is an *ideal* if and only if it meets (108):

(108) $\forall X,Y \subseteq E(X \cup Y \in Q \Leftrightarrow (X \in Q \wedge Y \in Q))$

⟦No children⟧ is an ideal, whereas the quantifier (30f) ⟦not all children⟧ is not. This is because it does not meet (102): both {b} and {a,c,d} are members of Q, but their union E is not. It is also possible to sharpen the notion of ideal into the notion of a *prime ideal*, but it turns out that this notion (which does not play an important role) coincides with the notion of an ultrafilter.

The property of conservativity in (97) $D_E AB$ iff $D_E A(A \cap B)$ is often called the property of 'living on A'. In Barwise and Cooper (1981) this property is defined as follows: Q lives on A if for any $X \subseteq E$, $X \in Q$ iff $X \cap A \in Q$. All sets X of Q have an intersection with A. They prove that if Q lives on A, then $A \in Q$ iff $E \in Q$. The notion of *strength* is defined as follows:

DEFINITION 9:
D_E is *positive strong* if for every A, $E \in D_E(A)$; otherwise weak
D_E is *negative strong* if for every A, $E \notin D_E(A)$; otherwise weak

For convenience, an NP with a strong determiner is called a strong NP. Strength plays an important role in the discussion about the well known distinction between weak and strong determiners originated in Milsark (1977). The latter cannot occur in existential sentences, as shown in (109)–(114).

(109) There is a/some child in the house
(110) *There is the/this/my/every child in the house

(111) There are two/three, etc. children in the house

(112) *There are these two/three, etc. children in the house

(113) There are few/many/several children in the house

(114) *There are /all/both/the many, etc. children in the house

Milsark proposed that [+DEF] be interpreted as universal quantification (over individuals) and [–DEF] as existential quantification. According to Barwise and Cooper, the semantic characterization of positive strong and weak in DEF 9 coincides at a higher order level with Milsark's first-order classification of [+DEF]-determiners and [–DEF]-determiners. The (incomplete) list (115) captures Milsark's position.

(115)

+DEF	–DEF
the	*a*
demonstratives	*some*
possessives, etc.	*few*, *several*, *many*, etc.
each, *all*, *every*	*two*, *three*, *four*, etc.
any, etc.	

His position is that a determiner can be either [+DEF] or [–DEF]. In Verkuyl (1981), it was argued that this position is untenable and that numerals and *few*, *several*, *many*, etc. be removed from the [–DEF]-category. I will discuss this proposal in chapter 6 in more detail, but here it suffices to point out that (115) shows that strength ([+DEF]) and weakness ([–DEF]) do not coincide with the opposition between [+SQA] and [–SQA].

Let Q=⟦NP⟧ be a quantifier. Then, in general, one may say that Q is to cut $\wp$(E) in two parts: the subsets of E satisfying the definition of Q (they are sent to 1) and those not satisfying it (they are sent to 0). The latter are collected in the complement of Q, Q'. If Q is a non-empty proper subset of $\wp$(E), then Q is called a *sieve*. If $Q=\wp$(E) or if $Q=\varnothing$, then Q is a non-sieve (Barwise and Cooper 1981: 179f.). In $\mathbf{M}_1$, the quantifiers in (51) are *proper* (they cut $\wp$(E) properly), but ⟦all⟧(⟦dog⟧) is a non-sieve. The same applies to ⟦no⟧(⟦dog⟧)=$\varnothing$, where $Q'=\wp$(E).

There is a relation between strength and properness. NPs with strong determiners are always proper if they are defined. This concludes the survey of properties of quantifiers potentially relevant for the research into the nature of [+SQA]-information.

Table 10 *This survey shows how standard notions of the theory of generalized quantification such as monotonicity, filter, ultrafilter, strength and properness relate to the [±SQA]-feature*

Monotone↑	*Filter*	*Ultrafilter*	↑*Strength*	*Proper*	[SQA]
Judith	+	+	+	|N|=1	+
the_{sg} N	+	+	+	|N|=1	+
this N	+	+	+	|N|=1	+
the_{pl} N	+	–	+	|N|>1	+
both N	+	–	+	|N|=2	+
the n N	+	–	+	|N|=n	+
all of the N	+	–	+	|N|>1	+
some of the N	–	–	+	|N|>1	+
most N	–	–	+	N≠∅	+
all N	+	–	+	N≠∅	+
every N	+	–	+	N≠∅	+
many N	–	–	–	|N|=many	+
several N	–	–	–	|N|≥2	+
not only N	–	–	–	N≠E	–
at least n N	–	–	–	|N|≥n	+
n or less N	–	–	–	|N|≥n	+
more than n N	–	–	–	|N|≥n	+
some N	–	–	–	N≠∅	+
a(n)	–	–	–	N≠∅	+
Monotone↓	*Ideal*	*Prime Ideal*	↓*Strength*	*Proper*	[SQA]
not Judith	+	+	+	|N|=1	+
not the_{sg} N	+	+	+	|N|=1	+
not the_{pl} N	+	–	+	|N|>1	+
none of the N	+	–	+	|N|>1	–
none of the n N	+	–	+	|N|=n	–
neither N	+	–	+	|N|=2	–
no N	+	–	–	N≠∅	–
not all N	–	–	+	N≠∅	+
not every child	–	–	+	N≠∅	+
only N	–	–	–	N≠E	–
at most n N	–	–	–	|N|>n	+
few N	–	–	–	|N|=few	+
n or less	–	–	–	|N|>n	+
less than n of the m	–	–	–	|N|>n	+
at most n of the m	–	–	–	|N|>n	+
Non-monotone			*Strength*	*Proper*	[SQA]
exactly n N			–	|N|≥n	+

In Table 10, a summary is given of how the properties discussed above relate to [±SQA]. The + under the heading [SQA] means that the NP in question is 'basically' [+SQA]. They will all be discussed in more detail shortly. The way in which the term 'basically' should be interpreted will be made more precise gradually. The idea is that their 'lowest-level'-use (type-logically) makes certain NPs [+SQA], but for all of them there are apparent counterexamples of different sorts: [+SQA]-NPs may appear in durative sentences as well, losing their [+SQA]-nature, so to say. Even proper names can be interpreted [–SQA], as will be pointed out below.

The counterexamples are not real, however, because there appears to be a system involved that can be characterized type-logically. The sentences in which otherwise [+SQA]-NPs occur as [–SQA] have characteristics which fully justify maintaining the distinction between [+SQA] and [–SQA]. There is so much system in this durative behaviour that it is fruitful to associate the [+SQA]-characterization as tied up with a particular type-logical level, which is crucially involved in the definition of terminative aspect. Moreover, there is no way to get from a 'basic' [–SQA]- to a [+SQA]-interpretation.

Table 10 illustrates that one cannot expect much explanatory power from the property of positive strength and properness and the monotonicity properties. It looks as if the notion of [+SQA] is square with any of the well-established notions of GQT. Undoubtedly this is due to the origin of GQT, which makes it difficult to deal with the notion of [+SQA] in which the atemporal structure expressed by the NP is somehow dependent on temporal structure expressed by the verb, given certain conditions. GQT does not have a tradition in which attention is paid to the interaction between these two different sorts of structure, so it is worthwhile to undertake a trip through a relatively unreclaimed area across the frontiers of the atemporal theory. While proceeding, a more clear picture of [+SQA] will emerge.

As a final remark, it is necessary to point out that the list in Table 10 is by no means exhaustive. For example, it is clear that a subset of the so-called comparative quantifiers like *fewer than, a greater number of-than, a greater percentage of-than, fewer ... at John's party-than*, as discussed in Beghelli (1992) can be characterized as [+SQA]-quantifiers. However, I shall restrict myself here to the list in Table 10, because a discussion of more complicated quantifiers would not add anything substantial to the analysis of the [+SQA]-notion.

4.3 Is SQA a constraint on Quantifiers?

In this and the following section, GQT will be confronted with a set of empirical problems raised from the point of view of aspectual theory. Certain observations need to be dealt with properly before GQT may qualify itself as a theory of aspectuality. In section 4.1, three situations were investigated:

(116) $|A \cap B| = m$ (where $m \in \mathbf{N}$) ⇒ [+SQA]
(117) $|A \cap B| = 0$ ⇒ [–SQA]
(118) $|A \cap B| =$ undetermined ⇒ [–SQA]

Though it does not work out satisfactorily, it is worthwhile to take it as a point of departure for further discussion. The notion of cardinality is crucial in (116)–(118), though in different ways for each of the situations. In order for atemporal NP-denotations to be structurally related to temporal structure so that the result expresses temporal boundedness, they should have some cardinality, say m, even though speakers and hearers need not know the exact value of m, dependent on the quantifying expression being used. Impressionistically: to denote a Specified Quantity of A is to denote a set whose members can be counted given an omniscient entity doing the counting, or to denote a bounded mass of A, where *bounded* is to mean 'having a value m as the output of a measure function'.

To say that the intersection $A \cap B = \varnothing$ is to say that its cardinality is zero. So in the representation of NPs meeting (117) this information should be present. It is present in, for example, (58) where $[\![no]\!](A) = \{X \subseteq E: A \cap X = \varnothing\}$. However, in GQT it is not very well possible to say that the cardinality of $A \cap B$ in sentences like (119)–(121) cannot be determined.

(119) Judith ate sandwiches
(120) Judith ate from the sandwiches
(121) Judith ate

Why are these sentences durative? And how is this captured in GQT? Here we meet a problem for GQT not solved by DEF 1–3: the problem of how to account for bare plurals and for implicit arguments. Chapter 6.3 tackles the problems with bare plurality. There, the unclear status of *only* N as a quantifier will be discussed too. The question of how to represent implicit arguments will be taken up in chapter 14. Till then it will simply be assumed that the absence of an argument can be equated with the presence of [–SQA]-information.

It is not only (118) which raises problems for a GQT-approach to [+SQA]: (116) is also not as clear-cut as one would like to have it. I shall demonstrate this with a discussion of four problems involved in establishing cardinality: (A) contrastive quantification; (B) *at least*-quantification; (C) *at most*-quantification; and (D) *not*+Q-quantification.

(A) Contrastive quantification

In certain contexts it is possible to use quantifiers even without using them as quantifiers in the strict sense. That is, even though on the face of it the NPs are [+SQA], they do not behave properly as [+SQA]-quantifiers:

(122) Judith ate few sandwiches compared with Jessica
(123) Judith took many sandwiches from THAT tray
(124) Judith ate her sandwiches grudgingly
(125) Judith took the sandwiches from the tray, but left the toast

There are different problems at issue, most of them having to do with contrast. What they have in common seems to be the fact that it is not the quantificational information which is important but rather the way a set of sandwiches is related to Judith: in (122) her set is smaller than Jessica's, in (123) the set of sandwiches from that tray is compared to sets of sandwiches from other trays. In (124), it is assumed by context that sandwiches are structurally part of some meal, say breakfast, and that Judith took an unspecified number of sandwiches. In (125), the article *the* seems to be used to make an opposition between two categories which are already introduced or known in the discourse domain. Its paraphrase is: the things she took from the tray were *sandwiches* rather than toast. In chapter 6.3, it will be pointed out in more detail that and how this sort of use of the definite article makes sentences like (125) durative rather than terminative. It appears more adequate to do this by treating NPs as denoting semantic objects of type $<<<e,t>,t>,t>$ rather than of type $<<e,t>,t>$.

(B) At least-quantification

Under this heading we have to consider a set of quantifying expressions ranging from the n they mention (possibly) to and including ∞.

(126) a. some (=sm) b. a(n) c. several
d. at least n e. more than n f. n or more

The problem is whether they have the mathematical meaning of '$\geq$' so that they could express infinite cardinality (or measure). This opens up the question of whether quantifying NPs of this category may express a Specified Quantity of A, given the fact that $A \cap B$ may be not finite. In (127) and (128)

(127) *At least three* children came in
(128) Mary has mailed *more than three* letters

the mathematical meaning of the ≥-sign does not seem to require that the intersection A∩B be finite: the set {x: x≥y} is an infinite subset of **N**. Are quantifiers which are defined in terms of an 'open end' less suitable to express [+SQA] than those which give an exact numerical value? Evidence to the contrary is given in (129)–(131):

(129) #*Some* (*of the*) *children* came in for hours
(130) #Judith has eaten *at least three sandwiches* for hours
(131) #For hours Mary has mailed *more than three letters*

Here, the sentences (minus the durational adverbials) are all terminative. They must pertain to situations in which the italicized constituents refer to finite, non-empty sets. It is not unreasonable to assume that the introduction of the temporal adverbial *for hours* enforces the presupposition that the cardinality statement |A∩B|≥n should count as the assertion that there is a certain natural number m larger than n (but not given to the hearer) which is taken as the cardinal number of the intersection. If this carries over to (126), we may say that we accept the possible use of ≥ in mathematical statements making the NP denotation ⟦at least n⟧(A) infinite. However, as soon as we interpret (127) as sentences *expressing temporal structure*, the NP-denotation becomes finite. Note that modal statements like (132) do not show this behaviour,

(132) At least three children will come in

if we make the sets ⟦child⟧ and ⟦come in⟧ infinite. Sentences like (132) allow for a [–SQA]-interpretation, but they are terminative if they are used with a temporal adverbial.

(133) #At least three children will come in for hours

Their NP shows the well known [+SQA]-behaviour, which can only be explained on the assumption of a presupposition of finiteness of the intersection A∩B induced by the temporal structure presupposed by *for hours*.

(C) At most-quantification

Under this heading we will consider a set of quantifying expressions ranging from the n they mention to and including 0.

(134)
a. at most n
b. n or fewer/less
c. less than n of the m
d. at most n of the m
e. less than
f. n or less

The problem is again whether they have the mathematical meaning of the $\leq$–sign so that they might express a cardinality in the range $0 \leq x \leq n$ rather than in the range $1 \leq x \leq n$. This opens up the question of whether NPs of this category may express a Specified Quantity of A, given the fact that $A \cap B$ might be empty in a given model. Sentences like

(135) *At most three* children came in
(136) *Three or fewer* cats came in

are terminative in their most natural interpretation. Natural language seems to require **N** here, as can be deduced from the aspectual behaviour of their NPs in (137)–(139).

(137) #*At most three* children came in for hours
(138) #Judith has eaten *fewer than four sandwiches* for hours
(139) #For hours Mary has mailed *fewer than three letters*

I find it impossible to interpret these sentences as pertaining to a state or process. They simply block the single-event reading and they express the well known odd aspectual repetition. That one has to do with terminative aspect also becomes clear from the fact that the NPs under consideration are happy to occur with *in an hour*, as exemplified in (140) and (141).

(140) *At most three* children came in in an hour
(141) Judith has eaten *fewer than four sandwiches* in an hour

Again it is not unreasonable to assume that the introduction of the temporal adverbials *for hours* and *in an hour* enforces the presupposition that the cardinality statement $|A \cap B| \leq n$ should count as the assertion that $A \cap B$ is a non-empty set and that this carries over to a temporal interpretation of sentences like (135) and (136).

(D) Not + Q-quantification

What about sentences like (142) and (143)?

(142) Not Judith ate three sandwiches
(143) Not the cat came in

These sentences are strange unless they are interpreted contrastively.

(144) Not Judith ate three sandwiches, but Mary
(145) Not the cat but a child came in

Note that *not Judith* falls under (116) rather than under (117). This becomes clear by having a look at its denotation in the model $\mathbf{M}_1$: it would contain any subset of E not containing Judith (see (50) for *not all children*). In general, the need to define quantifiers of the form *not* NP in GQT seems to be due to a certain over-measure of logical perfection. But given their definitions, the analysis of sentences like (142) and (143) is to be restricted to their contrastive behaviour, either in sentences like (144) and (145) or in a context. With this proviso in mind consider (146) and (147).

(146) #Not Judith ate three sandwiches for hours (but Mary)
(147) #For hours not the cat but a child came in

Here terminative aspect is clearly expressed: (146) means that it is not Judith who repeatedly ate three sandwiches but someone else. This interpretation differs from sentences like (148) and (149).

(148) For hours nobody ate three sandwiches
(149) For hours the cat did not come in

However, if *Judith* is replaced by *not a child*, or *not every child* the same applies: there is contrastive repetition. The same holds good for (150).

(150) #Not all children came in for hours (some did)

An interesting phenomenon shows up: the fact that it is sometimes possible to escape from a [+SQA]-interpretation because, due to contrastive or other factors the determiner is primarily focussed on the nature of the denotation of the head Noun rather than on the quantification over its members. This cannot be expressed easily in terms of an <<*e*,*t*>,*t*>-analysis as it involves a representational distinction between introduction or identification of a set and quantification over its members. In the course of Part II, this aspect of [+SQA]-identification will become more and more important, in particular in chapter 8.1.

This concludes the discussion of the quantifying expressions in Table 10 in terms of DEF 1–3. It might be useful to summarize what can be captured. First of all, it seems as if [+SQA] cannot be systematically related to the properties mon$\uparrow$, filter or ultrafilter nor to their mon$\downarrow$ counterparts. It also cannot be related to strength in a significant way, although typically strong quantifiers such as *Judith, both children, the three children* are clearly [+SQA]. So we have to have a further look at properness. This seems to be more rewarding. For example, the weak quantifiers *at least n* and *at most n* allow a [+SQA]-interpretation if we can make sure that the range of *at least n* does not include zero and the range of *at most n* does not express infinity. This amounts to saying that properness is penetrating the concept of [+SQA], in the sense that certain conditions on this sort of quantification make it possible for a quantifier Q to act as a sieve. In other words, a sieve can only operate properly as a splitting function in a power set if it is able to distinguish a specified quantity of elements in its domain.

Looking further into the notion of properness is not only rewarding, it is also necessary because intriguing problems arise with the aspectual interpretation of sentences with universal quantification. Aspectually, the analysis of universal quantification is difficult, because in first-order predicate logic there is a standard interpretation of the universal quantifier allowing it to range over the empty set. This is the case if in an NP of the form *all* N, $[\![N]\!]=\varnothing$. So the question is: what happens aspectually in sentences having such an NP? In other words, does it express [+SQA]? A more precise look into the complex notion of properness is called for in order to see how it relates to [+SQA]. The picture emerging will be that properness bears on the cardinality expressed by the quantifier: properness will be argued to be a necessary condition for [+SQA].

4.4 Properness and terminativity

In the approach advocated by Bertrand Russell, the interpretation function $[\![.]\!]$ is total. This means that a sentence like (151) would be true in $\mathbf{M}_1$, because it is analysed basically as (152).

(151) All dogs came in

(152) $\forall x(\text{dog}(x)\rightarrow\text{came\_in}(x))$

There are no dogs in $\mathbf{M}_1$, so the truth definition of the connective $\rightarrow$ makes (151) always true, as for all x, $x\notin[\![\text{dog}]\!]$. The first-order analysis in (152) carries over to second-order truth definitions like (153).

(153) $[\![\text{all}]\!](A)(B)=1 \text{ iff } B\in\{X\subseteq E\text{: } A\cap X=A\}$

This is always true when $A=\varnothing$. This can be seen in $\mathbf{M}_1$, where $[\![\text{all}]\!]([\![\text{dog}]\!])=\wp(E)$, because the intersection of any subset X of E with the empty set will yield $\varnothing$ itself. So $[\![\text{all}]\!]([\![\text{dog}]\!])$ is improper in $\mathbf{M}_1$.

Strawson (1950) was the first to attack Russell on this position.[25] On his approach, the interpretation of an NP should be partial, which means that one should allow models in which no truth value can be yielded if A in (153) is the empty set. In that case, it is necessary to add the presupposition to (153) that it should hold only if A is non-empty. For Strawson, the NP *all dogs* cannot be interpreted in a model without dogs, because the function ⟦all⟧(⟦dog⟧) does not find an argument, so it cannot yield a truth value, and the NP-denotation is undefined in that model. Even though they observe that it is hard to interpret *all N* as a non-sieve, Barwise and Cooper (1981) do not follow Strawson, but they allow partial functions, for example, for *neither* N, and *the n* N.

In De Jong and Verkuyl (1985), it was argued that one may also interpret *all* N partially in view of there being two uses of *all*: (a) a lawlike use as in (154); and (b) a contingent use as in (155).[26]

(154) All ravens are black
(155) All the seats are taken
(156) All men are ill

The former use is considered 'marked' in the sense that it has the status of a law and does not seem to refer to a particular model. Basically it is lexical knowledge (knowledge of the world) which is expressed; (154) talks about what the speaker knows about ravens, for example a parent informing her child (synthetically) about an analytical property of ravens.[27] In this use of *all*, ⟦all⟧(A) may be taken totally. However, the contingent use of *all* can be distinguished from the lawlike use, for example because it is not possible to drop *all* in (155) without a change of meaning, whereas it can be dropped in (154): *All ravens are black* means the same as *Ravens are black*, but *All seats are taken* does not mean the same as *Seats are taken*. If one drops *all* in (156) without a change of meaning, it will mean that there is a (psycho-biological) law saying that men are ill. Thus, it was proposed to follow the Strawsonian line by restricting definitions like in (157) to just those models in which $|A|\neq 0$.

	Quantifiers	*Definition*	*Restriction*
(157)	⟦all⟧(A)	$\{X\subseteq E: A\subseteq X\}$	$\|A\|\geq 1$
	⟦both⟧(A)	$\{X\subseteq E: A\subseteq X\}$	$\|A\|=2$
	$[\![\text{the}_{sg}]\!]$(A)	$\{X\subseteq E: A\subseteq X\}$	$\|A\|=1$
	$[\![\text{the}_{pl}]\!]$(A)	$\{X\subseteq E: A\subseteq X\}$	$\|A\|\geq 2$
	⟦not all⟧(A)	$\{X\subseteq E: A\cap X\neq A\}$	$\|A\|\geq 1$

Lawlike sentences are not applied directly to a model. From the aspectual point of view, this position seems to be enforced by the following data:

(158) #All children came in for hours
(159) #All dogs came in for hours
(160) #The three children were let in for hours
(161) #The three dogs were let in for hours

These sentences show the blocking of a single-event reading and the triggering of a forced repetition. Sentence (158), for example, means that for each child it was such that it came in repeatedly during the period mentioned. But exactly the same happens to (159): it says that all dogs came in repeatedly for hours, the single-event reading being blocked. This is even more so in (161). How is it possible that one can talk about dogs which do not exist but which were able to come in repeatedly?

The observations with respect to (158)–(161) seem to shed a new light on the Russell-Strawson controversy. In these sentences, Strawson appears to trump Russell: if sentences like (159) and (161) are undefined in $\mathbf{M}_1$, one need not worry about their aspectual properties. These are acknowledged but they may not play a role in $\mathbf{M}_1$. Russell would be forced to account for the forced repetition in (159) and (161) in terms of their truth conditions.[28] Whatever the outcome of an evaluation between Russell and Strawson may be, it is clear that what is at issue in (158)–(161) is the question of whether the construal of terminative aspect is dependent on the truth conditions. This is what is inherent to Russell's approach: its wish to draw certain phenomena into the realm of semantics. As far as I can see, there is an unexpected but feasible compromise between Russell and Strawson on the basis of an analysis of NPs at the $<<<e,t>,t>,t>$-level, so I return to the controversy in chapter 5.2, after having introduced the required formal machinery in chapter 5.2.

As far as definite descriptions are concerned, it is well known that Russell would qualify sentence (162) as false because (163) is false in any model in which there is no dog:

(162) The dog came in
(163) $\exists x(\forall y(dog(y) \leftrightarrow y{=}x) \wedge came\_in(x))$

This is because the first conjunct which says that x is a dog and that there is no individual y besides x that is a dog is false in $\mathbf{M}_1$ so the whole proposition must be false, even though there is an x which came in. It is aspectually important to see how sentences like (164) are treated. Russell's answer is: (164) is taken to be ambiguous between (165) and (166).

(164) The dog did not come in
(165) $\neg\exists x(\forall y(dog(y) \leftrightarrow y{=}x) \wedge came\_in(x))$
(166) $\exists x(\forall y(dog(y) \leftrightarrow y{=}x) \wedge \neg came\_in(x))$

Formula (165) makes (164) true because it is not the case that there is a unique individual which is a dog and which came in; formula (166) makes it false because it says that there is a unique individual which is a dog and did not come in (for a more detailed description, see Gamut 1991, I: 163).

In my view, Russell's answer is more than unsatisfactory. Firstly, because it levies a heavy toll on the notion of ambiguity. For example, suppose that *stay outside* is fully synonymous with *not come in*, then sentences like (167) would not be ambiguous at all.

(167) The dog stayed outside
(168) The dog hesitated but didn't come in

Also, in (168) the presence of a positive predicate and a negative predicate would require some reduction mechanism on ambiguity (think of what happens if we change the order of the two predicates). It would be much simpler to assume that *hesitated* and *did not come in* would be treated similarly. In general, ambiguity only makes sense given a model if the model provides means for a verifying test of both readings. So, it looks as if the ambiguity of (164) is an artefact of the logical system being used. Secondly, and not unrelated, Russell's solution is so unnatural: it gives the positive sentence (162) priority over the negative sentence (164) which it does not deserve: both (162) and (164) should be treated on a par.

At this point many will expect me to confess myself pro Strawson and to turn my back on Russell, but the question under discussion is more complicated. It is at the <<<*e*,*t*>,*t*>,*t*>-level that we find an unexpected complication of the discussion between Russell and Strawson, which allows us to improve on Russell. An <<<*e*,*t*>,*t*>,*t*>-analysis treats (162) and (164) in the same way by not allowing the negative sentence to be ambiguous. Moreover, it also treats (162), (164) and (151) in the same way as far as their truth value is concerned, the crucial point being that it is the NP rather than the VP that causes the controversy. However, it will be striking to see that by this Russell ends up far closer to Strawson than on lower-level analyses.

As far as the aspectual properties of the NPs in sentences like (151) and (162) are concerned, it was shown that they behave in the same way. In general, if they are proper, they pertain to [+SQA] and hence can contribute to terminative aspect. In the next chapter, more attention will be paid to the properties that *all* and *the* have in common.

4.5 Conclusion

The present chapter has served two purposes. The first was to show by an analysis of well-established GQT-notions that [+SQA] has to do with cardinality information. However, there is no systematic connection between the GQT-constraints and [±SQA]. All the same, there are points of attachment. For example, the notion of strength is intuitively related to [+SQA]: a strong quantifier denotes something which is bounded. For some monotone-decreasing quantifiers this does not hold good, because ⟦no⟧(A), ⟦none of the⟧(A), ⟦none of the n⟧(A) and ⟦neither⟧(A) are ruled out by (117). Moreover, there are weak quantifiers which are [+SQA]. Although it is not possible to relate properness directly to [+SQA], there are certainly strong indications that what is expressed by this constraint also relates to [+SQA]-information. If monotone-increasing quantifiers are proper, their most natural interpretation is to pertain to a Specified Quantity of A, even if one does not possess the means to establish the cardinality number, as in ⟦some⟧(A), ⟦at least n⟧(A), etc. This means that the other quantifiers, if proper, qualify themselves as [+SQA]-quantifiers unless they fall under DEF 2, that is, (117) and (118). Hence an investigation into the conditions under which [+SQA]-information is expressed overlaps considerably with an investigation of the conditions under which NPs are interpreted as proper quantifiers. It will be argued below that the presence of cardinality information at a specific type-logical level acts as a sieve, and that its absence at that level (and its possible presence at a higher level) leads to [–SQA]. It will also be shown that there are different ways in which cardinality may be left unexpressed.

The second purpose was to prepare for the argument that [+SQA] and especially [–SQA] are notions that may be captured by GQT, though not, or only in a forced way, at the level of $<<e,t>,t>$. To get a clear view of these things it is necessary to go up one level by looking at NPs as denoting semantic objects of type $<<<e,t>,t>,t>$. This will lead to the introduction or identification of a subset W of A, where A is the set presumed by Specified Quantity of A, and to the systematic expression of the presence or absence of cardinality information about W, with respect to which aspectual properties of the sentences in question are determined. More specifically, we will see below in chapters 6, 7 and 8 that there is a systematic way of expressing cardinality information about the members of W (i.e. [+SQA]) but also a systematic way of preventing this cardinality information to be present at that level in order to obtain a [–SQA]-interpretation.

5 *Numerals and quantifiers: one level up*

5.0 Introduction

There is a line of analysis of NP-quantification in GQT in which NPs are taken to be of type $<<<e,t>,t>,t>$. Scha (1981) and Verkuyl (1981) are among the earliest publications in this tradition, both building further on Bartsch (1973) and Bennett (1975). The main goal of Verkuyl (1981) was to build a sort of bridge between the framework of Montague Grammar and the Chomskian pre-Government-Binding X-bar Syntax. Its descriptive purpose was not to find out what [+SQA] stands for, rather it was focussed on the treatment of numerals and quantifiers. Yet, somewhat to my own surprise, some of its results turn out to bear directly on the issue of quantification in aspect construal, especially as the sort of NP-representations proposed (recall: at the $<<<e,t>,t>,t>$-level)[29] offer a quite workable point of departure for more sophisticated extensions in the area of temporality. Therefore, a short summary of my 1981 grammar is in order. The present chapter is divided into two sections: section 5.1 gives a description of an X-bar grammar *à la* Montague, in which syntactically and semantically two structural positions are available for the Standard GQT-determiners, whereas section 5.2 shows that this grammar has certain concrete things to say and solutions to offer about the Russell-Strawson controversy. Apart from the contribution it may have to the solution of the philosophical controversy, it is also relevant for the question of whether or not it is necessary to exclude terminative aspect from occurring in tautological sentences.

5.1 NP = [DET [NUM … N^0]]

The Montagovian-styled X-bar syntax proposed in Verkuyl (1981) is a variable binary branching categorial syntax having rules of the following form:

(169) If $\alpha \in X^i$ and $\beta \in X^{i+1}/X^i$ (or $X^i \backslash X^{i+1}$), then $F(\alpha,\beta) \in X^{i+1}$ and $F(\alpha,\beta) = \beta\alpha$ (or $\alpha\beta$)

It is a binary branching system, in which a functor β takes a value α on the projection line of X to yield either the same type as their input or a different type. X^0 is a lexical category of type <*e*,*t*>, X^{max} the maximal category of the projection induced by X^0. For NPs, X^{max} (=NP) is a fixed category in the sense that it denotes a semantic object of type <<<*e*,*t*>,*t*>,*t*> and it is obtained by a rule requiring a fixed type-logical characterization of N^{max-1} as being of type <<*e*,*t*>,*t*>, in order for it to qualify as the input of the NP-forming rule. This gives a special role to the determiner as providing NP-hood to a noun. Between N^0 and N^{max-1} there is a variable part, which accommodates the adjectival substructure of NPs, that is for adjectives of type <<*e*,*t*>,<*e*,*t*>>.[30] Thus, the general scheme for the structure of NPs looks as in (170).

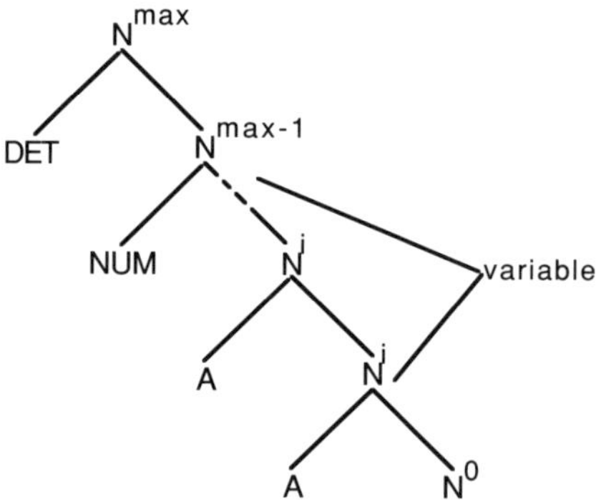

(170) $[N^{max}$ DET $[N^{max-1}$ NUM $[_{N}i$ A* $N^{0}]]]$

The asterisk in (170) represents the possibility of having a series of stacked adjectival modifiers such as in *The twelve nice red wooden boxes*. In the figure this is indicated by the dots. NUM and DET are taken as operations bringing about a change of type. NUM takes a semantic object of type <*e*,*t*> and brings it to <<*e*,*t*>,*t*>, whereas DET takes an object of type <<*e*,*t*>,*t*> to yield an <<<*e*,*t*>,*t*>,*t*>-type. In its most simple form, an NP has the form in (171):

(171) $[_{NP}$ DET $[N^1$ NUM $N^0]]]$

where NP=N^{max} and N^1=N^{max-1}. For convenience, I shall often use the simple structure to clarify certain points.

The semantic rules corresponding to (169) have the traditional PTQ-format of grammar, though the grammar was kept extensional. Numerals like *two*, *three*, etc. are seen as the lexicalized forms of the category to which Singular and Plural belong as abstract elements. In some languages they are grammaticalized as morphemes. As a consequence, the lexical category *child* in sentences like *The child walked* and *The children walked* is neutral between Singular and Plural: *the child* is now analysed as [the[SG[child]]] and *the children* as [the[PL[child]]].[31] The relevant semantic specifications of members of the lexical category NUM are:

	Element	*Category*	*Type*	*Denotation*
(172)	SG	NUM	$<<e,t>,<<e,t>,t>>$	$\lambda Y \lambda X[X \subseteq Y \wedge \lvert X \rvert = 1]$
(173)	PL	NUM	$<<e,t>,<<e,t>,t>>$	$\lambda Y \lambda X[X \subseteq Y \wedge \lvert X \rvert > 1]$
(174)	*three*	NUM	$<<e,t>,<<e,t>,t>>$	$\lambda Y \lambda X[X \subseteq Y \wedge \lvert X \rvert = 3]$

Here, the EL-conventions of DEF 3.3 are used: X and Y are variables of type $<e,t>$. N^0 in (171) was restricted to Count Nouns only.

The members of NUM are semantically interpreted as functions relating sets, just like the standard GQ-determiners.[32] In (175), the function ⟦three⟧ applied to a set, say ⟦child⟧, yields the collection of all sets X where X⊆⟦child⟧ and where each X contains three members.

(175) $\lambda Y \lambda X[X \subseteq Y \wedge \lvert X \rvert = 3](⟦child⟧) \Leftrightarrow \lambda X[X \subseteq ⟦child⟧ \wedge \lvert X \rvert = 3]$

The same applies to SG and PL. The numeral SG denotes the function ⟦SG⟧ which yields the set of all singletons X of a set Y. In our model $\mathbf{M}_1$, ⟦SG⟧ applied to ⟦child⟧ yields the collection $\lambda X[X \subseteq ⟦child⟧ \wedge \lvert X \rvert = 1]$, which is the set of singletons {{b},{c},{d}}. Thus, in the NP *the child*, the collection of sets ⟦SG⟧(⟦child⟧) is the semantic interpretation of $N^1 = \text{SG}(N^0)$. In major approaches to the semantics of plural NPs, such as Scha (1981) and Link (1983), it is standard to distinguish the set AT(⟦N⟧), that is, the set of all atoms in the power set of ⟦N⟧ in the model. This is done by introducing a separate operator. It is clear that ⟦SG⟧(⟦N⟧) is exactly this set, which is to say that (172) is quite a natural way of introducing the set of atoms.

One of the linguistic motivations for a scheme like (170) is that it accounts for the data in (176):

(176) a. nice quiet children
b. three nice children
c. *nice three children
d. *four three children

which suggest that the general rule is that adjectives should follow numeral elements. Some apparent counterexamples such as *the following two children* will be discussed in chapter 6.1. They may be seen as modifications of the numerals rather than of the Noun.

DET is defined as a function of type <<<*e*,*t*>,*t*>, <<<*e*,*t*>,*t*>,*t*>> operating on members of N^{max-1} and yielding a category of type <<<*e*,*t*>,*t*>,*t*>. Thus, determiners are taken as relations between collections of sets of individuals, in particular between $[\![N^{max-1}]\!]$ and $[\![VP]\!]$. Note that a part of the quantificational information, which in GQT is associated with determiners, is now transferred to the NUM-part of the NP. This has far-reaching linguistic consequences because on an <<<*e*,*t*>,*t*>,*t*>-analysis some of the determiners have to be made dependent on the information provided by SG and PL. *Some*, for example, will be given the lexical subcategorization information of the form $[—N^{max-1}]$, which says that it can take both SG and PL; *all* needs to be marked as taking only a plural N^{max-1}, *every* being subcategorized for SG. This does not sound unreasonable as this is what speakers have to learn lexically. *Some boys* is analysed as some(PL(boy)) and *some boy* as some(SG(boy)). So, agreement is governed by SG and PL.

The lexical specifications of *the*, *all*, *some*, *a* and ø are given in (177)–(181), which is based on the simplified (177), which means that N^1 is to be read as N^{max-1}.

(177)	*the*	$[—N^1]$	$\lambda Q\lambda P\exists!W[Q(W)\wedge P(W)]$
(178)	*all*	$[—N^1_{pl}]$	$\lambda Q\lambda P\exists!W[Q(W)\wedge P(W)]$
(179)	*some*	$[—N^1]$	$\lambda Q\lambda P\exists W[Q(W)\wedge P(W)]$
(180)	*a*	$[—N^1_{sg}]$	$\lambda Q\lambda P\exists W[Q(W)\wedge P(W)]$
(181)	ø	$[—N^1_{pl}]$	$\lambda Q\lambda P\exists W[Q(W)\wedge P(W)]$

Underlying this analysis is the conviction that whatever a determiner may be, it signals whether the referent of the NP is existentially introduced or whether it is given, that is identified by deixis, context or anaphoric reference as pertaining to something introduced. This is why in (177)–(181) the set W is either introduced by the existential quantifier ∃ or is given by the definiteness operator ∃! which is defined as follows:

(182) $\exists!W[\alpha(W)]=1$ iff there is a W such that $W\in\alpha$ and W is deictically or contextually or anaphorically given

Here it suffices to say that the operator ∃!W was meant to provide for identifying reference in the sense of Strawson's notion 'identifying description' (Strawson 1959, 1964). In Verkuyl (1981: 586f.), the term 'identifying' was used in this sense, in particular if it is strengthened by Löbner's (1985) treatment of definiteness in terms of a function picking out a unique (i.e. unambiguously identified) value. Löbner's position is compatible with the Strawsonian position on identification, just like Kadmon's (1987) position. In this sense, the notion of givenness used here is more closely associated with *unique identification* than with *familiarity*, the latter based on Heim (1982). However, a choice between the two approaches to definiteness does not affect the identification of [+SQA]-properties.[33]

Compositionally, the general type-logical structure of a simple NP of the form (177) can be characterized as follows:

(183)	N^0	$\langle e,t\rangle$
	NUM	$\langle\langle e,t\rangle,\langle\langle e,t\rangle,t\rangle\rangle$
	N^1	$\langle\langle e,t\rangle,t\rangle$
	DET	$\langle\langle\langle e,t\rangle,t\rangle,\langle\langle\langle e,t\rangle,t\rangle,t\rangle\rangle$
	N^2	$\langle\langle\langle e,t\rangle,t\rangle,t\rangle$

The structure is given bottom-top. To give some examples, sentences like *The three children came in* are derived as in (184).[34]

(184)

N^0	child	$[\![child]\!]$
NUM	three	$\lambda Y\lambda X[X\subseteq Y\wedge \lvert X\rvert=3]$
N^1	three(child)	$\lambda Y\lambda X[X\subseteq Y\wedge \lvert X\rvert=3]([\![child]\!])$
		$\lambda X[X\subseteq[\![child]\!]\wedge \lvert X\rvert=3]$
DET	the	$\lambda Q\lambda P\exists!W[Q(W)\wedge P(W)]$
N^2	the(three(child))	
		$\lambda Q\lambda P\exists!W[Q(W)\wedge P(W)](\lambda X[X\subseteq[\![child]\!]\wedge \lvert X\rvert=3])$
		$\lambda P\exists!W[\lambda X[X\subseteq[\![child]\!]\wedge \lvert X\rvert=3](W)\wedge P(W)]$
		$\lambda P\exists!W[[W\subseteq[\![child]\!]\wedge \lvert W\rvert=3]\wedge P(W)]$
V	came in	$[\![came\_in]\!]$
VP	came in	$\lambda X.X\subseteq[\![came\_in]\!]$
S	the three children came in	
		$\lambda P\exists!W[[W\subseteq[\![child]\!]\wedge \lvert W\rvert=3]\wedge P(W)](\lambda X.X\subseteq[\![came\_in]\!])$
		$\exists!W[[W\subseteq[\![child]\!]\wedge \lvert W\rvert=3]\wedge\lambda X.X\subseteq[\![came\_in]\!](W)]$
		$\exists!W[W\subseteq[\![child]\!]\wedge \lvert W\rvert=3\wedge W\subseteq[\![came\_in]\!]]$

NPs like *a child* and *three children* are derived as (185) and (186), respectively:

(185)

N^0	child	$[\![child]\!]$
NUM	SG	$\lambda Y\lambda X[X\subseteq Y\wedge \lvert X\rvert=1]$
N^1	SG(child)	$\lambda Y\lambda X[X\subseteq Y\wedge \lvert X\rvert=1]([\![child]\!])$
		$\lambda X[X\subseteq[\![child]\!]\wedge \lvert X\rvert=1]$
DET	a	$\lambda Q\lambda P\exists W[Q(W)\wedge P(W)]$

N^2	a(SG(child))	$\lambda Q\lambda P\exists W[Q(W)\wedge P(W)](\lambda X[X\subseteq[\![child]\!]\wedge\lvert X\rvert=1])$
		$\lambda P\exists W[[\lambda X[X\subseteq[\![child]\!]\wedge\lvert X\rvert=1](W)\wedge P(W)]$
		$\lambda P\exists W[W\subseteq[\![child]\!]\wedge\lvert W\rvert=1\wedge P(W)]$

(186)

N^0	child	$[\![child]\!]$
NUM	three	$\lambda Y\lambda X[X\subseteq Y\wedge\lvert X\rvert=3]$
N^1	three(child)	$\lambda Y\lambda X[X\subseteq Y\wedge\lvert X\rvert=3]([\![child]\!])$
		$\lambda X[X\subseteq[\![child]\!]\wedge\lvert X\rvert=3]$
DET	ø	$\lambda Q\lambda P\exists W[Q(W)\wedge P(W)]$
N^2	ø(three(child))	
		$\lambda Q\lambda P\exists W[Q(W)\wedge P(W)](\lambda X[X\subseteq[\![child]\!]\wedge\lvert X\rvert=3])$
		$\lambda P\exists W[\lambda X[X\subseteq[\![child]\!]\wedge\lvert X\rvert=3](W)\wedge P(W)]$
		$\lambda P\exists W[W\subseteq[\![child]\!]\wedge\lvert W\rvert=3\wedge P(W)]$

Note that N^1 in (185) yields a set of all singletons from the set of children in E, as N^1 in (184) and (186) yields the set of all triples of children.

There is a problem, not discussed in Verkuyl (1981), with respect to the analysis of *the* (and of *all*). One might be inclined to demand for *The three children came in* that the last line of the derivation (184) would be (187) on the presumption that $W=[\![child]\!]$ in the model, say $\mathbf{M}_i$:

(187) $\exists!W[W=[\![child]\!]\wedge\lvert W\rvert=3\wedge W\subseteq[\![came\_in]\!]]$

I leave this matter here and will continue to use $\subseteq$ rather than = in the representation of *the* N, but the issue will be taken up again in chapter 6.2 and in chapter 7.5.

In order to compare the above analysis with the standard GQT-analysis, some relevant semantic analyses are given:

(188)

a. $[\![the_{sg}\ child]\!]([\![VP]\!])$	=	$[\![VP]\!]\in\{X: [\![child]\!]\subseteq X\wedge\lvert[\![child]\!]\rvert=1\}$
b. $[\![the_{pl}\ children]\!]([\![VP]\!])$	=	$[\![VP]\!]\in\{X: [\![child]\!]\subseteq X\wedge\lvert[\![child]\!]\rvert>1\}$
c. $[\![all\ children]\!]([\![VP]\!])$	=	$[\![VP]\!]\in\{X: [\![child]\!]\subseteq X\}$
d. $[\![three\ children]\!]([\![VP]\!])$	=	$[\![VP]\!]\in\{X: \lvert[\![child]\!]\cap X\rvert=3\}$
e. $[\![some\ children]\!]([\![VP]\!])$	=	$[\![VP]\!]\in\{X: \lvert[\![child]\!]\cap X\rvert\geq 1\}$

(189)

a. $[\![the(\text{SG}(child))]\!]([\![VP]\!])$	=	$\exists!W[W\subseteq[\![child]\!]\wedge\lvert W\rvert=1\wedge W\subseteq[\![VP]\!]]$
b. $[\![the(\text{PL}(child))]\!]([\![VP]\!])$	=	$\exists!W[W\subseteq[\![child]\!]\wedge\lvert W\rvert>1\wedge W\subseteq[\![VP]\!]]$
c. $[\![all(\text{PL}(child))]\!]([\![VP]\!])$	=	$\exists!W[W\subseteq[\![child]\!]\wedge\lvert W\rvert>1\wedge W\subseteq[\![VP]\!]]$
d. $[\![ø(three(child))]\!]([\![VP]\!])$	=	$\exists W[W\subseteq[\![child]\!]\wedge\lvert W\rvert=3\wedge W\subseteq[\![VP]\!]]$
e. $[\![some(\text{PL}(child))]\!]([\![VP]\!])$	=	$\exists W[W\subseteq[\![child]\!]\wedge\lvert W\rvert>1\wedge W\subseteq[\![VP]\!]]$

The difference is clear: the analyses in (188) amount to saying that ⟦VP⟧ is an element of a collection of sets meeting some conditions on the intersection between ⟦child⟧ and ⟦VP⟧, whereas the corresponding analyses in (189) amount to characterizing a set W which is a subset of both ⟦child⟧ and ⟦VP⟧. It is this set that we will become increasingly interested in as it may be given structure that can be made dependent on time expressed by the verb.

Representations like (189) will have to be extended into more complex ones. This is because the [+SQA]-notion is quite complex indeed, but also because in Verkuyl (1981) I restricted myself to intransitive verbs only.

5.2 ⟦N^0⟧ = ∅: Strawson vs. Russell

It is interesting to see what happens with the problematic sentences of the preceding chapter, such as (151) *All dogs came in.* It would be derived as follows:

(190)	dog	⟦dog⟧
	PL	$\lambda Y \lambda X[X \subseteq Y \wedge \lvert X \rvert > 1]$
	PL(dog)	$\lambda Y \lambda X[X \subseteq Y \wedge \lvert X \rvert > 1](⟦dog⟧)$
		$\lambda X[X \subseteq ⟦dog⟧ \wedge \lvert X \rvert > 1]$
	all	$\lambda Q \lambda P \exists ! W[Q(W) \wedge P(W)]$
	all(PL(dog))	$\lambda Q \lambda P \exists ! W[Q(W) \wedge P(W)](\lambda X[X \subseteq ⟦dog⟧ \wedge \lvert X \rvert > 1])$
		$\lambda P \exists ! W[\lambda X[X \subseteq ⟦dog⟧ \wedge \lvert X \rvert > 1](W) \wedge P(W)]$
		$\lambda P \exists ! W[W \subseteq ⟦dog⟧ \wedge \lvert W \rvert > 1 \wedge P(W)]$

Due to the definition of PL something is going wrong at the level of N^1. It is at this point that the function $\lambda Y \lambda X[X \subseteq Y \wedge \lvert X \rvert > 1]$ is applied to the set ⟦dog⟧, that is, to the empty set ∅. It yields the weird function $\lambda X[X \subseteq \varnothing \wedge \lvert X \rvert > 1]$. This characteristic function is not only improper in the sense that it does not split the collection of sets, ⟦PL⟧(⟦dog⟧) is also ill-defined because it contains a contradiction. This is different from the situation in which in standard GQT a quantifier becomes improper. For example, (66f) ⟦no⟧(A) with A=⟦dog⟧ applied to subsets of E would yield in $\mathbf{M}_1$ ⟦no⟧(⟦dog⟧)=$\lambda X.$⟦dog⟧$\cap X = \varnothing$. In the definition of $\lambda X.$⟦dog⟧$\cap X$ there is no contradiction involved, whereas in (190) *all* is applied to a node N^1, PL(dog) denoting a weird function.

Now, given the controversy between Russell and Strawson, there are two lines of thought on which one could proceed. I will argue that at the end of these lines the same sort of conclusion must be drawn so that one may reach a final compromise there between two conflicting strategies, because we end up with a terminological debate. One needs type logic to see this.

On the Strawsonian line one might say: well, given a derivation like (190) one is obliged to stop after PL(dog), that is, at the level of N^1, because weird functions should not be allowed to be the input of some other semantic rule. The derivation simply stops, because whatever happens to the derivation, once a weird function always a weird function. The syntactic machinery delivers a well-formed sentence, but semantics refuses to give it a well-formed reading. Strawson and his associates were obliged to assume a truth-value gap because in a first-order representation the weirdness inevitably turns up at the point at which truth must be assigned. Due to the type logic involved in (190), the ill-formedness turns up 'earlier' in the form of a blocking of the interpretation of the NP.

This reasoning may not convince Russellians. They do not let pass the cup of weirdness of $\lambda X[X \subseteq \varnothing \wedge |X| > 1]$ because they want to go on to the end of the derivation where truth values are waiting. So the weirdness is carried over to the level of the NP, where one ends up with a function identifying a set which is described both as empty and non-empty by the contradictory conjunction $[W \subseteq \varnothing \wedge |W| > 1]$. That is, all(PL(dogs)) will be interpreted as:

(191) $\lambda P \exists ! W[W \subseteq \varnothing \wedge |W| > 1 \wedge P(W)]$

and this function applied to $[\![VP]\!]$ brings about the fiercely desired truth value. However, the presence of a contradiction suggests that one ends up with *All dogs came in* being always false in case there are no dogs in a domain. This would be quite different from what Russell wants universal sentences to mean: he wants them to be true.

There is perhaps a more adequate way of handling this contradictory information. The derivation (190) may be characterized metalinguistically as a case of *Ex falso sequitur quod libet* (EFSQ), a tautological argument of the form $\neg p \rightarrow (p \rightarrow q)$. That is, if $[\![dog]\!] = \varnothing$, one must assume that $|W| = 0$. Call this assumption $\neg p$. Then it follows that if $|W| > 1$ – call this assumption p – by picking out the numeral PL, one obtains the falsum $\perp$. By this, we may derive any value α for the open place P, provided it is of the right logical type. In other words, the EFSQ (192) is present in the derivation itself.

(192) $\lambda P \exists ! W[W \subseteq \varnothing \wedge |W| > 1 \wedge P(W)](\alpha)$

$\neg p \qquad p \qquad q$

In my view, this is not an unreasonable thing to argue. What it does is to make *All dogs came in* tautologically true in any model in which there are no dogs. So, here Russellians may feel comfortable again.

However, a quite unexpected compromise appears to be feasible or at least a situation in which Strawsonians and Russellians may find themselves back in a terminological debate. The main ingredient of the EFSQ is present in the NP itself, so the problem arises before the derivation has reached the stage at which the truth value is to be determined. So the matter can be settled before any possible truth-value gap is in sight, that is, before the point at which the function (191) is applied to an α. In other words, the EFSQ-structure of (191) makes it possible to settle the matter completely independent of the value or content of the VP. This sounds Strawsonian and indeed it is, but the difference of opinion can now be reduced to the question of whether or not Strawsonians would accept that the Russellian verdict 'tautologically true' resulting from an EFSQ is equivalent to their own judgment 'undefined': one may call sentences which are tautologically true *undefined* with respect to one particular model.

One of the reasons for pursuing this train of thought is, of course, the simple fact that in GQT the definitions of *all* and *the* are so congenial: $[\![\text{the}]\!](A)=[\![\text{all}]\!](A)$ plus some additional constraint concerning the cardinality. Yet, for Russell the universal sentences like *All unicorns are white* are always true if $[\![\text{unicorn}]\!]=\varnothing$, whereas *The unicorn is white* is false. In my view, the gap between *all* and *the* is unnecessarily wide and yawning. The present analysis predicts that it can be bridged. Consider the following sentences:

(193) The dog came in
(194) The dog did not come in
(195) At most two dogs did not come in
(196) At most two cats did not come in

For Strawson, the sentences (193) and (194) are in the same category as (151) *All dogs came in.* For Russell they were not, as pointed out in section 4.4. Under the present type-logical analysis, they will now also fall in the same category, so here we find in (197) again the ESFQ-format (198).

(197)	dog	$[\![\text{dog}]\!]=\varnothing$	$\neg p$
	SG	$\lambda Y\lambda X[X\subseteq Y\wedge\lvert X\rvert=1]$	p
	SG(dog)	$\lambda Y\lambda X[X\subseteq Y\wedge\lvert X\rvert=1](\varnothing)$	
		$\lambda X[X\subseteq\varnothing\wedge\lvert X\rvert=1]$	$\bot$

(198) $\lambda P\exists!W[W\subseteq\varnothing\wedge\lvert W\rvert=1\wedge P(W)](\alpha)$

$\qquad\qquad\neg p \qquad p \qquad\qquad q$

This makes (193) tautologically true rather than false. The same applies to (195) but it also applies to (196) because the cardinality of $[\![\text{cat}]\!]$ in E is 1. In this sense, all improper use of quantifiers is brought under one heading and in the compositionally driven bottom-top interpretation it remains essentially a matter of the NP rather than of the VP.

One may make an even stronger claim: the present analysis makes both (193) and (194) tautologically true (for the Russellians) or uninterpretable (for the Strawsonians). This needs to be shown to Russellians. Recall that Russell said that (194) is ambiguous because of the two positions available for the negation sign.

(199) $\neg\exists x(\forall y(\text{dog}(y) \leftrightarrow y=x)\wedge \text{came\_in}(x))$

(200) $\exists x(\forall y(\text{dog}(y) \leftrightarrow y=x)\wedge\neg \text{came\_in}(x))$

On the $<<<e,t>,t>,t>$-analysis of sentence negation, however, the negation sign $\neg$ will not appear in front of $\exists$W (see chapter 7.6 below). It will show up at the place at which the VP comes in. For example, the derivation of *The cat did not come in* is:

V	came in	$[\![\text{came\_in}]\!]$
VP	came in	$\lambda X.X\subseteq[\![\text{came\_in}]\!]$
$\overline{\text{VP}}$	not came in	$\lambda X.X\not\subseteq[\![\text{came\_in}]\!]$
S	the cat did not come in	
		$\lambda P\exists!W[[W\subseteq[\![\text{cat}]\!]\wedge\lvert W\rvert=1]\wedge P(W)](\lambda X.X\not\subseteq[\![\text{came\_in}]\!])$
		$\exists!W[[W\subseteq[\![\text{cat}]\!]\wedge\lvert W\rvert=1]\wedge\lambda X.X\not\subseteq[\![\text{came\_in}]\!](W)]$
		$\exists!W[W\subseteq[\![\text{cat}]\!]\wedge\lvert W\rvert=1\wedge W\not\subseteq[\![\text{came\_in}]\!]]$

whereas the analysis of *Nobody came in* results in:

V	came in	$[\![\text{came\_in}]\!]$
VP	came in	$\lambda X.X\subseteq[\![\text{came\_in}]\!]$
$\overline{\text{VP}}$	not came in	$\lambda X.X\not\subseteq[\![\text{came\_in}]\!]$
NP	nobody	$\lambda P\neg\exists W[[W\subseteq[\![\text{human}]\!]\wedge\lvert W\rvert\geq 1]\wedge P(W)]$
S	nobody came in	
		$\neg\exists W[W\subseteq[\![\text{human}]\!]\wedge\lvert W\rvert\geq 1\wedge W\subseteq[\![\text{came\_in}]\!])]$

In the former case the *P* remains 'positive' in the sense that the NP takes the λX-construction of the VP without 'seeing' the negation.[35] The NP takes $\overline{\text{VP}}$ the way it takes a positive VP. It is in this sense that an analysis along the lines of (170) and (177)–(181) correctly expresses that (193) and (194) are in the same way true or false or uninterpretable. This is how native speakers react if they are confronted with them.

Finally, let us have a second look at *at most*.

(201) At most two dogs came in

(202) At most two dogs did not come in

At the level of NP we have the following:

(203) $\lambda P \exists W[W \subseteq \varnothing \wedge |W| \leq 2 \wedge P(W)]$

In my view, these sentences are as weird as the above with *all*, *the* and *at least*. This seems to show that the information expressed by $|W| \leq n$ covers a range in the set {1,2, …, n} and not in the set {0,1,2, …n}. For if the latter were the case, then (201) and (202) would have truth values. As far as I can see, they have not. But note that the strength or weakness of the analysis does not depend on this judgment.

Summarizing, as far as *all* is concerned, sentences like (35) *All children came in* and (151) *All dogs came in* express [+SQA]-information as soon as the set A is presupposed to be non-empty. If not, the sentences in question do not pertain to a model and cannot be interpreted terminatively due to contradictory information. From this an important aspect of the notion of terminativity can be derived: it is extensional in that it pertains to just one model. It needs a properly quantifying NP as defined in the Strawsonian sense. Thus it seems that the notion of properness is needed to make warrant that an NP may express [+SQA]. We will see later on, however, that an NP may be proper and still be lacking the power to express cardinality at the proper extensional level. So we have to penetrate more deeply into the nature of the quantification involved in expressing [+SQA]-information.

5.3 Conclusion

The present chapter has introduced the X-bar $\langle\langle\langle e,t\rangle,t\rangle,t\rangle$-machinery developed in Verkuyl (1981) and it has demonstrated some of its properties. On the basis of this, it has been argued that the formalism being employed is adequate for dealing with representing [+SQA]-information at the right type-logical level. An $\langle\langle\langle e,t\rangle,t\rangle,t\rangle$-analysis produces for a number of determiners a clear cardinality expression of the form $|W|$ r n, where r is a member of the set of relations $\{<, \leq, >, \geq, =\}$ and where n is a certain value, either identified or not. This format will prove valuable later on, as it makes it possible to treat formally the notion of [–SQA]. In this respect, the present chapter has laid the foundation for the construction of an aspectual theory in which the [±SQA]-notion can be formally articulated. However, it will also be shown that the above framework is in need of revision at certain points.

6 *Some problems of prenominal NP structure*

6.0 Introduction

In view of our strategy to get at the interaction between atemporal NP structure and temporal VP structure stepwise, it is appropriate to discuss some problems of NP-structure that bear on the issue, but which did not receive attention or not enough attention in the grammar based on (169) and (170). It is also necessary to discuss some of the consequences of an <<<*e*,*t*>,*t*>,*t*>-analysis before we proceed. In particular, the division of labour between elements of the prenominal structure of an NP needs to be explored in more detail.

Let us have a look again at the lexical specifications of the determiners in (177)–(181), which I shall repeat for convenience (recall that N^1 is in fact N^{max-1}).

(177)	*the*	$[\text{—}N^1]$	$\lambda Q\lambda P\exists!W[Q(W)\wedge P(W)]$
(178)	*all*	$[\text{—}N^1_{pl}]$	$\lambda Q\lambda P\exists!W[Q(W)\wedge P(W)]$
(179)	*some*	$[\text{—}N^1]$	$\lambda Q\lambda P\exists W[Q(W)\wedge P(W)]$
(180)	*a*	$[\text{—}N^1_{sg}]$	$\lambda Q\lambda P\exists W[Q(W)\wedge P(W)]$
(181)	ø	$[\text{—}N^1_{pl}]$	$\lambda Q\lambda P\exists W[Q(W)\wedge P(W)]$

Clearly there is a bipartition, setting (177) and (178) apart from the other three determiners. It is also clear that *the* and *all* receive the same semantic characterization, and that this also holds for *some*, *a* and ø. The differences between the determiners are brought out by their different subcategorial information with respect to the N^1 they take.

In a sense, the reduction of the information expressed by determiners to either $\exists!W[Q(W)\wedge P(W)]$ or $\exists W[Q(W)\wedge P(W)]$ seems to be an impoverishment of their expressive power. Recall that the definiteness operator $\exists!$ was defined as (182); the existential quantifier can now be defined as (204).

(182) $\exists!W[\alpha(W)]=1$ iff there is a W such that $W\in\alpha$ and W is deictically or contextually or anaphorically given

(204) $\exists W[\alpha(W)]=1$ iff $W\in\alpha$ and W is existentially introduced in E

This means that the function of the determiner is restricted here to two things: (a) relating the (subject) NP-denotation (a collection *Q* of sets) to the VP-denotation (a collection *X* of sets); (b) expressing either definiteness (in the sense of identifying a set W), or indefiniteness (in the sense of introducing a set W). In this way, a determiner does not express directly any quantificational information (indirectly it does so by introducing or identifying sets).

In this chapter, some of the consequences of this analysis will be surveyed. The division of labour restricts the role of the determiner to expressing an intersection relation (in intransitive sentences between N^1 and VP) and to existentially introducing or identifying the intersection W. The most urgent question is: what happens to the other standard GQT-determiners? This question is raised in section 6.1 in an empirical setting: we have to look at the data in order to see which of the quantifying expressions fall under the heading of Determiner and which under the heading of Numerals. This problem is for a large part syntactic in the sense that one has to account for certain syntactic peculiarities of prenominal structure, in particular for the patterning of determiners, numerals and adjectivals. The semantic part of it is: where exactly is the [+SQA]-information located?

A second set of problems is: how to deal with *all*, *the* and *every* given the fact that we characterize W in, for example, $\exists!W[W \subseteq [\![\text{child}]\!] \ldots]$ in terms of a subset relation of $[\![N^0]\!]$. Would we not expect $\exists!W[W = [\![\text{child}]\!] \ldots]$? Moreover, how does one obtain a set of singletons 'child' in the case of *every child*? Should *every* not be interpreted as $\forall W[Q(W) \rightarrow P(W)]$? And how do we have to treat *all the children*? These problems are discussed in section 6.2. The third problem, discussed in section 6.3, is the issue of bare plurals. It will be argued that there are arguments for distinguishing indefinite and definite bare plurals. The fourth problem shows up in the use of the existential quantifier in the definitions of *some*, *a* and ø. The problem is that $\exists W[\ldots W \ldots]$ may pertain to more than one set W. It will be discussed below in chapter 7.1.

6.1 DET-NUM-problems

From the list in (205) it may be concluded that *the*, *all*, *my*, *some* belong to DET and not to NUM, DET being characterized as the most prominent node in the NP-structure of the form (170):

(170) $[N^{max}\ \text{DET}\ [N^{max-1}\ \text{NUM}\ [_{N^i}\ A^*\ N^0]]]$

(205) a. the many children c. my three children
b. all three children d. some nice children

e. eight tall children
f. *many the children
g. *three all children
h. *three my children
i. *nice some children
j. *tall eight children

These data are well known from the literature, in particular on English and Dutch (Jackendoff 1977; Klein 1980; Coppen 1991; De Jong 1983, 1987, 1991, among others).

As observed above, the difference between (205e) and (205j) was an argument for Verkuyl (1981) to assign NUM a more prominent place in prenominal structure than the adjectival category A. This point has been debated extensively by De Jong (1991). She argues that the pattern of phrases like (206a) and (206b), in which adjectives are freely permuted, is also present in (206c) and (206d):

(206) a. the long yellow daffodils
b. the yellow long daffodils
c. the eight yellow daffodils
d. the yellow eight daffodils

De Jong observes that it is necessary to put heavy stress on the numeral of (206d), and that this weakens the argument, but she then uses the examples in (207a)–(207c), from Klein (1980), and (207d), from Jackendoff (1977), to support her claim firmly.

(207) a. the following two pages
b. the remaining few survivors were hungry
c. the many and glorious achievements of the People's Revolution
d. a beautiful three weeks

Except for (207c), however, there are remarkably simple solutions for an X-bar syntax in dealing with these apparent counterexamples to scheme (170).

The first one is to allow the category DET to have the internal structure of regular X-bar syntactic categories. That is, we would have (208)–(211).

(208) $[_{N^2}\,[_{DET'}\,[_{DET}$ the] $[_{ADJUNCT}$ following]] $[_{N^1}[_{NUM}$ two] $[_{N^0}$ page]]]
(209) $[_{N^2}\,[_{DET'}\,[_{DET}$ the] $[_{ADJUNCT}$ remaining]] $[_{N^1}[_{NUM}$ few] $[_{N^0}$ survivor]]]
(210) $[_{N^2}\,[_{DET'}\,[_{DET}$ the] $[_{ADJUNCT}$ yellow]] $[_{N^1}[_{NUM}$ eight] $[_{N^0}$ daffodil]]]
(211) $[_{N^2}\,[_{DET'}\,[_{DET}$ a] $[_{ADJUNCT}$ beautiful]] $[_{N^1}[_{NUM}$ three] $[_{N^0}$ week]]]

This means that semantically *following, remaining, last, next, even, odd, final, first*, but also *yellow* and *beautiful* are treated as modifying adjuncts of the determiner. Type-logically, the ADJUNCT-operation would involve a modification of type <a,a>, where a=<<<*e*,*t*>,*t*>,<<<*e*,*t*>,*t*>,*t*>>. This seems a rather complex operation, but technically there are no problems. The solution makes sense as soon as one realizes that the presence of the prenumeral adjectivals is dependent on the presence of a definite determiner in some of the cases:

(212) I bought eight yellow daffodils
(213) *I bought yellow eight daffodils
(214) *I wanted to read following two pages

The second solution is to apply ADJUNCT-modification to NUM:

(208′) $[_{N^2}[_{\text{DET}}$ the$]$ $[_{N^1}[_{\text{NUM}'}[_{\text{ADJUNCT}}$ following$]$ $[_{\text{NUM}}$ two$]]$ $[_{N^0}$ page$]]]$
(209′) $[_{N^2}[_{\text{DET}}$ the$]$ $[_{N^1}[_{\text{NUM}'}[_{\text{ADJUNCT}}$ remaining$]$ $[_{\text{NUM}}$ few$]]$ $[_{N^0}$ survivor$]]]$
(210′) $[_{N^2}[_{\text{DET}}$ the$]$ $[_{N^1}[_{\text{NUM}'}[_{\text{ADJUNCT}}$ yellow$]$ $[_{\text{NUM}}$ eight$]]$ $[_{N^0}$ daffodil$]]]$
(211′) $[_{N^2}[_{\text{DET}}$ a$]$ $[_{N^1}[_{\text{NUM}'}[_{\text{ADJUNCT}}$ beautiful$]$ $[_{\text{NUM}}$ three$]]$ $[_{N^0}$ week$]]]$

In (207a), *following* would not say anything about pages, but rather something about the cardinality expressed by the numeral: it would restrict the meaning of *two* to ‘following two’, the meaning of *few* to ‘(the) few that are left’, and the meaning of *eight* to ‘(the) eight-tuples of X’ each of which intersect with the set of yellow things, along the lines of (215), where *eight* belongs to NUM:

(215) eight $\lambda Y\lambda X[X\subseteq Y\wedge|X|=8]$
yellow(eight) $\lambda Y\lambda X[X\subseteq Y\wedge X\subseteq[\![\text{yellow}]\!]\wedge|X|=8]$

The <a,a>-modification involved in (208′)–(211′) is not really counterintuitive: it simply adds a clause $X\subseteq Z$ to the numeral information. The technical details of this operation would only require an extension of the list of variable types in DEF 3.3.

I do not want to make a motivated choice between the two alternatives now, although intuitively the second is more appealing. But I do not want to exclude the possibility of having both available for solving different empirical problems. Anyhow, both protect (170) in a not *ad hoc* way against exceptions to the rule that numerals are more prominent in prenominal structure than adjectives, a more careful wording of this rule being: numerals are more prominent than noun-modifying adjectives. In chapter 7, the choice between the two options will have to be made again given a different syntactic constituency of the NP.

That the extension of the syntactic structure to NUM or DET is not *ad hoc*, can be shown by the comparison of the following phrases in (216).

(216) a. the two following interesting examples
b. the following two interesting examples
c. ?the following interesting two examples

The (a) and (b) phrases are much better than the (c) phrase. Theoretically, the latter one should be interpretable and it is, because if we allow modification of NUM, *interesting* is a potential modifier and why should it not occur as a specifier of a numeral? However, it becomes sortally harder and harder to make sense of the modification itself. But whatever meaning can be construed, it will be either [following(interesting)(two)], in which the adjective *following* modifies the adjective *interesting*, or [the(following(interesting))(two)], in which [following(interesting)] is an adjunct of *the*. That is, an analysis along the lines of [following(interesting(two(examples)))] is not what is expressed by (216c).

As far as the conjunction in (207c) is concerned, I do not have a definite answer. However, note that this example could be used to argue that *many* (like *few*) is not a numeral and that constructions like *her youngest and adult son* do not mean the same as *her youngest adult son.*

6.2 Problems with *all, the* and *every*

The following data show that the analysis based on (170) correctly predicts the behaviour of *all* in NPs like (217).

(217) a. all the children — *the all children
b. almost all children — nearly all children
c. nearly all the children — *nearly the children

The structures proposed are given in Figure 11. The data in (217) strongly suggest that the English *all* may occur both as a determiner and as a modifier of a determiner, as in Figure 11b. The evidence that *all* is a modifier of *the* is not overt in English, but it is in Dutch, which has ***alle*** *kinderen* (lit.: all children)

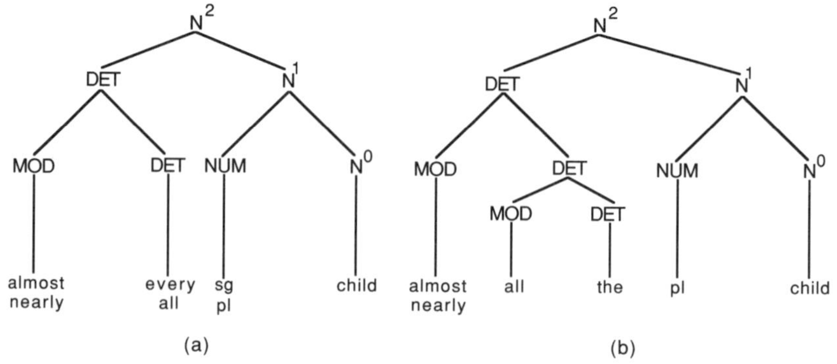

Figure 11 The type-logical X-bar approach of Verkuyl (1981) makes it possible to assign complex determiner structure to NPs

as well as ***al** de kinderen* (lit.: all the children) but not *****alle** de kinderen.* The data in (217) suggest that *all* and *the* are not always in complementary distribution.[36]

At this point it is necessary to have a look again at another problem with (170) and (177)–(181): the problem of the definition of all(PL(N)) and the(NUM(N)) presenting the set W which is involved in the predication as a subset of ⟦N⟧. The choice is between (218) and (219).

(218) all(PL(child)) $\lambda X\exists!W[W=[\![child]\!]\wedge|W|>1\wedge X(W)]$
the(SG(child)) $\lambda X\exists!W[W=[\![child]\!]\wedge|W|=1\wedge X(W)]$

(219) all(PL(child)) $\lambda X\exists!W[W\subseteq[\![child]\!]\wedge|W|>1\wedge X(W)]$
the(SG(child)) $\lambda X\exists!W[W\subseteq[\![child]\!]\wedge|W|=1\wedge X(W)]$

In (219), a technical solution would be to introduce $[\![child]\!]\subseteq W$ somewhere in the derivation so that the conjunction of $W\subseteq[\![child]\!]$ and $[\![child]\!]\subseteq W$ gives the desired result. A second one is to draw on making the N^0 a neutral stem by treating the N^0 as a basically lexical element in a syntactic structure, a place in which information about the model has not yet penetrated, so to say. This would mean that the applications of members of the category NUM have the effect of making model-dependent choices from the conceptual 'reservoir':

(220) $[\![N^0]\!] = \bigcup_{i\in\mathbf{N}} [\![N_i^0]\!]$

that is, from the union of all the sets $[\![child_i]\!]$, where $[\![child_i]\!]$ is the set of children in $\mathbf{M}_i$. For the cases in (219) it would mean that W is identified as $[\![child_i]\!]$ in $\mathbf{M}_i$. As said before, it is not *a priori* unreasonable to think of ⟦child⟧ as the set correlating with the concept CHILD constituting our lexical knowledge of the word *child.*[37] This information is present in the lexicon and N^0 is the point at which this information is brought into syntactic structure with respect to a certain model. It is worth the effort to continue thinking along these lines, but I shall not do so here.

In (177)–(181), the determiner *every* of Figure 11a is not present, so it is necessary to say something about it. There are three options: (221)–(223).

(221)

N^1	SG(child)	$\lambda X[X\subseteq[\![child]\!]\wedge|X|=1]$
DET	every	$\lambda Q\lambda P\exists!W[Q(W)\wedge P(W)]$
N^2	every(SG(child))	$\lambda Q\lambda P\exists!W[Q(W)\wedge P(W)](\lambda X[X\subseteq[\![child]\!]\wedge|X|=1])$
		$\lambda P\exists!W[\lambda X[X\subseteq[\![child]\!]\wedge|X|=1](W)\wedge P(W)]$
		$\lambda P\exists!W[W\subseteq[\![child]\!]\wedge|W|=1\wedge P(W)]$

(222)

N^1	SG(child)	$\lambda X[X \subseteq [\![child]\!] \wedge \lvert X \rvert = 1]$
DET	every	$\lambda Q \lambda P \forall W[Q(W) \rightarrow P(W)]$
N^2	every(SG(child))	$\lambda Q \lambda P \forall W[Q(W) \rightarrow P(W)](\lambda X[X \subseteq [\![child]\!] \wedge \lvert X \rvert = 1])$
		$\lambda P \forall W[\lambda X[X \subseteq [\![child]\!] \wedge \lvert X \rvert = 1](W) \rightarrow P(W)]$
		$\lambda P \forall W[W \subseteq [\![child]\!] \wedge \lvert W \rvert = 1 \rightarrow P(W)]$

(223)

N^1	SG(child)	$\lambda X[X \subseteq [\![child]\!] \wedge \lvert X \rvert = 1]$
DET	every	$\lambda Q \lambda P \exists W[Q(W) \wedge P(W)]$
N^2	every(SG(child))	$\lambda P \exists W[W \subseteq [\![child]\!] \wedge \lvert W \rvert = 1 \wedge P(W)]$

If *every* were given the analysis of (221), one would end up with a singleton *child*, whereas the set AT($[\![child]\!]$) of singletons is needed. This is what is correctly expressed by (222). The price paid for this is that one loses the attractive bipartition based on the distinction between ∃! in (182) and ∃W in (204). This could be unfortunate and it would be tempting to assign to *every* the status of a numeral defined as $\lambda Y \lambda X[X = Y \wedge \lvert X \rvert = 1]$, assuming that the NP *every child* has the structure [ø[every[child]]], as in (222). This will not do, however, because *every child* is a strong NP and 'strong' is identified with 'definite'. Moreover, the analysis in (223) depends on stretching out the meaning of ∃W as covering all singletons: though (223) is compatible with the meaning of *every child*, it does not express it.

A second look at (222) shows that for all atoms of a non-empty set $[\![child]\!]$ the predicate holds. One might now argue that *every child* is neither definite nor indefinite. As is well known from the literature, the anaphoric behaviour of *every* and *each* differs from *all*:

(224) All children came in. They were late
(225) Every child came in. *She was late
(226) Each child came in. *She was late.

In other words, in terms of definiteness and indefiniteness *every* and *each* have their own deviant place among the determiners of (177)–(181), because *all* behaves like *the*, *these*, *some* and *a* in this respect. On the other hand, the first sentences of (224)–(226) are all terminative and the three determiners involved are all strong. Yet there is a difference. This problem will be solved in chapter 7.5.

6.3 Indefinite and definite bare plurals

Sentences like (227) and (228) are problematic in so far as we have to state that they are durative:

(227) Children came in
(228) Judith ate sandwiches

because, due to DEF 4.3, the condition (118) $A \cap B$=undetermined holds. But what is undetermined in GQT? This is a real problem for an $<<e,t>,t>$-analysis of NPs to express properly. On an $<<<e,t>,t>,t>$-analysis, it would not be unreasonable to have (229) as the denotation for the bare plural NP *children*.

(229) $\lambda P \exists W[W \subseteq [\![\text{child}]\!] \wedge P(W)]$

This function deviates from the non-bare plurals by the lack of any information about the cardinality of W. It would make W completely dependent on the set $[\![\text{child}]\!]$ in the sense that (229) expresses that whatever entities from E came in they were children. Definition (229) makes (227) true even though in $\mathbf{M_1}$ the cat also came in. Applying (229) to the VP $[\![\text{came in}]\!]$, we would end up with:

(230)

VP	came in	$\lambda X.X \subseteq [\![\text{came in}]\!]$
S	children came in	
		$\lambda P \exists W[W \subseteq [\![\text{child}]\!] \wedge P(W)](\lambda X.X \subseteq [\![\text{came in}]\!])$
		$\exists W[W \subseteq [\![\text{child}]\!] \wedge \lambda X.X \subseteq [\![\text{came in}]\!](W)]$
		$\exists W[W \subseteq [\![\text{child}]\!] \wedge W \subseteq [\![\text{came in}]\!]]$

which means that W can be identified as any of the non-empty members of $\wp([\![\text{child}]\!])$. This does not appear unreasonable, as both (227) and (228) allow other entities in E to come in and to eat sandwiches.

However, there is a problem connected with this analysis. This is immediately revealed by the complete derivation of *children* in (231).

(231)	child	$[\![\text{child}]\!]$
	PL	$\lambda Y \lambda X[X \subseteq Y \wedge \lvert X \rvert > 1]$
	PL(child)	$\lambda Y \lambda X[X \subseteq Y \wedge \lvert X \rvert > 1]([\![\text{child}]\!])$
		$\lambda X[X \subseteq [\![\text{child}]\!] \wedge \lvert X \rvert > 1]$
	ø(PL(child))	$\lambda Q \lambda P \exists W[Q(W) \wedge P(W)](\lambda X[X \subseteq [\![\text{child}]\!] \wedge \lvert X \rvert > 1])$
		$\lambda P \exists W[\lambda X[X \subseteq [\![\text{child}]\!] \wedge \lvert X \rvert > 1](W) \wedge P(W)]$
		$\lambda P \exists W[W \subseteq [\![\text{child}]\!] \wedge \lvert W \rvert > 1 \wedge P(W)]$

One cannot get (229), unless we make some stipulation: by the definition of PL the information about cardinality of the set W is included at the level of N^1. So either one has to throw out this information as a step of the derivation or to introduce a bare 'numeral' which would have to be defined as (232).

(232) $[\![\text{BARE}]\!] := \lambda Y \lambda X[X \subseteq Y]$

This means that the bare plural NP *children* would be derived as in (233).

(233)

child	$[\![\text{child}]\!]$
BARE	$\lambda Y \lambda X[X \subseteq Y]$
BARE(child)	$\lambda Y \lambda X[X \subseteq Y]([\![\text{child}]\!])$
	$\lambda X.[X \subseteq [\![\text{child}]\!]$
ø(BARE(child))	$\lambda Q \lambda P \exists W[Q(W) \wedge P(W)](\lambda X[X \subseteq [\![\text{child}]\!])$
	$\lambda P \exists W[\lambda X.X \subseteq [\![\text{child}]\!](W) \wedge P(W)]$
	$\lambda P \exists W[W \subseteq [\![\text{child}]\!] \wedge P(W)]$

The advantage of having an 'empty' numeral is that NPs may express explicit lack of cardinality information. The semantic interpretation of ø(bare(child)) in (233) just says that the set W of entities which came in is a subset of the set $[\![\text{child}]\!]$. This seems to be a correct representation of its meaning, at least promising enough for an aspectual exploration of the notion of bareness. More generally, it would mean that [–SQA] could be defined in terms of the absence of the information about the cardinality of W in formulas like (229) and (233).

I would like to go one step further and argue that sentences like

(234) The children came in

taken in a non-quantificational sense might be analysed analogously as in (235).

(235) the(BARE(child)) $\lambda P \exists ! W[W \subseteq [\![\text{child}]\!] \wedge P(W)]$

This would be a situation in which (234) is used contrastively or as an announcement that during a certain period whoever came in was a child, where the category of entities coming in is already identified. I am tempted to think that in sentences like (236)–(238)

(236) The swallows are back early this year
(237) She fears the worst for the whales
(238) The civil servants form the backbone of bureaucracy

no quantification takes place. One may say (236) this year without any swallow being back here for the second time in its life, and even without seeing them as we might deduce their presence indirectly. Her concern for the whales may apply to whales scores of generations from now because (237) is about long-term effects. Note that the singular may be used here too:

(236′) The swallow is back early this year
(237′) She fears the worst for the whale
(238′) The civil servant forms the backbone of bureaucracy

Of course, there is some difference between the plural and the singular here, but it is so minimal that (236′) can be used to express the content of (236). If *the swallows* in (236) pertained to a specified quantity, it would not be possible to use (236′) as an alternative. Note also that the definite article in (238) can be dropped without any loss of content. The use of the definite article can be explained only by the fact that the category of civil servants is uniquely identified by the context; the indefinite bare plural would have introduced the category as new into the domain of interpretation.

It is important to observe that in the 'definite bare plural'-interpretation of (234), and of (236)–(238), it is not possible to get a [+SQA]-interpretation. Note also the difference between the two interpretations in (239)–(241).

(239) When soldiers came into town, the girls stayed indoors
(240) When the soldiers came into town, the girls stayed indoors
(241) When three soldiers came into town, the girls stayed indoors

Sentence (240) is ambiguous between the following two readings: (a) there is a specified quantity of soldiers, say, Harry, Bruce and Timmy, and when this group of soldiers came into town, the girls stayed inside; (b) given our knowledge of a near-to-town permanent NATO base, when soldiers of this base came into town – and not the sailors – the girls stayed inside. It is important to see the different aspectual behaviour of these readings. On the former, the sentence (242):

(242) The soldiers came into town

is terminative, on the latter it is not. Thus sentences like (243):

(243) For weeks the soldiers came into town

may either mean that for weeks it was such that Harry, Bruce and Timmy came into town repeatedly, or it may mean that for weeks the situation was such that soldiers – in this example already identified at the category-level as coming from the NATO base – came into town, where it is possible that none of the soldiers came into town twice. Note also that *the girls* in (239) and (240) in the (b) reading receive the same 'bare' interpretation. And finally, note that a (relatively light sort of) contrast is implied in (243) as if the category of soldiers is set alongside another one. Thus, the (b) interpretation is very natural in sentences like *For a couple of hours the general dropped the infantry soldiers behind the enemy and after that the marines.* We are talking then at the level of categories rather than at the level of individuals making up these categories. The only use for the definite article here is to identify the given category. The sentence would become very strange indeed if it pertained to Harry, Bruce and Timmy.

In GQT, there has been discussion about the question of whether or not *only* is a determiner. The present analysis makes it plausible to ban *only* from this set. The argument has two steps and it makes use of the ambiguity of (242). The first step is to observe that *only* occurs in front of both indefinite and definite NPs, as in (244) and (245).

(244) When only soldiers came into town, the girls stayed indoors
(245) When only the soldiers came into town, the girls stayed indoors

Note that the ambiguity of (240) remains intact in (245): it may mean (a) when it was only the specified group of soldiers that came into town, the girls stayed indoors; or (b) when (given our knowledge of a near-to-town permanent NATO base), only an unspecified quantity of an identified category, that is, the category of soldiers of this base came into town, the girls stayed inside. The second step of the argument is to observe that (244) is not ambiguous between an (a) and a (b) reading. Hence *only* should either have the effect of preventing the (b) reading, which is not true in view of (245), or it does not have any effect. But in that case, it is only the article *the* in (245) which allows for a choice between a [+SQA]- and a [–SQA]-interpretation to be involved. As such a choice can only be explained in terms of properties of determiners, it follows that *only* is not a determiner. In my view, this is an independent argument against *only* as a determiner on top of Thijsse's argument (1983: 24f.).

Are there bare singulars? Yes, there are. An otherwise definite singular [+SQA]-NP may receive a [–SQA]-interpretation in sentences like:

(246) This cat sold well
(247) This cat sold well for years
(248) For years I came across this cat in $1 million flats

On the durative reading of (246), the speaker does not have in mind a particular cat but rather a specific sort of cat an unspecified number of members of which has been sold. It is terminative in $\mathbf{M}_1$ if ⟦this cat⟧ = {a} and {a} is in the extension of the predicate ⟦sold well⟧. Sentences like (247) and (248) show that *this* does not always act as a strong and proper [+SQA]-determiner as it is not sufficient to trigger terminative aspect. There is some notion of unspecified plurality involved here, for (248) may mean that every time I came into a $1 million flat, I happened to come across a new specimen (or new specimens) of this sort of cat. The two sentences (249) and (250):

(249) For centuries, the mafia boss stabbed his rival with a knife
(250) For centuries, a mafia boss stabbed his rival with a knife

share the meaning that it was customary for whoever was the mafia boss (or a mafia boss) to stab his rival with a knife. So (249) and (250) express durativity even though *the mafia boss* and *a mafia boss* are [+SQA]-quantifiers in sentences pertaining to an individual.

In my view, the term *generic* does not cover these cases adequately: the interpretation of sentences involves individuals to which the predicate applies. The sentences are marked by the fact that the speaker refers at the category-level and does not quantify at the membership-level, which means that the NP is [–SQA]. One way to account systematically for the [+SQA]/[–SQA]-variation of NPs in (246)–(250), is to assume that *this cat* in (246) is structurally ambiguous between SG(cat) and BARE(cat). This would begin to explain why sentences like (247) and (248) have both a clear terminative and a clear durative reading, dependent on the level at which these sentences are used. If one would like to call the sentences under analysis *generic* in their durative interpretation, then the present aspectual theory would indeed cover phenomena falling under the term *genericity*. However, I do not claim that the present theory is a theory of genericity. Rather, there are reasons to take the cases under analysis here away from the core of genuine genericity: *be vigilant* is a quite different predicate from *stab a rival* and *come across*.

The problem at issue has many intricate knots. To begin with, it seems as if the relationship between knowledge of the world and structural factors inherent to linguistic information is central to the behaviour of the sentences like (249) and (250). We know that mafia bosses do not live for centuries, so we force ourselves into speaking about a plurality of them. Sentences like

(251) For hours, the mafia boss stabbed his rival with a knife
(252) For hours, a mafia boss stabbed his rival with a knife

are 'most normally' interpreted as meaning that a certain person who is the or a mafia boss (#–)repeatedly stabbed his rival with a knife. Our knowledge of the world says that mafia bosses have a lifetime considerably longer than a day which makes it more normal for us to assume that the mafia boss stabbed his rival in a certain period. This amounts to saying that there is one particular model containing a pair consisting of a mafia boss and his rival, and having a time axis with an interval of a certain length during which the mafia boss stabbed his rival repeatedly. However, there are lots of means to interpret (251) and (252) in exactly the same way as (249) and (252), respectively. One may think of a cartoon: *for hours* is now to be taken as a period during which several new films were shown, each movie containing new mafia bosses and new rivals.[38]

To defend the position that both *the mafia boss* and *a mafia boss* may pertain to an unspecified number of mafia bosses (possibly spread over completely different models) the bare numeral defined in (232) may explain its semantic properties. Taken in the durative reading, a sentence like (249) distinguishes the category of mafia bosses from other categories, without 'paying attention' to the cardinality of the set of mafia bosses. The same would hold for (250), which would lead to (provisional) representations like (253) and (254).

(253)	the(BARE(mafiaboss))	$\lambda P\exists!W[W\subseteq[\![\text{mafiaboss}]\!]\wedge P(W)]$
(254)	a(BARE(mafiaboss))	$\lambda P\exists W[W\subseteq[\![\text{mafiaboss}]\!]\wedge P(W)]$

Note, however, that (255) expresses about the same as (249), and (256) about the same as (250).

(255) For centuries, the mafia bosses stabbed their rival with a knife
(256) For centuries, mafia bosses stabbed their rival with a knife

It is hard to establish the exact semantic overlap between these four sentences because there is a difference involved between the possessive pronouns *his* and *their* in the direct object NPs. But also in other cases it is not very well possible to distinguish the meanings of (a) and (b) sentences in (257) and (258), and it is even hard to tell all four sentences apart.

(257) a. For centuries the mafia boss died in bed
b. For centuries the mafia bosses died in bed
(258) a. For centuries a mafia boss died in bed
b. For centuries mafia bosses died in bed

At this point the scope of the analysis may be extended again, because the list in (259) indicates that a large set of NPs which are [+SQA], may have the property of being able to apply to an unspecified series of tokens of a certain type.

(259) a. the saucer
b. John's saucer
c. both saucers
d. these saucers
e. three of the four saucers
f. all saucers
g. some saucers
h. some of the saucers

Consider a sentence of the form (260), in which NP is realized as one of the options in (259):

(260) Mary sold $[_{NP} \ldots]$ for years

It is easy to think of a situation in which Mary has been a saleswoman of many years' standing, selling saucers designed by one or more designers including John. In each of the cases exemplified in (259), it is possible to think of a *sort* of saucer. For example, if Mary bought a hundred (token) saucers of one design made by John and she sold them successfully over the years, (260) plus (259b) may pertain to the situation which is characterized by dozens of transactions in which Mary was the seller to possibly dozens of people. However, (260) plus the NP *John's saucer* may also mean that there is one particular concrete saucer made by John, which has been sold by Mary repeatedly. This sort of terminative reading is possible in the other cases as well. None of the NPs seems to resist a 'sort'-reading, even if one drops the durational adverbial.

The systematic choice between a [+SQA](one token)-reading and a [–SQA]-(type/tokens)-reading strongly suggests that we have to do with a systematically encoded meaning structure. In my view, the bare element in our syntax might serve as a node indicating the explicit absence of cardinality-information. However, there is a problem with applying the bare function (232) to the NPs in (261).

(261) a. three saucers
b. at most three saucers
c. fewer than three saucers
d. a few saucers
e. several saucers
f. many saucers

These NPs are [+SQA] if they express cardinality information, just like the NPs with strong determiners. They also may operate at the [–SQA]-category level, just like the cases in (260). If sentences like (262)

(262) For years Mary sold several saucers

(263) For years Mary sold three saucers

are used to say that Mary sold several types of saucer, then it says that Mary sold an unspecified quantity (in fact, the union) of tokens from different categories of saucers. In that case, (262) is clearly durative. The same applies to (263): as a durative sentence it says that Mary sold three sorts of saucers.

Throughout the present chapter it has been assumed that the determiners in (261) express cardinality information on the basis of a type-logical categorization given in (178). However, the abstract morpheme BARE is defined in (232) as belonging to the same category as *three*, *a few*, *several*, *many*, etc. Therefore, it cannot be used to account for the cases in (261), because members of the same category are in complementary distribution. Hence something must have gone wrong somewhere. In my view, the idea of treating (227), (228), (234)–(245) and (246)–(259) in terms of the concept of bareness remains attractive, because there is a clear-cut systematicity involved in the durative interpretations as opposed to the terminative interpretations.

So, let us try and save the essence of the present analysis by reconsidering derivation (186), but now abbreviated as (264).

(264)

N^0	saucer	$[\![\text{saucer}]\!]_{<e,t>}$
NUM	three	$\lambda Y \lambda X[X \subseteq Y \wedge \lvert X \rvert = 3]$
N^1	three(saucer)	$\lambda Y \lambda X[X \subseteq Y \wedge \lvert X \rvert = 3]([\![\text{saucer}]\!])$
		$\lambda X[X \subseteq [\![\text{saucer}]\!] \wedge \lvert X \rvert = 3]$
DET	ø	$\lambda Q \lambda P \exists W[Q(W) \wedge P(W)]$
N^2	ø (three(saucer))	$\lambda Q \lambda P \exists W[Q(W) \wedge P(W)](\lambda X[X \subseteq [\![\text{saucer}]\!] \wedge \lvert X \rvert = 3])$
		$\lambda P \exists W[\lambda X[X \subseteq [\![\text{saucer}]\!] \wedge \lvert X \rvert = 3](W) \wedge P(W)]$
		$\lambda P \exists W[W \subseteq [\![\text{saucer}]\!] \wedge \lvert W \rvert = 3 \wedge P(W)]$

This is the derivation for the [+SQA]-NP *three saucers*, whose denotation is a set of three token saucers. Suppose now that we want to talk about three categories of saucers. It is evident that one needs to operate at the $<<e,t>,t>$-level: in the [–SQA]-use of *three saucers* we are talking about three elements of $[\![\text{saucer}]\!]_{<<e,t>,t>}$, that is, about a collection of sets of saucers, without knowing or taking into account the cardinality of each of these sets.

Suppose that N^0 enters syntax as an object of type $<<e,t>,t>$. This would imply that the meaning of *three* would have to be adapted. In fact, rather than $<<e,t>,<<e,t>,t>>$, it would have to be $<<<e,t>,t>,<<<e,t>,t>>$. So BARE would be a modifier of a numeral rather than a numeral itself. If we allow for these two modifications, which need more motivation than I shall give here, the derivation in (265) is feasible:

(265)

N^0	saucer	$[\![\text{saucer}]\!]_{<<e,t>,t>}$
NUM	BARE(three)	$\lambda Q \lambda X[X = \bigcup Q \wedge \lvert Q \rvert = 3]$
N^1	BARE(three)(saucer)	
		$\lambda Q \lambda X[X = \bigcup Q \wedge \lvert Q \rvert = 3]([\![\text{saucer}]\!])$
		$\lambda X[X = \bigcup [\![\text{saucer}]\!] \wedge \lvert [\![\text{saucer}]\!] \rvert = 3]$
DET	ø	$\lambda Q \lambda P \exists W[Q(W) \wedge P(W)]$

N^2 $\varnothing$(BARE(three)(saucer))

$$\lambda Q\lambda P\exists W[Q(W)\wedge P(W)]$$
$$(\lambda X[X=\bigcup[\![\text{saucer}]\!]\wedge|[\![\text{saucer}]\!]|=3])$$
$$\lambda P\exists W[\lambda X[X=\bigcup[\![\text{saucer}]\!]\wedge|[\![\text{saucer}]\!]|=3](W)\wedge P(W)]$$
$$\lambda P\exists W[W=\bigcup[\![\text{saucer}]\!]\wedge|[\![\text{saucer}]\!]|=3\wedge P(W)]$$

The derivation begins with $[\![\text{saucer}]\!]_{<<e,t>,t>}$. BARE is now to be taken as an operator on Numerals, which has the effect of giving information about how many categories within the set $[\![\text{saucer}]\!]_{<e,t>}$ one is talking. The bottom line of the derivation now says that there is a set W which is the union of a three-membered collection of sets. This seems to express what *three saucers* in the durative interpretation of (263) means: Mary sold a set W of token-saucers having an unknown cardinality and this set can be split up into three (sub-)categories each having an unspecified number of members.

BARE could also be taken as an operator having SG and PL as its input as shown in (266) and (267).

(266) BARE(SG) $\lambda Q\lambda X[X=\bigcup Q\wedge|Q|=1]$
(267) BARE(PL) $\lambda Q\lambda X[X=\bigcup Q\wedge|Q|>1]$

Note that (266) restricts the number of Q to 1, which is to say that W is restricted to just one set. This appears to be correct, as demonstrated by *Mary sold John's saucer for years* given (260) and (259). This sentence says on the durative reading of *Mary sold John's saucer* that there is one set of saucers with an unspecified number of token-saucers sold by Mary. (On its terminative reading (260) plus *John's saucer* would express aspectual #-repetition.)

Unfortunately, a slight blemish is discerned: (267) requires that there be more than one set in the collection Q. This means that in (7), *Judith ate sandwiches*, we are bound to assume that the set of sandwiches eaten by Judith is the union of at least two (sub)sets. However, bare plurals tend to express plurality, not only at the token-level but also at the type-level. If someone says *Mary sold saucers for years*, it would be awkward if it turned out to be the case that she sold only specimens of just one type of saucer. If people insist upon removing blemishes, a remedy would be to change $|Q|>1$ into $|Q|\geq 1$ in (267), as suggested by Ojeda (1990).[39]

In this connection, it may be revealing that in Slavic languages like Polish a sentence like (263) would have two versions, the ungrammatical perfective one and the grammatical imperfective one:

(268) *Przez lata Maria sprzedała 3 spodki
For years Mary sold (perf.) 3 saucers

(269) Przez lata Maria sprzedawała 3 spodki
For years Mary sold (imperf.) 3 saucers

The former excludes the single-event reading in which Mary sold three token saucers. It cannot express the above (b) interpretation in which Mary sold three types of saucer. On the other hand, (269) may say that Mary was selling three token-saucers, but it may also mean that Mary sold an unspecified number of tokens from three saucer types. Likewise, the Polish translations of (240) clearly show that the opposition between the (a) and the (b) interpretations can be framed in terms of aspectual differences:

(270) Kiedy żołnierze *przyszli* do miasta, to dziewczęta chowały się do domów
When the soldiers came (perf.) into town the girls stayed indoors

(271) Kiedy żołnierze *przychodzili* do miasta, to dziewczęta chowały się do domów
Whenever the soldiers came (imperf.) into town, the girls stayed indoors

It is only in (270) that (240) may pertain to a specific group of soldiers coming into town on one occasion. In that case the perfective verbal form is used. In (271), one needs the imperfective form to get the (b) interpretation. In my view, these observations about Polish are additional evidence (over and above (242) and (243)) that the differences between the (a) and (b) interpretation in English and Dutch are of an aspectual nature.[40]

The same applies to data made available to me by Aone van Engelenhoven (pers. comm.) about Leti, a Malayan-Polynesian language spoken on the west coast of Leti in East Indonesia. Here the two interpretations of (240) are clearly separated by the use of a successive or a simultaneous temporal clause construction. In the former case, the definite interpretation of a group of soldiers is imposed, in the latter the bare interpretation:[41]

(272) Sɔldatɛ r– pasar–ma–kɔt –nɛm=bɔ puata:n–ɛ r–dentaru
soldier 3p– hit –to –city –PRP=SQ girl –i 3p–remain

lo – ruma nain –ø
at – house under –PRP–FIN

lit.: The soldiers came into town, and then the girls stayed inside

(273) Sɔldatɛ r –pasar–ma –kɔt –ɛde puata:n–ɛ r–dentaru
soldier 3p–hit –to –city –PRP=A3 girl –i 3p–remain

lo – ruma nain – ø
at – house under –PRP–FIN

lit.: As/if soldiers come/came into town, the girls stayed/will stay inside

In (273), the 'bare' interpretation is marked by nominalization due to the temporal anaphoric suffix *de*, whereas the [+SQA]-interpretation is obtained by the sequence clitic b⊃. In both cases, the definiteness is expressed by the index suffix ∊. So, here again we see a language in which the two interpretations are grammaticalized. Note that in both cases the crucial distinctive information is expressed by the verbal complex and that it involves temporal structure.

An advantage of the present extension of bareness to definites is that the (existential) bare plural is no longer an isolated phenomenon. It is more general: bare plurals, either definite or indefinite, express that no cardinality is expressed of the set W in the determiners given in (177)–(181). We use them because we wish to say something about the category to which individuals belong rather than about the individuals themselves. We want to speak about swallows, whales and soldiers without any wish to quantify over the members of these categories. This can be done on the basis of $\exists!W$ (uniquely identified) and on the basis of $\exists W$(new). A possible disadvantage is, of course, that in Dutch and in English we end up now with three empty elements in our syntax, two at the NUM-level, one at the DET-level. This point will be discussed in chapter 8.1. In chapter 8.2, a solution also will be proposed by a change in the definition of the BARE-operator. It will also eliminate the need to introduce the Noun at two different type-levels into the syntax. Due to a restructuring of the syntax in (170), an important drawback of (265) will be taken away, namely that the three types of saucer are the only saucers in the domain of interpretation.

Technically, though not in spirit, the present analysis differs considerably from the well known bare-plural theory in Carlson (1978, 1979, 1989), which would analyse the bare plural *saucers* as in (274):

(274) $\lambda P^{\vee}P(\iota x^{k}\Box\forall y^{o}[R(y^{o},x^{k}) \Leftrightarrow \text{saucer}(y^{o})])$

that is, as a set of properties defining a unique kind x such that necessarily the entities (objects) which realize the kind x belong to the set of saucers and the entities which are saucers are realizations of that kind.[42] In (274), there is modality involved as well as other forms of intensionality, but apart from that, Carlson had to make an ontological distinction between objects and kinds, expressed by the use of sorted variables. Moreover, Carlson (1978) introduced a Realization-relation R. In the present approach, the difference between object and kind is expressed by two things: (a) a difference of type-level; and (b), by the presence or absence of cardinality information at the level of the set W.[43] It should be pointed out, however, that the 'bareness'-analysis is not to replace existing theories about genericity; rather, it isolates in the area of genericity in its broad sense certain phenomena which on closer scrutiny do not or should not fall under the exclusive label of genericity. One might say that between contingent sentences and (lawlike) generic sentences there is a whole gamut of interpretational varieties. Certainly, the above bare-sentences are 'on their way' to fully fledged generic sentences, but the predicates used keep them sufficiently tied up with temporal structure so that they are at best only partially generic.[44] In chapter 13.8, I return to this point in view of habitual sentences.

The present analysis of bareness accounts for the possibility for NPs systematically to have a [–SQA]-interpretation beside their [+SQA]-interpretation. In the former case, they pertain to an unspecified quantity of individuals, whereas in the latter they pertain to a specified quantity of individuals. This difference corresponds with a type-logical difference between levels at which cardinality information is given. The systematic occurrence of the [–SQA]-interpretations beside [+SQA]-interpretations in the four syntactic categories involved ([±definite], [±plural]) supports the thesis defended here, namely that it is possible for GQT to achieve a precise delineation of the notion of (Un-)Specified Quantity, provided that the $<<<e,t>,t>,t>$-level of analysis is maintained. This makes it possible to define two levels at which cardinality information can be expressed, $<e,t>$ (cardinality of W) and $<<e,t>,t>$ (cardinality of Q). At the highest level, the cardinality of the individuals is no longer determinable and this provides the explanation for the durative behaviour of sentences containing NPs with a bare plural reading, as discussed in this section. In chapter 13, a detailed analysis will be given of why it is that the verb cannot 'see' the cardinality information at the level of Q.

6.4 Conclusion

The discussion of NP-structure at the $<<<e,t>,t>,t>$-level has shown, in my view, that the ingredients for [+SQA]-assessment can be made more precise than in the 1987 attempt sketched in chapter 4: the representations now introduce or identify a certain set W at the DET-level after which W goes through a series of inspections, with three different check points:

the relation of W to the head noun N^0;
the relation of W to the VP;
the cardinality of W.

The relation between W and the head noun N^0 is a subset relation. This relation makes W dependent on the size of $[\![N^0]\!]$. There are two special situations here: (a) $[\![N^0]\!] \subseteq W$, invoking the problem of whether or not identity relation must be given (see (218)); (b) $[\![N^0]\!] = \varnothing$, which implies that W should also be the empty set, which might conflict with information about the cardinality of W. This situation excludes a set of sentences from having terminative aspect, namely those which are undefined in the model (see chapter 5.2). The present framework made it possible to unify Russell's judgments on sentences with *the* and *all.*

The relation between W and the VP-denotation is also a subset relation: W must be an element of $\wp([\![VP]\!])$ in order for the sentence to be true. Of course, there is no problem at all if W is specified as consisting of, say, three children, and the application of the NP to the VP would yield $W \subseteq \varnothing_{VP}$ or $W \subseteq \{c,d\}_{VP}$. It would simply mean that the sentence is false. The cardinality of W is basically the contribution of NUM, the sister of N^0, which is taken as a functor yielding N^1. This information percolates via lambda-application to the final representation. In other words, there is a separation between cardinality information (coming from the N^1-node) and determiner-information introducing W itself (coming from the sister node of N^1). There are six sorts of cardinality information ($n \geq 1$): (i) $|W|=n$, (ii) $|W|>n$, (iii) $|W|<n$, (iv) $|W|\leq n$, (v) $|W|\geq n$, (vi) $|W|=0$. Dependent on the tenability of the bare plural analysis, one may add a seventh: (vii) no cardinality information is given. Given the unique identification ($\exists!W$) or the introduction ($\exists W$) of W via (182) or (204), on the basis of determiners like (177)–(181), the presence of cardinality information of types (i)–(v) is sufficient to provide for [+SQA]. If no cardinality information about W is given, an NP is [–SQA]. If $|W|=0$, then an NP is [–SQA].

It is perhaps necessary to underline that the five sorts of cardinality information (i)–(v) convey basically the same type of information. The statement $|W|=n$ deviates from (ii)–(v) only in that it gives a specific value, it identifies a particular number in **N**, because a speaker wants to give this information or is able to do that. The other cases deviate from (i) only in that the specific value m is not given directly. Rather, the speaker uses the value n to indicate a certain unknown value m plus the position of n with respect to m. This is at least the case when sentences express temporality. One cannot tie up $<$, $>$, $\leq$, and $\geq$ with unboundedness or infiniteness, because NPs with *at least* and *at most* happen to be used to express cardinality information plus some uncertainty about the exact value, whereas bare NPs of the type discussed in chapter 6.3 are used to prevent the transfer of cardinality information.

It may be concluded, then, that the <<<*e*,*t*>,*t*>,*t*>-analysis along the lines of (170) provides a good basis for the definition of the [+SQA]-notion in terms of either of the schemes for NPs in (275)

(275) a. $\lambda P \exists W[W \subseteq [\![N^0]\!] \wedge |W|\ r\ n \wedge P(W)]$
b. $\lambda P \exists ! W[W \subseteq [\![N^0]\!] \wedge |W|\ r\ n \wedge P(W)]$

where r is one of the relations and n one of the values in (i)–(v). Formulas of the form (275) are denotations of [+SQA]-NPs if n is one of the options (i)–(v). In those cases, the presence of information of the form |W| r n yields exactly the [+SQA]-properties we are looking for. In my view, it is the <<<*e*,*t*>,*t*>,*t*>-analysis and not the <<*e*,*t*>,*t*>-analysis of NPs which brings out the notion of Specified Quantity of A at its sharpest.

7 *Determiner structure*

7.0 Introduction

The NP-grammar (170) falls short in a number of respects. First of all, it does not deal with NPs which occur as direct object of transitive verbs, with bare plurality, negation and other important areas in which an aspectual theory must be tested. Secondly, there is a fundamental problem inherent in (170) and discussed below in section 7.1 that was signalled in the mid-eighties by Van Benthem (1986). Thirdly, it does not deal with the relation between temporal and atemporal forms of quantification. In this chapter the first two problems will be brought together and their solution will result in a change of the prenominal structure with the preservation of the advantages of working at the $<<<e,t>,t>,t>$-level. This will contribute to the solution of the third problem.

In Verkuyl and Van der Does (1991), a grammar was proposed for plural NPs as an alternative to Scha's and Link's theories on plurality. This grammar, called PLUG, will be included in the present chapter, as it provides the basis for a temporal extension resulting in PLUG$^+$, a formal grammar which will be discussed in chapter 13. Rather than having (170) as a syntactic pattern splitting DET-information from NUM-information, PLUG operates with structures like (276) or its simplified version (277), where $0 \leq i \leq max-1$.

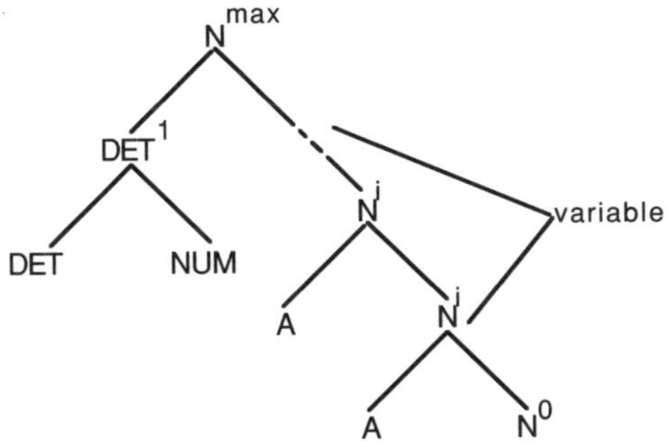

Figure 12 The NP-structure proposed in PLUG

(276) $[_{N^{max}} [_{DET} \text{DET NUM}] [_{N^i} [A^* N^0]]]$
(277) $[_{N^{max}} [_{DET} \text{DET NUM}] N^0]$
(170) $[_{N^{max}} \text{DET} [_{N^{max-1}} \text{NUM} [_{N^i} A^* N^0]]]$

The differences between PLUG and the grammar based on (170) and (177)–(181) concern the following points. Firstly, in PLUG the determiner has got a structure whose NUM is modified by a specifier (there will be a relabelling shortly, but here the old terms will be used to keep track of what is involved in the change). Secondly, the PLUG-proposal is more comprehensive because transitive sentences are taken into account, which makes it possible to be more explicit as to the asymmetry involved in aspectual construal: the VP is taken as a unit, as argued for in chapter 1. One of its corollaries is that there needs to be no scopal change of quantifiers in sentences with multiple quantification, in the absence of a theory about focus. Thirdly, the problem raised by Van Benthem is a problem for a grammar based on (170) + (177)–(181) but not for PLUG. Finally, PLUG provides for a point of attachment between temporal and atemporal structure by assigning the NP-denotation set-theoretical structure. A cardinality statement about a set W is not sufficient for an aspectual theory dealing with the [+SQA]-notion, as [+SQA]-information is only relevant *given the interaction between NP-structure and the temporal structure contributed by a* [+ADD TO]-*verb*. More structure will be needed.

In section 7.1, the adjectival approach to numerals underlying (170) is considered in some detail in view of the problem raised by Van Benthem. It will be shown that the root of the problem lies in the inclusion relation in NUMs, for example, for *three* in the information expressed by $X \subseteq Y$ in $\lambda Y \lambda X[X \subseteq Y \wedge |X|=3]$. In section 7.2, the notion of a partition will be introduced. It will be argued that it is necessary to provide for structure in the NP-denotation that can be made sensitive to temporal structure. In section 7.3, the rules of the PLUG-grammar resulting from the change of (170) into (276) will be given. Some aspectually relevant features of PLUG will be tested in the sections 7.4–7.6.

7.1 A problem with ø

There is an innocent-looking but nasty problem with (181). It is signalled in Van Benthem (1986: 52) and it shows up in (278), which is derived along the lines of (184) and (186).

(181) ø $[-N^1_{pl}]$ $\lambda Q \lambda P \exists W[Q(W) \wedge P(W)]$

(278)

N^0	child	⟦child⟧
NUM	three	$\lambda Y \lambda X[X \subseteq Y \wedge |X|=3]$
N^1	three(children)	$\lambda X[X \subseteq [\![child]\!] \wedge |X|=3]$
DET	ø	$\lambda Q \lambda P \exists W[Q(W) \wedge P(W)]$
N^2	ø(three(children))	
		$\lambda P \exists W[W \subseteq [\![child]\!] \wedge |W|=3 \wedge P(W)]$
VP	came in	$\lambda X.X \subseteq [\![came\_in]\!]$
S	three children came in	
		$\exists W[W \subseteq [\![child]\!] \wedge |W|=3 \wedge W \subseteq [\![came\_in]\!]]$

N^1 denotes a function sending all subsets of child containing three members to a collection of sets containing exactly three children. This set $\{X: [X \subseteq [\![child]\!] \wedge |X|=3]\} = \{\{b,c,d\}, \{b,c,m\}, \{b,d,m\}, \ldots, \{d,m,j\}\}$ in, say, an extended $\mathbf{M}_1$. Call it $\wp^3([\![child]\!])$, that is, the power set of the set ⟦child⟧ restricted to sets having three members. The set corresponding to $\lambda X.X \subseteq [\![came\_in]\!]$ is the set $\wp^+([\![came\_in]\!])$ of all non-empty subsets of the V-denotation ⟦came_in⟧. So, the bottom line of (278) says that if *Three children came in* is true, W is a member of both $\wp^3([\![child]\!])$ and $\wp^+([\![came\_in]\!])$.

Now, the problem is that the existential quantifier fronting W overrules the exactly-three condition in $|W|=3$, because the bottom line of (278) is compatible with the situation in $\mathbf{M}_1$ that there are four sets W with exactly three children. This is simply the meaning of $\exists$. This implies that *Three children came in* may mean that all members of $\wp^3([\![child]\!])$ came in. The same applies to, for example, *at most two*: here one would also end up with more than two children having come in. This is a serious problem indeed: *exactly three* is going to mean 'at least three'. Can it be solved?

One possible solution is to stipulate for all the indefinite determiners in (177)–(181) that $\exists W$ in $\lambda Q \lambda P \exists W[Q(W) \wedge P(W)]$ should be read as: there is just one W existentially introduced in the model. But this is not satisfactory because in many cases one needs the $\exists$ to assure an *at least*-interpretation. A better solution is to analyse the adjectival approach inherent to (278) in some detail in order to see where the root of the trouble is hidden. The NUM-node in (170) turns out to be the result of applying a more complex operation involving an adjectival modifier. The numeral *three* is defined along the lines of (174) as $\lambda Y \lambda X[X \subseteq Y \wedge |X|=3]$. However, this implies the application of an operation in which an adjectival operator, say ADJ, is involved. The adjectival view on determiners consists in the conviction that quite generally the familiar determiners of type <<*e*,*t*>, <<*e*,*t*>,*t*>> from Barwise and Cooper (1981) can be turned into adjectives of type <<*e*,*t*>,<<*e*,*t*>,*t*>>, by means of the ADJ-operator. Thus if ADJ is defined as in (279) and the determiner *three* as (280), the result of applying ADJ to *three* will be (281).

(279) ADJ $=_{df}$ $\lambda D_{<<e,t>,<<e,t>t>>}\lambda Y\lambda X[X\subseteq Y \wedge D(Y)(X)]$

(280) ⟦three⟧ $=_{df}$ $\lambda Y\lambda X[|X\cap Y|=n]$

(281) ADJ(⟦three⟧) $\lambda D\lambda Y\lambda X[X\subseteq Y\wedge D(Y)(X)](\lambda Y\lambda X[|X\cap Y|=3])$

$\lambda Y\lambda X[X\subseteq Y\wedge\lambda Y\lambda X[|X\cap Y|=3](Y)(X)]$

$\lambda Y\lambda X[X\subseteq Y\wedge|X\cap Y|=3]$

$\lambda Y\lambda X[X\subseteq Y\wedge|X|=3]$

Here the conventions of DEF 3.3 are observed, so X and Y are of type <*e*,*t*>. In the NUM of (278), the ADJ-operator was made 'invisible' by simply assuming that a numeral like *three* is the result of applying ADJ to some more basic form. In other words, not only is (281) the more sophisticated variant of numerals defined on the basis of (174), it is also the only way to bring about the change we envisage. There is no other way out but to restructure the prenominal structure such that the cardinality information is not immediately associated with the N-projection line. This appears to work for all NPs, regardless of the monotonicity behaviour of the original determiners, as will be shown in the remainder of this chapter.

The reorganized NP-structure of (278) is given in Figure 13, where DET^1 is no longer analysed as (281), that is, as ADJ(NUM), but rather along the lines of (280), that is, as expressing purely cardinality information without incorporating the inclusion relation $\subseteq$. In view of my wish to stay as close as possible to accepted principles of X-bar syntax in GB-syntax, the Specifier node SPEC now modifies a DET^1-node, yielding a complex determiner DET^2. DET^1 transmits

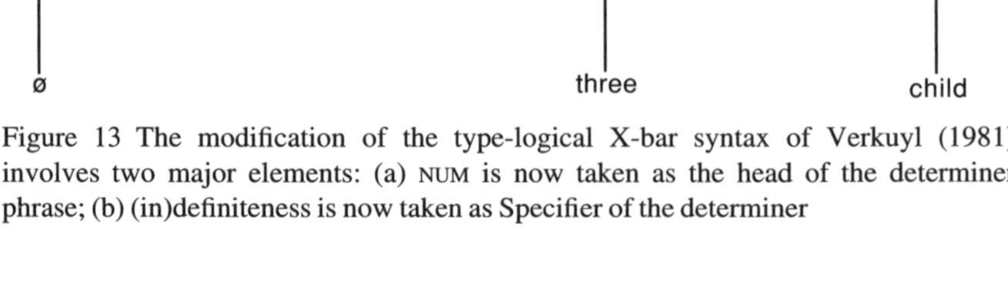

Figure 13 The modification of the type-logical X-bar syntax of Verkuyl (1981) involves two major elements: (a) NUM is now taken as the head of the determiner phrase; (b) (in)definiteness is now taken as Specifier of the determiner

purely quantificational information, which may be linked with the VP as soon as SPEC turns DET^1 into a determiner DET^2 of the proper (lifted) type, whereas SPEC contains 'referential' information, introducing a set or identifying it. Thus, a division of labour in the determiner DET^2 is obtained. As said, the information contained by ADJ above is now incorporated in SPEC. This means that there is no need to distinguish DET^1 from DET^0 as long as DET^1 is not branching. One might wish to assume a DET^0 at the syntactic level and indeed it is plausible to derive DET^1 [[three]] on the basis of the derivation (282):

(282) $[\![\text{three}]\!] = \lambda n \lambda X \lambda Y.|X \cap Y| = n(3)$

that is, in terms of a function $\lambda n \lambda X \lambda Y.|X \cap Y| = n$ applying to the number 3 (Scha 1981; Krifka 1989a). However, one might also assume that (282) is a lexical operation, so that (280) is inserted as a DET^0. In that case, GB-syntacticians would read the determiner structure in Figure 13 as being of the form $[_{\text{DET2}}$ SPEC $[_{\text{DET1}}$ $\text{DET}^0]]$, as in Figure 14. DET^0 will not be included in figures

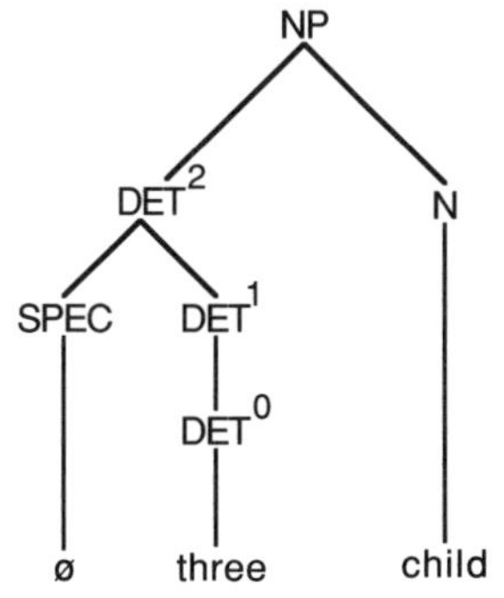

Figure 14 Considerations of GB-syntax could require that Figure 13 be fine-grained so as to contain a DET^0-level

unless there is branching involved that is of a syntactic nature, or unless it is relevant to do so. Moreover, I shall write DET rather than DET^0, as I shall also mostly write N rather than N^0.

In short, Figures 13 and 14 meet the requirements of an X-bar syntax in the standard GB-sense, though it should be said that the PLUG-grammar assumes only binary branching, as in Verkuyl (1981), whereas it is also syntactically more parsimonious. The claim is that an analysis of the NP based on Figure 13 does not meet the problem inherent to the adjectival analysis. This claim will be substantiated in the next section, in which the determiner structure of NPs will be investigated with a view on the contributions made by DET^1 and SPEC.

7.2 Scalarity, partitions and pseudo-partitions

As observed in chapter 1, an aspectual theory should account for the terminative behaviour of sentences like (284), as:

(283) Four men lifted three tables
(284) #Four men lifted three tables for hours
(285) Four men lifted three tables in an hour

Verkuyl (1987a, 1987b, 1988) argued that (284) is not multiply ambiguous. PLUG also holds that all NPs are of the same type and no NP is ambiguous between a collective and distributive reading. Rather, an NP like *four men* allows the whole range of interpretations between the extremes of the scale exemplified in Figure 15.[45] A scalar approach to quantification in sentences with plural NPs circumvents the proliferation of readings which is so typical of the logical or the logically oriented literature. In fact, in PLUG each sentence is given just one meaning. It is convenient, though, to have names for two situations covered by this meaning: the purely distributive and the purely collective interpretation of a sentence, as a distinction between atoms and a unit set seems to be a universal of language. It will be argued, though, that languages do not express this distinction structurally but rather lexically: some items have a distributive meaning, whereas others do not have it. For example *every* N denotes a distributive quantifier in English, *jede* N in German and *elke* N in Dutch.

Gillon (1987) argues that members in the range between Collective and Distributive be given a separate reading. He uses (286) to make his point.[46]

(286) Hammerstein, Hart and Rodgers wrote musicals

This sentence may well be true if, as in fact, Rodgers wrote both with Hammerstein and Hart. And a most straightforward analysis of this would be

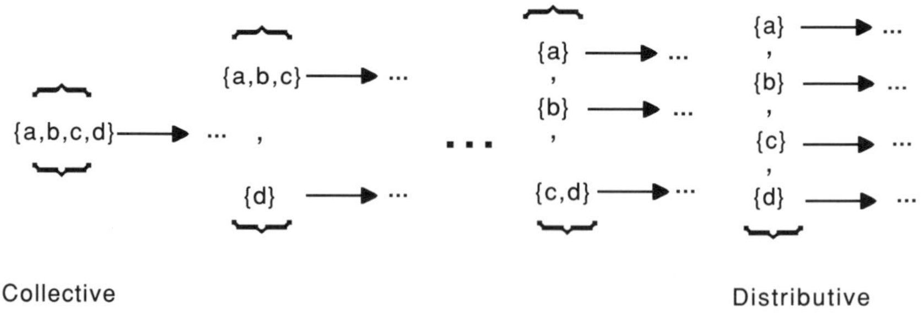

Figure 15 One way to look at the collective/distributive distinction is to see it in terms of a scale with 'collective' at one extreme and 'distributive' at the other extreme

that (286) may be used in a situation where to write musicals holds of two overlapping subsets of the set denoted by *Hammerstein, Hart and Rodgers*. More precisely, Gillon states that the truth conditions of (286) are:

> (286) is true iff there is a minimal cover of the set denoted by the NP which is a subset of the VP.

According to Gillon, this should be understood as saying that each minimal cover will yield a separate reading of (286), where the notion of minimal cover is defined by:

DEFINITION (MINIMAL-COVER) A set $Q \subseteq \wp(X)$ is a minimal cover of X, iff Q covers X, that is, $\bigcup Q = X$, but Q does not contain covers as a real part.

That is, $\neg \exists Z.\ Z$ covers X $\wedge$ $Z \subset Q$. In other words, each element in a minimal cover Q of X contributes at least one element in covering X not contributed by any of the other elements of Q.

Although one may agree with Gillon (and Scha for that matter) that intermediate interpretations exist, they do not induce a combinatorial explosion in the number of readings.[47] As it stands, (286) is simply vague as to which minimal cover will verify it, a vagueness which may be eliminated in a particular context of use.[48]

From 1983 onwards, I have been arguing that NP-denotations involved in terminative aspect should be taken in terms of partitions.

DEFINITION (PARTITIONS) A set $Q \subseteq \wp(X)$ is a partition of X, if $\bigcup Q = X$ and for all $U, V \in Q$: $U \cap V = \varnothing$.

A partition is a minimal cover whose elements do not overlap. The reason why one might like to have them is that for the interpretation of sentences like (287)

(287) Three children crossed the street

it is relevant to know that each of the members of the NP-denotation satisfies the predicate 'crossed the street', so that there is some relation between the cardinality of the NP and the number of configurations in which the children satisfied the predicate. That is, they may have crossed the street together, one by one or in a 1–2 or 2–1 configuration. It is essential that it is left in the dark how they did it. The need for partitions is guided by the empirical observation that if one extends this sentence with ... *and they did so one after the other*, we should be able to relate the temporal structure assumed by the use of *one after the other* to the representation of (287) by relating the cells of the partition to time units; similarly if one had proceeded with ... *first Judith crossed it, and then David and Jessica*, or with ... *together*.

The use of partitions in the analysis of sentences like (287) is inspired by the set-theoretical theorem (288) which says:

(288) every set X can be mapped canonically onto the quotient set X/E, where E is an equivalence relation

For if the thematic relation, that is, the way an argument relates to the verb, is conceived of as the equivalence relation 'being involved in the verbal predication at the same index', it is natural to use the theorem (Verkuyl 1987a, 1988). That is, the above set of three children may be partitioned on the ground of the equivalence relation 'having crossed the street at the same index . In this way, a partition of the set of three children into {{Judith}, {Dav d, Jessica}} expresses the fact that the two cells of the partition are related to different indices which make up the event described by (287). For the interaction between atemporal quantifiers and time intervals which make up an event, the notion of partition seems to be called for.

However, Van der Does pointed out that (287) can be understood in the following way: Judith crosses the street first, she observes David and Jessica at the other side, she walks back and then the three of them cross it all together. That (287) can be applied to this situation cannot be denied and plainly in an atemporal semantics this would result in a non-partitional set of sets. To take another (real-life) example, Max, Henk and Hans are playing chess in the following way: Max and Henk play together against Hans and so do Hans and Henk against Max, all at the same time. So *Max, Henk and Hans played two chess games* is a perfect sentence for this situation, though it describes many others as well.

These considerations led Verkuyl and Van der Does (1991) to incorporate the numerical upper-bound given by the atemporal NPs, especially by the external argument NP_1, into the definition of the sort of cover which they called pseudo-partition.

DEFINITION (PSEUDO-PARTITION) A set $Q \subseteq \wp(X)$ is a pseudo-partition of X, if $\bigcup Q = X$ & $|Q| \leq |X|$.

A pseudo-partition Q of X will exhaust all the elements in X, but the members of Q itself may overlap.[49] Both Van der Does and I have decided that this sort of cover does not work well, though for different reasons. Van der Does (1992) wishes to allow that the three children in (287) may have crossed the street repeatedly more than three times – this is excluded by the definition – and I myself considered the notion of pseudo-partition the next-best solution due to the fact that our analysis did not take into account temporal structure. As soon as one does, there are arguments to take the equivalence relation in (288) as basic for the assignment of thematic roles and to solve Van der Does' objections with regard to (196) in a different way.

In general, it seems as if interpretations in which we have to assume partitioning are often more normal than the other forms, for example in sentences containing VPs like *eat five sandwiches*, *kill three soldiers*, *fly to three cities*, etc. Both lexical and temporal information might be relevant for a particular choice. Moreover, it seems as if the problems with partitioning occur mainly with intransitive sentences and with external argument NPs. As far as the internal argument NPs are concerned, there seem to be no problems in having partitions as part of the meaning of an NP. Furthermore, it seems as if it is possible to maintain partitioning for the external argument NPs as well because their semantics will be argued to require a partitioning into singletons. In view of this, it seems appropriate in a study on aspectuality to take the strongest position – that of a partition – and see what sort of problems we meet on that assumption. In chapter 13, I will come back to this issue in much more detail.

For the time being, the following convention will be used: that Q partitions X will be written as QpsX, where ps is a relation between a set of sets and a set. It would be simpler to write Xpd$Q$ (X is partitioned by Q), but for the analysis of aspectuality the more elaborate 'active' form will be required. Partitions will create the structure necessary for dealing with temporal structure.

7.3 PLUG

The PLUG-grammar consists of the following rules:

Grammar:

1. $\mathrm{S} : [\![\mathrm{NP}]\!]([\![\mathrm{VP}]\!]) \quad \Leftarrow \quad \mathrm{NP} : [\![\mathrm{NP}]\!], \mathrm{VP} : [\![\mathrm{VP}]\!]$

2. $\begin{cases} \mathrm{VP} : \lambda X.[\![\mathrm{V}_1]\!](X) \\ \mathrm{VP} : \lambda X.[\![\mathrm{NP}]\!](\lambda Y.[\![\mathrm{V}_2]\!](Y)(X)) \quad \Leftarrow \quad \mathrm{V}_2 : [\![\mathrm{V}_2]\!], \mathrm{NP} : [\![\mathrm{NP}]\!] \end{cases}$

3. $\mathrm{NP} : [\![\mathrm{DET}^2]\!]([\![\mathrm{N}]\!]) \quad \Leftarrow \quad \mathrm{DET}^2 : [\![\mathrm{DET}^2]\!], \mathrm{N} : [\![\mathrm{N}]\!]$

4. $\mathrm{DET}^2 : [\![\mathrm{SPEC}]\!]([\![\mathrm{DET}^1]\!]) \quad \Leftarrow \quad \mathrm{SPEC} : [\![\mathrm{SPEC}]\!], \mathrm{DET}^1 : [\![\mathrm{DET}^1]\!]$

Lexical entries are of the form:

5. SPEC : $[\![\text{SPEC}_i]\!]$
6. DET[1] : $[\![D_i]\!]$
7. N : $[\![P_i]\!]$
8. $V_1 : [\![T_i]\!]$
9. $V_2 : [\![R_i]\!]$

The following notational conventions are used:

(289)

Variables	*Constants*	*Types*
x, y, z	–	*e*
X, Y, U, V, W, Z	P_i, T_i	*<e,t>*
–	R_i	*<e,<e,t>>*
P, Q, R, S	–	*<<e,t>,t>*
D	D_i	*<<e,t>,<<e,t>,t>>*

The expressions P_i, T_i, R_i, D_i ($i \in \mathbf{N}$) are treated as lexical constants receiving their interpretation from an underlying model $\mathbf{M} = \langle E, [\![-]\!]\rangle$ left implicit in the sequel. Furthermore, $E = [\![\text{thing}]\!]$.

The rules of PLUG are stated using the format (290).

(290) $\text{SYN} : F(\text{SEM}_1, \ldots, \text{SEM}_n) \quad \Leftarrow \quad \text{SYN}_1 : \text{SEM}_1 , \ldots , \text{SYN}_n : \text{SEM}_n$

SYN_i denotes a syntactic category and SEM_i its semantic denotation. The symbol '$\Leftarrow$' indicates that SYN is built from $\text{SYN}_1, \ldots , \text{SYN}_n$ and that its semantic denotation is $F(\text{SEM}_1, \ldots, \text{SEM}_n)$. If SYN_i is basic (that is, a lexical category, as in rules 5–9), the rules reduce to SYN : SEM, where SEM is given by the lexical definition. Most of the time, F is simply a functional application, but for convenience F in $VP \Leftarrow V_2$ NP, in rule 2 is a more complex, though standard, operation.

In the formulation of the semantic analysis of a syntactic expression of the form [V NP] an asymmetry is expressed between the internal argument and the external argument of the verb. That is, an NP in the direct object position is treated differently from an NP in the subject position. Impressionistically, an NP is 'sensitive' for the position in which it occurs. The fusion of a verb and its internal argument (in the sentences under analysis occurring as a direct object NP) requires a semantic operation of matching the *<<e,t>,<<e,t>,t>>*-type of the V_2 and the *<<<e,t>,t>,t>*-type of the NP. This is now done syncategorematically by rule 2, along familiar lines, but it can also be done categorematically by the type-lifting operator (291):

(291) $\lambda V_{2<<e,t>,<<e,t>,t>>} \lambda NP_{<<<e,t>,t>,t>} \lambda X_{<e,t>}.NP(\lambda Y_{<e,t>}.V_2(Y)(X))$

As this operation does not play a role in the analysis of the quantificational structure of all NPs, rule 2 is sufficient, but in the analysis of the temporal structure built up from the verb and its internal argument, it is not unreasonable to think of the verb as contributing an operator of this sort, as will be pointed out in chapter 13.4.

Rule 3 says that, in general, NPs are of the form DET^2 N. Actually, we could have written DET^{max} rather than DET^2 to underscore the X-bar nature of PLUG. Rule 4 represents the splitting up of quantificational information (DET^1) and referential information (SPEC).

For the definition of SPEC some requisite notions have to be given first. To begin with, an operator $|$ is to be defined, restricting type $<<e,t>,t>$-objects to objects of type $<e,t>$:

$$(292) \quad | \;=_{df}\; \lambda X_{<e,t>} \lambda Q_{<<e,t>,t>} \lambda Z_{<e,t>} \exists W \in Q[Z=W \cap X]$$

We shall write $Q|_X$ rather than $|(X)(Q)$. In set notation, (292) amounts to:

$$(293) \quad Q|_X =_{df} \{X \cap Z: Z \in Q\}$$

Thus if $Q=\{\{a_1,a_2,c_1\}, \{a_3,c_2,c_3\}\}$ and $[\![\text{child}]\!]=\{c_1,c_2,c_3\}$, then $Q|_{[\![\text{child}]\!]}= \{\{c_1\}, \{c_2,c_3\}\}$. If Q is thought of as the denotation of a VP (a set of collections), then $Q|_X$ contains exactly those parts of the collections in Q which consist of Xs.[50] The definition of the empty SPEC is now:

$$(294) \quad [\![_{\text{SPEC}}\, \emptyset]\!] =_{df} \quad \lambda D \lambda X \lambda P. \exists W[W \subseteq X \wedge D(X)(W) \wedge \exists Q \text{ps} W[Q=P|_X]]$$

In (294), D is a variable of type $<<e,t>,<<e,t>,t>>$, whereas $\exists Q\text{ps}W[\phi]$ is short for $\exists Q[Q\text{ps}W \wedge \phi]$. As said, the symbol 'ps' stands here for *partitions*.

SPEC itself is of type $<<<e,t>,<<e,t>,t>>, <<e,t>,<<<e,t>,t>,t>>>$. This type is quite different from the type of the empty determiner ø in Figures 13 and 14 which was of type $<<<e,t>,t>, <<<e,t>,t>,t>>$. Underlying this type change is the idea that a specifier should modify a determiner of type $<<e,t>,<<e,t>,t>>$ rather than an N′ of type $<<e,t>,t>$. It is this part of the definition of SPEC which enables us to incorporate into SPEC the information, previously associated with ADJ, which selected the sets W and X such that $W \subseteq X$ (and $W \in D(X)$). In this way a determiner structure is obtained in which the cardinality information expressed by an NP is located in DET, whereas the information about uniquely identified and newly introduced and other contextually determined information is located in SPEC. In fact, SPEC is the bridge between propositional information expressed by the sentence and the context in which this sentence is used. Below, we shall differentiate between the indefinite and definite use of SPEC. It should be observed that (294) is the instantiation of a scheme for a number of lexical items. As far as (278) is concerned, it may now be changed into (295).

(295)

N^0	child	$[\![\text{child}]\!]$
DET[1]	three	$\lambda Y \lambda X.\lvert X \cap Y \rvert = 3$
SPEC	ø	$\lambda D \lambda X \lambda P.\exists W[W \subseteq X \wedge D(X)(W) \wedge \exists Q \text{ps} W[Q = P\rvert_X]]$
DET[2]	ø(three)	$\lambda X \lambda P.\exists W[W \subseteq X \wedge \lvert W \rvert = 3 \wedge \exists Q \text{ps} W[Q = P\rvert_X]]$
NP	(ø(three))(child)	
		$\lambda P.\exists W[W \subseteq [\![\text{child}]\!] \wedge \lvert W \rvert = 3 \wedge \exists Q \text{ps} W[Q = P\rvert_{[\![\text{child}]\!]}]]$
VP	came in	$\lambda X.X \subseteq [\![\text{came\_in}]\!]$
S	three children came in	
		$\lambda P.\exists W[W \subseteq [\![\text{child}]\!] \wedge \lvert W \rvert = 3 \wedge \exists Q \text{ps} W[Q = P\rvert_{[\![\text{child}]\!]}]]$
		$(\lambda X.X \subseteq [\![\text{came\_in}]\!])$
		$\exists W[W \subseteq [\![\text{child}]\!] \wedge \lvert W \rvert = 3$
		$\wedge \exists Q \text{ps} W[Q = \{X \cap [\![\text{child}]\!] \mid [\![\text{came\_in}]\!](X)\}]]$

The last line of (295) says, given (293): inspecting the collections X containing children having come in, one finds that all these collections are formed out of a particular group consisting of exactly three children. In $\mathbf{M}_1$ this would be {b,c,d}. Thus, the problem raised by Van Benthem (1986) has been solved.

The semantic innovation of PLUG with respect to a derivation like (186) in chapter 5.1 is that the simple predication *P*(W) in expressions like (184) is now replaced by structured conditions on *P*. Compare, for example, the denotation of [ø(three)(child)] in (295), with the bottom line of derivation (186).

(186) $\lambda P \exists W[W \subseteq [\![\text{child}]\!] \wedge \lvert W \rvert = 3 \wedge P(W)]$

The difference is clear: (186) says that W is a subset of the VP-denotation, whereas (295) says that W is divided up into a finite number of sets each of which contains children involved in the predication. The heart of the matter is that (295) covers a number of possible combinations in which three children may be involved in the predication. In particular, (295) covers situations in which three children came in one by one, all together or in different groups. This is as it should be: *Three children came in* does not say anything about the way they came in. So we should be able to remain sufficiently vague in order to account for the many misunderstandings made possible by the use of a sentence without sufficient knowledge of its context of use. In other words, we want to let a speaker say *Three children came in*, intending to express that three children came in together but not saying it explicitly, whereas we want to give the hearer on the basis of contextual information the room of being misled into thinking that three children came in one after the other.

The lexicon of PLUG will contain entries like those in (296).

(296)
Lexicon:

SPEC

⟦the⟧:	$\lambda D\lambda X\lambda P[D(X\cap C)(⟦thing⟧)\wedge\exists Rps X\cap C[R=P|_{X\cap C}]]$
⟦ø⟧:	$\lambda D\lambda X\lambda P.\exists W[W\subseteq X\wedge D(X)(W)\wedge\exists Q ps W[Q=P|_X]]$

DET[1]

⟦SG⟧:	$\lambda X\lambda Y.|X\cap Y|=1$
⟦PL⟧:	$\lambda X\lambda Y.|X\cap Y|>1$
⟦n⟧:	$\lambda X\lambda Y.|X\cap Y|=n$
⟦many⟧:	$\lambda X\lambda Y.|X\cap Y|>k\bullet|X|$[51]
⟦several]:	$\lambda X\lambda Y.|X\cap Y|\geq 2$
⟦INC⟧	$\lambda X\lambda Y.|X\cap Y'|=0$

The derivation for the NP *the child* is given in (297). Its last line (298) can be translated into the notation of (182) as (299).

(297)

the	$\lambda D\lambda X\lambda Q[D(X\cap C)(⟦thing⟧)\wedge\exists R ps X\cap C[R=Q|_{X\cap C}]]$
SG	$\lambda X\lambda Y[|X\cap Y|=1]$
the(SG)	$\lambda D\lambda X\lambda Q[D(X\cap C)(⟦thing⟧)\wedge\exists R ps X\cap C[R=Q|_{X\cap C}]]$
	$(\lambda X\lambda Y[|X\cap Y|=1])$
	$\lambda X\lambda Q[|X\cap C|=1\wedge\exists R ps X\cap C[R=Q|_{X\cap C}]]$
the(SG)(child)	$\lambda X\lambda Q[|X\cap C|=1\wedge\exists R ps X\cap C[R=Q|_{X\cap C}]](⟦child⟧)$
	$\lambda Q[|⟦child⟧\cap C|=1\wedge\exists R ps ⟦child⟧\cap C[R=Q|_{⟦child⟧\cap C}]]$

(298) $\lambda Q[|⟦child⟧\cap C|=1\wedge\exists R ps ⟦child⟧\cap C[R=Q|_{⟦child⟧\cap C}]]$
(299) $\lambda Q.\exists!W[W\subseteq⟦child⟧\wedge|W|=1\wedge\exists R ps W[R=Q|_{⟦child⟧}]]$

Similarly, the last line of the derivation of ⟦the⟧(⟦PL⟧)(⟦child⟧), that is (300), can be written as (301):

(300) $\lambda Q.[|⟦child⟧\cap C|>1\wedge\exists R ps ⟦child⟧\cap C[R=Q|_{⟦child⟧\cap C}]]$
(301) $\lambda Q.\exists!W[W=⟦child⟧\wedge|W|>1\wedge\exists R ps W[R=Q|_{⟦child⟧}]]$

In (298) and (300), the definiteness of the NPs is given directly in terms of a context set. The cardinality of the context set intersected with the head noun is constrained by PL and SG. In this way, the SPEC *the* expresses definiteness. I will use (299) and (301) as synonymous with (298) and (300), respectively.

One might wish to evade abstract syntactic elements like ø, SG, PL and INC, but there are reasons for not doing so. Firstly, there are languages in which singularity and plurality are grammaticalized. Secondly, assuming one syntactic form *the* which is ambiguous between our DET^2-meanings ⟦the⟧(⟦SG⟧) and ⟦the⟧(⟦PL⟧) would cost two determiners. Thirdly, one would miss a generalization which makes plain how different DET^2-meanings are systematically related to each other. However, in the discussion about this matter, it is crucial to determine the syntactic level at which lexicalization takes place. One might argue that lexicalization takes place at the DET^2-level, which would mean that rather than ⟦the⟧, one would have [+definite], which together with SG would lexicalize as *the* at the DET^2-level. Other options are available. I will come back to this point in chapter 8.1.

The indefinite singular NP will be discussed at the close of section 7.5. The indefinite plural NP *three sandwiches* is analysed as (ø(three))(sandwich) and interpreted as ⟦ø⟧(⟦three⟧)(⟦sandwich⟧), which results in (302).

(302) $\lambda P.\exists W[W\subseteq[\![\text{sandwich}]\!]\wedge|W|=3\wedge\exists Q\text{ps}W[Q=P|_{[\![\text{sandwich}]\!]}]]$

Thus, the PLUG-rule 2, which combines the V_2-denotation ⟦eat⟧ and ⟦ø⟧(⟦three⟧)(⟦sandwich⟧), yields for the VP *eat three sandwiches*:

⟦eat three sandwiches⟧
$\lambda X.\lambda P\exists W[W\subseteq[\![\text{sandwich}]\!]\wedge|W|=3\wedge\exists Q\text{ps}W[Q=P|_{[\![\text{sandwich}]\!]}]](\lambda Y.[\![\text{eat}]\!](Y)(X))$
$\lambda X.\exists W[W\subseteq[\![\text{sandwich}]\!]\wedge|W|=3\wedge\exists Q\text{ps}W[Q=\lambda Y.[\![\text{eat}]\!](Y)(X)|_{[\![\text{sandwich}]\!]}]]$
$\lambda X.\exists W[W\subseteq[\![\text{sandwich}]\!]\wedge|W|=3\wedge\exists Q\text{ps}W[Q=\{U\cap[\![\text{sandwich}]\!]:$
$[\![\text{eat}]\!](U)(X)\}]]$

Proper names pertaining to individuals are treated without an appeal to partitions. There are two ways: (303) and (304).

(303) $[\![\text{Judith}]\!]=\lambda P.P(\{\text{j}\})$
(304) $[\![\text{(the) Judith}]\!]=\lambda P\exists!V[V=[\![\text{Judith}]\!]\cap\{\text{j}_i\}\wedge P(V)]$

In the former case, the NP *Judith* denotes the set of collections *P* such that {j} is an element of *P*. This is simply a type-lifted version of Montague's treatment of proper names. In (304), the NP *Judith* is treated as having a definite determiner, and the Noun denotation ⟦Judith⟧ is the set of those individuals called *Judith*. The singleton $\{j_i\}$ is the unique entity singled out in a specific context (Löbner 1985). Due to the presence of SG, one might extend (304) with cardinality information, or assume that this is captured by the context set $\{j_i\}$. I will assume the latter to be the case, so (304) will be used for the representation of (68) *Judith ate three sandwiches*, which is derived as in (305).

(305)
VP ⟦eat three sandwiches⟧
NP $[\![\text{(the)Judith}]\!]=\lambda P\exists!V[V=[\![\text{Judith}]\!]\cap\{\text{j}_i\}\wedge P(V)]$

S $[\![(\text{the})\text{Judith}]\!]([\![\text{eat three sandwiches}]\!])$

$\lambda P\exists!V[V=[\![\text{Judith}]\!]\cap\{j_i\}\wedge P(V)](\lambda X.\exists W[W\subseteq[\![\text{sandwich}]\!]\wedge|W|=3$
$\wedge\exists Q\text{ps}W[Q=\{U\cap[\![\text{sandwich}]\!]: [\![\text{eat}]\!](U)(X)\}]])$

$\exists!V[V=[\![\text{Judith}]\!]\cap\{j_i\}\wedge\lambda X.\exists W[W\subseteq[\![\text{sandwich}]\!]\wedge|W|=3$
$\wedge\exists Q\text{ps}W[Q=\{U\cap[\![\text{sandwich}]\!]: [\![\text{eat}]\!](U)(X)\}]](V)]$

$\exists!V[V=[\![\text{Judith}]\!]\cap\{j_i\}\wedge\exists W[W\subseteq[\![\text{sandwich}]\!]\wedge|W|=3$
$\wedge\exists Q\text{ps}W[Q=\{U\cap[\![\text{sandwich}]\!]: [\![\text{eat}]\!](U)(V)\}]]]$

This says that there is a uniquely identified Judith and that there is a set W of three sandwiches such that W is partitioned (by a collection *Q*) into subsets U which are eaten by Judith.

7.4 Multiple quantification

How can PLUG be put to work to provide the syntax and semantics of sentences with multiple quantification without having to specify the multitude of readings discerned by Link and Scha? This question will be answered by showing in detail how PLUG deals with (306), the syntactic structure of which is given in Figure 16.

(306) Two girls ate five sandwiches

As to the semantics of (306), we have the following bottom–top derivation:

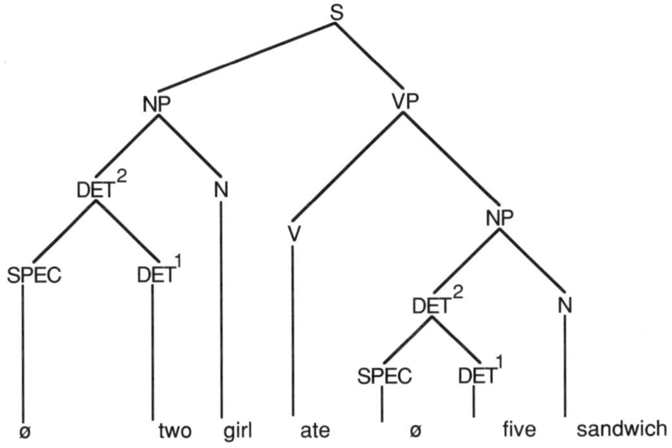

Figure 16 PLUG assigns this syntactic X-bar structure to *Two girls ate five sandwiches*

(307)

VP $[\![\text{eat five sandwiches}]\!]$

$\lambda X.\exists W[W\subseteq[\![\text{sandwich}]\!]\wedge|W|=5\wedge\exists Q\text{ps}W[Q=\{U\cap[\![\text{sandwich}]\!]: [\![\text{eat}]\!](U)(X)\}]]$

NP $[\![\emptyset\ (\text{two})]\!]([\![\text{girl}]\!])$

$\lambda Q.\exists Z[Z\subseteq[\![\text{girl}]\!]\wedge|Z|=2\wedge\exists P\text{ps}Z[P=Q|_{[\![\text{girl}]\!]}]]$

S $[\![\emptyset(\text{two})]\!]([\![\text{girl}]\!])([\![\text{eat five sandwiches}]\!])$

$\lambda Q.\exists Z[Z\subseteq[\![\text{girl}]\!]\wedge|Z|=2\wedge\exists P\text{ps}Z[P=Q|_{[\![\text{girl}]\!]}]]([\![\text{eat five sandwiches}]\!])$

$\exists Z[Z\subseteq[\![\text{girl}]\!]\wedge|Z|=2\wedge\exists P\text{ps}Z[P=[\![\text{eat five sandwiches}]\!]|_{[\![\text{girl}]\!]}]]$

$\exists Z[Z\subseteq[\![\text{girl}]\!]\wedge|Z|=2\wedge\exists P\text{ps}Z[P=\{V\cap[\![\text{girl}]\!]: [\![\text{eat five sandwiches}]\!](V)\}]]$

$\exists Z[Z\subseteq[\![\text{girl}]\!]\wedge|Z|=2\wedge\exists P\text{ps}Z[P=\{V\cap[\![\text{girl}]\!]: \exists W[W\subseteq[\![\text{sandwich}]\!]$
$\wedge|W|=5$
$\wedge\exists Q\text{ps}W[Q=\{U\cap[\![\text{sandwich}]\!]: [\![\text{eat}]\!](U)(V)\}]]\}]]$

This says that there is a set Z of two girls which can be subdivided into subcollections $V\cap[\![\text{girl}]\!]$, that is, the members of *P*, and for each of the collections V there is a set W of five sandwiches which is partitioned by *Q* into subcollections $U\cap[\![\text{sandwich}]\!]$ which are eaten by V. As above, the derivation makes use of the notational convention $\lambda X(R(V))|_X=\{V\cap X|R(V)\}$.

The *collective* extreme obtains in a model in which a set $\{\text{girl}_1,\text{girl}_2\}$ induces the partition $X=\{\{\text{girl}_1,\text{girl}_2\}\}$. In this case, $\{\text{girl}_1,\text{girl}_2\}$, say G_2, is assigned a set $\{s_1,s_2,s_3,s_4,s_5\}$, say S_5, of five sandwiches which in turn induces the partition $\{S_5\}$, so that G_2 stands in the eat-relation to S_5. The *distributive* extreme occurs in a model in which the set $\{\text{girl}_1,\text{girl}_2\}$ induces the partition $\{\{\text{girl}_1\},\{\text{girl}_2\}\}$. And to each of the sets $\{\text{girl}_1\}$ and $\{\text{girl}_2\}$ is assigned a set S^1_5 and a set S^2_5 respectively. They induce the partitions $\{\{s_1\},\{s_2\},\{s_3\},\{s_4\},\{s_5\}\}$ and $\{\{s'_1\},\{s'_2\},\{s'_3\},\{s'_4\},\{s'_5\}\}$ such that girl_1 eats s_i $(1\leq i\leq 5)$ and girl_2 eats s'_i $(1\leq i\leq 5)$.

The semantics of PLUG allows for all intermediate situations, like those in which girl_1 relates to $\{s_1,s_4,s_5\}$ and girl_2 to $\{s_2,s_3\}$. It even allows for a situation like the one depicted in Figure 17. One way to make sense of this is to interpret Figure 16 as the situation in which the girls had two sandwiches each and shared the fifth one. One may safely assume that all two-place predicates satisfy this regularity, except for those verbs which are to be marked as strictly distributive in one of their arguments. In general, this expresses the intuition that two-place verbs remain vague as to whether the individuals making up their arguments are involved strictly individually or in groups. Even the intransitive *die* might be argued to be vague in this respect, and one need

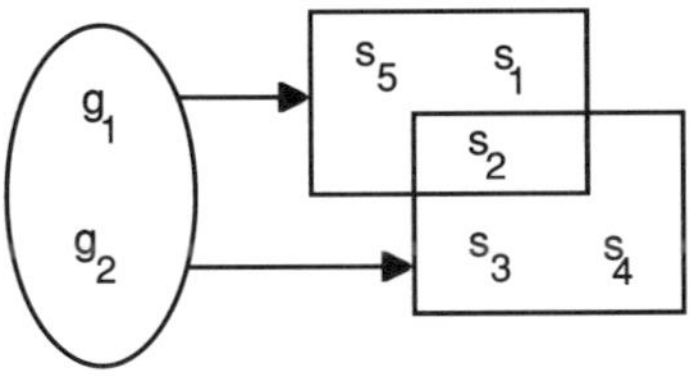

Figure 17 The semantics assigned to the sentences in Figure 16 allows the situation in which two girls share a sandwich

not to have travelled on the Orient Express to realize that a killing may be collective.

Our analysis of (283) *Four men lifted three tables* results in:

(308) $\exists Z[Z \subseteq [\![man]\!] \wedge |Z|=4 \wedge \exists P \text{ps} Z[P=\{V \cap [\![man]\!]:$
$\exists W[W \subseteq [\![table]\!] \wedge |W|=3$
$\wedge \exists Q \text{ps} W[Q=\{U \cap [\![table]\!]: [\![lift]\!](U)(V)\}]]\}]]$

This formula captures all the so-called readings of Scha and Link at once. We can even go one better than that, as exemplified in Figure 18, which makes (308) and hence sentence (283) true. It plainly shows that among the lifting collections there may be entities other than men and among the collections lifted entities other than tables. In other words, also if three politicians lifted three desks (and there are two tables among the desks) and if four professors lifted three pieces of furniture (among which one table) and two of the politicians and three of the professors are male (one being a politician and a professor), (283) will be a true sentence. Both (307) and (308) clearly fulfil a necessary condition for terminativity as their NPs are [+SQA], due to the presence of cardinality information on the sets W and Z. The sufficient condition will be contributed by the fact that the collections *P* and *Q* are finite (and non-empty) due to the partitioning of W and Z.

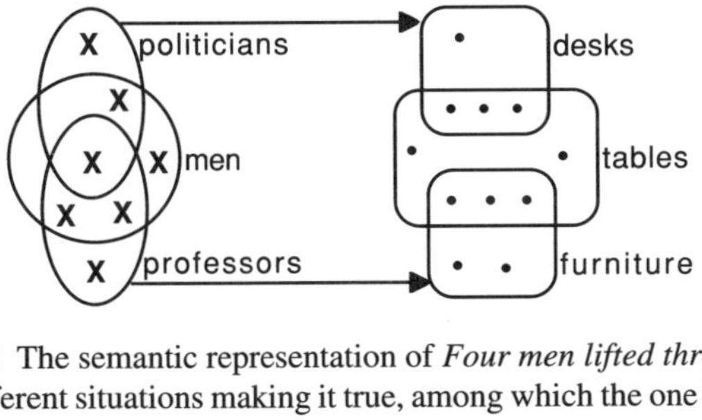

Figure 18 The semantic representation of *Four men lifted three tables* leaves room for many different situations making it true, among which the one in this figure

7.5 *All* and *every* again

The distinction between *all* and *every* is not made in the PLUG-rules 1–5. Without further lexical specifications, PLUG would not be able to give a satisfactory treatment of (309)–(312).

(309) All children dispersed
(310) ?*Every child dispersed
(311) All children came in
(312) Every child came in

There is a solution in which inherently distributive determiners can be uniformly distinguished from their default unmarked counterparts, which cover both collective and distributive interpretations. Instead of having a uniform lift from type $\langle\langle e,t\rangle,\langle\langle e,t\rangle,t\rangle\rangle$ to type $\langle\langle e,t\rangle,\langle\langle\langle e,t\rangle,t\rangle,t\rangle\rangle$, a distinction can be made between lifts for the distributive and for the default determiners. The latter, among which *all*, are assigned the node SPEC as defined in rule 5 of PLUG. For *all children* this means the derivation (313).

(313)

INC	$\lambda X\lambda Y[\lvert X\cap Y'\rvert=0]$
	$\lambda X\lambda Y.X\subseteq Y$
ø	$\lambda D\lambda X\lambda Q.\exists W[W\subseteq X\wedge D(X)(W)\wedge\exists P\mathrm{ps}W[P=Q\vert_X]]$
ø(INC)	$\lambda D\lambda X\lambda Q.\exists W[W\subseteq X\wedge D(X)(W)\wedge\exists P\mathrm{ps}W[P=Q\vert_X]]$
	$(\lambda X\lambda Y.X\subseteq Y)$
	$\lambda X\lambda Q.\exists W[W\subseteq X\wedge\lambda X\lambda Y.X\subseteq Y(X)(W)\wedge\exists P\mathrm{ps}W[P=Q\vert_X]]$
	$\lambda X\lambda Q.\exists W[W\subseteq X\wedge X\subseteq W\wedge\exists P\mathrm{ps}W[P=Q\vert_X]]$
	$\lambda X\lambda Q.\exists W[W=X\wedge\exists P\mathrm{ps}W[P=Q\vert_X]]$
	$\lambda X\lambda Q[\exists P\mathrm{ps}X[P=Q\vert_X]]$
child	$[\![\mathrm{child}]\!]$
ø(INC)(child)	$\lambda X\lambda Q[\exists P\mathrm{ps}X[P=Q\vert_X]]([\![\mathrm{child}]\!])$
	$\lambda Q\exists P\mathrm{ps}[\![\mathrm{child}]\!][P=Q\vert_{[\![\mathrm{child}]\!]}]$

This analysis of the NP *all children* appears to solve the problems discussed in chapter 6.2. The cardinality information $\lvert X\cap Y'\rvert=0$, expressed by INC, is equivalent to saying that $X\subseteq Y$. This leads to the information at the bottom line which says that the noun extension is partitioned. The definiteness of *all children* is now explained in terms of the presupposition about the unique identification of $[\![\mathrm{child}]\!]$. This explains the definiteness effect: *all* is the lexicalization ø(INC) which combines the $W\subseteq[\![N]\!]$ information with the $[\![N]\!]\subseteq W$-information, so that [+SQA] is secured on the basis of the finite cardinality of $[\![N]\!]$.

If a language has determiners with only a distributive interpretation, such as *every*, then they denote their usual relation (for *every* this is inclusion), but in a restricted way. In order to define this, one needs a function AT, which is of type $<<e,t>,<<e,t>,t>>$, defined in (314).

(314) $\text{AT} =_{df} \lambda X\lambda Y[Y\subseteq X\wedge|Y|=1]$

In this way, the set AT(X) of all atoms which can be formed out of X can be obtained. The AT-function (315) is used to lexically define, for English, a function $[\![_{SPEC}\emptyset_d]\!]$, or $[\![_{SPEC}\text{every}_d]\!]$ dependent on lexicalization, which is of type $<<<e,t>,<<e,t>,t>>,<<e,t>,<<<e,t>,t>,t>>>$.

(315) $[\![_{SPEC}\emptyset_d]\!] =_{df} \lambda D\lambda X\lambda Q\exists W[W\subseteq X\wedge D(X)(W)\wedge\exists P\text{ps}W[P=\text{AT}(X)\cap Q]]$

This would yield for *every child* the derivation in (316).

(316)

INC	$\lambda X\lambda Y[\|X\cap Y'\|=0]$
	$\lambda X\lambda Y.X\subseteq Y$
$\emptyset_d$	$\lambda D\lambda X\lambda Q.\exists W[W\subseteq X\wedge D(X)(W)\wedge\exists P\text{ps}W[P=\text{AT}(X)\cap Q]]$
$\emptyset_d$(INC)	$\lambda D\lambda X\lambda Q.\exists W[W\subseteq X\wedge D(X)(W)\wedge\exists P\text{ps}W[P=\text{AT}(X)\cap Q]]$
	$(\lambda X\lambda Y.X\subseteq Y)$
	$\lambda X\lambda Q.\exists W[W\subseteq X\wedge\lambda X\lambda Y.X\subseteq Y(X)(W)$
	$\wedge\exists P\text{ps}W[P=\text{AT}(X)\cap Q]]$
	$\lambda X\lambda Q.\exists W[W\subseteq X\wedge X\subseteq W\wedge\exists P\text{ps}W[P=\text{AT}(X)\cap Q]]$
	$\lambda X\lambda Q[\exists P\text{ps}X[P=\text{AT}(X)\cap Q]]$
child	$[\![\text{child}]\!]$
$\emptyset_d$(INC)(child)	$\lambda X\lambda Q[\exists P\text{ps}X[P=\text{AT}(X)\cap Q]]([\![\text{child}]\!])$
	$\lambda Q\ [\exists P\text{ps}[\![\text{child}]\!][P=\text{AT}([\![\text{child}]\!])\cap Q]]$
	$\lambda Q.\text{AT}([\![\text{child}]\!])\subseteq Q$

Here again the 'definiteness effect' of *every child*, discussed in (110), is due to the fact that the Noun extension $[\![\text{child}]\!]$ is presupposed to be given in the domain of interpretation.

Verkuyl and Van der Does (1991) propose to interpret all *distributive* NPs by use of the lexical format $[\![\text{SPEC}_d]\!]$, dependent on whether or not a language has this sort of constituents. This is a matter of the lexicon rather than of syntax itself. If a language contains, say, SPEC_c-elements, which express collectivity only, one has to provide for an appropriate lexical definition. *All* in English and *alle* in Dutch do not belong to SPEC_d: they range over collective and distributive interpretations and so they capture (316) as just one of their possible interpretations. English and Dutch do not appear to have simple SPEC_c-determiners, that is, no determiners where in all models the partition P necessarily contains just one member X where $|X|>1$. In contrast, both English and Dutch contain SPEC$_d$-determiners, just like some languages have a dualis, whereas other languages have more general forms.

Simplifying, it may be assumed that the intransitive verb phrase *disperse* satisfies the meaning postulate (317) and *come in* postulate (318):

(317) $X \in [\![\text{disperse}]\!]_{<<e,t>,t>} \quad \Rightarrow \quad |X|>2$

(318) $X \in [\![\text{come in}]\!]_{<<e,t>,t>} \quad \Rightarrow \quad$ X is an atom

Thus, the truth conditions of (309)–(312) are respectively:

(319)	$\exists P ps[\![\text{child}]\!][P=[\![\text{disperse}]\!]\|_{[\![\text{child}]\!]}]$	all children dispersed
(320)	$\text{AT}([\![\text{child}]\!]) \subseteq [\![\text{disperse}]\!]$	*every child dispersed
(321)	$\exists P ps[\![\text{child}]\!][P=[\![\text{came in}]\!]\|_{[\![\text{child}]\!]}]$	all children came in
(322)	$\text{AT}([\![\text{child}]\!]) \subseteq [\![\text{came in}]\!]$	every child came in

Plainly, (320) cannot obtain, for (317) stipulates $[\![\text{disperse}]\!]$ to be atomless. On the other hand, (319), (321) and (322) are satisfiable. In (321), the distributivity explicitly present in (322) is the 'extreme' case of a scale. The partition stated to exist is forced by (318) to be the unique finest possible in the case of (312). Consequently, we see that for all (lexically) distributive predicates D we have $[\![\textit{every}\ \text{N D}]\!] \subseteq [\![\textit{all}\ \text{N D}]\!]$. Note that the desirable result is accomplished without imposing ambiguity on the NPs involved.

The indefinite article in *a child* can be analysed as (323) and *one child* as (324):

(323) $[\![\text{SPEC}_d]\!]([\![\text{SG}]\!])([\![\text{child}]\!])$
$=\lambda Q.\exists W[W \subseteq [\![\text{child}]\!] \wedge |W|=1 \wedge \exists P psW[P=\text{AT}([\![\text{child}]\!]) \cap Q]]$

(324) $[\![\text{SPEC}\emptyset]\!]([\![\text{one}]\!])([\![\text{child}]\!])$
$=\lambda Q.\exists W[W \subseteq [\![\text{child}]\!] \wedge |W|=1 \wedge \exists P psW[P=Q|_{[\![\text{child}]\!]}]]$

In contrast to (324), (323) allows the presence of more than one child, be it that the other children present should be part of non-atomic collections. However, one could also reconsider the definition of SG by allowing ≥ 1 rather than $=1$. Then *one child* would correspond to the situation in which there is exactly one child, whereas *a child* would allow for more children.

7.6 Negation

For several reasons an aspectual theory should be interested in the interaction between quantification and negation. One of them is that the aspectual behaviour of sentences having terminative aspect changes under negation. Thus, there is a crucial difference between (325) and (326) on the one hand and (327)–(332) on the other:

(325) Two girls ate five sandwiches
(326) The three men lifted four pianos

(327) Two girls ate no sandwich
(328) The three men lifted no pianos

(329) No girl ate five sandwiches
(330) Nobody lifted four pianos

(331) Two girls did not eat five sandwiches
(332) The three men did not lift four pianos

The sentences (325) and (326) are terminative, whereas the other ones have a durative reading; they pertain to a state or an unbounded situation.

The second reason is the observation in Verkuyl (1987a, 1987b) that the intuitive distinction between collective and distributive interpretations is neutralized under negation. In terms of Figure 15: the two extremes of the scale no longer seem to matter under negation. Above, the collective and distributive extremes in (326) were characterized in terms of an opposition between $\{\{man_1, man_2, man_3\}\}$ and the set containing only singletons, $\{\{man_1\}, \{man_2\}, \{man_3\}\}$ for the subject NP. It makes no sense at all to do that for (328) nor for (330). The intuitive reason for this is: if no(ne of the) men in a model lifted pianos, why should one be interested in structuring the set of men? And, if two girls ate no sandwich, why should one be interested in the way they did not eat them?

In the literature on collective and distributive quantification virtually no attention has been given to its link with aspect and negation. The connection is that in (325) and (326) both the nature of aspectuality and the nature of quantification change, dependent on the sort of negation. Lønning (1989) argued that I wrongly opposed sentences like (326) to (330), rather than (332), to make its point on the blurring of the distinction between collectivity and distributivity. However, it is very hard to determine the meaning of a negative sentence like (332) without taking into account intonation, because the negation element may operate dependent on the place where contrastive stress is put. The blurring is visible if (329) and (330) are chosen not so much in terms of a contradictory or contrary opposition to (325) and (326) but rather in terms of their proper paraphrases: (329) and (330) form the clearest examples in which an

NP does not express a quantity and they do not like to be paraphrased with an appeal to the notion of distributivity or collectivity. An NP without reference to a specified quantity makes it impossible for (325) and (326) to express terminative aspect. Likewise, NPs like *no girl* or *nobody* do not pertain to a collectively or distributively taken empty set. Finally, if a sentence like (331) is read non-contrastively (if that is possible at all), we do not feel forced to assume that there is a set of distributive and collective readings. The presence of *not* immediately affects the function covering the scale between the two extremes in Figure 15. Thus, there will be no partition of the set of no girls such that for each of its members there is a set of five sandwiches etc. Likewise, (332) should not have, for example, a reading in which the three men each did not lift four different pianos on different occasions. If they did not lift or eat, how do we know how they did not do this? Or are we to speak about intentions in dealing with quantification?

The present PLUG-approach allows for *two girls* in (325) and (331) to be partitioned. As observed, (331) and (332) may be used contrastively, particularly if they are continued as in (333). The continuations in (333) make (331) and (332) terminative.

(333) a. … but they ate FOUR sandwiches
b. … but they lifted four HARPSICHORDS

Sentences like (327)–(333) form a litmus-test for the present analysis (see also Lønning 1989). Therefore we shall give their derivations in some detail. We shall start out with (329) *No girl ate five sandwiches*.

(334)

VP $[\![\text{eat five sandwiches}]\!]$

DET[1] $\text{NO}=_{df} \lambda U\lambda V.|U\cap V|=0$

DET[2] $[\![\text{no}]\!]=[\![\emptyset]\!](\text{NO})$

$\lambda D\lambda X\lambda P.\exists W[W\subseteq X\wedge D(X)(W)\wedge\exists Q\text{ps}W[Q=P|_X]](\lambda U\lambda V.|U\cap V|=0)$

$\lambda X\lambda P.\exists W[W\subseteq X\wedge|X\cap W|=0\wedge\exists Q\text{ps}W[Q=P|_X]]$

$\lambda X\lambda P.\exists W[W\subseteq X\wedge|W|=0\wedge\exists Q\text{ps}W[Q=P|_X]]$

$\lambda X\lambda P.\{\varnothing\}=P|_X$

NP $[\![\text{no}]\!]([\![\text{girl}]\!])$

$\lambda X\lambda P.\{\varnothing\}=P|_X([\![\text{girl}]\!])$

$\lambda P.\{\varnothing\}=P|_{[\![\text{girl}]\!]}$

S $[\![\text{no}]\!]([\![\text{girl}]\!])([\![\text{eat five sandwiches}]\!])$

$\{\varnothing\}=[\![\text{eat five sandwiches}]\!]|_{[\![\text{girl}]\!]}$

$\{\varnothing\}=\{V\cap[\![\text{girl}]\!]|\exists W[W\subseteq\text{sandwich}]\!]\wedge|W|=5$

$\wedge\exists Q\text{ps}W[Q=\{U\cap[\![\text{sandwich}]\!]: [\![\text{eat}]\!](U)(V)\}]]\}$

That is: looking for girls in the sets which eat five sandwiches you find none. As to (327) *Two girls ate no sandwich*, one obtains (335).

(335)

VP $\llbracket\text{eat no sandwich}\rrbracket$

$\lambda X.\{U\cap\llbracket\text{sandwich}\rrbracket: \llbracket\text{eat}\rrbracket(U)(X)\}=\{\varnothing\}$

NP $\llbracket\text{ø}\rrbracket(\llbracket\text{two}\rrbracket)(\llbracket\text{girl}\rrbracket)$

$\lambda S.\exists Z[Z\subseteq\llbracket\text{girl}\rrbracket\wedge|Z|=2\wedge\exists Q\text{ps}Z[Q=S|_{\llbracket\text{girl}\rrbracket}]]$

S $\llbracket\text{NP}\rrbracket(\llbracket\text{VP}\rrbracket)$

$\lambda S.\exists Z[Z\subseteq\llbracket\text{girl}\rrbracket\wedge|Z|=2\wedge\exists Q\text{ps}Z[Q=S|_{\llbracket\text{girl}\rrbracket}]](\llbracket\text{eat no sandwich}\rrbracket)$

$\exists Z[Z\subseteq\llbracket\text{girl}\rrbracket\wedge|Z|=2\wedge\exists Q\text{ps}Z[Q=\llbracket\text{eat no sandwich}\rrbracket|_{\llbracket\text{girl}\rrbracket}]]$

$\exists Z[Z\subseteq\llbracket\text{girl}\rrbracket\wedge|Z|=2\wedge\exists Q\text{ps}Z[Q=\{V\cap\llbracket\text{girl}\rrbracket: \llbracket\text{eat no sandwich}\rrbracket(V)\}]]$

$\exists Z[Z\subseteq\llbracket\text{girl}\rrbracket\wedge|Z|=2$
$\wedge\exists Q\text{ps}Z[Q=\{V\cap\llbracket\text{girl}\rrbracket|\{U\cap\llbracket\text{sandwich}\rrbracket|\llbracket\text{eat}\rrbracket(U)(V)\}=\{\varnothing\}\}]]$

This says that there is a set of two girls such that if you look at the collection of things eaten by them, either collectively or individually or both, you will find no sandwiches.

The relevant part of the derivation of (330) *Nobody lifted four pianos* is:

VP $\llbracket\text{lift four pianos}\rrbracket$

NP $\llbracket\text{nobody}\rrbracket=\lambda Q.\{\varnothing\}=Q|_{\llbracket\text{human}\rrbracket}$

S $\llbracket\text{nobody}\rrbracket(\llbracket\text{lift four pianos}\rrbracket)$

$\{\varnothing\}=\llbracket\text{lift four pianos}\rrbracket|_{\llbracket\text{human}\rrbracket}$

$\{\varnothing\}=\{V\cap\llbracket\text{human}\rrbracket|\exists W[W\subseteq\llbracket\text{piano}\rrbracket\wedge|W|=4$
$\wedge\exists Q\text{ps}W[Q=\{U\cap\llbracket\text{piano}\rrbracket: \llbracket\text{lift}\rrbracket(U)(V)\}]]\}$

The bottom line of the derivation of the non-contrastive (331) *Two girls did not eat five sandwiches* is:

(336) $\exists Z[Z\subseteq\llbracket\text{girl}\rrbracket\wedge|Z|=2\wedge\exists P\text{ps}Z[P=\{V\cap\llbracket\text{girl}\rrbracket: \neg\exists W[W\subseteq\llbracket\text{sandwich}\rrbracket$
$\wedge|W|=5\wedge\exists Q\text{ps}W[Q=\{U\cap\llbracket\text{sandwiches}\rrbracket: \llbracket\text{eat}\rrbracket(U)(V)\}]]\}]]$

Here the negation-sign shows up in front of the object-NP. Note that it is in the scope of the subject-NP.

As far as the contrastive continuations in (333) are concerned, they make (325) terminative, as pointed out in Verkuyl (1987b), which used the model-theoretic negation theory of Jacobs (1982) to account for contrastive negation. Though I do not want to go into all the details of contrastive negation, it might be helpful to give more than a glimpse of how (331) has to be interpreted if it is continued by (333a). Following Jacobs (1982), one would have to add a 'correctness predicate' CORR (of type $<t,t>$), which is (roughly) defined as:

DEFINITION:
CORRα is true iff α is true and α has a sufficient adequacy value *ad*

where *ad* is determined by an adequacy value assignment made dependent on standards in the domain of discourse. We would now obtain:

(337) $\exists Z[Z \subseteq [\![girl]\!] \wedge |Z|=2 \wedge \exists P ps Z[P=\{V \cap [\![girl]\!] \mid \neg \text{CORR} \exists W[W \subseteq [\![sandwich]\!] \wedge |W|=5 \wedge \exists Q ps W[Q=\{U \cap [\![sandwich]\!] \mid [\![eat]\!](U)(V)\}] \wedge \text{CORR}\ \exists W'[W' \subseteq [\![sandwich]\!] \wedge |W'|=4 \wedge \exists R ps W'[R=\{U' \cap [\![sandwich]\!]: [\![eat]\!](U')(V)\}]]]]\}]]$

which says that there is a partition *P* of ⟦two girls⟧ such that for each of its cells V it is not correct to say that there is a set W of five sandwiches such that they were eaten by V but that it is correct to say that there is a set W′ of four sandwiches of which it is correct to say that they were eaten by V.

In all cases considered in the present section, it is intuitively clear why (regular) negation and terminative aspect cannot go together: there is no domain for a possible mapping between atemporal and temporal structure. That is, in (221) and (222) the cardinality of the negative NPs is zero. In the non-contrastive interpretation of (331), the cardinality information in *five sandwiches* is affected by the negation. As far as contrastive negation is concerned, it turns out to be the case that the negation element operates on CORR bringing us indirectly to [+SQA]-interpretations. That is, if we had to interpret (313a) 'on its own' contrastively, we would interpret it in terms of the correction predicate without giving the correction itself.

(338) $\exists Z[Z \subseteq [\![girl]\!] \wedge |Z|=2 \wedge \exists P ps Z[P=\{V \cap [\![girl]\!]: \neg \text{CORR} \exists W[W \subseteq [\![sandwich]\!] \wedge |W|=5 \wedge \exists Q ps W[Q=\{U \cap [\![sandwich]\!]: [\![eat]\!](U)(V)\}]]\}]]$

This makes (331) somewhat odd, just like (339) which is made 'normal' in (340); see also (142) and (144) and the other sentences discussed there.

(339) Not Judith ate three sandwiches

(340) Not Judith ate three sandwiches, but Mary

Aspectually, it appears to be adequate to treat the terminative (340) exactly like (331) plus (333a), that is, in terms of a correction predicate. As far as sentences like (341) are concerned,

(341) #For hours not all children came in (some did)

it may be observed that *Not all children came in* is terminative. This can also be explained in terms of contrastivity:

(342) $\neg$CORR[$\exists P$ps⟦child⟧[P=⟦came_in⟧$|_{⟦child⟧}$]]$\wedge$CORR$\exists$W[W$\subseteq$⟦child⟧ $\wedge$|W|>1$\wedge\exists Q$psW[Q=⟦came_in⟧$|_{⟦child⟧}$]]

We have to assume that the [+SQA]-specification is here due to the correctness-predicate which represents the quantificational information expressed by *not all children.*

It is important to see that the treatment of NPs at the level of <<<*e*,*t*>,*t*>,*t*> makes it more natural to deal with negation. On the standard <<*e*,*t*>,*t*>-approach we are interested in whether the intersection A$\cap$B contains elements or not and [–SQA] could be defined in terms of the absence of elements. Now, negation can be expressed in terms of emptiness of the partitioned collection. Given the fact that in chapter 13 the partition is taken as the domain or the co-domain of a function, it simply follows that the function in question cannot operate, because its domain or co-domain is empty. In this sense, the [+ADD TO]-information expressed by the verbs in (325)–(332) is neutralized.

7.7 Conclusion

In this chapter, a grammar called PLUG has been introduced. It was proposed in Verkuyl and Van der Does (1991) in order to account for sentences with multiple quantification. The shift from the grammar based on (170) and (177)–(181) to PLUG has yielded some advantages:

The NUM-information in (170) is now made head of the determiner, which is considered a determiner phrase DET^2, having internal structure directed by principles of X-bar syntax. This has led to the solution of a problem raised by Van Benthem against <<<*e*,*t*>,*t*>,*t*>-approaches.

PLUG treats NPs as displaying internal (collection) structure in their interaction with the main predicate whose arguments they are: multiple quantification made it necessary to replace λQ...[...Q(W)] by λQ...[...$\exists P$psW[P=Q]]. This modification also prepares the ground for a formal treatment of the interaction between the verb and its arguments, and for the extension of PLUG.

Thirdly, PLUG is able to deal with the negation facts presented in this study. It explains why it is that terminative negative sentences like (327) and (329) are durative, whereas their positive counterparts are terminative. It also explains why in contrastive negation, terminativity is maintained.

8 *Some explorative issues*

8.0 Introduction

In this chapter, some issues will be discussed that may be considered natural extensions of the line followed above. In chapter 1, the syntactic considerations underlying the compositional aspectual machinery were married to generative syntax (in a rather broad sense). Now, given the fact that PLUG partly originates from work in the generative X-bar theory, it might be useful after the drastic change of the determiner structure in PLUG, to relate the treatment of noun phrases to those in more recent versions of X-bar theory. In particular, to the very popular DP-analysis as proposed in Abney (1987). This will be done in section 8.1.

Furthermore, it seems necessary to pick up the line of chapter 6.3 by paying attention to the question of how the notion of bare-ness should be treated, given PLUG. This will be done in section 8.2, which is followed by a section of mass terms. This section is in fact not explorative: it roughly indicates how on the basis of the relevant literature the [+SQA]-notion can be used in the realm of mass nouns. In section 8.4, I will test the present theory by discussing the question of how a dumb computer may recognize a [+SQA]-NP.

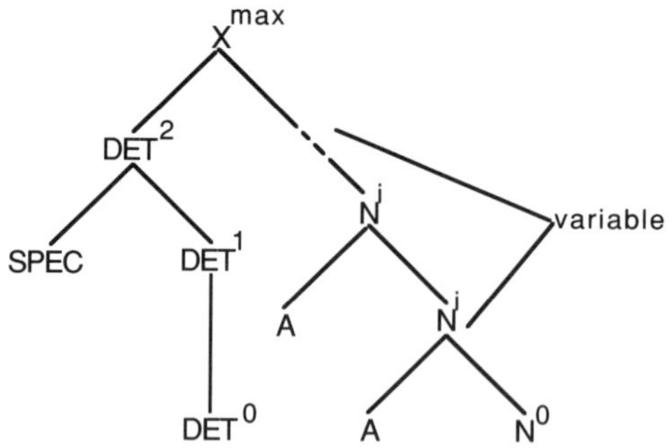

Figure 19 The NP-structure of Figure 12 can be relabelled so as to make specific requirements of X-bar syntax more visible

8.1 X-bar theory and PLUG

After the relabelling of some nodes in (276), the general scheme for NP-structure will be Figure 19, i.e. (343), which is the PLUG-successor to (170).

(343) $[_{N^{max}} [_{DET^1}$ SPEC $DET^0] [_{N^i} [A^* N^0]]]$

The difference between (343) and (170) is that on the projection line between N^0 and N^{max}, there is no type shift, assuming that A is of type <<*e*,*t*>,<*e*,*t*>>. This means that DET^2 takes an expression of <*e*,*t*> and yields an <<<*e*,*t*>,*t*>,*t*>. Also new is that the cardinality information expressed by NUM is now located in DET^1, as explained above. Recall that the lowest element occurring in the determiner structure in (343) is strictly speaking DET^0. This makes it possible to use the label SPEC in the same way as in standard X-bar syntax. As said earlier, DET^0 will often be left out if no branching is involved. Figure 20a is the simplified (343). N is the head of the NP, DET^2 is the (complex) Specifier making an NP out of a Noun projection, say N′. A further look at the syntax involved might establish how it relates to the D(eterminer) P(hrase)-analysis along the lines of Abney (1987). In the DP-analysis (Fig. 20b), the DET is the head of the DP, where the N (or more precisely, N^{max}) is taken as the complement of DET. Like Verkuyl (1981), Abney (1987) interprets X-bar nodes in terms of type-logical semantic objects; however, in his DP-analysis NPs are taken as in Barwise and Cooper (1981), that is, as denoting semantic objects of type <<*e*,*t*>,*t*>. Thus, DET is of type <<*e*,*t*>,<<*e*,*t*>,*t*>>, DET^1 is of type <<*e*,*t*>,*t*> and DP is also of type <<*e*,*t*>,*t*>, SPEC being a node just necessary for Poss-*ing* gerundive noun phrases like *John's building a spaceship* and absent in 'regular' NPs (so in the latter case DET^1 is the top node). The type-logical difference makes it hard to compare the two approaches. There are two ways to go for DP if it would go one level up. The first

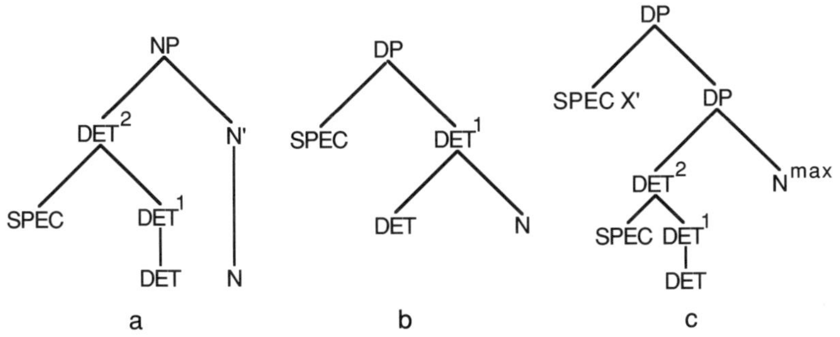

Figure 20 It appears to be possible to interpret the PLUG-grammar as a DP-analysis of noun-phrase structure along the lines of Abney (1987), but it might also be argued that PLUG allows both an NP-analysis and a DP-analysis

one is to retain Figure 20b and to redefine DET as *<<e,t>, <<<e,t>,t>,t>>*, so that DET^1 becomes of type *<<<e,t>,t>,t>*. This would amount to analysing DET as DET^2 in Figure 20a and giving SPEC in Figure 20b a different interpretation from that in PLUG. The second way would be to follow PLUG on the issue of determiner structure and to end up with something like Figure 20c. At first sight, this would not qualify as a DP-structure in its present sense, because the N (or N^{max}) would be the complement of DET^2. Note, however, that if DET in Figure 20b were seen as DET^2 in Figure 20a, there should be no problem in accepting Figure 20c. SPEC X′ would be the node Abney needs for his gerundive analysis. It would be a modifier of type <a,a>. If such a node were added to Figure 20a, one could even argue that PLUG allowed both for the DP-analysis and the NP-analysis, a possible choice being dependent on the agreement system of a particular language.

In the remainder of this study, Figure 20a will be adopted as the most simple structure for Dutch and English. Note that *the* in Figure 20a may be seen as a lexicalization of SPEC. This would mean that *the* in *the child* is to be analysed as

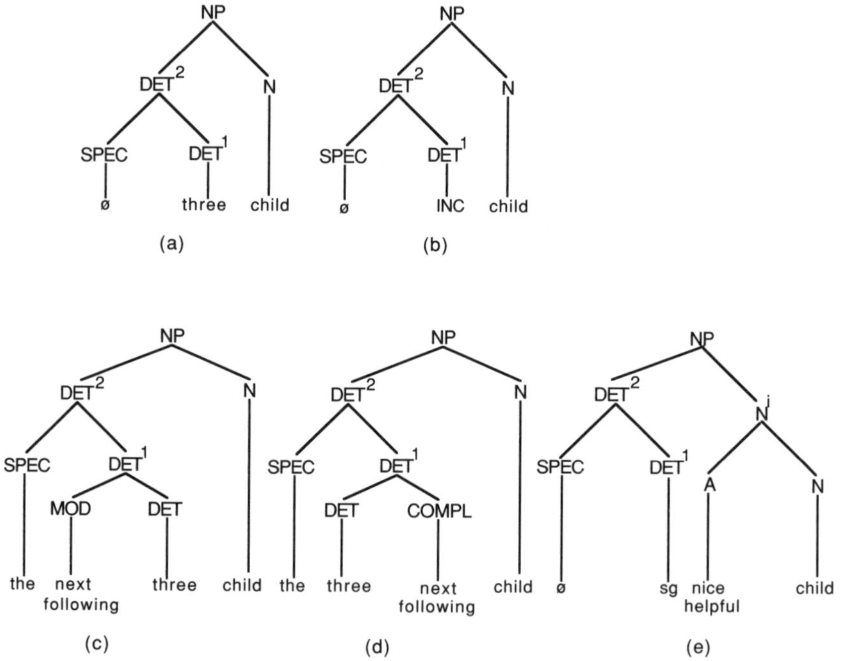

Figure 21 These examples illustrate the different ways in which PLUG handles 'adjectival' (modifying) information in relation to the quantificational information expressed by DET

[the(SG)]. SG and PL are thus taken as abstract markers. I will come back to this point shortly. It is perhaps useful to give some more illustrations of structures that are generated by the X-bar version of PLUG. In Figure 21, the structure is given of the NPs in (344)–(348).

(344) three children
(345) all children
(346) the next/following three children
(347) the three next/following children
(348) a nice/helpful child

Due to X-bar rules of the form (169) it is possible to analyse *following* and *next* in (346) as a modifier of the DET^0 *three* rather than as an adjective on the head Noun. The same applies to *following* and *next* in (347), where they are taken as complements of the DET^0 numeral *three*. Succinctly: there are beautiful and helpful children; there are no next children and following children. The differences between (346) and (347) are accounted for in Figure 21. For (346), the choice between Figure 21c and a structure like Figure 21e in which A takes N to yield N^i might depend on ontological convictions and on sortal correctness. If people allow for the intersection of ⟦following⟧ and ⟦child⟧ as some do, we have to assume (reluctantly) that in their lexicon *following* is labelled as an adjective taking nouns. In my own lexicon, *following* in (346) and (347) is located in the determiner structure. Differences of opinion do not bear on PLUG, as its syntax is not interested in lexical options. Note, however, that there is an argument in favour of Figure 21c for (346): *the following three children* does not have an 'at least three' meaning. This implies that *following* (or *next*) modifies *three* at the same place at which *exactly* or *at least* modifies *three* in *exactly three children* or *at least three children.*

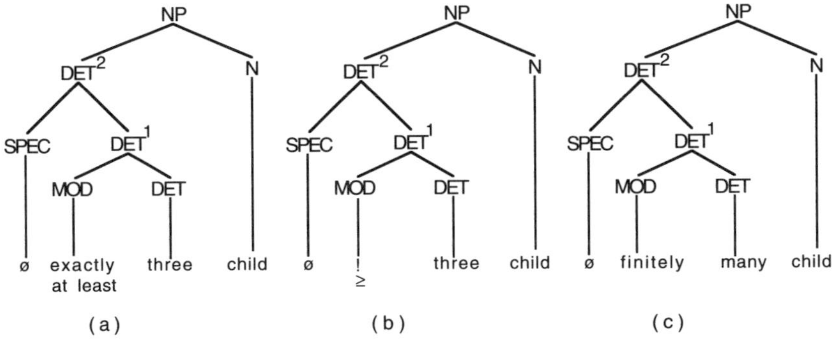

Figure 22 'Mathematical modifiers' like *exactly*, *at least*, *finitely*, etc. can be taken as modifiers on the DET-projection line

Let us have a closer look at the difference between *exactly three children* and *three children*. Their syntactic structure is given in Figure 22a and Figure 22b, respectively. The idea is that if *exactly* is lexically realized, it occurs in a position given in Figure 22a. The same applies to *at least*. In both cases *exactly* and *at least* are taken as modifying DET. The same applies to *finitely* in Figure 22c: it modifies *many*. In these cases, we profit from the X-bar nature of our grammar: DET being the head of DET^1 can be modified adjectivally, whereas SPEC takes a MOD(DET) yielding DET^2. It should be observed, however, that MOD in Figure 22 is not as prolific as A in structures like (170): cardinality does not call for many modifying restrictions, but one might think of *The perhaps finitely many children …*, *presumably infinitely many stars*, or *my by a miracle exactly three children*, which have unusual but interpretable meanings.

Implicit or context-dependent interpretations of *three* in *three children* may be represented as in Figure 22b as an alternative to Figure 21a. Let ! and ≥ stand for the implicit information 'exactly' and 'at least'. The question is now whether or not one may assume 'empty' modifying structure as in Figure 22b or just Figure 21a. There are reasons for not rejecting Figure 22b out of hand. In many contexts, the interpretation of *three children* is determined by information not expressed verbally but by other means (visually, deictically, by making inferences, by previous information, etc.). Figure 22b represents the view that this sort of information is implicitly present in *three children* modifying the head of the determiner structure [$_{DET^0}$ three]. Syntactically there is no surface element carrying the information, but there is an empty node; semantically, of course, one would have to provide for a contextual 'slot' for this node. However, the alternative route is also defensible: contextual information about the degree of preciseness could be located in the SPEC-node. In that case, Figure 21a would be sufficient and the difference between (implicitly exactly) *three* and (implicitly at least) *three* would have to be regulated by a contextual slot in the SPEC-node. Another option on this route would be simply to assume that by default a structure like Figure 21a is always interpreted in terms of a set W whose cardinality is =, allowing for the more sloppy interpretation ≥, if the context makes it clear that the =-meaning does not work. A choice between the three options is not really important for the present study, so I leave this matter unresolved.

It is tempting to explore some more possibilities of the categorial X-bar system, because it is important to know how the [+SQA]-NP (349)

(349) two of the three children

is to be analysed. I shall not yield to the temptation as it would lead too far astray (see however, Keenan and Stavi 1986 and De Jong 1991). In general, the

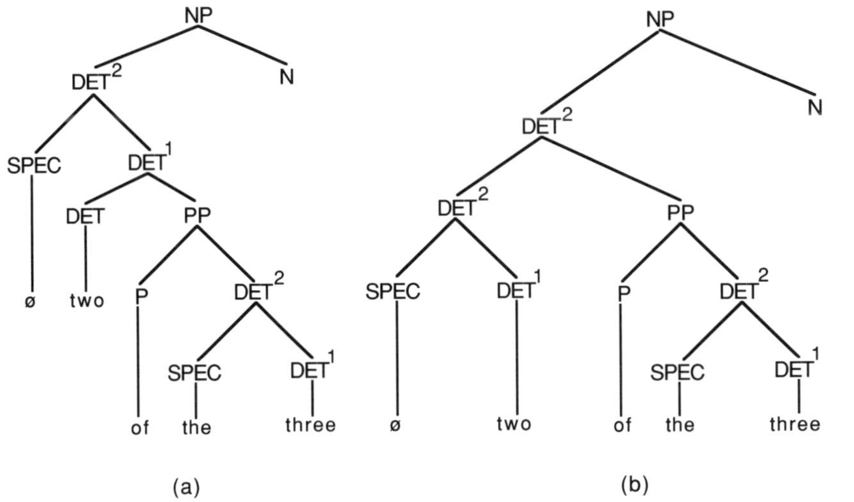

Figure 23 The determiner structure of partitive constructions may be quite complex, but from the point of view of X-bar syntax it is well organized

X-bar system makes it attractive to assign it one of the structures in Figure 23. It is attractive in view of the fact that attributive PPs can be analysed either as $[_{NP}$Spec $[_{N'}$N [P NP_2]] or as $[_{NP}NP_1$ [P NP_2]. In Figure 23, this patterning is visible, but now on the basis of the more general schemes $[_{XP}$Spec $[_{X'}$X [P XP_2]] or $[_{XP}XP_1$ [P XP_2]]. This suggests that the principles of X-bar syntax penetrate into the determiner structure. In my view, Figure 23a is to be preferred to Figure 23b. I have no clear arguments for a choice, but for the fact that the information gathered under DET^1 is essentially cardinality information: it gives the cardinality of a subset of an identified set of triples. This fits well as an argument for the SPEC-function as defined in PLUG.

Finally, I come back to the question of how lexicalization proceeds in the present grammar. The answer given by Barwise and Cooper (1981) would have been: at the level of DET^2. This would imply that the X-bar grammar used here would be partially lexical, as SPEC and DET^1 would have to be taken as abstract non-lexicalized elements. From the categorial point of view there would be no problem at all: why not use the compositionality principle 'below the surface' of a lexical item? However, from the GB point of view there might be syntactic arguments against considering DET^2 as the point at which lexical information is inserted into syntax. The matter can be settled by comparing languages having overt markers for cardinality information and for the definiteness/indefiniteness opposition. The strategy followed here is: lexicalize as early as you can (seen from bottom to top). In this way, *the* in English is a lexicalized SPEC, allowing for SG and PL, whereas *een* (a) in Dutch may be the result of combining ø with SG. As the issue does not bear on the analysis of aspectual properties of sentences, I will leave the matter here.

8.2 Bareness again

It is necessary to return to the notion of bareness, explored in some detail in chapter 6.3, because we face the problem of being confronted with structures like ø(BARE(PL))(child) containing three abstract elements two of which are not grammaticalized at all in languages like English and Dutch. Can we reduce this syntactic abundancy? There is a second consideration which makes it necessary to reject representations like (266) and (267)

(266) BARE(SG) $\lambda Q\lambda X[X=\bigcup Q \wedge |Q|=1]$
(267) BARE(PL) $\lambda Q\lambda X[X=\bigcup Q \wedge |Q|>1]$

The problem connected with the transition from (170) to (267) is that BARE(SG) or BARE(PL) – being of type $\langle\langle\langle e,t\rangle,t\rangle,\langle\langle e,t\rangle,t\rangle\rangle$ – are not fed by a semantic object of type $\langle\langle e,t\rangle,t\rangle$: there is no argument of the appropriate type, because in PLUG the head noun of the NP is of type $\langle e,t\rangle$.

It is possible, however, to reformulate the BARE-operator within the PLUG-framework capturing the essence of the bareness analysis in chapter 6.3. It leads to NP representations like the following:

(350) saucers
(351) $\lambda Q.\exists W\exists S[W\subseteq\bigcup S\subseteq[\![\text{saucer}]\!]\wedge|S|>1\wedge\exists P\text{ps}W[P=Q|_{[\![\text{saucer}]\!]}]]$

(352) three saucers
(353) $\lambda Q.\exists W\exists S[W\subseteq\bigcup S\subseteq[\![\text{saucer}]\!]\wedge|S|=3\wedge\exists P\text{ps}W[P=Q|_{[\![\text{saucer}]\!]}]]$

(354) the saucers
(355) $\lambda Q.\exists W\exists!S[W\subseteq\bigcup S=[\![\text{saucer}]\!]\wedge|S|>1\wedge\exists P\text{ps}W[P=Q|_{[\![\text{saucer}]\!]}]]$

(356) the saucer
(357) $\lambda Q.\exists W\exists!S[W\subseteq\bigcup S=[\![\text{saucer}]\!]\wedge|S|=1\wedge\exists P\text{ps}W[P=Q|_{[\![\text{saucer}]\!]}]]$

Note that in all four representations a set W is existentially introduced. This seems to be correct in view of the intuition that sentences like (358)–(361) in their 'bare'-reading pertain to some set which is not identified itself.

(358) Mary sold saucers
(359) Mary sold three saucers

(360) Mary sold the saucers
(361) Mary sold the saucer

This is natural for (358) and (359), but it can also be defended for (360) and (361): W is introduced as part of the identified *S*. This is not necessary, because one might represent (356) as (362) rather than as (357).

(362) $\lambda Q.\exists!S[\bigcup S=[\![\text{saucer}]\!]\wedge|S|=1\wedge\exists P\text{ps}\bigcup S[P=Q|_{[\![\text{saucer}]\!]}]]$

More in line with Westerståhl (1984) would be (363) instead of (357).

(363) $\lambda Q[|[\![\text{saucer}]\!]\cap C\,|=1\wedge\exists P\text{ps}\bigcup[\![\text{saucer}]\!]\cap C)[P=Q|_{\bigcup[\![\text{saucer}]\!]}]]$

However, this would commit us to introducing the Noun *saucer* at the <<*e*,*t*>,*t*>-level: both [[saucer]] and *C* are of type <<*e*,*t*>,*t*>. As said, in the PLUG-grammar, N retains its <*e*,*t*> status. A possible advantage of (357) over (362) and (363) would be that a sentence like (361) will never mean that Mary sold all the tokens of the saucer-type. It is said that she sold an indefinite number of tokens from a uniquely identified type. This holds for the other representations in (350)–(357) as well: the subset relation $\subseteq$ appears to express correctly that Mary did not necessarily sell all the tokens of the types. Another advantage of the representations in (350)–(357), but one that cannot yet be seen at this stage of the exposition, is that they structurally resemble the representation of habituality (see at the close of chapter 13).

Returning to the first problem, one might hold that the analysis in terms of (170) plus (177)–(181), namely ø(BARE(SG)(child)), was already an improvement on existing theories of bareness. The revision of this structure in PLUG to (ø(BARE(SG))(child) inherits this improvement, but it would not solve the problem of having three empty elements: ø, BARE and SG. This problem might be a pseudo-problem in view of languages where they are overt. But we might try to reduce the number of empty categories by holding that BARE is analysable as making up a system of grammar (partially) shown in (364).

(364)

SG_{bare}	$\lambda Y\lambda X\exists S[X\cap Y=\bigcup S\wedge|S|=1]$
PL_{bare}	$\lambda Y\lambda X\exists S[X\cap Y=\bigcup S\wedge|S|>1]$
n_{bare}	$\lambda Y\lambda X\exists S[X\cap Y=\bigcup S\wedge|S|=3]$
$\ldots_{\text{bare}}$	$\lambda Y\lambda X\exists S[X\cap Y=\bigcup S\wedge|S|=\ldots]$

For (350) *saucers* this would mean the derivation in (365).

(365)

PL_{bare}	$\lambda Y\lambda X\exists S[X\cap Y=\bigcup S\wedge|S|>1]$
ø	$\lambda D\lambda X\lambda Q.\exists W[W\subseteq X\wedge D(X)(W)\wedge\exists P\text{ps}W[P=Q|_X]]$

$\emptyset(\text{PL}_{bare})$	$\lambda D\lambda X\lambda Q.\exists W[W\subseteq X\wedge D(X)(W)\wedge\exists P ps W[P=Q|_X]]$
	$(\lambda Y\lambda X\exists S[X\cap Y=\bigcup S\wedge|S|>1])$
	$\lambda X\lambda Q.\exists W[W\subseteq X\wedge\lambda Y\lambda X\exists S[X\cap Y=\bigcup S\wedge|S|>1](X)(W)$
	$\wedge\exists P ps W[P=Q|_X]]$
	$\lambda X\lambda Q.\exists W[W\subseteq X\wedge\exists S[X\cap W=\bigcup S\wedge|S|>1]\wedge\exists P ps W[P=Q|_X]]$
	$\lambda X\lambda Q.\exists W\exists S[W\subseteq X\wedge X\cap W=\bigcup S\wedge|S|>1\wedge\exists P ps W[P=Q|_X]]$
	$\lambda X\lambda Q.\exists W\exists S[W\subseteq\bigcup S\subseteq X\wedge|S|>1\wedge\exists P ps W[P=Q|_X]]$
saucer	$[\![\text{saucer}]\!]$
$\emptyset(\text{PL}_{bare})(\text{saucer})$	$\lambda X\lambda Q.\exists W\exists S[W\subseteq\bigcup S\subseteq X\wedge|S|>1$
	$\wedge\exists P ps W[P=Q|_X]]([\![\text{saucer}]\!])$
	$\lambda Q.\exists W\exists S[W\subseteq\bigcup S\subseteq[\![\text{saucer}]\!]\wedge|S|>1$
	$\wedge\exists P ps W[P=Q|_{[\![\text{saucer}]\!]}]]$

In other words, (364) would represent one part of a two-level system: all members α of DET^0 can occur as α or as α_{bare}. In other words, NPs are taken as systematically conveying two sorts of cardinality information at DET^0, one at the <*e*,*t*>-level leading to [+SQA]-information, one at the <<*e*,*t*>,*t*>-level leading to [–SQA]-information. Note that the SPEC need not be adapted on this view. In the derivation, the 'higher level' with respect to which cardinality is expressed is introduced via the DET-node. The SPEC-node just takes this information. The advantage of such a duplicate system is considerable, the price for it is that people can misunderstand each other, which they often seem to do.

The analysis of BARE-ness in (364) seems to carry over to all elements which are defined as DET in the PLUG-grammar. It might be held against (364) that for it to be a real system all determiners need to be doubled, among which PL. However, it is an empirical fact in the languages under investigation that a bare plural NP can never be [+SQA]. So, PL cannot express cardinality information at the level of W. Of course, one might wish to interpret *Judith ate sandwiches* with *sandwiches* pertaining to a finite number of sandwiches (which is normally the case), but this is not what the sentence expresses. It expresses the lack of cardinality information at the <*e*,*t*>-level. So, in this respect, the bare plural would remain the exceptional category in a two-level system under the present BARE-analysis. As it is under any analysis.

The notion of specificity may be tied up to the SPEC-node of the determiner phrase. It seems reasonable to allow a modification of the indefiniteness information expressed by ø in (323). That is, due to the context one may modify ø such that one speaks about a specific entity not yet introduced into the domain of discourse. This carries over to the 'BARE-level'. At the 'token'-level, *A medal went to all winners* may be analysed terminatively as: a specific medal went to all winners (all together or consecutively). It may also be analysed BARE-ly as: an unbounded number of token medals went to all winners. However, in the latter case one may have a specific medal category in mind, say the gold.[52]

Summarizing, the approach to bareness in the present study contributes to a better understanding both of why it is that certain apparently clear cases of [+SQA]-NPs have a [–SQA]-interpretation, and of how quantification over individuals and reference to categories relate to each other. The definitions in (364) do not give cardinality information at the level of $\mathcal{U}_S$. This is how it can be explained that NPs in (350)–(357) in their bare interpretation are [–SQA], whereas there is a systematic way to interpret the NPs as [+SQA].

8.3 Mass terms

As observed in the introduction to Part II, an aspectual theory should be able to deal with the aspectual difference between sentences like (9) and (10):

(9) Judith ate a slice of bread
(10) Judith ate bread

In Verkuyl (1972), also sentences were discussed like:

(366) They ate cheese
(367) They ate from the cheese

(368) They drank whisky
(369) They drank a litre of whisky

(370) De Machula played music
(371) De Machula played a piece of music

However, in later work on aspectual theory I have never tried to deal with mass terms formally. Neither will I do this here beyond the minimum that is required to extend the coverage of the [+SQA]-notion to mass terms. This is possible due to interesting work on the relation between mass and plurality done in the past years: Bunt (1981), Hoepelman and Rohrer (1980), Link (1983, 1984), Krifka (1989a, 1989b), Lønning (1987a), Ojeda (1990), Pelletier and Schubert (1989), Schubert and Pelletier (1989), among others. This enables me to make just an ontological choice and to restrict myself to showing that the machinery developed so far can be used for the analysis of sentences like (9), (10) and (366)–(371), without forced adaptations.

The most natural choice for the present framework is to look for points of contact in Bunt's work, because this is in its turn closely associated with the framework of Scha (1981) to which the present formal machinery is congenial in many respects. This means that I will not make use of the formal machinery developed by, for example, Krifka, because his ontological assumptions have led him into a first-order approach: he makes use of join semi-lattices in which {David, Jessica} in (287) *Three children crossed the street* would be treated as an individual of type *e* rather than as a set <*e*,*t*>. So, even though this work is attractive from the point of view of dealing with the relation between discrete and continuous matter as expressed in language, the formal approach to sentences like (9) will be modelled after Bunt (1979, 1981, 1985). Bunt (1981) proposed a so-called 'ensemble theory', which is an extension of the Zermelo-Fraenkel (ZF) set-theory, which is based on the primitive relation of membership $\in$. Mass terms are taken as referring without individuating their parts (as atoms).

Staying close to representations in which set theory makes it possible for a determiner to identify or introduce a set W as in (177)–(181) and PLUG, ensemble theory makes it possible to identify or introduce a semantic object W_0 with a part-whole structure, where W_0 does not necessarily have minimal parts like W which has atoms. In other words, the standard primitive relation of set theory $x \in W$, in which x is a minimal part of W, does not hold for W_0: one cannot say $x \in W_0$. What Bunt does is to generalize over the part-whole relation in W and W_0, by calling them ensembles and defining the part-whole relation such that sets are ensembles with deviating properties. In short, the relation $\subseteq$ is taken as primitive and the $\in$-relation is derived from it for the ZF-part of his theory.

For our purposes, this generalization would mean the following. Recall that in the grammar based on (169), (170) and (177)–(181) in chapter 5.1 (to which I will restrict myself here, for convenience) a representation for sentences like (372) would be interpreted as (374):

(372) The child came in

(373) The snow came in

(374) $[\![\text{the (SG(child))}]\!]([\![\text{came\_in}]\!])$
$\Leftrightarrow \exists! W[W \subseteq [\![\text{child}]\!] \wedge |W|=1 \wedge W \subseteq [\![\text{came\_in}]\!]]$

and also recall that $W \subseteq [\![\text{child}]\!]$ is short for (375):

(375) $\forall x(x \in W \rightarrow x \in [\![\text{child}]\!])$

(376) $\forall x(x \subseteq W \rightarrow x \subseteq [\![\text{child}]\!])$

Bunt's adaptation would mean that we have to read $W \subseteq [\![\text{child}]\!]$ in (374) as (376). As $[\![\text{child}]\!]$ is a set containing discrete elements, (376) will turn out to be equivalent to (375). For *the snow* in (373), however, this equivalence does not hold, because ⟦snow⟧ is lexically identified as an atomless set of snow particles. At the level of representation (374) the difference between sets and ensembles does not show up, but it should be realized that it is present via (375).

Given the analysis of bareness in chapter 6.3, it stands to reason to assume that the BARE operator for count terms is similar to or at least closely related to the semantic element responsible for the absence of cardinality in mass terms. Along these line one would expect interpretations like (377) or even (378) for (373), BARE being taken as a modifier of SG along the lines of (170):

(377) $[\![\text{the}(\text{BARE}(\text{SG})(\text{snow}))]\!]([\![\text{came\_in}]\!])$
$\Leftrightarrow \exists!W[W{=}\bigcup[\![\text{snow}]\!]\wedge|[\![\text{snow}]\!]|{=}1\wedge W{\subseteq}[\![\text{came\_in}]\!]]$

(378) $[\![\text{the}(\text{BARE SG})(\text{snow}))]\!]([\![\text{came\_in}]\!])$
$\Leftrightarrow \exists W\exists!S[W{\subseteq}\bigcup S{\subseteq}[\![\text{snow}]\!]\wedge|S|{=}1\wedge W{\subseteq}[\![\text{came\_in}]\!]]$

if the account of bareness in section 8.2 is correct in view of sentences like (379):

(379) This snow must be swept away but the snow here may stay

The function | | in (377) and (378) should not be seen as yielding a cardinal value. It is standard to use measure functions. For the present theory, the difference between the two sorts of function is one of secondary importance. Primary is the fact that the value of measure function can be expressed in terms of a numerical value. The outline of the extension of the present theory of NP-structure into the realm of mass terms will be clear: the presence of a measure function yielding a numerical value, in representations like (377) and (378) makes an NP [+SQA], just as the presence of a cardinality function did with count NPs.

Bunt (1985) argues that NPs like *a litre of whisky* in sentences such as (369) should be analysed in terms of a measure function which, applied to an ensemble, yields finite amounts of a certain dimension, as exemplified in (380):

(380) $\lambda P\exists W[W{\subseteq}[\![\text{whisky}]\!]\wedge\mu(W){=}{<}1,\text{litres}{>}_V\wedge P(W)]$

That is, the amount of W is 1 litre, where V indicates the Volume-dimension of μ. This is also essentially the approach in Link (1983) and Krifka (1989a; 1989b). Likewise, *a slice of bread* in (9) would be represented as (381) where the subscript S denotes the standard Sandwich-slicing dimension:

(381) $\lambda P\exists W[W{\subseteq}[\![\text{bread}]\!]\wedge\mu(W){=}{<}1,\text{slice}{>}_S\wedge P(W)]$

(382) $\lambda P\exists W[W{\subseteq}[\![\text{bread}]\!]\wedge|W|_{\text{slice}}{=}1\wedge P(W)]$

One might wish to reformulate (381) as (382). If one does so, it will be clear how we may generalize over mass terms and count terms as far as the notion of [+SQA] is concerned. A mass NP is [+SQA] iff its representation contains a cardinality or measure function concerning the members or parts of W.

The partition analysis of PLUG can be extended to mass NPs. For example, *three slices of bread* would become:

(383) $\lambda P\exists W[W\subseteq[\![\text{bread}]\!]\wedge|W|_{\text{slice}}=3\wedge\exists Q\text{ps}W[Q=P|_{[\![\text{bread}]\!]}]]$

Finally, the NP *bread* can be analysed as (384). It is assumed that no cardinality information is expressed by mass nouns, though it is possible to do so by treating them in terms of bareness. In that case, one would have (385), where α would determine the sort of measuring function applied:

(384) $\lambda P\exists W[W\subseteq[\![\text{bread}]\!]\wedge\exists Q\text{ps}W[Q=P|_{[\![\text{bread}]\!]}]$

(385) $\lambda P\exists W\exists \mathcal{W}[W\subseteq\bigcup\mathcal{W}\subseteq[\![\text{bread}]\!]\wedge|\mathcal{W}|_{\alpha}=1\wedge\exists Q\text{ps}W[Q=P|_{[\![\text{bread}]\!]}]$

The former would give the semantic interpretation (386) for (10) *Judith ate bread.* Note that in both (384) and (385) no equivalent of cardinality information is given, which explains why (386) is durative.

(386) $\exists!V[V=[\![\text{Judith}]\!]\cap\{j_i\}\wedge\exists W[W\subseteq[\![\text{bread}]\!]$
$\wedge\exists Q\text{ps}W[Q=\{U\cap[\![\text{bread}]\!]\text{: }[\![\text{eat}]\!](U)(V)\}]]]$

This says that there is a unique Judith in $\mathbf{M}_i$ such that there is a set which is the union of all bread particles and there is a partition Q of W such that Judith ate subsets U of Q. This allows for Q to be both finite and infinite. Or more precisely: in (10) it is left in the dark whether Judith ate a finite amount of bread, though in many cases it may be implied conversationally. This is what seems to be called for: there is no information on cardinality, so she may have done something bounded or not. The simple fact is that we will never know, if (10) is the only information given by a speaker.

8.4 Conclusion

In this section, I will take up the question put at the beginning of Part II: can Generalized Quantification Theory account for the well-established but intuitive notion of [+SQA]? This question turns out to be quite complex because there appear to be circumstances under which a clear [+SQA]-NP behaves as if it were [–SQA]. So, before getting to an answer summarizing the findings of Part II, I would like to eliminate any misunderstanding what the question is about. The best way to avoid it is to take the minimal position of a dumb computer being able to read English sentences and to recognize NPs on the basis of their having determiners and instructed to distinguish NPs with [+SQA]-determiners from NPs having [–SQA]-determiners, say on the basis of the list in Table 10. This capacity, as well as its ability to recognize verbs marked [+ADD TO], should enable such a computer to mark the following sentences as terminative:

(5) Judith ate those three sandwiches
(6) Judith ate three sandwiches
(8) Judith ate that sandwich
(35) All children came in
(39) Several children came in
(242) The soldiers came into town
(306) Two girls ate five sandwiches

on the ground of their fitting in the terminative mould (387) discussed in chapter 1.2:

(387) $[_{T}[+\text{SQA}] + [_{TVP}[+\text{ADD TO}]+[+\text{SQA}]]]$

It should also recognize durative sentences like (119) and (120).

(119) Judith ate sandwiches
(120) Judith ate *from* the sandwiches

Let us call this the simple compositional strategy. It has become evident in the preceding chapters that we need a more sophisticated one, because sentences superficially fitting into (387) sometimes turn out to have durative interpretations. This means that the computer has to get beyond the point of checking only surface forms and that it has to take into account semantic information, some of which may be dependent on contextual information or more generally, on information concerning the domain of discourse, such as a set of presuppositions available on the basis of preceding sentences.

So, the more sophisticated question is: can Generalized Quantification Theory account for the well-established though intuitive notion of [+SQA] on the basis of a more sophisticated strategy? In the present section, an answer will be given by going once again through the list of determiners collected in Table 10 and by checking under which circumstances a sentence may contain 'degenerate' [+SQA]-NPs. The suggestive term 'degenerate' only counts from the point of view of quantificational information expressed by sentences having terminative aspect: in degenerate cases there is no way to specify, to delineate a set on the basis of the cardinality of its membership. (Whoever is fond of durativity may change *degenerate* into its opposite.)

Before we get to the list, it is necessary to point out that there is no way in which [–SQA]-NPs may be receive a [+SQA]-interpretation. That is, in sentences like (388)

(388) Judith ate sandwiches. She had all five of them in her box

them clearly has some anaphoric relation to *sandwiches*. Yet (119) *Judith ate sandwiches* is durative and remains so even if later information makes it clear that Judith ate a finite amount of sandwiches. Our analysis of the bare plural makes it even more plausible that (388) gives the information in the way it does. Its (119)-part introduces a category of entities in the domain of discourse E and identifies them as sandwiches without any information on the cardinality. This is added in the second clause. However, this increase of information does not change the aspectual nature of the first sentence in (388). The principles underlying the effect of new information on old information are outside the scope of the present study.

Let us now go through Table 10 again and summarize under which conditions [+SQA]-NPs remain [+SQA] and under which conditions they allow for durative leakage.

Proper names

Proper names pertaining to individuals are clearly [+SQA] and it seems as if they remain so under all circumstances. There are, however, interesting contexts of use for a proper name in which we obtain durative interpretations:

(389) For weeks she turned off Dallas

(390) I sold Ronald for a couple of years

Sentence (389) means that for weeks she turned off issues of *Dallas*, whereas (390) may pertain to a situation in which I sold statues or pictures of Reagan. In both cases, one may assume that the proper name refers to a type or to a set of tokens with an unspecified membership, as discussed in chapter 6.3.

From the point of view of model theory, there is no real problem here. If ⟦Dallas⟧ is a first-order individual of type *e*, just like ⟦Judith⟧ in $\mathbf{M}_1$, (389) will show aspectual repetition, which becomes clearer if we replace *Dallas* by *Dallas 215* (which is the 215th issue of *Dallas*). There is no doubt that this sentence is terminative: it gets an odd interpretation. The same applies to *Ronald*. If it is the name of a specific dog, (390) means that Ronald repeatedly got a new boss. It is only when proper names do not have a clear type-logical status, that is, are treated as definite bare singulars, that they manage to get a durative interpretation expressing unbounded plurality of tokens of a definite type. So, our computer must require that the denotation of a proper name can be given in terms of a specific cardinality, before it would assign [+SQA] to *Dallas* and *Ronald*.

The$_{sg}$ N, this N, the$_{pl}$ N, both N, the n N, all of the N, some of the N, most N, all N, every N
The same applies to the definite NP. Under this heading we may capture the definite article, possessives, *Judith's*, and demonstratives. For *all* and *every* the situation is slightly more complex. Apart from 'lawlike' statements not applying to a particular model, *all* and *every* behave properly: they belong to the definite determiners (though there are differences as pointed out in chapter 6.2 and chapter 7.6) and so they are bound to express [+SQA]-information.

The general picture is that if strong NPs pertain to individuals they are clearly [+SQA], given the non-emptiness of the head noun, as pointed out with respect to sentences like:

(162) The dog came in

which cannot be interpreted in models like $\mathbf{M}_1$. So, definite singular NPs are [+SQA], if they are defined. Sentences like (162) are simply not interpretable in $\mathbf{M}_1$. The same applies now to *all* and *every* as pointed out in chapter 4.4 and chapter 5.2: on our analysis *The dog came in*, *All dogs came in* and *Every dog came* in are EFSQ-true in $\mathbf{M}_1$, which is to say that they are undefined.

In chapter 6, the exact circumstances are given under which our computer would fail to recognize [–SQA]-information expressed by strong NPs. Consequently, the computer must be enriched so as to be able to read the formal representations, so that it will see whether or not information about cardinality is present or not. If it is not present, there is no way to 'get at' a specified quantity of individuals; if cardinality information is present, the NP expresses [+SQA]-information.

Some N, a(n) N,
The same applies for *some* N and for *a*(*n*) N. If no cardinality information is given in the representation, the NP refers 'barely' at a higher level, to a category, so that it is not able to give a specified quantity of its members.

Several N, many N, few N
These NPs are [+SQA] if they express cardinality information, just like the NPs with strong determiners. As pointed out, they may fail to behave as proper [+SQA]-NPs. If they are bare, as exemplified in (260), they operate at the category-level. That is, if sentences like (391)

(391) For years Mary sold several saucers

are used to say that Mary sold several types of saucer, then it says that Mary sold an unspecified quantity (in fact, the union) of tokens from different categories of saucers. In that case, *Mary sold several saucers* is clearly durative.

As far as *many* N and *few* N is concerned, it should be observed that they behave aspectually like *several* N, *some* N, etc.

At least N, n or less N, more than n N, at most n, few N, n or less N, less than m of the m N, at most n of the m, exactly n N
The notion of cardinality cuts across the notion of (non-)monotonicity. In other words, the [+SQA]-notion cannot be reduced to monotonicity. As long as the NPs are properly functioning as sieves, there is no problem in getting a [+SQA]-interpretation. It is possible, however, to have sentences like (392)

(392) For years Mary sold three saucers

meaning that she sold an unspecified quantity of three different types of saucer. Here there are [–SQA]-interpretations on the ground that the NP does not give information about the cardinality of the set W but rather about the cardinality of the collection of subsets of the head noun denotation A whose union constitutes W.

Not Judith, not the N, not all N, not every N, nobody
As far as these NPs are concerned, they were dealt with in chapter 4.3 and chapter 7.6: they express [+SQA] due to the fact that they are involved in contrastive negation, but they may receive a [–SQA]-interpretation like the above quantifiers.

If our computer were also instructed to recognize measure functions, it would also be able to predict exactly the circumstances under which mass NPs are [+SQA] or [–SQA].

CONCLUSION TO PART II

This concludes the analysis of atemporal quantificational structure as expressed by NPs. It may be convenient to give the PLUG-grammar here again. Its extension PLUG⁺ will be given at the end of Part III, so that both versions can easily be compared.

PLUG

PHRASE STRUCTURE RULES

1. $S : [\![NP]\!]([\![VP]\!]) \Leftarrow NP : [\![NP]\!], VP : [\![VP]\!]$

2. $\begin{cases} VP : \lambda X.[\![V_1]\!](X) \\ VP : \lambda X.[\![NP]\!](\lambda Y.[\![V_2]\!](Y)(X)) \Leftarrow V_2 : [\![V_2]\!], NP : [\![NP]\!] \end{cases}$

3. $NP : [\![DET^2]\!]([\![N]\!]) \Leftarrow DET^2 : [\![DET^2]\!], N : [\![N]\!]$

4. $DET^2 : [\![SPEC]\!]([\![DET^1]\!]) \Leftarrow SPEC : [\![SPEC]\!], DET^1 : [\![DET^1]\!]$

SPEC

$[\![the]\!] = \lambda D\lambda X\lambda P[D(X\cap C)([\![thing]\!])\wedge\exists R ps X\cap C[R=P|_{X\cap C}]]$

$[\![\o]\!] = \lambda D\lambda X\lambda P.\exists W[W\subseteq X\wedge D(X)(W)\wedge\exists Q ps W[Q=P|_X]]$

DET¹

$[\![SG]\!] = \lambda X\lambda Y.|X\cap Y|=1$

$[\![PL]\!] = \lambda X\lambda Y.|X\cap Y|>1$

$[\![n]\!] = \lambda X\lambda Y.|X\cap Y|=n$

$[\![many]\!] = \lambda X\lambda Y.|X\cap Y|>k\bullet|X|$

$[\![several]\!] = \lambda X\lambda Y.|X\cap Y|\geq 2$

$[\![INC]\!] = \lambda X\lambda Y.|X\cap Y'|=0$

Recall that rule 2 is given syncategorematically to evade a type-logically rather complicated derivation. Also, for reasons of convenience the representation of context sets as given in Westerståhl (1984) will be simplified by the use of ∃!, as exemplified in (299), so that the rule for $[\![the]\!]$ is replaced by its equivalent:

$[\![the]\!] = \lambda D\lambda X\lambda P.\exists!W[W\subseteq X\wedge D(X)(W)\wedge\exists Q ps W[Q=P|_X]]$

The results of the PLUG-analyses of the sentences important for the present aspectual theory will be collected here:

(393) Judith ate a sandwich

(394) $\exists!V[V=[\![Judith]\!]\cap\{j_i\}\wedge\exists W[W\subseteq[\![sandwich]\!]\wedge|W|=1$
$\wedge\exists Q ps W[Q=AT([\![sandwich]\!])\cap\{U: [\![eat]\!](U)(V)\}]]]$

(6) Judith ate three sandwiches

(305) $\exists!V[V=\llbracket\text{Judith}\rrbracket\cap\{j_i\}\wedge\exists W[W\subseteq\llbracket\text{sandwich}\rrbracket\wedge|W|=3$
$\wedge\exists Q\,\text{ps}\,W[Q=\{U\cap\llbracket\text{sandwich}\rrbracket: \llbracket\text{eat}\rrbracket(U)(V)\}]]]$

(306) Two girls ate five sandwiches

(307) $\exists Z[Z\subseteq\llbracket\text{girl}\rrbracket\wedge|Z|=2$
$\wedge\exists P\,\text{ps}\,Z[P=\{V\cap\llbracket\text{girl}\rrbracket: \exists W[W\subseteq\llbracket\text{sandwich}\rrbracket\wedge|W|=5$
$\wedge\exists Q\,\text{ps}\,W[Q=\{U\cap\llbracket\text{sandwich}\rrbracket: \llbracket\text{eat}\rrbracket(U)(V)\}]]\}]]$

(7) Judith ate sandwiches

(395) $\exists!V[V=\llbracket\text{Judith}\rrbracket\cap\{j_i\}\wedge\exists W\exists S[W\subseteq\bigcup S\subseteq\llbracket\text{sandwich}\rrbracket\wedge|S|>1$
$\wedge\exists Q\,\text{ps}\,W[Q=\{U\cap\llbracket\text{sandwich}\rrbracket: \llbracket\text{eat}\rrbracket(U)(V)\}]]]$

(10) Judith ate bread

(386) $\exists!V[V=\llbracket\text{Judith}\rrbracket\cap\{j_i\}\wedge\exists W[W\subseteq_m\llbracket\text{bread}\rrbracket$
$\wedge\exists Q\,\text{ps}\,W[Q=\{U\cap\ \llbracket\text{bread}\rrbracket: \llbracket\text{eat}\rrbracket(U)(V)\}]]]$

(327) Two girls ate no sandwich

(335) $\exists Z[Z\subseteq\llbracket\text{girl}\rrbracket\wedge|Z|=2$
$\wedge\exists P\,\text{ps}\,Z[P=\{V\cap\llbracket\text{girl}\rrbracket: \{U\cap\llbracket\text{sandwich}\rrbracket|\llbracket\text{eat}\rrbracket(U)(V)\}=\{\varnothing\}\}]]$

(329) No girl ate five sandwiches

(334) $\{\varnothing\}=\{V\cap\llbracket\text{girl}\rrbracket: \exists W[W\subseteq\text{sandwich}\rrbracket\wedge|W|=5$
$\wedge\exists Q\,\text{ps}\,W[Q=\{U\cap\llbracket\text{sandwich}\rrbracket: \llbracket\text{eat}\rrbracket(U)(V)\}]]\}$

Recall that these representations can be simplified by taking *Judith* standardly rather than in terms of an intersection of an individual and a set of those who bear the same name. In that case, (393) could be read as $\exists W[W\subseteq\llbracket\text{sandwich}\rrbracket\wedge|W|=1\wedge\exists Q\,\text{ps}\,W[Q=\text{AT}(\llbracket\text{sandwich}\rrbracket)\cap\{U|\llbracket\text{eat}\rrbracket(U)(\{j_i\})\}]]$. The fact that it does not seem to make very much sense to partition a set consisting of one element into a collection consisting of one singleton is not harmful. This is the result of trying to deal with singularity and plurality by the same rules.

The sentences (393), (6) and (306) are terminative. This cannot be seen by inspecting (394), (305) and (307). The only aspectually relevant information is the [+SQA]-information expressed by the presence of the cardinality statements $|W|=1$ in (394), $|W|=3$ in (305), and $|Z|=2$ plus $|W|=5$ in (307). This cardinality information is, of course, also present in $\exists!V[V=\llbracket\text{Judith}\rrbracket\cap\{j_i\}$. The other sentences are durative. In (7), (10) and (327), there is no cardinality information about the set W itself; in (334) this information is stacked 'too low'. To explain the aspectual behaviour of terminative and durative sentences it is necessary to have more information in their representations. In particular, the temporal contribution of the verb is not visible.

In the next part of the present study, the question will be central of how the atemporal information expressed by NPs interacts with temporal information introduced by verbs. It will be argued that for [+ADD TO]-verbs the collection of sets formed by the partition is the co-domain of a particular function. This means that the atemporal representations of terminative sentences like (6), (7) and (10) and (306) have to undergo a process of adaptation so that they are fit to express temporal structure. Furthermore, it will be shown that such an extension will be required to deal with other sentences listed in chapter 1, among which are the sentences (396)–(400):

(396) John pushed the cart
(397) John walked to the store
(398) Judith ate (=used to eat) three sandwiches
(399) Judith was eating a sandwich
(400) Judith ate up a sandwich

The interaction between temporal and atemporal structure of the sentences under investigation will be the central topic of Part III.

III Temporal structure

INTRODUCTION TO PART III

In this part, the interaction between temporal structure and atemporal structure in sentences expressing terminative and durative aspect will be under investigation. In particular, our compositional aspectual theory will be set out to give an explanation for why it is that the unbounded progress expressed by [+ADD TO]-verbs, for example *walk*, *eat* and *play*, can be brought to an end by the [+SQA]-nature of their arguments, and it will try to give a formal account of how complex sentential meanings are formed out of the temporal and atemporal meanings of their constituents.

Some would even like to say that an atemporal grammar like PLUG in chapter 7.3 might be sufficient if one could agree upon the simple observation that the number of elements of a partition never exceeds the cardinality of the set underlying it. However, this would amount to refusing to take into account the role of temporal structure. It might take Part III to convince those who want to stick to atemporal representations. It is only after going through four separate issues crucially involved in theory formation about temporal structure of sentences that in chapter 13 a formal account can be given because its ingredients and the choices behind them are built up stepwise in the preceding sections. In view of this, the organization of Part III is as follows.

In chapter 9, the notion of homogeneity will be analysed critically. If it is used, a terminative sentence like *John walked home* is analysed in terms of a walk-home interval (event) W_H which is called heterogeneous because an arbitrary subinterval of W_H is not itself a walk-home-interval. On the same ground, *John walked* was considered homogeneous because the complete walk-interval has the same structure as any of its subintervals. Working in the localistic additive tradition, I have always found the discussion about homogeneity ill-motivated and leading away from the real aspectual issues involved. What went wrong, in my view, is that the notion of interval became tied up with the notion of evaluation, however understandable this was at first sight, given the developments in Montague Grammar at the time. It will be shown that by comparing *John walked* and *John walked home* in this way, one is bound to make a 'holistic mistake' by treating a VP as if it were a complex verb.

In chapter 10, it will first be pointed out that the notion of homogeneity discussed in chapter 9 conflated two issues: (a) lexical homogeneity, which is not of interest to aspectual theory; and (b) the notion of a structured path. The latter issue will bring the need to elucidate the localistic background of the present study. It is placed in the localistic framework developed by Gruber (1976) in which change is conceived of as a movement of the so-called Theme from a

Source to a Goal, along a Path. Gruber's work has developed in (at least) two directions: (a) Conceptual Semantics, developed by Jackendoff; (b) the PLUG-grammar proposed in chapter 7. It should be underscored that the localistic notions of PLUG are very hard to recognize, certainly in its atemporal version. At this stage it suffices to say that, for example, the asymmetry inherent to PLUG has to do with the fact that the VP can be theoretically interpreted as a 'Path' on which the temporal change takes place. Due to considerations like these, it is necessary to pay attention to the localistic framework in order to see which notions are at issue, and to get points of attachment for the redrafting of too concretely taken localistic notions into more neutral set-theoretical constructs. One of the goals of Part III is to relate the localistic tradition to the more standard type-logic framework of Generalized Quantification. This implies a more abstract treatment of localistic notions. My strategy will be to bring about the translation in two steps: (a) an extrapolation of Jackendoff's framework in which the Path-notion has been articulated, in terms of set-theoretical formalism. This is of interest for a generalization which will be one of the leading goals of Part III: one and the same account for the terminative aspect of *John walked to three stores* and *Judith ate three sandwiches*; (b) the temporal extension of PLUG into PLUG^{+} based on this localistic excursion.

In chapter 11, attention will be paid to event semantics. The massive transition from interval semantics to event semantics in the late seventies/early eighties was in my view not an improvement at all, events being taken as primitives. A compositional approach to sentential aspect construal is very hard to be reconciled with events as primitives. The rise of event semantics co-occurred with the rise of Discourse Representation Theory (DRT). In my view, event semantics can be very well combined with the study of text structure but not so much with the study of sentential aspect construal. In more than one sense a compositional approach to aspect in which events are seen as semantic objects compositionally formed on the basis of [+SQA]- and [+ADD TO] information relates to the DRT-approach in the way micro-economics relates to macro-economics: from the DRT-point of view events are to be taken individually, as primitives, so that they play a role in explaining intersentential linguistic phenomena, such as temporal anaphoric reference. However, from the aspectual micro-point of view one has to look at events molecularly, that is, construed as 'dividuals' from more elementary information. The present aspectual theory operates at the micro-level. Preparatory for the discussion on aspectual perspective, some arguments in favour of events as primitives will be critically examined. Attention will also be paid to Krifka's event semantics, which is congenial to the present framework as far as the additive approach is concerned, but which differs in several respects.

In chapter 12, a major ingredient of traditional aspectual theory will be investigated: the fact that in our language use we are able to shift perspectives. It will be demonstrated that terminative aspect is a way to indicate that one wishes to speak about a bounded event given a unique temporal structure. One sentence will be analysed with respect to three levels of organization in a computer game. At the lowest level – a document (a world) with its own unique time structure – the sentence is terminative: it describes the movement of some object in the document. Shifting to a higher perspective is shifting to a durative interpretation of the same sentence: it now pertains to an unbounded set of situations in a number of sortlike documents each having its own temporal structure: it describes my bringing about changes in documents. By compressing the different time structures of the documents into one 'desktop' time structure (overruling them, as it were), the sentence again becomes terminative, though differently from the first situation: it now describes a change in all documents at the same desktop time. Thus, terminative aspect can be shown to be a form of event construal on the basis of a compositional machinery.

In chapter 13, event construal will be formalized by an extension of PLUG, that will be called PLUG$^+$. The partitions in the atemporal version of PLUG must be justified and the asymmetry involved will be explicated. That is, the partition of the internal argument NP will be made dependent on indices by a mapping, so that the denotation of this NP can be conceived of as a (low-level intensional) 'slice', allowing speakers to modify (that is, to select) the partition (for example, *one-by-one*, *all together*, etc.). As the application of this function is made dependent on the cardinality of the argument-NP, an explanation of terminative aspect follows immediately. The partition of the external argument NP is subjected to different constraints. In this way, the difference between the thematic roles of an internal argument and an external argument can be accounted for. It is also argued that the thematic role expressed by the direct object NP of two-place predicates is expressed by the preposition of directional complements. In this way a generalization can be made with respect to the aspectual behaviour of *Mary walked to Rome* and *Judith ate a sandwich*. On the basis of the presence of the partitioning information in the NP-representation, it is possible to define the notion of total and partial affectedness. This accounts for the indeterminacy expressed by certain prepositions, such as *naar* (towards) in Dutch and *nach* in German.

In chapter 13, a theory about the Progressive Form will also be developed which does not use (overt) modality. The index system expressed by [+ADD

TO]-verbs is based upon a ‘rounding off’ function relating the set of natural numbers **N** to the set of reals **R**. This system can be used to explain the durative behaviour of sentences with a Progressive Form.

In the final chapter 14, the Plus-principle sketched in chapter 1 is tested with respect to sentences like *Mary walked* and *John pushed the cart*, which constitute counterexamples. Their aspectual behaviour can be explained in terms of a so-called Complex Predicate analysis. It will be argued that verb (stems) are to be specified as to the argument frame in which they may appear. For example, *walk* will not be called an intransitive verb but rather a verb which may be used intransitively (*Mary walked*) or transitively (*Mary walked a mile*, *Mary walked to Rome*). Likewise, *die* in *the patient died* is marked for an ergative frame, explaining its terminative aspectuality. In this way, and by localizing the information concerning partial or total affectedness in the thematic role associated with a complex predicate, the difference between *John pushed the cart* and *John pushed the cart away* can be accounted for.

In the beginning of the present study a set of sentences was given and it was claimed that these sentences should fall within the scope of investigation. At the end of Part III these sentences again as well as their PLUG^{+}-representations are given. In this way, terminativity as well as nine different forms of durativity can be characterized. The Conclusion to Part III also contains the PLUG^{+}-grammar.

9 Homogeneity

9.0 Introduction

In the mid-sixties, the philosopher G.H. von Wright proposed to analyse change in terms of a transition operator T ('and next') from a certain state described by the proposition $\neg\phi$ to a certain state described by the proposition ϕ. Independently, the linguist J. Gruber proposed to analyse change in terms of a 'moving' entity, the Theme, which 'goes' from a Source- to a Goal-position.[1]

In both approaches, change is analysed in terms of an initial state and an end state which are related to points of time with respect to which these states are said to hold. However, there is a fundamental difference between the two. On the Von Wright approach, the interval being defined in terms of the initial state and the end state leaves the stretch between them as a sort of no man's land. No information is given by T, so a natural question is: what happened between the two states? All sorts of detailed questions arise, such as: at what point does the transition take place if there is such a point? What does the interval structure look like? What about subintervals? Is there a smallest interval?, etc. (Kamp 1979, 1980; Van Benthem 1983a). This approach put the concept of homogeneity at the centre of attention in the seventies and early eighties. The notion of homogeneity is closely tied up with the notion of monotone-decreasing structure, as defined in DEF 4.7: if the temporal interval I defined by the operator T is taken as a collection I of its subintervals, then for each $i_j,i_k \subseteq I$, if $i_j \in I$ and $i_k \subseteq i_j$, then $i_k \in I$.

On the Gruberian approach, the two points corresponding to $\neg\phi$ and ϕ are systematically connected by a Path taken by the Theme to bridge the distance between Source and Goal. Here the interval structure is built up additively and as the Theme arrives at the Goal, there is no need to go into the question of whether or not the interval was homogeneous. On this approach, the notion of additivity or cumulativity emerged, quite ponderously in the seventies, much more easily in the eighties after the introduction of algebraic techniques in the wake of the Theory of Generalized Quantification. Cumulativity can be defined in terms of closure: if the temporal interval I defined by the operator T is taken as a collection I of its subintervals, then for each $i_j, i_k \subseteq I$, if $i_j \in I$ and $i_k \in I$, then $i_j \cup i_k \in I$. The notion of cumulativity is weaker than the notion of monotone increasing structure in DEF 4.4: for all $i_j, i_k \subseteq I$, if $i_j \in I$ and $i_j \subseteq i_k$, then $i_k \in I$ If a structure is monotone increasing, it is also cumulative, but not conversely. As argued in Verkuyl (1987a, 1988, 1989), both cumulativity and homogeneity – defined as: if $i_j \in I$ and $i_k \in I$, then $i_j \cap i_k \in I$ – follow from the stronger notion of a filter in DEF 4.5: $i_j \cap i_k \in I$ iff $i_j \in I$ and $i_k \in I$. This point will be elaborated in the present study in chapter 10 and in chapter 13.

The present section will give an account of some of the issues involved in a choice between the two approaches. Recently, there has appeared a doctoral dissertation written by Alex Lascarides in which the main proposals based on the Von Wright approach are critically examined on their logical consistency: Dowty (1979, 1986), Taylor (1977, 1985), Bennett (1981), and Cooper (1983). Lascarides (1988) is really the fatal blow to any idea of homogeneity as an explanatory notion. Though I shall have the opportunity to summarize some of her arguments now and then, most of Lascarides' analyses are so detailed that I must simply refer to her excellent study.[2] The obvious question of whether there is still room left for a critical discussion of the concept of homogeneity can be answered affirmatively. Lascarides' view is also primarily logical and she is focussed on the Progressive Form and on Punctual Adverbials like *at three o'clock*. But the more principled reason for discussing some of the proposals of the seventies is to see where it went wrong. It went wrong because the concept of homogeneity is not a structural notion at all. It is either a lexical notion or a hybrid holistic notion applied to the VP. It does not leave room for a compositional approach. So the homogeneity approach will be approached from quite a different angle, viz. from the point of view of additivity as a sort of conceptual Cinderella. Bach (1981, 1986) is often taken as the prince who recognized the additivity shoes. But Cinderella's natural place is the prosperous Gruberian localistic republic founded in the early sixties.

9.1 Homogeneity and truth at intervals

As already said, for the logicians extending atemporal logic so as to deal with properties of a two-step evaluation of the transition proposition $\neg\phi T\phi$, a huge problem appeared. What happened between the states corresponding to $\neg\phi$ and ϕ? This problem haunted tense-logicians and linguists working on tense-logic in the seventies. The natural solution for this problem seemed to be: to fill the gap between the two points with conditions that would be able to guarantee a sort of permanency of truth during the passage from the states corresponding to

$\neg\phi$ and ϕ. So certain conditions concerning the internal structure of intervals were added to the truth conditions of sentences expressing change. A case in point is Bennett and Partee (1978), who tried to improve on Montague's treatment of tense by pointing out that his truth conditions (1c) of sentences like (1a) fail.

(1) a. John built a house
b. John builds a house
c. (a) is true at t iff there is a t′ such that t′ <t and (b) is true at t′

Bennett and Partee observed: 'Intuitively it seems that the truth condition for (a) should concern some past interval of time during which John is building a house and eventually completes it. Instead the condition is that (b) is true at some past moment of time and this is unintuitive' (1978: 11).

To remedy this problem, Bennett and Partee distinguish between subinterval VPs such as *walk*, *breathe*, *walk in the park* and *push a cart*, etc. and non-subinterval VPs such as *die*, *walk to Rome*, *build a house*, *catch a fish*, etc. If a sentence ϕ of the form [NP VP] is true at some interval i, then ϕ is true at every subinterval i′ of i, if VP is a subinterval VP. This is not the case for non-subinterval VPs. The truth conditions for sentences like (1a), according to Bennett and Partee (1978: 35), should be formulated as (2).

(2) $[\![\text{John built a house } \alpha]\!]_{M,i} = 1$ iff i is a moment of time, α refers to a time interval i′ and there is a time interval i″ (i″ a subinterval of i′) such that i″ precedes i and $[\![\text{John builds a house}]\!]_{M,i''} = 1$

The value of α may be temporal adverbials like *yesterday*, but in (1a) it is empty, so it may refer to an unidentified stretch of time including the interval at which John was building his house.

By their proposal, precedence was given to a holistic treatment of aspectuality in which questions of knowledge of the world were allowed to intrude deeply in the semantic analysis of what already had been shown to be a structural semantic phenomenon. The interest was focussed on the difference between (in Montague's terms) the Intransitive Verb Phrases *walk*, *walk in the park* and *walk to Rome*. In Verkuyl (1972), the focus of the aspectual analysis of *walk in the park* and *walk to Rome* also included the similarity between the two phrases as expressed by the verb *walk*; as well as the difference between *walk in the park* and *walk to Rome* on the one hand and *be in the park* and *be in Rome* on the other hand. It is exactly this part of the analysis – both the role of the verb and its interaction with its complements – that disappeared from the view of interval semanticists to the credit of the analysis of the differences between verb phrases as a whole. The clue to the shift to a holistic treatment can be found in the statement that 'it is important to focus on the intransitive verb phrases rather than simply verbs. For instance, *walk* is the main verb in both subinterval verb phrases (for example, *walk*, *walk in the park*) and in non-stative, non-subinterval verb phrases (*walk to Rome*, *walk out in front of the car*)' (1978: 14). In short, a holistic approach emerged rather than a compositional one (recall also Ter Meulen's approach in chapter 2.9: her aspectual classes concern VPs).[3]

The dominant term emerging from this sort of analysis in the seventies is *homogeneity*. An interval is considered homogeneous if its structure does not deviate from the structure of its arbitrarily chosen subintervals, that is, if it has the subinterval property. On the basis of this concept, aspectuality of sentences was tackled: the distinction between being homogeneous and heterogeneous became equated with the distinction between durative and terminative (verb) phrases. Verb phrases like *walk in the park* were considered durative because they are homogeneous: the durative *Mary walked in the park*, being true at an interval i, is also true at any subinterval of i. On the other hand, *walk to Rome* was said to be terminative because *Mary walked to Rome* being true at i cannot be true at any proper interval of i. So, *walk to Rome* is heterogeneous. Hence, the opposition between durative and terminative aspect was explained in terms of having or not having the property of homogeneity.

In particular, Taylor's concept of temporal homogeneity, which is a modification and elaboration of Bennett and Partee's ideas, has been very influential. As it also plays a role in Dowty's interval semantics as well as in further discussions, I shall discuss its main features briefly here. According to Taylor, gold is homogeneous because '*every* three-dimensional area within a homogeneous lump of gold is occupied by a lump of gold' (1977: 209). Homogeneous stuff 'fills' space, whereas a heterogeneous substance 'delimits' it. A fruit-cake is heterogeneous because a sultana cannot count as a lump of fruit-cake, so there are areas in the cake that do not count as lumps of fruit-cake though they certainly belong to it and constitute part of it. According to Taylor, the same goes for the difference between the heterogeneous *chuckle* and the homogeneous *fall*. A microsecond of a fall-movement can be reckoned to be falling because a fall is homogeneous. However, a microsecond during a chuckle would be too short to give enough information about what is going on: it might not be sufficiently representative, so to speak, for the chuckling event. Thus, his temporal concept of homogeneity is based on a spatial analogy.

Taylor distinguishes three verb classes: State-predicates, Energeia-predicates and Kinesis-predicates. The opposition between homogeneity and heterogeneity is made between the latter two. Sentences with state predicates meet condition (3), with i an interval and t a moment, that is, a singleton interval.

(3) *State*

$[\![\phi]\!]_i=1$ iff for all t: $t \subset i$, $[\![\phi]\!]_t=1$

State predicates do not take time, the other two classes of predicates do. They meet the condition that if they hold in time, they hold for an interval. The Energeia-predicates are split up into two subclasses. The first one is given in (4):

(4) *Energeia* (1)

if $[\![\phi]\!]_i=1$, then $\exists i'$: $i \subseteq i'$ & i' contains within it no earliest moment & $[\![\phi]\!]_{i'}=1$ & $\forall i'' \subseteq i$, $[\![\phi]\!]_{i''}=1$. Pictorially:

$$\text{\_\_\_\_}(_{i'}\text{\_\_\_\_}(_{i}\text{\_\_}(_{i''}\text{\_\_ }_{i''})\text{\_\_}_{i})\text{\_\_\_\_\_\_}_{i'})\text{\_\_\_\_}$$

$$\text{\_\_\_\_\_\_\_\_\_\_\_\_true\_\_\_\_\_\_\_\_\_\_\_\_}$$

In (4), the conditions are given for sentences with verbs like *fall*, *move*, *ponder*, *blush*, etc. If *John fell* is true at i, then i is contained by a larger (left-)open interval i′ at which *John fell* is also true and for all subintervals of i *John fell* is also true. Dowty (1979) adopted it but later it was weakened to ‘most subintervals of time’ (1986: 42). The second sub-class is given in (5).

(5) *Energeia* (2)

if $[\![\phi]\!]_i=1$, then $\exists i'$: $i \subseteq i'$ & $[\![\phi]\!]_{i'}=1$ & $\exists i''$: $i'' \subseteq i'$ & $[\![\phi]\!]_{i''}=1$ & $\forall i'''$: $i'' \subseteq i''' \subseteq i'$ & $[\![\phi]\!]_{i'''}=1$. Pictorially, e.g.:

$$\text{\_\_\_\_\_\_\_\_\_\_\_\_\_\_true\_\_\_\_\_\_\_\_\_\_\_\_\_\_}$$

$$\text{\_\_\_}(_{i'}\text{\_\_}(_{i'''}\ldots(_{i}\text{\_\_}(_{i''}\text{\_\_ }_{i''})\text{\_\_}_{i/i'''})\text{\_\_}_{i'})\text{\_\_}$$

$$\text{\_\_\_\_\_\_\_\_\_\_true\_\_\_\_\_\_\_\_\_\_}$$

This says that there should be minimal parts that are not counted as predicable and which makes interval structure look like fruit-cakes containing sultanas (represented here as ...). It applies to verbs like *talk*, *chuckle*, *stroke* (a dog), *walk*, etc. If *John walked* is true of the stretch i this interval can be embedded in a larger interval i′, for which it is true that *John walked*, but for each arbitrary subinterval there are always minimal intervals, temporal sultanas so to speak, that is short rests, for example (i‴,i), or the like, I presume.

The real heterogeneous predicates like *discover* (America), *polish* (the boot), *build* (a house) meet the condition given in (6).

(6) *Kinesis*

if $[\![\phi]\!]_i=1$, then for all i' such that $i' \sqsubset i$: $[\![\phi]\!]_{i'} = 0$. Pictorially e.g.:

$$
\begin{array}{c}
\text{———————false———————} \\
\text{\_\_}(_{i}\text{\_\_}(_{i'}\text{\_\_\_\_\_\_\_\_\_\_}_{i'})\text{\_\_\_\_}_{i})\text{\_\_} \\
\text{———————true———————}
\end{array}
$$

This is the non-subinterval property, now formulated at the sentential level.

Lascarides (1988: 31–41) points out that there is a huge problem for Taylor (1977, 1985) with respect to this classification. She compares the sentences (7a) and (8a).

(7) a. Max won the race at 3 pm
b. $(\exists t)(t<\text{now} \wedge \text{WIN\_THE\_RACE}(\text{max}',t) \wedge \text{AT}(3\text{pm}, \text{ST}[\text{WIN\_THE\_RACE}(\text{max}',t)]))$

(8) a. Max ran at 3 pm
b. $(\exists t)(t<\text{now} \wedge \text{RUN}(\text{max}',t) \wedge \text{AT}(3\text{pm}, \text{ST}[\text{RUN}(\text{max}',t)]))$

Basically and simplified, Taylor's representations boil down to (7b) and (8b), where $\text{ST}[\phi,t]$ means that the state of affairs ϕ obtains during t. So, (7a) is accounted for by the definition of Kinesis: the state of affairs [Max win the race] took place at the singleton $\{t_{3pm}\}$. But here is the problem: (8a) does not mean that the state of affairs [Max run] obtains at $\{t_{3pm}\}$. It means that Max *started* to run at 3 o'clock. Lascarides proves that there is no way for Taylor to remedy this shortcoming, which is really inherent to his wish to differentiate structurally between homogeneity and heterogeneity.

More generally, I would like to point out that Taylor distinguishes his classes in a clear and in a diffuse way. The clear part is that he takes verbs as lexical items and partitions them into three main classes. This interest in the lexical properties of verbs may be an important enterprise, or not. A fact is that Taylor speaks about properties of verbs that are of interest for the lexicographer, the lexicologist or the ontologist, as follows from his analysis of *stroke* and *chuckle*. The diffuse part is that verbs are also classified together with their (internal) argument, so that the notion of verb is sometimes equated with V+NP, sometimes not. The problem with his approach becomes urgent at the moment at which he treats a V+NP-combination as if it were a verb. What can be the explanatory value of a Kinesis-predicate if its internal structure is not taken into account?

9.2 Three problems for Dowty

Bennett and Partee did the only proper thing they could do from the point of view of developments in Montague Grammar of the time. They tried to find out the restrictions of the PTQ-framework and to remedy these shortcomings by staying as close as possible to PTQ. As their discussion about aspectuality started with the definition of tense, evaluation-at-an-interval became the central notion in terms of which the discussion took place. Hence, the heavy stress on the problem of closing the truth value gap between the initial state at which $\neg\Phi$ is true and the end state at which Φ is true. Thus, they developed the notion of 'truth at an interval'.[4]

Dowty (1979, 1986) incorporated insights both from Bennett and Partee and Taylor in his system. Criticisms have been raised against Dowty's treatment of interval semantics, in particular against his treatment of the Progressive Form (Abusch 1985; Krifka 1989b; Lascarides 1988; Parsons 1989). But I will focus on some aspects of the analysis of change, which are still relevant and which have gone unnoticed in the literature, as far as I know. Compare the following sentences and their analyses.

(9) a. Mary walked to Rome
b. walk′(m)∧BECOME be–at′(m,r)

(10) a. Mary died
b. BECOME dead′(m)

The truth definition of BECOME ϕ, based on Bennett and Partee, is formulated as follows (Dowty 1979: 140ff.):[5]

DEFINITION 1
$[\![\text{BECOME }\phi]\!]_{M,i,g}=1$ iff
a. for some interval $j\in I$ containing the lower bound of i, $[\![\phi]\!]_{M,j,g}=0$
b. for some interval $k\in I$ containing the upper bound of i, $[\![\phi]\!]_{M,k,g}=1$.

Thus, (9) is true with respect to interval i iff (a) Mary was not in Rome during interval j, (b) Mary was in Rome during interval k. The BECOME-operator is supposed to bridge the gap between the interval j at which it is not true that Mary was in Rome and the interval k at which it is true that Mary was in Rome, as illustrated in Figure 24. Dowty was very much aware of the difficulties with DEF 1, so he tried some additional conditions, such as:

c. there is no non-empty $i'\sqsubset i$ such that a and b hold for i' and i

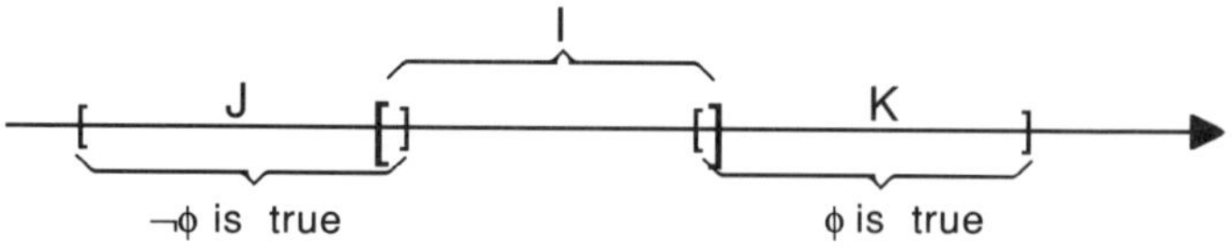

Figure 24 Change defined in terms of a transition between the truth values of propositions evaluated at two different points of time leads to the problem of having a truth-value gap

which introduces the notion of 'smallest interval'. It solves the problem of the predication be–at′(m,r) being true during i itself. However, this solution triggers another problem: requirement (c) is too strong because now the process of becoming must be shortened to just two moments, viz. the lower bound of i and the upper bound of i. This is, of course, out of the question. Dowty (1979: 144) also considers and rejects the solution for change offered by Cresswell (1977).

DEFINITION 2

$[\![\neg\phi T \phi]\!]_{\mathbf{M},i,g}=1$ iff

a. there is an interval j containing the lower bound of i such that ¬ϕ is true at j, and there is an interval k containing the upper bound of i such that ϕ is true at k;

b. (a) does not hold for any non-empty proper subset of i.

where $[\![\neg\phi T\phi]\!]_{\mathbf{M},i,g}$ – or in Cresswell's terms $[\![\phi \text{ AND } \psi]\!]_{\mathbf{M},i,g}$ – would take over the job of $[\![\text{BECOME } \phi]\!]_{\mathbf{M},i,g}$. However, Dowty does not want a two-place operator for change. So he takes (c) as a sort of pragmatic conversational principle which is not part of the truth conditions. This makes it possible for him to allow for some gaps between j and k.[6]

Now, having said this in order to introduce the minimum of equipment to deal with the issues at hand, I would like to look at sentences (9) and (10) from the point of view of aspectuality. First of all, it should be observed that the role of *walk* in (9) is extremely limited. Even the fact that *walk* is an activity verb as distinguished from a mental state verb, for example *long* (*for*), does not really matter for the representation itself. The aspectual 'load' is with the intransitive preposition *to*, which has got a sort of verbal characterization because it is defined as:

(11) a. to ⤳ $\lambda \mathcal{Y} \lambda Y \lambda x \mathcal{Y}(\lambda y[Y(x) \wedge \text{BECOME be–at}'(x,y)])$

b. to Rome ⤳ $\lambda Y \lambda x(Y(x) \wedge \text{BECOME be–at}'(x,r))$

c. walk to Rome ⤳ $\lambda x(\text{walk}'(x) \wedge \text{BECOME be–at}'(x,r))$

where the proper name r being of type $\langle\langle e,t\rangle,t\rangle$, substitutes for $\mathcal{Y}$ by lambda-conversion, so that the PP *to Rome* ends up as (11b). Which is of type

<<*e*,*t*>,<*e*,*t*>>. So it takes *walk* to form (11c). This shows that BECOME is part of *to*, not of *walk* itself. This means that if there is any sense of progress in time it is not put into *walk* but rather into *to*. In (10b), however, the BECOME-operator is inherent to the verb *die* itself, just as in the verbs *cool* and *open*.[7]

(12) a. John opened the door
b. ιx(door′(x)∧CAUSE BECOME (j,open′(x)))

Now, the tense evaluation of sentence (9a) is based on the so-called Past Tense rule which replaces the main verb with its past-tense form (1979: 330). Even though there are modernized versions of it in Dowty's later work, the basic idea remains that ϕ in PASTϕ is the proposition *Mary walk to Rome*. It works smoothly in (10) and (12) but not in (9). The result is (9c).

(9) c. ∃i[PAST(i)∧AT(i,(walk′(m)∧BECOME be–at′(m,r)))]

Strikingly, this evaluation of *Mary walked to Rome* does not occur in Dowty (1979). This is just bad luck, as it would have revealed a fundamental shortcoming of his analysis. For (9a) to be true, it would be required to assert both walk′(m) and BECOME be–at′(m,r) to be simultaneously true at the interval i.[8] However long one makes the interval i, the two propositions making up the second argument of the AT-predicate should hold for exactly the same time interval. One cannot stipulate that walk′(m) should be evaluated first and then the other proposition without making the ∧-connective temporal.[9]

The second main problem with Dowty's system as a theory of aspectuality is that any precise formal account of sentences like (13)–(18) is absent in Dowty (1979, 1982b, 1986).

(13) Judith ate her sandwich
(14) She knitted a sweater
(15) Nick played that concerto
(16) John swam a mile
(17) Joop drank a glass of whisky
(18) Barbara drove in a Cordoba

All these sentences contain verbs that behave like *walk* in that they lexically express an unbounded process, as pointed out sufficiently in the preceding chapters, if not in Verkuyl (1972). Certainly, Dowty gave a precise formal representation of the verb *drive*, but he did that only in sentences like:

(19) John drove the car from Boston to Detroit

where *drive* is inserted in the BECOME-frames provided by the prepositions *from* and *to*, comparable with the way *walk* was inserted in (11). Also, Dowty (1979: 221) gives (schematic) representations of sentences with verbs like *hammer, wipe, drink, sleep*, etc., but these are resultative sentences: *John hammered the metal flat, John drank himself silly*, etc. Likewise, the technical, formal details of transitive verbs like *open, appoint, cool, kill, find, discover* and some other verbs are given, but these verbs all express terminative aspect inherently. Inherently? Yes and no. *Yes*, because to kill someone is to cause a transition and that is lexically expressed by the verb *kill* itself (it can only be undone, for example, by the choice of a bare plural). *No*, because the matter is more complicated, as these verbs all require the presence of a direct object. Given his restricted choice of verbs, Dowty's characterization of these verbs in terms of BECOME is quite understandable. But what can we know about a transitive verb itself (*per se, sui generis*) if it always demands a direct object? Nothing. The BECOME-information could just as well be attributed to the direct object, in the way it is associated with *to Rome* in Dowty's analysis of *walk to Rome*.

So, why did Dowty not pay attention to sentences that were central in Verkuyl (1972), that is, sentences with *eat, play, swim, drink, drive*, etc.? These are verbs clearly expressing unbounded processes, which may or may not be bounded by the particular choice of their complements. Certainly, one may throw at me that I did not pay much attention to the set of *kill*-verbs, but at least it is less dangerous and even defensible, as pointed out below, to model the *kill*-verbs after the *drive*-verbs, rather than the other way around. I guess that Dowty fell into the trap of thinking that there is a clear lexical difference between *eat* and *kill*. Stereotype has it that *eat* is unbounded and that *kill* expresses something bounded. However, is this correct? And if correct, is it structurally relevant? It can only be partly correct: as soon as the complement of verbs like *kill, discover*, etc. is plural, they start to behave like verbs such as *eat, play*, etc. The question boils down to one of whether *kill* means 'to end the life of one animate entity' or 'to end the life of'. I will come back to this point in more detail in chapter 10.1. By his one-sided choice of verbs, Dowty in fact returns to a traditional analysis of aspect in terms of just verbal properties, but now at the level of a holistically taken Montagovian IV. This concludes my second objection.

There is a third one. Compare the following sentences and their formal Dowty-like representations without and with *for hours*:

(20) a. John opened a door

b. $\exists x(\text{door}'(x) \wedge \text{CAUSE BECOME}\ (j,\text{open}'(x)))$

c. #John opened a door for hours
d. $\exists i[\text{PAST}(i_1) \wedge \text{AT}(i_1, [\text{hours}'(i_1) \wedge \forall i_2(i_2 \subseteq i_1 \rightarrow \text{AT}(i_2, \exists x(\text{door}'(x) \wedge \text{CAUSE BECOME}(j, \text{open}'(x))))))])]$

(12) a. John opened the door
b. $\iota x(\text{door}'(x) \wedge \text{CAUSE BECOME}(j, \text{open}'(x)))$
c. #John opened the door for hours
d. $\exists i[\text{PAST}(i_1) \wedge \text{AT}(i_1, [\text{hours}'(i_1) \wedge \forall i_2(i_2 \subseteq i_1 \rightarrow \text{AT}(i_2, \iota x(\text{door}'(x) \wedge \text{CAUSE BECOME}(j, \text{open}'(x))))))])]$

(21) a. John opened doors
b. $\exists x(\text{door}'(x) \wedge \text{CAUSE BECOME}(j, \text{open}'(x)))$
c. John opened doors for hours
d. $\exists i[\text{PAST}(i_1) \wedge \text{AT}(i_1, [\text{hours}'(i_1) \wedge \forall i_2(i_2 \subseteq i_1 \rightarrow \text{AT}(i_2, \exists x(\text{door}'(x) \wedge \text{CAUSE BECOME}(j, \text{open}'(x))))))])]$

Operating within Dowty's own assumptions, we have to observe that the means available to define the difference between the three (a) sentences are restricted to a difference between the existential quantifier and the iota-operator, as shown in the (b) representations. This may account for the difference between *a door* and *the door* in (20a) and (12a). It may even account for the difference between (20c) and (12c), because the definite description $\iota x(\text{door}'(x))$ is not subjected to the universal quantifier $\forall i_2$, as Dowty (1979: 79) explains. So the difference between (20c) and (12c) might be explained in terms of a difference in scopal behaviour. However, the problem for Dowty is that (20c) and (12c) show aspectually the same behaviour, as against (21c): (12a) and (20a) are terminative, (21a) is durative. Dowty (1979: 80) proposes (21d) as the representation for the durative (21a) occurring in (21c). Dowty can make no difference between (12a) and (21a) as far as I can see. Actually, Dowty (1979) does not formally represent one single terminative sentence with a singular indefinite direct object NP nor one with a definite NP.[10] The only way for him would be to work with scopal differences, for example by getting $\exists x.\text{door}'(x)$ out of the scope of $\forall i_2$. But would this have explanatory value?

Summarizing, I would like to conclude that on close scrutiny there is something quite striking in Dowty's treatment. He does not treat quantified NPs (*three sandwiches*, *some sandwiches*, *all sandwiches*, *many sandwiches*). Of course, in his explanation of Montague Grammar, some of these quantifying expressions occur, but they do not play a role in his aspectual analysis. Heavy emphasis is put on sentences with proper names, indefinite and definite singular

NPs and on prepositional complements. However, apart from proper names only the last category receives a formal treatment. For example, much attention is paid to the sentence *John is drawing a circle*, but we do not get a representation of the terminative sentence *John drew a circle*. As already said, there is no single sentence in which the role of a quantifier in a sentence expressing terminative aspect is given attention, except for sentences like (20c) and (21c). There we find some attempt to use scope as an explanatory means, but only rudimentary and with the exclusion of sentences like (12c). The root of these troubles is the holistic approach and the focussing on a restricted class of lexical predicates, which happen to block a direct view on aspectuality.

9.3 Homogeneity and the alleged Imperfective Paradox

The existence of the Imperfective Paradox appears to be taken for granted in the literature. Dowty (1979: 133) discusses the following examples from Vendler (1957) and Kenny (1963):

(22) John was drawing a circle
(23) John drew a circle

(24) John was pushing a cart
(25) John pushed a cart

He characterizes the Imperfective Paradox as the problem of accounting for the fact that (22) '*does not* entail that he brought a circle into existence', whereas (24) entails (25).

Dowty uses the Imperfective Paradox as a test separating aspectual classes. There are two versions: *Homogeneity* and *Imperfective*, which were discussed in chapter 2.3. Both are supposed to separate Vendler's Accomplishments (and Achievements) from Activities (and States). They are repeated here:

DEFINITION 3: *Homogeneity*
If V is an activity verb, then *x V-ed for y time* entails that at any time *x V-ed* was true. If V is an accomplishment verb, then *x V-ed for y time* does not entail that *x V-ed* was true during any time within y at all.

DEFINITION 4: *Imperfective*
If V is an activity verb, then *x is (now) V-ing* entails that *x has V-ed*. If V is an accomplishment verb, then *x is (now) V-ing* entails *x has not (yet) V-ed.*

DEF 3 says that if *draw* is an Accomplishment verb, *John drew a circle for an hour* does not entail that *John drew a circle* was true during any time in that hour. In chapter 2.3, I made some objections against *Homogeneity*, but here it may be added that there is something wrong with the Imperfective Paradox itself. What is unclear in its formulation is the phrase *does not entail that*. Dowty (1979: 57) says: 'If John walked for an hour, then, at any time during that hour it was true that John walked. But if John painted a picture for an hour, then it is not the case that he painted a picture at any time of that hour.' The idea is that if (22) is true for a certain interval, there is no proper interval during which (23) is true.

Now, interestingly enough, this criterion applies only to a certain set of cases: it does not always differentiate between Accomplishments and Activities. Consider the sentences in (26) and (27).

(26) a. John has drawn some circles
b. John has eaten a piece of fruit-cake
c. Judith had taken at most three sandwiches

(27) a. John has drawn three circles
b. John has eaten a pound of fruit-cake
c. Judith had taken at least three sandwiches

The two sets of sentences are all terminative, and according to Dowty they contain Accomplishment verbs, as shown in (28) and (29).

(28) a. John has drawn some circles in an hour
b. John has eaten a piece of fruit-cake in an hour
c. John has polished at most three pairs of boots in an hour

d. John has drawn three circles in an hour
e. John has eaten a pound of fruit-cake in an hour
f. Judith had taken at least three sandwiches in an hour

(29) a. #John has drawn some circles for hours
b. #John has eaten a piece of fruit-cake for hours
c. #For hours Judith ate at most three sandwiches

d. #John has drawn three circles for hours
e. #John has eaten a pound of fruit-cake for hours
f. #For hours Judith had taken at least three sandwiches

So it is predicted by Dowty that all sentences in (26) and (27) should have the same behaviour with respect to *Homogeneity*. However, in (26a) but not in

(27a) one can 'go into' the interval i and meet a proper subinterval i′ which satisfies the same predication as i itself. This goes for *a piece of fruit-cake* as well, even more compellingly. It also holds for (26c): if you have mailed two out of three letters you satisfy the predicate 'to mail at most three letters'. And if Mary happened to have mailed fifty letters in consecutive heaps of about five or ten, then after the fourth mailing the predicate 'mail many letters' can be applied. It is intriguing why *a pound of* deviates so strongly from *a piece of*, whereas they do not show any aspectual differences. Note that the property of monotone decrease or increase does not explain the phenomenon, because *at most* is monotone decreasing and *some* is monotone increasing.

As to DEF 4, we encounter similar difficulties. It says that if *John is drawing a circle* is true for the period i, then it (necessarily) follows that *John has not yet drawn a circle* is true for a period i′, where $i' \subseteq i$. Are there Accomplishments which fail the basic type test? Indeed there are, as shown by the sentences in (30)–(33).

(30) a. John is drawing some circles
b. John is eating a piece of fruit-cake
c. John is taking at most five sandwiches

(31) a. John has not yet drawn some circles
b. John has not yet eaten a piece of fruit-cake
c. Judith has not yet taken at most five sandwiches

(32) a. John is drawing three circles
b. John is eating a pound of fruit-cake
c. Judith is taking at least three sandwiches

(33) a. John has not yet drawn three circles
b. John has not yet eaten a pound of fruit-cake
c. Judith has not yet taken at least three sandwiches

For example, it is not the case that (30a) entails the truth of (31a): John may have drawn some circles at the final point of i′ and has thereby satisfied the requirement for (30a) to be true, so even if he would be interrupted, (31a) would be true. The same applies *mutatis mutandis* to the (b) and the (c) cases. *Imperfective* works only for the cases in (32) and (33).

These data are somewhat startling. People believed adamantly in the existence of the Imperfective Paradox (people will continue to refer to it even though they know that there is something wrong with it), whereas a more careful treatment of the data would have pointed in another direction. Which direction?

Well, Vendler, Dowty and all the others who have discussed the Imperfective Paradox have been restricting themselves to sentences like (34), so the discussion about the Imperfective Paradox has been restricted mainly to sentences with a singular direct object or to examples with directional PPs.

(34) a. John drew a circle
b. Mary walked to Rome
c. She painted a picture
d. The sheriff of Nottingham jailed Robin Hood
e. He built a house

In these sentences, the paradox appears to work. But does this mean that it is the property of homogeneity of an interval which is the decisive factor? Of course not. It does not even mean that there is a paradox. There are other explanations, certainly within an additive approach in which the Progressive Form is nothing but a means to express that one is involved in building up structure. A formal description of the Progressive Form will be given in chapter 13.8, where it will be shown that it is possible to give an explanation of the difference between sentences like (30) and (32).

9.4 Homogeneity and quantification

Taylor (1977) and Cresswell (1977, 1979b) have extended the discussion about evaluation at intervals by asking themselves what would happen in sentences with logical quantifiers like *every*, *all*, etc. Some of their views will be discussed here, because their work has been influential, but also because it shows that they impeded the discussion by focussing too much on (naive) physics and too little on the linguistic side of the problems.

In view of sentences like (35), Taylor adjusted his Kinesis-concept (6) of heterogeneity:[11]

(35) John is polishing all the boots

This sentence can be true if John polished the boots consecutively. The temporal condition corresponding to this is (36):

(36) if $[\![\phi]\!]_{i}=1$, then $\exists i'{:}i \subseteq i'$ & $[\![\phi]\!]_{i'}=1$ & $\exists i''{:}i'' \subseteq i'$ & $[\![\phi]\!]_{i''}=1$ & $\forall i'''$: $i''' \subset i''$ $([\![\phi]\!]_{i'''}=1 \rightarrow \exists\, i''''{:}\ i''' \subset i'''' \subset i'$ & $[\![\phi]\!]_{i''''}=0)$
Pictorially, e.g.:

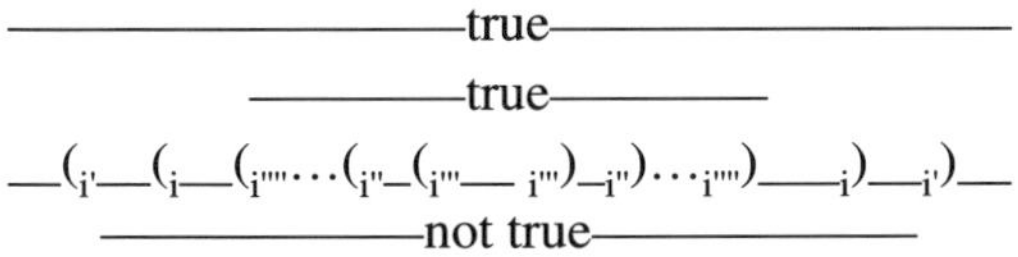

Applied to a verb like *build* or *polish*, this means that (6) is more or less relaxed; (36) expresses (roughly) that there are falsity-holes, indicated by '...' in the interval i′, as well as truth-lines. It says that there may be proper subintervals for which the predication holds, though there must be larger proper intervals for which the predication is not true. Thus, i′ may contain several of such subperiods i‴ which together constitute the event.

To ensure that all individuals involved in the predication, that is, the boots, are related to the subintervals constituting the interrupted event, Taylor added a postulate to (36), which applied to (35) says that if (37) is true, for all boots y, the assertion Polish(j, y) is true at i.

(37) For all y∈Boot, there is an i′ (i′⊂i) and Polish(j,y) is true at i′ and for all moments t (t⊂i), there is a boot y and there is an i″ (t⊂i″) such that Polish(j,y) is true at i″.

> even when John's polishing of the boots is consecutive, there will be a time – viz. the time stretching from his applying the first lick of polish to the first boot, up to his laying aside of the last – which meets the condition imposed in (37) (assuming, as seems reasonable, that we are prepared to count any moment in a pause between his laying aside the n-th boot and his first brush-stroke on the (n+1)th as belonging either to the time of his polishing the n-th boot, or to that of his polishing the (n+1)th). (p. 216)

If the whole period t of John's consecutive boot-polishing performance would count as the period in which it is true that he polished a certain boot b_i, then it should be true that 'at any moment within t it is true that John is polishing boot b_i _ even for example, at a moment when he has laid b_i aside as finished, and begun applying to polish boot b_{i+1}' (1977: 217). A pragmatic principle says that a speaker must not assert that John is polishing b_i 'on his belief that the current moment falls with a time t of John's polishing every boot ..., since the testimony of his senses informs him that the current moment falls within a minimal period of John's polishing of boot b_{i+1} but not of boot b_i' (Taylor 1977: 218).

Taylor's argument is given in some detail in order to illustrate how deeply Taylor is committed to accounting for knowledge of the world rather than for the interplay between the constituents making up a sentence. It is part of the task of linguists to explain why it is that sentences like (38)–(42)

(38) John polished all the boots
(39) John polished the three boots
(40) John polished three boots
(41) John polished three pairs of boots
(42) John polished six boots

are suitable, without being ambiguous, to apply to situations in which he either polished all the boots simultaneously (think of an electric machine) or in all sorts of groups or one by one. What about cases like (39)–(42)? Here exactly the same applies as to (38). One might argue that (41) is more homogeneous than (40), because there may be a certain structural repetition involved which is lacking in (40): there being pairs of boots. So if he polished them pairwise, there was some sense of structural repetition after the second pair. But now what about (42)? Here both possibilities seem to be included.

So, the problems are: when exactly is something going on during a period structurally similar? And what counts as such? They boil down to: how relevant would it be for linguistic purposes? The answer to these questions is: it is not a linguistic (structural) problem, but rather a problem of our knowledge of the world and of our cognitive structure. I agree in this respect with Cresswell, who observes that it is doubtful whether the concept of polishing can be analysed: 'We learn what polishing is by watching and seeing; and so I assume that my readers have been observant enough to be able to recognize in any situation when over a period of time a polishing is taking place' (1977: 11).

In general, the difference between the homogeneity of *fall*, *polish* and *chuckle* is not of interest to the present aspectual theory. The PLUG-grammar of chapter 7 simply identifies the set W whose members are in the intersection of the set of boots and the set of polished entities such that W is partitioned. This account is not interested at all in last licks or first brush-strokes.

As a last example of the homogeneity tradition, consider the two following sentences from Cresswell (1977) and their (simplified) tenseless analyses.

(43) a. Every student left
b. $\forall x[\text{student}'(x)\rightarrow\exists i'[i'\subseteq i\wedge\text{leave}'(i')(x)]\wedge\forall i''[\forall x(\text{student}'(x)\rightarrow \exists i'[i'\subseteq i''\wedge\text{leave}'(i')(x)]\rightarrow i\subseteq i'']]]$

(44) a. John polished every boot
b. $\forall z[\text{boot}(z)\rightarrow\exists i'[i'\subseteq i\wedge\text{polish}(z)(j)(i')]\wedge\forall i''[[\forall z[\text{boot}'(z)\rightarrow \exists i'[i'\subseteq i''\wedge\text{polish}'(z)(j)(i')]\rightarrow i\subseteq i'']]]$

Sentence (43a) is true at i just in case i is the smallest interval such that for each student x there is a subinterval i′ of i during which x leaves.[12] However, Krifka (1989b: 120f.) raises a serious problem with regard to Cresswell's analysis: it does not work for sentences like *Every girl sings*. Suppose Anna, Barbara and Caecilia sing during the intervals [9,10], [10,11], and [11,12], respectively. Cresswell's definition of *every* makes i=[9.59,11.01] the smallest interval (if we restrict ourselves to minutes). This makes *Every girl sings* only true at i, as exemplified in Figure 25. According to Krifka, the sentence should also be true

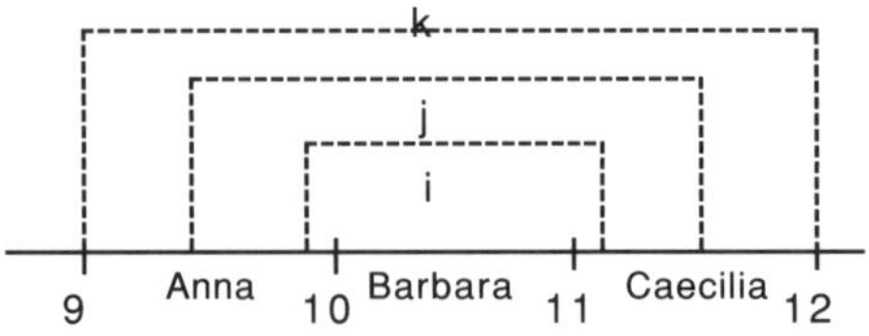

Figure 25 This picture shows the problem raised by an analysis based on the notion of 'smallest interval': *every girl sings* is true only at i

at j and k. Note that Cresswell did not treat *Every girl sings*. His definition of *every* only applies to Taylor's Kinesis-predicates.

Even though objections like these can be made, it must be observed that the interesting part of Cresswell's analysis does not lie in his attempt to suit Taylor's purpose with respect to homogeneity. Its real value lies in the idea that there is a correspondence between atemporal entities (girls, boots) and subintervals of a larger interval. This is the feature which makes Cresswell's analysis of change still useful in spite of his DEF 2. Logically it is independent of the property of homogeneity. So, if (39b) and (40b) would be reduced to

(45) $\forall x[\text{student}'(x) \rightarrow \exists i'[i' \subseteq i \wedge \text{leave}'(i')(x)]]$

(46) $\forall z[\text{boot}(z) \rightarrow \exists i'[i' \subseteq i \wedge \text{polish}'(z)(j)(i')]]$

one would have a small bridge from the realm of homogeneity to the partition analysis advocated in chapter 7 and extended temporally in chapter 13.

9.5 Breaking up a notion

Homogeneity in Taylor's sense is basically a notion that has structurally nothing to do with aspect construal, the very simple reason being that the verbs *eat*, *walk*, *buy* and *discover* in spite of their obvious differences with respect to homogeneity, do the same job with respect to the composition of terminative and durative aspect in (47)–(58):

(47) Judith ate a sandwich
(48) Judith ate three sandwiches
(49) Judith ate sandwiches
(50) John walked to the store
(51) John walked to three stores
(52) John walked to stores

(53) Judith bought a sandwich
(54) Judith bought three sandwiches

(55) Judith bought sandwiches
(56) John discovered a treasure
(57) John discovered three treasures
(58) John discovered treasures

The question is whether it is advisable to distinguish a Kinesis-predicate ‘eat three sandwiches’ from an Energeia-predicate ‘eat sandwiches’, if it is clear that the predicate ‘eat’ itself is a constant factor. As observed before, it would have been better if more attention would have been paid to the behaviour of terminative sentences with plural NPs rather than with the definite singular NP only. It is easy to be led into the concept of the non-subinterval property if you deal with (56) rather than with (57), or with (12a) *John opened the door* rather than with *John opened three doors*. It is clear that whatever (56) pertains to, it is less partible than (57) in the same way as one coin is less partible than three coins. The sequence (56) *a treasure* (singleton) < (57) *three treasures* (finite collection) < (58) *treasures* (unbounded collection) corresponds to the increasing degree of divisibility, and with this an increasing degree of homogeneity. This holds for the other sentences as well. So the question is whether or not the requirement that the complex predicate ‘eat three sandwiches’ be applicable to a subinterval is an artefact.

It is not unreasonable to call *walk* in itself more homogeneous than *buy*, as the discussion about a split-up in the Energeia-class has shown. But it means that there are two separate issues involved, which are wrongly interwoven in the approaches to homogeneity discussed above. The first one is that speakers of English will by and large agree on the following scale (with a certain degree of overlap between neighbouring items):

fly – fall – polish – walk – dial – buy – discover

One may say that the more to the left a verb is located on the scale the more it pertains to a homogeneous eventuality. This is what one may call *lexical* homogeneity, which will be discussed in chapter 10.1. This concept is and is not relevant for aspect construal: it is not, as long as one keeps thinking about cakes and sultanas (though this may be interesting for philosophers); it is, as it opens the way to the additive dynamic approach. The second issue is the property of divisibility of the VP-denotation, the leading idea being that ⟦discover three treasures⟧ is a minimal semantic object in the sense that a proper subpart of it cannot be called *discover three treasures*. However, the issue of divisibility is clearly related to the direct object NPs in (47)–(58). To say that (56) and (57) are heterogeneous (Kinesis-)predicates is to ignore two important facts:

(a) that John in (57) may have discovered his three treasures one after the other, or simultaneously, or in groups; this means that the notion of plurality is involved, in the sense that a certain bounded event-type 'discover a treasure' is actualized more than once but at most three times; (b) related to this is the fact that exactly the same holds for (58), only one cannot determine the cardinality of the set of events 'discover a treasure'. In other words, it is not the count-mass distinction that is at issue, it is rather the count ([+SQA])-noncount ([–SQA])-distinction, as pointed out in Verkuyl (1972).

9.6 Conclusion

Of course, one likes to know what happens between Von Wright's $-\phi$ and ϕ. There are two ways to deal with it: (a) a 'top-down' approach correlating $-\phi$ and ϕ with the begin-point and end-point of an interval and asking questions about its internal structure; (b) the 'bottom-top' approach inherent to, for example, the localistic framework, building up a structure resulting into a structure having a begin-point and an end-point at which $-\phi$ and ϕ hold, respectively. The notion of homogeneity was given a central place in the first approach. From the point of view of aspectual composition, this approach boils down to a holistic treatment in which the VP is taken as a sort of complex verb having a variable open place very much comparable with the English complex verb *call* X, where X may be *up*, *off*, *forth*, *forward*, etc. VPs like *walk to Rome*, *walk home* and *walk in the park* are treated in this way. My conclusion is that it is only by taking the elements of this sort of complex verb in their own right that one may have the hope of finding out what the verb contributes and what is contributed by its complement.

10 *Localism and additive structure*

10.0 Introduction

In this chapter, three issues are central. The first one follows naturally from the line of argument in chapter 9. It will be argued in section 10.1 that the notion of homogeneity may apply to verbs but that this notion then is no longer of interest for aspectual theory. In terms of Taylor's sultana metaphor: the VP *walk to Rome* should not bear comparison with a fruit-cake, nor the VP *walk* in *John walked* with gold, or cake for that matter. By dealing with the sultana-issue at the level of lexical knowledge, one clears the way for a different approach in which the verb and its complement have different contributions to make.

This opens up the second issue: the verb induces temporal structure to which the information associated with its complement systematically relates. As a result, the notion of Path emerges: the fusion of temporal and atemporal structure which can be bounded (terminative) or unbounded (durative). The contribution of verbs expressing change to the construction of temporal structure will be discussed in section 10.2 as a first leg up to formalization in chapter 13.

The third issue is built on top of the others: the question is what the terminative (47), (48), (50) and (51) have in common, and what the durative sentences (49) and (52). For (48) and (51) this question can be made more concrete: if there is a mapping between the temporal structure induced by *eat* and the set of three sandwiches, what is the mapping relation between the walk-structure and the denotation of the PP-complement (including the preposition)? This question will emerge as one of the central questions of this chapter because it obliges us to show formally how the PLUG-grammar deals with this correspondence. Note that the question is put with respect to (48) and (51). In my view, this gives a much better view of (47) and (50), in particular of (50): the strategy will be to bring (48) and (51) on a (terminative) par and then apply the correspondence to the other two sentences.

In Jackendoff (1983, 1990, to appear), which also belongs to the localistic tradition resuscitated by Gruber (1976), the question about what the sentences (47)–(49) have in common with (50)–(52), has been dealt with in sufficient detail to justify a principled discussion between localistic and non-localistic approaches. Also, as chapter 2 did not deal with sentences of the form (50)–(52), it will be profitable to discuss Jackendoff's analysis. First, a general picture is given of Jackendoff's notion of Path in section 10.3; then, a model-theoretic extrapolation of his aspectual analysis of sentences like (47)–(52) will be given in section 10.4 along the lines of Verkuyl and Zwarts (1992). This makes it possible to apply the [+SQA]-notion also to NPs in PP-complements. As a result, VP-aspectuality, called $[\pm T]_{VP}$ in chapter 1.2, for both (47)–(49) and (50)–(52) can be characterized in a precise way. So, these sections serve two purposes: (a) to give a good view of the virtues of a localistic approach; (b) to indicate how localism can be 'neutralized' by capturing it in more standard set-theoretical representations. In this sense, chapter 10 as a whole prepares the formal ground for the extension of PLUG in chapter 13.

10.1 Lexical homogeneity

It is not unreasonable to assume that some information about the manner of motion should be included in the verbal entry. Thus, in order to distinguish *John walked home* from *John flew home* one might include predicates such as THROUGH THE AIR in the entry for *fly* as restrictive modifiers of the function expressing positional change, as for example, in Gruber (1976), Miller (1972), Miller and Johnson-Laird (1976), Jackendoff (1976, 1983, 1990). That is, these modifiers are taken as expressing properties of the Path of the Theme, that is, as the 'space' connecting Source and Goal, as in (59) and (60), which occur in Jackendoff (1976).[13]

(59) walk
$\text{GO}(NP_{Theme}, NP_{Source}, NP_{Goal})$
BY LAND

(60) fly
$\text{GO}(NP_{Theme}, NP_{Source}, NP_{Goal})$
THROUGH THE AIR

For those not acquainted with the thematic formalism, it might be helpful to first explain the GO-predication in terms of Jackendoff (1972, 1976), where the expression of change in sentences like (47)–(58) is represented as (61).

(61) $\text{GO}_{\alpha}(X,Y,Z)$

The change-predicate GO is taken as a three-place move-relation between a Theme, a Source and a Goal. The values for X, Y and Z fulfil specific so-called thematic roles. They constitute the argument structure associated with the verb. In this sense, the logical standard form of n-place predication $P^n(a_1,\ldots,a_n)$ differs crucially from the localistic format in (61) in that in the latter X, Y and Z fulfil specific so-called thematic roles in a three-place pattern. The basic idea is that X is the Theme (the moving entity), Y is the Source (where the movement begins) and Z the Goal (where the movement ends): X moves from Y to Z, where Y and Z are connected in the sense that they are the initial point and terminal point of the Path of the Theme. For example, in (50) John (X) moves from an unspecified position (Y) to the store (Z), whereas in (48) three sandwiches 'go' from some unspecified position to Judith. Thus, the localistic approach underscores the idea that arguments of an n-place predicate have specific semantic roles in a three-place scheme, specific in the sense that they express positions in temporal structure. For example, the (simplified) logical predication E(x,y) for (48) is rejected in favour of (61).

If *walk* and *fly* should be distinguished from one another by these sorts of restrictive predicates, it might be appropriate to introduce a predicate HOMOGENEOUS as well in order to be able to distinguish between predicates. To this end, Verkuyl (1978) developed the notion 'Path of the Theme' based on the observation that if one says (62),

(62) John walked home

the path traced in Figure 26 may have been followed.[14] John started his walk at his office P_1; at a bookshop P_2 he realized that he had forgotten something, so at t_2 he was back at P_1; then he found himself at P_3 at t_3 after having taken a slightly different route by taking a parallel street, P_3 being a bar, where he stayed longer than the sum total of (t_0,t_3) and (t_3,t_n), and finally he reached his home. My conclusion at the time was that the notion of a Path turns out to apply to an essentially spatio-temporal unit, and that a Path of the Theme should be defined on the basis of this semantic object being *at* a series of certain spatio-temporal positions.

So, for the analysis of an event like John's walking home described by the sentence *John walked home* (63) turned out to be more appropriate to work with than (59).

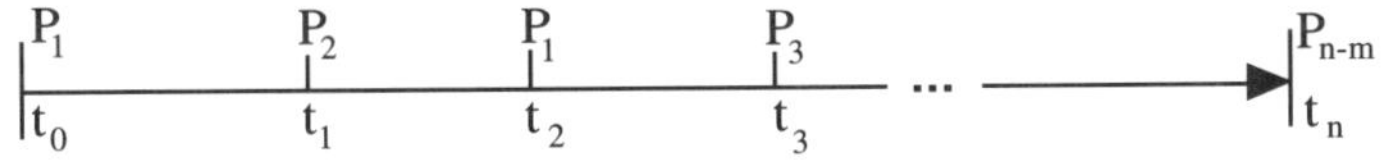

Figure 26 John may have gone back and yet he is on his way home

(63) walk
GO(NP_{Theme}, NP_{Source}, NP_{Goal})
BY LAND ($\pi(NP_{Theme})$)

The function π is taken as mapping the denotation of the NP_{Theme} to the set of spatio-temporal positions which it goes through. In terms of model-theoretic domains, the definition used in Verkuyl (1978) would be something like:

DEFINITION 1. The Path of a Theme x is assigned to an entity x by the partial function π: $\mathbf{D}_e \rightarrow \mathbf{D}_L{}^{\mathbf{DT}}$ defined by:[15]

(64) $x \mapsto \ell$, where $\ell = \{<t,p>: [\![AT(p)(x)]\!]_{\mathbf{M},t}=1\}$

where $\mathbf{D}_T$ is a discretely ordered set of moments of time, $\mathbf{D}_L$ is the domain of spatial coordinates p. The path ℓ itself was taken as a function from $\mathbf{D}_T$ into $\mathbf{D}_L$. $\mathbf{D}_L$ can be taken as the set of (either mental or 'real-world') coordinates at which certain entities are located. It could be points, but one might think of regions as well, or even of three-dimensional spaces. In this way, ℓ was taken as a sequence of the spatio-temporal positions whose spatial positions $p=\ell(t)$ are positions in one of the semantic fields specified by the V, viz. Position, Possession, Identification and Circumstance. Below, this picture will be modified, in particular by taking $\mathbf{D}_T$ more neutrally as a set of indices.

The basic idea underlying DEF 1 is that x 'goes through' a function ℓ in which spatial positions are dependent on temporal indexed times. So, as the set of natural numbers from which the time indices are taken is well ordered, in (62) π(John) is an ordered sequence of spatio-temporal positions, say ℓ_{walk}, which by the information of its complement *home* becomes:

(65) $\ell_{walk\ home}$={<t_0, office>, <t_1, book shop>, <t_2, office>, ..., <t_4, bar>, ..., <t_n, home>}

In the next section, I will return to the distinction between ℓ_V, that is, the unbounded function associated with the verb V, and ℓ_{VP}, in which information coming from the complement of the verb is inserted.

It is important to observe that $\mathbf{D}_T$ was taken as a discrete structure, whereas the underlying temporal structure itself is dense: the union of all intervals between the counting points from $\mathbf{D}_T$ is an interval. In Verkuyl (1978), the use of two different temporal systems was clarified with the help of a spatial analogy in a chessboard situation. Consider a situation in which a chess player moves the queen from d2 to d7 on the seventeenth move. And suppose that he does so by moving the queen on the board itself without lifting it. From the point of view of spatial particles, the fields form the (discretely) ordered sequence of sets of particles $\text{Move}_{17}=\{d_i: \textsc{at}(d_i)(\text{queen})\}$, each d_i representing a set of spatial particles. The union of the fields d_i (66)

(66) $$\bigcup_{i\in 8} d_i$$

is, in fact, the piece of wood (or cardboard) occupied by the d-fields. It has a dense structure as the queen physically moved from its position on d2 to its position on d7 uninterruptedly. However, from the point of view of chess, what really happens is that the queen operates in a discretely ordered structure which is part of a coordinate system, say $\textsc{chessboard}\subset\textbf{Alphabet}\times\textbf{N}$. From this point of view, the movement from d2 to d7 takes place in a structure which is discretely ordered, just as we move discretely in our diary from 2 April to 7 April by jumping over the intermediate stretch even though we know that underlying the calendar system, time is dense. It is indices which create the fields, so to say. It is also indices which create the feeling of progress in time by counting. This view on temporal structure is supported by psychological studies such as Miller and Johnson-Laird's (1976) which observes that 'there are psychological studies to support the assumption that time is experienced in quantized moments' (1976: 76).

In order to assign internal structure to the walk, one often takes as walking positions stretches between shops, bars or some other elements which can help to divide the path of the moving object into subintervals that can be used as reference points. Imagine yourself sitting in a car driving on an endless motorway: your position is changing in accordance with the properties of the system **R** of real numbers: density and convexity are warranted (Van Benthem 1983a). However, the path covered by the movement is assigned structure in terms of **N**: one counts the mileage, or the number of exits, or the number of towns, and so on. The only method to obtain this structure is to count discretely. This is what aspectuality seems to be about. I think the analogy between this chess situation and John's walking situation is quite striking in important respects. What we are basically doing is extracting from a dense structure some part that is equivalent to the structure inherent to the set of natural numbers. In particular, we use its well-ordering property. This enables us to jump from one position to another without having gaps, given means to connect **R** and **N**. These means will be incorporated into the formalism in chapter 13.

This being said about John's walk home, the question was raised: how homogeneous is *walk*? And what does this property contribute to aspect? My answer in 1978 was to construct a set $\mathcal{P}_{\text{walk}}$ of all possible ordered pairs of arbitrarily chosen walking positions in the walking Path of a Theme which is part of $\ell_{\text{walk home}}$, as shown in (67):

(67) $\mathcal{P}_{walk} = \{<\ell(t_0),\ell(t_1)>, <\ell(t_0),\ell(t_2)>, <\ell(t_0),\ell(t_3)>, \ldots ,<\ell(t_1),\ell(t_3)>, <\ell(t_1),\ell(t_4)>,\ldots, <\ell(t_{m-1}),\ell(t_m)>\}$

Each pair $<\ell(t_k),\ell(t_n)>$, where $k < n$, represents the movement of the Theme through the spatial interval $(\ell(t_k),\ell(t_n))$. The idea was that it should be possible to compare the intervals structurally. The best analogy is to put John's walk as part of his walking home on a film tape, and to see $\mathcal{P}_{walk}$ as the set of all possible partial replays, given a certain minimum (at least one step or at least two steps). In this way, homogeneity was defined in terms of the notion of Path:

DEFINITION: ℓ is homogeneous iff all members of the set $\mathcal{P}_{walk}$ constructed from it are structurally similar.

There are two obvious problems with this definition. The first one is that it is not really clear what a structural similarity between members of $\mathcal{P}_{walk}$ is. The second (not totally unrelated) problem is that verbs expressing change allow for a variety of ways in which the change can take place. To begin with the latter: John's walk is less homogeneous if he takes drinks in bars on his way to the store than if he had walked straight home. It is very important to observe that this has nothing to do with *home*, it is a property of *walk* itself. On the other hand, if we analyse the content of a verb like *fall* with respect to a paratrooper jumping from a plane, we have to allow that his path can be less homogeneous by horizontal gliding, certainly if compared with the path of an apple falling from a tree. The path of the falling paratrooper is less homogeneous than the path of the falling apple. Again, this is a lexical property, determined by our knowledge of the world. (People who do not know about paratroopers might take *fall* as being much more homogeneous than people who do know about horizontal gliding.) Given these considerations, Verkuyl (1978) introduced a relativized notion of (lexical) homogeneity.

DEFINITION: ℓ is α-homogeneous iff the majority of members of the associated set $\mathcal{P}_V$ are structurally similar.[16]

This definition led to entries like (68) and (69), where $\ell = \pi(NP_{Theme})$:

(68) *walk*

GO(NP_{Theme}, NP_{Source}, NP_{Goal})
α-HOMOGENEOUS($\pi(NP_{Theme})$)
BY LAND($\pi(NP_{Theme})$)

(69) *buy*
GO(NP_{Theme}, NP_{Source}, NP_{Goal})
HETEROGENEOUS($\pi(NP_{Theme})$)
POSSESSIONAL($\pi(NP_{Theme})$)

and where the value of α is a value on a scale determined by our stereotypes or by the particular needs of the situation we are speaking about. The first problem was solved by the consideration that native speakers happen to have some idea of homogeneity which they agree upon on the basis of their lexical knowledge of verbs. So, this problem is captured under the wide cloak of α.

The verb *buy* is, given these assumptions, heterogeneous because stereotypically the majority of intervals in $\mathcal{P}_{buy}$ is dissimilar. This amounts to saying that *buy* is α-HOMOGENEOUS($\pi(NP_{Theme})$) with α below a certain point on a homogeneity scale. In other words, lexical homogeneity is a sliding scale like a thermometer with heterogeneity below a certain degree. Many so-called heterogeneous predicates can be applied to quite homogeneous situations. A verb like *tear apart* looks quite inhomogeneous when applied to a relation between a human person and an object. When applied to continents it seems to become more homogeneous.

Summarizing, aspectually the property of lexical homogeneity which sneaked into the holistic treatment of the VP as a sort of verb in chapter 9, turns out to be a dead end. There is nothing of interest in the difference between the degrees of homogeneity of *eat*, *walk* and *discover* for aspectual theory. However, the analysis of lexical homogeneity turned out to be rewarding in quite a different way: the notion of Path that was used to define lexical homogeneity, is useful for the analysis of aspect. So, we will turn now to the notion of Path from an aspectual point of view.

10.2 The Verb as odometer

Given the linguistic tradition of localism, it is conceptually very tempting to think of the verb *walk* in *walk home* in terms of an odometer indicating the 'mileage' counted from a point zero. However wild this metaphor might seem at first glance, it is a very natural one in the tradition of localism in which change in a domain of interpretation is conceptualized in terms of a movement along a Path (ὁδος) from a point zero to or towards an end-point. Taken this way, progress in time must be expressed by a sort of numerical index contributed by the verb, which is to be 'tuned to' its internal argument. That is, complement denotations like ⟦home⟧ and ⟦to the store⟧ are to be connected

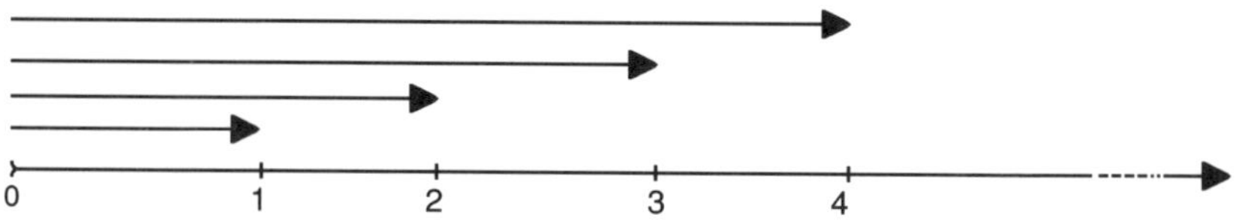

Figure 27 This figure expresses what underlies an odometer in a driving car: each natural number k that appears on the odometer represents the stretch (0,k). Verbs expressing change can be compared with an 'active' odometer: their semantics represent stretches (Paths) having an origin

with the unbounded index system induced by the verb. Of course, there are many complications involved in getting this picture clear, but I will put these aside temporarily to get the main issue involved in the right conceptual focus. A way to think of an odometer is in terms of a picture like Figure 27. Each number indicates the sum total of units which have been covered from point zero. Figure 27 captures the possibility of relating the interval structure to the use of two different interactive temporal systems. One is based on **N**, which allows us to 'jump' in time. It would cover our mental experience of progress in time. The other one is based on **R**. One may think of [+ADD TO]-verbs as exactly expressing this sort of structure. It captures the notion of progress in time and space connected with these verbs. More formally, this sort of structure can be captured in terms of a successor function operating on intervals, taken here in their most neutral (mathematical) sense. So, one might think of a function s: $I \to I$, where $I=\{(0,n): n \in \mathbf{N}\}$, and defined as:[17]

DEFINITION 2:
$\forall i \in I$, if $i=(0,n)$, $s(i)=(0,n+1)$

This function provides the 'real time' in a model, either directly (by taking $\mathbf{R} \subseteq \mathbf{T}$, as part of the time axis) or indirectly (by mapping **R** into **T**). If we use the daily odometer in a car driving from A (where we have put it at 0) to B, we look at natural numbers (more precisely ordinals) passing by. These natural numbers 'compress' the dense structure of the path we are covering into the discrete structure we are used to handle. If we see a number m we know that we have driven m miles from point zero. So m is an ordinal short for the m-th position in the structure of the interval (0,m). It is obvious that the function s as defined in DEF 2 may be used in the construction of the Path by the path function π in (64).[18]

It is important to see that interval structures of the sort exemplified in Figure 27 are defined by DEF 2 as filters in the sense of the Theory of Generalized Quantification, as pointed out in Verkuyl (1987a, 1989). That is, they are closed under intersection: for any $i,j \in I$, $i \in I$ & $j \in I \Rightarrow i \cap j \in I$ (see DEF 4.7, (107)). This deals effectively with the Von Wright problem of a truth value gap. There is no problem at all if the valuation takes place with respect to (0,n), because this automatically includes the valuation with respect to (0,n–1), provided that the information yielded by the internal argument of the verb is dealt with in terms of being related to n.

In Van Benthem (1983a: 195), a postulate is discussed regarding the possibility of interpreting the Von Wrightian operator T in interval structure as a conjunction so as to provide for a 'durational flavour in many ordinary contexts'. Given a model **M** with a period structure, Van Benthem's principle is formulated as (70).

(70) $\mathbf{M} \models \phi T \psi[i]$, if $\mathbf{M} \models \phi[i]$ & for some immediate successor j of i, $\mathbf{M} \models \psi[j]$

This says that **M** makes $\phi T \psi$ true at i just in case ϕ is true in **M** at interval i and ψ is true in **M** at some immediate successor j of i. Van Benthem suggests that (70) brings about directionality.

If the domain $\mathbf{D_T}$ were relabelled $\mathbf{D_I}$, to underscore the use of times as indices, the Path-notion inherent to DEF 1 and Figure 27 may be linked to (70) by assuming that ϕ and ψ are propositions of the form AT(p)(x) and that AT(p)(x)[k] is true if $p = \ell(k)$ that is, if the function value of ℓ applied to a temporal index k, slightly generalizing (64), such that for all x (71) holds good:

(71) $\mathbf{M} \models \phi T \psi[i]$, if $\exists p,p' \in \mathbf{D_L}$ such that $\mathbf{M} \models [_\phi AT(p)(x)][i]$ and for some immediate successor j of i, $\mathbf{M} \models [_\psi AT(p')(x)][j]$

In this way, the Von Wrightian transition operator is redefined additively within the localistic framework. Note that the information from the arguments of the verb is now tied up with the Path-function. So, technically, the valuation proceeds on the indices i and j and the function values at a given j can be used as the last index. Principle (71) plus DEF 1 and DEF 2 formalize the additivity contributed by verbs expressing change, such as *eat*, *walk*, *buy, die* and *discover.*

At this stage of our exposition, however, it is more important to discuss underlying theoretical assumptions involving the localistic view on change in time than to give a precise formal account. It should be noted that an analysis based on (71) differs from the interval semantic approaches of the seventies: in the analysis of the [+ADD TO]-verbs we do not deal directly with temporal intervals, but rather with well-ordered numerals representing them. This is done on the basis of our capacity to compress sets to points taking for granted their internal **R**-structure. This means that the property of being closed under intersection is warranted.

At this point it is perhaps useful to return to (65), the Path of John with respect to *walk home* in (62). As the notion of Path is defined on the verb itself, (65) is part of an unbounded set, which in our example should look like (72):

(65) $\ell_{\text{walk home}} = \{\langle t_0, \text{office}\rangle, \langle t_1, \text{book shop}\rangle, \langle t_2, \text{office}\rangle, \ldots, \langle t_4, \text{bar}\rangle, \ldots, \langle t_m, \text{home}\rangle\}$

(72) $\ell_{\text{walk}} = \{\langle t_0, \text{office}\rangle, \langle t_1, \text{book shop}\rangle, \langle t_2, \text{office}\rangle, \ldots, \langle t_4, \text{bar}\rangle, \ldots\}$

The set ℓ_{walk} is unbounded as there is no maximal indexed time in $\mathbf{D}_T$. However, at the VP-level the maximal index of *walk home* is n, so the Path is bounded. Hence the denotation of *home* should provide for the maximal pair $\langle t_m, \text{home}\rangle$, the contribution of the verb being to induce the unbounded series of pairs in which $\langle t_m, \text{home}\rangle$ is 'inserted' to make John's walk bounded at the VP-level. In Verkuyl (1978) this problem was not solved. We have to look for a formal mechanism which yields a transition from ℓ_V to ℓ_{VP}.

10.3 The thematic role of the internal argument

A difficult question for the thematic system is: how can one determine unequivocally which thematic roles are fulfilled by which NPs? In sentences like (73)–(77), for example, it is very hard to determine what sort of thematic role should be attributed to the NPs.

(73) Judith ate five sandwiches

(74) a. ... and when she had finished, she was relieved
b. ... and when the sandwiches were gone, she was relieved

(75) a. Mary mailed the letters
b. Mary brought the letters

(76) a Mary dropped the letters
b. Mary picked up the letters

(77) a. The meteorite hit the earth
b. The earth hit the meteorite

Suppose that one makes *Judith* the Theme NP, then (73) is localistically interpreted in terms of Judith going from one state to another by moving from a point zero along an eating-Path and ending at the moment at which she had eaten five sandwiches. This interpretation has (74a) as a natural continuation.

But what about taking *five sandwiches* as Theme NP instead? These can be taken as moving from some place into the mouth of Judith, as suggested by the continuation in (74b). Also, what about (75b), if *the letters* is the Theme NP in (75a)? Why is Mary not also a Theme, as she is physically moving along with the letters? Likewise if *the letters* is the Theme NP in (76) – the letters move from some position to the ground – why exclude Mary from being a theme NP? She moved towards the ground and back. And finally, what about two moving objects which hit each other? There are two major strategies to escape from going bust thematically: the first one is syntactic, the second lexical. Surprisingly, they end up sharing some important features, so they will both be discussed here.

In Verkuyl (1988), it was proposed to replace the Gruberian interpretation of thematic roles by a more abstract pattern very much modelled after the distinction between external and internal argument as proposed in Williams (1980, 1981). Here *Judith* in (48) *Judith ate three sandwiches* is assigned a Θ-role different from the thematic role of *three sandwiches*, the latter being assigned by V, the former by VP. The semantic interpretation of these roles is marginal. Following Chomsky's thematic parsimony (for example, Chomsky 1981), many generative syntacticians simply call them Θ_1 and Θ_2 just to distinguish the two roles. Lexically, this information can be attached in the form of a thematic 'grid' (78a), where Θ_{ext} indicates that the NP is the external argument, and Θ_{int} that the NP is internal.

(78) a. V:(Θ_{ext}, Θ_{int}) b. NP_{ext} [V NP_{int}]

In sentences like (73)–(77), the roles are matched with the two NPs. The subject NP is external argument, the object NP internal argument. These arguments are not equipollent as they would be in logical formulas of the form $V(NP_1,NP_2)$. A structure of the form (78b) expresses a closer structural relationship between the internal argument and the verb than between the external argument and the verb. In my 1988 paper, aspectual asymmetry was tied up with the asymmetry between internal and external argument. It should be stressed again, as in chapter 1.3, that the need for aspectual asymmetry has been argued for quite independently from the syntactic considerations having led to (78b). It should also be underscored that the interpretation of thematic roles along the lines of (78b) hinges on the compositional strategy underlying the present aspectual theory.

Structures like (78b) require binary branching, so it says that a two-place verb – indicated as V – in a structure like Figure 28 combines at the lexical level with an argument NP to form a one-place predicate VP which combines

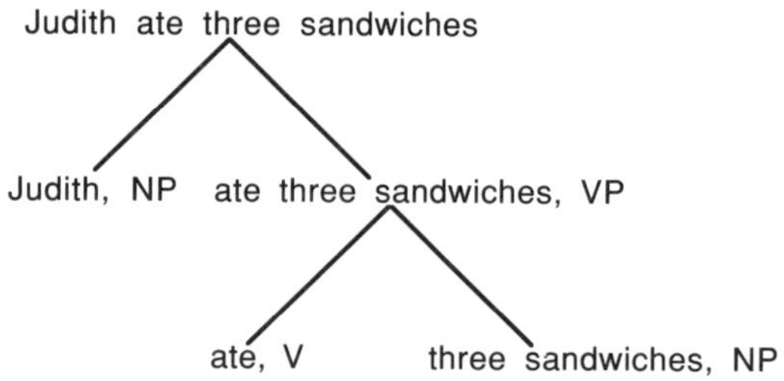

Figure 28 The fundamental NP–VP distinction involves a basic asymmetry underlying aspectual construal

with an argument NP to yield a zero-place predicate, that is, a proposition. In Verkuyl (1988) it was proposed to analyse the thematic structure of sentences like (73)–(77) simply in terms of Θ_{ext} and Θ_{int}, where all direct object NPs are given the same thematic role Θ_{int}, which is the first argument to be related to the temporal structure expressed by the verb, dependent, of course, on the verb. The subject NPs of the sentences are all external arguments, and in that sense they 'come into the picture later'. Their thematic role is to operate on the VP-structure which has been assembled. This view is compatible with the architecture of PLUG-representations in the sense that the partitioned structure of the internal-argument denotation happens to be always in the scope of the external-argument denotation. It will be made formally more precise in chapter 13 after a comparison with the second strategy for dealing with thematic roles, as in Jackendoff's lexical-conceptual approach, which will be discussed first now.

The structural (and parsimonious) approach to thematic structure has as an immediate consequence that the internal argument of the sentences in (47)–(49) and (50)–(52) can be assigned the same thematic role: it provides for the function values of the function ℓ as defined in (64). That is, *three sandwiches* in (48) *Judith ate three sandwiches* and *to three stores* in (51) *John walked to three stores* should be given the same sort of thematic role. This is what will be formalized in chapter 13 on the basis of PLUG: the complements of *eat* and *walk* will be treated as providing the 'space' through which Judith and John are 'going'. Still metaphorically, in both cases one may think of the external argument 'going through' a bounded set of indexed entities. This idea will be made more concrete in two steps: the first one is taken in the remainder of this section, the second in chapter 13.3 and chapter 13.4.[19]

The first step starts at the point at which it turns out to be necessary to consider Jackendoff's more recent contributions to the localistic framework. In

Jackendoff (1978, 1983, 1990) a drastic modification of the GO-scheme (61) took place. Rather than by (61), the change-predication in sentences like (48) and (50) is now represented by:

(79) GO($[_{\text{Thing}}\ ]$, $[_{\text{Path}}\ ]$)

where GO is a function mapping the Theme-argument and the Path-argument into the set of events. The basic idea is simple: the Theme (the moving entity) relates now to a region in which it moves as part of the event. Representation (79) incorporates 'the claim that there has taken place an event consisting of the motion of some object *x* along some path *p*. In other words, the first variable of GO corresponds to the theme, the second to the path' (1978: 218f.).

The motivation behind this change is both syntactic and semantic. One syntactic argument is that Source and Goal are often expressed by a PP and that PPs share a lot of properties with NPs, as exemplified by Table 11. Jackendoff concludes that the ontology should be enriched with locations and paths. Some entities are measured, referred back to, pointed to, and individuated, without their being things or stuff. In type-theoretic terms: if *into the air* is a PP, its denotation ⟦into the air⟧ is an entity of the type of individuals *e*, just like ⟦John⟧ or ⟦the store⟧.[20] There is another argument. Jackendoff (1978: 208) rejects (80a) as a representation for (50).

(80) a. walk(John)∧ to(John, the store)
b. walk(John,(to(the store))

Why? Because it presents a 'patent complication of the syntax-semantics mapping'. The conceptual structure of the form (80b) has, according to Jackendoff, the 'property of much more closely preserving the syntactic integrity of the construction in its semantics. Thus the projection rules are a simpler mapping than if prepositions are predicates' (*ibid.*).

Table 11 *PPs and NPs share important properties*

	NP	**PP**
modification	*nearly three* sandwiches	*quite far* into the air
anaphoric reference	John ... and *he*	in the room...and *there*
deictic reference	*This* sandwich	*Here*
individuated	*Which* sandwich	*Where*

Finally, given this notion of Path, the parallelism between the sentences in (81) is accounted for:

(81) a. The train travelled from Detroit to Cincinnati
b. The hawk flew over the prairie
c. A meteor hurtled towards the earth

Over the prairie, for example, is easier to conceive of as a Path than as a Goal, whereas the meteor might even miss the earth. 'The semantic similarity between these sentences can be described by saying that the concepts they express are all instances of the general concept GO(X,P)' (1978: 218f.).

Generative grammar makes uses of different components in a grammar. Hence it is possible to treat *eat* in (48) *Judith ate three sandwiches* both as a two-place verb (in syntax) and as expressing a 'stacked' argument structure in a different component. In Jackendoff (1990) this is done by indexing *Judith* and *three sandwiches* in syntax, and by using the same indices in the thematic structure, as exemplified in (82).

(82) a. Judith^1 ate $[\text{three sandwiches}]^2$

b. $[_{\text{Event}}\ \text{CAUSE}([_{\text{Thing}}\ \text{JUDITH}\ ]^1, [_{\text{Event}}\ \text{GO}([_{\text{Thing}}\ 3\ \text{SANDWICHES}]^2, [_{\text{Path}}\ \text{TO}([_{\text{Place}}\ \text{IN}([_{\text{Thing}}\ \text{MOUTH\_OF}([_{\text{Thing}}\ \text{JUDITH}\ ]^1)])])])])])]$

The conceptual representation (82b) says that Judith causes some event which consists of three sandwiches moving into the mouth of Judith. The direct object NP *three sandwiches* is the Theme NP. Scheme (79) is clearly visible in the second argument of the cause-predication in (83).[21]

(83) $[_{\text{Event}}\ \text{GO}([_{\text{Thing}}\ ]^2, [_{\text{Path}}\ \text{TO}([_{\text{Place}}\ \text{IN}([_{\text{Thing}}\ \text{MOUTH\_OF}([_{\text{Thing}}\ ]^1)])])])]$

The Theme-Path pattern is here restricted to the direct object NP in its relation to some part of the subject. Thus, the entries for verbs like *eat* and *drink* contain selectional information about what sort of things may be eaten and drunk.

There is a huge abyss between (82b) and its PLUG-counterpart (84).

(84) $\exists! V[V = [\![\text{Judith}]\!] \cap \{j_i\} \wedge \exists W[W \subseteq [\![\text{sandwich}]\!] \wedge |W| = 3$
$\wedge \exists Q \text{ps} W[Q = \{U \cap [\![\text{sandwich}]\!] : [\![\text{eat}]\!](U)(V)\}]]]$

However, even though (84) is not *a priori* localistic, it will be possible to give it a localistic interpretation. It is the purpose of this section to let valuable insights from the localistic tradition into the mainstream of logical-semantic research which might need such a supply as it still bears so much the traces of its atemporal origin.

There is hardly any need to convince people that representations like (82b) deviate substantially from representations like (84), but there is also no need to burden the exposition by further discussing Jackendoff's arguments for having the functions making up Places, Paths and Events. It is much more interesting to see which are the correspondences that make it necessary and worthwhile to go deeper into the implications of using the scheme (79). It turns out that it is at least compatible with the asymmetric approach expressed by Figure 28. The correspondences that will be singled out are the following:

The GO-function in (79) yields events. This is compatible with a compositional approach in which the notion of event is derivative in the sense that it is made up of contributions of the [+ADD TO]-verb and its [+SQA]-arguments.

The Path itself is to be located in the VP. This is compatible with the approach in which an [+ADD TO]-verb and its [+SQA]-internal argument make up a partitioned structure whose mapping to temporal structure can be taken localistically.

Terminativity can be expressed in terms of a function having a finite domain or co-domain; roughly, a mapping 'goes through' its domain and stops if there are no values available.

These correspondences do not impose themselves naturally, as Jackendoff's formalization is neither articulated enough nor phrased in standard logical expressions. To achieve sufficient insight into Jackendoff's view on aspectuality, it will be necessary to discuss his conceptual approach in some detail. Though in some sense the discussion of his non-model-theoretic framework is a deviation on our way to a precise formalization of the temporal extension of the PLUG-grammar, it is worth its while because it will enable us to make the aspectual generalization with respect to (47)–(49). Some valuable insights into the semantics of sentences like (50)–(52) can be transferred to the PLUG-framework, via a translation into its basis: set theory. Moreover, it will lead to a lot of interesting aspectual problems faced by Jackendoff, but also by Declerck (1979), which are mostly ignored by others (including myself), such as the question of how to deal with sentences like *She walked along the river* and *He walked through the tunnel*. Actually, these are sentences which also made Gruber (1964) so fascinating.

10.4 The notion of Path: dimension, direction, boundedness

In 'Parts and Boundaries' (Jackendoff, to appear), Jackendoff develops a system of aspectual features, which will be briefly described in this section on the

Table 12 *Jackendoff's Conceptual Semantics can be characterized in terms of a number of features*

	Features	*Entity*, for example,
Thing		
substance	[–internal structure, –bounded]	bread
individual	[–internal structure, +bounded]	Judith
aggregate	[+internal structure, –bounded]	sandwiches
aggregate	[+internal structure, +bounded]	three sandwiches
group:	[+internal structure, +bounded]	committee
Space		
place	[–directional, 0–dimensional,]	at this point
	[–directional, 1–dimensional,]	along the river
	[–directional, 2–dimensional,]	in the circle
	[–directional, 3–dimensional,]	in the cup
path	[+directional, 1–dimensional, –bounded]	towards the store
	[+directional, 1–dimensional, +bounded]	into the house
Situation		
state	[–bounded, 1–dimensional]	be in the store
event	[+bounded, 0–dimensional]	flash
	[+bounded, 1–dimensional]	walk to the store, eat 3 sandwiches

basis of the set-theoretical interpretation of Jackendoff's Conceptual Semantics in Zwarts and Verkuyl (1991) and Verkuyl and Zwarts (1992). The list in Table 12 gives an idea of how different entities can be characterized by means of a small set of basic features, consisting of the features [±internal structure], [±bounded], [±directional] and [n–dimensional] (for 0≤n≤3), the most important ones of which are given for a particular category. In order to understand what the features mean and what role they play in aspect construal, a model-theoretic interpretation of conceptual structure will be given. For the purpose of the present section, it is sufficient as well as more enlightening to assume that the interpretation of conceptual structure consists of the construction of partial models, couched in a simplified set-theoretical formalism that is meant to provide insight into the nature of aspectuality. For example, the denotation of the concept $[_{\text{Thing}}$ THREE STORES] can be interpreted as the set of all sets (or individual sums) of three stores in the domain or as the set of three stores that the concept denotes under a particular assignment. These two levels can also be distinguished in the more complex interpretation of situation-concepts. The concept that corresponds to (50) *John walked to the store* is either interpreted as a set of events, or as one particular event (where events are not taken as primitives but as mathematical constructions from time, space and other entities). In this way, the interpretation of a conceptual structure can be seen as the construction of a partial model. On these assumptions, made explicit in Verkuyl and Zwarts (1992), Jackendoff's features [n-DIMENSIONAL], [HETEROGENEOUS], [BOUNDED] and [DIRECTIONAL] can be interpreted as sets of model-theoretic structures.

What does it mean for an object to have a certain dimension? The notion of dimensionality in Jackendoff may be taken as follows: the dimensionality of an object is the number of spatial orderings that can be imposed on the material parts of that object. Thus, a river can be seen as 1-dimensional, because it can be partitioned into a set of parts ordered by one spatial relation indicating that one slice of the river follows another one. A sheet of paper is 2-dimensional because it can be partitioned into a set of pieces on which two orthogonal spatial relations are imposed. A globe is 3-dimensional because its partition into parts is ordered by three orthogonal spatial relations. A river might also be viewed as 2- or 3-dimensional, if width or depth are taken into account. In this case, every slice of the river is itself materially partitioned and its parts spatially ordered. Every object is basically 0-dimensional, and whether it has other dimensionalities depends on the number of spatial orderings that can be imposed on its material partition. Meaning postulates can be used to impose suitable restrictions on models.

There are clear empirical arguments that plural entities can also be regarded as 1-dimensional, in the sense informally used by Jackendoff. The preposition *along* in (85) demands a 1-dimensional Thing as its argument:

(85) a. the road along the river
b. the road along the stores

This Thing can be either a singular Thing with a 1-dimensional shape like [RIVER] or a plural Thing that is conceptualized as a row of Things of arbitrary dimension, in other words, a 1-dimensional plurality like [STORES]. Analysing [STORES] as a 1-dimensional Thing makes it the reference-object of *along*.[22] In our account, the elements of any set can also be spatially ordered by one, two or three spatial orderings. In this way, it follows naturally from our account that the plural [STORES]-concept can be 1-dimensional.

An entity is [+internal structure] if it has clearly discernible individual parts. A [+internal structure]-concept can be interpreted as denoting a mapping from a subset of **N** into the set of entities falling under that concept. In other words, it is possible to count the members of the set. A concept is [–internal structure] if it denotes a mapping from a subset of **R** into the set of entities falling under the concept and it is therefore impossible to enumerate the elements of that set.

Along these lines the denotation of the concept [$_{\text{Thing}}$STORE] for *the store* can be given as the entity s. The concept [$_{\text{Thing}}$STORES] is [+internal structure] because it denotes a mapping from **N** to the set of stores, which can be represented as $\{s_1, s_2, \ldots\}$. The concept [$_{\text{Thing}}$WINE] denotes a mapping from a subset of **R** to the set of portions of wine (Link 1983; Krifka 1989a, 1989b).

An entity is [+bounded] for Jackendoff if it is conceptualized as having a clear boundary in time and/or space; an entity is [–bounded] if it is not bounded in time and space by a particular shape, like portions of matter. An interpretation of the [±bounded]-feature will be pursued here along the lines of Part II, that is, in terms of [±SQA]-information about cardinality, without committing Jackendoff to such a view. The [±bounded]-feature for the EVENT-concept in the top of a conceptual structure assigned to sentences depends on the features of the concepts from which it is derived. This is illustrated below, where a (partial) conceptual representation is given of the meaning of the sentence (50) *John walked to the store*:

$$\begin{bmatrix} \text{EVENT} \\ \text{+bounded} \\ \text{GO}\left(\begin{bmatrix}\text{THING}\\ \text{+bounded}\\ \text{JOHN}\end{bmatrix}, \begin{bmatrix}\text{PATH}\\ \text{+ bounded}\\ \text{TO}\left(\begin{bmatrix}\text{THING}\\ \text{+bounded}\\ \text{STORE}\end{bmatrix}\right)\end{bmatrix}\right) \end{bmatrix}$$

The EVENT is bounded because it is the result of applying the two-place GO-function to a bounded thing and a bounded Path. The Path is bounded because it is defined as the value of a one-place TO-function applied to a bounded entity, that is, store. It should be observed that Jackendoff's formal notation does not meet the rigorous standard of a model-theoretic semantics, but it is shown in Zwarts and Verkuyl (1991) that, given some extrapolations, the representation above can be translated into a formal-logical language. So, Jackendoff's own notation can be used for clarifying the points at issue.

That Jackendoff's notion of boundedness by and large can be interpreted in terms of [+SQA] and [+ADD TO] also follows from an inspection of (86)–(91).

(86) John walked to that store
(87) John walked to *stores*
(88) *Children* walked to the store
(89) John walked *towards* the store
(90) John *was walking* to the store
(91) John *hated* the store

Five times an 'aspectual leak' has been made in the terminative sentence (86), resulting in a change of aspect for the whole sentence. In Jackendoff's terminology, the conceptual structure of the situation becomes [–bounded], as on the italicized position a [–bounded] concept now replaces a [+bounded] one, or in the case of (91) a [–ADD TO]-verb. Thus, the composition of terminative aspect appears to be based on a general principle saying that a concept is [+bounded], if it is the result of a function taking concepts that are all [+bounded], and otherwise [–bounded].[23] This is very much related to the Plus-principle (plus + plus = plus) introduced in chapter 1.2, which is the basis for the present study.[24] As in mass terms, the notion of cardinality does not seem to fit; boundedness can certainly be treated in terms of picking out a natural number n representing the denotation of an NP as bounded, for example, by applying a measure function in the sense of Bunt (1981) or Krifka (1989a, 1989b), as said in chapter 8.3.

Finally, the feature [+directional] is interpreted in terms of a linear ordering of the elements of a set. A set is directional if it is linearly ordered in one direction, yielding one unique begin-point and a potential end-point. Localistically taken, directionality is interpreted as the movement of the Theme through a Path which consists of a set of Things. The movement involves counting. That is, directionality imposes a certain order on an unordered set whose members receive numerical indices: $\{s_i, s_j, s_k\} \Rightarrow <s_1, s_2, s_3>$. Table 13 illustrates which type of set-theoretical constructs corresponds to a particular combination of features. The Path-function TO maps its argument [STORE] into a directional set representing a Path leading to s.[25] There will actually be a set of possible Paths to the store, but we talk about one of these paths.[26] The concept $[_{Path}$TO([STORE])] denotes the linearly ordered homogeneous set of points of space $L_{TO}=<p_1,..., p_i,...,p(s)>$, closed off by the spatial position of the store,

Table 13 *Conceptual Semantic features can be interpreted model-theoretically*

NP	**Concept**	**Model**
the store	$[_{Thing}$STORE] [–int. str., +bounded, 0–dim]	s
stores	$[_{Thing}$STORES] [+int. str., –bounded, 1–dim]	$\{s_1,...,s_i,...\}$
three sandwiches	$[_{Thing}$3 SANDWICHES] [+int. str., +bounded]	$\{s_1,s_2,s_3\}$
bread	$[_{Thing}$BREAD] [–int. str., –bounded]	$\{b_1,...,b_i...\}$

p(s), and conceptualized as a point in Space. Likewise, the concept $[_{Path}$FROM([STORE])] denotes a linearly ordered set of spatial points starting with the store $L_{FROM}=<p(s), \dots , p_i,\dots,p_n>$.[27] Path-functions may lack such a termination. $[_{Path}$TOWARDS ([STORE])] denotes a part of the path L_{TO} having no fixed end-point. AROUND can have both a bounded and a non-bounded meaning: $[_{Path}$AROUND([STORE])] may denote a single bounded round $<p_1,\dots,p_i, \dots ,p_1>$, where i≥1, or an unbounded iteration round and round: $<p_1,\dots,p_1, \dots,p_1,\dots>$.[28]

A reference-object like ⟦the river⟧ can sometimes be conceptualized as 0-dimensional, as in *to the river*, or as 1-dimensional, as in *along the river*. $[_{Path}$TO([RIVER])] is bounded, whereas $[_{Path}$ALONG([RIVER])] is not. In the latter case, the river is taken as an unbounded 1-dimensional entity, representable as a linearly ordered homogeneous and unbounded set of slices of that river: $<r_1,\dots,r_i,\dots,r_j,\dots>$. Each of these pieces constitutes a reference-object for ALONG, so the concept $[_{Path}$ALONG([RIVER])] can be represented as $<p'(r_1),\dots, p'(r_i), \dots , p'(r_j),\dots>$. In this way, the unboundedness of the river carries over to the unboundedness of the Path 'along the river'.

Summarizing, the excursion into Jackendoff's system makes it clear that the notion of Path defined in terms of his aspectual features is important as a unifying concept over apparently disparate structures, such as ⟦three sandwiches⟧ and ⟦to the store⟧. The interpretation of the features which are part of the syntax of his Conceptual Structure is less geometric than Jackendoff (pers. comm.) would like to have it.[29] For the present aspectual theory, set theory is taken as its basis. It is clear that the differences between phrases like *to the store*, *along the river*, *along the store*, *to the river*, etc. will have to be included in an aspectual theory. In my view, this can be done set-theoretically, as will become clear in chapter 13.

10.5 A localistic construction of Path structure

In this section, we shall analyse the contribution of Path-concepts and Thing-concepts to the construction of events, and other situations. This will be done on the basis of the set-theoretical interpretation of Jackendoff's aspectual features in chapter 10.4. Jackendoff's semantic representation of (50) is given in (92).

(50) John walked to the store

(92) $[_{Event}$ GO($[_{Thing}$JOHN],$[_{Path}$TO($[_{Thing}$STORE])])]

In a model-theoretic interpretation of this structure, reference should be made to time, because John's movement to the store involves a bounded sequence of moments of time $<t_1,...,t_n>$. At each of these moments of time $t_1 \leq t_i \leq t_n$, John is also at a spatial position p_j of the Path. Our representation will be extended to include pairs of entities: $<t_i,p_j>$, representing a spatio-temporal position, and $<j,\ell>$ representing the situation of John being mapped onto the spatio-temporal function ℓ, defined in (64). Staying as close as possible to Jackendoff, we will treat the introduction of a temporal parameter as part of the Path-notion in the sense of (64) as an extension of Jackendoff's system.

The asymmetry in the composition of the terminative aspect of sentences like (50) consists of the verb first taking its internal argument to form a VP, after which the VP relates to the external argument. This means (92) must be reformulated as (93).

(93) $[_{\text{Event}}$ GO($[_{\text{Path}}$TO([STORE])])($[_{\text{Thing}}$JOHN])]

This can be done by simply applying here the Montagovian notation convention by which a two-place predicate $\gamma(\alpha,\beta)$ is written as $\gamma(\beta)(\alpha)$. This means that GO will take its arguments in two steps. First it will apply to the Path-argument $[_{\text{Path}}$TO([STORE])], and then to the Thing-argument$[_{\text{Thing}}$JOHN]. Each of these two functional applications can be considered as a structure-building operation, the result of which is a Situation, that is, a (terminative) Event. The foundation of this situational structure is a temporal structure provided by the GO-function itself, which is defined in terms of the successor function s in DEF 2.

Given the fact that dimensionality plays a prominent role in Jackendoff's system, it is tempting to illustrate the compositional procedure pictorially, as in Figure 29a, where $<t_1,..., t_i,...>$ is represented as a dense arrow and $<p_1,..., p_i,..., p(s)>$ as a discrete arrow. The result of the application of GO to the spatial Path will be a mapping from the temporal Path into a spatio-temporal Path consisting

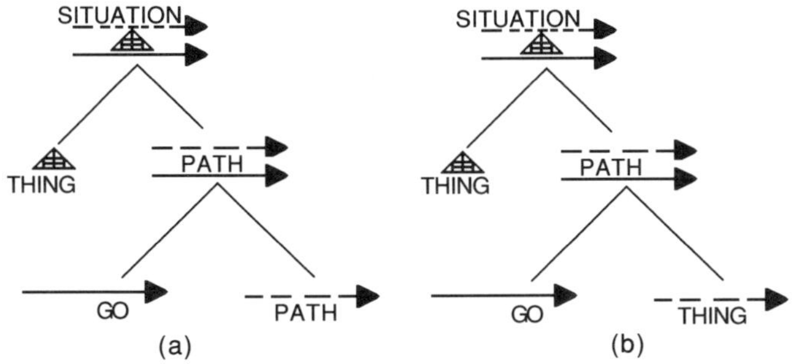

Figure 29 Jackendoff generalizes over the Path structure in the domain of things and in the domain of spatio-temporality

of pairs of points in time and spatial positions. The boundedness of this spatio-temporal Path is completely dependent upon whether or not the spatial Path is bounded, because the mapping stops as soon as its co-domain is exhausted. Therefore, the VP-path $<<t_{1},p_{1}>,\ldots, <t_{i},p_{i}>,\ldots, <t_{n},p(s)>>$ corresponding to GO([TO([STORE])]) will be bounded, whereas the VP-Path $<<t_{1},p_{1}>,\ldots,<t_{i},p_{i}>,\ldots>$ which corresponds to GO([ALONG([RIVER])]) will be unbounded. The next compositional step will then be to relate the theme of GO to the spatio-temporal path that is already built up. This step will result in a situational Path, because it expresses what sort of position in space a thing occupies at a given time. In the case under discussion, *John walked to the store*, this will be associated with the sequence: $<j,<<t_{1},p_{1}>,\ldots,<t_{n},p(s)>>>$ which is short for $<<j,<t_{1},p_{1}>>, \ldots, <j,<t_{n},p(s)>>>$, if one wants to underscore the intuition that John is the moving object going through the VP-Path. The derivations 1 and 2 for (50) and (94):

(94) John walked along the river

show how a model-theoretic interpretation of Jackendoff's conceptual structures leads to a compositional treatment of aspectual phenomena.

Derivation 1 (50) *John walked to the store*

[$_{Thing}$ STORE,0-dim]	s
[$_{Path}$ TO([STORE])]	$<p_{1},\ldots,p(s)>$
GO([TO([STORE])])	$<<t_{1},p_{1}>,\ldots,<t_{n},p(s)>>$
[$_{Event}$ GO([TO([STORE])])(JOHN)]	$<<j,<t_{1},p_{1}>>,\ldots,<j,<t_{n},p(s)>>>$

Derivation 2 (94) *John walked along the river*

[$_{Thing}$ RIVER, 1-dim,–b]	$<r_{1},\ldots,r_{i},\ldots>$
[$_{Path}$ ALONG([RIVER])]	$<p'(r_{1}),\ldots,p'(r_{i}),\ldots>$
GO([ALONG([RIVER])])	$<<t_{1},p'(r_{1})>,\ldots,<t_{i},p'(r_{i})>,\ldots>$
[$_{Event}$GO([ALONG([RIVER])])([JOHN])]	$<<j,<t_{1},p'(r_{1})>>,\ldots,<j,<t_{i},p'(r_{i})>>,\ldots>$

Up to now the mapping relations between the sets involved have been kept rather simple. The situation becomes much more complex when sentences like those in (86)–(91) are considered. Intuitively, what happens in (52) *John walked to stores* must allow that the bounded situation of John walking to a store is multiplied an unbounded number of times, because there is an unbounded number of stores. In other words, the plurality of the stores is somehow lifted up to the level of a plurality of situations, though it is certainly possible that (87) applies to one walk and to an unspecified quantity of stores.

The same is true for (88) *Children walked to the store.* Except for the quite natural possibility of distributing functions over the members of a set, it is not necessary to introduce any new complications into the system to account for the durative aspect in (52) and (88). The conceptual structures of *stores* and *children* will carry the feature [–bounded, +internal structure, 1-dimensional]. Therefore they can be represented as unbounded sets $\{s_1,...,s_i,...\}$ and $\{c_1,...,c_i,...\}$, respectively. The Path-function TO, however, cannot be applied to these sets, because TO needs a single 0-dimensional Thing to bound a Path. So one needs to assume that TO distributes over the elements of the set, yielding not one Path but an unbounded set of bounded Paths, as represented in (95b) and pictorially represented as in Figure 30a. It is possible that each of these Paths has a different origin.

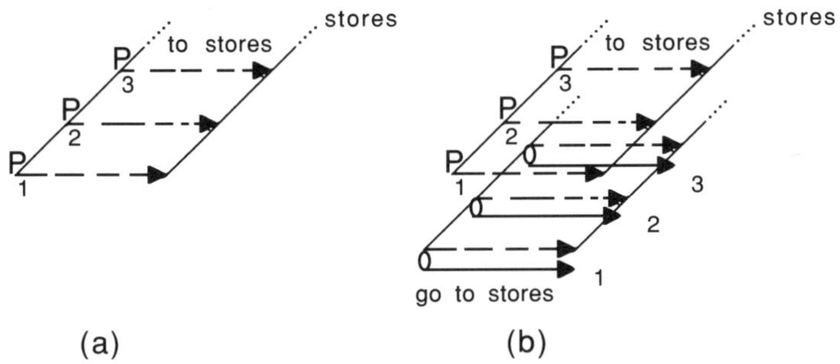

Figure 30 *Go to stores* is formed from *go* and *to stores* by a distributive function

(95) a. $[_{Path}$ TO($[_{Thing}$ STORES])]
b. $\{P_1,...,P_i,...\}$, where each P_i=<$p_1,...,p(s_i)$>

When GO is applied to this structure, it will also distribute over this set. This results in an unbounded set of spatio-temporal paths $\{\Pi_1,...,\Pi_i,...\}$, where each Π_i=<$(t_1,p_1),...,(t_n,p(s_i))$>. This results in a situation depicted in Figure 30b.

Finally, John is mapped to each of these sets, resulting in $\{E_1,...,E_i,...\}$ where each E_i is a situational Path, <<j,<t_1,p_1>>,...,<j,<t_n,p_n>>>, on its own. The unboundedness in the case of (52) does not arise from an unbounded temporal or spatial path but from an unbounded set of situations. The compositional interpretation of this conceptual structure is given in derivation 3.

Derivation 3 (52) *John walked to stores*

$[_{Thing}$ STORES, 1-dim,–b]	$\{s_1,...,s_i,...\}$
$[_{Path}$ TO([STORES])]	$\{P_1,...,P_i,...\}$

GO([TO([STORES])])	$\{\Pi_1,...,\Pi_i,...\}$
[$_{Event}$GO([TO([STORES])])([JOHN])]	$\{E_1,...,E_i,...\}$

where each P_i=<p_1, ..., $p(s_i)$>, each Π_i=<<t_1,p_i>, ..., <t_n,$p(s_i)$>>, and each E_i=<<j,<t_1,p_i>>, ..., <j,<t_n,$p(s_i)$>>>. A somewhat different account can be given of the unboundedness of (88) *Children walked to the store*. In this case, there is an unbounded set of children, but a bounded spatio-temporal Path along which each of these children has to move. However, this does not need to be the same Path for each child. Different children may have taken different routes at different times to the same store. One needs a set of different Paths to the store: $\{\Pi_1,..,\Pi_i,...\}$, each Π being defined as <<t_1,p_1>,...,<t_n,p(s)>>. The set of children is mapped into this set of possible spatio-temporal Paths. What results is an unbounded set of situations $\{E_1,..,E_i,...\}$, each of them being a linearly ordered set <<c_k,<t_1,p_1>>,...,<c_k,<t_n,p(s)>>>, expressing the movement of one particular child. Again we have a compositional construction of a set of events, as shown in derivation 4.

Derivation 4 (88) *Children walked to the store*

[$_{Thing}$ STORE]	s
[$_{Path}$TO([STORE])]	<p_1,...,p(s)>
GO([TO([STORE])])	<<t_1,p_1>,...,<t_n,p(s)>>
[$_{Thing}$CHILDREN]	$\{c_1,...,c_i,...\}$
[$_{Event}$GO([TO([STORE])])([CHILDREN])]	$\{E_1,..,E_k,...\}$

where each E_k=<<c_k,<t_1,p_1>>, ..., <c_k,<t_n,p(s)>>>. This set is unbounded, so durative aspect is predicted.

We now arrive at the analysis of (48) *Judith ate three sandwiches*. This sentence can be treated in almost the same way as (51). The composition of its meaning proceeds in a way illustrated in Figure 29b. The three sandwiches constitute an atemporal partition and, by the mapping relation between GO and the NP-denotation, the eating of three sandwiches constitutes a VP-Path. In some sense, Judith ate herself 'through' a set of three sandwiches. The partial conceptual structure of this sentence involves the GO-function, so (96) is the proper Jackendoffian representation.

(96) [$_{Sit}$GO([$_{Path}$ 3 SANDWICHES])([$_{Thing}$ JUDITH])]
(97) [$_{Sit}$GO([$_{Thing}$3 SANDWICHES])([$_{Thing}$ JUDITH])]

However, this would force us to characterize the NP *three sandwiches* as a Path *sui generis*. This is an unnatural thing to do, because the NP should be a Thing at the beginning of the derivation. It is only at the very moment that it is drawn into the predication to form a VP, that it is necessary to structure it linearly. The GO-function cannot apply to a spatial Path in the literal sense. Rather it should apply to a 'Thing-Path', that is, a set having linear structure.

The concept [$_{\text{Thing}}$SANDWICHES,1-dimensional], which corresponds to the common noun *sandwiches*, is interpreted as $\{s_1,...,s_i,...\}$. The addition of the numerical information in [$_{\text{Thing}}$3 SANDWICHES] leads to the bounded set $\{s_1, s_2, s_3\}$. The GO-function supplies a temporal Path $<t_1,...,t_k,...>$ into which this set of three sandwiches can be mapped. However, there is an important difference between spatial paths and the set $\{s_1,s_2,s_3\}$, because this set is not inherently ordered; it is not yet a real Path. We will assume that this set is structured and linearized in virtue of its participation in the situation. It is Judith, the eater of the sandwiches, who determines the order in which the sandwiches are eaten. The result of applying the function GO to [$_{\text{Thing}}$3 SANDWICHES] yields the following spatio-temporal object: $<<t_1,s_2>,<t_2,s_1>,<t_3,s_3>>$. This is 'the going through three sandwiches'. The interpretation of the whole conceptual structure of (48) is $<<j,<t_1,s_2>>, <j,<t_2,s_1>>,<j,<t_3,s_3>>>$. The event of Judith eating three sandwiches consists of three subevents in this particular model. The stepwise interpretation of the conceptual structure is given in derivation 5.[30]

Derivation 5 (48) *Judith ate three sandwiches*

[$_{\text{Thing}}$ SANDWICHES]	$\{s_1,...,s_i,...\}$
[$_{\text{Thing}}$ 3 SANDWICHES]	$\{s_1,s_2,s_3\}$
[GO([$_{\text{Thing}}$3 SANDWICHES])]	$<<t_1,s_1>,<t_2,s_2>,<t_3,s_3>>$
[$_{\text{Thing}}$ JUDITH]	j
[$_{\text{Event}}$EAT([3 SANDWICHES])([JUDITH])]	$<<j,<t_1,s_1>>,<j,<t_2,s_2>>, <j,<t_3,s_3>>>$

However, to obtain a better parallelism between (48) and (51) one might think in terms of the p-function applied in the construction of $\Pi=<p_1,...,p(s)>$, which brings the store s into a position. Likewise one could think of p in the case of (48) as a participancy-function covering the way in which members of the denotation of the internal argument are involved in the predication. To obtain this, the GO-function may be allowed to take an unordered set (Thing) as part of its input, because the unordered nature of $\{s_1, s_2, s_3\}$ is compatible with any ordered choice from it. From a finite set S one may compute a set of sets S/E containing all partitioned subsets of S, as in Verkuyl (1987a, 1988). So, if the GO-function is permitted to range over this set S/E, it may be defined as a function mapping anything that is compatible with the feature specification [$_{\text{Entity}}$1-dimensional,+directional] into a function mapping a [THING] into [SITUATION]. For (48) this amounts to the following derivation:

Derivation 6 (48) *Judith ate three sandwiches*

$[_{Thing}$ SANDWICHES] $\{s_1,\ldots,s_i,\ldots\}$

$[_{Thing}$ 3 SANDWICHES] $\{s_1,s_2,s_3\}$

[GO($[_{Thing/Path}$3 SANDWICHES])] $<<t_1,p(\{s_1\})>,\ldots, <t_n,p(\{s_1,s_2,s_3\})>>$

[JUDITH] j

$[_{Event}$EAT([3 SANDWICHES])([JUDITH])] $<<j,<t_1,p(\{s_1\})>>,\ldots,$
$<j,<t_n,p(\{s_1,s_2,s_3\})>>>$

It is obvious that [GO($[_{Thing}$3 SANDWICHES])] can be interpreted as expressing the information that the set $\{s_1,s_2,s_3\}$ is partitioned and that the cells of the partition are added cumulatively along the VP-Path. Note as well that [GO($[_{Thing/Path}$3 SANDWICHES])] represents a set of possible interpretations due to the fact that the indices may or may not be identical. In the case of eating sandwiches, this is quite unnatural, but *to drop three dimes* may mean that one can drop one and the same dime three times. (This point will be discussed in some detail in chapter 13.5.) If Judith ate two sandwiches at once and after that the remaining third, $t_1=t_2$. If she ate the three all together the temporal index n=1.

What about sentences like (98)?

(98) Two girls ate three sandwiches

Their derivation would be as follows:

Derivation 7 *Two girls ate three sandwiches*

$[_{Thing}$ SANDWICHES] $\{s_1,\ldots,s_i,\ldots\}$

$[_{Thing}$3 SANDWICHES] $\{s_1,s_2,s_3\}$

[GO($[_{Thing/Path}$3 SANDWICHES])] $<<t_1,p(\{s_1\})>,\ldots, <t_n,p(\{s_1,s_2,s_3\})>>$

$[_{Thing}$2 GIRLS] $\{g_1, g_2\}$

[EAT([3 SANDWICHES])([2 GIRLS])] $\{E_1,E_2\}$

where each $E_i=<<g_i,<t_1,p(\{s_1\})>>,\ldots,<g_i,<t_n,p(\{s_1,s_2,s_3\})>>>$. Again, for each i, the indices of the VP-structure may or may not be different. If all are different, then we have a complete distributive interpretation; if all indices are the same a collective one; if some are identical, one obtains 'mixed' interpretations. In the derivations 6 and 7, the interpretation of Jackendoff's representations is evidently bent into the direction of the PLUG-grammar of chapter 7.

10.6 Conclusion

This present section has been included in order to promote familiarity with the localistic way of thinking. It brings forward the additive approach to change in time as an alternative to the top-down treatment in the homogeneity-tradition. However informal localism might seem to be, conceptually it is a very interesting branch of linguistic analysis, in my view. I have first tried to offer a way of looking at the contribution of the verb to the interpretation of sentences: verbs expressing change should be seen in terms of an odometer. They provide for a natural number (taken as an ordinal), which represents dense structure. The argument structure of the verb operates at the level of the available odometer structure, that is, basically in terms of the system of natural numbers **N**. Tense will be taken later on as operating on underlying **R**-structure. The notion of Path, which has been important from the start of the Gruberian branch of localism, is taken as expressing the notion of aspectual asymmetry as pleaded for in chapter 1.

The transformation from the localistic framework to the PLUG-grammar takes two steps. The first one leads through (an interpretation of) Jackendoff's work in order to clear up certain notions central to localism and to show that they relate straightforwardly to relatively simple set-theoretical constructs. In my view, the transformation is sufficiently meaning-preserving to give a reliable idea about theoretical concepts that have always been prominent in the localistic tradition, such as the notion of Path and the dynamicity expressed by the verb. The second step will be to extend the PLUG-grammar such that the notion of Path can be built into the formal machinery of EL without enforcing an identity crisis on those who happen to work in the GQT-framework. This will be done in chapter 13.5.

11 *Event semantics and aspect construal*

11.0 Introduction

An important issue emerging from the discussion so far is the status of events. In the present aspectual theory, events – here taken as eventualities in Bach's sense – are not primitive: they are construed. In the above extrapolation of Jackendoff's theory, events result from a mapping of Things and Paths into the set of events. There are also theories in which they are taken as primitives.

Let me underscore here the pointlessness of a debate about whether or not events *are* primitive individuals or complex dividuals. That matter can be settled by belief, or maybe by purely philosophical arguments. However, a debate about events as possible denotations of expressions in a natural language is meaningful if the debate is focussed on the question of whether or not they explain things that cannot be explained otherwise. I would like to operate on this assumption, which is another way of saying that it makes no sense to explain the notion of terminativity in sentences like (47), (48), (50) and (52) in terms of expressions like ∃e(...e...), where e is a variable over eventualities or events. Of course, it is very handy to speak about events or eventualities but this does not mean that one is committed to their existence. It is just handy to have terms for things whose nature we do not understand well and whose existence we cannot be sure of. In fact, I shall adopt the position that an aspectual theory may very well be able to speak about events as if they exist in the 'real world' without referring to them in representations. Thus, one might say that (47) *Judith ate a sandwich* pertains to an event, but this does not mean that in its representation room must be made for event-variables or constants.

Perhaps the best way to characterize the position I will defend is to look for an analogy in statehood. The twelve members of the European Community are individuals only in terms of some perspective relevant at that level of operating, for example in casting votes. New members will be allowed only in terms of their meeting criteria which need investigation into their internal structure. In that respect, they are to be treated as dividuals, as illustrated in Figure 31.

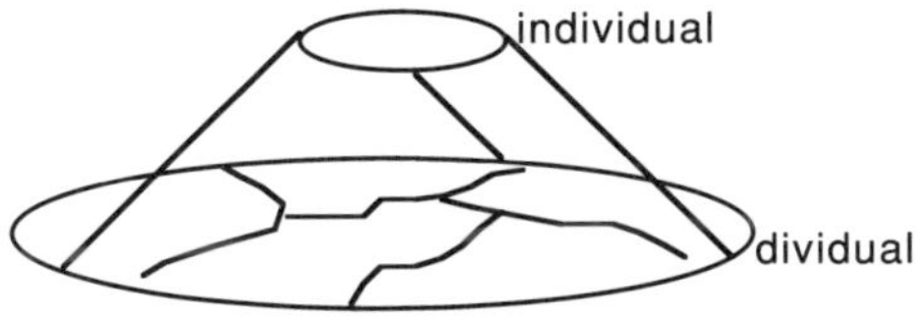

Figure 31 The notion of individual is highly relative in natural language: we shift from treating entities as individuals to treating them as 'dividuals'

Sentences can best be compared with candidates for membership: they have to meet certain criteria to become individuals at the highest level at which they form a unit. The position taken here is that it does not make sense to use the format ∃e(…e…) if you try to establish criteria for eventhood. Another aspect of Figure 31 is that we constantly change from the level of individuality to the level of dividuality and that aspect has to do with this perspectival shift, as will be argued for below in chapter 12.

It should be observed that there are in fact two sorts of event semantics: the first one is the Davidsonian branch (as from 1967); the second one is the Kamp branch (as from Kamp 1979, 1980). The latter is primarily part of the study of discourse. Abundant quantification over events has settled itself in the DRT-tradition stemming from Kamp (1981).[31] In this respect, it is perfectly understandable that events are taken as primitives which play a role in the construction of Discourse Representations. It is a matter of focus, just as in the distinction between macro-economy and micro-economy. The entities which are analytically dissected at the micro-level can be taken as indivisible units at the macro-level. So expressions like ∃e(…e…) are fully legitimate as they explicate certain properties of text structure. As said earlier, it may be doubted whether they do at the micro-level, which the present study is committed to. Given a structure of the form in Figure 32, one can easily imagine that there is

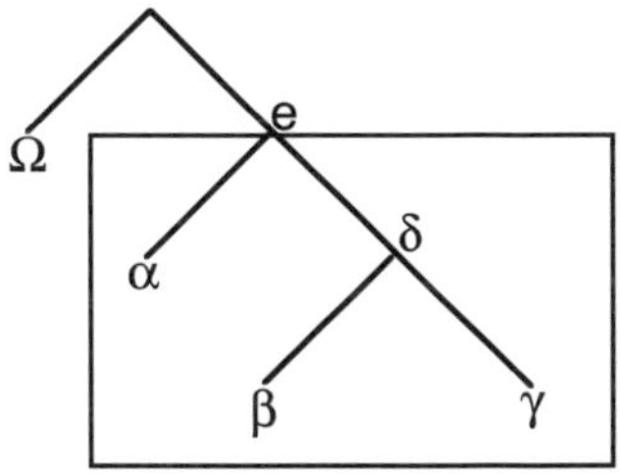

Figure 32 An existential quantifier over events is not to be taken absolutely. For the analysis of aspectuality ∃e should be allowed only if certain conditions are fulfilled by the presence of aspectual information, which is in the box

a level e at which certain linguistically relevant conditions concerning α, β and γ are met such that they enable us to talk about an event, whereas at δ or lower in the tree it would be senseless to use this term. Suppose that Figure 32 corresponds to the structure assigned to a sentence like *Judith ate a sandwich*, where α stands for *Judith*, β for *eat* and γ for *a sandwich*. Then it is at a level at which α, β and γ are structurally, that is compositionally, interpreted that one might start to say that there is an event e. In this sense, the structure inside the box – the bottom of Figure 32 – could be taken as an event structure e which can be quantified over by predicates like Ω (such as *often*, *twice*, *every day*, *for hours* and so on), and which is subject to anaphoric reference. But it means that events are not primitives in the Davidsonian sense.

In section 11.1, the entailment arguments by which Davidsonian event semanticists try to defend the use of events for the analysis of internal sentential structure will be critically examined. A possible motivation for the use of events at the micro-level would be to say that, given Figure 32, a predication of the form $\exists e\phi$ should have the structure $\exists e(\beta(e) \wedge \Theta_1(\alpha,e) \wedge \Theta_2(\gamma,e))$ in order to be qualified as a well-formed expression allowing entailments, where β is a predicate having e as its argument or one of its arguments, and where Θ_1 and Θ_2 are taken as (thematic) predicates, along the lines of, for example, Carlson (1984). In section 11.2, it will be shown that aspectual properties of sentences cannot be explained in terms of frames like $\exists e(\beta(e) \wedge \Theta_1(\alpha,e) \wedge \Theta_2(\gamma,e) \wedge \xi(e))$ where ξ stands for aspectual predicates such as 'Hold' for durative aspect, or 'Culm' (= culminate) for terminative aspect. In section 11.3, some attention will be paid to the treatment of thematic roles in event semantics and it will be argued that this is not encouraging. In section 11.4, Krifka's event semantics will be attested on its explanatory power for aspectuality. This will be done in view of the fact that in spite of his event semantics some of his basic assumptions (notably, on additivity) are so congenial to assumptions underlying the present theory that it is interesting and necessary to see what the differences and correspondences are.

11.1 Entailment arguments and monotonicity

In this section, I will review some of the arguments of some event semanticists in order to show that from the point of view of the analysis of sentential structure they systematically fail to ask the right linguistic questions. This may be due to the fact that these semanticists are philosophical logicians so that their main interest is focussed on the entailment relations of sentences, but the fact is that they leave important questions not only unanswered but even unraised.

In Davidson (1967) it was argued that verbs like *break*, *eat*, *lift*, etc. should be analysed as three-place rather than two-place predicates, the third argument being a so-called event-place e. Thus (47) would be represented as ∃e∃x (sandwich(x)∧eat(j,x,e)). This says that there is an event and there is an x such that x is a sandwich and e is j's eating of x. His article has become a landmark: it has generated what is called the Davidsonian tradition, which is characterized by two things: (a) events are taken as primitive individuals; (b) his approach is basically first order. The former property of the Davidsonian approach is purely ontological: the universe of discourse is enriched with a new sort of entities, events. They constitute a 'fundamental ontological category' on a par with material objects such as glasses, humans, and so on (see 'The Individuation of Events' and 'Events as Particulars' in Davidson 1980). As to first order: ir some way this feature of Davidson's framework seems to be related to the ontological status of events. By simply taking them as individuals, you need not construct them as complex semantic objects.[32]

Davidson (1980: 163ff.) discusses some arguments for taking events as entities. One of them is based on entailment and on the logical form of sentences and it is this argument which is linguistically relevant.[33] Davidson (1980: 166) gives the following pair of sentences:

(99) Sebastian strolled through the streets of Bologna at 2 am
(100) Sebastian strolled through the streets of Bologna

saying that (99) entails (100) 'by virtue of its logical form'. According to him, if (101) is the logical form of (99), and (102) the logical form of (100),

(101) Strolled_through_at(Sebastian, the streets of Bologna, 2 am)
(102) Strolled_through(Sebastian, the streets of Bologna)

then it is impossible formally to relate these two forms in terms of entailment because the two predicates have a different arity. Attempts to treat the binary predicate 'Strolled_through' as an elliptical form of the ternary predicate 'Strolled_through_at' fail because if one allows this, there is no theoretical upper bound to the number of ellipted arguments. So, why not do it the simple way and assuming events? This leads to the well-known Davidsonian logical form (103):

(103) ∃e(Strolled(Sebastian,e)∧Through(e,the streets of Bologna)
∧At(e,2 am))
(104) ∃e(Strolled(Sebastian,e)∧Through(e,the streets of Bologna))

which entails (104), as it also entails that Sebastian strolled and that something was through the streets of Bologna.

Parsons (1985, 1989) supports Davidson's analysis and considers the fact that a series of entailments from sentences like (99) to (100) can be made one of the major virtues of Davidson's contribution to the analysis of action sentences. Parsons modifies Davidson's analysis in that he would analyse (99) as:

(105) $\exists e(\text{Strolling}(e) \wedge \text{Agent}(\text{Sebastian}, e) \wedge \text{Through}(e, \text{the streets of Bologna}) \wedge \text{At}(e, \text{2am}))$.

This is called the neo-Davidsonian approach, which does away with the idea that an n-place verb should be analysed as an n+1 predicate in favour of the idea that the verb and its n arguments are all taken as predicates of e. This makes it possible to take grammatical functions (Subject, Object) or argument roles (Agent, Patient) as relations between events and individuals. For the rest there is no difference with Davidson, so both variants can be treated in the same way as far as the entailment arguments are concerned.

One of Parsons' examples, plus analysis, is (106).

(106) a. Brutus stabbed Caesar in the back with a knife
b. $\exists e[\text{Stabbing}(e) \wedge \text{Subject}(b,e) \wedge \text{Object}(c,e) \wedge \text{In}(\text{the\_back}, e) \wedge \text{With}(\text{a\_knife}, e)]$

which entails the truth of the sentences in (107).

(107) a. Brutus stabbed Caesar in the back
b. Brutus stabbed Caesar with a knife
c. Brutus stabbed Caesar
d. Brutus stabbed
e. There was some stabbing

The idea is simple: a set of atomic conjoined propositions entails its members.

I am deeply convinced about the fact that if something happened at a certain time something happened, and that if something happened with a knife, it happened. But the question is, of course, whether the observations made are empirically relevant and sufficient for the theory at hand. First of all, it must be observed that both Davidson and Parsons restrict themselves to cases in which they can make use of the monotone-increasing property of the generalized quantifiers ⟦Sebastian⟧ and ⟦Brutus⟧. The question of whether one needs events should also be raised in view of pairs like:

(108) At most three girls strolled through the streets of Bologna at 2 am
(109) At most three girls strolled through the streets of Bologna
(110) Not all girls strolled through the streets of Bologna at 2 am
(111) Not all girls strolled through the streets of Bologna

There appears no way to defend (108) ⊨ (109), because it is evident that at 2 a.m. the number of girls strolling through the streets of Bologna is at most three, but it does not hold for the larger period of which 2 am is part. So, the relation between (108) and (109) is different from the one between (99) and (100). In terms of GQT, *at most three girls* and *few girls* are monotone-decreasing quantifiers, so it is predicted that (109) ⊨ (108) and (111) ⊨ (110) are the proper entailments.[34] However, one may achieve (108) ⊨ (109) as follows:

(112) $\exists e(\text{Strolled}(\leq 3 \text{ girls,e}) \wedge \text{Through(e, the streets of Bologna)}$
$\wedge \text{At(e,2 am)})$

(113) $\exists e(\text{Strolled}(\leq 3 \text{ girls,e}) \wedge \text{Through(e, the streets of Bologna)})$

(114) $\exists e(\text{Strolled}(\leq 3 \text{ girls,e}))$

The fact that there is an event in which at most three girls strolled through the streets of Bologna at 2 am entails that there is an event in which at most three girls strolled through the streets of Bologna and also that there is an event in which at most three girls strolled. This analysis is radically different from the one in which at most three girls would be fronted, as in (115) and (116).

(115) $\exists{\leq}3x$(x a girl$\wedge\exists$e(e is a strolling by x$\wedge$e is through the streets of Bologna$\wedge$e is at 2 am))

(116) $\exists{\leq}3x$(x a girl$\wedge\exists$e(e is a strolling by x$\wedge$e is through the streets of Bologna))

The entailment (116) ⊨ (115) says that if one or two or three girls walked through the streets of Bologna, it is true that they walked through the streets of Bologna at 2 am. Here one can safely conclude from the truth of (116) to the truth of (115). However, the relation between (113) and (112) can only be understood if we talk about (113) as being of a completely different category from (112). That is, (116) may pertain to two different events, say one taking place with one girl in 1985, the other one also with one girl in 1986. In this way, (116) makes (115) true if one of the strolls was at 2 am. However, this is not the sort of entailment we are interested in, given the temporal structure of sentences like (108) and (109). In other words, Davidson's analysis is basically atemporal. We ought to be interested in the entailment in which the denotation of *at most three girls* and *stroll through the streets of Bologna* are kept constant, so that (108) and (109) are sentences in the same semantic category.

In my view, Davidson has in fact collapsed two sorts of analyses, which is not visible because he used a proper name to make his point and proper names do not participate in scopal differences. If one replaces the proper names by a monotone-increasing quantifier like *at least three girls*, the appropriate paraphrases are given pairwise:

(117) $\exists e$(e is a strolling by at least 3 girls$\wedge$e is through the streets of Bologna$\wedge$e is at 2 am))
(118) $\exists e$(e is a strolling by at least 3 girls$\wedge$e is through the streets of Bologna)
(119) $\exists{\geq}3x$(x a girl$\wedge\exists e$(e is a strolling by x$\wedge$e is through the streets of Bologna$\wedge$e is at 2 am))
(120) $\exists{\geq}3x$(x a girl$\wedge\exists e$(e is a strolling by x$\wedge$e is through the streets of Bologna))

Here we find both (117) $\models$ (118) and (119) $\models$ (120), but these are different sorts of entailments: (117) $\models$ (118) is the one we should be interested in from the point of view of temporal structure expressed by a sentence, not (119) $\models$ (120), even though they happen to fall together in this case. They do not in the case of (108) and (109). It is only in the monotone-increasing sentences that the logical form with the event-quantifier in front is logically equivalent to the logical form having the atemporal individual-quantifier in front. So, Davidson suggests via the equivalence of (117)/(118) and (119)/(120) that (112)/(113) is the pair we are looking at. We are not.

After all, the most simple solution for someone who is interested in the temporal structure of sentences like (99) and (100) would be simply to analyse them as:

(121) At(Strolled_through(Sebastian, the streets of Bologna), 2 am))
(122) $\exists i$(At(Strolled_through(Sebastian, the streets of Bologna), i))

In this case, the entailment relation (99) $\models$ (100) would be interpreted as a form of existential generalization over time indices, not events. In other words, (122) expresses that (100) is the existential generalization of (99), so there is a valid entailment even though there is a monotone-decreasing quantifier involved, as shown by (123) and (124).

(123) At(Strolled_through($\leq$3girls, the streets of Bologna), 2 am))
(124) $\exists i$(At(Strolled_through($\leq$3girls, the streets of Bologna), i))

The point I am trying to make is that, in spite of Davidson's conviction, temporal adverbials behave differently from other adverbials: they constitute domains in which eventualities take place and in that respect they differ considerably from manner adverbials, instrumental adverbials, etc. So, after all, I am not really convinced that we should not treat sentences like (100) as elliptical in the contexts in which we use these sentences related to temporal structure. If we use (100) 'out of the blind', then an analysis of (122) would be the unnatural burden which Davidson tried to escape. However, if we use the sentence to talk about a certain eventuality like the strolling of Sebastian or girls at a certain time, we should be able to guarantee that time structure is present even though it is not visible as in (100). I will come back to this point shortly.

Other entailments are not so valid either. Parsons discusses the following valid argument:

(125) a. In every burning, oxygen is consumed
b. Agatha burned some wood
c. Oxygen was consumed

The idea is that (125a) quantifies over burnings, and this is not the case in (125b) and (125c). Yet there must be some relation between (125a) and (125b) and between (125a) and (125c), because of the entailment relation. Parsons solves this problem by assuming that (125b) and (125c) involve (existential) quantification over burning-events. The logical forms are given in (126).

(126) a. $\forall$e(e is a burning$\rightarrow\exists$e'(e' is a consuming$\wedge$Object(oxygen,e') $\wedge$In(e,e')))
b. $\exists$e(e is a burning$\wedge\exists$x(x is wood$\wedge$Agent(agatha,e)$\wedge$Object(x,e)))
c. $\exists$e(e is a consuming$\wedge$Object(oxygen,e))

It is easy to find counterexamples by which the importance of having event-variables is reduced considerably, for example (127).

(127) a. In every blessing, the pope speaks twelve languages
b. The pope blessed Agatha
c. The pope spoke twelve languages (to bless Agatha)

Even though (127a) and (127b) are true, (127c) need not follow, for example because Agatha may have left the church right after the blessing in her own language. Note that (127c) must be understood as pertaining to Agatha's blessing because (125c) can only be understood by assuming that it should be read as: oxygen was consumed for the burning of some wood. So logical forms like (128) along the lines of (125) will not do.

(128) a. $\forall$e(Blessing(e)$\rightarrow\exists$e'(Speaking(e')$\wedge$Object(12_languages,e') $\wedge$Agent(the pope,e')$\wedge$In(e,e')))
b. $\exists$e(Blessing(e)$\wedge$Object(agatha,e)$\wedge$Agent(the pope,e))
c. $\exists$e(Speaking(e)$\wedge$Object(12 languages,e'))

It should be pointed out that I do not deny the validity of (125); I only deny its status as an argument for eventhood on the basis of logical forms containing event variables. The simple truth is that representations like (126) tend to conceal rather than reveal the intricacies of quantificational structure involved in the sentences under analysis.

The same applies to the way temporal adverbials are treated, that is, simply as a predicate over e. This can be demonstrated as follows. Davidson warns us repeatedly not to treat sentences like (129a) as referring to a particular event. Doris may have capsized twelve times and this uncertainty is what (129b) really expresses, and what justifies the ∃e in (129c):

(129) a. Doris capsized the canoe yesterday
b. Doris capsized the canoe
c. $\exists e(\text{Capsizing}(e) \wedge \text{Agent}(doris,e) \wedge \text{Object}(her\_canoe,e) \wedge \text{Yesterday}(e))$

Thus, he concludes, there is no singular term which uniquely determines an event.[35] However, there are problems with sentences like (130).

(130) a. Doris capsized her canoe yesterday and the day before
b. Doris capsized her canoe
c. $\exists e(e \text{ is a capsizing} \wedge \text{Agent}(doris,e) \wedge \text{Object}(her\ canoe,e) \wedge \text{Yesterday}(e) \wedge \text{The\_day\_before}(e))$
d. $\exists e \exists e'(\text{Capsizing}(e) \wedge \text{Agent}(doris,e) \wedge \text{Object}(her\ canoe,e) \wedge \text{Yesterday}(e) \wedge \text{Capsizing}(e') \wedge \text{Agent}(doris,e') \wedge \text{Object}(her\ canoe,e') \wedge \text{The\_day\_before}(e'))$

As observed in Verkuyl (1972), sentences like (130a) must mean that Doris capsized her canoe (at least) twice, once yesterday, the other time the day before.[36] Note that we cannot obtain in (130c) the entailment we need to have, namely that Doris capsized at least two canoes, unless we distinguish between two events e and e′. So one is forced to assign the logical form (130d) to (130a). Apart from its high degree of artificiality, suppose that Davidsonians commit themselves to (130d). Then they have to explain why sentences like (131a) do not lead to event splitting:

(131) a. Doris capsized her canoe quickly and unexpectedly
b. $\exists e(\text{Capsizing}(e) \wedge \text{Agent}(Doris,e) \wedge \text{Object}(her\_canoe,e) \wedge \text{Quick}(e) \wedge \text{Unexpected}(e))$

In other words, one should explain the difference between manner adverbials and temporal (domain) adverbials.

There is a second problem for them. Sentences like (132a) may pertain to two sailings or to one. This is allowed for by the existential quantifier in (132c):

(132) a. Doris sailed on Lake Erie yesterday and the day before
b. Doris sailed on Lake Erie
c. $\exists$e(Sailing(e)$\wedge$Agent(doris,e)$\wedge$On(lake_erie,e) $\wedge$Yesterday+The_day_before(e))
d. $\exists$e$\exists$e′(Sailing (e)$\wedge$Agent(doris,e)$\wedge$Object(her_canoe,e) $\wedge$On(lake_erie,e)$\wedge$On(lake_erie,e′)$\wedge$Yesterday(e)$\wedge$Sailing(e′) $\wedge$Agent(doris,e′)$\wedge$Object(her_canoe,e′)$\wedge$The_day_before(e′))

However, if (132a) pertains to two sailings, it should locate one event in the domain ⟦yesterday⟧ and the other one in the domain ⟦the day before yesterday⟧. So again, one is forced to allow something like the monstrous (132d).

It is important to see that aspectual properties play a role here: (129b) is a terminative sentence, whereas (132b) is a durative sentence. Note that if Davidson is right in observing that (129b) should be analysed in terms of existential quantification over events, because (129b) may pertain to more than one capsizing, the quantifier must range over entities whose aspectual properties have already been established. This means that aspectual properties are determined at the level at which the entities e are dividuals rather than individuals. It also shows at least that there is a more demanding structural relation between temporal adverbials introducing temporal domains and the events located in them. The representations given by Davidson are in no way fit for expressing the difference in entailment behaviour between the sentences in (130) and (132). So, let us see what Parsons' extension of Davidson's framework will have to say on this topic.

11.2 Development and Culmination

Parsons introduces two 'key technical notions': (a) the notion of culmination; and (b) the notion of holding. In Parsons (1985: 240), Culm(e,t) is 'to mean that *e* is an event that culminates at *t*', whereas Hold(e,t) means 'that the eventuality in question is holding at *t*, that is, that *e* is a state and *e*'s agent is in state *e* at *t*, or *e* is a process which is going on at *t*, or *e* is an event which is in development at *t*'. Thus the difference between (133a) and (134a) is accounted for in terms of a difference between these two predicates.

(133) a. Mary saw Fred
b. $\exists t(t < now \wedge \exists e[Seeing'(e) \wedge Subject(m,e) \wedge Object(f,e) \wedge Hold(e,t)])$

(134) a. Mary built the bookcase
b. $\exists t(t < now \wedge \exists e[Building'(e) \wedge Subject(m,e) \wedge Object(c,e) \wedge Culm(e,t)])$

It is necessary to give some of the relevant rules of the grammar used by Parsons. The syntactic categories distinguished are: NAME (=proper noun), V, VP, CL (=sentential clause), Adv, Prep and S. The translations are added on the line(s) following the syntactic rule.

PG-Rules

R1: If $\alpha \in V_{Intr}$, then $\alpha \in VP$
$\alpha \rightsquigarrow \lambda e[\alpha'(e)]$

R2: If $\alpha \in V_{Trans}$ and $\beta \in$ NAME, then $\alpha\beta \in VP$
$(\alpha\beta)' \rightsquigarrow \lambda e[\alpha'(e) \wedge Object(\beta',e)]$

R3: If $\beta \in$ NAME and $\alpha \in VP$, then $\beta\alpha \in$ (untensed) CL
•if α is a state or a process VP:
$(\beta\alpha)' \rightsquigarrow \lambda e \lambda t[\alpha'(e) \wedge Agent(\beta',e) \wedge Hold(e,t)]$
•if α is an event VP:
$(\beta\alpha)' \rightsquigarrow \lambda e \lambda t[\alpha'(e) \wedge Agent(\beta',e) \wedge Culm(e,t)]$

R4: If $\alpha \in$ CL, then Past(α), Pres(α), Fut(α)$\in CL_{Tensed}$
$Past(\alpha)' \rightsquigarrow \lambda e \lambda t(\exists t'[t'<t \wedge \alpha'(e,t')]$,
$Pres(\alpha)' \rightsquigarrow \alpha'$, and
$Fut(\alpha)' \rightsquigarrow \lambda e \lambda t(\exists t'[t'>t \wedge \alpha'(e,t')]$

R5: If $\alpha \in CL_{Tensed}$, then $\#\alpha\# \in S$
$(\#\alpha\#)' \rightsquigarrow \lambda t.\exists e(\alpha'(e,t))$

R6. If α is a non-stative VP, then be α-ing is a Stative VP
be α'-ing $\rightsquigarrow \lambda e[\alpha'(e)]$, or
be α'-ing $\rightsquigarrow \lambda e[\alpha'(e) \wedge Object(\beta',e)]$

R7: If $\alpha \in$ Adv and $\beta \in$ VP, then $\beta\alpha \in$ VP
$(\beta\alpha)' \rightsquigarrow \lambda e[\beta'(e) \wedge \alpha'(e)]$

R8: If $\alpha \in$ Prep and $\beta \in$ NAME, then $\alpha\beta \in$ Adv
$(\alpha\beta)' \rightsquigarrow \lambda e[\alpha'(\beta',e)]$

In her analysis of this rule system – she discusses the complete version as well as earlier variants of rule 3 – Lascarides (1988) demonstrates a number of logical inconsistencies. In my opinion, she is right and so I shall briefly summarize her main points by way of introduction, but only because it sheds some light on the basic shortcoming of an enterprise based on lame predicates like Culm and

Hold. So, my own criticism is independent and focussed on other aspects of the system.

The main problem according to Lascarides is that the predicates Culm and Hold are logically independent of one another. She makes this visible by a detailed comparison of the difference between the clauses (135) and (136):

(135) a. Max won a race
b. $\lambda t(\exists e)(\exists t')[t'<t \wedge Winning'(e) \wedge Agent(max',e) \wedge Object(race',e) \wedge Culm(e,t')]$

(136) a. Max was winning a race
b. $\lambda t(\exists e)(\exists t')[t'<t \wedge Winning'(e) \wedge Agent(max',e) \wedge Object(race',e) \wedge Hold(e,t')]$

There is no way to relate these logical forms, so the Progressive Form in (136) is not logically related to the non-progressive form in (135), whereas (135a) entails (136a).

Evidently, Parsons' PG has some difficulties with the 'development' part of a terminative phrase. Lascarides points out that sentences like (137a), which have the logical form (137b),

(137) a. Max ran across the street
b. $\lambda t(\exists e)(\exists t')[t'<t \wedge Running'(e) \wedge Agent(max',e) \wedge Across'(street',e) \wedge Culm(e,t')]$

are always false, the problem being that *run* translates as $\lambda e.running'(e)$, which is a process. Hence *running* cannot culminate. Hence (137) is always false.

Parsons (1989) himself is also not content about the treatment of Processes along with States. He proposes to treat Process verbs as denoting events. This would change rule 3 to R3′.

R3′: If $\beta \in$ NAME and $\alpha \in$ VP, then $\beta\alpha \in$ (untensed) CL
if α is a state VP:
$(\beta\alpha)' \rightsquigarrow \lambda e \lambda t[\alpha'(e) \wedge Agent(\beta',e) \wedge Hold(e,t)]$
if α is a process or event VP:
$(\beta\alpha)' \rightsquigarrow \lambda e \lambda t[\alpha'(e) \wedge Agent(\beta',e) \wedge Culm(e,t)]$

An advantage would be that sentences like *Max was running across the street* do not entail *Max ran across the street*, so that the Imperfective Paradox is avoided. According to Lascarides, however, this is not the whole story. For the whole story one also has to look at (138) and (139), the latter obtained by R6, which makes a stative VP out of a non-stative VP.

(138) a. Max ran

b. $\lambda t(\exists e)(\exists t')[t' < t \wedge Running'(e) \wedge Agent(max',e) \wedge Culm(e,t')]$

(139) a. Max was running

b. $\lambda t(\exists e)(\exists t')[t' < t \wedge Running'(e) \wedge Agent(max',e) \wedge Hold(e,t')]$

The two sentences are logically unrelated. There is no logically valid entailment, where there should be. Lascarides shows that other revisions do not lead to the desired result. Her conclusion is that there is something fundamentally wrong with the whole approach of dealing with aspect in terms of the predicates Hold and Culm.

My own objections are more linguistic. The first one concerns the rules R3 and R3′. They smuggle in a lot of information which should be dealt with more carefully. Let us focus on R3′ because this is evidently the latest version (but my remarks apply to R3 as well). How do we know that α is a State VP or an Event (=Process or Event) VP? As a philosopher Parsons has the right to speak about States and Events as discernible entities, but it is a different matter to speak about a State VP and an Event VP. The question, then, is simply: how do you know that you are justified to introduce predicates like Hold and Culm? What are the linguistic means to provide for such a justification? If the answer would be that there are linguistic clues, then the question is: why do you not proceed by construing?

The second objection is that in Parsons' PG there is no systematic way to relate the Agent- and Patient-predicates to the Culm/Hold-predicates and to the main predicate. This has several consequences, one of them being that the aspectual asymmetry cannot be accounted for. All propositions making up the representation have an equal status, so there is no way to account for a phenomenon that is empirically established. That is, Parsons' representation cannot deal with the fact that the VP *run across the street* is terminative and should 'contain' the Culm-predicate, dependent on the [+SQA]-nature of the NP *the street*. In short, there is no way to express that the Culm-predicate has much closer ties to the complement of the verb than to its subject. Of course, Parsons cannot deal with *run across streets* and with *Children ran across the street* simply because he has no mechanism to replace Culm by Hold dependent on the [–SQA]-nature of the NP involved. That is, there is no way to account for the contribution of [+SQA]-information to Culm.

The third related objection is that nothing in Parsons' representations could possibly point into the direction of an explanation. A logical form like (137b) contains the culmination information expressed by Culm, but it also contains the 'culmination' information expressed by Across′ as opposed to Along′. The question is, of course, why for sentences like (140a)

(140) a. Max ran along the street
b. $\lambda t(\exists e)(\exists t')[t'<t \wedge Running'(e) \wedge Agent(max',e) \wedge Along'(street',e) \wedge Culm(e,t')]$
c. $\lambda t(\exists e)(\exists t')[t'<t \wedge Running'(e) \wedge Agent(max',e) \wedge Along'(street',e) \wedge Hold(e,t')]$

(140b) is not appropriate, whereas (140c) would be correct (in Parsons' system, that is). It means that *along* must be characterized lexically as being involved in the choice of Hold. This is not the story told by the PG-rules, which says that Hold and Culm are introduced by R3 (or R3′) and that R7 takes a VP and combines it with an Adverbial Phrase formed by R8. I know of no detailed description of the meaning of prepositions in Parsons' work (nor in Davidson's work), which might hint at a solution. Suppose that by R3 (141a) is chosen and that R8 is to be applied.

(141) a. $\lambda e \lambda t[Running'(e) \wedge Agent(\beta',e) \wedge Hold(e,t)]$
b. $\lambda e \lambda t[Running'(e) \wedge Agent(\beta',e) \wedge Culm(e,t)]$

It should make a difference whether Across′(street′,e) or Along(street′,e) is selected, because the former should not be allowed to enter into (141a), whereas the latter may be allowed. So, some context-sensitive rules are needed to account for the difference. Parsons does not give them, and as long as they are not given, the lack of any rule must count as a counterargument against PG. The same problem shows up for R3′. In (141b), Along(street′,e) must be blocked. So, in either alternative there is an unsolved problem, and no way to go for a reasonable solution without taking into account the root of the problem: the lack of interaction between the different propositions making up the logical form. And this is exactly what is wrong with Parsons' approach: there is no principled way to deal with the variety of factors determining terminative and durative aspect. Summarizing, Parsons' PG rules fall short of dealing adequately with sentences as in (142).

(142) a. Max ran across the street
b. Max ran along the street
c. Max ran across streets
d. Children ran across streets

This problem is rooted deeply in the abundant use of $\wedge$ in the logical forms resulting from the quantification over e: the analysis in terms of atomic propositions blocks any deep understanding of the relationship between Running′, Agent, Object, Along′ on the one hand and Culm or Hold on the other hand. The only way to bring some system is to work with a set of coherent postulates defining the relation between the members of the complex proposition, as in Krifka's work discussed in section 11.4. Parsons does not have such a system.

11.3 Thematic structure and eventology

The fifth objection is the poor argumentation for the choice of the specific roles. It is clear that Parsons is wavering between several options. In Parsons (1985) he uses Agent and Object, in Parsons (1989) Subject and Object. It is evident that he did not pay much attention to the question of what exactly the predicates Agent, Object, Subject, etc. stand for.

Dowty (1989) goes a long way to seeing whether this part of the Davidsonian approach can be improved upon. I shall discuss his analysis in some detail because it is important for the assessment of the issues involved. Moreover, he tries to make a sort of compromise between the Davidsonian and non-Davidsonian treatment of argument structure. Dowty sees three important consequences and advantages of the (neo-)Davidsonian analysis. First of all, completeness is obtained, because the only way to say that an individual participates in an event is by relating it to an event by a thematic predicate. Secondly, each thematic role is distinct: there is no verb assigning the same thematic role to different arguments. And thirdly, the thematic roles are characterized independently from the meaning of the verb, which means that the predication Agent(β',e) is the same for *run* and for *kill*.

One could object to the first point by saying that representations like (135b), (138b) and (140b) do not reveal how many arguments a verb has, but this problem is solved by postulates, like (143)–(145).

(143) $\forall e \Box[\text{giving}(e) \rightarrow \exists x.\text{Theme}(x,e) \wedge \exists y.\text{Source}(y,e) \wedge \exists z.\text{Goal}(z,e)]$

(144) $\forall e \forall x \Box[[\text{singing}(e) \wedge \text{Agent}(x,e)] \rightarrow \text{Moving\_vocal\_chords}(x)]$

(145) $\forall \Theta_i \forall e \forall x \Box[\Theta_i(x,e) \rightarrow \forall y[\Theta_i(y,e) \rightarrow x=y]]$

Postulate (143) assures that events of giving always have three participants, (144) exemplifies entailments about singing Agents, and (145) warrants the uniqueness of the individual role-bearer, by stipulating that no other individual has the same role in a certain event.[37] Note, by the way, that Dowty uses quite different thematic roles from Davidson and Parsons, but even though it is an improvement, it does not take away the drawbacks concerning the relation between elements in these propositions. That is, if Parsons' PG-system would be equipped with thematic roles like Theme, Source, Goal, it would gain nothing.

The point where Dowty raises doubts as to the neo-Davidsonian approach is the way it deals with argument reduction. Consider (146)–(148).

(146) a. Mary gave a book to John
b. Mary gave a book
c. Mary gave

(147) a. Judith ate a sandwich
b. Judith ate

(148) a. John drove from Chicago to Boston
b. John drove to Boston
c. John drove

Dowty compares the neo-Davidsonian approach with what he calls the Ordered-Argument Approach, in which a verb is given a fixed number of argument places for arguments. Standardly, for an n-place predicate, the denotation of the arguments is a n-tuple, such that (149) holds:

(149) $[\![P(x_1, \ldots, x_n)]\!]=1$ iff $<I(x_1), \ldots, I(x_n)> \in [\![P]\!]$
(150) $[\![P(x_1, \ldots, x_{n-1})]\!]=1$ iff $\exists y: <I(x_1), \ldots, I(x_{n-1}), I(y)> \in [\![P]\!]$

Dowty observes that on the Ordered-Argument Approach, if a verb appears without one of its arguments, as for example in the (b) and (c) cases of (146)–(148), the semantic interpretation follows (150). Thus, (146b) would be represented as (151), which is a form of existential quantification, whereas neo-Davidsonians would represent it as (152):

(151) $\exists y \in \text{Book} \exists z.\text{Give}(\text{mary},y,z)$,
(152) $\exists e[\text{giving}(e) \wedge \text{Theme}(\text{the\_book},e) \wedge \text{Source}(m,e)]$

For (151), the lexical postulate (143) would warrant the existence of the missing participant having the Goal-role. Dowty (1989: 89) does not really choose between these mechanisms, but continues to observe that verbs

> characteristically exhibit subcategorization – i.e. each verb has one or more fixed sets of complements – and this subcategorization is independent of the matter of what event participants are entailed to exist by the meaning of the verb. The verbs *dine*, *eat* and *devour*, for example, all entail the consumption of some quantity of food, but the first is obligatorily intransitive, the third obligatorily transitive and the second belongs to both subcategories.

On the neo-Davidsonian approach (143) allows for a series of entailments:

(153) a. Mary gave a book to John
b. $\exists e[\text{giving}(e) \wedge \text{Theme}(\text{a\_book},e) \wedge \text{Source}(m,e) \wedge \text{Goal}(j,e)]$
(154) a. Mary gave a book
b. $\exists e[\text{giving}(e) \wedge \text{Theme}(\text{a\_book},e) \wedge \text{Source}(m,e)]$

(155) a. A book was given
b. $\exists e[giving(e) \wedge Theme(a\_book,e)]$
(156) a. Mary gave to John
b. $\exists e[giving(e) \wedge Source(m,e) \wedge Goal(j,e)]$
(157) a. A book was given to John
b. $\exists e[giving(e) \wedge Theme(a\_book,e) \wedge Goal(j,e)]$
(158) a. Mary gave
b. $\exists e[giving(e) \wedge Source(m,e)]$
(159) a. John was given
b. $\exists e[giving(e) \wedge Goal(j,e)]$
(160) a. There was a giving
b. $\exists e[giving(e)]$

However, as Dowty points out, it meets a lot of difficulties with many constructions, such as *John dined* vs. **John dined his lunch* and **John devoured* and *John devoured his lunch.* It might be added that in (153)–(160) there are problems too. One is inclined to allow (160b) as an entailment, but it is interesting only if the sentence were *Gave* and if (160a) were not the form used to express that entailment. So there are more restrictions involved, even in a well-behaving *give*-pattern. Moreover, (156a) may mean that Mary gave different things to John at different times and different places, whereas (154a) is more close to the one-event reading expressed by (153).[38]

Dowty observes that the sort of restrictions on verbs like *dine* and *devour* do not occur in NPs whose head noun denotes an event, such as *The gift of a book from Mary to John would surprise Helen.* This sentence freely allows all possible entailments like *the gift of a book to John*, *the gift to John*, *the gift*, etc. So Dowty concludes that there are many reasons to assume that the neo-Davidsonian approach is to be restricted to the realm of nouns denoting events and to adjuncts.

At this point, it is important to have a look again at the sentences in (146)–(148), which I repeat here, adding aspectual information:

(146)	a. Mary gave a book to John	terminative
	b. Mary gave a book	terminative
	c. Mary gave	durative
(147)	a. Judith ate a sandwich	terminative
	b. Judith ate	durative
(148)	a. John drove from Chicago to Boston	terminative
	b. John drove to Boston	terminative
	c. John drove	durative

The transition from terminative to durative is a problem both for (143) as well as for the alternative scheme (161), which is the one which Parsons would have to use.

(161) $\forall e \Box[\text{giving}(e) \rightarrow \exists x.\text{Theme}(x,e) \wedge \exists y.\text{Source}(y,e) \wedge \exists z.\text{Goal}(z,e) \wedge \text{Culm}(e)]$

Of course, it is possible to make stipulations, but this is an artefact of the decision to work in terms of event-arguments. It would be a bad thing to put this into meaning postulates, because then one might be tempted to try and explain these meaning postulates and then we are back at page 1 of the present study. In my view, the absence of a mapping making the VP-Path bounded explains the data in (146)–(148). As long as there are NPs which may fulfil the role of making a Path bounded, a VP becomes terminative. The (c) cases can be dealt with in terms of the bare-plural analysis and not in terms of an existential introduction of entities. That is, *Mary gave* means 'Mary gave things', where things being taken as of type *<<e,t>,t>* denotes an unbounded collection of entities (see chapter 14.3).

11.4 Krifka's event semantics

After Krifka (1987, 1989a, 1989b) it has become impossible to assess event semantics without taking into account Krifka's contributions. He offers a theory of 'temporal constitution' in which both count and mass terms are accounted for. Following Link's lattice-theoretical approach, he uses lattices maintaining a first-order ontology because a join of two individuals is taken as an individual itself (see chapter 2.7).[39]

The model structure for the representational language and its partly formalized metalanguage is a six-tuple $M_K = \langle O, E, \sqcup_O, \sqcup_E, \sqsubseteq_O, \sqsubseteq_E \rangle$, where O is the domain of objects (atomic or complex individuals) and E the domain of events (atomic or complex individuals). The structure in O and E is that of a join semi-lattice without a zero element (so atoms are the lowest-level entities in the structures). If the join-operator $\sqcup_O$ applies to two individuals, say z and z′, then $z \sqcup_O z'$ is also an individual (in O). Likewise $z \sqsubseteq_E z'$ means that z is a part of z′ in E.[40] Furthermore, P, Q, etc. are one-place predicates applying to individuals. The same applies to predicates R, which, being of type *<e,<e,t>>*, express relations between entities. There are many postulates, formulated in a higher-order (meta-)language, which constrain the behaviour of predicates and relations. When necessary, they will be given in a definition at the relevant places. Krifka also makes use of measure functions so as to be able to deal with

NPs like *five ounces of gold*. Therefore he also includes names for real numbers and arithmetic operations in his representations.

A brief summary of the main features of Krifka's system is in order, to make it possible to compare his approach with the present approach. In a number of ways there is congeniality between the two. There are also a number of differences, as will become clear when we proceed. Let us see how Krifka derives sentences like (162), (163) and (47)–(49):

(162) Judith ate bread
(163) Judith ate the sandwich
(47) Judith ate a sandwich
(48) Judith ate three sandwiches
(49) Judith ate sandwiches

Krifka (1989a) is not sufficient, as follows from (164):

(164)

a.	eat	$\rightsquigarrow \lambda e[eat'(e) \wedge Ag(e,x) \wedge Pat(e,y)]$
b.	bread	$\rightsquigarrow \lambda P \lambda e \exists y[P(e) \wedge bread'(y)]$
c.	eat bread	$\rightsquigarrow \lambda e \exists y[eat'(e) \wedge Ag(e,x) \wedge Pat(e,y) \wedge bread'(y)]$
d.	Judith	$\rightsquigarrow \lambda P \lambda e \exists x[P(e) \wedge Ag(e,x) \wedge x{=}j]$
e.	Judith eats bread	$\rightsquigarrow \lambda e \exists x \exists y[eat'(e) \wedge Ag(e,x) \wedge Pat(e,y) \wedge bread'(y) \wedge x{=}j]$

In (164a), the verb *eat* is lexically characterized as a two-place verb (1989a: 108f.), whose arguments are Agent and Patient, respectively. The variable x is a fixed variable for the subject NP and y a fixed variable for the object NP.[41] In (164c), ⟦bread⟧ has been applied to ⟦eat⟧, yielding a set of events. In (164e), ⟦Judith⟧ defined in (164d) is applied to the VP-denotation (164c). The derivation is not spelled out, but on applying lambda-conversion it should be clear that something is wrong with (164), or simply missing. For example, the application of (164d) to (164c) proceeds as in (165):

(165) $\lambda P \lambda e \exists x[P(e) \wedge Ag(e,x) \wedge x{=}j](\lambda e \exists y[eat'(e) \wedge Ag(e,x) \wedge Pat(e,y) \wedge bread'(y)])$

and this makes it clear that there are at least two problems: (a) the doubling of Ag(e,x); and (b) the fact that the free variable x in (164a) is bound by ∃x, which is, of course, not allowed.

There is another problem with the introduction of Ag and Pat: they must be introduced with free variables. It cannot be done with lambda-abstraction, as shown in (166):

(166)

a. eat $\rightsquigarrow$ $\lambda e\lambda x\lambda y[eat'(e)\wedge Ag(e,x)\wedge Pat(e,y)]$

b. bread $\rightsquigarrow$ $\lambda P\lambda e\exists y[P(e)\wedge bread'(y)]$

c. eat bread $\rightsquigarrow$ $\lambda P\lambda e\exists y[P(e)\wedge bread'(y)](\lambda e\lambda x\lambda y[eat'(e)\wedge Ag(e,x)\wedge Pat(e,y)])$
$\lambda e\exists y[\lambda e\lambda x\lambda y[eat'(e)\wedge Ag(e,x)\wedge Pat(e,y)](e)\wedge bread'(y)]$
$\lambda e\exists y[\lambda x\lambda y[eat'(e)\wedge Ag(e,x)\wedge Pat(e,y)]\wedge bread'(y)]$

There is no way to get rid of λx and λy. This is, of course, another way of saying that P is not of the right type to perform lambda-conversion. But this raises the question: why a different treatment for the variables x, y and e in *eat*?

In a personal communication about these two problems, Krifka pointed out that the representation in Krifka (1989a) is indeed not correct, but that the (earlier) Krifka (1989b) and Krifka (1990) contain a solution to both problems, or at least a way out. This would lead to (167) rather than to (164).

(167)

a. eat $\rightsquigarrow \lambda e[eat'(e)]$

b $\emptyset_{obj/pat}$ $\rightsquigarrow \lambda Q\lambda P\lambda e\exists y[P(e)\wedge Pat(e,y)\wedge Q(y)]$

c. bread $\rightsquigarrow \lambda x.bread'(x)$

d. ø bread $\rightsquigarrow \lambda P\lambda e\exists y[P(e)\wedge Pat(e,y)\wedge bread'(y)]$

e. eat bread $\rightsquigarrow \lambda e\exists y[eat'(e)\wedge Pat(e,y)\wedge bread'(y)]$

f. Judith $\rightsquigarrow \lambda P\lambda e\exists x[P(e)\wedge Ag(e,x)\wedge x=j]$

g. Judith eats bread $\rightsquigarrow \lambda e\exists x\exists y[eat'(e)\wedge Pat(e,y)\wedge bread'(y)\wedge Ag(e,x)\wedge x=j]$

That is, the direct object NP *bread* will be marked syntactically as being both Object and Patient. The Patient-information is translated via the determiner into the presence of the role-information Pat(e,y) in the NP *bread*, the variable y now being bound by the existential quantifier introduced in the determiner. The same applies *mutatis mutandis* to the subject NP. The machinery necessary to accomplish this is shown in (168), which is the general definition of the indefinite determiner, as suggested by Krifka (pers. comm.):

(168)

$$[\![[NP\begin{bmatrix}ARG: v\\ \Theta: w\end{bmatrix}/N]]\!] = \lambda Q\lambda P\lambda e\exists f: f(v)[P(e)\wedge f(w)(e,f(v))\wedge Q(f(v))]$$

It says that ø takes a Noun (*bread*) to form an NP; v is an argument-variable and w is a variable over the thematic-role predicates. Krifka assumes a function f mapping the syntactic information PAT to the role-information Pat. So, f(PAT)=Pat. Given (168), and dependent on the syntactic position of the NP, the variables in the indefinite determiner of *bread* in *eat bread* are given the values y and Pat, by application of f to v and to w, respectively. The existential quantifier binds the syntactic variable y and it also binds the variable y in the Pat(e,y)-predicate. Note in passing that the verb *eat* in (167) is now totally deprived of its arguments and that the information about its arguments is taken over by syntax and by the determiners of the argument-NPs which are to be identified syntactically. Assuming, however, that (167) is really an improvement on (164), we must also assume that the derivation of a sentence like (47) proceeds as in (169):

(169)

a.	eat	$\rightsquigarrow$	$\lambda e[eat'(e)]$
b	$a_{obj/pat}$	$\rightsquigarrow$	$\lambda R\lambda P\lambda e\exists y[P(e)\wedge Pat(e,y)\wedge R(y, 1)]$
c.	sandwich	$\rightsquigarrow$	$\lambda n\lambda x.sandwich'(x,n)$
d.	a sandwich	$\rightsquigarrow$	$\lambda P\lambda e\exists y[P(e)\wedge Pat(e,y)\wedge sandwich'(y,1)]$
e.	eat a sandwich	$\rightsquigarrow$	$\lambda e\exists y[eat'(e)\wedge Pat(e,y)\wedge sandwich'(y,1)]$
f.	Judith	$\rightsquigarrow$	$\lambda P\lambda e\exists x[P(e)\wedge Ag(e,x)\wedge x=j]$
g.	Judith eats a sandwich		
		$\rightsquigarrow$	$\lambda e\exists x\exists y[eat'(e)\wedge Pat(e,y)\wedge sandwich'(y,1)$ $\wedge Ag(e,x)\wedge x=j]$

Note that the quantificational information inherent in *a sandwich* is dealt with in two ways: the noun *sandwich* is analysed as a relation between an entity and a number, whereas the determiner contains the information that this number is 1. So λnλx.sandwich′(x,n), being of type <*e*,<*e*,*t*>>, may replace the variable R. For sentences like (48) *Judith ate three sandwiches*, this would mean (170), for (163) *Judith ate the sandwich* it would mean (171):

(170) $\lambda e\exists x\exists y[eat'(e)\wedge Pat(e,y)\wedge sandwich'(y,3)\wedge Ag(e,x)\wedge x=j]$

(171) $\lambda e\exists x\exists y[eat'(e)\wedge Pat(e,sup(\lambda y.sandwich'(y,1))\wedge Ag(e,x)\wedge x=j]$

Here, the supremum SUP is taken as SUP(P)=x iff P(x)∧x=FU(P), and FU is the fusion operation mapping a set to its lowest upper bound.[42] As to (49), *Judith ate sandwiches*, Krifka's (shortened) derivation would be (172).[43]

(172)

a.	sandwiches	$\rightsquigarrow$	$\lambda m\lambda x.sandwich'(x,m)$
b.	$\emptyset_{obj/pat}$	$\rightsquigarrow$	$\lambda R\lambda P\lambda e\exists y[P(e)\wedge Pat(e,y)\wedge\exists n(R(y)=n)]$
c.	ø sandwiches	$\rightsquigarrow$	$\lambda P\lambda e\exists y[P(e)\wedge Pat(e,y)\wedge\exists n(sandwich'(y,n))]$

d. eat sandwiches $\rightsquigarrow$ $\lambda e\exists y[eat'(e)\wedge Pat(e,y)\wedge\exists n(sandwich'(y,n))]$

e. Judith eats sandwiches

$$\rightsquigarrow \lambda e\exists x\exists y[eat'(e)\wedge Pat(e,y)\wedge\exists n(sandwich'(y,n)) \wedge Ag(e,x)\wedge x=j]$$

The bare plural is treated in terms of an existential quantification over numerals. This is not adequate in the light of the analysis of bare NPs in chapter 6.3 and chapter 8.2.

Now, the question is: what makes (47), (48) and (163) terminative, and what makes (162) and (49) durative? Krifka's answer is: durative VPs like *eat bread* and *eat sandwiches* are cumulative, whereas terminative VPs like *eat a sandwich* are quantized. When is an expression cumulative? According to Krifka, an expression ϕ of the form:

(173) $\phi \rightsquigarrow \lambda e\exists y[\alpha(e)\wedge\ldots\wedge\Theta(e,y)\wedge\delta(y]$

is cumulative if α and δ are cumulative and Θ is summative.

DEFINITION 1: CUMULATIVITY

$\forall P(\textbf{CUM}(P) \quad \Leftrightarrow \quad \forall x\forall y[P(x)\wedge P(y)\rightarrow P(x\sqcup y)])$

DEFINITION 2: SUMMATIVITY

$\forall R(\textbf{SUM}(R) \quad \Leftrightarrow \quad \forall e\forall e'\forall z\forall z'[R(e,z)\wedge R(e',z')\rightarrow R(e\sqcup_E e',z\sqcup_O z')])$

Cumulativity says that if you join two events, the result will be a complex event and if you join members of a set of object individuals, the result will be a complex individual. If Θ holds between an event and an individual, *Summativity* warrants that it will hold for all the joins in O and E. Given these definitions, the difference between the durative (162) and the terminative (47) and (48) must be a difference in the relation between α (=eat), δ (=bread or a sandwich) and Θ. Krifka says that a ϕ with a cumulative α expresses a durative predicate, that is, is cumulative, if δ is cumulative and Θ is summative.

For terminative VPs like *eat a sandwich* and *eat three sandwiches* the following seems to hold: an expression of the form (171) represents a terminative VP if α is cumulative, δ has *Quantized reference* and Θ satisfies the constraints *Uniqueness of objects*, following Dowty's (145), and *Mapping to objects*.[44]

DEFINITION 3: Quantized reference

$\forall P(\textbf{QUA}_O(P) \quad \Leftrightarrow \quad \forall z\forall z'[P(z)\wedge P(z')\rightarrow\neg z'\sqsubseteq z])$

DEFINITION 4: Uniqueness of objects

$\forall R(\textbf{UNI–O}(R) \quad \Leftrightarrow \quad \forall e\forall z\forall z'[R(e,z)\wedge R(e,z')\rightarrow z=z'])$

DEFINITION 5: Mapping to objects
$\forall R(\text{MAP-O}(R) \Leftrightarrow \forall e\forall e'\forall z[R(e,z)\wedge e'\sqsubseteq_E e\rightarrow\exists z'[z'\sqsubseteq_O z\wedge R(e',z')]])$

A sandwich has the property of Quantized reference, which means that it is the smallest individual satisfying what Krifka calls the nominal predicate *a sandwich.* Furthermore, Θ satisfies the condition that there is just one individual which has the relation to the eating event (Uniqueness of objects), and it satisfies the condition that every part of a sandwich is eaten as part of the eating event (Mapping to objects).

At this point, it is appropriate to give some comment on Krifka's representations. First of all, the problems signalled with respect to derivation (164) are not solved satisfactorily. The advantage of giving *eat* its argument structure (164a) has disappeared in (142a): the information that the verb *eat* is of type *<e,<e,t>>* is in (142a) no longer available. Semantically it is of type *<e,t>*. The problem for (164) was that the arguments may not be introduced by free variables.

Secondly, Krifka needs to harbour a lot of information in the determiner. Consider, for example, the derivation (175) of sentences like (174):

(174) Judith ate fewer than three sandwiches

(175)

a. fewer than three $\rightsquigarrow$
$\lambda R\lambda P\lambda e\exists y[MXE(e)\wedge max(\lambda n\lambda y\exists e'[P(e')\wedge Pat(e',y)$
$\wedge R(y,n)\wedge e'\subseteq e])\leq 3]$

b. fewer than three sandwiches $\rightsquigarrow$
$\lambda P\lambda e[MXE(e)\wedge max(\lambda n\lambda y\exists e'[P(e')\wedge Pat(e',y)\wedge sandwich'(y,n)$
$\wedge e'\subseteq e])\leq 3]$

c. eat fewer than three sandwiches $\rightsquigarrow$
$\lambda e[MXE(e)\wedge max(\lambda n\lambda y\exists e'[eat(e')\wedge Pat(e',y)\wedge sandwich'(y,n)$
$\wedge e'\subseteq e])\leq 3]$

d. Judith $\rightsquigarrow \lambda P\lambda e\exists x[P(e)\wedge Ag(e,x)\wedge x=j]$

e. Judith ate fewer than three sandwiches $\rightsquigarrow$
$\lambda e\exists x[[MXE(e)\wedge max(\lambda n\lambda y\exists e'[eat(e')\wedge Pat(e',y)$
$\wedge sandwich'(y,n)\wedge e'\subseteq e])\leq 3]\wedge Ag(e,x)\wedge x=j]$

Here the notion of maximal event (MXE) is to be defined as well as the notion of highest number (max). The predicate MXE is defined as in DEF 6, where $\tau(e)$ is the running time of the event, τ being a temporal 'trace function' mapping an event to its temporal trace, its running time (Krifka 1989a: 97).

DEFINITION 6: Maximal event at some time
$\forall e(\text{MXE}(e)\Leftrightarrow\exists t(e=FU_E(\lambda e[\tau(e)\subseteq_T t])))$

Clause (175e) expresses that the event in (174) consists of there being an entity Judith who is the agent of a maximal event such that there is an e′ being part of e in which the sandwich relation between numbers and entities is sent to the highest number for which the relation holds. Note that the information about the maximality of the event as well as about the maximal number is put into the numeral *fewer than three*. One can live with the presence of λe(… e…) in the determiners but, as argued in chapter 10, it is the verb which is decisive for the question of whether or not arguments are involved in temporal structure. In other words, in *Judith hated fewer than three sandwiches* the representation is unnecessarily complicated by the presence of the MXE-predicate, which is not (or should not be) needed for *hate*. Note also that sentences like *At least three girls ate fewer than three sandwiches* should contain two MXE-predicates, one for the subject-NP and one for the object-NP.

Thirdly, the treatment of the bare plural in (172) is not satisfactory. First of all, if there is a number n such that R(y)=n, then the set of sandwiches in (172) is bounded. Krifka has to assume that δ is cumulative. Now this holds for the nominal predicate sandwich in (172) because if the sandwiches s_1 and s_2 are members of the set of sandwiches in (147a), their join also belongs to this set. This would not apply to sandwich′(y,1), as it falls under DEF 3. So, Krifka considers ∃y[…sandwich′(y,1)] as quantized and ∃y∃n[…sandwich′(y,n)] as not quantized. This is unnatural because the existential generalization over the number 1 cannot or should not represent an unbounded set: given an assignment in a given model, it should represent an unidentified entity.

Fourthly, I think that the equilibrium between what is expressed by the representations and what is expressed by postulates is out of balance. For example, DEF 3 is just an artefact of the assumption that thematic roles are expressed as relations between events and arguments. In PLUG-representations there is no need to do this because the thematic role follows from the position of the verb with respect to its arguments. Krifka needs tens of postulates to get his system working. *Mapping to objects*, for example, is a sophisticated way of saying that verbs and direct objects are related. It is not built into the representations themselves, but it serves as a postulate. Krifka puts too much information into postulates, which can be directly incorporated in the representations of the expressions themselves. The need for them is proportionate to the number of conjuncts making up representations.

Fifthly, it is counterintuitive to define (argument) NPs as modifiers of type <<*e*,*t*>,<*e*,*t*>>. At least, there is no empirical motivation for it.

Finally, with respect to aspectual composition the problem is that terminativity is determined on the basis of **QUA**$_O$(P), **UNI–O**(R) and **MAP–O**(R), and that durativity is determined on the basis of **CUM**(P) and **SUM**(R). But note that the bold metapredicates apply to entities of type $<e,t>$ and $<e,<e,t>>$, that is, to predicates and relations corresponding to nouns rather than to NPs. At a number of places in Krifka (1989a) *a sandwich* and *the sandwich* are called nominal predicates, where the term *nominal predicate* clearly refers to Q in, for example, $\lambda Q \lambda P \lambda e \exists y[P(e) \wedge Q(y,1)]$. For example, Krifka (1989a:95) speaks about quantized nominal predicates like *a sandwich.* Yet it is $\mathbf{QUA}_O(Q)$, given DEF 3. But Q stands here for the Noun and not for the NP *a sandwich*, represented as $\lambda P \lambda e \exists y[P(e) \wedge Pat(e,y) \wedge sandwich'(y,1)]$, which is of type $<<e,t>,<e,t>>$. It might be conjectured that Krifka lets his postulates apply to phrases which would correspond with N′ = [NUM N] in Verkuyl (1981). If the function $\lambda n \lambda x.sandwich'(x,n)$ were applied to a number, say 3, then one would obtain $\lambda x.sandwich'(x,3)$, which is of type $<e,t>$. But is $\lambda x.sandwich'(x,3)$ a quantized nominal predicate? No, it never shows up in any of the derivations. And as said, if it did show up, there would be problems with $\lambda x.\exists n(sandwich'(x,n))$ which would also be quantized. So something is wrong here, or wrongly formulated, or unnecessarily complicated. The question is: how does one match the semantic information expressed by NPs to the predicates occurring in postulates like 1–6? This question is not satisfactorily answered in Krifka (1989a, 1989b, 1990).

There are more problems, such as the question of what exactly is expressed by DEF 1 (for example, is a join of two consecutive events to be interpreted in the same way as a join between two non-consecutive events?) and whether this is what one would like to have, but I shall not go into these details here. In general, the problems discussed above point sufficiently to the artificiality of postulating events as primitive entities. The introduction of new entities may solve a lot of problems, but it creates new problems too, for example more complex representations whose conjoined members must be related to the syntactic structure of the sentences under analysis. The main conceptual differences between Krifka's and my own approach are the following:

The representational language is different due to a difference of ontology. Krifka uses predominantly first-order language for his representations, due to his wish to quantify over sums, given his model structure M.

Krifka's grammar is based on events as primitives, whereas in my approach events are construed, so that Krifka does not capture the importance of aspect expressing the perspective of speakers (see chapter 12).

Krifka's constraints are not derived from the information contained by linguistic constituents in the sentences under analysis; they are merely descriptive devices.

11.5 Conclusion

In this section, it was argued that event semantics along the lines of Davidson and Parsons fails to be of interest for linguistic purposes, in particular the study of aspectuality. Their representations may be valuable to warrant a certain set of entailments, but evidently these sets are not involved in the study of temporal properties of sentences. Krifka's event-semantic analysis of aspectuality can be judged more positively, at least in my view, because it is put on the same foundations as my 1972 theory was grounded. Krifka has accepted three leading ideas which have proved to be necessary for the analysis of aspect: (a) the additive contribution of the verb; (b) the [+SQA]-contribution of NPs; and (c) the compositional approach to aspect. These three elements can easily be traced back in the characterization of (173): (a) the property of cumulativity is comparable with the [+ADD TO]-information expressed by the verb and interpreted in terms of the successor function s in DEF 10.2; (b) the notion of Quantized reference as being inherent to NPs is comparable with the idea that only [+SQA]-NPs may contribute to terminative aspect; and (c) the meaning of a sentence is built up compositionally. The fourth correspondence, the existence of a mapping relation between the verb and its object, has been given quite a different form in our work during the eighties. Finally, in my view the GQT-representations tend to be more perspicuous and simpler than Krifka's.

12 *Aspect and perspective*

12.0 Introduction

The visual connotation of the English term *aspect* is surpassed in Slavistic circles by that of the term *vid*, which means 'appearance', or 'view'. The need to formalize exactly the representations of our basic stock of examples, such as the sentences in (47)–(52), cannot but lead into a position in which a visual connotation is appropriate, in particular by an appeal to the notion of *perspective*. This is partly due to the technical decision to make the extensional logic underlying the PLUG-representations partly intensional. In particular, the notion *world* in Intensional Logic (IL) makes it possible to admit intensional objects into the domain: they are defined as functions from worlds to entities of some sort, whose extension can be obtained by applying this function at a given world-index w. It is not difficult and even illuminating to make this characterization of these abstract semantic objects concrete by imagining oneself to have a look from w into the domain where this extension is present.[45]

In my view, aspect construal should indeed be analysed in terms of perspective, in the sense that indices are playing a crucial role in determining sentential aspect, where *index* is the neutral term for semantic entities on which other semantic entities are made dependent. To the set of indices belong numbers, worlds, models, intervals, situations, points, etc. Perspective comes in at the moment at which it depends on the choice of an index whether or not a sentence is used to express terminative aspect or durative aspect. So the main issue of this section is: is aspect a way of organizing reality by the use of language? And does language provide us systematically with clues to indicate in terms of which category a speaker wants to talk about the domain of discourse? And at which level of abstraction? The general answer will be that the distinction between terminative and durative aspect gives speakers the means to encode their wish to speak about (terminative) events, or (unbounded) processes, or about states. In other words, if speakers use a certain combination of [±SQA]-NPs and a [±ADD TO]-verb, the choices they make provide them with the means to construe bounded events, or processes or states for the purpose of interpretation. They cast an aspectual net over reality, so to say. If philosophers wish to distinguish between different ontological categories such as events, processes or states, they may do so, but one should always have in mind that these categories do not have an independent life *an sich*: they are made up dependent on the context of use. So I prefer them as filters – in the non-technical sense – on the domain of discourse.

In earlier work, I have often stayed more or less neutral with respect to ontological questions. The mentalistic way of thinking about aspect has become articulated more and more strongly during the writing of the present study, due to the observations with respect to the cats, saucers and mafia bosses discussed in chapter 6. In this section, I would like to continue the analysis of these NPs in terms of a plea to relate the different levels at which we are able to speak and hear to the different levels at which indices can be used. In section 11.1, a fascinating desktop phenomenon will be discussed which is due to the Tarski courseware game invented by Barwise and Etchemendy. It will relate the bare plural/singular analysis to David Lewis' (1975) analysis of donkey-sentences which has laid the foundation for the Kamp/Heim semantics. In section 11.2, a phenomenon will be discussed which can only be explained in terms of perspective: the fact that without warning one may shift from quantification over events to quantification over subevents. This phenomenon also points in the direction of events being construed rather than being there. This will prepare the ground for chapter 13.

12.1 Models, worlds, indices and shifting perspectives

Consider the situation in which I am sitting in front of my Apple Macintosh window looking at the set of icons representing the documents of the well-known Tarski courseware designed by J. Barwise and J. Etchemendy. Its goal is to let students familiarize themselves with the syntax and semantics of standard first-order logic. By double-clicking on a world-document one opens up a world consisting of a quadrangle on which mathematical objects such as cubes, pyramids and tetrahedrons can be placed and replaced. These objects have different sizes. By double-clicking on a language document one gets access to a syntax. By clicking on buttons of the syntax table, one may produce first-order expressions. Correct formulas pertain to a chosen domain: they are interpreted standardly given a variable assignment. There is a way to check whether or not the formulas are syntactically correct and whether or not they are true.

Figure 33 shows the icons of a set of unopened world-documents (the language documents are not made visible). Each of these worlds has a temporal

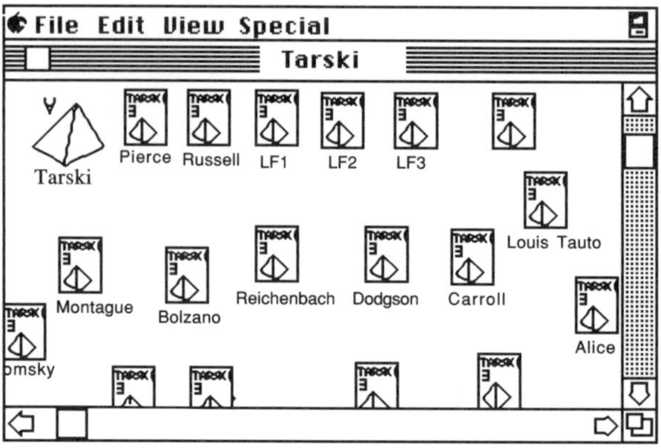

Figure 33 This figure shows the application called Tarski and a number of documents, some of which are Tarski worlds

structure in the sense that one can talk about a particular domain in terms of things that happened there, because the cursor picked up some object and manipulated it. For example, by double clicking the Carroll document, I have just opened w_{12} (say, Carroll's world) so that Figure 33 has disappeared and is replaced by a view of a quadrangular floor on which several objects are put. As I have performed manipulations with these objects, I might say to the person who just came in and who is looking over my shoulder:

(176) I moved the small cube to the left of the largest tetrahedron

This means that I am speaking about the past of w_{12} with respect to now. Note that w_{12} is a model in the formal sense of the word: there is a domain of entities; there is a language (partly translatable into the formal language) of which (176) is a well-formed expression; and there is an interpretation function. The variable assignment in w_{12} may differ drastically from the assignments in other worlds. In fact, we may assume that all assignments in the set W of worlds on the window are different from one another. This means that we may take the icons as representing different models, each model consisting of a domain and an interpretation function. From the desktop point of view, however, it is possible to think in terms of a union of all domains, as we shall see. Now, if sentence (177a) is interpreted with respect to w_{12},

(177) a. #For half an hour I moved the small cube to the left of the largest tetrahedron

b. I moved the small cube to the left of the largest tetrahedron in a minute then we obtain the odd aspectual repetition in (177a), which shows that (176) is terminative when applied to w_{12}. There is a specific cube and a tetrahedron and it is impossible to speak about just one completed move. If (177a) is interpreted, then I moved the cube repeatedly to the left of the tetrahedron, or moved the cube around in a prolonged attempt to get it to the left of the largest tetrahedron.[46] The aspectual test with *in a minute* also applies, as shown in (177b). What happened was that I managed to bring about an event which took place in w_{12} within the bounds of an interval of one minute.

Now, let us return to the desktop situation as depicted in Figure 33 and suppose that I got back to it after having gone through all world-documents in order to make all sorts of changes in the set of worlds, possibly making new worlds and doing things there. Given this task, and with Figure 33 now on the screen, (176) can be used to report to someone about my work on the Tarski worlds during the period in which I was busy. The hearer and I have to share the common knowledge that if I operated on cubes, there was always one cube per world unequivocally identified by the use of *the small cube*. Now, in this context (176) says that I placed the small cube to the left of the tetrahedron in all those worlds in which there was a small cube and a tetrahedron. It is telling that now (177a) does not express the odd aspectual repetition when interpreted in this way, as can be seen from the continuation in (178):

(178) … but then I changed my mind and decided to put it/them there

This means that (176) is to be interpreted if it pertains to my activity of doing the same sort of thing in different worlds. In (177a), the durative interpretation pertains to an unbounded series of movements, one for each word containing one (identified) specimen of a (sort of) cube such that I moved it to the left in a minute. This is not the queer aspectual repetition to be marked with #. In short, I am reporting about a process rather than about a terminative event.

The present discussion is not a simple remake of the bare-plural analysis in chapter 6.3; it is an extension. The old ingredient is the observation that a singular NP like *the cube* may pertain to an unbounded series of different token-specimens and that under those circumstances its [+SQA]-properties are affected. The new element is that the Tarski example makes it clear that there is structure involved in the difference between type and token: we go from world to world meeting a specimen of the required category to which the predicate applies. In the Tarski setting, (176) expresses terminative aspect in a specific world w_i. If we generalize over worlds, (176) expresses durative aspect. In this way, it becomes clear that terminative aspect can be seen as connected with the 'lowest-level index' present. With this, I mean to say that if a sentence

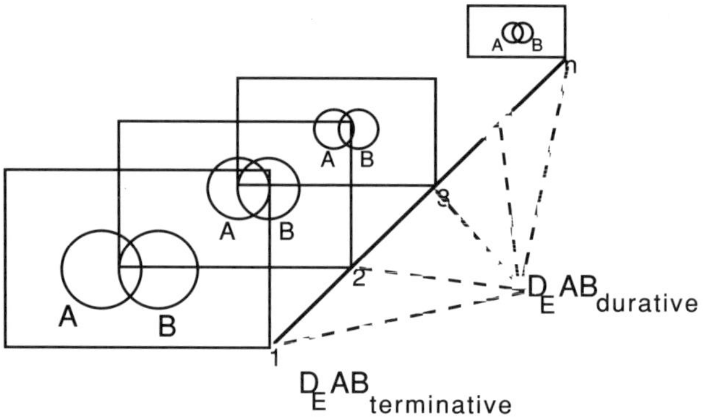

Figure 34 In principle, terminativity can never be attributed to a sentence ϕ if ϕ pertains to a series of different models

like (176) allows for a terminative and a durative interpretation, the terminative one is fully extensional as compared with the durative one. This point can be made more perspicuous visually, by embedding the well-known basic intersection scheme for NPs (of type $<<e,t>,t>$) in GQT, as given in Figure 10 in chapter 3.2, in a series as shown in Figure 34. Recall that (176) can be analysed in terms of the (simplified) basic scheme $D_E AB$, standing for something like 'The cube was moved (by me) to the left of the tetrahedron.' So (176) applied to Tarski word w_{12} would be terminative. However, (176) applied to the set of words $\{w_1, w_2, \ldots, w_n\}$ would be durative, as we do not get access to the cardinality of the token-cubes in the different words (we might even have got into a loop).

There are two important issues involved in Figure 34. The first one is that we have got into a situation in which a sentence like (176) taken duratively is going to be interpreted in the scheme by which genuine donkey-sentences are interpreted:

(179) a. Every farmer who owns a donkey killed it
b. For all cases, if x is a farmer and y is a donkey and if x owns y, x kills y
c. For all inspected words (cases) w if x is a small cube and y a tetrahedron, and if x was moved by me, x was moved to the left of y

So, Lewis' (1975) analysis of quantification over 'cases' is in this way connected to the study of aspect. How? Note that (177), if taken as durative, that is, ranging over the set of words, would provide an interesting extension of the Lewis analysis. The essence of his analysis is that quantification in sentences like (179) ranges over cases, but what does *range over* mean? And what exactly are cases? In my view, it means that in interpreting we mentally go over different cases, worlds or the like. If our mind had to deal with (179a) the way a dumb computer has to do it, it would have to inspect all cases, worlds or the like individually, and it would end up with being able to evaluate (179a) properly after having checked the n-th world of Figure 34. As said earlier, if we take the inspection procedurally it cannot but take (mental) time. Suppose that we were to confirm the truth of (179a) with the help of an inspection of all cases related to a time stretch. Then we could say, for example, (180a):

(180) a. For hours every farmer who owns a donkey killed it
b. For hours, if x is a man, if y is a donkey, and if x had y, x killed y

This means, if the (179a)-part of (180) is taken terminatively, that for hours it was such that all members of a group of farmers in a certain domain E_{wi} having a donkey killed it repeatedly, or it cannot be interpreted. If the (179a)-part of (180) is taken duratively it means that (180a) is interpreted at a highly abstract level, in particular a level at which we report about an unspecified set of models containing sets whose cardinality cannot be settled, which we were inspecting for hours. It means on this interpretation that for hours one was proceeding along the line of models (say, in Figure 34) such that at each index the situation was such that if one found the statement that a farmer having a donkey killed it, it would be true. One is not really talking here about farmers killing their donkeys, but rather one is claiming the truth of (179a) for an unspecified number of models. This sort of meaning for donkey-sentences is generally left out of consideration, but I think that an aspectual theory should deal with them, as durative aspect is closely tied up with the structure we are to give to mental time. A sentence like *For centuries Socrates has been mortal* may report about what we know about a well-known example in the philosophical literature rather than directly about Socrates. Compare *For centuries, the sun rotated round the earth, but it's the other way ever since Copernicus.*

The second important issue is the sophistication of the indexing machinery involved in dealing with the Tarski worlds. It is obscured in (177) but it shows up in sentences like (181):

(181) Three times the cube was put at the extreme left

(182) a. In w_{12}, there are three time indices j_1, j_2, j_3 such that the cube was put at the extreme left at each of the indices j

b. For each world w_i, there are three time indices $j_{i,1}$, $j_{i,2}$ and $j_{i,3}$ such that if the cube is in w_i it was put at the extreme left at $j_{i,1}$, $j_{i,2}$ and $j_{i,3}$
c. There are three time indices J_1, J_2, J_3 such that for all worlds w if the cube is in w it was moved to the extreme left, at J_1, J_2, and J_3

If (181) applies to one world, say w_{12}, it means that within the history of this world, there were three times at which the cube was put at the extreme left. In this case (182a) is a proper paraphrase. However, (181) may also report on my moving the cubes three times in all relevant worlds (so *three times* might amount to say 20 × 3 movements), as paraphrased by (182b). There also appears to be a 'desktop time' which is the time at which I perform operations on all worlds simultaneously, while suppressing the internal time structure of each of the documents.[47] On this interpretation, (181) now expresses that I have operated simultaneously on all (relevant) worlds with respect to desktop time indices J_1, J_2 and J_3, amounting to 3 × 20-at-once movements. Let J_1 at desktop stand short for all the first indices per model, the second index for the second per world, etc. Then we can use it mentally as part of our speech time by abstracting over all indices of the worlds themselves. Under this interpretation *three times* in (181) stands for three different sets of world-times compressed into three times of the desktop time, that is, the time I am executing commands getting all documents on the computer into one domain. Consider the more specific sentence (183), in which a temporal adverbial is added to (181):

(183) #For a minute the cube was put at the extreme left three times

Can it mean that in a minute (desktop time), say in the interval (11:01,11:02), the computer went through all the documents such that at 11:01:24 it put the cube in all world-documents at the extreme left simultaneously, and that it did so at 11:01:35 and at 11:01:56? In this case, we are forced to speak about a terminative event at the desktop level due to the fact that we are now concentrating on the highest level, pressing down the lower-level structure. Thus, as far as (181) itself is concerned in the context of the situation given in Figure 34, it may express (a) three events in a given world, say w_{12}; (b) k × 3 events, where k is the cardinality of the set of worlds which were opened; and (c) three desktop events in which the worlds remained closed and compressed to individual entities.

I have led the analysis to a point where two things are visible:

(a) the subtlety and sophistication of our cognitive system: we are able to shift from 'going into' a particular world to talking about it at a higher level, as the Tarski example demonstrates sufficiently;

(b) this shift has no absolute grounding: our second example showed that we were able to take a w_i as the aspectual 'rock-bottom' which we were able to determine because (176) is terminative with respect to this world (which has its own time structure). In contrast, (176) was durative with respect to the whole set of worlds W observed from a higher level. At this higher level there is no place for terminativity.

However, by robbing the worlds w of their own time structure, so to speak, we may reduce them to a set of entities on which changes can be performed simultaneously at 'desktop time'. As demonstrated with the help of (183), one now can make the desktop situation into the lowest level and so we may interpret (176) as terminative with respect to W, whose elements w are no longer temporally accessible.

12.2 Events and shifting perspective: the Guns of Navarone

Parsons (1989) rejects an interval-based approach and proposes to take events as ontological primitives.[48] Critical to his decision appears to be English sentence (184):

(184) Miles was wounded twice (by a bullet) yesterday
Miles werd gisteren twee keer geraakt door een kogel

Parsons says that 'the natural treatment of [(184)] within interval semantics would be to propose something like:

(185) For two distinct intervals, i_1 and i_2, Miles was in the extension of "be wounded by a bullet yesterday" at both i_1 and i_2' (1989: 233)

and says that (185) would entail that the wounds in (184) were not simultaneously inflicted upon Miles, the problem for interval semantics being that there is a natural reading of (184) saying that Miles got his wounds simultaneously. So, for Parsons it seems to be necessary to have a one-to-one relation between an interval and an event. I do not want to defend interval semantics as it was developed in the literature of the seventies, as should be clear from chapter 9. Here, I simply want to show that there is something dubious about Parsons' argument against (184).

To begin with, (184) is in the passive. It is clear that Parsons cannot make the same point with the active sentence *A bullet hit Miles twice yesterday*. That the passive form is the only way to construct an alleged counterexample to interval semantics is quite suspicious, because whatever is known about the semantics of the passive, it is strongly suggested that it expresses a mixture of an event-like and a state-like description (for example, Beedham 1982). This is correct for the Dutch gloss of (184): it can be understood as giving the sum total of the times Miles was hit (in which case the hits are counted atemporally) or it may report about the result of two consecutive events. Hence, (185).

Let us suppose, however, that the linguistic observation leading to (185) as the proper analysis for (184) was correct. In that case, Parsons' notion of event turns out to fail for two reasons: the first one is that frequency adverbials do not behave the way he thinks they do; the second one is that it sneaks in agency as a factor where it should not. As for the first point, frequency adverbials have an interesting property: in pseudo-clefts they can occur before and after the copula, yielding quite different interpretations. Consider the sentences (186)–(190):[49]

(186) He hit Miles six times
(187) What he did was hit Miles six times
(188) What he did six times was hit Miles
(189) What happened was that he hit Miles six times
(190) What happened six times was that he hit Miles

Sentence (186) is ambiguous. The first reading is expressed by (187) and (189), the second by (188) and (190). In (187) and (189), there is one event in which there are subevents (most probably six). So one event can have substructure: it can consist of subevents. In (188) and (190), there are six events. During each of these six events Miles can have been hit many times.

Frequency adverbials like *twice*, *six times* appear to operate on events as well as on subevents. Assuming that the intervals out of which events are construed have filter structure (see DEF 4.5), it is easy to explain why (162) and (163) display the behaviour of frequency adverbials as they do. Technically, this means that an interval is taken as a generalized quantifier, that is, as a set I of intervals where the internal structure of I is defined such that the interval (0,1) is contained in (0,2), (0,2) in (0,3), as in DEF 10.2. The numbers 1, 2, 3, etc. are 'counting points', that is, points at which substructural units (pairs of intervals and hits, in this case) are counted as having been processed. At point 2 a certain number m of hits have been related to time and at point 3 the number is m+k. Figure 35a represents a possible realization of (189): in (0,1) he had hit Miles once, in (0,2) 1+3=4 times, in (0,3) 4+2=6 times. Figure 35b expresses that as far as (190) is concerned, we need six intervals, each relating to at least one hit, but there can be more than one hit per interval.

1 hit 3 hits 2 hits

(a) 0_______1_________2________3

1 hit 10 hits 7 hits 1 hit 2 hits 1hit

(b) 0_____1___________2_____3_____4______5____6

Figure 35 Frequency adverbials can be interpreted as assigning cardinality to generalized quantifiers, that is, collections of intervals built up by the successor function given a point of origin 0

As said earlier, the advantage of taking 1, 2, 3 etc. as counting points in the structuring of progress in time is that this makes it unnecessary to take into account the dense structure of intervals. The numbers associated with the intervals belong to our mental organization: they can treat dense time discretely by using two different ordering systems at once. We can map two hits into the same interval without being forced to assume that they took place at exactly the same time within this interval. They can follow one another in time without forcing us to say that two events are involved. At the level of subevents we are simply not interested in too much structure, as shown by (190), which abstracts away from the possible many hits that he gave Miles each time.

For the second objection against Parsons' analysis, I shall create a simple 'Gedankenexperiment' by promoting Miles to the rank of the commanding officer of an American ship sailing in the range of the guns of Navarone during the Second World War. Let *Miles was hit* stand short for *Miles' ship was hit* and let us assume, for the sake of coming close to (184), that if a ship is hit by a cannonball, it is wounded.

According to the well-known movie, the guns of Navarone consisted of two parallel guns, each of which was able to produce a cannonshot on its own, having its own crew. Both crews were commanded by a (German) officer. I will now discuss some hypothetical situations.

Situation 1. The German officer says *Feuer*, the guns fire and Miles is hit by two projectiles at exactly the same time (Figure 36a). One can speak here of one event involving two subevents, that is, two hits. So, if one says (191), it will be interpreted as (192).

(191) Miles was hit twice
(192) Miles got two hits

The use of (191) is forced because *twice* cannot quantify over the main event. A natural situation is when in the well-known game 'Battleships', I have to

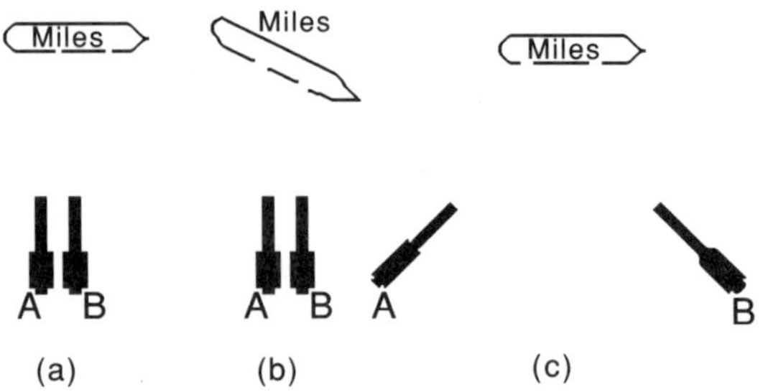

Figure 36 These three situations illustrate the point that one and the same situation can be experienced as one event or as more than one event, depending on a 'span of control' not provided by the sentence itself, but rather by the context

report about how many times a ship occupying two, three or fou squares was hit in one salvo. So it is on inspection that one may quantify ove times, taken in the mathematical rather than temporal sense. For Figure 36a, (192) is far more correct. It would be strange to say *He is going to hit Miles now for the third time*, whereas it would be normal to say *He is going to give Miles his third hit*. If it is not strange for the German officer to say *for the third time*, it is because he is taken as counting the hits. And if you count, you may quantify over mathematical times. But then you quantify over cases, not over intervals.

Situation 2. The German officer says *Feuer*, the guns fire at exactly the same moment and hit Miles one after the other, say a second later as depicted in Figure 36b. For the Germans their salvo counts as one event: the hits are placed in the same time span. Some English engineer Jones on the lower deck on Miles' ship may have experienced what happened as two separate events, not knowing where the hits came from. Or if this sounds strange, if some electronical device on the leading battleship miles away from Miles can only register Jones' observations sequentially, that is, by registering only one datum after the other, it becomes even more appropriate for someone on this ship to use (191). He could certainly add: ... *and we are now waiting for the third hit*, or ... *and we are now waiting for the third time.*

Situation 3. The guns were taken apart and put on a different location, say one mile from each other (Figure 36c). They have now different commanders shooting independently from one another, according to their own judgment. The two commanders are ordered by a general to sink Miles. Now, the guns happen to fire one after the other and Miles is hit by two projectiles at exactly the same time. Is it reasonable to speak of one event? It depends on the observer. For Miles (not being able to tell the sound of the two guns apart from that of other guns) it is reasonable to think of one event consisting of receiving two hits at the same time. For those who do not know about the span of control of the German general, there are two events: they do not take into account coordination of the gun. For the general it is one event.

The three situations make it clear that the notion of agency is essential to Parsons' judgment. His interpretation of (184) as pertaining to two events seems dependent on whether or not there are two different agents inflicting wounds upon Miles. Indeed, for each individual inflicting a wound upon Miles this can be seen as an event. But from other points of view, there may be just one event. This is shown in situation 3, where it is not the agency that counts (the guns each have the same crew in all three situations), but rather a far more abstract span of control. One and the same situation can be experienced as one event or as more than one event, without there being thematic roles to express whether or not the speaker wishes to speak about one event or not. Parsons' analysis is based upon secretly taking into account the role of agency.

Let us now consider sentences with a plural subject in order to see how much agency is involved in the need to work with events rather than with intervals. The point with respect to (193):

(193) John and Miles hit the wall

is that interval semantics cannot distinguish between a situation in which John and Miles hit the wall one after the other and the situation in which John hit the wall and Miles hit the wall simultaneously without their being involved collectively.[50] The same applies to:

(194) Two men hit the wall

where the only way to get a simultaneous reading would be to assume that the two men were involved in the hit-action together, sharing a common goal, in this case to hit the wall. This is the counterpart of the distributive reading in which each of the men is supposed to hit the wall independently of the other.

The only way to get a reading in which there are two men hitting the wall at the same time such that it is reasonable to speak about two events, is to assume that the hits are unrelated to one another, in some sense of that word. So there is a hit-event e_1 and a hit-event e_2, where $e_1 \neq e_2$ and both e_1 and e_2 occur at i. This means that in the notion of event a sort of agency must be included which makes e_1 different from e_2 even though they take place at the same time. What if the two men are dead bodies? Can there be two hit-events? Yes, a lot of people would say, because dead bodies can be seen as 'derived' agents, because inanimate objects may be treated analogously to animate ones. So, one may stretch the argument role of *two men* so that it includes their bodies.

Suppose that a gust of wind lifted the bodies one after the other against the wall, say with half a minute intermission? Then one has clearly two different times, so $i_1 \neq i_2$, and yet we might wish to speak of one event, for example, if the gust of wind is much longer than half a minute. It is the gust that provides the time span for the decision whether or not we speak about one or two events. So (194) reports about a hurricane gust smashing the two men against the wall. One is free to take the gust as the unifying factor providing for the notion of simultaneity or precedence. But the wind stays completely out of view in (194): there is no thematic role for it. In other words, speakers are able to provide for unifying time spans if they wish to present something as an event. From the point of view of eventhood, it should be irrelevant whether or not the entities fulfilling the role of external argument of *hit* acted as agents and whether or not they cooperated. In my view, collective quantification should abstract away from agency by dealing with (194) irrespective of the question of whether the two men are alive or dead. It is possible to analyse (194) as saying that the two men are assigned to an index on the basis of a (participancy) equivalence relation which can be circumscribed as 'hit the wall in the same index I', where I can have *internal temporal structure.*

To see that neither spatial nor temporal distance are involved in determining whether one has to do with one or more event, consider (195):

(195) Mary and John crossed the border

which may pertain to at least five different classes of situations:

(a1) Mary crossed the border at San Diego and John at Buffalo at exactly the same time i_k, as part of a master plan directed by someone in New York without any awareness of this on their side; (a2) the same as (a1) but now at clearly different times i_k and i_m.

(b1) Mary crossed the border at San Diego and John crossed the border at Buffalo, both crossings taking place separately without any span of control, at i_1; (b2) the same as (b1) but at different times i_k and i_m.

(c1) Mary and John crossed the border at Buffalo at the same time as part of a joint enterprise (they wanted to walk to the Canadian part of the Niagara Falls, say) at i_1; (c2) the same but at different times i_k and i_m.

(d1) Mary and John (who do not know each other) crossed the border at Buffalo at i_1 (at the same time entering Canada via different customs points); (d2) the same but at different times i_k and i_m.

(e1) Mary and John crossed the border at Buffalo (at the same time entering Canada via different customs points) as part of a master plan directed by someone in New York without any awareness of this on their side; (e2) the same but at different times i_k and i_m.

Here we see that these situations cannot be dealt with adequately in terms of events. We need a more neutral notion to deal with it. Let us have a closer look at the following statement: 'A natural treatment of (195) within Parsons' event semantics would be to propose something like (196).

(196) For two distinct events e_1 and e_2, the border was in the extension of 'was crossed by Mary and by John' in e_1 and e_2'

The problem for Parsons' event semantics is that there is a natural reading of (195) saying that the border was crossed at the same event, for example (a1) or (e1). Here we clearly have two different crossing events in which Mary and John are involved which happen to constitute one crossing event. If one says that this is quite natural for events, there is no reason why intervals should not show the same behaviour. This is shown by (a2): here the intervals are consecutive and yet they can form a union which expresses that one is speaking about one event made up of two subevents, as in (e2). Thus, the apparent counterexample (184), felt by Parsons as crucial and deadly for interval semantics, fails to be convincing: it is possible to analyse (184) in such a way that two hits are assigned to an interval i leaving unspecified whether or not they were counted as simultaneous. In certain situations (184) may be understood as pertaining to two events, in other situations it may pertain to just one event having internal interval structure. The notion of event is extremely flexible in the sense that it may comprise semantic objects which also may be called events if the perspective is more restricted. Strikingly, this holds for intervals too. In other words, Parsons' move from intervals to events is ill-motivated as both intervals and events show exactly the same behaviour in terms of their allowing substructure. So there is no reason to reject intervals in favour of events.

The general conclusion is that intervals do play a decisive role in the structure of events, but not in the way of the interval semantics which dominated the scene in the seventies.

12.3 Conclusion

One of the main conclusions of the present section is that terminative aspect has a special status as compared with durative aspect. In earlier work, I have called durative aspect the aspectual 'garbage can' in the sense that a lot of different phenomena fall under this notion. A more traditional way of characterizing the opposition is, of course, to call terminative aspect marked. In the Slavistic literature the *communis opinio* is that perfective aspect is marked, whereas imperfective aspect is unmarked.[51] The notion of markedness has now been extended and can be made more concrete regarding the notional category of aspectuality: terminative aspectuality in English and Dutch is the marked category because it signals the 'extensional rock-bottom'. That is, by giving a sentence of a natural language a terminative form, speakers may signal that they want to operate at an extensional level, where the level chosen may be dependent on contextual information. The Tarski example (176) made it clear that one sentence may be used terminatively in a document, duratively at desktop level if the temporal structure of the documents is not suppressed and terminatively at desktop level if the documents are subjected to desktop time. This makes aspectuality a highly intricate and sophisticated property of natural language, but there is system in it. And the system is determined by the requirement that [+SQA]- and [+ADD TO]-information be determinable as part of the reality about which we want to speak. Durative aspect means that some part of the information conveyed by the sentence is presented at a more abstract level at which it is not possible or desirable to quantize.

As observed during the discussion of bare plurals in chapter 2, speakers may shift their perspective by making a type-logical shift from a certain type to a higher type, and conversely. For example, one may talk about saucers and cats in terms of (a set of) individuals as well as in terms of (a collection of) sets of saucers and cats. This point was dealt with in our discussion of bare plurals in chapter 6.3, where, for example, the sentence *The soldiers came into town* may pertain to one event in which say three soldiers came into town, but also to a situation in which unspecified members of a given category came into town. The difference between the two interpretations also corresponds with the difference between terminative aspect and durative aspect. This can also be explained in terms of perspective if one realizes that different indices, that is, different points of perspective, may be used, leading to different interpretations for apparently similar structures. *In concreto*, speaking about the category of soldiers is to take a different perspective from speaking about some specified group of its members. As said above, indices are quite useful for articulating a position from which a domain is given structure.

13 *Event construal*

13.0 Introduction

Chapter 13 has three goals. The first one is comparable with the goal of chapter 3.1: to introduce machinery and explain some basic technical type-logical notions for those readers who may find it convenient to go through it in order to refresh their logical memory.[52] This will be done in section 13.1. This goal has been combined with the need to justify each step formally. This is necessary because the EL-logic which has been employed up to now will be extended with some intensional rules. In many formal semantic analyses, intensionality is given by making use of the rules of IL, the intensional logic used in Montague's PTQ. However, the PLUG-grammar of chapter 7.3 will only be partially intensionalized and not by IL-rules but rather by rules of the system called Ty2. As IL and Ty2 can be translated into each other, I will first introduce the relevant IL-rules, and then make a transition to the more generally formulated two-sorted logic Ty2, which has become increasingly standard because it turns out to be an easier language to work with, especially in the GQT direct representation of PLUG. In section 13.2 the second goal becomes visible: making a weak intensional version of PLUG on the basis of Ty2, that is, a version which is intensionally weaker than Ty2. This is to say that we do not need the full intensional capacity of IL and Ty2 to deal with the varied forms of index-dependency discussed in chapter 12. These two goals justify the amount of formal machinery to get to the point at which we can expand PLUG to PLUG$^+$. In the sections 13.3 and 13.4, the third goal is to account formally for the index structure induced by [+ADD TO]-verbs and for the interaction between these verbs and the semantics of the internal argument. After a discussion of the semantics of the external argument in section 13.5, the analysis of the thematic role of the internal argument of sentences like (47) and (48) is generalized in section 13.6 into an account of the interaction between verbs and their PP-complements. In this way, the promise of a similar formal treatment of sentences like (47)–(49) and (50)–(52) is fulfilled. In section 13.7, the issue of bare plurality is taken up again. In section 13.8, a formal description of Tense and the Progressive Form is given. Also, habituality is taken into account. By then the formal machinery required to describe and explain aspectual properties of sentences has been sufficiently developed so as to fulfil the requirements of a theory: to predict and to be falsifiable. In chapter 14, the theory will be tested in view of apparent counterexamples.

13.1 Index-dependency in IL and Ty2

As IL is an extension of EL as defined in DEF 3.1–3.6, we simply add the relevant intensional rules, adapting the system where it is needed:

DEFINITION 1

T, the set of types, is the smallest set in IL such that:

a. $e, t \in \mathbf{T}$

b. if $a,b \in \mathbf{T}$, then $<a,b> \in \mathbf{T}$

c. if $a \in \mathbf{T}$, then $<s,a> \in \mathbf{T}$

Standardly, intensionality is expressed by means of the notion of possible world. So expressions of type <*s*,a> are generally taken as functions from possible worlds to semantic objects of type a, where worlds are primitives. The vocabulary of EL in DEF 3.2 is extended with a clause introducing four intensional operators: $\Box$ (necessary that), $\Diamond$ (possible that), ^ (intensionalizer) and $^\vee$ (extensionalizer). The syntax of EL is modified and extended by:

DEFINITION 2

Syntax of IL:

a. if $\alpha \in CON_a$, then $\alpha \in ME_a$
   if $\alpha \in VAR_a$, then $\alpha \in ME_a$

...

g. if $\phi \in ME_t$, then $\Box\phi, \Diamond\phi \in ME_t$

h. if $\alpha \in ME_a$, then $^\wedge\alpha \in ME_{<s,a>}$

j. if $\alpha \in ME_{<s,a>}$, then $^\vee\alpha \in ME_a$

k. Every meaningful expression in L is constructed by (a)–(j) in a finite number of steps.

The two modal operators are introduced in clause (g). By clause (h) the ^-operator makes an intensional expression out of an extensional expression, and in (j) the $^\vee$-operator yields the extension of an intensional expression at a given world.

The semantics of DEF 2 presumes a domain of interpretation $\mathbf{D}_a$ which is defined as follows for the different types:

DEFINITION 3

a. $\mathbf{D}_e$=E   b. $\mathbf{D}_t$=$\{1,0\}$

c. $\mathbf{D}_{<a,b>}=\mathbf{D}_b^{\mathbf{D}_a}$ d. $\mathbf{D}_{<s,a>}=\mathbf{D}_a^{W}$

The semantics of the expansion of DEF 3.6 is given in DEF 4.

DEFINITION 4

Semantics:

a. if $\alpha \in CON_a$, then $[\![\alpha]\!]_{\mathbf{M},w,g}=I(\alpha)(w)$
if $\alpha \in VAR_a$, then $[\![\alpha]\!]_{\mathbf{M},w,g}=g(\alpha)$

...

g. if $\phi \in ME_t$, then
$[\![\Box\phi]\!]_{\mathbf{M},w,g}=1$ iff for all $w' \in W$: $[\![\phi]\!]_{\mathbf{M},w',g}=1$
$[\![\Diamond\phi]\!]_{\mathbf{M},w,g}=1$ iff there is at least one $w' \in W$: $[\![\phi]\!]_{\mathbf{M},w',g}=1$

h. if $\alpha \in ME_a$, then
$[\![{}^\wedge\alpha]\!]_{\mathbf{M},w,g}$=that function $h \in \mathbf{D}_a^W$ s.t. $\forall w' \in W$: $h(w')=[\![\alpha]\!]_{\mathbf{M},w',g}$

j. if $\alpha \in ME_{<s,a>}$, then $[\![{}^\vee\alpha]\!]_{\mathbf{M},w,g}=[\![\alpha]\!]_{\mathbf{M},w,g}(w)$

The interpretation of IL-expressions now proceeds with respect to a model **M**, a world w and an assignment g.

As far as clause (a) is concerned, when applied to the constants of the language IL, it says that $I(\alpha)$ is an intensional object (a function from worlds into the set of entities of type α) which applied to w yields the extension of α in w. Let w_1, w_2 and w_3 be worlds in W in the standard IL-sense, that is, taken as primitives. If *sandwich* is of type <*e*,*t*>, $[\![\text{sandwich}]\!]_{\mathbf{M},w2,g}$ is the result of applying I(sandwich) to w_2. This yields the set of sandwiches in w_2. Being a function from W into the collection of sets of type <*e*,*t*>, I(sandwich) is the intensional object $[\![{}^\wedge\text{sandwich}]\!]_{\mathbf{M},w,g}$ of type <*s*,<*e*,*t*>>, defined in clause (h) as the function h such that for each w′, $h(w')=[\![\text{sandwich}]\!]_{\mathbf{M},w',g}$, which is itself of type <*e*,*t*>. In this way, $I(\alpha)(w)$ is equivalent to $[\![{}^\vee{}^\wedge\text{sandwich}]\!]_{\mathbf{M},w,g}$, as can be seen from clause (j). Clause (a) says that, given world-indices, *sandwich* would have to be taken as denoting a function of type <*s*,<*e*,*t*>> applied to a world-index and yielding its extension in that world. The function value may be different for each w. As all constants are captured by clause (a), the verbal predicate constant *walk* in *John walked* is treated as I(walk)(w). In this way, IL accounts for the fact that interpretations of expressions may vary from world to world. In our extension of PLUG, we shall adopt an intermediate position between DEF 4 and the EL-clause (a) in DEF 3.4 by which predicate constants such as *sandwich* and *walk* are of type $<e,t>$:

DEF 3.4a. if $\alpha \in CON_a$, then $[\![\alpha]\!]_{M,g}=I(\alpha)$

In our extension, PLUG^{+}, only [+ADD TO]-verbs will be given an index-dependency, because they meet clause (a) in DEF 4, whereas nouns are treated extensionally, by DEF 3.4a.

The language IL has been simplified and regimented by Gallin (1975), who developed a language Ty2 (see Janssen 1983 for an extensive description; Muskens 1989).

DEFINITION 5

Ty2, the set of types, is the smallest set such that:

a. $e, t, s \in$ **Ty2**

b. if $a,b \in$ **Ty2**, then $<a,b> \in$ **Ty2**

This introduces a new basic type *s*. Expressions of type *s* denote possible worlds. Clause (b), in which a and b are metavariables, makes it possible to derive types like $<s,e>$ (individual concepts), $<s,<e,t>>$ (properties), $<s,t>$ (propositions), etc. Correspondingly, DEF 3 needs to be modified:

DEFINITION 6

a. $\mathbf{D}_e=E$ b. $\mathbf{D}_t=\{1,0\}$

c. $\mathbf{D}_s=W$ d. $\mathbf{D}_{<a,b>}=\mathbf{D}_b{}^{\mathbf{D}_a}$

Ty2 itself is introduced here just to exemplify how the PLUG-grammar of chapter 7 is to be extended. We only need the Ty2-equivalents of the four operators:

IL:	$\Box\phi$	$\Diamond\phi$	$^\wedge\alpha$	$^\vee\alpha$
Ty2:	$\forall a\phi$	$\exists a\phi$	$\lambda a\alpha$	$\alpha(a)$

In this way $[\![^\wedge walk_{<e,t>}]\!]_{M,w,g}$ is translationally equivalent to the interpretation $[\![\lambda a.walk_{<s,<e,t>>}(a)]\!]_{M,g[a/w]}$, where g[a/w] means 'the assignment g′ which is like g except for the possible difference that g(a)=w'; a is a variable of type *s*. In view of our wish to 'intensionalize' verbal predicates like *walk* and *eat*, it is appropriate to make more clear how the interpretation proceeds. *Walk*, for example, is lexically characterized as a predicate, say Walk*(a), where Walk* is of type $<s,<e,t>>$. Now, $[\![Walk^*(a)]\!]=I(Walk^*)(g(a))$. In this way, the index-dependency of *walk* is made dependent on the assignment g.

13.2 An intensional extension of PLUG

Let us start our remodelling of the PLUG-grammar into PLUG⁺ by repeating the rules of PLUG at this place. Recall that it was designed as a GQT-grammar, which means that we use direct rather than indirect representations:

Grammar:

1. $\mathrm{S} : [\![\mathrm{NP}]\!]([\![\mathrm{VP}]\!]) \quad \Leftarrow \quad \mathrm{NP} : [\![\mathrm{NP}]\!], \mathrm{VP} : [\![\mathrm{VP}]\!]$

2. $\begin{cases} \mathrm{VP} : \lambda \mathrm{X}.[\![\mathrm{V}_1]\!](\mathrm{X}) \\ \mathrm{VP} : \lambda \mathrm{X}.[\![\mathrm{NP}]\!](\lambda \mathrm{Y}.[\![\mathrm{V}_2]\!](\mathrm{Y})(\mathrm{X})) \quad \Leftarrow \quad \mathrm{V}_2 : [\![\mathrm{V}_2]\!], \mathrm{NP} : [\![\mathrm{NP}]\!] \end{cases}$

3. $\mathrm{NP} : [\![\mathrm{DET}^2]\!]([\![\mathrm{N}]\!]) \quad \Leftarrow \quad \mathrm{DET}^2 : [\![\mathrm{DET}^2]\!], \mathrm{N} : [\![\mathrm{N}]\!]$

4. $\mathrm{DET}^2 : [\![\mathrm{SPEC}]\!]([\![\mathrm{DET}^1]\!]) \quad \Leftarrow \quad \mathrm{SPEC} : [\![\mathrm{SPEC}]\!], \mathrm{DET}^1 : [\![\mathrm{DET}^1]\!]$

The weakening of Ty2 to PLUG⁺ as a weak intensional language consists of dropping clause (a) in DEF 4 in favour of DEF 3.4a, and of stipulating lexically whether verbal predicates denote intensional entities of type <*s*,<a,t>>, or not. So, let us first adapt some of the type-logical definitions:

DEFINITION 7

$\mathbf{T}_{\mathrm{PLUG+}}$, the set of types, is the smallest set such that:

a. $e, t, i \in \mathbf{T}_{\mathrm{PLUG+}}$

b. if $\mathrm{a,b} \in \mathbf{T}_{\mathrm{PLUG+}}$, then $<\mathrm{a,b}> \in \mathbf{T}_{\mathrm{PLUG+}}$

This introduces a basic type *i*. Clause (b) makes it possible to derive types like <*i*,*e*> (index-dependent entities), <*i*,*t*> (index-dependent truth values), etc., but also a type like <*i*,<<*e*,*t*>,*t*>>, that is, relations between indices and sets. Expressions of type *i* denote indices. It will be argued that if indices are treated as *representatives* of certain semantic objects (say, intervals in **R**, temporal intervals, etc.), they can be taken as numerals, in particular ordinals. Accordingly, DEF 3 needs to be adapted:

DEFINITION 8

a.	$\mathbf{D}_e=\mathrm{E}$	c.	$\mathbf{D}_i=\mathbf{N}$
b.	$\mathbf{D}_t=\{1,0\}$	d.	$\mathbf{D}_{<\mathrm{a,b}>}=\mathbf{D}_{\mathrm{b}}^{\mathbf{D}_{\mathrm{a}}}$

The list of notational conventions is extended with (at least) the list in (197). The extension concerns bold-face variables which are used for intensionalizing substructure of an otherwise extensional NP-denotation.

(197)

	Variables	*Constants*	*Types*
	x, y, z	–	e
	i, k, m		i
	I, J		$<i,t>$
	X, Y, U, V, W, Z	P_i, T_i	$<e,t>$
	–	R_i	$<e,<e,t>>$
	P, Q, R, S	–	$<<e,t>,t>$
	D	D_i	$<<e,t>,<<e,t>,t>>$
	X, Y, W		$<i,<<e,t>,t>>$

It should already be noted here that the distinction between type i and $<i,t>$ might turn out to be somewhat artificial, though perhaps it is more perspicuous to make it during the exposition. When taken as ordinals, natural numbers may include each other, so $1\subseteq 2$ because taken as ordinal numbers one may read $\{0\}\subseteq\{0,1\}$. In this way the variable I might be dropped from the list because we could write $i\subseteq j$ rather than $i\in J$, but I will not do so, in order to keep a better view of things with variables like I and J as ranging over sets of indices, and i, k and m ranging over their members.

The point of departure for a change of PLUG into PLUG$^+$ is the atemporal PLUG-formula (198), which is of type $<<e,t>,t>$.

(198)

$$\lambda X\lambda P\exists W[W\subseteq[\![\text{sandwich}]\!]\wedge|W|=3\wedge\exists Q\text{ps}W[Q=P|_{[\![\text{sandwich}]\!]}]](\lambda Y.[\![\text{eat}]\!](Y)(X))$$

It stands for the VP *eat three sandwiches* before lambda-application has been applied and it represents an example of rule 2. If the λX in front is dropped so that X is treated as a free variable, we can simplify the exposition: the remaining formula is, as in (199):

(199)

$$\lambda P.\exists W[W\subseteq[\![\text{sandwich}]\!]\wedge|W|=3\wedge\exists Q\text{ps}W[Q=P|_{[\![\text{sandwich}]\!]}]](\lambda Y.[\![\text{eat}]\!](Y)(X))$$

It is of the form $[\![\text{NP}]\!](\lambda Y.[\![\text{eat}]\!](Y)(X))$. The variable NP is used here to abbreviate semantic objects of type $<<<e,t>,t>,t>$.

The need for a departure is motivated by our wish to match the progress expressed by [+ADD TO]-verbs to the structure of the NP-denotation. Although a partitioned collection provides for some structure, its cells are intrinsically unordered, when considered apart from temporal considerations. If we see five letters on the table, we may assign any atemporal partition by grouping them into cells, given the right equivalence relation. At a given point some more information might be added, in particular, information about the intention to act upon the group of letters. One may group them and decide that they are *going to* be sent in groups. At that point an equivalence relation is introduced imposing ordered structure. So one obtains in a completely arbitrary way, say, three groups of letters {letter to Antoinette, letter to Mary}, {letter to Judith}, {letter to Jessica, letter to David}. Nothing in this situation says anything yet about the *order* in which they were actually sent (later on). This is why I did not use numerals in this example, because they impose an ordering even if one does not want it. Here is also where intentionality (or telicity) is coming in, but it should be seen that telicity crucially differs from temporality: we may well-order the three groups telically so that we get the linear order {letter to Antoinette, letter to Mary}$_1$, {letter to Jessica, letter to David}$_2$, {letter to Judith}$_3$, representing the intended order, but the actual temporal order induced by the use of verbs like *mail* might be $2<1<3$.

Now, there turns out to be an instructive element in this example. Suppose that I mailed the set {letter to Antoinette, letter to Mary}$_1$ and I did that on day 1. On day 2 my wife mails the letter to Judith in one post box and I mail the remaining two in another box in Jaujac, so that the three letters are shipped simultaneously (there is one shipping per day). In that case, I think, we would be forced to assume a partially ordered temporal structure associated with the partition, because there are clearly two different sets involved but they are sent on the same day. The instructive thing is that the need for a linear order is closely tied up with the thematic structure involved: the partition requires that there be a constant first argument (in this case, sender) engaged in the actualization of the partition. Note that this is important in view of our thesis that there is a fundamental asymmetry in aspect construal: at the level of VP we need 'constant first argument' mappings, expressing a linear order of the elements of the partition.

The question now is how fine-grained one ought to be. Let us assume that (48) pertains to a situation in which Judith ate three sandwiches one by one. According to PLUG, the direct object NP contains the information that there is some partition Q containing three singletons, as in Figure 37a. It is not really spectacular if three sandwiches happen to be involved in a 1+1+1-structure, but, as observed, *Jessica ate three sandwiches* may pertain to an event in which Jessica first ate one sandwich and later two together, the corresponding 1+2 partition given in Figure 37b. On the assumption that the domain of interpretation is structured both temporally and atemporally, access is obtained to the 'history' of the internal argument of *eat* in (48) in a particular model, so that it is compatible with modifiers like *one by one*. Whatever we may say about the meaning of *one by one*, we are certainly allowed to say that it

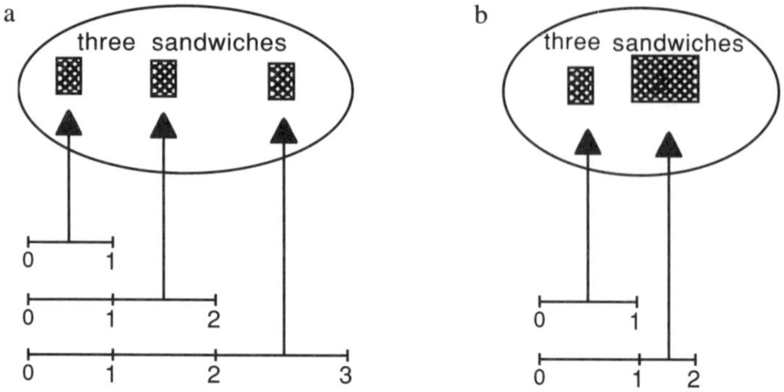

Figure 37 These two situations are among a combinatorially defined number of situations denoted by the VP *to eat three sandwiches*

requires that the structure of the denotation of the internal argument of the verb be built up stepwise. This is done by making the singletons of the partition index-dependent, where the indices belong to a well-ordered set. However, it is not the set ⟦three sandwiches⟧ which is made index-dependent; it is rather the collection of sets which is induced by the partition. In terms of chapter 7, the cardinality of $Q|_{[\![\text{sandwich}]\!]}$ is 3 as in Figure 37a or at most 3 as in Figure 37b. So, Figure 37 does represent semantic objects of type <*i*,a>, but in both cases the union of the sets making up the 'intensional slice' is the extensional set ⟦three sandwiches⟧ itself.

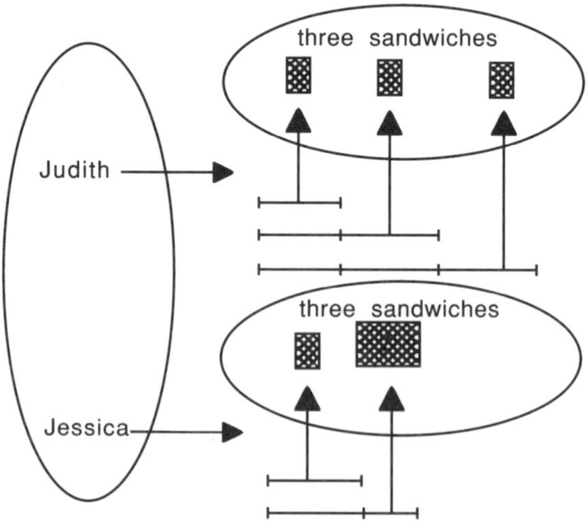

Figure 38 *Judith and Jessica ate three sandwiches* can be made true by a (finite) number of quite different situations including the situation given here

The same carries over to sentences like *Judith and Jessica ate three sandwiches*, for which Figure 38 would be a correct representation, given the two situations of the particular model chosen. Note that the intervals of each of the two subevents may, but need not, overlap in real time. This is what was also expressed in derivation 7 at the end of chapter 10.5. The partitioning of the argument-NPs – different for the internal and external argument – opens the way for a more detailed account of how the argument is involved in the predication, and this more fine-grained analysis is necessary for an insight into the interaction between temporal and atemporal structure. As pointed out in Verkuyl (1987a, 1988), the index structure involved may be interpreted in terms of a thematic equivalence relation. That is, the function values of the index-dependent mapping in Figure 37 are members of a subset of the NP-denotation which distinguish themselves from other members on the ground of their getting involved at a particular index.

At this point, we have to discuss the problem of whether we have to take the partitioning physically or mentally. In terms of Figure 37a: is it necessary for Judith to finish her first sandwich s_1, which she has on her plate, as a whole before the mapping from i_1 to $\{s_1\}$ may take place? Or is she allowed to eat a sandwich by collecting parts of sandwiches, for example by having all three sandwiches on her plate and taking a part of s_1, then a part of s_2 and finally a part of s_3, so that her first sandwich is actually composed of the stuff of different sandwiches? I think a choice between the two alternatives (physical or in terms of measuring units) is more philosophical than linguistic and either alternative will lead us to a point where it joins onto the main road on which we proceed. I am inclined to think that in saying (48) one need not always take the partitioned set corresponding to ⟦three sandwiches⟧ physically. We may think of it more abstractly in terms of a set of equivalents of physical objects. That is, if one uses cardinality expressions, the information $|\alpha|=k$ may be taken as pertaining to k members of the set α, but the criteria for membership of α may be loosened, dependent on the verb, and/or the context of use. Perhaps the general system of quantification always operates in terms of membership projected into abstract measuring units. That this is not visible might be due to the fact that in most of the cases it happens to be that measuring unit and physical member fall together. I leave this matter as it is, concluding that the mapping of indices onto the partitioned NP-denotation proceeds with the help of naturals. As a last remark on this issue: one may eat halves of sandwiches, but if we say *Judith ate six halves* the halves are taken as units. In section 13.5, I will come back to this issue.

As follows from the existential introduction of the partitioned set Q in (199), it is not correct to say that Figure 37a is *the* visual representation of the meaning of the VP of (48), because we want to let (48) be compatible with any member of a *set* of which Figures 37a and 37b are just two of the combinatorial possibilities. However, Figure 37 has the virtue of illustrating quite clearly why it is that (48) expresses terminative aspect: the set of three sandwiches is partitioned into a collection *S* of three singletons and there is a mapping from the set of indices {1,2,3, ...} into the finite *S*. It would explain why the mapping shown in Figure 37 'comes to a stop': the mapping function would become ill-defined.

How does one temporalize partitions like *Q*? The first clue is given by the fact that the structure generated by the verb can be represented in terms of numerical indices. That is, an index is a counting point at which certain entities are counted as belonging to a set whose members are eaten (up), as discussed in chapter 12.3. The second clue is given by the fact that the cardinal number of *Q* is dependent on the cardinality of the partitioned set W: for any non-empty sets W and any partition *Q*, $|Q| \leq |W|$. These two clues will provide the answer to the question of how to temporalize *Q*.

13.3 The index structure induced by [+ADD TO]-verbs

Let us first become more technical about the contribution of the verb. We have assumed that in the localistic framework the Von Wrightian transition operator T should be defined additively on the basis of DEF 10.1, which will be repeated here for convenience.

DEFINITION 10.1. The Path of a Theme x is assigned to an entity x by the partial function π: $\mathbf{D}_e \rightarrow \mathbf{D}_L{}^{\mathbf{D}_T}$ defined by:

(64) $x \mapsto \ell$, where $\ell = \{<t,p>: [\![AT(p)(x)]\!]_{\mathbf{M},t} = 1\}$

where $\mathbf{D}_T$ is a discretely ordered set of moments of time, $\mathbf{D}_L$ is the domain of spatial coordinates p.

If we want to build this into the PLUG-grammar, we have to keep in mind that its rule for sentence formation requires that the NP of type $<<<e,t>,t>,t>$ take the VP, which is of type $<<e,t>,t>$. Likewise, a two-place predicate is something which is taken by the internal argument NP to yield the VP.[53] I shall do two things: (a) build in the functional scheme $x \mapsto \ell$ as expressing the relation between the external argument NP and its VP; (b) build in the function ℓ in the internal structure of the VP itself. In order to accomplish this, the function π must be adapted:

DEFINITION 9. The (partial) participancy function π: $\mathbf{D}_e \rightarrow \mathbf{D}_L{}^{\mathbf{N}}$ is defined by:

(200) $x \mapsto \ell$,where $\ell = \{<i,p>: [\![AT(p)(x)]\!]_{\mathbf{M},i}=1\}$

N is the set of indices representing intervals (of any sort), $\mathbf{D}_L$ is the domain of spatial coordinates p and $\ell \in \mathbf{D}_L{}^{\mathbf{N}}$. It is my purpose to show that given a sentence of the form NP_1 $[_{VP}V\ NP_2]$, the function π takes the denotation of NP_1 as its domain and has as its co-domain a set of pairs ℓ consisting of indices and 'locations', in particular the cells of the partitioned NP_2-denotation. In this way, the results of our reanalysis of the localistic (Jackendoffian) system in terms of the schemes in Figure 29 (chapter 10.5) can be transplanted into the standard model-theoretic framework. It is assumed that the type-logical relation between NP and VP remains as in PLUG, that is, as a functional relation in which $NP_{<<<e,t>,t>,t>}$ takes the $VP_{<<e,t>,t>}$. However, the co-domain of the π-function is built in in the relation between the verb and its internal argument NP_2. Accordingly, (71) will also be adapted:

(201) $\mathbf{M} \models \phi T \psi[i]$, if $\mathbf{M} \models [_{\phi}AT(\ell(i))(x)]$ and for some immediate successor j of i, $\mathbf{M} \models [_{\psi}AT(\ell(j))(x)]$

In (64), ℓ was defined as a set of pairs whose first members are elements of the set of moments **T**, whereas they now belong to **N**. In (201), the function ℓ is defined in terms of indices i, which are taken as *representatives* for spatio-temporal positions. If this generalization of ℓ is pressed into a more abstract pattern, ℓ can be defined as a function, whose domain is **N** or a subset thereof and whose co-domain is a set of locations $\mathbf{D}_L$. The term 'location' is taken in a very broad sense, covering all sorts of semantic fields (position, possession, etc.) along the lines of, for example, Jackendoff (1990). In this way, (65) would be a temporalized instance of the more generally defined VP-path (202):

(65) $\ell_{\text{walk home}} = \{<t_0$, office>, $<t_1$, book shop>, $<t_2$, office>, ..., $<t_4$, bar>, ..., $<t_n$, home>}

(202) $\ell_{\text{walk to X}} = \{<0,\ell(0)>, <1,\ell(1)>, <2,\ell(2)>, \ldots, <4,\ell(4)>, \ldots, <m,\ell(m)>\}$

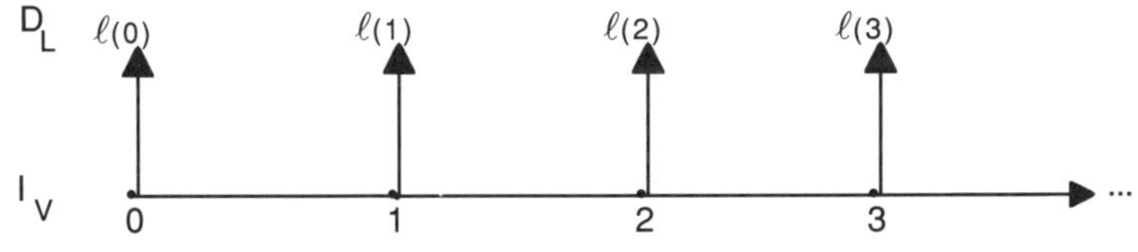

Figure 39 The Path-structure of *John walked home* can be represented by a function from indices (natural numbers) into a domain of locations, in particular a domain of spatio-temporal locations

where $X=\ell(m)$. The resulting Path-structure is illustrated in Figure 39. Correspondingly, we obtain three sets: (a) I_V, the set of intervals $\{(0,1), (0,2), (0,3), \ldots\}$; (b) I, the set of (designated) representatives of these intervals; and (c) Ran(ℓ), the set of function values of ℓ.[54]

DEFINITION 10: $I_V := \{(0,k) \subseteq \mathbf{R}: k \in \mathbf{N}\}$ and $I := \{k | (0,k) \in I_V\}$
Let $0,1,2, \ldots \in \mathbf{N}$ and $\ell(0), \ell(1), \ell(2), \ldots \in \mathbf{D_L}$ as defined in (200). Then membership of I_V is induced recursively by (i) $i_1 \in I_V$; (ii) if $i_n \in I_V$, then $i_{n+1} \in I_V$, where for any k, i_k is short for (0,k). Note that $(0,0) \in I_V$; also that $I=\text{dom}(\ell)$.

I_V belongs to **R** and it represents the [+ADD TO]-dynamicity of 'going densely through' $\mathbf{D_L}$. The conditions (i) and (ii) say that $i_1=(0,1)$ is the first interval of I_V. Its successor is $i_2=(0,2)$. The third interval $i_3=(0,3)$, etc. The set I of representatives of the intervals in I_V is well ordered as it is isomorphic to **N**.[55] As I is completely representative for I_V, we shall need only I and its members for the representation of [+ADD TO]-verbs.

One might wish to stipulate that **T**, that is, the set of moments of time, should appear in DEF 9. We must assume, however, that there is some degree of freedom left in the choice of **R** as underlying I. Most normally, **T** will be taken, but one might wish to consider and interpret sentences more abstractly, for example in mathematical contexts. This is what is meant by our statement that I represents all sorts of interval: it may represent atemporal **R** itself, if we wish to use a sentence without reference to time.

As observed earlier, when we measure the length of a road, we assume the presence of **R**-properties of the object which is being measured, but we express ourselves in **N** by counting in kilometres or miles. We proceed from the zero point to a final point by marking certain intermediate points by numerals. If I am driving from Amsterdam to Jaujac in order to play pétanque with Mr Bertrand and Mr Prat, and I see on the daily odometer the number 978, it indicates the 978th kilometre driven so far: it represents the dense interval $(0,978+k)$, where $0 \leq k < 1{,}000$ metres. What we are basically doing is imposing ordinal **N**-structure on **R**, but due to the property of well-ordering of **N** we may take the indices assigned to the Path-intervals as ordinal numbers. This is what we do if we go dynamically from point zero to some place indicated by a natural number. In much the same way, we assign temporal structure to the interpretations of verbs expressing change in natural language. If members of **N** are used to represent certain intervals from **R**, it is always possible to reconstruct from a given representative n its 'underlying' **R**-interval. In other words, if we analyse a verb in terms of members of I, we have I_V as a 'safety net'.

There is a natural mathematical device to relate I_V and I in the way **R** relates to **N** if natural numbers are used to represent subsets of **R**. This is the so-called *Entier-function*:[56]

DEFINITION 11: Ent: $\mathbf{R} \rightarrow \mathbf{N}$ is a function defined as: for all $x \in \mathbf{R}$, Ent(x)=y such that $y \in \mathbf{N}$ and $y \leq x < y+1$.

This well-known truncation function enables us to deal with both dense and discrete structure at once, expressing our capacity to use two time orderings at once, as demonstrated with the chess field example (66) in chapter 10.1. In DEF 9 the Entier-function is built into ℓ, which is defined in DEF 10. We shall use a variant of Ent below in dealing with Tense, because in the present approach it is Tense which brings us from **N**-representations to **R**. In other words, and still metaphorically, we will need something like Ent to get from index representations to 'real-time representations'.

Let us now make three assumptions about the index set I:

(a) I as a whole is determined by the context (and so is I_V);

(b) the number of indices taken from I is determined by the cardinality of the internal argument NP-denotation, if there is one;

(c) I is the value of a variable inside the NP VP-proposition bound by tense, thus accounting for its actualization.

These assumptions are not unreasonable. The first one is supported by the fact that we may change our perspective on what is going to be represented by the choice of a verb. A sentence like *He walked to school* may be taken as pertaining to one walk or to a set of walks. Depending on the context, we may have to do with one I taken as just one set of indices or with a collection of Is. In the latter case, *He walked to school* may pertain to his habit of walking to school. This point will come back in section 13.8. The context-dependency is also manifest in the fact that the co-domain of the function ℓ is clearly selected depending on the context. If we say *She gave him the parcel* we do not know whether she did so by handing him the parcel or by ordering someone to do so. By making I_V context-dependent, we make sure that we are free as to our particular choice of the co-domain $\mathbf{D_L}$. The first assumption is nothing but the warrant that underlying I we can always place a structure (time, worlds, models, situations, and the like) which is or is isomorphic to the interval structure of I_V.

On the second assumption, the lexical definition of [+ADD TO]-verbs provides information about I and its members: each cell of the partition is related to a different index belonging to I. The cardinality of a partition Q is 'tuned to' (in a sense to be formalized) the index set I, which is to say that in this way the interdependency of the direct object NP and the verb is (partly) accounted for. The third assumption expresses the fact that in PLUG$^+$, a structure of the form NP VP will be analysed as being of type $<<i,t>,t>$, that is, as semantically of the form $\lambda I.\phi[I]$, where I is of type $<i,t>$ and I is associated with the main verb.

On the assumption that the function ℓ should be built into the relationship between the verb and its internal argument and that I be accommodated as well to provide access to the tense structure of the sentence as a whole, we may define the verb *eat* in terms of the argumental scheme (203).

(203) $\lambda I\lambda X\lambda i\lambda Y.[\![eat]\!](I)(i)(Y)(X)$

This says that $[\![eat]\!]$ is of type $<<i,t>,<i,<<e,t>,<<e,t>,t>>>>$. Here $<i,t>$ ranges over semantic objects like I, whereas i ($i \in \mathbf{N}$) ranges over numeral indices expressed by the [+ADD TO]-verb *eat* in order to 'address' its internal argument. So, *eat* is taken to express a relation between sets of entities and semantic objects of type $<i,t>$ and type *i*. In other words, to achieve an extension from the atemporal PLUG to the temporal PLUG$^+$ by taking into account the temporal structure expressed by a verb like *eat*, we build in two argument places: I for being able to make the proposition dependent on an I which can be actualized in real time, and i for expressing the progress in time expressed by a [+ADD TO]-verb. It is important to underscore the fact that in PLUG the rule for the VP is given syncategorematically in order to save on tedious and unnecessarily complex derivations. This means that the $\lambda I\lambda X$-part of the formula in (203) is to be ignored until the subject NP takes the VP and the tense fills in the appropriate value for I. As far as the internal structure of the VP is concerned, it is the $\lambda i\lambda Y.[\![eat]\!](I)(i)(Y)(X)$-part of (203), which is of type $<i,<<e,t>,t>>$, that will play a role in the derivations below.

The two following meaning postulates for *eat* express some properties which distinguish this verb from verbs like *hate*.

MP1: $\forall I \forall X \forall k,m[k \leq m \Rightarrow \lambda Y^1.[\![eat]\!](I)(Y^1)(k)(X) \subseteq \lambda Y^2.[\![eat]\!](I)(Y^2)(m)(X)]$
MP2: $\forall I \forall X \forall Y.[\![eat]\!](I)(Y)(0)(X) = \varnothing$

MP1 makes sure that the eating-Path is incremental; MP2 says that at the zero-point the VP-predication does not hold. Both postulates follow straightforwardly from the discussion above, but, as we shall see shortly, they can be drawn into a more general definition of [+ADD TO]-verbs.

There are two alternative ways of distinguishing *eat* from the intransitive verb *walk*:

(204) $\lambda I \lambda X.[\![walk]\!](I)(X)$

(205) $\lambda I \lambda X \lambda i.[\![walk]\!](I)(i)(X)$

In (204) *walk* would be without an index i, which means that it would not be analysed in terms of the function ℓ. In (205), $\lambda i.[\![walk]\!](I)(i)(X)$ would be of type *<i,<<e,t>,t>>>*, just like $\lambda i \lambda Y.[\![eat]\!](I)(i)(Y)(X)$, but in this case there would be no Y available for constraining the 'odometer' i, because the co-domain of ℓ is left unspecified, so that the verb will never be able to get a terminative sentence. Of course, (204) cannot yield terminative aspect, because there is no way for the verb to express progress in the sense of DEF 9 and DEF 10. In chapter 14, I will discuss these alternatives in more detail, also in view of the fact that verbs like *walk* may often be used transitively as in *She walked a mile* and as I shall point out, (50) *John walked to the store*. In that connection, I shall also discuss the verb *eat* when used intransitively as in *Judith ate*.

So-called unaccusative verbs like *die*, *arrive*, *depart*, *succeed*, etc. will be treated as (206).

(206) $\lambda I \lambda i \lambda Y.[\![die]\!](I)(i)(Y)$

So, $[\![die]\!]$ will be defined as belonging to type *<<i,t>,<i,<<e,t>,t>>>*, just like *walk* in (205), but in this case the argument has a different thematic role, viz. the role of internal argument. Recall from chapter 1.4 that sentences like (207) are syntactically treated as (208). That is, *John* is analysed as the internal argument of *die* 'moved' from its position of the internal argument to the external argument position.

(207) John died

(208) $[[_{NP}\text{John}]_i\ [_{VP}\text{die } e_i]]$

In this way, (207) will be treated as expressing the function ℓ in (200). In other words, the problem will be to find an appropriate value for x. I will return to the treatment of these verbs in chapter 14.

That the treatment of unaccusative verbs and verbs like *walk* is postponed is due to the fact that the system inherent to [+ADD TO]-verbs is optimally visible in two-place verbs when occurring with their arguments. So, I will first discuss the semantics of the internal Θ-role in sentences like (48) *Judith ate three sandwiches* and then proceed to discuss the semantics of the external Θ-role, thereby explaining the π-function in terms of a difference between the two thematic roles.

13.4 The semantics of the internal Θ-role

Turning now to the interaction between the verb and its internal argument, let us consider the VP *eat three sandwiches* in more detail to see which modifications are to be made. After that, we shall deal with the transition from NP-structure *an sich* to NP-structure as the internal argument, whose interpretation is determined by the verb with which it is occurring. By this, I mean to say that the relation between a verb like *eat* and its internal argument is quite different from the relation between *hate* and its internal argument. In the former but not in the latter relation there must be room for the construal of temporal structure and for the tuning of the information conveyed by the verb and the information expressed by the internal argument NP.

In PLUG the VP-rule for two-place verbs was (209).

(209) $\mathrm{VP} : \lambda X.[\![\mathrm{NP}]\!](\lambda Y.[\![\mathrm{V}_2]\!](Y)(X))$

In view of (203) we need to extend this to something like (210):

(210) $^{*}\mathrm{VP} : \lambda I \lambda X.[\![\mathrm{NP}]\!](\lambda i \lambda Y.[\![\mathrm{V}_2]\!](I)(i)(Y)(X))$

where, as already said, λIλX are positioned outside the VP. It is immediately obvious that there is a type-clash problem in (210), because the type of the NP is $<<<e,t>,t>,t>$, which is not the type of the argument it is to take. This is also visible on inspection of the internal structure of the NP itself. The place of interest in the NP in (211) is the position P, as this is where the verbal information comes in.

(211) $\lambda P \exists \mathrm{W}[\mathrm{W} \subseteq [\![\mathrm{sandwich}]\!] \wedge |\mathrm{W}| = 3 \wedge \exists Q \mathrm{ps} \mathrm{W}[Q = P|_{[\![\mathrm{sandwich}]\!]}]]$

However, P is not of the right type to receive (203). As the λI and λX front the VP, we may peel away the $<i,t>$ and the first $<e,t>$ of [[eat]] in (203), so that we can reduce the type-clash problem to the fact that P is of type $<<e,t>,t>$, whereas we need a variable of type $<i,<<e,t>,t>>$ for the expression $\lambda i \lambda Y.[\![\mathrm{eat}]\!](I)(i)(Y)(X)$. This also follows from (210) itself, of course.

In the list of notational conventions for PLUG^{+} the appropriate variable **W** has been included, resulting in the first modification of (211):

(212) $\lambda \mathbf{W} \exists \mathrm{W}[\mathrm{W} \subseteq [\![\mathrm{sandwich}]\!] \wedge |\mathrm{W}| = 3 \wedge \exists Q \mathrm{ps} \mathrm{W}[Q = \ldots \mathbf{W} \ldots]]$

The blanks in the formula after = should contain means to get a subformula including **W** which is of the same type as Q, namely $<<e,t>,t>$. It is exactly at this place that the fusion of the information conveyed by the verb and its internal argument is taking shape. This fusion is in some way dependent on the cardinality of the internal argument, as for any partition Q of W, $|Q|\leq|W|$. So, the following solution for the right-hand side dots in (212) may do:

(213) $\lambda\mathbf{W}\exists W[W\subseteq[\![sandwich]\!]\wedge|W|=3\wedge\exists Q ps W[Q=\bigcup_{I}\mathbf{W}|_{[\![sandwich]\!]}]]$

where $\bigcup_I\mathbf{W}$ abbreviates $\bigcup_{i\in I}\mathbf{W}_i$. It is the union of the set of function values of ℓ from numeral indices to collections of sets applied to members of the set I. $\bigcup_{i\in I}\mathbf{W}_i$ is a collection of sets obtained by taking **W** as the function ℓ such that at any index i it gives us a collection of sets to which the predicate applies at i. The index i fulfils the same sort of role with respect to **W** as the index *a* to Walk* in the expression Walk*(*a*) discussed in our introduction of Ty2. Thus, **W**(i) is of type <<*e*,*t*>,*t*>, just like $\bigcup_I\mathbf{W}$. Also, **W**(i) can be written as $\mathbf{W}_i$. That the cardinality of Q, $|Q|$, is a subset of I follows straightforwardly from the information that $Q=\bigcup_I\mathbf{W}$, as defined below in DEF 12. In this way, the terminativity induced by the internal argument [+SQA]-NP is accounted for.

Let us have a more detailed look at the formal machinery given in DEF 12. A collection of sets P is constructed by **W** because **W** is defined as a function determining exactly which sets are in P at each construction step, as follows:[57]

DEFINITION 12: $\mathbf{W}$: $I\rightarrow\mathbf{D}_L$, where $\mathbf{D}_L=\{1,0\}^{(\{1,0\}^{D_e})}$ and **W** is defined as follows:

(i) for all U, **W**(0)(U)=0
(ii) for all U, **W**(m)(U)=1 ⇒ **W**(m+1)(U)=1
(iii) for at most one U, **W**(m)(U)=0 & **W**(m+1)(U)=1
(iv) for all U, **W**(m)(U)=**W**(m+1)(U) ⇒ for all n>m, **W**(n)=**W**(m)

In this way, **W** constructs the collection of sets $P=\bigcup_I\mathbf{W}=\bigcup_{i\in I}\mathbf{W}_i$, as exemplified in Figure 40. Suppose that Judith happened to have eaten three sandwiches in two parts, first sandwich s1, and then the sandwiches s2 and s3 together (recall the discussion in section 13.2). In that case, Figure 40 would be compatible

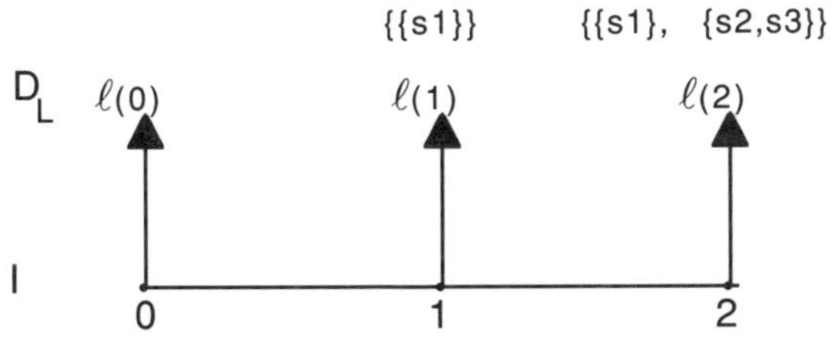

Figure 40 Like Figure 39, this figure illustrates Path-structure, where the domain of locations is now a collection of sets, whose structure is built up cumulatively

with that situation: at counting point 1, $\mathbf{W}_1$ applied to {s1} would warrant that {s1}∈ *P* and at counting point 2, $\mathbf{W}_2$ would warrant that both {s1} and {s2,s3} are elements of *P*. The equation *Q*=*P* in ∃*Q*psW[*Q*=*P* ...] makes sure that the partition *Q* introduced by ∃*Q*psW in (213) is equated with *P*. This will turn out to become non-trivial below in section 13.6, where the equation sign is going to be interpreted as 'totally affected'. Note that $\mathbf{D}_L$, the co-domain of the function ℓ in its newly adapted form **W**, is constructed from the types *e* and *t*, so we need not introduce new entities in our model.[58]

Let us have a brief look at (i)–(iv) in DEF 12. The first rule makes sure that one starts from scratch, and (ii) ensures that any continuation is incremental; (iii) says that from one counting point we go to the next one, whereas (iv) is a stop condition. That is, if the domain of the function does not contain elements to operate on, its last image is taken as a constant. The four rules together do not only fit the recursive DEF 9 and the meaning postulates MP1 and MP2 given above, they also ensure that **W** has the following three desired properties.

> *Property* 1: for each countable collection *P* there is an interval I and a constructor **W** such that **W** constructs *P* during I.
>
> *Property* 2: a collection of sets *P* will generally have more than one constructor. A partition can be constructed in more than one way.
>
> *Property* 3: if **W** constructs *P*, then ∀m>|*P*|, **W**(m)=*P* & ∀m<|*P*|, **W**(m)⊂*P*. The stopping point is the cardinality of *P*, or *Q*, for that matter.

The main question is now: how does one obtain (213) from (211)? This question has two answers: the first concerns the change of the <<<*e*,*t*>,*t*>,*t*>-NP (211) into an NP of type <<*i*,<<*e*,*t*>,*t*>>,*t*>; the second one pertains to the information if $\mathbf{W}_i$, then i∈|*Q*|. How does this come in?

The answer to the first question is important in view of the problem of elucidating the theoretical notion of assigning a Θ-role to an NP. This notion plays a role in the GB-framework, but also in other branches of generative grammar. The transition from (211) to (213) assumes the following syntactic operation: a verb like *eat* is specified as taking an NP on the basis of a specific Θ-instruction whose exact nature is determined by the lexical properties of *eat*. In other words, rather than specifying *eat* in terms of the frame [—NP] it is specified in terms of [—[$_{NP'}$ Θ NP]], where Θ contains verb-dependent information. This means that the Θ-information associated with *hate* is different from the Θ-information of *eat*. Members of the set of [+ADD TO]-verbs have a thematic role which prepares the atemporal information expressed by the argument NP such that it can be tuned to the nature of the verb. In this way, the dependency of the

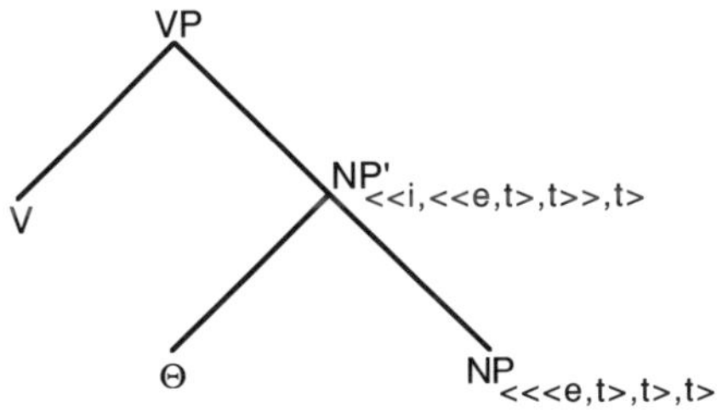

Figure 41 The Θ-role assigned by the verb V to its internal argument can be seen as the 'thematic lubricant' between the verb and the NP

direct object NP *three sandwiches* on the verb *eat* is given form. Formally, the interpretation of Θ_{int} for [+ADD TO]-verbs is defined as:

DEFINITION 13: $[\![\Theta_{int}]\!]=\lambda NP\lambda\mathbf{W}[NP(\bigcup_I\mathbf{W})]$

Or, in the other notation: $\lambda NP\lambda\mathbf{W}[NP(\bigcup_{i\in I}\mathbf{W}_i)]$. For convenience, the variable NP will be used for semantic objects of type $<<<e,t>,t>,t>$. The structure underlying this operation is given in Figure 41. Applied to (211), Θ_{int} yields (213) as follows:

$$[\![\text{three sandwiches}]\!]$$
$$\lambda P\exists W[W\subseteq[\![\text{sandwich}]\!]\wedge|W|=3\wedge\exists Q\text{ps}W[Q=P|_{[\![\text{sandwich}]\!]}]]$$

$$[\![\Theta_{int}]\!]([\![\text{three sandwiches}]\!])$$
$$\lambda NP\lambda\mathbf{W}[NP(\bigcup_I\mathbf{W})](\lambda P\exists W[W\subseteq[\![\text{sandwich}]\!]\wedge|W|=3\wedge\exists Q\text{ps}W[Q=P|_{[\![\text{sandwich}]\!]}]])$$
$$\lambda\mathbf{W}[\lambda P\exists W[W\subseteq[\![\text{sandwich}]\!]\wedge|W|=3\wedge\exists Q\text{ps}W[Q=P|_{[\![\text{sandwich}]\!]}]](\bigcup_I\mathbf{W})]$$
$$\lambda\mathbf{W}.\exists W[W\subseteq[\![\text{sandwich}]\!]\wedge|W|=3\wedge\exists Q\text{ps}W[Q=\bigcup_I\mathbf{W}|_{[\![\text{sandwich}]\!]}]]$$

The introduction of a Θ-element into the syntax of the VP may appear artificial. Another empty element seems to be introduced. However, there are arguments to defend this move. The first is that the Θ-information can be syntactically associated with application of rules assigning case. In GB-syntax it is quite standard to assume a case-marking operation at the very point at which Θ is located in Figure 41. For German, but not for English or Dutch, this would amount to looking at Θ-role assignment as co-occurring with overt case assignment. The second argument is that in directional phrases like *to the store*, the Θ-information can be associated with the preposition. This will be worked out in more detail in section 13.6.

By (213), one obtains a point of attachment in the NP for temporal information contributed by the verb. Let us write the NP in (213) as NP′. Then ⟦NP′⟧, being of type *<i,<<e,t>,t>>*, can now be applied to (203). This is done by rule 2 of PLUG$^+$, resulting in (214).

(214) $\text{VP}: \lambda I\lambda X.[\![\text{NP}']\!](\lambda i\lambda Y.[\![\text{V}]\!](I)(i)(Y)(X))$

For (203), recall that the operators λI and λX are 'peeled off' from the rest of the verbal information: they precede the application of the operation inside the VP. Hence the argument of the NP′ in the VP *eat three sandwiches* is the verb which is at that stage of the derivation of type *<i,<<e,t>,t>>*.

(215) $\lambda \mathbf{W}\exists W[W\subseteq[\![\text{sandwich}]\!]\wedge|W|=3\wedge\exists Q\text{ps}W[Q=\bigcup_I \mathbf{W}|_{[\![\text{sandwich}]\!]}]]$
$(\lambda i\lambda Y.[\![\text{eat}]\!](I)(i)(Y)(X))$

This argument replaces the variable **W**, which means that for every $i\in I$, the function $\lambda Y.[\![\text{eat}]\!](I)(i)(Y)(X)$ yields a collection of sets, namely the set of sets eaten at index i.

(216)
$\exists W[W\subseteq[\![\text{sandwich}]\!]\wedge|W|=3\wedge\exists Q\text{ps}W[Q=\bigcup_{i\in I}\{\lambda Y.[\![\text{eat}]\!](I)(i)(Y)(X)|_{[\![\text{sandwich}]\!]}\}]]$

As said above, Q is the union of a collection of collections of sets, because at every index the function $\lambda Y.[\![\text{eat}]\!](I)(i)(Y)(X)$ yields a collection of sets for which it is true that Y is eaten by X, and Q is defined as the union of an indexed family of these function applications. In set notation, this results in the final line of (217) which is short for (218).

(217) $\exists W[W\subseteq[\![\text{sandwich}]\!]\wedge|W|=3$
$\wedge\exists Q\text{ps}W[Q=\bigcup_{i\in I}\{U\cap[\![\text{sandwich}]\!]: [\![\text{eat}]\!](I)(i)(U)(X)\}]]$

(218) $\exists W[W\subseteq[\![\text{sandwich}]\!]\wedge|W|=3$
$\wedge\exists Q\text{ps}W[Q=\bigcup\{\{U\cap[\![\text{sandwich}]\!]: [\![\text{eat}]\!](I)(i)(U)(X)\}_{i\in I}\}]]$

Both (217) and (218) say that Q is the (finite) collection of sets U intersected with the set of sandwiches such that for each U_k, the intersection $U_k\cap[\![\text{sand-}$ $\text{wich}]\!]$ is eaten by X at index k, given a contextually given I, where $k\leq|Q|\leq|W|$. I will continue to use (217).

So, sentence (48) *Judith ate three sandwiches* will be represented as:

(219) $\lambda I.\exists!V[\,V=[\![\text{Judith}]\!]\cap\{j_i\}\wedge\exists W[W\subseteq[\![\text{sandwich}]\!]\wedge|W|=3$
$\wedge\exists Q\text{ps}W[Q=\bigcup_{i\in I}\{U\cap[\![\text{sandwich}]\!]: [\![\text{eat}]\!](I)(i)(U)(V)\}]]]$

which can be understood as expressing that the unique individual (singleton) V who bears the name *Judith*, had an eat-relation to an indexed family of sets Q, such that she ate at most three subsets of the set $[\![\text{sandwich}]\!]$. The terminativity of (48) follows from the fact that 'going through' Q is bounded because the number of sets U is at most 3.

There are some interesting and potentially vexing problems concerning the nature of quantification in sentences like (220):

(220) Ole lifted three tables

In (220), the situation could have been something like (221):

(221) $\lambda I.\exists !V[V=[\![Ole]\!]\cap\{j_i\}\wedge\exists W[W\subseteq[\![table]\!]\wedge|W|=3$
$\wedge\exists Q ps W[Q=\bigcup_{i\in I}\{U\cap[\![table]\!]: [\![lift]\!](I)(i)(U)(X)\}]]]$

The problem is that (221) requires, due to $|W|=3$, that there be three different tables involved in (220), just as in (218). However, (220) may be used to describe a situation in which Ole performed some medical task, namely lifting three tables, like doing a couple of deep knee bends. So, *three tables* means here 'three times a table'. There are several ways out of this marked case. One is to declare *lifted three tables* a one-place predicate. Another, perhaps more convincing, possible way out might be to loosen the criteria for set membership by allowing for certain predicates like *lift* (but not for *sell*, *eat* and *destroy*) to let ∃W range over index-dependent tokens. For (220), this is equivalent to observing that there are three index-dependent occurrences of one and the same table and to decide that these occurrences are counted as different members of W. This ontological decision might sound forced, but it is in fact what happens if one interprets (220) and is confronted with the marked interpretation that (220) concerns the same table. Note also sentences like (222):

(222) Three theatres have a Sol LeWitt-painting in the main hall

Sentence (222) seemingly excludes the interpretation that two theatres have the same Sol LeWitt-painting and a third theatre a different one. This would come out even more clearly if we talked about three original Rembrandt paintings. But as Sol LeWitt is a conceptual artist, it is perfectly acceptable to interpret (222) as being about two paintings. In other words, a difference between the NPs *Sol LeWitt-painting* and *Rembrandt-painting* may be involved in the judgment about partitioning in (222). Thus, it may be concluded that the way we are involved in quantification is not a structural matter but a matter of all sorts of restrictions involving lexical knowledge among other things. In general, it seems affirmed by the fact that sentences like *This salesman sold fourteen Peugeots 309* may be true even if this salesman sold five Peugeots twice because these were sold back on part exchange. A genuine partition is only possible if one quantifies over index-dependent Peugeots. In fact, this is the only way to get fourteen events, which is necessary in view of the continuation *… and fourteen times he made his customers happy.*[59]

A formal characterization of the problem of what sort of entities we quantify over might proceed along the lines of extending representations like (221) to (223):

(223) $\exists \mathbf{W}[\mathbf{W} \subseteq (\mathbf{N} \times [\![\text{table}]\!]) \wedge |\mathbf{W}| = 3 \wedge \exists \boldsymbol{Q} \text{ps} \mathbf{W}[\boldsymbol{Q} = \ldots]]$

where the bold-faced **W** and ***Q*** are pairs of indices and sets (of individuals and sets respectively). It would add nothing to the present analysis to work out this extension here in detail. It would also not add to a better understanding of the [+SQA]-property of *three tables* in (220).

13.5 The semantics of the external Θ-role

The function π in (200) commits to aspectual asymmetry because x corresponds to NP_1 and ℓ, now **W**, to the pair [V NP_2]. Verkuyl (1988) called π a participancy function because π determines the way in which the members of the external argument denotation participate in the predication. Two functions π were distinguished: an injective function denoted by π_i and a constant function denoted by π_c. In this way, the extensional nature of the subject NP position was underscored by requiring that each *individual* belonging to the NP_{ext}-denotation be assigned its own unique image (its own Path, so to say), as in (224), where the function π is spelled out for each individual x:

(224) $x_1 \mapsto \ell_1 \text{: } \mathbf{N} \rightarrow \mathbf{D_L}$
$x_2 \mapsto \ell_2 \text{: } \mathbf{N} \rightarrow \mathbf{D_L}$
$x_3 \mapsto \ell_3 \text{: } \mathbf{N} \rightarrow \mathbf{D_L}$
...

When π is an injection, then for all i,j, $x_i \neq x_j \Rightarrow \ell_i \neq \ell_j$. When π is a constant function, then for all i,j, $x_i \neq x_j \Rightarrow \ell_i = \ell_j$. In the case of (48) there is no way to distinguish between π_i and π_c.

(48) Judith ate three sandwiches
(225) Judith $\mapsto \{\langle 1,s_1\rangle, \langle 2,s_2\rangle, \langle 3,s_3\rangle\}$
(226) Judith $\mapsto \{\langle 1,s_{1,2}\rangle, \langle 2,s_3\rangle\}$
(227) Judith $\mapsto \{\langle i_1,s_1\rangle, \langle i_2,s_2\rangle, \langle j_3,s_3\rangle\}$

Note that (225) is a simplified notation of one of the situations allowed by (218). It verifies a possible situation in which Judith would have eaten three sandwiches one after the other, whereas in the possible situation (226) she 'went through' her three sandwiches in two steps. In other words, the partition steps of the internal argument NP are made visible by the pair-notation. In

Verkuyl (1988), NPs were treated as denoting semantic objects of type $<<e,t>,t>$, so the domain of the functions π was a set of individuals x. In the present framework the functions will have to operate on singletons, as the NP is of type $<<<e,t>,t>,t>$. For convenience I shall not write, for example, $\{\text{Judith}\} \mapsto \{<1,\{s_1\}>,<2,\{s_2\}>,<3,\{s_3\}>\}$, or more accurately $\{\text{Judith}\} \mapsto \{<1,\{\{s_1\}\}>, <2,\{\{s_1\},\{s_2\}\}>, <3,\{\{s_1\},\{s_2\},\{s_3\}\}>\}$ as required by the function **W** in DEF 12. So, in explaining the working of π the notation which is not used for derivations but rather for explanation, will be kept simple. In the analysis of plural NPs it is convenient to write the natural numbers in the domain of l as subscripts of indices i, j and k in order to distinguish them properly, as in (227).

Let us now consider (228), interpreted with respect to a situation in which each of the four boys lifted a different table. This situation is covered among many others by π_i.

(228) Four boys lifted three tables

(229) $boy_1 \mapsto \{<i_1,table_1>, <i_2,table_{2,3}>\}$
$boy_2 \mapsto \{<j_1,table_{4,5}>, <j_2,table_6>\}$
$boy_3 \mapsto \{<k_1,table_7>, <k_2,table_8>, <k_3,table_9>\}$
$boy_4 \mapsto \{<m_1,table_{10,11,12}>\}$

For each boy there is a point of origin, the point zero of the function defined in DEF 10. Now, for each i_i, j_i, k_i and m_i it may be the case that they are identical or different. In fact, in (228) j_1 could be identical to i_1, and j_2 to i_2. Yet the function value of π_i would be different for (the singletons) boy_1 and boy_2, because the tables differ. The constant function requires that the function values all be identical.

The empirical motivation for the functions π is given by the fact noticed in Verkuyl (1988) that there is a certain arithmetical law determining the number of combinatorial possibilities in sentences like those of the form (230):

(230) $[_{NP1}\ k\ N]\ [_{VP}V\ [_{NP2}\ n\ N]]]$

On the face of it, the rule seems to be that, given a sentence like (228), the number of tables may vary between 3 and 12. However, given the index-dependence of the members of the internal argument denotation, the rule is more forceful and demanding: it requires there to be *either* 1×3 *or* 4×3 tables, if we count a table connected with index i different from the same table at index j. The rule introduces index-dependent cardinality which amounts to saying that the table-occurrence $<i_1, t_3>$ is different from the table-occurrence $<i_2, t_3>$, where t_3 is a table and where i_1 and i_2 are distinct indices. The token-rule can be made part of PLUG$^+$. In fact, it follows straightforwardly from the temporalization of PLUG, in which indices are incorporated (see also derivation 7 at the end of chapter 10.5).

The enlarged degree of freedom solves the problem of there being just three tables in (228), as exemplified by (231), where it is sufficient for π_i to be an injection if, for example, $i_1 \neq j_1$.

(231) $boy_1 \mapsto \{\langle i_1, table_1\rangle, \langle i_2, table_{2,3}\rangle\}$
$boy_2 \mapsto \{\langle j_1, table_1,\rangle, \langle j_2, table_{2,3}\rangle\}$
$boy_3 \mapsto \{\langle k_1, table_2,\rangle, \langle k_2, table_1\rangle, \langle k_3, table_3\rangle\}$
$boy_4 \mapsto \{\langle m_1, table_{1,2,3}\rangle\}$

This configuration meets the conditions of π_i because for each individual singleton boy $\{x\}$ in the NP domain, there is a different unique function value $\pi(\{x\})$. The configuration (232), abbreviated as (233), is yielded by π_c as one of a variety of interpretations in which all boys relate to the same function value.

(232) $boy_1 \mapsto \{\langle i_1, table_1\rangle, \langle i_2, table_{2,3}\rangle\}$
$boy_2 \mapsto \{\langle i_1, table_1\rangle, \langle i_2, table_{2,3}\rangle\}$
$boy_3 \mapsto \{\langle i_1, table_1\rangle, \langle i_2, table_{2,3}\rangle\}$
$boy_4 \mapsto \{\langle i_1, table_1\rangle, \langle i_2, table_{2,3}\rangle\}$

(233) $boy_{1,2,3,4} \mapsto \{\langle i_1, table_1\rangle, \langle i_2, table_{2,3}\rangle\}$

The constant function π_c also allows cases like (234).

(234) Three men bought two houses

It is very hard to get reliable judgments on its meaning: people differ in their opinions (even within themselves). In particular, the problem seems to be that the cardinality of the external argument is higher than that of the internal argument. Note that (234) cannot be interpreted as (235) because (235) cannot be obtained by an injective function, but π_c may yield (236).

(235) $man_{1,2} \mapsto \{\langle i_1, house_1\rangle\}$
$man_3 \mapsto \{\langle i_1, house_2\rangle\}$

(236) $man_{1,2,3} \mapsto \{\langle i_1, house_{1,2}\rangle\}$

In this way, joint ownership is not excluded because one may allow internal structure in which two of the three men were acting jointly. Essential for (236) is that there be something which brings the three men together in one collection: three men satisfy the predicate ‘buy two houses’, but whether they were involved as a set of three does not matter. The only way for me to interpret (234) in the way described here is the situation in which, for example, someone reports about the sum total of men with respect to a predicate 'buy two houses'. In this way, there is some cumulativity involved in a function π_c. This point is important enough to consider it again with an eye on the π_c-situation (238) verifying (237):

(237) Three policemen have transported (today's) two prisoners

(238) $\text{policeman}_{1,2,3} \mapsto \{<i_1,\text{prisoner}_{1,2}>\}$

In (237), three policemen were involved in the transportation of two prisoners, but the collective task may have spread out over, say, the whole evening as i_1 represents an interval. There are two interesting scenarios in this respect: (a) $\text{policemen}_{1,2}$ transported prisoner_1 at about 6.30 pm and policemen_3 transported prisoner_2 at about 11.45 pm; (b) $\text{policemen}_{1,2}$ transported prisoner_1 at about 6.30 pm, and $\text{policemen}_{1,3}$ transported prisoner_2 at about 11.45 pm. In the latter case, policeman_1 carried out two transports. Note that in this case, (238) also solves Gillon's problem mentioned in chapter 7.2, if it turned up in *Three men wrote two musicals* (Hammerstein = man_2, Rodgers = man_1, Hart = man_3, and i is an index covering a period of time).

In both cases considered, there is some shared property organizing the individual men and policemen into some set. This 'set-ting' property could be 'house buying', or 'transportation duty', or the like. It seems to be provided by contextual information about the index, not by the sentence itself. Recall that index i_1 *represents* an **R**-interval in which the prisoners are involved in the predication. Of course, one could require that the situation described in the preceding paragraph be covered by (239) rather than by (238), but this would ignore the nature of indices representing intervals.

(239) $\text{policeman}_{1,2,3} \mapsto \{<i_1,\text{prisoner}_1>, <i_2,\text{prisoner}_2>\}$

The representation of an interval by a natural number, which is what we do when we represent, for example, natural days by numbering them, should give sufficient room for the situation in which, given a group of three policemen, two of them relate to one prisoner and a third policeman to a second prisoner. In this perspective, it would be simply misleading to require for (237) a common transport activity on the part of all the men for the whole interval. The sentence underinforms us by using a representative (index) and thus provides for a lot of possible ways in which the transport relations are actualized.

It is important to underscore that the meaning of $\mapsto$ in the application of the functions π_i and π_c is not 'be completely involved in' but rather 'be involved in'. An adequate paraphrase for the verb *lift*, for example, would be something like 'execute lifting activities'. The sense of completeness is not inherent to *lift* itself, it is contributed by the cardinality information expressed by the arguments of the verb in question.

(240) One boy lifted a table
(241) Four boys lifted a table

It is indeed hard to escape from the 'complete involvement'-interpretation which says that boy_1 is the only actor involved in the lifting of $table_1$ whereas $table_1$ is not lifted by other individuals (at the time with respect to which (240) is true). However, to assign such a 'one-to-one sense' to *lift* as part of its meaning would be misleading. The verb *lift* in (241) must be able to express that each of the four boys did just a part of the total activity needed to lift the table. (It may even be used to describe a situation in which three boys actually happened to lift the table whereas the fourth one opened the door, prevented scratching, and directed the lifting.) This also means for the table that it did not relate to just one lifting individual. Due to the fact that it should be used in sentences like (241), the verb *lift* must be characterized as being vague with respect to complete involvement of the individuals which make up the denotations of its arguments. More generally, the degree to which individuals which are part of the argument denotation are involved in the predication is left unspecified by the verb itself; it is filled in by the arguments (Carlson 1978; Roberts 1987). Hence $\mapsto$ means 'sufficiently involved in the predication to speak of participancy'.

The upshot of the above considerations leads to the conclusion that the two partitions in (242) are constrained differently.

(242) $\lambda I.\exists W[Z\subseteq[\![boy]\!]\wedge|W|=4\wedge\exists P\text{ps}Z[P=\{V\cap[\![boy]\!]: \exists W[W\subseteq[\![table]\!] \wedge|W|=3\wedge\exists Q\text{ps}W[Q=\bigcup_{i\in I}\{U\cap[\![table]\!]: [\![lift]\!](I)(i)(U)(V)\}]]]]$

That is, the external argument partition $\exists P$psZ is a partitioning of Z into singletons, whereas the internal argument partitioning of W by Q is defined by the interaction of the members of the internal argument NP denotation with indices as sketched in the previous section. A way to build in the function π into (242) would be (243):

(243) $\lambda I\exists W[Z\subseteq[\![boy]\!]\wedge|W|=4\wedge\exists P\text{ps}Z[P=\{\textsc{at}(V\cap[\![boy]\!]): \exists W[W\subseteq[\![table]\!] \wedge|W|=3\wedge\exists Q\text{ps}W[Q=\bigcup_{i\in I}\{U\cap[\![table]\!]: [\![lift]\!](I)(i)(U)(V)\}]]]]$

In this way, $\exists P$psZ is a partitioning of Z into singletons V (Van der Does 1992). I will not pursue this line further, as this was done in Verkuyl (1992). It suffices here to show that the specific requirements on π (injective or constant) can be easily built in.

Let us finally consider sentences like (244) in view of Van der Does' contention that it may allow the five children to have come in repeatedly.

(244) Five children have come in

Given a set of five children, one would not like to exclude the possibility for some children to have come in twice. Say Deborah came into the room but upon hearing Rosalie coming up the stairs, she left the room to welcome her and both went into the room. After this, three other children rang the bell; Rosalie and Deborah went out, greeted them at the staircase and all five came in. Suppose that (244) is uttered at i* (the index representing the point of speech), then (244) is true even if the evaluation covers the time from Deborah's very first entrance to i*. It is evident that the sentence is used with a focus on the information about the number of children satisfying the predicate rather than on the number of entrances.

In my view, this sort of consideration does not force us into weakening the notion of partition because the successor function involved in DEF 10 has been defined with the point zero as a constant. Thus (244) is compatible with the following incremental construction of the three-membered partition which made (244) true.

(245) $\{\{c1\}\}_1 + \{\{c1,c2\}\}_2 + \{\{c1,c2\}, \{c3\}, \{c4\}, \{c5\}\}_3$

It is arguable, then, that as soon as the sets of children {c1} and {c1,c2} are counted as falling under the extension of the verbal predicate *came in* at indices 1 and 2, one might allow for this predicate to apply to the whole monotone-increasing index structure, much in the way we might allow *John rang the bell* to pertain to a situation in which John pressed the bell twice, still considering it as one ring-event. In other words, given an atemporal partition, the desired weakening of the partition may be obtained by transmitting the information available at an index k to the index k+1. It should be observed that there are many empirical complexities involved, such as the choice of the predicate. Not all predicates substituted for *came in* allow internal repetitions, for example *were born* and *did not show up*. So, the choice between partitions and weaker forms such as covers or pseudo-partitions might be a marginal issue (for a detailed discussion on these options see Van der Does 1992).

This concludes the discussion about the external thematic role of two-place verbs like *eat*.

13.6 Indexed PP-complements

Turning now to sentence (51) *John walked to three stores* as compared with (48) *Judith ate three sandwiches*, let us consider the question of how to get a parallel story. It is obvious that the question is involved of how local one should take $\mathbf{D_L}$. For parsimonious reasons, I shall try to reduce $\mathbf{D_L}$ in (51) to a subdomain solely constructed from the basic types *e* and *t*. Firstly, it should be observed that (51) means that we may take it as pertaining to a partition, though stereotypically as a linearly ordered tripartition. Stereotypically, because John might have walked to a point where two stores are situated as neighbouring settlements, so that we may indeed talk about one walk having two stores at one counting point and one at the other. Loosening stereotyped reins on the meaning of *walk* and *fly*, we might even say that we would like the sentence *John flew to three cities* to be able to pertain to an eventuality in which just two flights were involved: on one flight John rented a car and visited two cities near the airport, Dallas/Fort Knox being a case in point. So, one should not press this sentence into covering only the flight part of it. If (as in daily life) some distance is taken from the flight and walking part of the events reported about, then (51) *John walked to three stores* does not really deviate much from (48) *Judith ate three sandwiches*. It is then easy to see that *to three stores* as the complement of *walk* appears to correspond with *three sandwiches* as the complement of *eat*, just like *to stores* after *walk* appears to correspond with *sandwiches* after *eat*. In other words, we would like to have (246), with the VP as in (218):

(246) $\lambda I.\exists!V[V=[\![\text{John}]\!]\cap\{j_i\}\wedge\exists W[W\subseteq[\![\text{store}]\!]\wedge|W|=3$
$\wedge\exists Q\text{psW}[Q=\bigcup_{i\in I}\{U\cap[\![\text{store}]\!]:\ [\![\text{walk}_{\text{to}}]\!](I)(i)(U)(V))\}]]]$

One can afford this generalization without losing grip on the more spatial location in which the event of (51) takes place: it is evident from the meaning of *walk* that the event has to do with some movement by foot over land. But this information is expressed by the verb itself, not by its complement.

Syntactically, the PP *to the store* is the complement of the verb *walk*. Assume that *walk* is lexically specified for $[\text{—}[_{PP}\Theta_{to}\ \text{NP}]$, then the interpretation of the preposition *to* includes assigning a specific semantic role to the NP *the store*. Hence, the lexical specification $[\text{walk}\ [_{PP}\Theta_{to}\text{—}]$ can be considered a complex verb taking the NP *the store* as the argument of the transitive verb *walk-to*, while leaving the verb *walk* semantically intact, so to speak. In this way, one evades the problem discussed with respect to Davidson's (101) and (102), that is, the problem that *walk to* is a predicate as different from *walk* as it

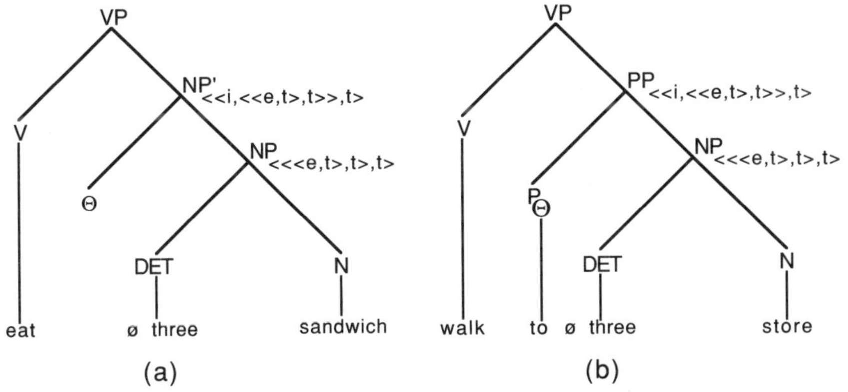

Figure 42 From an aspectual point of view it appears attractive to generalize over the thematic Path-structure of NPs and PPs

is from *eat*. On the present analysis, entailment relations are respected due to the fact that the verbal information expressed as ⟦walk⟧ remains 'visible', both in *walk to* and in *walk*. In chapter 14, this point will be worked out in detail.

The atemporal NP *three stores* is represented as (247), so the transition from (247) to (246) presumes a change from (247) to (248).

(247) $\lambda P\exists W[W\subseteq[\![store]\!]\wedge|W|=3\wedge\exists Q psW[Q=P|_{[\![store]\!]}]]$
(248) $\lambda \mathbf{W}\exists W[W\subseteq[\![store]\!]\wedge|W|=3\wedge\exists Q psW[Q=\bigcup_I \mathbf{W}|_{[\![store]\!]}]]$

This suggests that the directional preposition *to* may be analysed as accomplishing this. In other words, type-logically, *to* can be defined as a function of type *<<<<e,t>,t>,t>, <<i,<<e,t>,t>>,t>>*. This would open the way to an aspectual generalization over (48) and (51), as illustrated in Figure 42. In Figure 42a, the assignment of the Θ-role by the verb is taken as a semantic operation 'loading' the NP as the internal argument of a [+ADD TO]-verb. It yields the transition from (211) to (213) by transmitting information from *eat* to the NP. This can be seen as copying an index from the verb into the NP by Θ-marking, thus making it dependent. The same is done by *to* with respect to the internal argument of (51). It might be questioned whether *to* must be interpreted as in Figure 42b. One might wish to take it as a function *<<<<e,t>,t>,t>,<<i,<p,t>>,t>*, where expressions of type *p* denote places, spatial locations. This is not implausible in the case of (50) *John walked to the store*. In that case one would have to insert the NP-denotation into an ordered sequence of positions of which the store is the last one. However, as pointed out above, sentences like (51) strongly suggest that the internal structure of the set ⟦three stores⟧ should be taken into account.

The analysis of (47) *Judith ate a sandwich* and (50) *John walked to the store* in terms of Figure 42 may comfort those who are worried about the analysis of (62) *John walked home* in chapter 10.1, especially with regard to Figure 26 and (64) in DEF 10.2, and to DEF 9 and Figure 40 in the present section. They might find the essentially lexical analysis of *walk* too fine-grained. It should be noted that DEF 9 allows fine-grainedness, but it also allows tuning to more rough-grained structure. It might even be the case that the successor function in DEF 10 applied to (62) operates just once. In other words, $\bigcup_I \mathbf{W}$ might be just $\bigcup\{\{\mathbf{W}(m)\}\}$ at index m, where m=1 and $\mathbf{W}$(m)=home, because m is the only index. In this sense, the present analysis is less localistic in its concrete sense, but it retains the localistic perspective.

Terminative sentences like (249) are now aspectually analysed analogously to (50) as (250):

(249) John walked from the store

(250) $\lambda I.\exists!V[V=[\![John]\!]\cap\{j_i\}\wedge\exists W[W\subseteq[\![store]\!]\wedge|W|=3$
$\wedge\exists Q psW[Q=\bigcup_{i\in I}\{U\cap[\![store]\!]: [\![walk_{from}]\!](I)(i)(U)(X)\}]]]$

The difference between (50) and (249) is to be accounted for in terms of a lexical difference between *to* and *from*. In this way, (249) is analysed as expressing that *walk* is a two-place predicate by virtue of *from* making the denotation of *the store* index-dependent, where *from* contains the information that at the beginning of a mapping John is at the same place as the function value. So, structurally *from* does the same job as *to* (enforcing the complete mapping from indices into the NP-denotation, as opposite to *towards*, etc.), whereas lexically it gives information about the spatial position of the arguments with respect to one another.[60]

In Dutch, the preposition *naar* (to/towards) would be a natural translation for the preposition *to* in, for example, (50) *John walked to the store*, but there is a problem. There is a difference in meaning between (251) and (252):

(251) John liep naar de winkel
lit.: John walked towards the store

(252) John wandelde tot (aan) de winkel
lit.: John walked up to the store

The latter cannot but express that John walked till he reached the store, whereas the former does not make it necessary for John to have reached the store. This becomes clear if the sentences are continued with (253):

(253) ... maar halverwege veranderde hij van gedachten
... but halfway he changed his mind

The continuation is not possible for (252) or very forcedly, but it is possible for (251). Yet it should be observed that (251) may express that he reached the store, and it mostly does so. In German, the prepositions *nach* and *zu* show a similar difference between indeterminacy and requiring that the goal of the movement be reached.

Recall that at the beginning of this study an observation was made on the difference between the Dutch near-equivalents of sentences (51), (254) and (255):

(254) Judith at drie boterhammen
Judith ate three sandwiches

(255) Judith at drie boterhammen op
Judith ate three sandwiches up

Here the default interpretation for (254) is that Judith ate all three sandwiches, but for some native speakers though not for myself, (254) may be continued by (256), meaning that Judith was involved in eating three sandwiches, whereas this interpretation is not possible for (255).

(256) ...toen ik binnenkwam
...when I came in

In this case, (255) has to pertain to an event strictly following the event of my coming in (Hinrichs 1986a, 1986b; Kamp and Rohrer 1983). Here again there seems to be some sort of a lexically determined difference between indeterminacy – Judith may or may not have eaten three sandwiches (for those native speakers, that is) – and genuine completion.

How do we solve the indeterminacy problem in (251) and (254), taking into account that in both cases it is lexically defined, albeit idiolectically in (254)? Suppose that English speakers had the same judgment about the English (51) as some Dutch speakers have about the Dutch (254). The best way to look for a solution would then be the equation $Q{=}\bigcup_{I}\mathbf{W}$ in (213), the denotation of the internal argument NP *three sandwiches*:

(213) $\lambda\mathbf{W}\exists W[W\subseteq[\![\text{sandwich}]\!]\wedge|W|=3\wedge\exists Q\text{ps}W[Q=\bigcup_{I}\mathbf{W}|_{[\![\text{sandwich}]\!]}]]$

Recall that the terminativity of (51) was explained by the finiteness of $|Q|$. Now, what if we could obtain a situation in which (257) held?

(257) $\lambda\mathbf{W}\exists W[W\subseteq[\![\text{sandwich}]\!]\wedge|W|=3\wedge\exists Q\text{ps}W[Q\supseteq\bigcup_{I}\mathbf{W}|_{[\![\text{sandwich}]\!]}]]$

That is, in the application of (214) introducing the verb *eat*, it could be left indeterminate how the eating-part of the predication takes place: *eat* could have been defined as a verb requiring $\subseteq$ rather than =. In this connection, one could also explain Fillmore's observation, discussed in chapter 1.0, that *John read the book for an hour* and *John read the book in an hour* are both acceptable, whereas the standard aspectual tests should require that at least one be unacceptable. It can be explained by saying that in Fillmore's (and in Dowty's) lexicon the verb *read* is specified in terms of $Q \supseteq \bigcup_I \mathbf{W}$, because *for an hour* and *in an hour* are both compatible with the indeterminacy expressed by $\subseteq$. As said above, for Dutch this does not hold good for my own lexicon, but apparently it holds firmly for at least one speaker of Dutch (Wim Stokhof, pers. comm.). At any rate, the $\subseteq$-relation in (257) appears to be called for in (252), where *wandelen naar* (walk toward) clearly rules out the equation $Q=\bigcup_I \mathbf{W}$. So there is some firm ground to go by: directional phrases not requiring completion.

The question becomes: how do we obtain semantic objects of the form (257)? The technical answer proceeds as follows. We may assume that *naar* (to, towards) assigns the Θ-role defined in (258):

(258) $[\![\Theta_{\text{TOWARDS}}]\!] :=\lambda \text{NP}\lambda \mathbf{W}\exists R[\text{NP}(R)\wedge \bigcup_I \mathbf{W}\subseteq R]$

This function, when applied to (247), yields derivation (259):

(259)
$\lambda \text{NP}\lambda \mathbf{W}\exists R[\text{NP}(R)\wedge \bigcup_I \mathbf{W}\subseteq R](\lambda P\exists \text{W}[\text{W}\subseteq [\![\text{store}]\!]\wedge |\text{W}|=3$
$\quad\wedge \exists Q\text{psW}[Q=P|_{[\![\text{store}]\!]}]])$
$=\lambda \mathbf{W}\exists R[\lambda P\exists \text{W}[\text{W}\subseteq [\![\text{store}]\!]\wedge |\text{W}|=3\wedge \exists Q\text{psW}[Q=P|_{[\![\text{store}]\!]}]](R)\wedge \bigcup_I \mathbf{W}\subseteq R]$
$=\lambda \mathbf{W}\exists R\exists \text{W}[\text{W}\subseteq [\![\text{store}]\!]\wedge |\text{W}|=3\wedge \exists Q\text{psW}[Q=R|_{[\![\text{store}]\!]}]\wedge \bigcup_I \mathbf{W}\subseteq R]$

This will be written as:

(260) $\lambda \mathbf{W}.\exists \text{W}[\text{W}\subseteq [\![\text{store}]\!]\wedge |\text{W}|=3\wedge \exists Q\text{psW}[\bigcup_I \mathbf{W}|_{[\![\text{store}]\!]}\subseteq Q]]$

In this way, the vagueness of the Dutch sentence (261) is accounted for.

(261) John liep naar drie winkels
John walked to/towards three stores

John may have changed his mind but he may also have reached three stores. This is correctly expressed by (260).

If the line of thought is correct, a distinction is made between at least two sorts of Θ-roles, one exemplified by (262), the other by (263):[61]

(262) $[\![\Theta_{=}]\!]=\lambda \text{NP}\lambda \mathbf{W}\exists R[\text{NP}(R)\wedge \bigcup_I \mathbf{W}=R]$
(263) $[\![\Theta_{\subseteq}]\!]=\lambda \text{NP}\lambda \mathbf{W}\exists R[\text{NP}(R)\wedge \bigcup_I \mathbf{W}\subseteq R]$
(264) $[\![\Theta_{\subset}]\!]=\lambda \text{NP}\lambda \mathbf{W}\exists R[\text{NP}(R)\wedge \bigcup_I \mathbf{W}\subset R]$

It might even be argued that there is a third option: (264). This could be assigned in English, for example, to a preposition like *from* in (265):

(265) Judith ate from three sandwiches

which means that Judith ate a part of the three sandwiches but cannot mean that she ate all three of them. Also, (264) might be used to account for the difference between sentences like (266) and (267):

(266) Wúpwe wún ewe kkónik
I will drink the water
'I will drink some of the water'

(267) Wúpwe wúnúmi ewe kkónik
I will drink the water
'I will drink up the water'

– from the Micronesian language Trukese – mentioned in Hopper and Thompson (1980: 263), which says that the verb stem *wún* indicates a partitive internal argument, whereas the stem *wúnúmi* signals the totally affected argument. If *partially affected* here is unequivocally defined in terms of $\subset$ rather than $\subseteq$, this would be an example in favour of allowing the option (264).

However, (264) is debatable for (265) as one might wish to analyse *from three sandwiches* as $[_{NP}\ [_{N'}\emptyset]\ [_{PP}$from three sandwiches]], as in Verkuyl (1972). It could also be debatable for (266) if $\subset$ in (264) did not only express 'no completion', but also boundedness; (264) would then pertain to a proper (finite and non-empty) subset of *R* and hence one could argue that [+SQA]-cardinality is involved. However, this latter does not appear necessary due to the fact that [+SQA] can be defined in terms of the presence of the cardinality as expressed by the full NP and not by a part of it.[62] In my view, the matter should be settled empirically by comparing a number of languages in order to see whether the three options (262)–(264) are grammaticalized. At any rate, apart from the question of whether (264) can be defended, $\subseteq$ in (263) can certainly be interpreted as resulting in durativity due to the fact that it makes it impossible to decide what happened. In the remainder of this study, I shall assume that *eat*, like the Dutch *eten*, is to be specified in terms of (262) rather than (263). As said above, this may be debated by those who prefer (263), but this difference of opinion is a lexical matter, so a matter of taste. No theoretical issue depends on a choice between (262) and (263).

In Slavic languages, perfective affixes can be described in terms of (262) on the basis of the proposal in Baker (1988), who argues that these are incorporated in verbal forms coming from D-structure positions comparable with the Θ-position in Figure 42a. That is, a sentence like (268) may be derived from a D-structure like (269):

(268) Ja napisal pis'mo
I wrote a letter (and finished it)

(269) Ja pisal [$_{\Theta_=}$na [$_{NP}$pis'mo]]

after which *na* is moved to its position in front of the verb, as in (269). Those who reject such a 'movement'-analysis would be forced to assume that the verbal form *napisal* as a whole incorporates the information expressed by (262) lexically or via morphological rules of some sort. The same sort of consideration applies to Finnish, for instance, to the example taken from Heinämäki (1984: 156).

(270) Metsästäjä ampui vahingossa lehmän
hunter shot accident-in cow-acc.
'The hunter shot a cow by accident'

(271) Metsästäjä ampui vahingossa lehmää
hunter shot accident-in cow-part.
'The hunter shot (at) a cow by accident'

Heinämäki observes that the difference between these sentences is that in (270) the cow is dead as a result of the shooting, whereas in (271) this is not necessary. The difference can be explained in the present framework by assuming that $\Theta_=$ is expressed by the accusative case, whereas $\Theta_\subseteq$ is expressed by the partitive case.

13.7 Bare plurals again

In this section, attention will be paid to (49) and (52), which are durative due to the presence of a bare plural.

(49) Judith ate sandwiches

(52) John walked to stores

Recall from chapter 8.2 that bare plural NPs like *sandwiches* are analysed as (272):

(272) $\lambda R\exists W\exists P[W\subseteq \bigcup P\subseteq [\![\text{sandwich}]\!] \wedge |P|>1 \wedge \exists Q\text{ps}W[Q=R|_{[\![\text{sandwich}]\!]}]]$

On this assumption, and on the assumption that *eat* requires an equation, (49) will end up as (273):

(273) $\lambda I.\exists!V[V=[\![Judith]\!]\cap\{j_i\}\wedge\exists W\exists P[W\subseteq\bigcup P\subseteq[\![sandwich]\!]\wedge|P|>1$
$\wedge\exists Q psW[Q=\bigcup_{i\in I}\{U\cap[\![sandwich]\!]: [\![eat]\!](I)(i)(U)(V)\}]]]$

However, the cardinality of *Q* cannot be determined, because the cardinality of W is not determined. We know that $W\subseteq\bigcup P\subseteq[\![sandwich]\!]$, but as there is no information about the sets which are elements of [[sandwich]], there is no way of being sure that $\bigcup P$ is finite, unless the Fixed Context Assumption is applied to [[sandwich]]. Certainly, in many situations to which (49) applies it pertains to finite sets, but there is an indeterminacy which leads to a [–SQA]-interpretation: there is no highest index given by (49) itself. The same applies *mutatis mutandis* to (52).

The same carries over to sentences like *Judith ate bread*, discussed in chapter 8.3, which in the light of the revisions made above can be analysed as (274):

(274) $\lambda I.\exists!V[V=[\![Judith]\!]\cap\{j_i\}\wedge\exists W\exists P[W\subseteq\bigcup P\subseteq_m[\![bread]\!]$
$\wedge\exists Q psW[Q=\bigcup_{i\in I}\{U\cap_m[\![bread]\!]: [\![eat]\!](I)(i)(U)(V)\}]]]$

This says that Judith ate partitioned subsets of the union set of bread-particles, but the domain of the function **W** is not bounded. The subscript m indicates here that the ⊆-relation pertains to mass terms denotations.

In this connection, it might be useful to speculate a little on the relation between bare plurality (in the sense developed here) and habituality. The correspondence between the two notions is suggested by the fact that we may use sentences like (47) *Judith ate a sandwich* both as pertaining to a unique eventuality that can be located in time and as speaking about a habit. Also, (48) *Judith ate three sandwiches* may be used in a context in which it is clear that it refers to Judith's habit of eating three sandwiches, say at breakfast. And (50) *John walked to the store* may be used to say that John was in the habit of going to the store by foot. In this case it is natural to combine the sentences with adverbials like *always, sometimes, normally, habitually* and so on.

As it is not my intention to present a fully-fledged theory of habituality, I shall restrict myself here to discussing some formalizations of habituality which are part and parcel of the present aspectual theory. Recall that given a VP-representation like (217), the tenseless (51) can be represented as (275):

(275) $\lambda I.\exists!V[V=[\![Judith]\!]\cap\{j_i\}\wedge\exists W[W\subseteq[\![sandwich]\!]\wedge|W|=3$
$\wedge\exists Q psW[Q=\bigcup_{i\in I}\{U\cap[\![sandwich]\!]: [\![eat]\!](I)(i)(U)(V)\}]]]$

It might be argued that as bare plurality can be accounted for in terms of a shift from the *<e,t>*-level to the *<<e,t>,t>*-level, habituality may be analysed in terms of the same sort of type shift. In other words, rather than applying λI to a specific argument, one would have to apply Tense to some other interval which I is a member of. So Tense would have to operate on a set of structures like (275) rather than on the application of $\lambda I(\ldots I \ldots)$ to an argument which yields a unique eventuality. The issue of habituality will be picked up again more formally in the next section, after the treatment of Tense and of the Progressive Form.

13.8 Tense, Progressive Form and habituality

In this section, the role of Tense will be drawn into the analysis of aspectuality. It will be the tail-piece of the aspectual theory presented here in the sense that Tense is given a specific role in mapping the abstract representation of a sentence into real time. The best metaphor for me to express the underlying conceptualization is still the one used in Verkuyl (1972, 1976), namely that in which the realization of terminative aspect is seen in terms of the performance of (a part of) an abstract object, say a score of a musical phrase. The relation between the representation of the score of the first phrase of Beethoven's piano sonata in C sharp minor and its actual performance is comparable with the relation between the representation of, say, (275) and the performance of this sentence in real time. In the present theory, the use of Tense is comparable with the performance of the abstract score (275). It is along the lines of this metaphor that the analysis of Tense will proceed, the more so as the passage of natural numbers on an odometer of a car can also be seen as going through a score which is being performed at the **R**-level, notes being discrete representations of underlying dense structure.

The literature on tense is abundant.[63] I will assume some familiarity with the Reichenbachian (and Priorean) framework. For the purpose of this chapter it will not be necessary to go deeply into the treatment of the famous Reichenbachian point of reference R or into the need for another perspectival point. I will restrict myself simply to the Past and Present relation, assuming that, given the Reichenbachian framework, it will be easy to extend the machinery. The present analysis is congenial to the so-called Two-Track Theory of Time proposed by Oversteegen (1989) but formally it deviates substantially from the proposals made there. As in Oversteegen (1989) and Oversteegen and Verkuyl (1985), it is assumed that for Simple Tense it is sufficient to have Past and Present and that the auxiliaries *have* and *shall* or *will* provide for anteriority and posteriority relations. I shall not deal with the meanings of *have* and *shall/will*. Past and Present will be subsumed under the label INFL. As far as syntax is concerned, it is assumed that here Figure 43 will do.

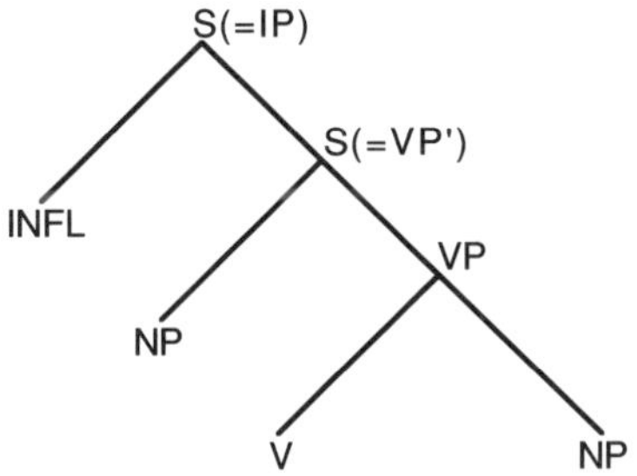

Figure 43 INFL is taken as an operator on a tenseless S

INFL operates on a tenseless 'sentence' to form a tensed one. For example, INFL would take (275) to form either (276) or (48).

(276) Judith eats three sandwiches
(48) Judith ate three sandwiches

In Figure 43, the part corresponding with the tenseless (275) is S (=VP′). There are two labels in order to indicate that a structure like (275) corresponds to what in GB-syntax is taken as a VP′, that is, as a projection of V. In older versions of generative grammar this node would simply be called S. In GB-syntax, INFL is taken as the head of the so-called IP. Actually, Figure 43 is part of a larger structure, but as this does not play a role in the analysis of tense, I shall not go into this. Figure 43 is compatible both with recent versions of GB-syntax and with more traditional versions in which structures like (275) are not taken as projections of the verb (e.g. Kerstens 1991).

Type-logically, it has been assumed that S (=VP′) is of type $<<i,t>,t>$ and that S (= IP) is of type *t*. This means that above IP no semantic information bearing on the truth value of (275) is present. This assumption is not only reasonable, it is quite standard to assume that tensed sentences like (276) and (48) end up having a truth value when interpreted in a certain model given an assignment and a time index i* (=now), as in Dowty (1982b). Given the fact that S (=VP′) is of type $<<i,t>,t>$, there are two possibilities for INFL: either it must be of type $<i,t>$ or it must be of type $<<<i,t>,t>,t>$. I will adopt the latter course, because on this analysis, INFL is taken as a relation between a set of indices $<i,t>$ and a truth value. This is exactly what is expressed in the provisional semantic characterization of INFL in (277), where $\alpha = <$ or $=$:

(277) $[\![\text{INFL}]\!] = \lambda S \exists I[S(I) \wedge \text{Tense}_{\alpha}(\ldots(I))(i^*)]$

S (=VP′) is of type $<<i,t>,t>$, and I of type $<i,t>$. $[\![\text{INFL}]\!]$ applied to (275) would yield derivation (278):

(278)

$\lambda S\exists I[S(I)\wedge \mathrm{Tense}_<(\ldots(I))(i^*)](\lambda I.\exists!V[V=[\![\mathrm{Judith}]\!]\cap\{j_i\}\wedge\exists W[W\subseteq[\![\mathrm{sandwich}]\!]$
$\wedge|W|=3\wedge\exists Q\mathrm{ps}W[Q=\bigcup_{i\in I}\{U\cap[\![\mathrm{sandwich}]\!]: [\![\mathrm{eat}]\!](I)(i)(U)(V)\}]]])$

...

$\exists I\exists!V[V=[\![\mathrm{Judith}]\!]\cap\{j_i\}\wedge\exists W[W\subseteq[\![\mathrm{sandwich}]\!]\wedge|W|=3$
$\wedge\exists Q\mathrm{ps}W[Q=\bigcup_{i\in I}\{U\cap[\![\mathrm{sandwich}]\!]: [\![\mathrm{eat}]\!](I)(i)(U)(V)\}]]$
$\wedge \mathrm{Tense}_<(\ldots(I))(i^*)]$

Here the <*i,t*>-variable I in (275) is bound by the existential quantifier in (277). So, (278) says that there is a set I of (well-ordered) indices which are structurally related to the 'score-structure' of the tenseless proposition 'Judith eat three sandwiches'. It continues to say that i* (the deictic constant 'now') is preceded by some semantic object in which I occurs. The question evoked by the three dots in (277) is: what sort of entity is the first argument of $\mathrm{Tense}_<$?

Assuming that any i* is a subset of **R** (a singleton or an 'extended now' in the Reichenbachian sense), it is necessary to assume that the other relatum is also in **R**. Recall that DEF 9–11 made clear that I is a subset of **N**. So this makes it necessary to assume that the empty dots in (277) stand for some operator (a function) mapping I from **N** into **R**. This sounds not only natural, but as it should be if one wants to obtain a truth value: I is actualized in real time by a mapping. As a first approximation, let us define the following function on the basis of DEF 9–11.

DEFINITION 14: The actualization function E: $\wp(\mathbf{N})\rightarrow\wp(\mathbf{R})$ is defined by $I \mapsto\{x\in \mathbf{R} \mid \exists k\in I: \langle x,k\rangle\in \mathrm{Ent}\}$.

E yields the set of all points in **R** involved in the Entier-function Ent. It gives an interval in real time during which I is realized. This seems to express correctly the actualization of the mental object associated with I: the tense relation holds between the actualization of I in real time and the point of speech. Type-logically, *E* is a function of type <<*i,t*>,<*i,t*>> provided that we allow entities of type i to be in the union of **N** and **R**. Hence we obtain the following representation in which $\mathrm{Tense}_<(E(I))(i^*)$ is of type t, $\mathrm{Tense}_<$ itself being of type <<*i,t*>,<<*i,t*>,*t*>, that is, a relation between a (singleton) set i* and a set of points.[64]

(279) $\exists I\exists!V[V=[\![\mathrm{Judith}]\!]\cap\{j_i\}\wedge\exists W[W\subseteq[\![\mathrm{sandwich}]\!]\wedge|W|=3$
$\wedge\exists Q\mathrm{ps}W[Q=\bigcup_{i\in I}\{U\cap[\![\mathrm{sandwich}]\!]: [\![\mathrm{eat}]\!](I)(i)(U)(V)\}]]$
$\wedge \mathrm{Tense}_<(E(I))(i*)]$

As said above, complex tenses with *will* and *have* require a more complicated analysis of the relation between I and i*, but as this can be done rather standardly with the help of intermediate reference points, I will refrain from discussing them. Here it suffices to underscore the role of tense in the actualization process of abstract semantic objects like (275).

It was pointed out that the characterization of INFL in (277) is provisional. This had to do with the analysis of the Progressive Form in cases like (280):

(280) Judith was eating three sandwiches

Syntactically the English Progressive Form is to be given a less prominent place than INFL. We shall assume that it is located 'between' INFL and S (= VP′) in Figure 42. Type-logically this amounts to saying that the syntactic element PROG is taken as a modifier: it takes something of type $<<i,t>,t>$ and it yields something of type $<<i,t>,t>$. In other words, it operates on a semantic object like (275) so that its result is the input to the INFL-operation. The first approximation would be something like (281):

(281) $[\![\text{PROG}]\!]=\lambda S\lambda I'\exists I[S(I)\wedge E(I')\subset E(I)]$

This captures an idea that will be pursued. If $[\![\text{INFL}]\!]$ operates on the result of applying $[\![\text{PROG}]\!]$ to an S(=VP′), the derivation proceeds as in (282):

(282) $[\![\text{PROG}]\!](S)$
$\lambda S\lambda J\exists I[S(I)\wedge E(J)\subset E(I)](S)$
$\lambda J\exists I[S(I)\wedge E(J)\subset E(I)]$

$[\![\text{INFL}]\!]([\![\text{PROG}]\!](S))$
$\lambda S\exists I'[S(I')\wedge \text{Tense}_<(E(I'))(i^*)](\lambda J\exists I[S(I)\wedge E(J)\subset E(I)])$
$\exists I'[\lambda J\exists I[S(I)\wedge E(J)\subset E(I)](I')\wedge \text{Tense}_<(E(I'))(i^*)]$
$\exists I'\exists I[S(I)\wedge E(I')\subset E(I)\wedge \text{Tense}_<(E(I'))(i^*)]$

Its last line says that there is a set I′ which is a proper subset of the set I (the odometer number of the proposition S) such that *E*(I′) is earlier than the point of speech. Note that *E*(I′) is a subset of **R**, so that the Past tense can be said to hold in **R**, that is, at the level of real time. *E*(I′) can be considered to be the actualized event associated with I.

The nice thing about this analysis is that the evaluation is restricted to that part of the eventuality that is actualized or realized in time. It does not speak out on *E*(I). The bad thing about it is that there are two compelling arguments against it. The first one is that it can be maintained that the existential quantifier ∃I commits us to the existence of *E*(I).[65] This can be questioned, but the problem is that this matter can only be settled in the area of belief or non-belief. We meet here the same problem as in *He builds a house*, where

$\exists x(\text{house}(x) \wedge \text{build}(\text{he},x))$ would only be allowed if the quantification is taken as ranging over abstract objects, in particular a blueprint of the house or an abstract representation of it (Verkuyl 1972: 87f.). There are many who demand the x to range over concrete objects, not over models of a house. However, any further speculation on this issue can be stopped by the consideration that there is another technical difficulty with (282): $E(I')$ will be an interval whose last point is a natural number.[66] So something must be wrong with (282) although it seems to express a basically sound idea by trying to characterize the Progressive in terms of a distinction between a mental numerical structure associated with an eventuality and the real-time interval expressing the actualization of the eventuality, relating it to the point of speech so that evaluation becomes possible.

It is possible to overcome these difficulties by replacing the E-function by its inverse and by quantifying both in **N** and **R**. Consider DEF 15:

DEFINITION 15: Let Ent^+: $\wp(\mathbf{R}) \rightarrow \wp(\mathbf{N})$ be defined as: for all $J \subseteq \mathbf{R}$, $\text{Ent}^+(J) = \{n \in \mathbf{N}: \exists x \in J \ \& \ n = \text{Ent}(x)\}$.

Ent^+ is in fact the Entier-function operating at a higher level. What it does is to assign to any arbitrarily long interval J from **R** an I in **N**. Suppose that $J=[0,1.75]$, then $\text{Ent}^+(J)=\{0,1\}$. Then DEF 15 warrants that an interruption of an eventuality in progress can be at any time. This is what we need.

Given the function Ent^+ the definitions of INFL and PROG can be revised as follows:

(283) $[\![\text{INFL}]\!] = \lambda S \exists I \exists I_R[S(I) \wedge I = \text{Ent}^+(I_R) \wedge \text{Tense}_\alpha(I_R)(i^*)]$
(284) $[\![\text{PROG}]\!] = \lambda S \lambda J' \exists J[S(J) \wedge J' \subset J]$

Sets of indices without a subscript are in **N**. Intervals in **R** have a subscript R. This is only necessary for INFL, where actualization of the eventuality takes place. The Progressive Form is defined as expressing a relation between two sets of indices in **N**: in this way we stay at the abstract 'score'-level. In (283), two sets of indices are introduced, one in **N** and one in **R**. The I in **N** is associated with the tenseless proposition, in the second conjunct it is said that I is the result of applying Ent^+ to I_R and finally the tense-relation (either $<$ or $=$) is asserted between the **R**-interval and the point of speech. In (284), we obtain the function yielding all proper subsets J' of a set J, where J is associated with tenseless propositions.

The derivation (282) can now be improved on, as shown in (285), where PROG has been applied to the tenseless sentence (275). I will not give the whole of (275) but only the relevant part of it. INFL is now taken as Past, so $\alpha = <$.

(285) $[\![\text{PROG}]\!]([\![(275)]\!])$
$\lambda S\lambda J'\exists J[S(J)\wedge J'\subset J](\lambda I\exists!V[\ldots(I)\ldots])$
$\lambda J'\exists J[\lambda I\exists!V[\ldots(I)\ldots](J)\wedge J'\subset J]$
$\lambda J'\exists J\exists!V[\ldots(J)\ldots\wedge J'\subset J]$

$[\![\text{PAST}]\!]\ ([\![\text{PROG}]\!]([\![(275)]\!]))$
$\lambda S\exists I\exists I_R[S(I)\wedge I=Ent^+(I_R)\wedge Tense_<(I_R)(i^*)](\lambda J'\exists[\exists!V[\ldots(J)\ldots\wedge J'\subset J])$
$\exists I\exists I_R[\lambda J'\exists J\exists!V[\ldots(J)\ldots\wedge J'\subset J](I)\wedge I=Ent^+(I_R)\wedge Tense_<(I_R)(i^*)]$
$\exists I\exists I_R\exists J\exists!V[\ldots(J)\ldots\wedge I\subset J\wedge I=Ent^+(I_R)\wedge Tense_<(I_R)(i^*)]$

The last line of (285) says with respect to (275) that there are two sets of indices I and J in **N** and a subset $I_R \subseteq \mathbf{R}$ such that the J is the set of indices associated with the tenseless [[Judith eat three sandwiches]] where I ($=Ent^+(I_R)$) is a proper subset of J and the truth is asserted for the interval I_R whose representative is I. This seems to capture exactly what we want to capture: the evaluation takes place with respect to that part of the eventuality that was actualized in real time. In this way, we leave open the possibility for Judith to have consumed all sandwiches between the interval I_R and i*. However, the English counterpart *Judith was eating three sandwiches* of the sentences (280) does not say anything about it: it just says that the operation of the function **W** defined in DEF 12 is only applied to a proper subset of the domain of indices. In this way, not reaching the end-point is expressed by ⊂. Note that Tense is taken here in terms of the commitment to warrant the truth only for that part of J which was actualized. This does not say anything about the possibility for Judith to have completed the eating of three sandwiches. Only, one is left in the dark about whether or not this happened. The only thing one can derive from the score-proposition associated with J is that had it been actualized in real time, it would have yielded a terminative eventuality. This is the telic part of the information. This seems to me what is expressed by a Progressive Form. Let us now return to sentences like (23a) and (25a).

(23a) John is drawing some circles
(24a) John has not yet drawn some circles
(25a) John is drawing three circles
(26a) John has not yet drawn three circles

The problem for Dowty was that his *Imperfective*-criterion in DEF 9.4 (right after (25)) fails to make the correct prediction. The sentence *John drew some circles* is terminative and yet (23a) does not entail (24a). The correct prediction is made, however, with respect to (25a) and (26a).

Note that the difference between (23a) and (25a) follows straightforwardly from the present analysis. As far as the tenseless sentences *John draw some circles* and *John draw three circles* are concerned, the relevant characterizations are given in (286) and (287):

(286) $\ldots \exists W[W \subseteq [\![\text{circle}]\!] \wedge |W| \geq 1 \ldots$

(287) $\ldots \exists W[W \subseteq [\![\text{circle}]\!] \wedge |W| = 3 \ldots$

(288) $\exists I \exists I_R \exists J \ldots \exists W[\ldots [\![\text{draw}]\!](J) \ldots] \wedge I \subset J \wedge I = \text{Ent}^+(I_R) \wedge \text{Tense}_=(I_R)(i^*)]$

Now, both (23a) and (25a) will occur in a structure containing substructure (288). In this case, J is the set of indices associated with the tenseless S-denotation. So, if I is a proper subset of J, then (26a) is entailed by (25a). On the other hand, the cardinality statement in (286) is indefinite and so the cardinality may be, say, 8 in a given situation. Any cardinality number i ($1 \leq i \leq 7$) is a proper subset of 8, so it may be true that (23a) is compatible with the sentence *John has drawn some circles*. The same holds good for the difference between *a piece of fruit-cake* in (23b) and *a pound of fruit-cake* in (25b), if we assume that the measure function μ defined in chapter 8.3 also differentiates between values specified in terms of ≥ and =, respectively. That is, *a piece of fruit-cake* could be characterized, for example, as $|W|_{\text{grains}} \geq m$ and, following Webster, *a pound of fruit-cake* as $|W|_{\text{grains}} = 7000$. In the latter case, it is impossible to take a proper subset, in the former case it is not.

The present analysis differs from a number of proposals in which modality plays a dominant role. As noted in chapter 2.10, it is congenial to the approaches of the Progressive Form in Moens (1987) and Lascarides (1988), though the formalism they use differs substantially from the one used here: they focus on properties of intervals, whereas in the present analysis the focus is on the relation between the internal argument denotation and the index structure generated by the verb.[67] The role attributed to modality is partly taken over here by the Ent^+-function, which is allowed to 'project forward' in **R**. It is also captured by the fact that the existential introduction of the set J does not commit us to the actualized existence of its counterpart J_R in **R** itself. We are only committed to the actualization I_R of the I-part of J in (224). I see no reason to introduce modal operators for dealing with the difference J–I.

The present analysis also predicts that there are two ways for expressing a 'Progressive-like meaning': the first one by $\Theta_{\subseteq}$ and the second one by PROG. In my view, this appears to be an empirically correct result, particularly in view of the fact that it is compatible with the systematic poly-interpretability of the Russian imperfective form in sentences like (289).

(289) On pisal pis'mo

(290) a. He was writing a letter

b. He wrote at a letter (He worked on a letter)

The imperfective sentence (289) may express a meaning equivalent to the English Progressive Form, but also a cumulative meaning which expresses that he wrote at a letter piecemeal (for example, every day some lines). There is a lot of overlap between the two translations, but there are also situations in which one is more appropriate than the other. For example, *He was writing a letter* is the natural continuation of the sentence *When I came in, I saw that...* and not *He wrote at a letter* if I want to report that he was actually engaged in writing. In the former case, he was actually writing, whereas on the (b) interpretation in (290) one may conclude from other things that he was involved in getting a (or the) letter ready. Perhaps, the difference between the (a) and the (b) interpretation of (290) is brought out more clearly by the sentences in (291) and (292).

(291) Tolstoi pisal *Vojnu i mir*

(292) a. Tolstoj was writing *War and Peace*

b. Tolstoj wrote at his *War and Peace*

On the (a) interpretation of (292), the speaker saw Tolstoj with a pen in his hand writing at his book, whereas on its (b) interpretation (291) can be used to say that at that time he was engaged in creating *War and Peace*. Tolstoj might even have been on holiday at the point of reference. It is as if the set of indices I on the (a) interpretation pertains to one situation, whereas in the (b) interpretation the I goes over a longer period.

The last section was closed off with a suggestion of how to deal with habituality. The problem was triggered by the idea that habituality may be accounted for in terms of a set of intervals I. A solution would be to assume an INFL_{hab} which acts as the unbounded plural of the regular INFL, as in (293).

(293) $[\![\text{INFL}_{hab}]\!]=\lambda S\exists \mathcal{I}\ \forall I[I\in \mathcal{I}\rightarrow\exists I_R[S(I)\wedge I=Ent^{+}(I_R)\wedge Tense_{\alpha}(I_R)(i^*)]]$

This would capture the idea of tense operating on each of the occurrences of (275). It says that there is a set $\mathcal{I}$ of intervals such that for each $I\subseteq\mathbf{N}$ if I belongs to $\mathcal{I}$, there is an **R**-interval I_R (for which I is a representative) such that Tense applies to each I_R. As the universal quantifier is involved the presence of [+SQA]-information is not existentially introduced; rather, it is derived on the basis of the existence of $\mathcal{I}$. Thus in sentences like (294)

(294) Judith ate (=used to eat) three sandwiches (at breakfast)

(295) $\exists \mathit{I}\forall I[I\in \mathit{I}\rightarrow\exists I_R\exists W[W\subseteq[\![\text{sandwich}]\!]\wedge|W|=3$
$\wedge\exists \mathit{Q}\text{psW}[\mathit{Q}=\bigcup_{i\in I}\{U\cap[\![\text{sandwich}]\!]: [\![\text{eat}]\!](I)(i)(U)(V)\}]]$
$\wedge I=\text{Ent}^{+}(I_R)\wedge\text{Tense}_{<}(I_R)(i^{*})]$

the presence of the information |W|=3 does not trigger [+SQA]-effects for the whole sentence. In other words, the cardinality information about W is too low down to be reached. However, its presence gives an interpretation in which each actualization of an event in which Judith ate three sandwiches would be terminative. Note also that the habit is anchored in a series of actualizations.

Carlson (1989: 181) discusses sentences like (296)–(298):

(296) A cat ran across my lawn every day
(297) A cat ran across my lawn on four days
(298) A cat runs across my lawn every day

Under (293), (296) would have to be analysed such that *every day* and *on four days* distributes over the members of the set *I*. For (297), one might even think of roughly something like (299):

(299) $\lambda S\exists \mathit{I}\exists 4I[(I\in \mathit{I}\wedge I\subseteq[\![\text{day}]\!])\rightarrow\exists I_R[S(I)\wedge I=\text{Ent}^{+}(I_R)\wedge\text{Tense}_{<}(I_R)(i^{*})]]$

The only problem with (293) is now the problem of how to account for (298). Actually, (298) is the example discussed by Carlson: he uses only the Present Tense. As the value for α in the Present Tense is defined as =, there is, so to speak, room enough to harbour all the actualizations. The only way to do this is to take i* as an extended now, so that = in $\text{Tense}_{=}$ covers actualizations that may be anterior or posterior. This is not an unreasonable move. In (296), the habit of the cat lies in the past and in that connection the i* might even be compressed to a singleton because the <-relation does not require a time stretch. However, if one describes a habit which still continues, the Present may be analysed as having the function of identifying the whole stretch in which a series of actualizations is to be located. An alternative might be to define the Present Tense as '$\leq$ or $\geq$' assuming that actualizations are located in a stretch or in stretches having just an overlap-relation with a (compressed) i*.[68]

Lascarides (1988: 114) takes the position that *Max ran* in (300):

(300) Max ran in four minutes (every day)
(301) $\lambda S\exists \mathit{I}\forall I[(I\in \mathit{I}\wedge I\subseteq[\![\text{day}]\!])\rightarrow\exists I_R[S(I)\wedge I=\text{Ent}^{+}(I_R)\wedge\text{Tense}_{<}(I_R)(i^{*})]]$

pertains to a culminated process in the sense of Moens (1987), as discussed in chapter 2.10, because *ran* can be combined with an *in*-adverbial (see chapter 2.3). Both take (300) to mean that Max used to run in four minutes, say every day. Both also agree on saying that ⟦Max ran⟧ should be taken as a culminated process, though they disagree on whether (Lascarides) or not (Moens) to take *Max ran* to be ambiguous between a process and a culminated process. Under the present analysis (301) would leave ⟦Max ran⟧ unbounded, but as the index I is taken as a subset of ⟦day⟧, ⟦Max ran⟧ is bounded indirectly, as it should be. Note that the presence of *in four minutes* is, of course, bounding too, but the problem at issue can be solved without appealing to outer aspect (see chapter 1.1): (301) also would apply to *Max ran* (every day). Note also that in (301), I⊆⟦day⟧ may naturally be extended to I⊆⟦4_minutes⟧⊆⟦day⟧, providing that adverbials are taken as operating on the I. This does not seem to be forced: after all, part of a temporal entity like ⟦day⟧ is a system of natural numbers.

Bache (1985: 71) observes that sentences like (302)

(302) Ivan p'et čaj
(303) Ivan is drinking tea
(304) Ivan drinks tea

with the imperfective form *p'et* have a Progressive Form meaning, expressed in (303), but that it may also be used 'to refer to situations which are so vague that they hardly qualify as *situations* but rather as *characterizations*' of the subject Ivan. In the present analysis, one might treat (302) in its (304)-interpretation as having a habitual tense. This tense predicts the durative aspect of (302), but it would have to be like (301) with I⊆⟦drinking occasion⟧, or some other abstract unit over which one may quantify given the context in which (304) is used.

13.9 Conclusion

In this chapter, the formal machinery for dealing with aspectuality in a variety of constructions has been developed. It deviates from event-semantic enterprises in that events are construed on the basis of information contained by parts of the sentence. It deviates from interval semantics in that intervals are no longer taken as temporal entities. Instead use is made of two number systems, **N** and **R**, and their interaction (by a variant of the Entier-function) is taken into account. Thus, just one feature of the interval semantics of the seventies is maintained, the use of indices, but until tense is drawn into consideration the notion of event remains at an abstract 'score' level at which things are made discrete as in **N**. By making use of numbers representing intervals rather than intervals themselves, the system evades a lot of problems inherent in interval semantics. At the level of tense, the actualization of the event scheme construed by a sentence takes place. The present machinery appears to account for Progressive Form and habituality as well.

The system PLUG^{+} developed in this chapter incorporates valuable localistic insights into the nature of change as expressed in natural language. Localism is incorporated by the π-function which maps members of the external argument NP denotation to structured members of the VP denotation. By interpreting thematic roles semantically it is possible to generalize over transitive verbs taking internal argument NPs and verbs taking directional phrases. As far as terminative aspectuality is concerned, the grammar accounts for the Plus-principle discussed in chapter 1: by the presence of indices contributed by the [+ADD TO]-verb, the cardinality information expressed by [+SQA]-NPs can be seen as constituting a finite, non-empty domain for the function which brings the progress in time to a stop.

14 *Testing the Plus-principle*

14.0 Introduction

In this chapter, attention will be given to cases adduced as counterexamples against the Plus-principle. The most famous one is undoubtedly anachronistic. Vendler's *John pushed the cart* looks like a counterexample to the Plus-principle: *John* is [+SQA], *the cart* is [+SQA], and it would be playing ostrich simply to call the verb *push* [–ADD TO]. Yet the sentence can be used duratively. How come? And how serious a counterexample is this against the Plus-principle, which is the real foundation of a compositional approach to terminative aspect? For an answer to this question, I will discuss a set of verbs like *push* and *stroke* which are a sort of hybrid between [+ADD TO] and [–ADD TO]. When generalizing over the behaviour of the verbs *push* and related verbs in English and *duwen* and related verbs in Dutch, I shall use the term 'PUSH-verbs'. Their properties bring their analysis into the realm of a controversy between adherents to the so-called Small Clause Analysis and the so-called Complex Predicate Analysis for (terminative) sentences like *John pushed the cart away*. This is explained in section 14.2 and I shall take sides in favour of the (syntactic) Complex Predicate Analysis. This makes it possible to devise a semantics for verb stems and their argument frames in section 14.3: I will distinguish between a transitive scheme, an unergative scheme and an unaccusative scheme in which verb stems are (non-compositionally) inserted to form the lowest syntactic verbal category, the verb. In section 14.4, an account is given of the aspectual behaviour of PUSH-verbs.

14.1 PUSH-verbs

There is a complication which has to do with grammar rather than with the empirical material itself. Semantically the PUSH-verbs in English and Dutch seem to show the same behaviour, as I shall show shortly. In English, however, a verb like *push* can be extended to a complex verb consisting of the original verb plus a particle. So, if *push* is a [–ADD TO]-verb or a [±ADD TO]-verb, then *push away* can be called a complex [+ADD TO]-verb, as it certainly may contribute to the construal of terminative aspect. In English, the complex verb, however, is what some grammarians call a 'multi-word verb' or a phrasal verb: *push* is not a verb stem but remains a verb in a larger verb. Due to the underlying OV-order in the VP, a Dutch PUSH-verb is extended by a particle or by a prefix, as *weg-* (away) in the (separable) compound verb *wegduwen*, in which *duwen* is the verb stem. It is this complication which I have in mind: the English and the Dutch data are by and large comparable, but the machinery involved in the transition from *duwen* to *wegduwen* is syntactically less complicated than the transition from *push* to *push away* in English.

In view of this, I will discuss the PUSH-verbs with the help of English data alongside the Dutch data. Then I shall discuss a syntactic machinery which is worked out for Dutch and I will connect to it the semantic machinery developed in the previous sections. On the basis of this marriage of syntactic and semantic insights, I shall work out the concept of a 'shimmer area' between the lexicon and syntax. After that I shall also briefly suggest a possible transfer of the results to the English VO-situation which apparently can be obtained without too many difficulties.

The first observation is that *push* and *duwen* are not the single exceptions: the category of PUSH-verbs is quite large.

(305)	draw	trekken	stroke	aaien	mow	maaien
	caress	strelen	paint	verven	beautify	verfraaien
	hit	slaan	knock	kloppen	rub	wrijven
	iron	strijken	drive	sturen	help	helpen
	turn	draaien	hammer	hameren	call	bellen

The second observation is that these verbs share the property that their complement behaves more like an indirect object than a direct object, semantically speaking. Certainly, *the cart* in (306) is a direct object NP, but on closer inspection *push* might be analysed as a complex verb paraphrased as 'to give one or more pushes to' or as 'to exert force to'.

(306)	John pushed the cart	Jan duwde de wagen
(307)	Jessica stroked Shlomie	Jessica aaide Shlomie
(308)	Roland painted the door	Roland verfde de deur
(309)	The council beautified the park	De raad verfraaide het plantsoen

In Dutch the underlying indirect object structure can be made transparent in paraphrases: *aaien* (stroke) can be paraphrased as 'een aai geven aan' or 'aaien geven aan', that is, as 'to give one or more strokes to', *verven* (paint) is often paraphrased loosely as 'een verfje geven', that is, 'to give a paint to', *verfraaien* (beautify) as 'verfraaiing(en) aanbrengen aan', that is, literally 'to make beautifications to', etc. The general rule is that in the paraphrases these verbs require prepositional circumscriptions typical of the indirect object. The typical [+ADD TO]-verbs do not allow this sort of paraphrase. In short, the thematic structure expressed by the PUSH-verb is somewhat irregular as compared with verbs like *eat, mail, send, kill, discover, play*, etc.

The thematic structure of the verbs in (305) also seems to express that the external argument and the internal argument 'stay together': some form of comitativity is involved. More generally, these verbs do not require a 'Source-Goal movement' in the traditional localistic sense. Someone may push without moving, or the one who pushes, moves along with the moved object, and the distance between Roland and the door remained the same while he was painting the door. Likewise, Jessica may have sat and stroked Shlomie on her lap. So, it seems as if these verbs waver between expressing a state and a process in the localistic sense in which the internal argument undergoes a change of location. As Galton (1984: 24–30) observes, one may describe something going on in time as a state of change or as a change of state. It occurs to me that the verbs under analysis express a state of change, as opposed to verbs like *hate, like, be warm*, etc., and as opposed to verbs like *eat, drink, play*, etc., which express a change of state. It seems as if the resultative particles operating on the verbs in (305) have the effect of forcing the verb into expressing a Path in the sense made explicit above. That is, it is arguable that the function **W** as defined above fails to be applied or be applied completely in cases like (306)–(309). In other words: PUSH-verbs can be treated in terms of the thematic indeterminacy expressed by [—$\Theta_{\subseteq}$ NP], and the extension of a PUSH-verb to a [+ADD TO]-verb may then be seen as the change into a [—$\Theta_{=}$ NP]-specification.

The third observation is that the sentences in (306)–(309) all allow for a bounded interpretation. That is, if we want, we are able to let (310) express a forced #-repetition as in (311). In that case, we single out the 'one-push' part of the interpretation of *push*, forcing (306) to be taken as terminative.

(310) For hours John pushed the cart
(311) #For hours John gave the cart a push

Also, in many discourses (308) will be interpreted as saying that Roland finished his job of painting the door. The same applies to (309). This indeterminacy observation is relevant in view of the above analysis of thematic roles. As observed above, an analysis of these verbs in terms of $\Theta_{\subseteq}$ would provide for exactly such an indeterminacy. Note that the indeterminacy may include the fact that *push* may be used in the sense of exerting force without any overt movement: an object may push against a larger object without being able to move it. So, the general picture of the PUSH-verbs is that they allow the whole range between expressing a statelike situation and a real [+ADD TO]-process, that is, a process in terms of a Path that is taken. Again, [—$\Theta_{\subseteq}$ NP] seems to be an appropriate way to express this, because it 'blocks' going through the structured NP-denotation.

The fourth observation is that most of the verbs in (305) occur in resultative constructions yielding a terminative reading as in (312) and (313):

(312)	John pushed the cart *away*	Jan duwde de wagen *weg*
(313)	Roland painted the door *blue*	Roland verfde de deur *blue*
(314)	John pushed three carts *away*	Jan duwde drie wagens *weg*
(315)	John pushed carts *away*	Jan duwde wagens *weg*
(316)	Roland did*n't* paint the door *blue*	Roland verfde de deur *niet blauw*

Note that on the assumption that *push away* and *paint blue* are [+ADD TO]-verbs, the Plus-principle operates smoothly, as can be seen in (312)–(314). Also, (315) and (316) are durative in the way predicted by the Plus-principle. So, the most convenient safeguard against the attack on the Plus-principle would be to assume that *push away* and *paint blue* act as 'regular' [+ADD TO]-verbs like *eat*, *buy*, *mail*, etc.

The fifth observation is that PUSH-verbs may all occur in resultative constructions even though the result may sound somewhat awkward, and that they do so in the same way as the so-called unergatives, that is, verbs like *work*, *play*, *bicycle*, *skate*, *bark*, *chirp*, *sneeze*, *cough*, *cry*, *breathe*, *cry*, *urinate*, *grumble*, *laugh*, *dance*, *ski, swim*, *play*, *speak*, *talk*, *mumble*, *grin*, *wrestle*, *cough*, listed in Tenny (1987). All these typically one-place verbs show the ability to behave like a two-place predicate under very restricted conditions.

(317)	Jessica caressed Shlomie asleep	He mowed himself to death
	He rubbed himself warm	He worked himself dead
	She wept herself asleep	He wrestled himself from the hold

Though the reflexive form seems to give the 'most natural' reading, it is possible to replace *himself* or *herself* by a constituent referring to other persons. If we analyse the newly formed predicates as *stroke to death*, *rub warm*, etc., we may explain the terminative aspect in all the sentences in (317) on the basis of the Plus-principle.

14.2 Small Clause vs. Complex Predicate

In the syntactic literature there are two ways of looking at sentences like (312)–(314). The first one is the so-called Small Clause analysis, which became more or less standard in GB-theory after Stowell (1981), in spite of Williams (1980, 1983b). For Dutch, the Small Clause (SC) analysis is advanced by Hoekstra (1984, 1988), Hoekstra, Lansu and Westerduin (1989), and Hoekstra and Mulder (1990), whereas Neeleman (1991) and Neeleman and Weerman (1991) proposed the so-called Complex Predicate (CP) analysis. The CP-analysis has some overlap with Williams' Predication Theory, and with, for example, Carrier-Duncan and Randall (1986), but it is based on different assumptions. Recall that for Dutch the SOV-order is assumed. The difference between the SC- and the CP-analysis can be illustrated with the help of the schemes (318) and (319).

(318) *Small Clause analysis*
NP_{ext} [NP XP] V

(319) *Complex Predicate analysis*
NP_{ext} NP_{int} [XP V]

As said above, I will discuss the Dutch OV-situation and then sketch the way in which the results can be transferred to the English VO-situation.

The SC-analysis (318) says that XP, that is, *weg* (away) in (312) and *blauw* (blue) in (313), is the main predicate of a small (that is, tenseless and always durative) clause of the form [NP XP]. Thus, in (312) the small clause [NP XP] would be *de wagen weg* (the cart away).

(320)	(dat)	Jan	[de wagen [$_{XP}$weg]]	duwt
	(that)	John	[the cart away]	pushes

and similarly for (313) *de deur blauw* (the door blue). Semantically, the small clause cannot but be durative: its interpretation is in terms of *be* XP. It represents a state, in particular an end state (the cart is away) of the pushing-activity or -process expressed by the verb.

Under an SC-analysis coupled to the PLUG$^+$-grammar, it follows that the meaning of change expressed by (312) is to be explained in terms of the combination of the verb *push* and a clause indicating the 'Goal of the movement'. In other words, the SC *de wagen weg* (the cart away) in (312) should behave with respect to *duwen* (push) as the direct object *drie boterhammen* (three sandwiches) behaves with respect to *eten* (eat) in (321).

(321)	(dat)	Judith	drie boterhammen	eet
	that	Judith	three sandwiches	eats

The difference between (312) and (315) can then be explained by the [+SQA]-nature of *de wagen* (the cart) as against the [–SQA]-nature of *wagens* (carts).

From the point of view of the aspectual theory developed in this study, there are two problems with an SC-analysis along these lines. The first one is that a PUSH-verb is not a real [+ADD TO]-verb in the sense of Figure 39: it does not seem to produce a Path with respect to which a mapping between time and direct object NP can take place. The second one is that if V were taken as a regular [+ADD TO]-verb, the semantic object corresponding to the small clause [NP XP] would not be appropriate for the application of the function **W**: its co-domain would not be in $\mathbf{D}_L$. This would become more visible in (322).

(322) Jan duwde drie wagens weg
John pushed three carts away

For **W** to be applied, it would be required to have a co-domain containing the partition of the set W, where W is a subset of carts and |W|=3. However, the SC-analysis offers the denotation of the small clause [NP XP] as part of the co-domain of the mapping. And the denotation of this clause cannot but belong to the set of truth values. Of course, we might wish to define this denotation such that this problem is solved, for example, by taking it to be a set of states with a cardinality equal to or less than three, but why should one wish to strain oneself semantically if the CP-analysis is available in which one may use the PLUG$^+$-machinery without any forced adaptation?

So, let us go more deeply into the reason why the CP-analysis (319) has been proposed as an alternative to the SC-analysis. There appear to be several problems for the SC-analysis which are solved quite naturally in the CP-analysis. Following Neeleman and Weerman (1991), I will discuss some of these problems here, because they bear on the issue discussed in the preceding sections. First of all, in SOV-sentences like

(323)	(dat) we drie deuren	in stukken	sloegen
	(that) we three doors	in pieces	beat

(324)	(dat) Jan	hen	sloeg
	(that) John	them	beat

(325)	(dat) Jan	drie deuren	bracht
	(that) John	three doors	brought

the SC-analysis says that within the small clause the NP *drie deuren* (three doors) must receive a Θ-role as the PP *in stukken* (in pieces) is a predicate which assigns a Θ-role to its argument. On the other hand, the main verb *slaan* (beat) also must assign Θ-roles to its arguments. Under the SC-analysis one must assume that the SC *drie deuren in stukken* (three doors in pieces) is also an argument of the verb. This cannot be the regular internal argument role assigned to an ordinary object like *hen* (them) in sentences like (324), because with Williams (1980) one cannot beat a proposition in the same way as some do with human beings. Recall that it was pointed out above that from the point of view of the present aspectual theory, the relation between the verb *slaan* (beat) and the SC *drie deuren in stukken* (three doors in pieces) is in no way comparable to the relation between the verb *eat* and *three sandwiches* in (51). This can also be brought out by a paraphrase. For (323), it is possible to paraphrase it as in (326):

(326) NP_{ext} V-ed such that at a given point NP_{int} XP

That is, we beat such that three doors were in pieces at a given point. Whatever paraphrase we have for sentences like (324), we can never use the phrase 'John beat such that ...'. Note that this paraphrase is also excluded on the assumption that the XP belongs to the V itself: *in stukken slaan* (to beat in pieces) behaves like *eten* (eat) and *brengen* (bring). Thus, in the SC-analysis there is no direct semantic relation between *in stukken slaan* (beat in pieces) and the NP *drie deuren* (three doors) comparable with the relation between *eten* (eat) and *drie boterhammen* (three sandwiches). Neeleman (1991) and Neeleman and Weerman (1991), Hoeksema (1991), Model (1991), Beeken (1991) contain many syntactic arguments against the SC-analysis. I shall not go into them here because this would force us into a detour through many intricacies of the syntax of GB-theory. Here it suffices to restrain ourselves to arguments bearing on the thematic structure of resultative constructions.

On the CP-analysis one has to make two crucial assumptions: (i) that it is possible to have complex predicates at D-structure in which the XP is adjoined to the V, as illustrated in Figure 44, which, apart from the SOV-order, is identical to Figure 43 except for the fact that the V has now got a complex structure; (ii) that the internal argument role for NP_{obj} is determined at the highest lexical V-level, to wit V^0. As far as the first assumption is concerned, it should be observed that it allows for the insertion of lexical material in a quasi-productive way. That is, at the lowest lexical V-level V_0 is introduced into D-structure with a variable position for a lot of possibly structured information: XP may be PPs like *in stukken* (into pieces), NPs like *een blauw oog* (lit.: a blue eye), APs like *blue* (blauw), particles like *weg* (away), prefixes, etc.

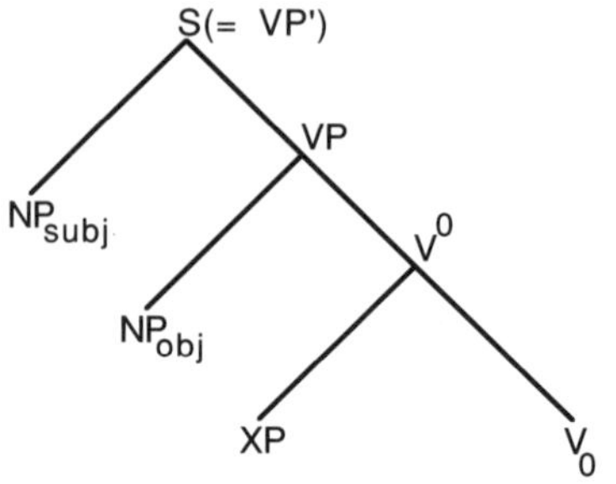

Figure 44 In this Complex Predicate structure V^0 is the verb as it enters into syntactic processes: it is syntactically the bottom element. V_0 is the lexical verb stem combining with the XP to form V^0 in a non-compositional way

Even though the information is syntactically structured, if an NP is XP or part of XP, then it is normally not referential:[69]

(327) ?Wij sloegen drie deuren in deze stukken
?We beat three doors into these pieces

(328) Zij sloeg Jan een blauw oog
lit.: She beat John a blue eye
She blacked John's eye

(329) ?Zij sloeg Jan zijn blauwe ogen
lit.: She beat John two blue eyes

(330) We zetten de vuilnisbak op straat
lit.: We put the trash can on street
We put the trash can on the street

(331) ?We zetten de vuilnisbak op straten
lit.: We put the trash can on streets

This strongly suggests that the 'regular' syntactic processes are not yet available at the level of V_0 (V sub zero). In other words, whatever thematic role is assigned by V^0 (V super zero) it does not assign the same sort of referential power as V_0.[70] In fact, one may be led to believe that it is only at the level of V^0 that the internal argument role can be assigned to NP_{obj}. In other words, in resultative sentences the Θ-role is to be assigned by V^0 rather than by V_0. This is visualized in Figure 45. According to Neeleman and Weerman (1991), the thematically relevant information expressed by the XP and the V_0 may percolate upwards. At the level of V^0 the information from the XP and the V_0 is com-

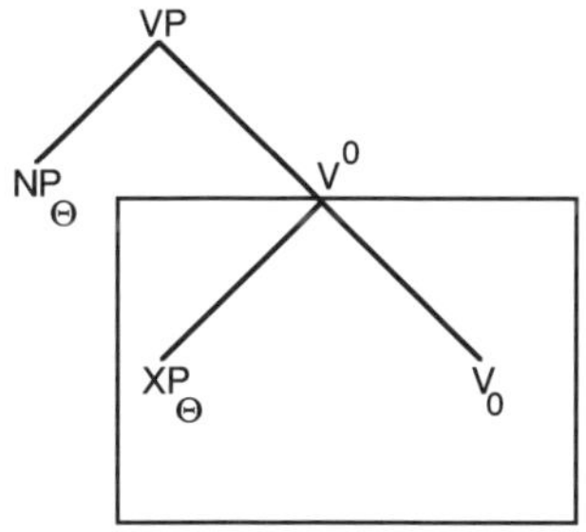

Figure 45 According to Neeleman and Weerman (1991), the thematic information expressed by the XP (which may act as a secondary predicate) percolates upwards. It amalgamates with the thematic information expressed by V^0

bined into a complex verb V^0, which assigns a Θ-role, the internal argument role, to the object NP.

The basic idea of Figure 45 is that the lowest-level thematic information may be incorporated below the V^0-level, but that it is expressed structurally at the level of V^0. In this way one gets around the so-called Principle of Lexical Integrity discussed in, for example, Booij (1990), which says that syntactic rules may not relate sublexical elements like XP to elements outside V^0. Compare the following sentences:

(332)	Jan duwde drie wagens	John pushed three carts
(333)	Jan duwde drie wagens voort	John pushed three carts on
(334)	Jan duwde drie wagens weg	John pushed three carts away

Both (332) and (333) are durative, whereas (334) is terminative. Given a CP-analysis, *wegduwen* (push away) but not *voortduwen* (push on) has an internal argument *drie wagens* (three carts) which constitutes a finite domain for the function **W**(i). The difference between (333) and (334) can now be explained in terms of a difference in thematic information: *voort* (on) contributes the $[\![\Theta_{\subseteq}]\!]$-information whereas *weg* (away) yields $[\![\Theta_{=}]\!]$-information. This is analogous to the difference between *naar* (towards) and *tot* (up to). The difference cannot be explained by information inherent to the verb *duwen* (push) itself: it is clearly located in the XP. So, it is not unreasonable to assume that *duwen* in (332) may also be explained in terms of $[\text{—}\Theta_{\subseteq}\ \text{NP}]$ being expressed at the V^0-position, but not at the V_0-position. So, there is no reason to burden the analysis with a discussion about the or a Θ-criterion which would stipulate that *drie wagens* (three carts) cannot receive a thematic role both from V^0 *wegduwen* (push away) and from the particle *weg* (away). In the present analysis, the specific lexical information about *weg* is incorporated into the (complex) lexical information expressed by the verb *wegduwen* (push away).

14.3 Argument Frames and Verbal Stems

Semantically, the above syntactic CP-analysis is compatible with the position adopted here, namely the position in which V_0 is taken to be the completely neutral verb stem, that is, stem-information without information about the argument structure in which the stem is going to be inserted. On this approach, the transition from V_0 to V^0 is not compositional, as it does not proceed by lambda-abstraction.[71] We assume that the area between V_0 and V^0 is not entirely lexical and not entirely syntactic: it is a twilight zone between (at super zero level) syntactic behaviour subjected to syntactic principles with respect to argument structure on the one hand, and verb-specific information (at sub zero level) on the other. As information about argument structure is essentially structural, the XP can be seen as the means to attach this to the otherwise neutral verbal stem. On the other hand, the difference between *duwen* (push) and *eten* (eat) cannot but be lexical, so these lexical items must be marked differently as to what sort of argument structure they may participate in.

More generally, one might think of the following frames which non-stative verbs may be specified for:

(335)	$\lambda I \lambda X \lambda i \lambda Y.[\![V_0]\!](I)(i)(Y)(X)$	transitive
(336)	$\lambda I \lambda i \lambda Y.[\![V_0]]\!](I)(i)(Y)$	unaccusative
(337)	$\lambda I \lambda X \lambda i.[\![V_0]\!](I)(i)(X)$	unergative

Scheme (335) provides for the transitive use of verbal stems, (336) and (337) for their intransitive use. The stem is non-compositionally inserted into the V_0-slot in a way discussed shortly. In this way, the notion of a [+ADD TO]-verb is formally tied up with the presence of i, where i>0: an odometer in action is the only way for a verb to express progress in time and space. The i-specification in non-stative verbs will be discussed later on.

To say that a verb is used *transitively* means now that the verb stem is inserted into a transitive frame requiring it to have a certain argumental structure. A transitive frame is a frame in which an internal argument occurs, so that a mapping between the verb and this argument can take place, through the application of the Θ-function. In the transitive use of *eat* the i is connected with the internal argument Y, so that the VP is terminative if the internal argument is [+SQA]. In this sense, *walk* in (50) *John walked to the store* is transitively used because the preposition *to* provides for the second argument. A verb is used *unaccusatively* if its only argument is an internal argument, that is, it is made dependent on i. So here the machinery involved in the VP [eat [three sandwiches]] fully applies to the structure [Δ [die [three patients]]], which in GB-syntax will become [three patients$_i$ [die [e$_i$]]], where e$_i$ is the trace of a movement of the subject NP *three patients* (see (94) and (95) in chapter 1.4). A verb is used *unergatively* if its only atemporal external argument is the subject NP. Recall that in fact two alternatives were offered: (337) and scheme (204): $\lambda I \lambda X.[\![V_0]\!](I)(X)$. I will discuss these options now.

It is important to see the advantages of saying that the verb *walk* can be used transitively and intransitively (unergatively) rather than saying that *walk* is an intransitive verb which can be used transitively. To say that the verb at the V_0-level is lexically not specified as belonging to the category of transitive or unaccusative or unergative verbs amounts to saying that its type-logical status is only syntactically 'visible' as soon as it occurs in syntactic expressions, that is, as a V^0-entity. In this way, XP is seen as making the verb suitable for entering syntax at V^0 (the lowest categorial X-bar level) as a lexical unit of a certain type by providing argument structure for V_0. As verbs like *walk* may occur in a transitive frame as well as in an unergative frame, it is lexically marked for these two options. The marking may be done very practically: one might, for example, lexically mark *walk* at the V_0-level simply as: 'occurring in XP-schemes (335) or (337)', distinguishing it in this way from the English *die* that would be marked as 'occurring in (336)'. A verb which is marked for more than one frame receives a different argument structure in each case, which leads to a different syntactic and semantic behaviour.

Suppose that one used scheme (204) $\lambda I \lambda X.[\![V_0]\!](I)(X)$ rather than (337) for the unergative use of *walk*. Then one could argue that due to the specification 'occurring in XP-schemes (335) or (204)' one keeps track of the fact that *walk* is used as a [+ADD TO]-verb. In other words, there would be no need for the index (i) as given in (337) because, when interpreting *John walked* in terms of scheme (204), one always has access to the information that *walk* also may occur in (335). This argument could even be strengthened by claiming that in a lot of cases (among which even *walk*) one is not focussed on progress in time, but on talking about the activity itself. Thus, *Icarus flew above the sea* may mean that the place where Icarus was engaged in flying was above the sea rather than that he went along a 'fly-path'. In other words, (204) does not appeal to the function ℓ in its interpretation **W**, whereas (337) assumes **W** but lets the context fill in its co-domain, yielding unboundedness. Some might wish to argue, however, that in some contexts *John walked* has an (i)-parameter and is to be interpreted as an [+ADD TO]-verb, whereas in other situations one is really focussed on the activity itself. In that case, (337) would do, because one may always 'neutralize' the i, that is, send all i to a fixed value, or to zero, depending on the context.

In the remainder of this study, I shall stick to (337), in view of the fact that indeed in certain contexts the 'odometer-use' of an intransitive verb may become relevant, whereas in other uses it is the activity-part of the meaning which is more important. Scheme (337) allows this. Hence, the unergative use of *walk* is specified in terms of the absence of an internal argument – there is no Y – whereas the transitive use of *walk* is specified for [—$\Theta_=$ NP] at the V^0-level. This explains the different aspectual behaviour of sentences like *John walked* (durative) on the one hand, and *John walked a mile* and *Mary walked to Rome* (terminative) on the other. The regular [+SQA]-feature algebra operates in these cases: witness the durative sentence *John walked miles*. Note also that there is no need to analyse *John walked* as having an implicit argument Δ which must be interpreted as [–SQA], as in Verkuyl (1972).

The inferential behaviour of a verb is accounted for in this proposal too. Basically, it takes place at or via the V_0-level: the difference in argument structure is not and must not be taken into account as part of the meaning of the verb itself, because there is no unique notion of verb. One lexical V_0 or V_0-stem may be used differently at the V^0-level. The fact that the truth of (50) entails the truth of (338) is due to the fact that the V_0 *walk* is marked for (335) and for (337). Both the V^0 *walk* in (50) and the V^0 *walk* in (338) imply the same V_0 *walk*.

(50) John walked to the store

(338) John walked

(47) Judith ate a sandwich

(339) Judith ate

The same applies to (47) and (339): what is entailed by (47) is strictly speaking not (339) itself, but rather what is entailed by both (47) and (339): Judith is engaged in an eating-activity. The well-known entailment from (47) that Judith ate something does not follow from properties of the verb *eat* itself. It is due to the fact that for any (positive) two-place predication the denotation of the (concrete) head noun of the argument NP can be described in terms of the set of things E, that is, the domain of discourse. In other words, for any sentence of the form *Judith* V-ed *a sandwich* one may entail *Someone* V-ed *a sandwich*, or *Judith* V-ed *something* or *Someone* V-ed *something*. It has nothing to do with properties specific to the verb *eat* itself, rather with the principle of existential generalization applied to subsets of E. If (339) implies that Judith ate something, it follows simply from the fact that the V_0 *eat* is positively specified for the transitive XP-frame (335). The use of a conditional here is motivated by the fact that *She called her mother* implies that she called someone (on the basis of existential generalization), whereas it would be wrong to infer from *She called* that she called someone.

Apart from (335)–(336), there must also be a lexical instruction about the Θ-role of the verb at the V^0-level. In transitive cases, the XP is as in (335), but now prefixes or particles in the XP can be combined with the verb stem, their Θ-information being established at the level of V^0 in the form of co-occurrence restrictions on the internal argument. The verb *eten* (eat) will be lexically specified for V^0 as $[—\Theta_{=}\,\mathrm{NP}]$, by default, as in (340), that is, without a prefix: the V_0 *eten* is simply inserted into the XP-frame (335) yielding V^0 (340).

(340) λIλXλiλY.⟦eten⟧(I)(i)(Y)(X) $[—\Theta_{=}\,\mathrm{NP}]$

It is important to underscore that each specification of the form $[—\Theta_{\alpha}\,\mathrm{NP}]$, where α is $\subseteq$, $\subset$ or $=$, is basically idiosyncratic. Recall that there are some speakers of Dutch who are hesitant to call *Judith at een boterham* (Judith ate a sandwich) terminative. In terms of the present theory, in their lexicon these speakers have $[—\Theta_{\subseteq}\,\mathrm{NP}]$ in (340) rather than $[—\Theta_{=}\,\mathrm{NP}]$. In general, however, the default specification for the Dutch [+ADD TO]-verbs is $[—\Theta_{=}\,\mathrm{NP}]$.

14.4 PUSH-verbs + particles

PUSH-verbs need the indeterminacy V^0-information $[—\Theta_{\subseteq}\,\mathrm{NP}]$, as shown in (341), or in (342):

(341) λIλXλiλY.⟦ø+duwen⟧(I)(i)(Y)(X) $[—\Theta_{\subseteq}\,\mathrm{NP}]$
(342) λIλXλiλY.⟦duwen⟧(I)(i)(Y)(X) $[—\Theta_{\subseteq}\,\mathrm{NP}]$

Note that (341) and (342) are alternative options. I prefer (341) to (342) because (341) makes the XP really the place where the decisive thematic information comes from, as in the regular cases such as (343):

(343) λIλXλiλY.⟦weg+V_0⟧(I)(i)(Y)(X) $[—\Theta_{=}\,\mathrm{NP}]$
(344) λIλXλiλY.⟦weg+duwen⟧(I)(i)(Y)(X) $[—\Theta_{=}\,\mathrm{NP}]$

(345) λIλiλY.⟦weg+V_0⟧(I)(i)(Y) $[—\Theta_{=}\,\mathrm{NP}]$
(346) λIλiλY.⟦weg+lopen⟧(I)(i)(Y) $[—\Theta_{=}\,\mathrm{NP}]$

The particle *weg* (away) requires $[—\Theta_{=}\,\mathrm{NP}]$ if it takes verbs like the V_0 *duwen* (push) to form a transitive V^0. Note that it also takes the V_0 *lopen* (walk) to form an unaccusative V^0 *weglopen* (walk away).

PUSH-verbs also take prefixes or particles such as *voort* (on, lit.: further) that do not lead to a [+ADD TO]-specification at the V^0-level.

(347) λIλXλiλY.⟦voort+V_0⟧(I)(i)(Y)(X) [—$\Theta_{\subseteq}$ NP]
(348) λIλXλiλY.⟦voort+duwen⟧(I)(i)(Y)(X) [—$\Theta_{\subseteq}$ NP]

In this way, the difference between

(349) #Jan duwde urenlang de kar weg
#For hours John pushed the cart away
(350) Jan duwde urenlang de kar voort
For hours John pushed on the cart

can be explained: the particle *voort* (on) simply may take the V_0 *duwen* to form a V^0 requiring a thematic role expressing indeterminacy.

XPs may seem to 'strengthen' a verb like *eten* (eat) which is already marked for [—$\Theta_{=}$NP] (in my lexicon), or for [—$\Theta_{\subseteq}$ NP] (in the lexicon of some speakers of Dutch).

(351) λIλXλiλY.⟦op+V_0⟧(I)(i)(Y)(X) [—$\Theta_{=}$NP]
(352) λIλXλiλY.⟦op+eten⟧(I)(i)(Y)(X) [—$\Theta_{=}$NP]

However, the appropriate analysis in terms of our schemes is that *op* (up) is defined in (351) as [—$\Theta_{=}$NP] and that it takes the V_0-verb stem *eten*, which at the sub zero level is not marked for the thematic specification [—$\Theta_{=}$NP]. So, in this sense the V^0 *opeten* is not a stronger version of the V^0 *eten*; it is, rather, a different verb. Both *opeten* (eat up) and *eten* (eat) have the V_0 *eten* in common. Note that the V_0 *eten* is only marked for the transitive scheme (351) and not for an unaccusative or unergative *op* (up) because **Judith at op* (Judith ate up) is ungrammatical.

Summarizing, the leading theoretical idea of stem-insertion is that a V_0 can now be specified as to the frames in which it may occur, either the 'regular' schemes (335), (336) and (337) or these schemes associated with particles and prefixes with which the verbs may combine into complex verbs. Traditionally, *walk* is treated lexically as an intransitive verb. The same applies *mutatis mutandis* to English. The behaviour of *walk* in sentences like (353):

(353) John walked a mile, the marathon, a stretch

is traditionally accounted for, in the form of the statement that intransitive verbs may sometimes take a complement, just like the sentences in (50). But, in this view, the verb remains fundamentally intransitive. In the present analysis, the verb *walk* is transitively used in (353) and in (50) and intransitively in

(338) *John walked*. Likewise, the verb *eat*, when used intransitively in (339) *Judith ate*, now simply means that Judith was involved in the (unbounded) activity of eating.

As observed earlier, in an unergative scheme like (337) there is no object Y present, which means that the i remains unbounded. This holds for some verbs that are used intransitively such as *duwen* in (354), but also for particles which occur in intransitive frames, like *voort* (on).

(354)	$\lambda I\lambda X\lambda i.[\![\text{duwen}]\!](I)(i)(X)$	no Θ_{int}–specification
(355)	$\lambda I\lambda X\lambda i.[\![\text{voort}+V_0]\!](I)(i)(X)$	no Θ_{int}–specification

Voort (on) may occur in a transitive scheme (348), specified as [—$\Theta_{\subseteq}$ NP], as in *voortduwen*, but that it may not take verbs like *lopen* (walk) and *eten* (eat) to form a transitive verb. Its most normal use is (355) as in (356) and (357).

(356)	*Hij liep een mijl voort	lit.: he walked on a mile
	*Judith at een sandwich voort	lit.: Judith ate a sandwich on
(357)	De boer, hij ploegde voort	The farmer, he ploughed on
	Hij liep voort	He walked on

The present analysis of stem-insertion is supported by the fact that the fronting prefixes and particles are often 'specialized'. That is, there are sentences like (358)–(360),

(358) Jan duwde de wagen *stuk*
Jan pushed the cart *out of order*

(359) Zij las het boek *uit*
lit.: She read the book *out*
She finished the book

(360) Judith at de boterham *op*
Judith ate the sandwich *up*

in which *stuk duwen* (push out of order), *uitlezen* (lit.: read out) become verbs at the V^0-level after their stems have been inserted in XP-schemes like (361).

(361)	$\lambda I\lambda X\lambda i\lambda Y.[\![\text{stuk}+V_0]\!](I)(i)(Y)(X)$	[—$\Theta_{=}$ NP]
	$\lambda I\lambda X\lambda i\lambda Y.[\![\text{uit}+V_0]\!](I)(i)(Y)(X)$	[—$\Theta_{=}$ NP]
	$\lambda I\lambda X\lambda i\lambda Y.[\![\text{op}+V_0]\!](I)(i)(Y)(X)$	[—$\Theta_{=}$ NP]

However, the italicized parts in (358)–(360) cannot occur in sentences like (362)–(364).

(362) *Jan duwde *stuk* — *Jan pushed *out of order*
(363) *Zij las *uit* — lit.: She read *out*
(364) *Judith at *op* — *Judith ate *up*

So there seems to be a general rule saying that no prefix or particle occurring in schemes like (361) can occur in scheme (337).

(365) If a transitivizing particle specified as $[—\Theta_{=}\,NP]$ occurs in the XP-scheme $\lambda I\lambda X\lambda i\lambda Y[\![\text{Particle}+V_0]\!](I)(i)(Y)(X)$, it cannot occur in an unergative XP-scheme of the form $\lambda I\lambda X\lambda i[\![\text{Particle}+V_0]\!](I)(i)(X)$

Whether the rule also holds for the unaccusative scheme (336) is not clear. It does in general, but there are sentences like:

(366) Ze heeft gelezen
She has read/has been reading
(367) Ze is uitgelezen
lit.: she is read out
She reads no more

(368) Ze heeft gegeten
She has eaten
(369) Ze is uitgegeten
lit.: she is eaten out
She finished (her) eating/ She eats no more

If (367) and (369) are in the scope of the present analysis, they are cases in which *uit* (out) is put into the unaccusative scheme (336): they have an ergative flavour.[72] However, neither can have a simple tense – for example, **Ze at uit* (She eats out) cannot mean that she finished eating – so there must be rather heavy constraints on these constructions. In general, particles and prefixes in XPs taking verb stems to form transitive verbs specified as $[—\Theta_{=}\,NP]$ do only occur in these frames. This fact supports, in my view, the present analysis in which verb stems are inserted in different sorts of XP-schemes. There is just one scheme leading to a $[—\Theta_{=}\,NP]$-characterization and it is predicted that V_0-stems plus the unergative scheme never bring about terminativity at the V^0-level. It is sometimes possible in the unaccusative scheme, but highly restricted as can be expected.

The above analysis of prefixes and particles as they occur in (Dutch) Complex Predicates is by no means exhaustive. For example, there is a famous connection in Dutch between terminative interpretation and the use of *zijn* (be) in sentences like *Hij is naar Prades gelopen* (lit.: He is walked to Prades) as opposed to *Hij heeft naar Prades gelopen* (He has walked to Prades). In the former case, he reached Prades, in the second case he might never have reached it. Indeed, the unaccusative scheme favours the use of the auxiliary *zijn* (be). On the other hand, sentences like *Hij is doorgelopen* (He has walked on, lit. He is walked on) are durative just like *Hij heeft doorgelopen met die ziekte* (He kept going despite being ill; lit.: He has walked on with his illness), so there is no one-to-one correspondence. In spite of these sorts of problems on the periphery of the present study, the main line is relatively clear: there is a principled way to distinguish the durativity of sentences like (338) *John walked* from the terminativity of sentences like (207) *John died* and (50) *John walked to the store* on the basis of (335)–(337), whereas these schemes also explain the behaviour of PUSH-verbs as opposed to regular [+ADD TO]-verbs in a principled way.

As far as [−ADD TO]- or stative verbs are concerned, a choice must be made between (370) and (371) for verbs with two arguments, like *hate*, *know*, etc. and between (372) and (373) for verbs with one argument such as *be mortal*, *hang*, etc.:

(370) $\lambda I\lambda X\lambda Y.[\![V_0]\!](I)(Y)(X)$
(371) $\lambda I\lambda X\lambda i\lambda Y.[\![V_0]\!](I)(i)(Y)(X)$

(372) $\lambda I\lambda X.[\![V_0]\!](I)(X)$
(373) $\lambda I\lambda X\lambda i.[\![V_0]\!](I)(i)(X)$

(374) Judith hated three yuppies
(375) $\exists I\exists I_R\exists!V[V=[\![\text{Judith}]\!]\cap\{j_i\}\wedge\exists W[W\subseteq[\![\text{yuppy}]\!]\wedge|W|=3$
$\wedge\exists Q\text{psW}[Q=\{U\cap[\![\text{yuppy}]\!]: [\![\text{hate}]\!](I)(U)(V)\}]]$
$\wedge I=\text{Ent}^+(I_R)\wedge\text{Tense}_<(I_R)(i^*)]$

In (370) and (372), stative verbs do not have indices i at all. On this analysis, it is only if transitive verbs have the i-index information that they may temporalize the internal argument. In other words, the direct object NP of (374) analysed on the basis of (370) is not temporalized: it would remain $<<<e,t>,t>,t>$, as in (375).

However, there are arguments for considering (371) and (373), so that stative verbs are just special cases of verbs fitting in (335) or (337). The idea would be to assume that [−ADD TO]-verbs are lexically characterized in terms of the same frames as [+ADD TO]-verbs, but that their temporal index is kept zero, because all arguments of **W** are mapped to point zero. Note that INFL has been defined in terms of the actualization function Ent⁺, so it could not apply if i is absent. This amounts to saying that the index system employed for [+ADD TO]-

verbs can be used, but that the actualization function Ent^{+} will yield one and the same value for *hate* in (374), for example by the lexical index stipulation requiring that $I_V=\{i_0\}$ and $I=\{0\}$.[73] The presence of the temporal system used for [+ADD TO]-verbs in the characterization of [–ADD TO]-verbs (so that the latter are a special case of the former) would explain why sometimes one may temporalize [–ADD TO]-verbs as in *He was ignoring me during the dinner, I was wondering why*, or *The village was lying in the valley*, discussed in chapter 2.2. This would simply mean that speakers put into use the available index-machinery to obtain temporalization effects for otherwise stative verbs. It would also mean that the transition from non-stative verbs to verbs expressing activity only is made more fluent. Who can tell us the difference between the activity expressed by *walk* in *John walked yesterday*, which may be intended to be very stative (it reports about a fact, say), and *hate* in *By that remark she hated that yuppy so much that she felt her hate creeping into mere frenzy*?

If the modelling of [–ADD TO]-verbs after the temporal format of [+ADD TO]-verbs is correct, then (375) would become (376)

(376) $\exists I \exists I_R \exists ! V[V=[\![\mathrm{Judith}]\!]\cap\{j_i\}\wedge\exists W[W\subseteq[\![\mathrm{yuppy}]\!]\wedge|W|=3$
$\wedge\exists Q\mathrm{psW}[Q=\bigcup_I\{U\cap[\![\mathrm{yuppy}]\!]: [\![\mathrm{hate}]\!](I)(0)(U)(V)\}]]$
$\wedge I=\mathrm{Ent}^{+}(I_R)\wedge\mathrm{Tense}_{<}(I_R)(i*)]$

where the lexical specification that i=0 is made visible in the formula itself, to mark the difference with [+ADD TO]-verbs.

14.5 Conclusion

This concludes the excursion into the realm of apparent counterexamples against the Plus-principle. As observed above, the present analysis is based upon the Dutch OV-order, but it should not be very difficult to develop a CP-analysis for English, even though the analysis for English is complicated by the fact that the complex verb 'wraps around' its internal argument, as in:

(312) John pushed the cart away
(313) Roland painted the door blue

In other words, the complex verb is discontinuous. In terms of Neeleman's work on complex predicates, this would require a structure like Figure 46, in which the particle *up* is moved from its XP-position to a higher (non-argument) position in the VP, by adjunction. In categorial grammar, different techniques are used to account for discontinuity, but basically the same idea is captured: a discontinuous constituent may be treated as a unit (e.g. Bach 1979,

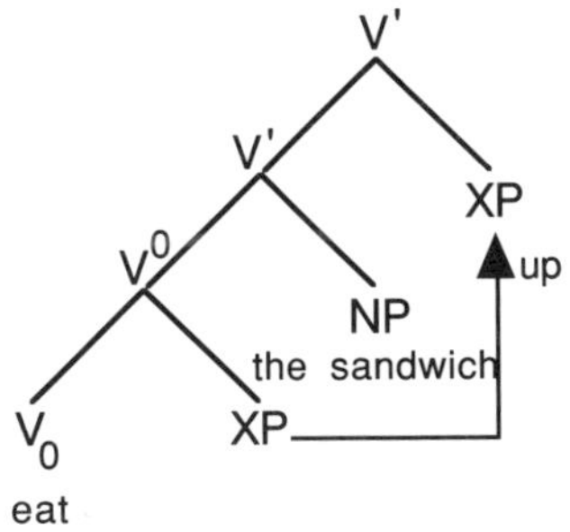

Figure 46 In English, Complex Predicate formation proceeds by adjunction of the XP to V′, due to its underlying SVO order

1984; Moortgat 1992). I am aware that the present discussion of complex predication is closely tied up with GB-syntax (the discussion about the option between Small Clause and Complex Predicate takes place there), but I see no reason why the idea of a non-compositional 'shimmer area' between V_0 and V^0 should not be compatible with the tenets of categorial grammar.

Perhaps this is the place to pay some attention to a possible compositional alternative to the above 'stem-insertion strategy'. In fact, this alternative would come closer to the standard reduction strategy. In the present context this strategy would amount to declaring that each verb is the argument of a scheme λVλIλXλiλY⟦V⟧(I)(i)(Y)(X) which applied to any V_k yields a four-place transitive verb of the form λIλXλiλY⟦V_k⟧(I)(i)(Y)(X). In this way, one would derive verbs like *eat*, *die*, *walk* and *hate*.

(203) λIλXλiλY.⟦eat⟧(I)(i)(Y)(X)
(377) λIλXλiλY.⟦die⟧(I)(i)(Y)(X)
(378) λIλXλiλY.⟦walk⟧(I)(i)(Y)(X)
(379) λIλXλiλY.⟦hate⟧(I)(i)(Y)(X)

The XP-procedure would, so to say, rig up the V-stem with its argument structure, which it does not need to express itself in the lexicon. Thus, the meaning of *away* would be roughly characterized as:

(380) λVλIλXλiλY.⟦V+away⟧(I)(i)(Y)(X) [—$\Theta_=$NP]

where the complex verb V+*away* is a (discontinuous) category of type *<<i,t>,<i,<<e,t>,<<e,t>,t>>>>*. Thus, *away* may be taken as a modifier operating on members of this type yielding semantic objects of the same type. The lexical information expressed by *away* and differentiating it from *on* is not visible in (380), but it is present, just like all the rest of the ⟦eat⟧-information is present in *eat*. Also, thematic information concerning the internal argument is assumed to be expressed.

The reductional strategy is compatible with the analysis in which the implicit argument in sentences like (381) would be analysed as in (382):

(381) Judith ate

(382) $\lambda I.\exists!V[V=[\![\text{Judith}]\!]\cap\{j_i\}\wedge\exists W\exists S[W\subseteq\bigcup S\subseteq[\![\text{edible}]\!]\wedge|S|\geq 1$
$\wedge\exists Q\text{psW}[Q=\bigcup_I\{U\cap[\![\text{edible}]\!]: [\![\text{eat}]\!](I)(i)(U)(V)\}]]]$

that is, in terms of an implicit bare plural. Just as in postulate (150), discussed by Dowty, a postulate could guarantee that the pseudo-intransitive *eat* is related to its transitive 'Ur-form' in which V is the transitive form (Zubizaretta 1987). The general scheme for such a detransitivization postulate would be (383):

(383) $[\![V]\!](I)(i)(X)=1 \text{ iff } \exists W\exists S[W\subseteq\bigcup S\subseteq[\![\text{V–ible}]\!]\wedge|S|\geq 1$
$\wedge\exists Q\text{psW}[Q=\bigcup_I\{U\cap[\![\text{V–ible}]\!]: [\![V]\!](I)(i)(U)(X)\}]]$

The difference between the reduction strategy and the stem-insertion strategy is clear: in the former the Principle of Compositionality applies below the level of V^0, whereas in the latter V^0 is the smallest syntactic building block which it applies to. The obvious disadvantage of the reduction approach is that it is highly unnatural to use postulates like (383) to get rid of argument structure in the case of verbs which can only occur as genuine ergatives or as genuine unergatives. For a verb like *tremble* this is very unnatural, even though one might form marked sentences like *She trembled herself to death*. Moreover, it assumes that inferences have to take into account information about argument structure, which they do not. And finally, a compositional approach to the formation of complex predicates does not take into account that there are clear differences between the simplex verb and its complex extension, as pointed out above.

As far as the last point is concerned, the composition of stem and XP into a complex predicate V^0 at which the eventual thematic structure is settled is indeed not always compositional. The question is therefore whether we may allow compositionality in the interface between lexicon and syntax, rather than whether we need it. There are some arguments for the position that *wegduwen* (push away) would be better treated as a verb whose meaning is not compositionally derived. For example, the meaning of the verb stem *–duwen* (push) in *wegduwen* comes closer to the meaning of 'give a push' than is expressed by the verb *duwen*. This seems to hold more generally, as pointed out in Booij and Van Haaften (1988) with respect to prefixes, which change the selection restrictions of the base verb.[74] They reject the so-called Inheritance hypothesis, which predicts that prefixations preserve the original selection restrictions. This can be seen as a strong argument for not applying the lambda-machinery below V^0 as part of the syntactic machinery.

In my view, the data considered strongly suggest that the Complex Predicate analysis makes room for a more subtle analysis of the linguistic facts than available if one simply tries to analyse sentences with verbs like (305) as counterexamples. The present analysis makes it possible to explain the behaviour of these verbs by paying attention to their internal structure in which thematic information is expressed by the XP-frame in which they occur in syntax. Dahl (1981: 81f.) says that sentences like (384)–(386)

(384)	I was writing	(–P,–T)
(385)	I was writing a letter	(–P,+T)
(386)	I wrote a letter	(+P,+T)

are to be partitioned into two oppositions: (i) (384) vs. (385)/(386); and (ii) (384)/(385) vs (386). The former is based on the opposition [±T], the latter on the opposition [±P], where T stands for 'telicity' (directed towards attaining a goal or limit, after which the process stops) and P for 'T + the goal is claimed to be reached'. Stambolieva (1989: 503f.) strongly opposes Dahl's view, arguing that in Slavic languages the English (386) is not necessarily translated into a sentence with a perfective verb form and that (384) and (385) are not aspectually opposed in any Slavic language. The present aspectual theory evades the problems raised by Stambolieva by assigning to *write* in (384) the scheme (337), by assigning (385) a Progressive Form based on $\subset$, and by treating (386) exactly along the lines of (47) *Judith ate a sandwich*, that is, with the possibility of taking the verb *eat* in terms of either $\Theta_{=}$ or $\Theta_{\subseteq}$, dependent on the private lexical definition of a speaker. In this way, it can be explained why the translation of the English sentence (386) into Bulgarian leads to the use of either an Aorist or an Imperfect.

CONCLUSION TO PART III

In chapter 1, the descriptive goal of the present study was to account formally for a number of sentences. In chapter 7 a grammar, called PLUG, was developed which accounted for the contribution of the atemporal NPs to the construal of terminative aspectuality. In chapter 13, an extension has been made resulting in a grammar which is called PLUG$^+$. This grammar has been developed on the basis of the grammar PLUG, proposed by Verkuyl and Van der Does (1991). PLUG$^+$ is a temporal extension of the atemporal PLUG. Its rules were discussed in chapter 13, but they are given now in the form of rules forming Phrase Structure and rules for Tense and Progressive Form. Perhaps a more general X-bar format could have been chosen, including rules for modification, but as this does not bear on the heart of the aspectual matter this has not been done.

PLUG$^+$

PHRASE STRUCTURE RULES:

$$1.\ \mathrm{S} : \lambda \mathrm{I}.\, [\![\mathrm{NP}]\!](\lambda \mathrm{X}.\, [\![\mathrm{VP}]\!](\mathrm{I})(\mathrm{X})) \quad \Leftarrow \quad \mathrm{NP} : [\![\mathrm{NP}]\!],\ \mathrm{VP} : [\![\mathrm{VP}]\!]$$

$$2.\ \begin{cases} \mathrm{VP} : \lambda \mathrm{X}.\, [\![\mathrm{V}_1]\!](\mathrm{X}) \\ \mathrm{VP} : \lambda \mathrm{X}.\, [\![\mathrm{NP'}]\!](\lambda \mathrm{i} \lambda \mathrm{Y}.\, [\![\mathrm{V}_2]\!](\mathrm{I})(\mathrm{i})(\mathrm{Y})(\mathrm{X})) \quad \Leftarrow \quad \mathrm{V}_2 : [\![\mathrm{V}_2]\!],\ \mathrm{NP'} : [\![\mathrm{NP'}]\!] \end{cases}$$

$$3.\ \mathrm{NP'} : [\![\Theta]\!]([\![\mathrm{NP}]\!]) \quad \Leftarrow \quad \Theta : [\![\Theta]\!],\ \mathrm{NP} : [\![\mathrm{NP}]\!]$$

$$4.\ \mathrm{NP} : [\![\mathrm{DET}^2]\!]([\![\mathrm{N}]\!]) \quad \Leftarrow \quad \mathrm{DET}^2 : [\![\mathrm{DET}^2]\!],\ \mathrm{N} : [\![\mathrm{N}]\!]$$

$$5.\ \mathrm{DET}^2 : [\![\mathrm{SPEC}]\!]([\![\mathrm{DET}^1]\!]) \quad \Leftarrow \quad \mathrm{SPEC} : [\![\mathrm{SPEC}]\!],\ \mathrm{DET}^1 : [\![\mathrm{DET}^1]\!]$$

TENSE AND PROG:

1. $\mathrm{S'} : [\![\mathrm{INFL}]\!]([\![\mathrm{S}]\!]) \quad \Leftarrow \quad \mathrm{INFL} : [\![\mathrm{INFL}]\!],\ \mathrm{S} : [\![\mathrm{S}]\!]$
2. $\mathrm{S} : [\![\mathrm{PROG}]\!]([\![\mathrm{S}]\!]) \quad \Leftarrow \quad \mathrm{PROG} : [\![\mathrm{PROG}]\!],\ \mathrm{S} : [\![\mathrm{S}]\!]$
3. $[\![\mathrm{INFL}]\!] = \lambda \mathrm{S} \exists \mathrm{I} \exists \mathrm{I_R}[\mathrm{S}(\mathrm{I}) \wedge \mathrm{I}{=}\mathrm{Ent}^+(\mathrm{I_R}) \wedge \mathrm{Tense}_\alpha(\mathrm{I_R})(\mathrm{i}^*)]$
4. $[\![\mathrm{PROG}]\!] = \lambda \mathrm{S} \lambda \mathrm{J'} \exists \mathrm{J}[\mathrm{S}(\mathrm{J}) \wedge \mathrm{J'} \subset \mathrm{J}]$
5. $[\![\mathrm{INFL_{hab}}]\!] = \lambda \mathrm{S} \exists I\ \forall \mathrm{I}[\mathrm{I} \in I \rightarrow \exists \mathrm{I_R}[\mathrm{S}(\mathrm{I}) \wedge \mathrm{I}{=}\mathrm{Ent}^+(\mathrm{I_R}) \wedge \mathrm{Tense}_\alpha(\mathrm{I_R})(\mathrm{i}^*)]]$

Θ-interpretation:

$[\![\Theta_=]\!] \quad = \quad \lambda \mathrm{NP} \lambda \mathbf{W} \exists R[\mathrm{NP}(R) \wedge \bigcup_\mathrm{I} \mathbf{W} = R]$

$[\![\Theta_\subseteq]\!] \quad = \quad \lambda \mathrm{NP} \lambda \mathbf{W} \exists R[\mathrm{NP}(R) \wedge \bigcup_\mathrm{I} \mathbf{W} \subseteq R]$

$[\![\Theta_\subset]\!] \quad = \quad \lambda \mathrm{NP} \lambda \mathbf{W} \exists R[\mathrm{NP}(R) \wedge \bigcup_\mathrm{I} \mathbf{W} \subset R]$

SPEC

$[\![\text{the}]\!] = \lambda D\lambda X\lambda P.[D(X\cap C)([\![\text{thing}]\!])\wedge\exists Q\text{ps}X\cap C\,[Q=P|_{X\cap C}]]$

$[\![\varnothing]\!] = \lambda D\lambda X\lambda P.\exists W[W\subseteq X\wedge D(X)(W)\wedge\exists Q\text{ps}W[Q=P|_{X}]]$

DET[1]

$[\![\text{SG}]\!] = \lambda X\lambda Y.|X\cap Y|=1$

$[\![\text{PL}]\!] = \lambda X\lambda Y.|X\cap Y|>1$

$[\![\text{n}]\!] = \lambda X\lambda Y.|X\cap Y|=n$

$[\![\text{most}]\!] = \lambda X\lambda Y.|X\cap Y|>1/2\bullet|X|$

$[\![\text{several}]\!] = \lambda X\lambda Y.|X\cap Y|\geq 2$

$[\![\text{INC}]\!] = \lambda X\lambda Y.|X\cap Y'|=0$

V_1, V_2

$[\![V^0]\!]$	=	$\lambda I\lambda X\lambda i.[\![V_0]\!](I)(i)(X)$	unergative scheme
	=	$\lambda I\lambda i\lambda Y.[\![V_0]\!](I)(i)(Y)$	unaccusative scheme
	=	$\lambda I\lambda X\lambda i\lambda Y.[\![V_0]\!](I)(i)(Y)(X)$	transitive scheme

PLUG^{+} makes it possible to fulfil the promise made in chapter 1. The sentences discussed there are now given, together with their formal representations. All of them have been treated in Part III and this will be indicated by their numbering. The sentences and their descriptions are:

(47) Judith ate a sandwich

(387) $\exists I\exists I_R\exists!V[V=[\![\text{Judith}]\!]\cap\{j_i\}\wedge\exists W[W\subseteq[\![\text{sandwich}]\!]\wedge|W|=1$
$\wedge\exists Q\text{ps}W[Q=\bigcup_{i\in I}\{U\cap[\![\text{sandwich}]\!]: [\![\text{eat}]\!](I)(i)(U)(V)\}]]$
$\wedge I=\text{Ent}^{+}(I_R)\wedge\text{Tense}_{<}(I_R)(i^{*})]$

(48) Judith ate sandwiches

(388) $\exists I\exists I_R\exists!V[V=[\![\text{Judith}]\!]\cap\{j_i\}\wedge\exists W\exists P[W\subseteq\bigcup P\subseteq[\![\text{sandwich}]\!]\wedge|P|>1$
$\wedge\exists Q\text{ps}W[Q=\bigcup_{i\in I}\{U\cap[\![\text{sandwich}]\!]: [\![\text{eat}]\!](I)(i)(U)(V)\}]]$
$\wedge I=\text{Ent}^{+}(I_R)\wedge\text{Tense}_{<}(I_R)(i^{*})]$

(51) John walked to three stores

(389) $\exists I\exists I_R\exists!V[V=[\![\text{John}]\!]\cap\{j_i\}\wedge\exists W[W\subseteq[\![\text{store}]\!]\wedge|W|=3$
$\wedge\exists Q\text{ps}W[Q=\bigcup_{i\in I}\{U\cap[\![\text{store}]\!]: [\![\text{walk}_{\text{to}}]\!](I)(i)(U)(V)\}]]$
$\wedge I=\text{Ent}^{+}(I_R)\wedge\text{Tense}_{<}(I_R)(i^{*})]$

(251) Jan liep naar de winkel
John walked to(wards) the store

(390) $\exists I\exists I_R\exists!V[V=[\![\text{John}]\!]\cap\{j_i\}\wedge\exists!W[W\subseteq[\![\text{store}]\!]\wedge|W|=1$
$\wedge\exists Q\text{ps}W[Q\ \bigcup_{i\in I}\{U\cap[\![\text{store}]\!]: [\![\text{walk}_{\text{towards}}]\!](I)(i)(U)(V)\}]]$
$\wedge I=\text{Ent}^{+}(I_R)\wedge\text{Tense}_{<}(I_R)(i^{*})]$

(280) Judith was eating three sandwiches

(391) $\exists I \exists I_R \exists J \exists ! V[V=\llbracket \text{Judith} \rrbracket \cap \{j_i\} \wedge \exists W[W \subseteq \llbracket \text{sandwich} \rrbracket \wedge |W|=3$
$\wedge \exists Q \text{ps} W[Q=\bigcup_{i \in J}\{U \cap \llbracket \text{sandwich} \rrbracket : \llbracket \text{eat} \rrbracket (J)(i)(U)(V)\}]]$
$\wedge I \subset J \wedge I=\text{Ent}^+(I_R) \wedge \text{Tense}_<(I_R)(i^*)]$

(49) Judith ate three sandwiches

(392) $\exists I \exists I_R \exists ! V[V=\llbracket \text{Judith} \rrbracket \cap \{j_i\} \wedge \exists W[W \subseteq \llbracket \text{sandwich} \rrbracket \wedge |W|=3$
$\wedge \exists Q \text{ps} W[Q=\bigcup_{i \in I}\{U \cap \llbracket \text{sandwich} \rrbracket : \llbracket \text{eat} \rrbracket (I)(i)(U)(V)\}]]$
$\wedge I=\text{Ent}^+(I_R) \wedge \text{Tense}_<(I_R)(i^*)]$

(306) John pushed the cart

(393) $\exists I \exists I_R \exists ! V[V=\llbracket \text{John} \rrbracket \cap \{j_i\} \wedge \exists ! W[W \subseteq \llbracket \text{cart} \rrbracket \wedge |W|=1$
$\wedge \exists Q \text{ps} W[Q \bigcup_{i \in I}\{U \cap \llbracket \text{cart} \rrbracket : \llbracket \text{push} \rrbracket (I)(i)(U)(V)\}]]$
$\wedge I=\text{Ent}^+(I_R) \wedge \text{Tense}_<(I_R)(i^*)]$

(314) John pushed three carts away

(394) $\exists I \exists I_R \exists ! V[V=\llbracket \text{John} \rrbracket \cap \{j_i\} \wedge \exists ! W[W \subseteq \llbracket \text{cart} \rrbracket \wedge |W|=3$
$\wedge \exists Q \text{ps} W[Q=\bigcup_{i \in I}\{U \cap \llbracket \text{cart} \rrbracket : \llbracket \text{push away} \rrbracket (I)(i)(U)(V)\}]]$
$\wedge I=\text{Ent}^+(I_R) \wedge \text{Tense}_<(I_R)(i^*)]$

(98) Two girls ate three sandwiches

(395) $\exists I \exists I_R \exists Z[Z \subseteq \llbracket \text{girl} \rrbracket \wedge |Z|=2$
$\wedge \exists P \text{ps} Z[\textsc{at}(V \cap \llbracket \text{girl} \rrbracket): \exists W[W \subseteq \llbracket \text{sandwich} \rrbracket \wedge |W|=3$
$\wedge \exists Q \text{ps} W[Q=\bigcup_{i \in I}\{U \cap \llbracket \text{sandwich} \rrbracket : \llbracket \text{eat} \rrbracket (I)(i)(U)(V)\}]]]$
$\wedge I=\text{Ent}^+(I_R) \wedge \text{Tense}_<(I_R)(i^*)]$

(162) Judith ate bread

(396) $\exists I \exists I_R \exists ! V[V=\llbracket \text{Judith} \rrbracket \cap \{j_i\} \wedge \exists W \exists P[W \subseteq \bigcup P \subseteq_m \llbracket \text{bread} \rrbracket$
$\wedge \exists Q \text{ps} W[Q=\bigcup_{i \in I}\{U \cap_m \llbracket \text{bread} \rrbracket : \llbracket \text{eat} \rrbracket (I)(i)(U)(V)\}]]$
$\wedge I=\text{Ent}^+(I_R) \wedge \text{Tense}_<(I_R)(i^*)]$

(339) Judith ate

(397) $\exists I \exists I_R \exists ! V[V=\llbracket \text{Judith} \rrbracket \cap \{j_i\} \wedge \llbracket \text{eat} \rrbracket (I)(i)(V)]$
$\wedge I=\text{Ent}^+(I_R) \wedge \text{Tense}_<(I_R)(i^*)]$

(294) Judith ate (=used to eat) three sandwiches (at breakfast)

(398) $\exists \mathit{I} \forall I[I \in \mathit{I} \rightarrow \exists I_R \exists W[W \subseteq \llbracket \text{sandwich} \rrbracket \wedge |W|=3$
$\wedge \exists Q \text{ps} W[Q=\bigcup_{i \in I}\{U \cap \llbracket \text{sandwich} \rrbracket : \llbracket \text{eat} \rrbracket (I)(i)(U)(V)\}]]$
$\wedge I=\text{Ent}^+(I_R) \wedge \text{Tense}_<(I_R)(i^*)]$

(374) Judith hated three yuppies

(399) $\exists I \exists I_R \exists ! V[V=\llbracket \text{Judith} \rrbracket \cap \{j_i\} \wedge \exists W[W \subseteq \llbracket \text{yuppy} \rrbracket \wedge |W|=3$
$\wedge \exists Q \text{ps} W[Q=\bigcup_{I}\{U \cap \llbracket \text{yuppy} \rrbracket : \llbracket \text{hate} \rrbracket (I)(0)(U)(V)\}]]$
$\wedge I=\text{Ent}^+(I_R) \wedge \text{Tense}_<(I_R)(i*)]$

The difference between PLUG^{+} and PLUG can be measured by comparing the representations of some of the sentences in this list with their counterparts at the close of Part II. The representations of the sentences in (387)–(399) now *explain* the terminativity of some of the sentences (47), (49), (51), (314) and (98), and the durativity of the others.

As argued in chapters 6–8, terminative behaviour is obtained straightforwardly on the basis of the presence of cardinality information on the sets V and W in the formulas, as well as on the basis of the appropriate thematic information $[\![\Theta]\!]_{=}$. The former information is present in the form of the expressions like |W| r n, where r∈ {<, ≤, >, ≥, =} and where n is a certain numerical value, either known to speaker and/or hearer, or not. The thematic information is made visible in the expression $\exists Q$psW[Q R ...], where R∈ {=, ⊒, ⊐} and where ... stands for information conveyed by the predicate. This has been discussed extensively from chapter 13.3 till the end of Part III. As the predicates of (47), (49), (51), (314), and (98) are all partitioned by =, the sentences are terminative.

The durative aspect of the sentences is of a diverse nature:

In (388), it is due to the presence of the bare plural information which makes it impossible to 'see' the cardinality of W, as explained in detail in chapter 8.2 and chapter 13.7.

In (390), the durative aspect is due to the fact that the thematic role of the preposition *naar* (towards) is defined as $[\![\Theta]\!]_{\subseteq}$. This was formally analysed in chapter 13.4.

In (391), the Progressive Form requires that there be only a proper subinterval whose actualization can be supported by the truth conditions of the Past tense. This has been discussed in chapter 13.8. So the function **W** cannot exhaust the partition.

In (393), the lexical definition of the verb *push* requires $[\![\Theta]\!]_{\subseteq}$ which leaves the partitioning of the internal argument NP indeterminate.

In (396), it is the measure function which cannot find the proper domain on which it has to apply, as pointed out in chapter 8.3 and chapter 13.7.

In (397), the stem-insertion strategy yields an intransitive verb. Due to the fact that there is no internal argument Y the i is unbounded. On the reduction-strategy, however, the implicit argument should be defined as bare, either directly or by a meaning postulate on verbs occurring with an overt internal argument, whose relevant part is represented as

$\exists W \exists P[W \subseteq \bigcup P \subseteq \text{Edible} \wedge |P| \geq 1 \wedge \exists Q \text{psW}[Q = \bigcup_{i \in I}\{U \cap \text{Edible}: [\![\text{eat}]\!](I)(i)(U)(V)\}]]$

In both cases, the result is durative.

In (398), there is no terminative aspect due to the fact that the habitual tense does not introduce or identify [+SQA]-information at the right level. This means that the information is below the level at which the tense operates.

In (399), it is the [–ADD TO]-verb *hate* which is lexically defined as having a zero-index, so that no progress can be expressed by the verb.

Recall from chapter 7.6 that durative aspectuality is also caused by negation: the negation sign ¬ cancels the possibility for the verb to have a mapping between its index and the internal argument NP-denotation, as, for example, in *Judith did not eat three sandwiches*. This sentence would be represented in PLUG⁺ as in (400).

(400) $\exists I \exists I_R \exists ! V[V = [\![\text{Judith}]\!] \cap \{j_i\} \wedge \neg \exists W[W \subseteq [\![\text{sandwich}]\!] \wedge |W| = 3 \wedge \exists Q \text{psW}[Q = \bigcup_{i \in I}\{U \cap [\![\text{sandwich}]\!]: [\![\text{eat}]\!](I)(i)(U)(V)\}]] \wedge I = \text{Ent}^{+}(I_R) \wedge \text{Tense}_{<}(I_R)(i^*)]$

The negation rules out the possibility for I to have been the set of indices during which it is true that Judith ate three sandwiches. Note that (400) does not exclude the existence of Judith (in fact, it is required), and that it does not exclude either that she might have eaten two sandwiches or different things. This appears to be empirically correct. The principles involved in the making of durative aspectuality hold as well as for other forms of negation discussed in chapter 7.6. It seems to me that there is some structure in the durative 'garbage can': there is no way to process the |W|-information temporally at the proper level.

Two ingredients of the NP-analysis are crucial to the present aspectual theory: (a) the treatment of NPs at the level of <<<*e*,*t*>,*t*>,*t*>; and (b) the notion of partition. Both were discussed in chapter 7 and in chapter 13. The <<<*e*,*t*>,*t*>,*t*>-analysis of NPs leads to the discrimination of a set with respect to which referential and quantificational information expressed by the NP is organized. Information about definiteness and indefiniteness – here interpreted as uniquely identified vs. introduced – identifies or introduces a set. Subsequently, information about the cardinality of this set is given: if it is present in some form, explicitly given or implicitly, then there is a cardinality statement and this is exactly where the [+SQA]-notion can be tied up. Next to these two information units, which are structurally present in the syntax of the NP as argued for in chapter 7, there is room for structured information about the arguments to which the NP being a function applies. Rather than being of the form $\lambda P\exists!W[\ldots P(W)]$ or of the form $\lambda P\exists W[\ldots P(W)]$, an array of structurings of W is put as a constraint on the semantic objects which are the values for P. In other words, the structural scheme $\ldots\exists Q\mathrm{ps}W[Q{=}P|_{[\![N]\!]}]$ is used to prepare the NP for its interaction with the verb. In this way, the representation captures the aspectual asymmetry argued for in chapter 1. This is because the structure of the representation is such that the information from the VP is embedded in the NP-information of the subject. It can be seen easily with the help of (398) when reduced to: $\exists V[\ldots\wedge\exists S\mathrm{ps}V[S{=}\{V\cap[\![N]\!]: \exists W[\ldots]\}]$. The VP-part starts with $\exists W$, but note that $\exists W$ is completely dependent on the set V. That is, if there are two sets V, each of them will have a W for which the predication holds.

It is somewhat ironical that the price for introducing machinery for dealing with complex cases complicates the simple issues. Singular proper names or singular definites or indefinites are treated as singletons, but these are hardly of interest for the concept of a partition. As pointed out, it is possible to simplify the partitioned representations if they apply to singletons, but in my view the issue is not empirically important at all. So *Judith* is analysed in terms of a choice from a set of persons bearing the name *Judith*. In this connection it is perhaps necessary to point out that sentences like (49) can be used very well in situations in which people do not know the Judith of (49), say at the beginning of a sort of conference when people are having their first lunch. The sentence may be used, for example, by the administrator as a conclusion from the information filled out on a form by Judith. However, after a second person called Judith is identified as a member of the group, the administrator will be forced to ask *Which Judith?* or *Judith who?* This is the reason why I prefer to give proper names in terms of an entity belonging to a set of name-bearers.

The terminative aspect of sentences is explained by the finiteness of the partition which is completely dependent on the presence of the cardinality information in the representation. It also presumes the mapping from indices into the partitioned NP-denotation. If there is no cardinality information about V or W in the above representations, as in the case of bare plurality, for example, there is no way to constrain the partition. In that case the function **W** defined in DEF 13.12, which is responsible for the tuning of the temporal information expressed by the verb to the partitioned structure of the NP, can operate indefinitely. Underlying the notion of such a mapping between time structure and atemporal structure is the concept of localism. That is, the function is taken to express progress in time, that is, dynamically. Mathematical functions are not dynamic *sui generis*, but there are two ways of looking at them: statically and dynamically. In the present theory the mapping between temporal structure and atemporal structure requires a dynamic view and therefore the basic ingredients of the functional machinery involved in the interpretation of [+ADD TO]-verbs are taken from the localistic tradition. This accounts for the apparent detour through the localistic framework in chapter 10, by which we got the tools for bringing (48) and (51) under the same label.

To bring two things under one label may be done in different ways: one may model one thing after the other, or one may change both. In the case of (48) and (51) the latter strategy has been chosen: *walk to three stores* is now not analysed as in Cresswell (1977) in terms of a going through a spatial region, but rather in terms of a going through a set. The physical spatial information is completely relegated to the lexical specification of *walk* itself, not to the relation between *walk* and its complement. The price to be paid at the other side is the partitioning of the atemporal set of three sandwiches. This price is an investment into a lot of insight into plurality. But it should be stressed here that the basic intuition underlying the notion of partition cannot but be localistic. This can only be seen at the moment at which a partition is made dependent on time structure.

The present study has dealt with phenomena such as the Strawson-Russell paradox, bare plurality, multiple quantification, the Progressive Form, habituality, tense, resultatives, etc. My 1972 book ended as follows: 'Whatever the formal apparatus necessary to describe the opposition between Durative and Nondurative Aspects may ultimately look like, I hope to have shown that the generalizations made in this study should be accounted for in grammar' (p. 178). The present book may end as follows: I hope to have shown that the generalizations made in this study are accounted for by the formal grammar developed here.

Notes

Part I Issues of compositionality

1 There is system behind the references to chapters, sections and definitions. If in chapter 1, for example, its second section is referred to, it is called 'section 1.2'. If it is referred to in chapter 2 or 3, it will be called 'chapter 1.2'. Likewise, definition 3 of chapter 3 will be referred to as 'DEF 3' in this chapter itself. In another chapter, it is called 'DEF 3.3'. The book is divided into three parts, each containing several chapters. The numbering of the sentences will start per part rather than per chapter, because many sentences are under analysis throughout a part.

2 The object language of the present book is predominantly English and partly Dutch. English is the object language only because it has a large aspectual overlap with Dutch, my native language. In some cases, in particular for the discussion of complex predicates in chapter 14, I shall analyse Dutch phenomena rather than English ones. I shall also discuss aspectual data from other languages.

3 They also learned that (2) and (3) could not be handled in predicate logic, so bare plurals and mass nouns were simply not treated in first-order logics. This situation changed drastically in the seventies and eighties.

4 There is a very rich tradition in linguistics in the nineteenth century and the first part of this century which focussed on the temporal properties of sentences. In Verkuyl (1972) this tradition was taken into account.

5 More recently attempts have been made to analyse sentences like (11) in terms of event structure (e.g. Krifka 1989a, 1989b); see chapter 13 below for a more detailed analysis of event semantics.

6 As the English counterparts show, the same phenomenon occurs in English. I shall discuss this phenomenon with the help of Dutch because in Dutch and not in English complex verbs are made rather than verbs followed by a particle. In view of the fact that Dutch is in this respect 'closer to' the situation in Slavic languages and due to the fact that there are subtle differences between the meanings of the Dutch verbs and their English counterparts, I shall describe the Dutch facts.

7 I would have preferred to discuss the English sentence *John walked to the store*, but for English native speakers this means that John must have reached the store, according to, for example, R. Quirk and S. Greenbaum's *A University Grammar of English* (1973).

8 For example, Bennett and Partee (1978), Dowty (1979), Taylor (1977), Cresswell (1977), Vlach (1981), Parsons (1985, 1989), Lascarides (1988).

9 Notably, Comrie (1976) does not make a difference between aspect and Aktionsart.

It is made by Bache (1985) and Barentsen (1985), among many others.

10 In the mid-sixties, there were two localistic branches: Gruber's Thematic Framework and somewhat later Fillmore's Case Grammar. Both emanated from generative grammar but both were kept outside the mainstream of syntactically oriented research. In both, the study of argument structure is central. That is, verbs are taken as n-place predicates and what linguistics has to offer to logicians as far as representations of the form $P^n(x_1, ...x_n)$ are concerned is information about the specific structurally semantic content of the role of an arbitrary x_i involved in the predication. Thus, x_1 may be the Agent and x_2 the Patient, for certain P^2, whereas for other P^2, x_1 should be an Experiencer and x_2 an Instrument. And so on. Fillmore (1968) sought alliance with the grammatical tradition in which case expressed by nouns and noun phrases is more central than subject and object; and he found it: generative grammar even became popular among classical grammarians, though for a very short period. Gruber's system was focussed more on temporal structure.

11 Actually, a distinction was made between durative and non-durative sentences. At that time, I still divided nondurative aspect into terminative and momentaneous aspect. This distinction was dropped in the eighties and rather than *non-durative* I am now using *terminative* as the opposite of *durative*.

12 Actually, in Verkuyl (1972: 14) it is also said that nodes like PERFORM, MOVEMENT, TAKE and CHANGE can be reduced to one primitive category ADD TO.

13 The problem was that in the sixties logical courses were mainly syntactic; courses including model-theoretic interpretation became fashionable around 1974, so semantic insights into generative grammar were expressed informally, or at best quasi-formally by Gruberian categories.

14 By the impossibility of finding convincing criteria for determining a systematic mapping between the thematic roles and their carriers, Gruber's work soon fell into disfavour with generative syntacticians, the more so after Chomsky (1970) cut short any discussion about this mapping in terms of lexical decomposition. Gruber's system was put aside, if it ever penetrated into the heart of the matter. Jackendoff (1972, 1976, 1978; 1983, 1990) is actually the only one in the main stream of MIT generative grammar of the seventies who has been constantly trying to stress the value of Gruber's system. He has now developed a cognitively based semantics, called Conceptual Semantics. It should be said that there was an important stream of related psycholinguistic work in this area in the 1970s (Miller 1972; Miller and Johnson-Laird 1976). Jackendoff's work tries to combine this sort of work in cognitive psychology with the generative tradition.

15 Figure 1 is somewhat misleading in the sense that the [–ADD TO, +SQA] combination is not given. However, it expresses the intermediate position of processes quite clearly. See Figure 8 in chapter 2.11 for the full picture.

16 So Vendler's well-known quadripartition is not used. One of the reasons for this is that the criteria separating his four aspectual classes were well known in the linguistic literature on Slavic aspect between 1875 and 1950. Moreover, it ignores the systematic contribution of information coming from the (argument) noun phrases. So, even though I appreciated Vendler's 'Verbs and Times' as a masterful essay, I consider it as an ontological study relevant at the level of lexical information rather than at a linguistically, that is structurally, relevant level. The terminological triple

State, Process and Event was used by Comrie (1976) and Mourelatos (1978), among others. Bach (1981) proposed to use the term *eventualities* as a cover term for the three categories.

17 In chapter 14, it will be argued that *Judith ate* is durative due to the fact that a two-place [+ADD TO]-verb not realizing its internal (second) argument should be analysed at the level of VP as [–T] because the verb stem selects an argument frame in which [+ADD TO]-verbs are unbounded.

18 It was defended for the first time at the fifth Amsterdam Colloquium in 1984. The asymmetry is compatible with dominant principles of GB-syntax: if the S-node is interpreted at the top without taking into account structure, every piece of information at the (lexical) bottom must percolate upwards. Given (67), this would not be possible because features have to percolate via non-heads; given (69), it is possible due to the presence of the VP-structure (Martin Everaert, pers. comm.).

19 Here the labelling is, of course, in terms of the generative grammar of the time. In current GB-analysis, the S of Figure 2 would be called VP.

20 However, there are also rules which apply both to idioms and their non-idiomatic counterparts. See, for example, Abeillé and Schabes (1990).

21 Coopmans and Everaert's analysis in the GB-framework assumes that *the bucket* is linked to the lexically absorbed internal (thematic) Θ-role of *kick*, where *the bucket* is a non-argument linked to *kick*. In other words, in the idiomatic VP *the bucket* has no argument role.

22 It seems to me that it should be more fruitful to report about the Dutch examples rather than to force myself into a description of corresponding English data. I presume that similar effects may be detected in English, but the judgments in the area of idioms are simply too subtle for non-native speakers. The examples (without the durational adverbials) are taken from Coopmans and Everaert (1988).

23 This type of argumentation seems to bear on the discussion about configurational and non-configurational languages. Suppose that there is a non-configurational language L where in two-place predicates the argument NPs are marked by cases, say c_1 and c_2 respectively, and one can show that aspectually the verb is related more closely to the NP having c_2 than to the NP having c_1. Now, if the NP with c_2 corresponds to direct object NPs in English, then it can be argued, as done in chapter 13.4–13.6, that aspect formation in L supports the view that L has some level at which V and the NP with c_2 form a VP-like unit (Chomsky 1981: 127ff.).

24 Most of the sections were part of 'Aspectual Classes and Aspectual Composition' which appeared in *Linguistics and Philosophy* 1989. Apart from minor stylistic and organizational changes, there are some major changes. Firstly, the discussion about Taylor (1977) is cut out and incorporated in chapter 9; secondly in section 2.4 a new argument against the distinction between Achievements and Accomplishments has been added; thirdly, a section about Carlson (1981) was added; finally a section was dedicated to Moens' system. The sketch of my own theory in section 6 of ACAC is of course left out.

25 In this connection, it seems fair and historically appropriate to give some quotes from a letter by Vendler written to me in 1987. He said: 'I wrote that paper as a third year grad. student 30 years ago. At that time I did not know anything about linguistics, and I did not even realize that what I am doing matches Aristotle. My aim was

at the time to refute Ryle's claim that seeing is always an achievement. This is the reason why I focussed on action verbs, i.e. what humans do (as you correctly point out).' … 'I am very amused at seeing my old paper being milked beyond its capacities. My four classes have acquired a life of their own, like grown up children. And the parent can only watch their career. I hope you treat them well.' In a postscript to the letter mentioned earlier, Vendler says: 'By the way, in my original manuscript I formulated the time schemata of those classes by quantifying over times, and producing neat formulae. Phil Review cut them out: at that time they refused to print logical formulae. Tempora mutantur…'

26 In his letter mentioned earlier, Vendler writes: 'By the way accomplishments vs. achievements, I always regarded the latter as a *terminus* of a process (e.g. winning *vis à vis* running, reaching the top *vis à vis* climbing, spotting *vis à vis* looking for, etc.). This (by and large) is not true of accomplishments (e.g. climbing the mountain or running the Marathon).'

27 For Comrie (pers. comm.) *Do you run?* can only be interpreted as a habitual. The answer *Yes* indicates that I do habitually run, but there is no intention involved. Maybe this is why Dowty did not have it.

28 An unexpected complication can be found in Wagner (1839), where Senta sings: *Vor Anker alle sieben Jahr', ein Weib zu frein, geht er ans Land* , which means 'At anchor every seventh year, he goes ashore to seek a wife'. Aspectually, the sentence *Er geht ans Land* (He goes ashore) has terminative aspect, but *alle sieben* does not mean 'all seven' but rather 'every seventh'.

29 In chapter 11.1, this criterion will be discussed as a means to raise objections against the Davidsonian approach.

30 Kenny (1963), Taylor (1977), Mourelatos (1978), Galton (1984).

31 My contention that stereotypes are involved is confirmed by Vendler in his letter: 'Again, I did not consider esoteric or special circumstances (e.g. computer use, sport-commentator's reports, etc.). I took, say, writing, or drawing or winning, in their stereotypes (as current in the 1950s): the "folk"-idea of them.' However, Vendler continues: 'Nevertheless, I still think that the fourfold classification is ~~still~~, useful as an abstract schema in discussing the actual behavior of verbs: "… here the verb V behaves like an achievement but there (in another context) as an accomplishment…" and the like.' In this way, however, Vendler would use parameters rather than classes.

32 Comrie (1976) also uses this tripartition.

33 This formulation improves on the formulation I used in Verkuyl (1989: 59).

34 In Dik (1989: 98 ff.) a related tree is proposed, which contains in fact a doubling of the classes by an extra parameter [±control]. Thus, it is possible to distinguish between, for example, *dynamic* and *active*, as subclasses of Processes and Actions, respectively, which together constitute Events.

35 For a more detailed analysis of the five parameters involved see Verkuyl (1989: 64–67). I shall skip it here, because the other two parameters do not really matter in the present context.

36 There is a second objection, which does not bear directly on the question of whether or not Vendler-classes are useful for the study of aspect. Does Dowty really explain things here? I think he does not. Formula (173d) may be verified by $i_2=i_1$. In that

case, it would mean that there is a unique subinterval of i_1, namely i_1 itself at which sleep'(j) is true. But then it is hard to see why *John slept in an hour* is not well formed. Nothing in the formula prevents Statives and Activities from occupying the place reserved for Accomplishments and Achievements. The same sort of objection goes for (174d): it satisfies the situation in which i_2=i_1. Why should the interval corresponding to *an hour* have subinterval structure under all circumstances?

37 Hoeksema uses the symbol + instead of $\sqcup$ to represent the summation operation. For lattice-theoretical approaches, see Link (1983, 1984), Krifka (1987, 1989a, 1989b).

38 This move appears to be justified in view of the role of [–Count] in the characterization of States. Suppose that x=y, and x is an instant. Then, States would be instantaneous or punctual, and that is what Hoeksema does not want.

39 Thus I leave aside the category of Momentaneous sentences (– – +) to which *I hit him* belongs, and the Dynamic category (+ + +) exemplified by *The caravan stood in its own place*, the former being a 'refinement' of Achievements, the latter being intermediate between States and Actitivies.

40 I have actually given a mirror image of their scheme as their network can be projected into a scheme that will be discussed below in Figure 8.

41 For a quick survey and an extension of his work, see Lascarides (1988) and Caenepeel (1989).

42 Comrie (1976: 41–44) opposes punctuality and 'durativity', saying that punctual situations do not have internal structure, whereas non-punctual situations do have internal structure. He fails, however, to prove that this distinction is formally marked in some languages as he sets out to do, because the opposition between the Hungarian *zörren* (to give a knock) and *zörög* (to knock repeatedly) is not convincing: semelfactivity vs. repetition cannot be equated with 'having no length' and 'having length'.

Part II Noun phrase structure

1 For convenience, I shall often refer only to [+SQA], but it should be understood that its counterpart [–SQA] is also assumed in the *mutatis mutandis* mode.

2 The text is slightly adapted to a different numbering. Also, the original text had * rather than #, but there * had the same interpretation as now is given to #, which is used to unburden the asterisk.

3 Hence the use of the term *node* for the carrier of the semantic information 'Specified'.

4 They are rather unclear about how the lexicalization of *a* and *the* should take place. This was a general problem of the Gruberian polycategorial syntax of the time.

5 *Eat* would be an accomplishment verb in Dowty's terms. Activity verbs are verbs like *walk*, *sleep*, etc. See chapter 2 for this terminology. I do not take into account here my objections against the use of Vendler-classes as formulated in that chapter, so I will accept here the terms used by Dowty.

6 Actually, Dowty also gives four positive specifications, for example, $[_{VPdur}[_{V}$AGENTIVE$]$ + $[_{NP}[$INDEFINITE PLUR$]]$, but it is clear that (12) is the only device throwing out ill-formed expressions. All five representations were rejected explicitly in Verkuyl (1972).

7 Recall from chapter 1 that the verbal nodes represent semantic information (provisionally) represented by the node [+ADD TO], which expresses progress in time, or non-stativity. Scheme (13) is simplified by leaving out the indirect object NP and by representing (UN)SPECIFIED QUANTITY OF A as [±SQA].

8 In fact, it shows that Dowty had a look at page 52 of my book, from which (12) must have been taken. But on page 53, it says: 'I have said that the node AGENTIVE is provisionally introduced to account for a certain meaning element in the Verbs under discussion. It will be shown that there are reasons to describe the composition of Aspects in terms of more elementary semantic categories.'

9 Sentence (16) will be ignored here because the discussion of mass nouns would complicate the exposition. However, I will discuss sentences like (16) in chapter 8.3.

10 Note that the 'there is at least an x' meaning of $\exists x$ makes it possible to interpret (20) as saying that John discovered one flea. So one must assume that $\forall t$ requires that there are at least two times.

11 For example, Partee, Ter Meulen and Wall (1990) and Gamut (1991).

12 I assume some familiarity with the construction of the logical language based on DEF 1. In particular, I make use of Gamut (1991, II: 79ff.).

13 V_1, V_2, A, N and Det are treated as variables.

14 Thus, g[v/d] is the assignment which is like g but for the possible difference with respect to the variable v.

15 See the papers collected in Ter Meulen (1983), Van Benthem and Ter Meulen (1985) and Gärdenfors (1987); also Van Benthem (1986), Keenan and Stavi (1986), Keenan and Faltz (1985), Westerståhl (1985), Zwarts (1981, 1986), etc.

16 E will be used for a specific domain used in examples as well as more generally for any universe of discourse.

17 One may rewrite (45)–(47) and (50) in terms of cardinalities of the intersections but this is not necessary.

18 There are determiners which can be interpreted as three- or more-place relations, but I shall restrict myself here to two-place determiners. If there is no misunderstanding I shall write $[\![\alpha]\!]$ rather than $[\![\alpha]\!]_M$. Also, I shall write [[child]] if I refer to the denotation of the Noun *child* irrespective of its surface grammatical form. Thus, [[the children]] and [[the_{plur} child]] are the same semantic object.

19 For example, it is not common to write $\lambda x.\text{child}(x) \subseteq X$.

20 Note that also [[all children]] $\Leftrightarrow$ $\{X | [\![\text{child}]\!] \subseteq X\}$, so $\{X | [\![\text{child}]\!] \subseteq X\}$ will be used rather than $\boldsymbol{\lambda} X.[\![\text{child}]\!] \subseteq X$ when it is easier to treat a semantic object as a set rather than as a function.

21 Note that $\wp(E')$ is now considerably larger than $\wp(E)$. It means that $\mathbf{M}_1$-definitions like (51) must be adapted. It also shows why it is virtually impossible to construct manageable models. As the model is only intended to demonstrate certain aspects of GQT, I will continue to refer to E as the domain of discourse rather than to E' even though I sometimes deal with the extended E.

22 So, the direct object determiner [[three]] does not simply relate two sets, as in the general scheme $D_E AB$ of Figure 10, but rather a set and a relation. To generalize over the two different sorts of quantifying situation, one may apply the so-called Geach rule which says that if an expression is of type <a,b> it is also of type <<c,a>,

<c,b>>, for all categories c. This means that if an NP is of type <<*e*,*t*>,*t*>, it is also of type <<*e*,<*e*,*t*>>, <*e*,*t*>>, where a=<*e*,*t*>, b=*t* and c=*e*. In other words, the direct object NP may take a two-place verb to yield a unary predicate of type <*e*,*t*>, that is, the VP, in this case the set of sandwich-eaters.

23 Thus a difference is made between the N *Judith* and the NP *Judith*. For the latter it is assumed that it contains a definite determiner. Proper names will be discussed below in chapter 7. Here it suffices to use (44) for the sketch of the GQT-framework.

24 When a quantifier satisfies the constraint $X\cap Y\in Q \Rightarrow (X\in Q \;\&\; Y\in Q)$ it is monotone increasing; when it satisfies $(X\in Q \;\&\; Y\in Q) \Rightarrow X\cap Y\in Q$, it is monotone decreasing. So a filter is a conjunction of these two constraints.

25 In Strawson (1964) it is pointed out that Strawson shares his views with Quine (1960) and Austin (1961), among others. In this paper, Strawson strikes a conciliatory chord by trying to demonstrate that both points of views are reasonable and that 'it is more instructive to see how both are reasonable, how both represent different ways of being impressed by the facts'. In the sections to come I shall follow this strategy.

26 There seems to be a difference between English and Dutch pointed out by Jackendoff (pers. comm.). In both languages the universal quantifier may precede the definite article. So one has *all ravens are black* and *alle raven zijn zwart* as against *all the ravens are black* and *al de raven zijn zwart.* The sentences with the article are clearly to be interpreted as pertaining to a specified quantity. In Dutch, however, it is easier than in English also to interpret the universal quantifier without the definite article as pertaining to a specified quantity. Thus, the proper translation of the Dutch *alle plaatsen zijn bezet* is *all the seats are taken* rather than *all seats are taken*, though the latter is not impossible, especially in imperative sorts of statement. The subtle difference between Dutch and English is ignored here, but if the facts discussed in this section do not completely cover English they pertain to Dutch.

27 So, for De Jong and Verkuyl (1985) there is no difference between (154) and *Bachelors are unmarried.* It is not difficult to find the counterpart of the well-known white raven: it is the bachelor who married some foreign woman to get her into the country, but who continues to live as he did before: as a bachelor, the marriage contract being reduced to a formal technicality.

28 A plausible Russellian countermove would be to say that the use of a durational adverbial requires there to be temporal structure in the domain of discourse, which means that we speak more specifically about a particular model than in the case of sentences without these adverbials, so that the existential presuppositions increase as a function of the increase of domain structure. This could explain why we require there to be 'real' entities if we use *all* and *the three* in sentences like (158)–(161). This means that if someone says (159), we are bound to think of a domain in which there are dogs, whereas sentences like (151) might have insufficient structure for presuppositions to hold in a specific model. I do not find this way out very satisfactory.

29 For convenience I will speak about an a-analysis or an analysis at the a-level, when I speak about a GQT-analysis of NPs taken as denoting semantic objects of type a.

30 In generative syntax one would represent the X-bar syntax yielding (170) as:

(i) $N^{max} \rightarrow Det\ N^{max-1}$;
(ii) $N^{max-1} \rightarrow Num\ N^i$
(iii) $N^i \rightarrow \ldots N^i \ldots\ (0 \leq i \leq 1)$

In assuming a separate place for numerical information, it relates to Bresnan (1973) and Selkirk (1977). X-bar theoretically, it differs from Jackendoff (1977) as well as from Stowell (1981), and other X-bar systems developed in the eighties. The X-bar system in (169) was defined on the basis of an underlying type-logical characterization of syntactic categories, with binary branching. For a thorough analysis of different X-bar systems, see Van Eyck (1985) and Stuurman (1985). Abney's 1987 version can also be interpreted type-logically. It will be discussed in chapter 8.1. I assume that (169) fits in with the more flexible categorial systems discussed in, for example, Moortgat (1988).

31 The idea of a neutral Noun stem has already been around in linguistics for quite a long time (e.g., Jespersen 1909, 1924).

32 As they take $<e,t>$ to yield $<<e,t>,t>$, they are 'on top of' the adjectival structure. An N^1 like *little children* would be analysed as: [pl[little[child]]].

33 See Van Deemter (1991), Zeevat (1989) for some arguments against familiarity. In Verkuyl (1981), $\exists!W$ was written as ΘW to underscore the degree of identification expressed by *these*, *the* and *all*, but here this aspect of the analysis is left aside. The information in (112) will be dealt with in terms of Westerståhl's context sets in chapter 7.3. Ojeda (1990, 1991) discusses an interesting analysis of the definite article by taking it as denoting the function which assigns to each $F \subseteq E$ which has a greatest element, the family $\{X \subseteq E | \Gamma(F) \in E\}$, where $\Gamma = [\![the]\!]$ assigns the sum of all elements of X, that is, asserts the existence of a greatest element in X. Ojeda's analysis presumes a mereological framework, but his definition is intended to retain the virtues of the Russellian approach (existence, uniqueness) rather than to proceed on the Heim-line (by dropping the uniqueness-condition).

34 In Verkuyl (1981), $W \subseteq [\![child]\!]$ was written as $\forall x(W(x) \rightarrow Child(x))$.

35 This was worked out in Verkuyl (1987b), following Jacobs (1982). Hence, *not* is analysed as $\lambda\beta(\lambda p(\neg p)(\alpha(\beta)))$, where α and β range Geach-like over variable types. In the present case, one would obtain something like $\lambda X(\lambda p(\neg p)(\lambda Y.\mathit{came\_in}(Y)(X)))$. As the argument is of type *t*, it would convert into $\lambda X.\neg came\_in'(X)$, where came_in' is of type $<<e,t>,t>$. This is interpreted as $\lambda \mathbf{X}.\mathbf{X} \not\subseteq [\![came\_in]\!]$.

36 One might even argue that the English modifier *all* does 'in the plural mode' what *every* does in *every child* 'in the singular mode'. That is, *all* in *all the children* seems to strengthen the information already expressed by *the children* (which identifies a group of children by $\exists!$) by redundantly underscoring that all individuals are involved. I am hesitant whether this position can be defended, but it certainly is a plausible way of explaining the subtle difference between *the children* and *all the children.*

37 See, for example, Jackendoff (1983, 1987, 1990), Zwarts and Verkuyl (1991).

38 In my opinion the 'movie-interpretation' of sentences like (251) and (252) offers many interesting perspectives. Linguists are supposed to sort out which factors are

linguistic and which are not. One way out of the morass of knowledge of the world is to assume that what really is at issue here is a systematic difference between speaking about different models (each having its own temporal structure and its own assignments) in which mafia bosses occur on the one hand, and speaking about one particular model on the other. Suppose that we may assume that in the interpretation of (252) we do not take into account the time of a particular model, but that we move so to say discretely along a time axis which contains indices offering entrance to a specific model. One might argue that in sentences like (250), the adverbial *for centuries* applies — given our 'normal' knowledge of the world — to a period covering a set of models rather than to one particular model itself. (Think of this in terms of the series of movies in (251) or (252) which we have been watching, each movie being a model with its own assignments.) The speaker may offer a range of models over a certain period with respect to the statement *the mafia boss stabbed his rival with a knife*. In this case, there is no aspectual repetition involved. On the other hand, as soon as the temporal structure induced by the use of the durational adverbials is a part of one particular model, aspectual repetition is imperative. This leads to the thesis that terminative aspect as expressed by sentences meeting the *for an hour*– and the *in an hour*–tests, crucially involves denotation in a specific model. I will come back to this issue in more detail in chapter 12.

39 One might wonder whether $|X|>1$ the definition of PL in (173) $\lambda Y \lambda X[X \subseteq Y \wedge |X|>1]$ should not have been replaced by $|X|\geq 1$ right away, on the ground that it might have prevented the problem signalled in connection with the derivation (231). Note, however, that one might accept Ojeda's proposal without being forced to revise the bareness-analysis: any cardinality information at the level of W will be interpreted as [+SQA]-information.

40 Bernard Comrie (pers. comm.) pointed out that (271) may pertain to a specific group of soldiers coming into town periodically. This observation strengthens the point at issue, because its English counterpart (240) also has this habitual interpretation.

41 i = indexical definite marker; PRP = perfect of recent past; SQ = sequence marker; FIN = final suffix marking the end of a sentence; = symbolizes a clitic; – is a morpheme boundary; A3 = indirect anaphoric definite marker.

42 P is a variable of type $<s,<e,t>>$, so $^{\vee}P$ is of type $<e,t>$. See chapter 13.1 for the intensional logic made use of in this representation.

43 The present theory also differs from Krifka's (1988) approach to genericity, mainly due to the fact that he employs first-order techniques to deal with genericity. It should be pointed out that the above discussion of bare plurality might be seen as locating certain phenomena outside the realm of 'real' genericity, which have been included up to now.

44 The present analysis differs from Dik's treatment of genericity and specificity (1989: 143ff.). Dik makes a distinction between reference to 'any arbitrary token of the ensemble designated by the term' and reference to 'a particular token of the ensemble designated by the term'. His notion of specificity is more closely tied up with reference (and thus with assignment of a specific entity to a variable) than with cardinality information. In the present analysis, there seems to be no need for a separate 'specific' operator, due to the fact that NPs are treated at the $<<<e,t>,t>,t>$-level. I will come back to this point in chapter 8.2.

45 From here to section 7.6 the text follows the main line of Verkuyl and Van der Does (1991).

46 The issue of the existence of intermediate readings has resulted in a debate of Lasersohn against Gillon (see Gillon (1987, 1990) and Lasersohn (1989)).

47 See Lasersohn (1989) for arguments against intermediate readings, and Gillon (1990) for a reply.

48 Apart from this, Verkuyl and Van der Does (1991) have two more objections against Gillon (1987). Commonly it is understood that NPs denote sets of VP extensions and not just sets. So, how does Gillon's proposal extend to arbitrary NPs, and how does it deal with multiple quantification? Moreover, is the notion of minimal cover general enough?

49 In Van der Does (1992) it is proved that minimal covers are pseudo-partitions, but not conversely. The notions discussed here relate to one another as follows: partitions $\subset$ minimal covers $\subset$ pseudo-partitions $\subset$ covers.

50 This is more general than another kind of restriction which is often used implicitly: Y restr $X =_{df} Y \cap \wp(X)$. Here the restriction is to those groups in Y which consist of X's only (Van Benthem 1991).

51 Here, only one of the (at least) four meanings of *many* is treated. k is a (contextually determined) constant between 0 and 1. See Westerståhl (1985).

52 In this way a specific interpretation is taken as intermediate between purely indefinite and definite. Another intermediate case is *It was in a year in which he went to the US* (Verkuyl 1973).

Part III Temporal structure

1 For example, in Von Wright (1965). Gruber's dissertation is from 1965. Both turn out to be part of a tradition that is not very well described, historically. For example, Russell's analysis of change as expressed by sentences like *Brutus killed Caesar* in Russell (1940, chapter 2) strikes me as very congenial to what Von Wright and Gruber see as the essence of change. Gruber is part of the linguistic, so-called localistic tradition.

2 The present discussion of Lascarides' work is based on Lascarides (1988). Part of the main results of this work is given in Lascarides (1991).

3 In Montague Grammar intransitive verbs like *walk* are also called Intransitive Verb *Phrases*. So the difference between V and VP is somewhat diffuse in Montague Grammar.

4 Later in the seventies notions such as truth *for* an interval, truth *in* an interval emerged (Bach 1980).

5 Dowty's representations will be simplified. For example, intensions are left out because they do not play a role. I shall also write $]\!]_{M,i,g}$ rather than $]\!]_{M,w,i,g}$ as the world parameter does not play a role here.

6 This is exactly the point where Lascarides (1988: 46ff.) caught Dowty in the act of committing an inconsistency because his definition of the progressive operator PROG does not allow any gap, which prevents him from correctly describing sentences like *Max is winning the race*.

7 It would not really matter for the point being made if the representation were:

CAUSE BECOME (j,open′(ιx(door′(x)))).

8 Note that AT(i,X) means 'X holds for the interval i'. It does not mean simple inclusion. If Dowty's definition were changed in this sense, the problem with (9c) would not be solved. ∃i[PAST(i) ...] is to be interpreted as saying that i is earlier than i*, where i* is the point of speech.

9 Moreover, the situation is made more complicated by Dowty's condition c, which excludes both $\neg\phi$ and ϕ in the BECOME-part to be true at i. Now this has to be extended to the *walk*-part of the representation. Another objection that could be made is that the categorial system used by Dowty forced him into distinguishing a transitive preposition *to* which, due to another choice made by Dowty, must be specified as a CAUSE BECOME predicate. I shall not use this as an objection because I consider this as an artefact of the syntax which could be improved on and because I do comment on Dowty just on the line of thought about aspectual composition.

10 On page 225, we find the representation of the sentence *Mary made John wash the car*: ιx(car′(x)∧∃Q(Q(m) CAUSE wash′(j,x))). But here *wash the car* is obviously treated duratively.

11 It is remarkable that Taylor used the Progressive Form here to make his point.

12 Again I have left out all world-indices because they do not play any role at all for the argument.

13 Comrie (pers. comm.) would object against BY LAND because of sentences like *Jesus walked on the water* or *I felt as if I was walking on air*. I will take Jackendoff's definition as a rough approximation of the basic sense expressed by the verb, that is, the fact that some medium is strong enough to carry the body of the walker.

14 This paper appeared in 1976 as a publication of Nijmegen University. As it was partly written in 1975 (in Dutch) and 1976 (in English) I did not know of any discussion based on Bennett and Partee (1978) and Taylor (1977). So the lexical analysis of John's walk in terms of 'temporal sultanas' was made independent of Taylor's philosophical analysis which appeared in 1977. It will be evident that quite different conclusions were drawn. I was focussed on cognitive-psychological work. The English version was read at the Stirling conference on psycholinguistics in June 1976.

15 As I restricted my analysis to John's walk, the function is defined on individuals. In Verkuyl (1978), no attention was given to plurality; (50) is a simplified version of the definition used at the time.

16 As observed earlier, Dowty (1986: 42) also works with the notion of 'most subintervals' (though at a different level of analysis) but there *most* applies to time intervals.

17 The present definition deviates from, for example, Verkuyl (1987a) in that it keeps the point zero constant rather than, for example, $\forall i \in I$, if $i=(n-1,n)$, $s(i)=(n,n+1)$.

18 Metaphors can be telling but sometimes their source may contain elements leading to considerations that should not bear on the issue: a standard odometer also counts the tenths. However, this does not make the odometer an instrument indicating **R**-structure: the successor's function also applies to this part. However interesting this **N**-substructure may be, I leave it out of consideration and assume a simple odometer.

19 From here to section 10.5, the text follows Verkuyl and Zwarts (1992), though not literally.

20 This sort of ontology, however strange at first sight, is as plausible or implausible as, for example, Link's ontology. In general, a simpler type-theoretical construction of the domain of interpretation leads to a simplification of the formal language. The price for it: counterintuitive entities. The prize for it: more generalizations. See Zwarts and Verkuyl (1991) for a model-theoretic analysis of Jackendoff's framework.

21 As Jackendoff's theory does not include quantification, it is sometimes hard to compare representations. In Zwarts and Verkuyl (1991) a model-theoretic analysis of his Conceptual Semantics is given, in which it is pointed out that $[_{\text{Thing}}\ ]$ is to be taken as a sorted variable, without descriptive content.

22 We represent *the stores* here in a way Jackendoff would do. Thus, [STORES] rather than [THE STORES]. The treatment of quantifiers is still the Achilles' heel of his Conceptual Semantics. In Zwarts and Verkuyl (1991) it is assumed that the brackets around [STORES] represent (or abbreviate) determiner structure.

23 *The road leads to the store* is durative due to the function EXT, by which Jackendoff explains that the road does not move to the store, but that it extends along a path to the store. The application of EXT results in a state.

24 The Plus-principle raises a problem for Jackendoff: in (87) the noun *stores* is [–bounded], but the NP *three stores* is [+bounded]. In other words, the feature [–bounded] assigned to N must be of a different nature than the [–bounded] of the NP *stores*. So Jackendoff must distinguish between different sorts of boundedness.

25 Though it might be confusing to use the letter s both for *stores* and *sandwiches*, we do it to underscore the correspondence between the analyses of *John walked to the store* and *Judith ate three sandwiches*.

26 In a more precise logical formulation this means that we talk about the p in $\exists p[p \in [\![\text{TO(STORE)}]\!] \wedge \ldots]$ and not about $[\![\text{TO(STORE)}]\!]$.

27 This raises the question of how p_n is obtained. This question has not been discussed in Verkuyl and Zwarts (1992), but it will be taken up in chapter 13.5.

28 For a more detailed description of the German counterpart of *around* see Wunderlich (1990). Jackendoff points out that there is a third , 'detour', meaning of *around*, which is captured by the definition of *um* (around) in Wunderlich: $\lambda x\lambda y[\text{LOCATED}(x,\text{EXT}(y)) \wedge \text{ENCLOSED}(\Pi(x),y)]$, which expresses a relation between some x located within a region surrounding or neighbouring y where $\Pi(x)$, the path of x, (roughly) is or covers the border of a region enclosing y. The detour meaning is obtained by defining EXT(y) partially in the context of a goal-directed motion.

29 For an extension along these lines see Nikanne (1990).

30 In the last line of this derivation and the ones to follow, we will write EAT rather than GO in order to underscore that other semantic information is to be included as well. EAT subsumes GO.

31 Barwise and Perry (1983) are taken to Davidsonian quantification. However, in Situation Semantics event structure can be represented in terms of so-called infons (states of affairs, possible facts, consisting of a relation and a number of arguments) supported by situations (Cooper 1991). In general, the tendency is to prevent loss of information about event structure at discourse level. Infons would allow [±SQA]-information as defined in chapter 2, so it seems as if terminativity can be expressed by infons.

32 In 'The Logical Form of Action Sentences' several attempts are discussed to deal with the logic of change as expressed by sentences of natural language. Davidson argues against the Von Wrightian $\neg\phi T\phi$-analysis that it can make no difference between sentences like *He flew from New York to LA* and *He drove from New York to LA*, because there is no way to make a difference between *fly* and *drive*. This is not a very strong argument because lexical entries like (59) provide easily for restrictively modifying information on verbs.

33 There is a group of arguments based on the idea that it should be possible to characterize events in terms of identity statements. Thus, according to Davidson, it is very hard to think of a theory of action if you are not able to talk about a certain action with the help of different descriptions. If someone burned a paper which happens to be an important document the sentences *He burned a paper* and *He burned an important document* should refer to the same action (in that particular model). Another argument based on identity concerns explanation. If a catastrophe happened in the village last week, and we try to explain what happens, this description can be recast into a statement about an avalanche, and this statement again can be given a redescription. In all these different more precise formulations, there should be some constant and this constant can be conceived of as an event. A third argument in this group concerns the identity theory of mind which is said to require that mental events are identified with certain physiological events.

34 See Higginbotham (1983) for similar observations but different conclusions; see however Neale (1988).

35 For convenience, I shall use the neo-Davidsonian rather than the Davidsonian representation. Davidson would have $\exists e(\text{Capsizing}(\text{Doris},\text{her\_canoe},e) \wedge \text{Yesterday}(e))$.

36 See also chapter 2.3. Note that Doris may have capsized two different canoes (it might be easier to see this in view of sentences like *Martina broke her tennis racket yesterday and today*). Note also that one cannot make use of the fact that the conjunction of two NPs is involved, because the observation holds as well for *on Friday and on Saturday*.

37 See Carlson (1984) and Chierchia (1984), who have proposed the third postulate.

38 Comrie (pers. comm.) points out that *give* in (153)–(160) gets the specialized meaning 'donate'. I am not sure whether Dowty was aware of this, but there are verbs that do not show this specialization, such as *hand*.

39 See Landman (1989) for a criticism against the lattice-theoretical approach. See also Lønning (1989).

40 Subscripts on the operation symbols indicate the domain O or E; if there are no subscripts the operation applies to both domains.

41 In Krifka (1987), an earlier version of Krifka (1989a) an operator COMB was used to combine the direct object and its verb. So, *bread* translates to bread′ and $\forall x \forall P \forall Q[\mathbf{COMB}(x)(P)(Q) \equiv \lambda e \exists x[P(e) \wedge Q(x)]]$ provided for the information now contained in $\lambda P \lambda e \exists y[P(e) \wedge \text{bread}'(y)]$ itself.

42 Krifka (1989a: 77): $\forall x \forall P[FU(P) = x \Leftrightarrow \forall x'[P(x') \rightarrow x' \sqsubseteq x \wedge \forall x''[\forall x'[P(x') \rightarrow x' \sqsubseteq x''] \rightarrow x \sqsubseteq x'']]]]$.

43 This representation is from Krifka (1989b: 224 and 233).

44 It also should exclude iterativity but as this does not play a role here, I leave it out of consideration.

45 The standard modal notion of *accessibility* can be explained very well in terms of visibility: one can 'see' other worlds or not.

46 Rossana Petrova (pers. comm.) pointed out to me that in Bulgarian (176), when occurring with the durational adverbial, assumes two different forms to bring about an interpretation: (a) *As premestvah kubceto naliavo ot piramidata* which together with the durational adverbial conveys the idea of repetition; and (b) *As mestih kubceto naliavo ot piramidata* which together with the durational adverbial expresses a 'step-by-step' process not completed within half an hour. This distinction is not grammaticalized in Dutch, but in Bulgarian, secondary imperfectivization after prefixal perfectivization in the Imperfect tense yields the former effect, whereas the 'stretching' is effected by imperfective aspect in the Aorist tense.

47 This is not technically possible with the present Apple system 7.0 but System 8.0 or Big Blue Apple System 9.0 will certainly provide for this feature.

48 Most of the text of this section is taken from Verkuyl (1990), though some revisions have been made.

49 See Verkuyl (1972: 165ff.) for a detailed analysis of (186)–(188); see also Mourelatos (1978).

50 This point was made independently by Emmon Bach (pers. comm.) and Remko Scha (pers. comm.), so I consider it useful to discuss it in more detail.

51 A notable exception is Galton (1964).

52 I assume sufficient familiarity with the formal framework and refer to Dowty, Wall and Peters (1981), Partee, Ter Meulen and Wall (1990) and Gamut (1991).

53 Technically, this requires that the NP be lifted (by Geach's rule) to type $<<<e,t>,<<e,t>,t>>, <<e,t>,t>>$.

54 The intervals are represented here as open intervals. As the openness or closedness of intervals does not play a role in the present theory, the use of (and) should be seen as neutral between the two options.

55 Verkuyl (1987a) assumed isomorphism between I and **N*** which is like **N** except for the property of equidistance. In the present layout of the formal machinery this point is left aside, but our 'personal odometer' is less regular than mechanical ones. So, one may read **N*** for I and specify the relation between I and **N** given appropriate adaptations which are easy to make.

56 This was suggested to me by Ed Hoenkamp in 1975 and it led to the chess-field reflections in Verkuyl (1978). Van Benthem (1983a) pointed out **Q** is sufficient for dealing with the properties at issue. However, it does no harm to use **R**. The choice between **Z** and **N** looks less futile, but I do not think it is necessary to deal with 'negative time'.

57 This replaces a more simple looking non-constructive definition in an earlier version, which could not properly relate *P* to *Q*. The improvement is due to Kees Vermeulen. A further simplification is due to discussions with Jaap van der Does about PLUG⁺ (see also footnote 58).

58 Suppose that $\ell(0)=\varnothing$, $\ell(1)=\{s1\}$, and $\ell(2)=\{s1,s2,s3\}$. Then the following procedure would be sufficient to clear up the impact of DEF 12 with respect to Figure 40:

$X_0=\varnothing$

$X_{n+1}=X_n \cup \{\ell(n+1) \setminus \bigcup_{1\leq i\leq n} X_i\}$

This would give:

(i) $X_0=\varnothing$,

(ii) $X_1=X_0 \cup \{\ell(1) \setminus \bigcup_{i\leq 0} X_i\}=\varnothing\}=\varnothing \cup \{\{s1\}\setminus \varnothing\}=\{\{s1\}\}$, and

(iii) $X_2=X_1 \cup \{\{s1,s2,s3\}\setminus \bigcup_{1\leq i\leq 1} X_i\}=\{\{s1\}\}\cup\{\{s1,s2,s3\}\setminus\{s1\}\}$
$=\{\{s1\}\}\cup\{\{s2,s3\}\}=\{\{s1\},\{s2,s3\}\}$, etc.

59 Sentences like these have been discussed recently in Krifka (1990) in a different framework in which notions of event semantics are used to deal with token-occurrences. In Verkuyl (1984, 1988) a completely different route was taken. The relevant observations are made in Carlson (1978) and Gupta (1980), and in Verkuyl (1976) in which sentences like *For hours Den Uyl handed the Labour badge to congress-goers* was discussed. This sentence is durative if it expresses that Den Uyl handed an unspecified number of tokens of the Labour badge to anyone who was a congress-goer. Verkuyl (1984) discussed cases like *Hey, look there is my pen* pointing at a pen lying in the shop-window and similar to my own Waterman pen in my pocket. In all these seemingly disparate cases, 'blueprints' are used, but essentially two different ways of counting are involved: Boolean and arithmetical. For example, the Den Uyl sentence is about one badge *and* about many badges. See also Verkuyl (1992) for a more detailed discussion.

60 Θ-marking clearly differs per verb. *Walk* differs from *eat* in that *walk* is stereotypically 'by foot by land', along the lines of (84). This information is not transmitted but inevitably it will be involved in the interpretation of the 'going through' of the partitioned NP-denotation.

61 One might see $\Theta_=$ and $\Theta_\subseteq$ as formalizations of Hopper and Thompson's (1980) notion of total or partial affectedness, on which Tenny's (1987) notion of 'total (un)affectedness' seems to be based. If so, my work since 1972 has been focussed on total affectedness: the [+SQA]-notion as part of terminative aspect only makes sense in relation to the verb. The present analysis of Θ-roles is based on Verkuyl (1987a, 1985a, 1988).

62 An argument against this would be *to eat from some sandwiches*. But note that inherent to (262)–(264) is the working of the Entier-function. So, one could argue that a proper subset of representative indices does not warrant completion, because the Entier-function projects forward.

63 See, for example, Tedeschi and Zaenen (1981), Lascarides (1988), Richards (1982), Oversteegen (1989), Dowty (1979, 1982b, 1986), Kamp (1981), Kamp and Rohrer (1983), Partee (1984), Lo Cascio and Vet (1986), Bartsch (1989), Van Eynde (1987).

64 This stresses the correspondence between Tense and the atemporal determiners of GQT.

65 This was held against (281) by Nicholas Asher and Hans Kamp (European Workshop on Time and Space, Toulouse 1991).

66 The second problem was raised by Kees Vermeulen.

67 Thus, the relevant part of the definition of PROG(ϕ) in Lascarides (1988: 146) based on Moens (1987) amounts to: PROG(ϕ) is true with respect to (a world and) an index

iff $[\![\phi]\!]$ is a process and there is a closed interval j ($i \subset j$) and ϕ is true at j. Here the interval notion is taken strictly as temporal.

68 For the view that pragmatic factors may be involved, see Kasher and Manor (1980).

69 The only possible counterexample to this might be the example of the type found in Lansu (1988) *Ik rijd de brommer de sloot in* (I drive the motorbike into the ditch), because a sentence like *Ik reed de brommer deze sloot in* (I drove the motorbike into this ditch) is possible, but these directional phrases can be argued to have a different structure than Figure 40, as *in* may be taken to be a particle occupying the XP-phrase and forming the bitransitive verb *inrijden.*

70 In this sense, my present position deviates from Neeleman (pers. comm.) in that he allows freely phrases at the XP-position with their full referential capacity, for example directional phrases. I am hesitant and sceptical about that position, but as this area of investigation is still largely unknown, it seems better not to speak out on this issue and to leave it open. At any rate, the present treatment is more restrictive than Neeleman and Weerman's approach because I restrict myself here to particles and prefixes and to XPs characterized by a loss of referentiality as in the examples just given.

71 Kees Vermeulen (pers. comm.) convinced me of the impossibility of proceeding compositionally from V_0 to V^0, that is, by lambda-application, unless every verb is declared transitive, as discussed below. For several reasons this option is not attractive, one of them being that verb stems in complex verbs often lose their original meaning.

72 That they are ergative might be suggested by the difference between **Er werd uitgelezen* (lit.: there was read out) vs. *Er werd gelezen* (lit.: there was read), and by the fact that *de uitgelezen geleerde* (the read out scholar) is much better than the ungrammatical *de gelezen geleerde* (the read scholar). See Hoekstra (1984: 176ff.).

73 See Rozwadowska (1988: 151) for the suggestion that verbs like *hate*, *enjoy*, *know*, *understand* are to be lexically defined as having a neutral thematic role.

74 For example, *zwaaien* (wave) vs. *afzwaaien* (leave military service), *bijten* (bite) vs. *uitbijten* (erode), *studeren* (study) vs. *afstuderen* (do the final examination), etc.

References

Abeillé, A. and Y. Schabes (1990), 'Non-Compositional Discontinuous Constituents in Tree Adjoining Grammar'. Abstract Proceedings of the Symposium on Discontinuous Constituency. Tilburg, 85–96.

Abney, S. (1987), 'The Noun Phrase in its Sentential Aspect'. Dissertation, Massachusetts Institute of Technology.

Abusch, D. (1985), 'On Verbs and Time'. Dissertation, University of Massachusetts at Amherst.

Aristotle (1984), *Metaphysics*. In: J. Barnes (ed.), *The Complete Works of Aristotle* (The Revised Oxford Translation II), 1552–1728. Princeton University Press.

Austin, J.L. (1961), 'Performative Utterances'. In: *Philosophical Papers*. Oxford University Press, 233–252.

Bach, E. (1979), 'Control in Montague Grammar'. In: *Linguistic Inquiry* 4, 515–531.

(1980), 'Tenses and Aspects as Functions on Verb-Phrases'. In: C. Rohrer (ed.), *Time, Tense and Quantifiers*. Niemeyer: Tuebingen, 19–37.

(1981), 'On Time, Tense, and Aspect: An Essay in English Metaphysics'. In: P. Cole (ed.), *Radical Pragmatics*, Academic Press: New York, 62–81.

(1984), 'Some Generalizations of Categorial Grammars'. In: F. Landman and F. Veltman (eds.), *Varieties of Formal Semantics*. Foris: Dordrecht.

(1986), 'The Algebra of Events'. In: *Linguistics and Philosophy* 9, 5–16.

Bach, K. (1982), 'Semantic Nonspecificity and Mixed Quantifiers'. In: *Linguistics and Philosophy* 4, 593–605.

Bache, C. (1982), 'Aspect and Aktionsart; Towards a Semantic Distinction'. In: *Journal of Linguistics* 18, 57–72.

(1985), *Verbal Aspect; A General Theory and its Application to Present-Day English*. Odense University Press.

Baker, M. (1988), *Incorporation. A Theory of Grammatical Function Changing*. University of Chicago Press.

Barentsen. A.A. (1985), 'Tijd, Aspect en de conjunctie poka; Over betekenis en gebruik van enkele vormen in het moderne Russisch'. Dissertation, University of Amsterdam.

Bartsch, R. (1973), 'The Semantics and Syntax of Number and Numbers'. In: J.P. Kimball (ed.), *Syntax and Semantics*. Vol. II. Academic Press: New York.

(1989), 'Tenses and Aspects in Discourse'. In: *Theoretical Linguistics* 15, 133–194.

Barwise, J. and R. Cooper (1981), 'Generalized Quantifiers and Natural Language'. In: *Linguistics and Philosophy* 4, 159–219.

Barwise, J. and J. Perry (1983), *Situations and Attitudes*. The Massachusetts Institute of Technology Press: Cambridge, Mass.

Beedham, C. (1982), *The Passive Aspect in English, German and Russian*. Narr: Tubingen.

Beeken, J. (1991), 'Spiegelstructuur en variabiliteit: pre- en postposities in het Nederlands'. Dissertation, Catholic University of Leuven.

Beghelli, F. (1992), 'Comparative Quantifiers'. Unpublished Paper, University of California Los Angeles.

Bellert, I. (1989), *Feature System for Quantification Structures in Natural Language*. Foris: Dordrecht.

Bennett, M. (1975), *Some Extensions of a Montague Fragment of English*. Indiana University Linguistics Club.

(1981), 'Of Tense and Aspect: One Analysis'. In: P.J. Tedeschi and A. Zaenen (eds.), *Syntax and Semantics 14; Tense and Aspect*. Academic Press: New York, 13–29.

Bennett, M. and B. Partee (1978), 'Toward the Logic of Tense and Asp ct in English'. Indiana University Linguistics Club.

Bommer, J. (1989), 'Passief Aspect'. Master's Thesis, Utrecht University.

Booij, G.E. (1990), 'The Boundary between Morphology and Syntax: Separable Complex Verbs in Dutch'. In: G.E. Booij and Jaap van Marle (eds.), *Yearbook of Morphology* 3. Foris: Dordrecht, 45–63.

Booij, G.E. and T. van Haaften (1988), 'The External Syntax of Derived Words: Evidence from Dutch'. In: G.E. Booij and Jaap van Marle (eds.), *Yearbook of Morphology* 1. Foris: Dordrecht, 29–44.

Bresnan, J. (1973), 'Syntax of the Comparative Clause Construction in English'. In: *Linguistic Inquiry* 4, 275–343.

Bunt, H.C. (1979), 'Ensembles and the Formal Properties of Mass Terms'. In: F.J. Pelletier (ed.), *Mass Terms: Some Philosophical Problems*. Reidel: Dordrecht, 249–277.

(1981), 'The Formal Semantics of Mass Terms'. Dissertation, University of Amsterdam.

(1985), 'The Formal Representation of (Quasi-) Continuous Concepts'. In: R. Moore and G. Hobbes (eds.), *Formal Theories of the Common Sense World*, 37–70.

Caenepeel, M. (1989), 'Aspect, Temporal Ordering and Perspective in Narrative Fiction'. Dissertation, University of Edinburgh.

Carlson, G.N. (1978), 'Reference to Kinds in English'. Dissertation, University of Massachusetts at Amherst.

(1979), 'Generics and Atemporal When'. In: *Linguistics and Philosophy* 3, 49–98.

(1984), 'Thematic Roles and their Role in Semantic Interpretation'. In: *Linguistics* 22, 259–279.

(1989), 'English Generic Sentences'. In: G. Chierchia, B. H. Partee and R. Turner (eds.), *Property Theory, Type Theory and Natural Language*. Vol. II. *Semantic Issues*. Reidel: Dordrecht, 167–192.

Carlson, L. (1981), 'Aspect and Quantification'. In: P.J. Tedeschi and A. Zaenen (eds.), *Syntax and Semantics 14; Tense and Aspect*. Academic Press: New York, 31–64.

Carrier-Duncan, J. and J. Randall (1986), 'Derived Argument Structure; Evidence from Resultatives'. Milwaukee Morphology Meeting 1986.

Chellas, B. (1980), *Modal Logic; An Introduction*. Cambridge University Press.

Chierchia, G. (1984), 'Topics in the Syntax and Semantics of Infinitives and Gerunds'. Dissertation, University of Massachusetts at Amherst.

Chomsky, N. (1965), *Aspects of the Theory of Syntax*. The Massachusetts Institute of Technology Press: Cambridge, Mass.

(1970), 'Remarks on Nominalization'. In: R. A. Jacobs and P. S. Rosenbaum (eds.), *Readings in Transformational Grammar*. Ginn: Waltham, Mass., 184–221.

(1981), *Lectures on Government and Binding*. Foris: Dordrecht.

(1986), *Knowledge of Language. Its Nature, Origin and Use*. Praeger: New York.

Comrie, B. (1976), *Aspect*. Cambridge University Press.

Cooper, R. (1983), *Quantification and Syntactic Theory*. Reidel: Dordrecht.

(1991), 'Situation Semantic Grammar'. Collection of Course Readings. Third European Summer School in Language, Logic and Information. Saarbrücken.

Cooper, R. and T. Parsons (1976), 'Montague Grammar, Generative Semantics and Interpretive Semantics'. In: B.H. Partee (ed.), *Montague Grammar*. Academic Press: New York, 311–362.

Coopmans, P. and M. Everaert (1988), 'The Simplex Structure of Complex Idioms: The Morphological Status of *laten*'. In: M. Everaert, M. Trommelen and R. Huybregts (eds.), *Morphology and Modularity*. Foris: Dordrecht, 75–104.

Coppen, P.A. (1991), 'Specifying the Noun Phrase'. Dissertation, Catholic University of Nijmegen. Thesis Publishers: Amsterdam.

Cresswell, M.J. (1977), 'Interval Semantics and Logical Words'. In: C. Rohrer (ed.), *On the Logical Analysis of Tense and Aspect*. Narr: Tuebingen, 7–30.

(1979a), 'Adverbs of Space and Time'. In: F. Guenthner and S.J. Schmidt (eds.), *Formal Semantics and Pragmatics for Natural Languages*. Reidel: Dordrecht, 171–199.

(1979b), 'Interval Semantics for Some Event Expressions'. In: R. Baüerle, U. Egli and A. von Stechow (eds.), *Semantics from Different Points of View*. Springer: Berlin, 90–116.

Dahl, O. (1981), 'On the Definition of the Telic-Atelic (Bounded–Non-bounded) Distinction'. In: P.J. Tedeschi and A. Zaenen (eds.), *Syntax and Semantics 14; Tense and Aspect*. Academic Press: New York, 79–90.

Danchev, A. (1992), 'An Outline of Aspectuality in English within a Compromise Linguistic Model'. In: M. Stamenow (ed.), *Current Advances in Semantic Theory*. John Benjamins: Amsterdam, 321–337.

Davidson, D. (1967), 'The Logical Form of Action Sentences'. In: N. Rescher (ed.), *The Logic of Decision and Action*. Pittsburgh, 81–120. Also in: D. Davidson (1980), 105–122.

(1980), *Essays on Actions and Events*. 3rd Edition. Clarendon Press: Oxford.

(1984), *Inquiries into Truth and Interpretation*. 2nd Edition. Clarendon Press: Oxford.

Davies, Martin, (1989), '*Two Examiners Marked Six Scripts*. Interpretations of Numerically Quantified Sentences'. In: *Linguistics and Philosophy* 12, 293–323.

De Groot, C. and H. Tommola (eds.), *Aspect Bound; A Voyage into the Realm of Germanic, Slavonic and Finno-Ugrian Aspectology*. Foris: Dordrecht 1984.

De Jong, F.M.G. (1983), 'Numerals as Determiners'. In: H. Bennis and W.U.S. van Lessen Kloeke (eds.), *Linguistics in the Netherlands*. Foris: Dordrecht, 105–114.

(1987), 'The Compositional Nature of Indefiniteness'. In: E.J. Reuland and A.G.B. ter Meulen (eds.), *The Representation of (In)definiteness*. The Massachusetts Institute of Technology Press: Cambridge, Mass., 270–285.

(1991), 'Determiners: Features and Filters'. Dissertation, Utrecht University.

De Jong, F.M.G. and H.J. Verkuyl (1985), 'Generalized Quantifiers: the Properness of their Strength'. In: J. van Benthem and A. ter Meulen (eds.), *Generalized Quantifiers: Theory and Applications*. Foris: Dordrecht, 21–43.

Declerck, R. (1979), 'Aspect and the Bounded/Unbounded (Telic/Atelic) Distinction'. In: *Linguistics* 17, 761–794.

Dik, S.C. (1989), *The Theory of Functional Grammar*, Part 1: *The Structure of the Clause*. Foris: Dordrecht.

Dowty, D.R. (1979), *Word Meaning and Montague Grammar. The Semantics of Verbs and Times in Generative Semantics and in Montague's PTQ*. Reidel: Dordrecht.

(1982a), 'Grammatical Relations and Montague Grammar'. In: P. Jacobson and G. Pullum (eds.), *On the Nature of Syntactic Representation*. Reidel: Dordrecht, 79–130.

(1982b), 'Tenses, Time Adverbs and Compositional Semantic Theory'. In: *Linguistics and Philosophy* 5, 23–55.

(1986), 'The Effects of Aspectual Class on the Temporal Structure of Discourse: Semantics or Pragmatics?'. In: *Linguistics and Philosophy* 9, 37–61.

(1989), 'On the Semantic Content of the Notion "Thematic Role"'. In: G. Chierchia, B. H. Partee and R. Turner (eds.), *Property Theory, Type Theory and Natural Language*, Vol. II: *Semantic Issues*. Reidel: Dordrecht, 69–129.

Dowty, D.R., R.E. Wall and S. Peters (1981), *Introduction to Montague Semantics*. Reidel: Dordrecht.

Fillmore, C.J. (1968), 'The Case for Case'. In: E. Bach and R.T. Harms (eds.), *Universals in Linguistic Theory*. Holt, Rinehart and Winston: New York, 1–88.

(1971), 'Lectures on Deixis'. Indiana University Linguistics Club.

Freed, A. F. (1979), *The Semantics of English Aspectual Complementation* (Synthese Language Library 8). Reidel: Dordrecht.

Gallin, D. (1975), *Intensional and Higher-Order Modal Logic*. Mathem. Studies 17. North-Holland: Amsterdam.

Galton, A. (1984), *The Logic of Aspect; An Axiomatic Approach*. Clarendon Press: Oxford.

Galton, H. (1964), 'A New Theory of Slavic Verbal Aspect'. In: *Archivum Linguisticum* 16, 133–144.

Gamut, L.T.F. (1991), *Logic, Language and Meaning*. Vol. I. *Introduction to Logic*. Vol. II. *Intensional Logic and Logical Grammar*. The University of Chicago Press.

Gazdar, G., E. Klein, G. Pullum and I. Sag (1985), *Generalized Phrase Structure Grammar*. Blackwell: Oxford.

Gil, D. (1982), 'Distributive Numerals'. Dissertation, University of California Los Angeles.

Gillon, B.S. (1987), 'The Readings of Plural Noun Phrases in English'. In: *Linguistics and Philosophy* 10, 199–219.

(1990), 'Plural Noun Phrases and Their Readings: A Reply to Lasersohn'. In: *Linguistics and Philosophy* 13, 477–485.

Gruber, J.S. (1976), *Lexical Structures in Syntax and Semantics*. North-Holland: Amsterdam. Part I: Functions of the Lexicon in Formal Descriptive Grammars. (Revised) Doctoral Dissertation, Massachusetts Institute of Technology 1965; Part II: Functions of the Lexicon in Formal Descriptive Grammars. Internal Publication, System Development Corporation 1967.

Gupta, A. (1980), *The Logic of Common Nouns. An Investigation in Quantified Model Logic*. Yale University Press.

Heim, I. (1982), 'The Semantics of Definite and Indefinite Noun Phrases'. Dissertation, University of Massachusetts at Amherst.

Heinämäki, O. (1974), 'Semantics of English Temporal Connectives'. Dissertation, University of Texas.

(1984), 'Aspect in Finnish'. In: C. de Groot and H.Tommola (eds.), *Aspect Bound; A Voyage into the Realm of Germanic, Slavonic and Finno-Ugrian Aspectology*. Foris: Dordrecht, 153–178.

Higginbotham, J. (1983), 'The Logic of Perceptual Reports: An Extensional Alternative to Situation Semantics'. In: *The Journal of Philosophy* 80, 100–127.

(1985), 'On Semantics'. In: *Linguistic Inquiry* 16, 547–593.

Hinrichs, E. (1981), *Temporal Anaphora im Englischen*. Zulassungsarbeit. University of Tubingen.

(1986a), 'A Compositional Semantics for Aktionsarten and NP Reference in English'. Dissertation, Ohio State University.

(1986b), 'Temporal Anaphora in Discourses of English'. In: *Linguistics and Philosophy* 9, 63–82.

Hoeksema, J. (1983), 'Plurality and Conjunction'. In: A.G.B. ter Meulen (ed.), *Studies in Modeltheoretic Semantics*. Foris: Dordrecht, 63–83.

(1984), 'Categorial Morphology'. Dissertation, University of Groningen.

(1991), 'Complex Predicates and Liberation in Dutch and English'. In: *Linguistics and Philosophy* 14, 661–710.

Hoekstra, T.A. (1984), *Transitivity; Grammatical Relations in Government–Binding Theory*. Foris: Dordrecht.

(1988), 'Small Clause Results'. In: *Lingua* 74, 101–139.

Hoekstra, T.A., M. Lansu and M. Westerduin (1989), 'Complex Verba'. In: *Glot* 10, 61–77.

Hoekstra, T. A. and R. Mulder (1990), 'Unergatives as Copular Verbs: Locational and Existential Predication'. In: *The Linguistic Review* 7, 1–79.

Hoepelman, J. and Ch. Rohrer (1980), 'On the Mass–Count Distinction and the French Imparfait and Passe Simple'. In: Ch. Rohrer (ed.), *Time, Tense and Quantifiers; Proceedings of the Stuttgart Conference on the Logic of Tense and Quantification*. Niemeyer: Tubingen, 85–112.

Hopper, P.J. and S.A. Thompson (1980), 'Transitivity in Grammar and Discourse'. In: *Language* 56, 251–299.

Jackendoff, R.S. (1972), *Semantic Interpretation in Generative Grammar*. The Massachusetts Institute of Technology Press: Cambridge, Mass.

(1976), 'Toward an Explanatory Semantic Representation'. In: *Linguistic Inquiry* 7, 89–150.

(1977), *$\overline{\text{X}}$-Syntax: A Study of Phrase Structure*. The Massachusetts Institute of

Technology Press: Cambridge, Mass.
(1978), 'Grammar as Evidence for Conceptual Structure'. In: M. Halle, J. Bresnan and G.A. Miller (eds.), *Linguistic Theory and Psychological Reality*. The Massachusetts Institute of Technology Press: Cambridge, Mass. 201–228.
(1983), *Semantics and Cognition*. The Massachusetts Institute of Technology Press: Cambridge, Mass.
(1987), 'The Status of Thematic Relations in Linguistic Theory'. In: *Linguistic Inquiry* 18, 369–412.
(1990), *Semantic Structures*. The Massachusetts Institute of Technology Press: Cambridge, Mass.

Jacobs, J. (1982), *Syntax und Semantik der Negation im Deutschen*. Fink Verlag: Munich.

Jacobsohn, H. (1933), 'Aspektfragen'. In: *Indogermanische Forschungen* 51, 292–318.

Janssen, T.M.V. (1983), 'Foundations and Applications of Montague Grammar'. Dissertation, University of Amsterdam.

Jespersen, O. (1909), *A Modern English Grammar on Historical Principles*. Part II *Syntax* Vol. I, Allen and Unwin/Munksgaard: London/Copenhagen.
(1924), *The Philosophy of Grammar*. Allen and Unwin: London.

Kabakciev, K. (1984a), 'Verkuyl's Compositional Aspects in the Slavonic Languages'. In: *Linguistique Balkanique* 27, 77–83.
(1984b), 'The Article and the Aorist/Imperfect Distinction in Bulgarian; An Analysis Based on Cross-Language Aspect Parallelisms'. In: *Linguistics* 22, 643–672.

Kadmon, N. (1987), 'On Unique and Non-Unique Reference and Asymmetric Quantification'. Dissertation, University of Massachusetts at Amherst.

Kamp, H. (1979), 'Events, Instants, and Temporal Reference'. In: R. Baüerle, U. Egli, and A. von Stechow (eds.), *Semantics from Different Points of View*. Springer: Berlin, 376–416.
(1980), 'Some Remarks on the Logic of Change, Part 1'. In: Ch. Rohrer (ed.), *Time, Tense and Quantifiers; Proceedings of the Stuttgart Conference on the Logic of Tense and Quantification*. Niemeyer: Tubingen, 135–179.
(1981), 'A Theory of Truth and Semantic Representations'. In: J.A.G. Groenendijk, T.M.V. Janssen and M.J.B. Stokhof (eds.), *Formal Methods in the Study of Language* (Mathematical Centre Tracts 136, I). Amsterdam, 277–322.

Kamp, H. and C. Rohrer (1983), 'Tense in Texts'. In: R. Baüerle, C. Schwarze and A. von Stechow (eds.), *Meaning, Use and Interpretation of Language*. Walter de Gruyter: Berlin, 250–269.

Kasher, A. and Ruth Manor (1980), 'Simple Present Tense'. In: Ch. Rohrer (ed.), *Time, Tense and Quantifiers; Proceedings of the Stuttgart Conference on the Logic of Tense and Quantification*. Niemeyer: Tubingen, 315–328.

Keenan, E.L. (1976), 'Towards a Universal Definition of "Subject"'. In: C.N. Li (ed.), *Subject and Topic*. Academic Press: New York, 303–333.

Keenan, E.L. and L.M. Faltz (1985), *Boolean Semantics for Natural Language*. Synthese Language Library 23. Reidel: Dordrecht.

Keenan, E.L. and J. Stavi (1986), 'A Semantic Characterization of Natural Language Determiners'. In: *Linguistics and Philosophy* 9, 253–326.

Kempson, R. M. and A. Cormack (1981), 'Ambiguity and Quantification'. In: *Linguistics and Philosophy* 4, 259–309.

Kenny, A. (1963), *Action, Emotion and Will*. Routledge and Kegan Paul: London, New York.

Kerstens, J. (1991), *Phi-Features in Dutch. A Theory of Functional Projection and Functional Definition*. Walter De Gruyter: Berlin.

Klein, E. (1980), 'Determiners and the Category Q'. Unpublished paper, University of Sussex.

Krifka, M. (1987), 'Nominal Reference and Temporal Constitution: Towards a Semantics of Quantity'. In: J. Groenendijk, M. Stokhof and F. Veltman (eds.), *Proceedings of the 6th Amsterdam Colloquium 1987*, 153–173.

(1988), 'The Relational Theory of Genericity'. In: M. Krifka (ed.), *Genericity in Natural Language*. Proceedings of the 1988 Tuebingen Conference. Tuebingen.

(1989a), 'Nominal Reference, Temporal Constitution and Quantification in Event Semantics'. In: R. Bartsch, J. van Benthem and P. van Emde Boas (eds.), *Semantics and Contextual Expression*. Foris: Dordrecht 1989, 75–115. (A revised and extended version of Krifka 1987.)

(1989b), *Nominalreferenz und Zeitkonstitution. Zur Semantik von Massentermen, Pluraltermen und Aspektklassen*. Fink: Munich.

(1990), 'Four Thousand Ships Passed Through the Lock: Object-Induced Measure Functions on Events'. In: *Linguistics and Philosophy* 13, 487–520.

Landman, F. (1987), 'Groups, Plural, Individuals and Intentionality'. In: J. Groenendijk, M. Stokhof and F. Veltman (eds.), *Proceedings of the 6th Amsterdam Colloquium 1987*. Institute for Language, Logic and Information: Amsterdam, 197–217.

(1989), 'Groups'. In: *Linguistics and Philosophy* 12, I: 559–605; II: 723–744.

Lansu, M.E.M. (1988), 'De syntaxis van complexe verba'. Master's thesis, Leiden University.

Larson, R.K. (1985), 'Bare-NP Adverbs'. In: *Linguistic Inquiry* 16, 595–621.

Lascarides, A. (1988), 'A Formal Semantics of the Progressive'. Dissertation, University of Edinburgh.

(1991), 'The Progressive and the Imperfective Paradox'. In: *Synthese* 87, 401–447.

Lasersohn, P. (1989), 'On the Readings of Plural Noun Phrases'. In: *Linguistic Inquiry* 20, 130–134.

(1990), 'Group Action and Spatio-Temporal Proximity'. In: *Linguistics and Philosophy* 13, 179–206.

Leech, G.N. (1969), *Towards a Semantic Description of English*. Indiana University Press.

(1971), *Meaning and the English Verb*. Longman: Harlow.

Lindstedt, J. (1984), 'Nested Aspects'. In: C. de Groot and H.Tommola (eds.), *Aspect Bound. A Voyage into the Realm of Germanic, Slavonic and Finno-Ugrian Aspectology*. Foris: Dordrecht, 23–38.

(1985), *On the Semantics of Tense and Aspect in Bulgarian*. Helsinki.

Link, G. (1983), 'The Logical Analysis of Plurals and Mass Terms'. In: R. Baüerle, C. Schwarze and A. von Stechow (eds.), *Meaning, Use and Interpretation of Language*. Walter de Gruyter: Berlin, 302–323.

(1984), 'Plural'. In: D. Wunderlich and A. von Stechow (eds.), *Semantics. An International Handbook of Contemporary Research*. Walter de Gruyter: Berlin and New York, 1991.

(1987), 'Generalized Quantifiers and Plurals'. In: P. Gärdenfors (ed.), *Generalized Quantifiers. Linguistic and Logical Approaches*. Reidel: Dordrecht, 151–180.

LoCascio, V. and C. Vet (eds.), *Temporal Structure in Sentence and Discourse*. Foris: Dordrecht 1986.

Löbner, S. (1985), 'Definites'. In: *Journal of Semantics* 4, 279–326.

(1988), 'Ansätze zu einer integralen semantischen Theorie von Tempus, Aspekt und Aktionsarten'. In: V. Ehrich and H. Vater (eds.), *Temporalsemantik; Beiträge zur Linguistik der Zeitreferenz*. Niemeyer: Tuebingen, 163–191.

Lønning, J.T. (1987a), 'Mass Terms and Quantification'. In: *Linguistics and Philosophy* 10, 1–52.

(1987b), 'Collective Readings of Definite and Indefinite Noun Phrases'. In: P. Gärdenfors (ed.), *Generalized Quantifiers. Linguistic and Logical Approaches*. Reidel: Dordrecht, 203–235.

(1989), 'Some Aspects of the Logic of Plural Noun Phrases'. Cosmos Report 11. Department of Mathematics, University of Oslo.

Marantz, A.P. (1984), *On the Nature of Grammatical Relations*. The Massachusetts Institute of Technology Press: Cambridge, Mass.

Miller, G. (1972), 'English Verbs of Motion: A Case Study in Semantics and Lexical Memory'. In: A.W. Melton and E. Martin, *Coding Processes in Human Memory*. Winston: Washington, 335–372.

Miller, G.A. and P.N. Johnson-Laird (1976), *Language and Perception*. Cambridge University Press.

Model, J. (1991), 'Incorporatie in het Nederlands'. In: *Gramma* 15, 57–88.

Moens, M. (1987), 'Tense, Aspect and Temporal Reference'. Dissertation, University of Edinburgh.

Moens, M. and M. Steedman (1987), 'Temporal Ontology in Natural Language'. In: *Proceedings of the 25th Annual Meeting of the Association for Computational Linguistics*, Stanford University, July 1987, 1–7.

Montague, R. (1974), *Formal Philosophy; Selected Papers of Richard Montague*. Edited and with an Introduction by Richmond H. Thomason. Yale University Press.

Moortgat, M. (1988), *Categorial Investigations. Logical and Linguistic Aspects of the Lambek Calculus*. Foris: Dordrecht

(1992), 'Generalized Quantifiers and Discontinuous Type Constructors'. Research Institute for Language and Speech Working Paper CL 92–001. In W. Sijtsma and A. van Horck (eds.), *Discontinuous Constituency*. Walter De Gruyter: Berlin.

Mourelatos, A.P.D. (1978), 'Events, Processes and States'. In: *Linguistics and Philosophy* 2, 415–434.

Muskens, R. (1989), 'Meaning and Partiality'. Dissertation, University of Amsterdam.

Naumann, R. (1991), 'Aspectual Composition'. Unpublished paper, University of Duesseldorf.

Neale, S. (1988), 'Events and "Logical Form" '. In: *Linguistics and Philosophy* 11, 303–321.

Neeleman, A. (1991), 'Are there Small Clause Complements in Dutch?'. Research Institute for Language and Speech Prepublication Series.

Neeleman, A. and F. Weerman (1991), 'Case Theory and the Diachrony of Complex

Predicates in Dutch'. To appear in *Natural Language and Linguistic Theory*.

Nikanne, U. (1990), *Zones and Tiers; A Study of Thematic Structure*. Suom. Kirjallisuuden Seura: Helsinki.

Ojeda, A.E. (1990), 'Linguistic Individuals'. Dissertation, Linguistics Program, University of California at Davis.

(1991), 'Definite Descriptions and Definite Generics'. In: *Linguistics and Philosophy* 14, 367–397.

Oversteegen, E. (1988), 'Temporal Adverbials in the Two Track Theory of Time'. In: V. Ehrich and H. Vater (eds.), *Temporalsemantik. Beiträge zur Linguistik der Zeitreferenz*. Niemeyer: Tuebingen, 129–162.

(1989), 'Tracking Time. A Proposal for the Representation of Temporal Expressions in Dutch'. Dissertation, Utrecht University.

Oversteegen, E. and H.J. Verkuyl (1985), 'De temporele zinsstructuur van het Nederlands: twee tijdsbanden'. In: *Glot* 7, 257–297.

Parsons, T. (1980), 'Modifiers and Quantifiers in Natural Language'. In: *Canadian Journal of Philosophy*. Supplementary Series Volume 6, 29–60.

(1985), 'Underlying Events in the Logical Analysis of English'. In: E. Lepore and B.P. McLaughlin (eds.), *Actions and Events. Perspectives on the Philosophy of Donald Davidson*. Blackwell: Oxford, 235–267.

(1989), 'The Progressive in English: Events, States and Processes'. In: *Linguistics and Philosophy* 12, 213–241.

Partee, B.H. (1980), 'Montague Grammar, Mental Representation and Reality'. In: S. Kanger and S. Öhman (eds.), *Philosophy and Grammar*. Reidel: Dordrecht, 59–78.

(1984), 'Nominal and Temporal Anaphora'. In: *Linguistics and Philosophy* 7, 243–286.

Partee, B.H., A. ter Meulen and R.E. Wall (1990), *Mathematical Methods in Linguistics*. Kluwer: Dordrecht.

Pelletier, F. J. and L. K. Schubert (1989), 'Mass Expressions'. In: D. Gabbay and F. Guenthner (eds.), *Handbook of Philosophical Logic*. Vol. IV. Reidel: Dordrecht, 327–407.

Poutsma, H. (1926), *A Grammar of Late Modern English*, Vol. I: *The Parts of Speech*, Vol. II: *The Verb and its Particles*. Noordhoff: Groningen.

Pustejowsky, J. (1987), 'The Geometry of Events'. Working Draft, Brandeis University.

(1988), 'Event Semantic Structure'. Unpublished paper, Brandeis University.

Putnam, H. (1978), *Meaning and the Moral Sciences*. Routledge and Kegan Paul: London.

Quine, W.V.O. (1960), *Word and Object*. The Massachusetts Institute of Technology Press: Cambridge, Mass.

Quirk, R. and S. Greenbaum (1973), *A University Grammar of English*. Longman: London.

Richards, B. (1982), 'Tense, Aspect, and Time Adverbials I'. In: *Linguistics and Philosophy* 5, 59–109.

Roberts, C. (1987), 'Modal Subordination, Anaphora, and Distributivity'. Dissertation, University of Massachusetts at Amherst.

Rozwadowska, B. (1988), 'Thematic Restrictions on Derived Nominals'. In: W. Wilkins (ed.), *Syntax and Semantics 21*. Academic Press: New York, 147–165.

Russell, B. (1905), 'On Denoting'. In: *Mind* 14, 479–493.

(1940), *An Inquiry into Meaning and Truth*. Pelican A 500.

Ryle, G. (1949), *The Concept of Mind*. London.

Scha, R. (1981), 'Distributive, Collective and Cumulative Quantification'. In: J.A.G. Groenendijk, T.M.V. Janssen and M.B.J. Stokhof (eds.), *Formal Methods in the Study of Language*. Mathematical Centre Tracts: Amsterdam, 483–512.

Schubert, L.K. and F.J. Pelletier (1989), 'Generically Speaking, or, Using Discourse Representation Theory to Interpret Generics'. In: G. Chierchia, B. H. Partee and R. Turner (eds.), *Property Theory, Type Theory and Natural Language*. Vol. II: *Semantic Issues*. Reidel: Dordrecht, 193–268.

Selkirk, E.O. (1977), 'Some Remarks on Noun Phrase Structure'. In: P. W. Culicover, T. Wasow and A. Akmajian (eds.), *Studies in Formal Syntax*. Academic Press: New York, 285–316.

(1982), *The Syntax of Words*. The Massachusetts Institute of Technology Press: Cambridge, Mass.

Stambolieva, M. (1989), 'Notes on Aspect in Bulgarian and English'. In: M. J. B. Stokhof and L. Torenvliet (eds.), *Proceedings of the Seventh Amsterdam Colloquium. December 19–22, 1989*. Part II. Amsterdam, 495–508.

Stowell, T.A. (1981), 'Origins of Phrase Structure'. Dissertation, Massachusetts Institute of Technology, Cambridge, Mass.

Strawson, P.F. (1950), 'On Referring'. In: *Mind* 59, 320–344.

(1959), *Individuals; An Essay in Descriptive Metaphysics*. Methuen: London.

(1961), 'Singular Terms and Predication'. In: *Journal of Philosophy* 58, 393–412.

(1964), 'Identifying Reference and Truth–Values'. In: *Theoria* 30, 96–118.

Stuurman, F.J. (1985), *X-bar and X-plain: A Study of X-bar Theories of the Phrase Structure Component*. Foris: Dordrecht.

Taylor, B. (1977), 'Tense and Continuity'. In: *Linguistics and Philosophy* 1, 199–220.

(1985), *Modes of Occurrence; Verbs, Adverbs and Events*. Blackwell: Oxford.

Tedeschi, P.J. and A. Zaenen (eds.), *Syntax and Semantics 14; Tense and Aspect*. Academic Press: New York 1981.

Tennant, N. (1981), 'Formal Games and Forms for Games'. In: *Linguistics and Philosophy* 4, 311–320.

Tenny, C.L. (1987), 'Grammaticalizing Aspect and Affectedness'. Dissertation, Massachusetts Institute of Technology, Cambridge, Mass.

Ter Meulen, A. (1983), 'The Representation of Time in Natural Language'. In: Alice ter Meulen (ed.), *Studies in Modeltheoretic Semantics*. Foris: Dordrecht, 177–191.

(1984), 'Events, Quantities and Individuals'. In: Johan van Benthem and Alice Ter Meulen (eds.), *Generalized Quantifiers in Natural Language*. Foris: Dordrecht, 259–279.

Ter Meulen, A.G.B. (ed.) (1983), *Studies in Model-theoretic Semantics*. Foris: Dordrecht.

Thijsse, E. (1983), 'On Some Proposed Universals of Natural Language'. In: A.G.B. ter Meulen (ed.), *Studies in Modeltheoretic Semantics*. Foris: Dordrecht, 19–36.

Tichy, P. (1980), 'The Semantics of Episodic Verbs'. In: *Theoretical Linguistics* 7, 262–296.

(1985), 'Do we Need Interval Semantics?'. In: *Linguistics and Philosophy* 8, 263–282.

Van Benthem, J.F.A.K. (1980), 'Points and Periods'. In: C. Rohrer (ed.), *Time, Tense and Quantifiers. Proceedings of the Stuttgart Conference on the Logic of Tense and Quantification*. Niemeyer: Tuebingen, 39–57.

(1983a), *The Logic of Time. A Model–theoretic Investigation into the Varieties of Temporal Ontology and Temporal Discourse*. Reidel: Dordrecht.

(1983b), 'Determiners and Logic'. In: *Linguistics and Philosophy* 6, 447–478

(1986), *Essays in Logical Semantics*. SLAP 26. Reidel: Dordrecht.

(1989), 'The Fine-Structure of Categorial Semantics'. Paper, Institute for Language, Logic and Computation, University of Amsterdam.

Van Benthem, J.F.A.K. and A.G.B ter Meulen (eds.) (1985), *Generalized Quantifiers in Natural Language*. Foris: Dordrecht.

Van Deemter, K. (1991), *On the Composition of Meaning*. Dissertation, University of Amsterdam.

Van der Does, J. (1990), 'Among Collections'. To appear in *Linguistics and Philosophy*.

(1992), 'Applied Quantifier Logics'. Dissertation, University of Amsterdam.

Van Eyck, J. (1985), 'Aspects of Quantification in Natural Language'. Dissertation, University of Groningen.

Van Eynde, F. (1985), *Betekenis, vertaalbaarheid en automatische vertaling*. Dissertation, University of Leuven.

(1987), *Time. A Unified Theory of Tense, Aspect and Aktionsart*. Eurotra-Report. Leuven.

Van Riemsdijk, H.C. and E. Williams (1986), *Introduction to the Theory of Grammar*. The Massachusetts Institute of Technology Press: Cambridge, Mass.

Vendler, Z. (1957), 'Verbs and Times'. *The Philosophical Review* 66, 143–160.

(1967), *Linguistics in Philosophy*. Cornell University Press: Ithaca, New York.

Verkuyl, H.J. (1969), *De constituentenstatus van tijdsbepalingen*. University of Amsterdam.

(1971), 'Aspecten als kompositionele kategorieën'. In: S.C. Dik (ed.), *Taalwetenschap in Nederland 1971*. University of Amsterdam.

(1972), *On the Compositional Nature of the Aspects*. Reidel: Dordrecht. (Dissertation, Utrecht University 1971.)

(1973), 'Temporal Prepositions as Quantifiers'. In: F. Kiefer and N. Ruwet, *Generative Grammar in Europe*. Reidel: Dordrecht, 582–615.

(1976), 'Interpretive Rules and the Description of the Aspects'. In: *Foundations of Language* 14, 471–503.

(1978), 'Thematic Relations and the Semantic Representation of Verbs Expressing Change'. In: *Studies in Language* 2, 199–233.

(1980), 'On the Proper Classification of Events and Verb Phrases'. In: *Theoretical Linguistics* 7, 137–148.

(1981), 'Numerals and Quantifiers in Xbar-Syntax and their Semantic Interpretation'. In: J.A.G. Groenendijk, T.M.V. Janssen and M.J.B. Stokhof (eds.), *Formal Methods in the Study of Language* (Mathematical Centre Tracts 136). Amsterdam, 567–599.

(1984), *Verdiepingen in taal*. Veen: Utrecht.

(1985a), 'Temporal Insulation: On the Construction of Events'. In: *Dutch Crossing* 27, 22–45.

(1985b), 'On Semantics without Logic'. In: *Lingua* 68, 59–90.

(1987a), 'Nondurative Closure of Events'. In: J.A.G. Groenendijk, D. de Jongh and M.J.B. Stokhof (eds.), *Studies in Discourse Representation Theory and the Theory of Generalized Quantifiers*. Proceedings of the 5th Amsterdam Colloquium on Formal Semantics 1984. Foris: Dordrecht, 87–113.

(1987b), 'Aspect, Quantification and Negation'. In: J. Groenendijk, M. Stokhof and F. Veltman (eds.), *Proceedings of the 6th Amsterdam Colloquium, April 13–16 1987*. Institute for Language, Logic and Computation: Amsterdam, 353–372.

(1987c), 'Verbal Aspect in Russian and in English?' In: *Linguistics* 25, 403–420.

(1988), 'Aspectual Asymmetry and Quantification'. In: V. Ehrich and H. Vater (eds.), *Temporalsemantik. Beiträge zur Linguistik der Zeitreferenz*. Niemeyer: Tübingen, 220–259.

(1989), 'Aspectual Classes and Aspectual Composition'. In: *Linguistics and Philosophy* 12, 39–94.

(1990), 'Did the Guns of Navarone Hit Miles Twice?'. In: M. J. B. Stokhof and L. Torenvliet (eds.), *Proceedings of the 7th Amsterdam Colloquium. December 19–22, 1989*. Part 2. Amsterdam, 581–595.

(1992), 'Some Issues in the Analysis of Multiple Quantification with Plural NPs'. OTS–WP–TL–92–005. In: F. Hamm and E. Hinrichs (eds.), *Plural Quantification*. Kluwer: Dordrecht.

Verkuyl, H.J. and J. van der Does (1991), 'The Semantics of Plural Noun Phrases'. In: J.M. van der Does & J.A.N. van Eyck (eds.), *Generalized Quantifier Theory and Application*. Institute for Language, Logic and Computation: Amsterdam, 403–411.

Verkuyl, H.J. and J. Zwarts (1992), 'Time and Space in Conceptual and Logical Semantics: the Notion of Path'. In: *Linguistics* 30, 483–511.

Vet, C. (1976), 'Aspecten: een kwestie van tijd'. In: *Spektator* 6, 137–155.

(1980), *Temps, aspects et adverbes de temps en français contemporain*. Geneva.

Vlach, F. (1981), 'The Semantics of the Progressive'. In: P.J. Tedeschi and A. Zaenen (eds.), *Syntax and Semantics 14; Tense and Aspect*. Academic Press: New York, 271–292.

Wagner, R. (1839), *Der Fliegende Holländer*. Collected Works.

Westerståhl, D. (1984), 'Determiners and Context Sets'. In: J. van Benthem and A. ter Meulen (eds.), *Generalized Quantifiers: Theory and Applications*. Foris: Dordrecht, 45–71.

(1985), 'Logical Constants in Quantifier Languages'. In: *Linguistics and Philosophy* 8, 387–413.

Williams, E. (1977), 'Discourse and Logical Form'. In: *Linguistic Inquiry* 8, 101–139.

(1980), 'Predication'. In: *Linguistic Inquiry* 11, 203–238.

(1981), 'Argument Structure and Morphology'. In: *The Linguistic Review* 1, 81–114.

(1983a), 'Against Small Clauses'. In: *Linguistic Inquiry* 14, 287–308.

(1983b), 'Semantic vs. Syntactic Categories'. In: *Linguistics and Philosophy* 6, 423–446.

Wright, von, G.H. (1965), 'And Next'. In: *Acta Philosophica Fennica* XVIII, 293–304.

Wunderlich, D. (1990), 'On German *um*; Semantic and Conceptual Aspects'. Paper read at Max Planck Institut Nijmegen. University of Düsseldorf.

Zeevat, H. (1989), 'Realism and Definiteness'. In: G. Chierchia, B. H. Partee and R. Turner (eds.), *Property Theory, Type Theory and Natural Language*. Vol. II. *Semantic Issues*. Reidel: Dordrecht, 269–297.

Zubizaretta, M.L. (1987), *Levels of Representation in the Lexicon and in the Syntax*. Foris: Dordrecht.

Zwarts, F. (1981), 'Negatief polaire uitdrukkingen'. In: *Glot* 4, 35–132.

(1986), 'Categoriale grammatica en algebraïsche semantiek. Een onderzoek naar negatie en polariteit in het Nederlands'. Dissertation, University of Groningen.

Zwarts, J. and H.J. Verkuyl (1991), 'An Algebra of Conceptual Structure; an Investigation into Jackendoff's Conceptual Semantics'. Research Institute for Language and Speech. Paper, Utrecht University.

Index